WWDD

# What Would Dewey Do ?

# What Would Dewey Do ?

WWDD

an Unshelved™ collection
by Bill Barnes and Gene Ambaum

OVERDUE
MEDIA
Seattle

*Unshelved* is distributed internationally by Overdue Media LLC.

"Unshelved" is a trademark of Overdue Media LLC.



Reprinting *Unshelved* comic strips originally published on the Overdue Media LLC website from February 16, 2003 to February 15, 2004, the ALA Midwinter Meeting 2004 website, the ALA Midwinter Meeting 2004 *CogNotes* newspaper from January 9, 2004 to January 12, 2004, and a handout at Bumbershoot 2003. Comic strips copyright © 2003 or 2004 as noted individually.



ISBN: 0-9740353-1-9

Printed in Canada

# Introduction

I'm probably the only librarian in the world who doesn't belong to a listserv, where, I understand, chatter about the first daily cartoon devoted to life in a public library was ubiquitous, so I was probably the last librarian around to learn about the existence of *Unshelved*. Oh, I had heard my colleagues chatting about a Young Adult librarian named Dewey, but I thought they were referring to some new hotshot in the profession. It wasn't until the fall of 2003 that I finally became acquainted with the comic strip that's now become daily reading for me. One day I got 37 (that's right, I counted them) emails, all asking me if I'd seen the *Unshelved* about the Librarian Action Figure, for which I was the model. Many people helpfully included the URL, so I could take a look myself. Which I did, and was, of course, totally enchanted by what I saw. Being a good librarian (despite not belonging to any listservs), I immediately checked to see if my library owned *Unshelved* in book form, which it did. After waiting impatiently for my name to make its way up the rather longish holds queue, I took the book home and settled in for a treat: getting to know the staff and patrons of the Mallville Library – Dewey, the motorcycle riding YA librarian (so that's who he was!), Tamara, the children's librarian whose favorite letter is T (as a former children's librarian myself, my favorite letter happened to be S), Mel, the new library manager, Merv, the non-reading teenager, Buddy the Book Beaver (the summer reading program mascot who evidently works all year round), and various other characters.

It's clear that Bill Barnes and Gene Ambaum know libraries from the inside out – the good, the bad, and the needing to be weeded. And lucky us, who get to read, chuckle, and shake our heads over this slice of library life (the frightening thing is that it could easily be life in <u>our</u> library) that appears so conveniently in our inbox every day of the year.

I know you'll enjoy the second volume of *Unshelved* as much I do.

Nancy Pearl, librarian, author of *Book Lust: Recommended Reading for Every Mood, Moment, and Reason*, and action-figure model.

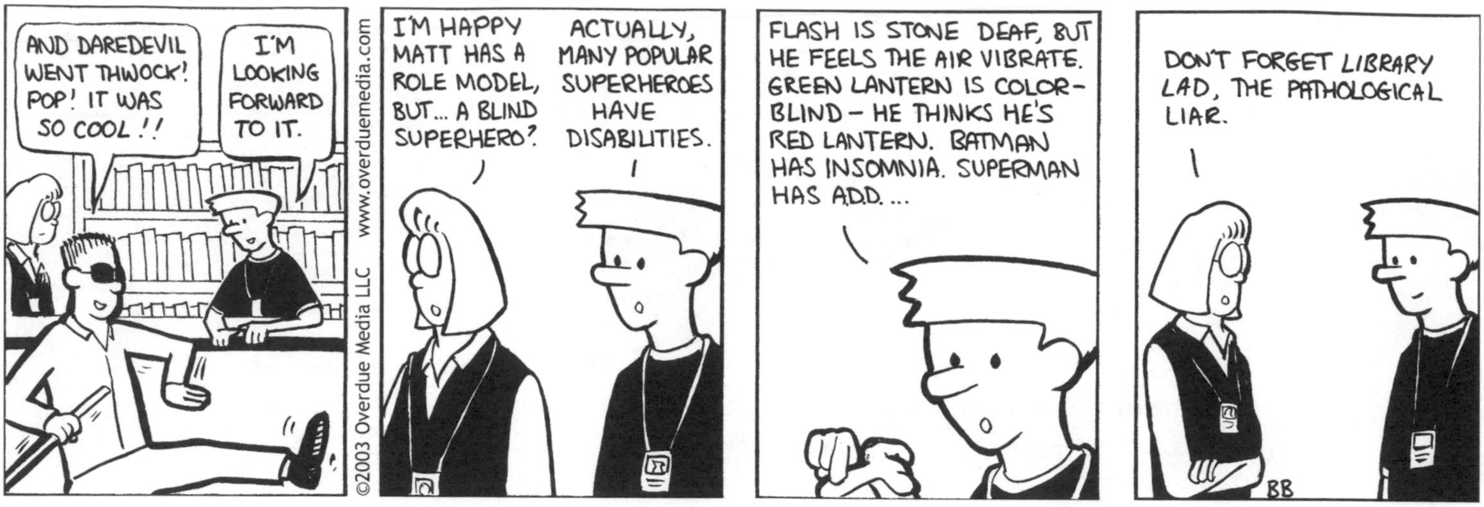
AND DAREDEVIL WENT THWOCK! POP! IT WAS SO COOL!!
I'M LOOKING FORWARD TO IT.
©2003 Overdue Media LLC www.overduemedia.com
I'M HAPPY MATT HAS A ROLE MODEL, BUT... A BLIND SUPERHERO?
ACTUALLY, MANY POPULAR SUPERHEROES HAVE DISABILITIES.
FLASH IS STONE DEAF, BUT HE FEELS THE AIR VIBRATE. GREEN LANTERN IS COLOR-BLIND – HE THINKS HE'S RED LANTERN. BATMAN HAS INSOMNIA. SUPERMAN HAS A.D.D. ...
DON'T FORGET LIBRARY LAD, THE PATHOLOGICAL LIAR.
BB

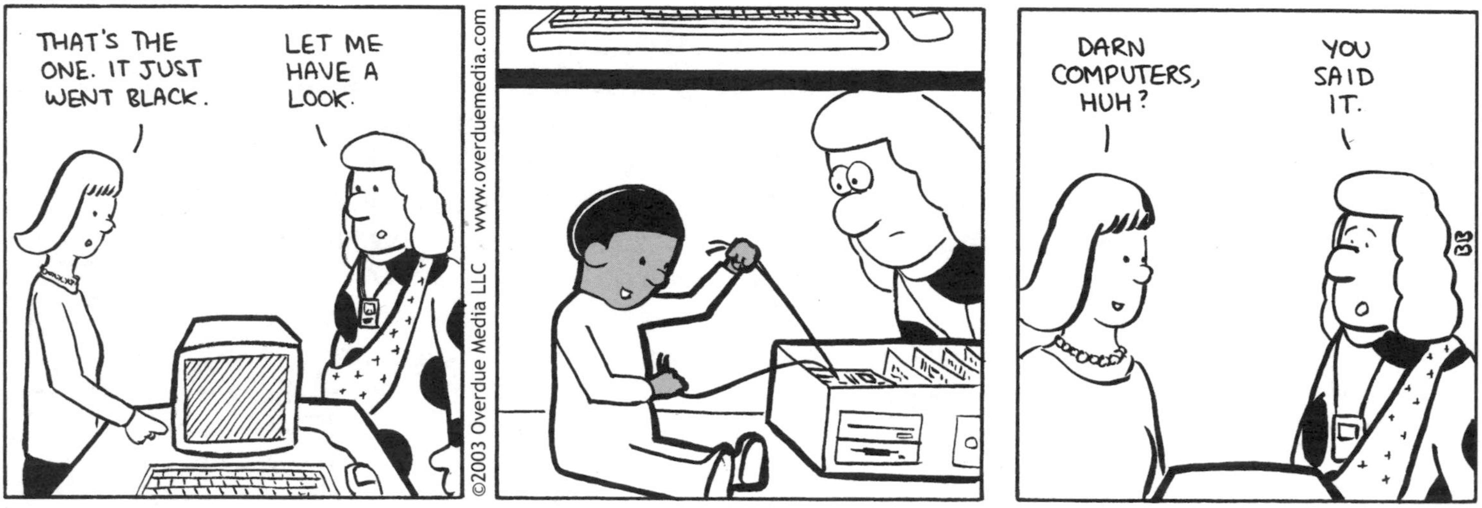
THAT'S THE ONE. IT JUST WENT BLACK.
LET ME HAVE A LOOK.
©2003 Overdue Media LLC www.overduemedia.com
DARN COMPUTERS, HUH?
YOU SAID IT.
BB

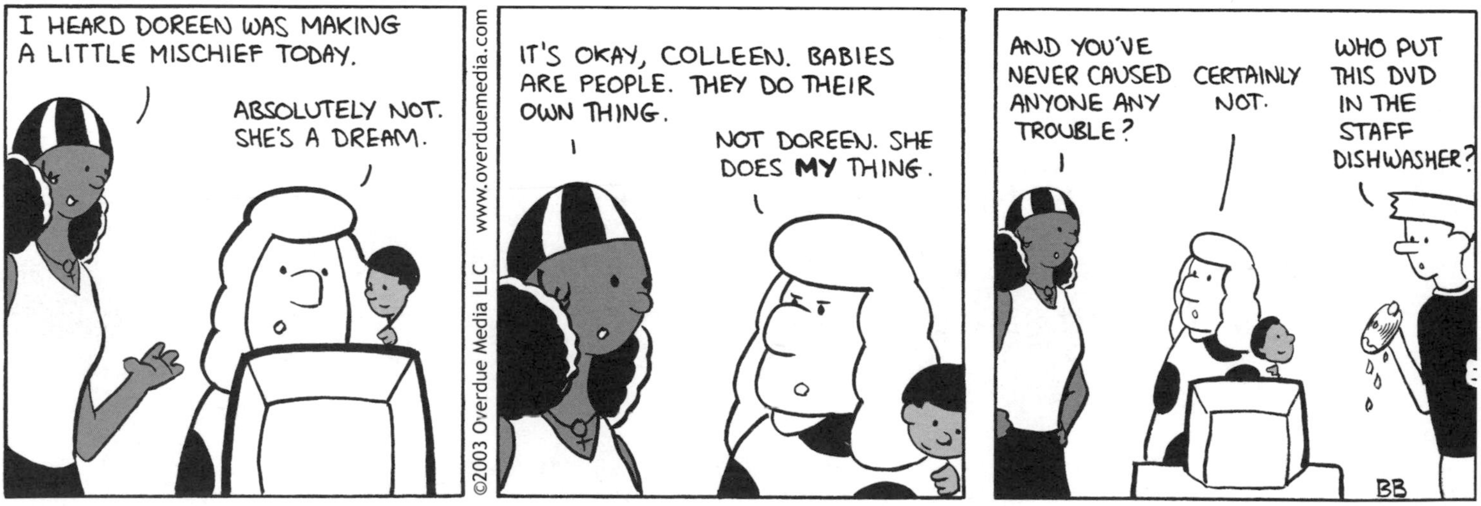
I HEARD DOREEN WAS MAKING A LITTLE MISCHIEF TODAY.
ABSOLUTELY NOT. SHE'S A DREAM.
©2003 Overdue Media LLC www.overduemedia.com
IT'S OKAY, COLLEEN. BABIES ARE PEOPLE. THEY DO THEIR OWN THING.
NOT DOREEN. SHE DOES MY THING.
AND YOU'VE NEVER CAUSED ANYONE ANY TROUBLE?
CERTAINLY NOT.
WHO PUT THIS DVD IN THE STAFF DISHWASHER?
BB

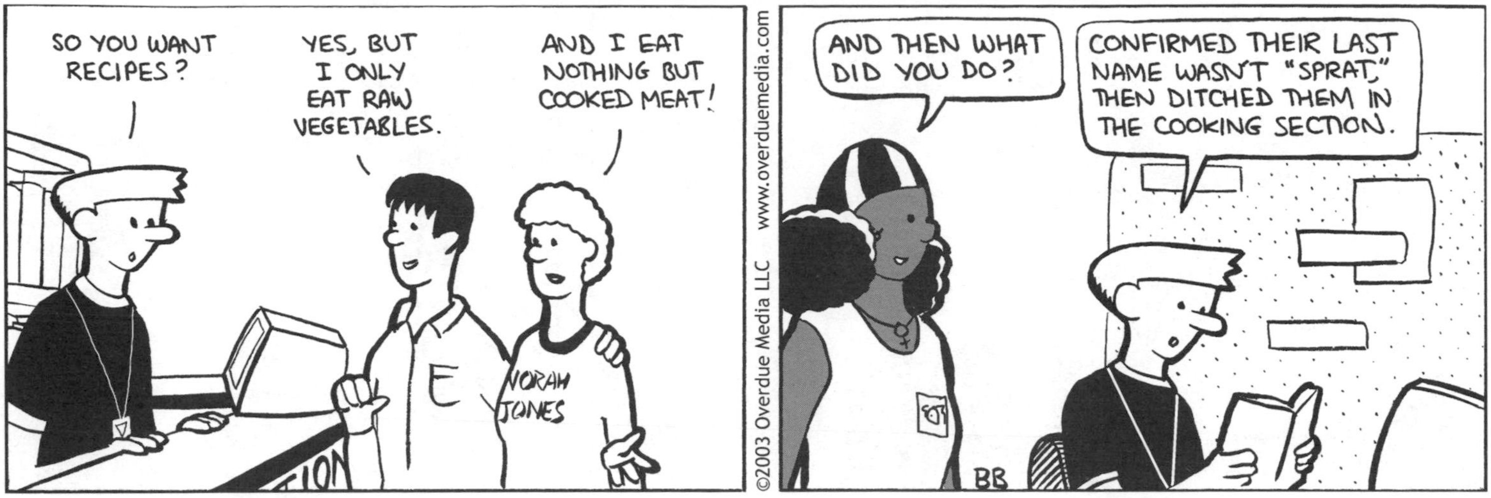
SO YOU WANT RECIPES?
YES, BUT I ONLY EAT RAW VEGETABLES.
AND I EAT NOTHING BUT COOKED MEAT!
NORAH JONES
AND THEN WHAT DID YOU DO?
CONFIRMED THEIR LAST NAME WASN'T "SPRAT," THEN DITCHED THEM IN THE COOKING SECTION.
BB


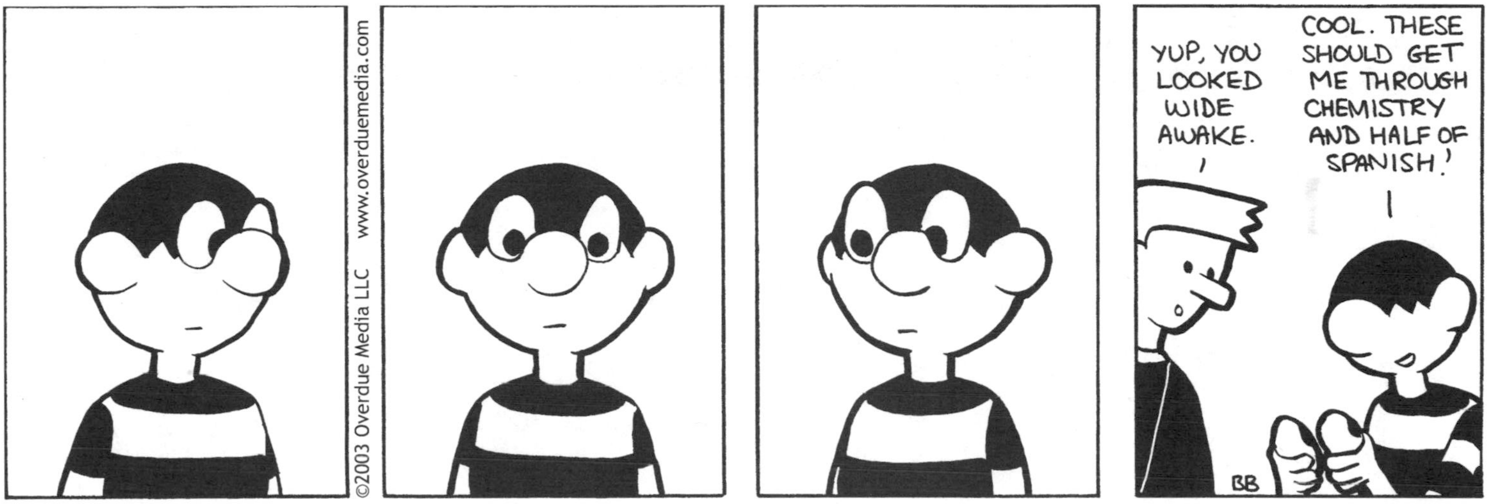
YUP, YOU LOOKED WIDE AWAKE.
COOL. THESE SHOULD GET ME THROUGH CHEMISTRY AND HALF OF SPANISH!
BB


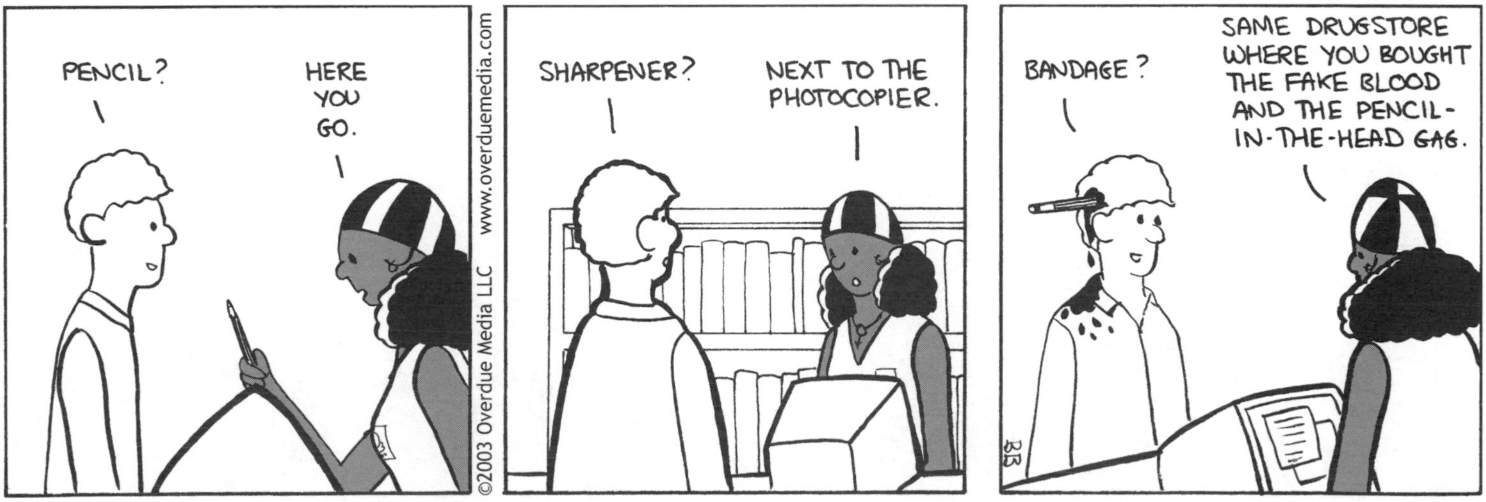
PENCIL?
HERE YOU GO.
SHARPENER?
NEXT TO THE PHOTOCOPIER.
BANDAGE?
SAME DRUGSTORE WHERE YOU BOUGHT THE FAKE BLOOD AND THE PENCIL-IN-THE-HEAD GAG.
BB

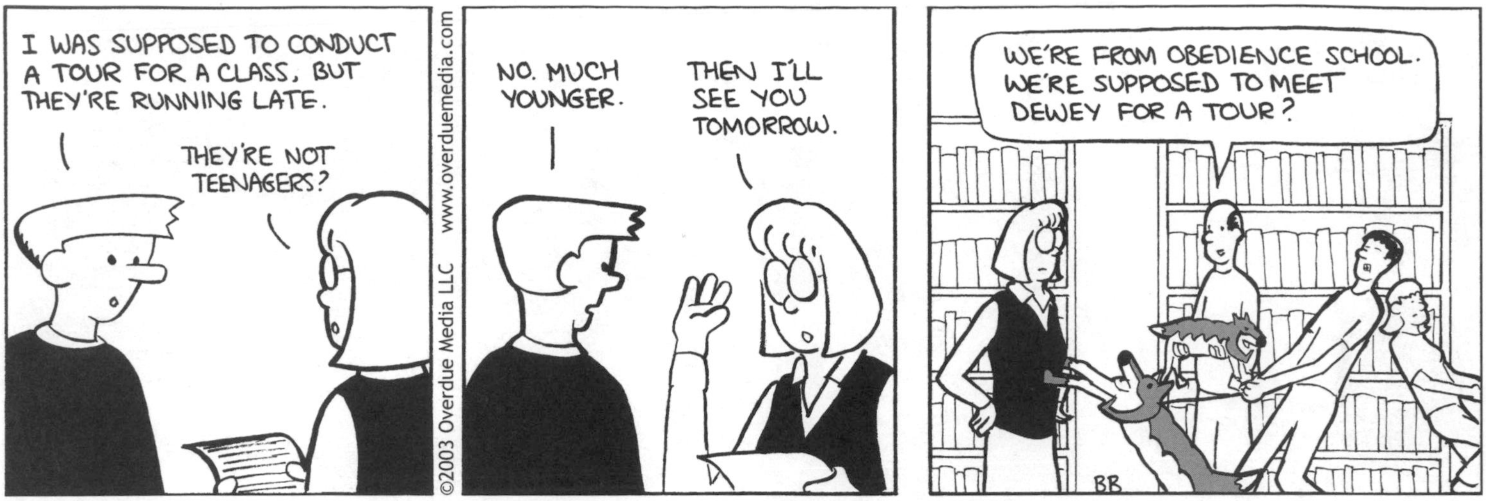
I WAS SUPPOSED TO CONDUCT A TOUR FOR A CLASS, BUT THEY'RE RUNNING LATE.
THEY'RE NOT TEENAGERS?
NO. MUCH YOUNGER.
THEN I'LL SEE YOU TOMORROW.
WE'RE FROM OBEDIENCE SCHOOL. WE'RE SUPPOSED TO MEET DEWEY FOR A TOUR?
BB
©2003 Overdue Media LLC www.overduemedia.com

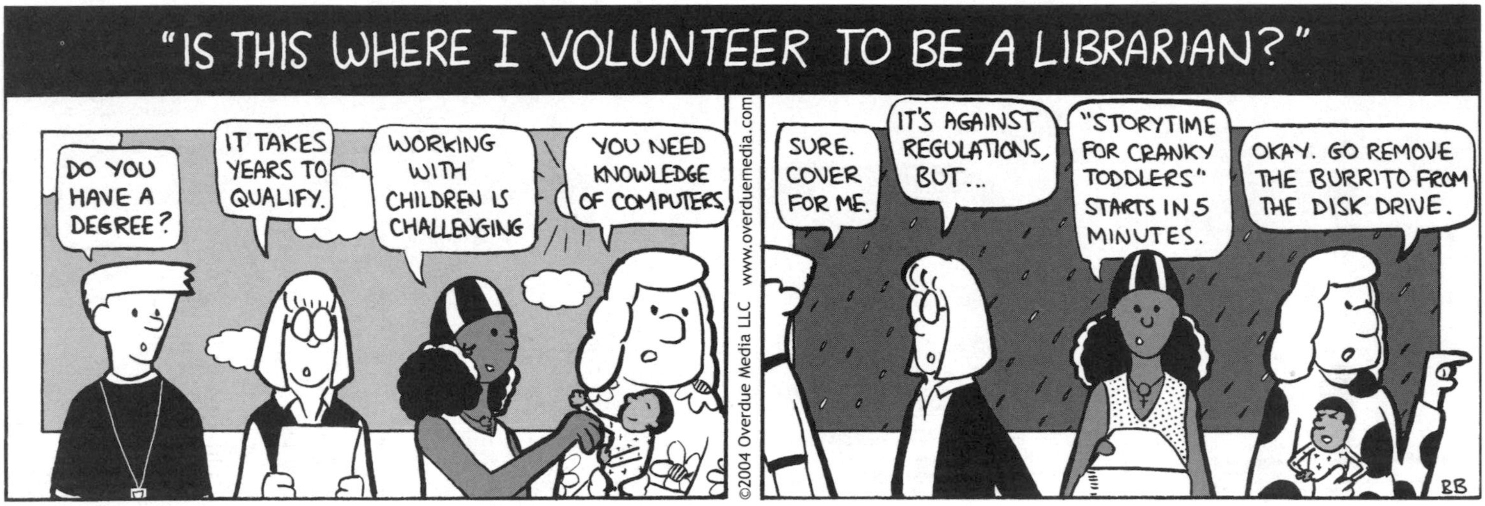
"IS THIS WHERE I VOLUNTEER TO BE A LIBRARIAN?"
DO YOU HAVE A DEGREE?
IT TAKES YEARS TO QUALIFY.
WORKING WITH CHILDREN IS CHALLENGING
YOU NEED KNOWLEDGE OF COMPUTERS
SURE. COVER FOR ME.
IT'S AGAINST REGULATIONS, BUT...
"STORYTIME FOR CRANKY TODDLERS" STARTS IN 5 MINUTES.
OKAY. GO REMOVE THE BURRITO FROM THE DISK DRIVE.
BB
©2004 Overdue Media LLC www.overduemedia.com

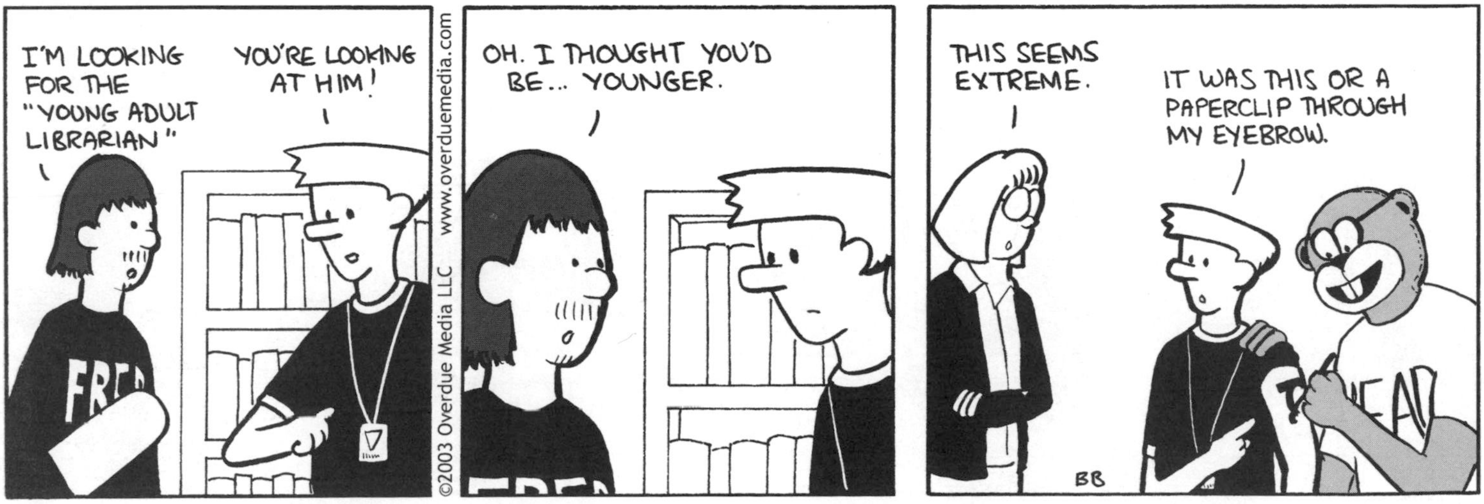
I'M LOOKING FOR THE "YOUNG ADULT LIBRARIAN"
YOU'RE LOOKING AT HIM!
OH. I THOUGHT YOU'D BE... YOUNGER.
THIS SEEMS EXTREME.
IT WAS THIS OR A PAPERCLIP THROUGH MY EYEBROW.
BB
©2003 Overdue Media LLC www.overduemedia.com

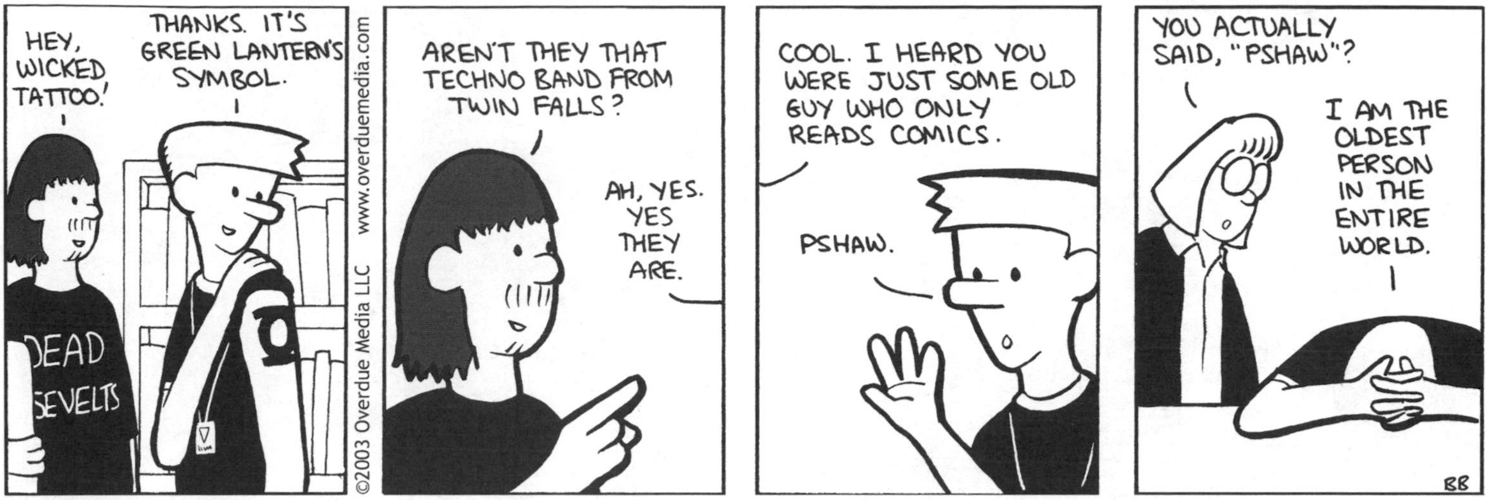
HEY, WICKED TATTOO!
THANKS. IT'S GREEN LANTERN'S SYMBOL.
DEAD SEVELTS
AREN'T THEY THAT TECHNO BAND FROM TWIN FALLS?
AH, YES. YES THEY ARE.
COOL. I HEARD YOU WERE JUST SOME OLD GUY WHO ONLY READS COMICS.
PSHAW.
YOU ACTUALLY SAID, "PSHAW"?
I AM THE OLDEST PERSON IN THE ENTIRE WORLD.
BB
©2003 Overdue Media LLC www.overduemedia.com

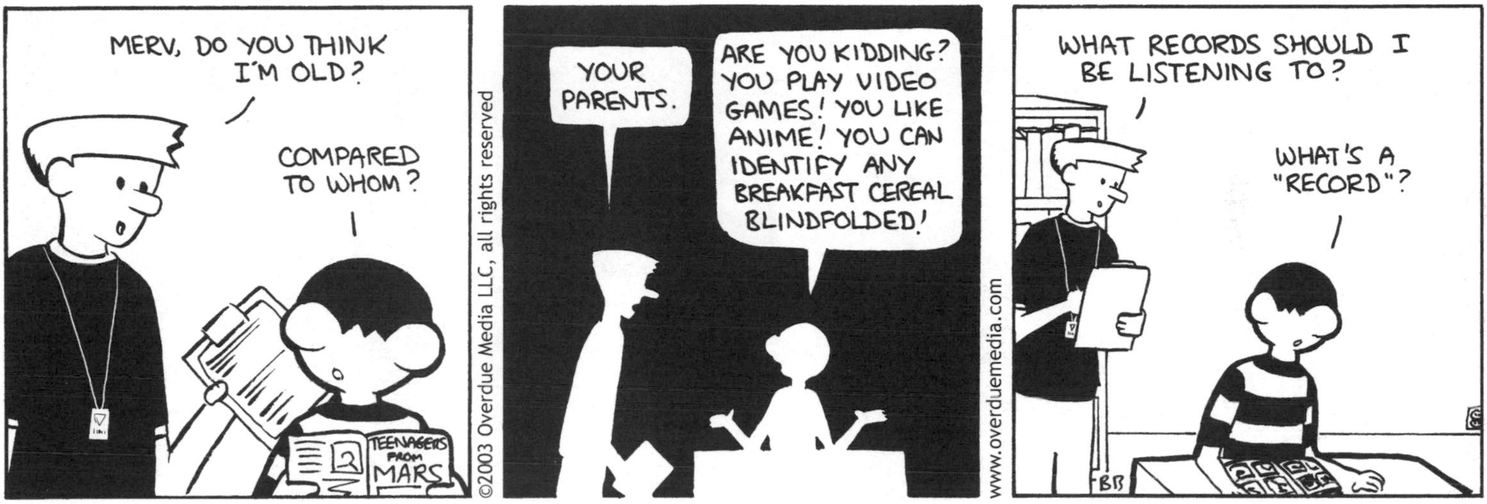
MERV, DO YOU THINK I'M OLD?
COMPARED TO WHOM?
TEENAGERS FROM MARS
YOUR PARENTS.
ARE YOU KIDDING? YOU PLAY VIDEO GAMES! YOU LIKE ANIME! YOU CAN IDENTIFY ANY BREAKFAST CEREAL BLINDFOLDED!
WHAT RECORDS SHOULD I BE LISTENING TO?
WHAT'S A "RECORD"?
BB
©2003 Overdue Media LLC, all rights reserved
www.overduemedia.com

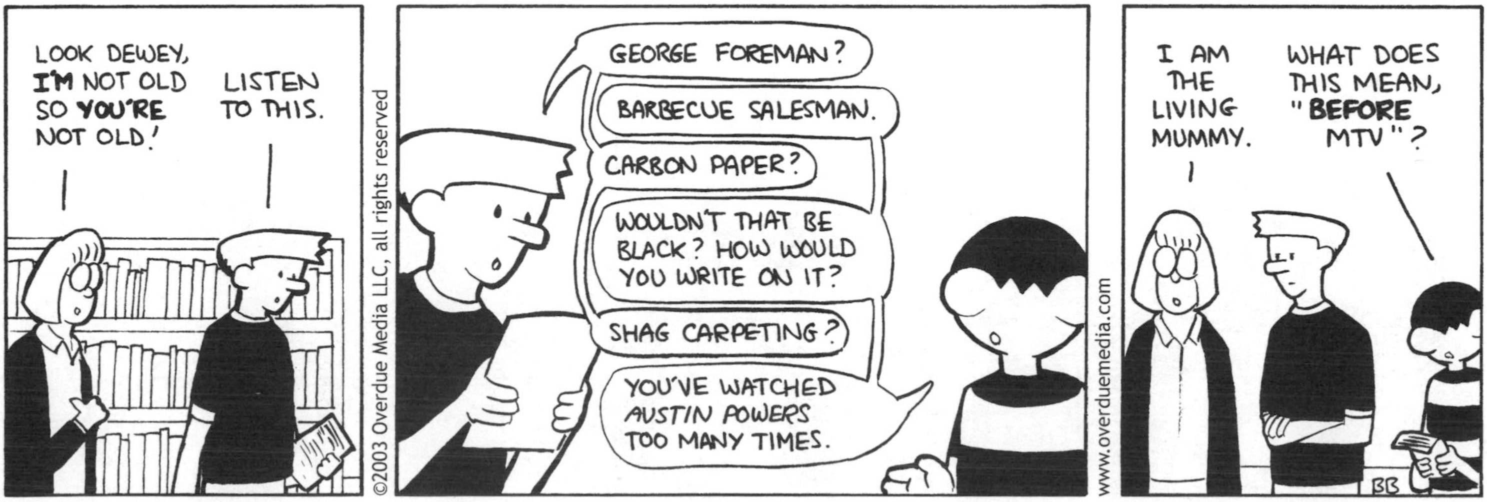
LOOK DEWEY, **I'M** NOT OLD SO **YOU'RE** NOT OLD!
LISTEN TO THIS.
GEORGE FOREMAN?
BARBECUE SALESMAN.
CARBON PAPER?
WOULDN'T THAT BE BLACK? HOW WOULD YOU WRITE ON IT?
SHAG CARPETING?
YOU'VE WATCHED *AUSTIN POWERS* TOO MANY TIMES.
I AM THE LIVING MUMMY.
WHAT DOES THIS MEAN, "**BEFORE** MTV"?
BB
©2003 Overdue Media LLC, all rights reserved
www.overduemedia.com

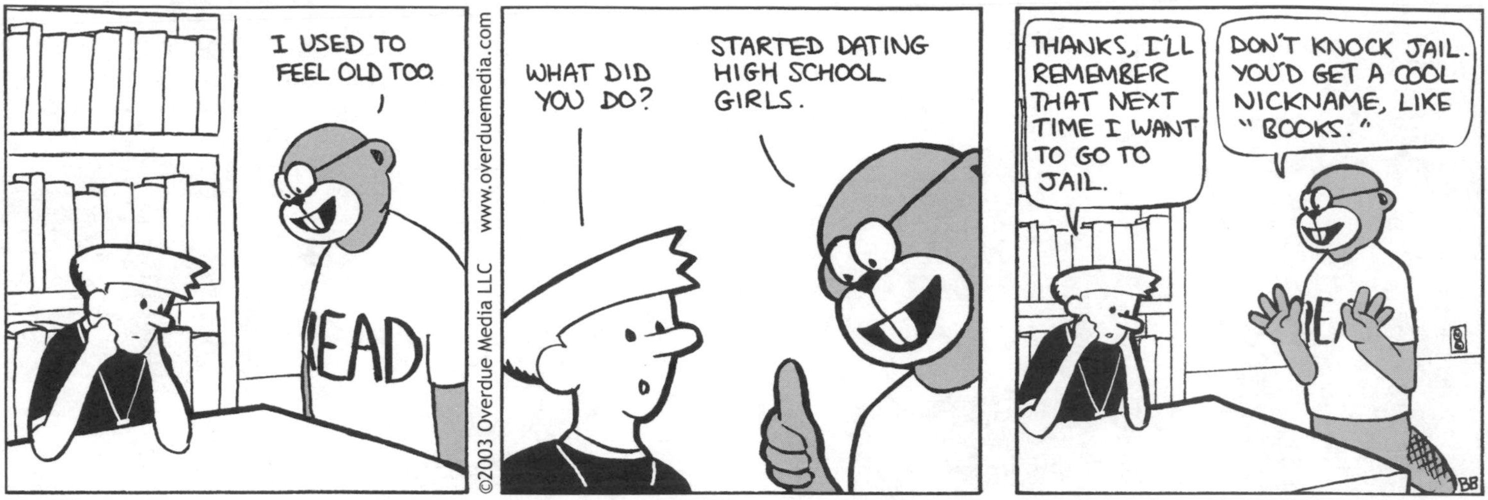
I USED TO FEEL OLD TOO.
WHAT DID YOU DO?
STARTED DATING HIGH SCHOOL GIRLS.
THANKS, I'LL REMEMBER THAT NEXT TIME I WANT TO GO TO JAIL.
DON'T KNOCK JAIL. YOU'D GET A COOL NICKNAME, LIKE "BOOKS."
READ
©2003 Overdue Media LLC www.overduemedia.com
BB

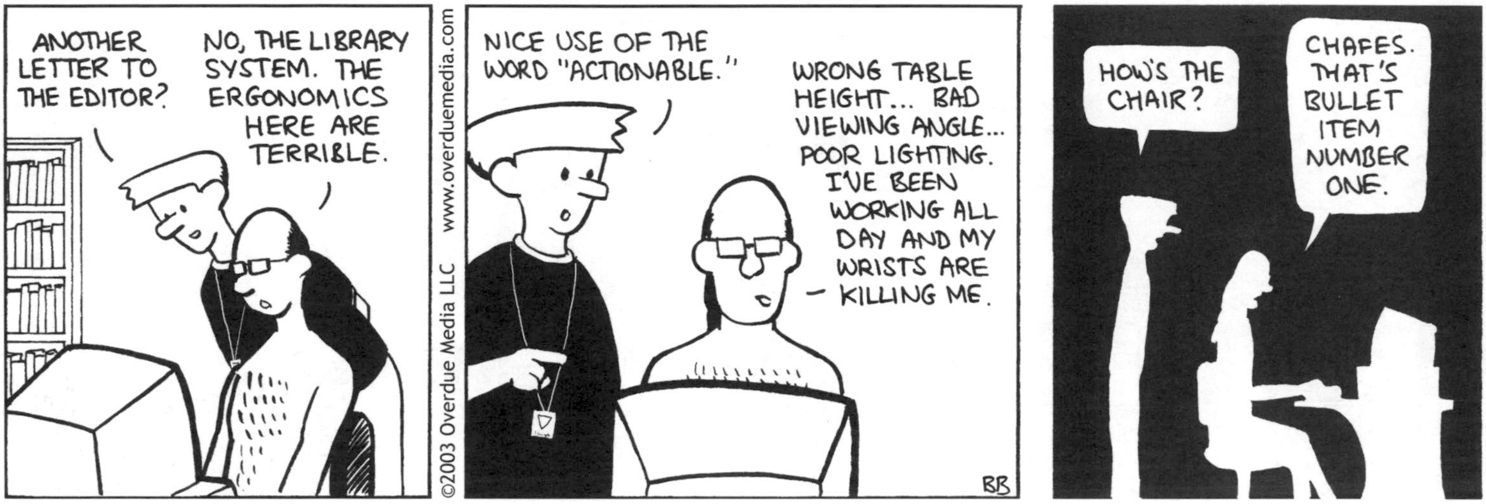
ANOTHER LETTER TO THE EDITOR?
NO, THE LIBRARY SYSTEM. THE ERGONOMICS HERE ARE TERRIBLE.
NICE USE OF THE WORD "ACTIONABLE."
WRONG TABLE HEIGHT... BAD VIEWING ANGLE... POOR LIGHTING. I'VE BEEN WORKING ALL DAY AND MY WRISTS ARE KILLING ME.
HOW'S THE CHAIR?
CHAFES. THAT'S BULLET ITEM NUMBER ONE.
©2003 Overdue Media LLC www.overduemedia.com
BB

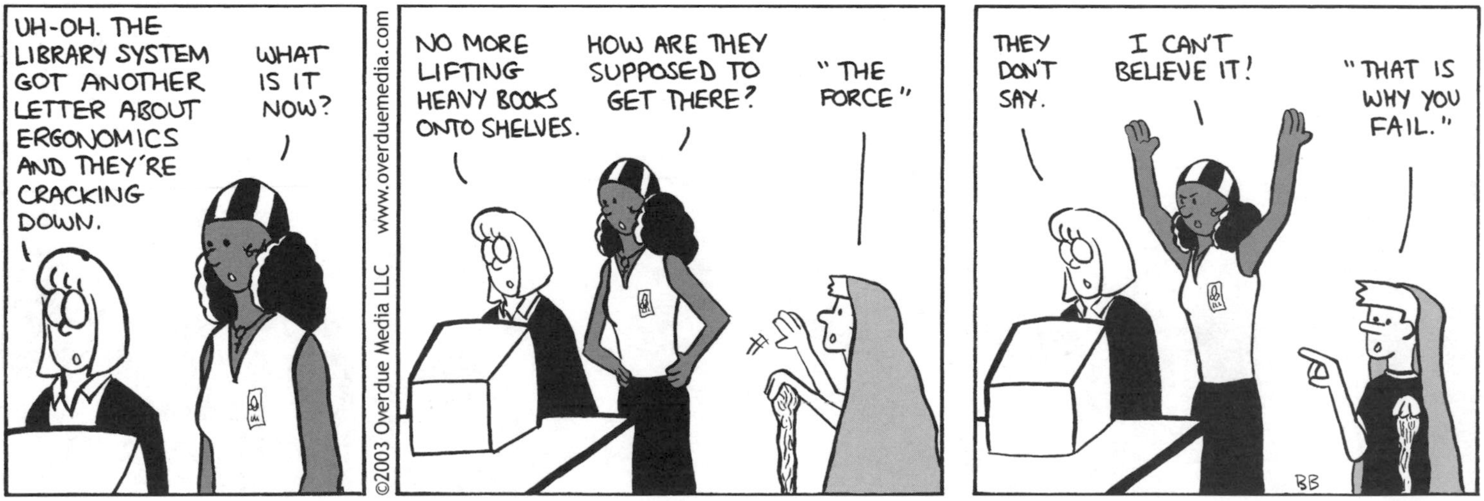
UH-OH. THE LIBRARY SYSTEM GOT ANOTHER LETTER ABOUT ERGONOMICS AND THEY'RE CRACKING DOWN.
WHAT IS IT NOW?
NO MORE LIFTING HEAVY BOOKS ONTO SHELVES.
HOW ARE THEY SUPPOSED TO GET THERE?
"THE FORCE"
THEY DON'T SAY.
I CAN'T BELIEVE IT!
"THAT IS WHY YOU FAIL."
©2003 Overdue Media LLC www.overduemedia.com
BB

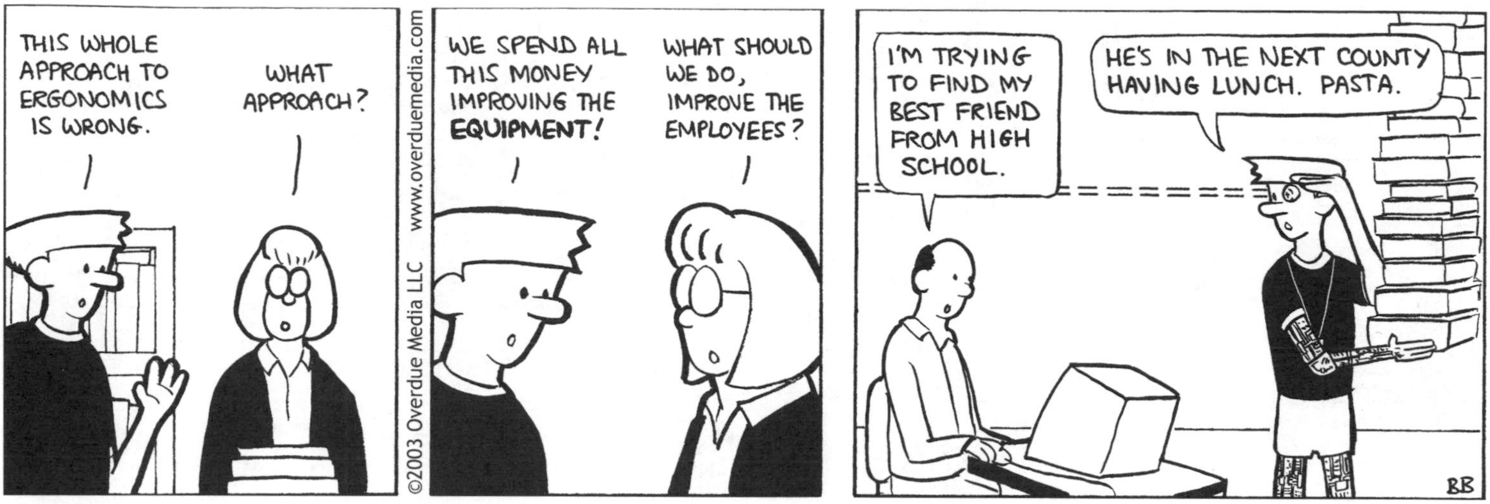
THIS WHOLE APPROACH TO ERGONOMICS IS WRONG.
WHAT APPROACH?
WE SPEND ALL THIS MONEY IMPROVING THE **EQUIPMENT**!
WHAT SHOULD WE DO, IMPROVE THE EMPLOYEES?
I'M TRYING TO FIND MY BEST FRIEND FROM HIGH SCHOOL.
HE'S IN THE NEXT COUNTY HAVING LUNCH. PASTA.
BB


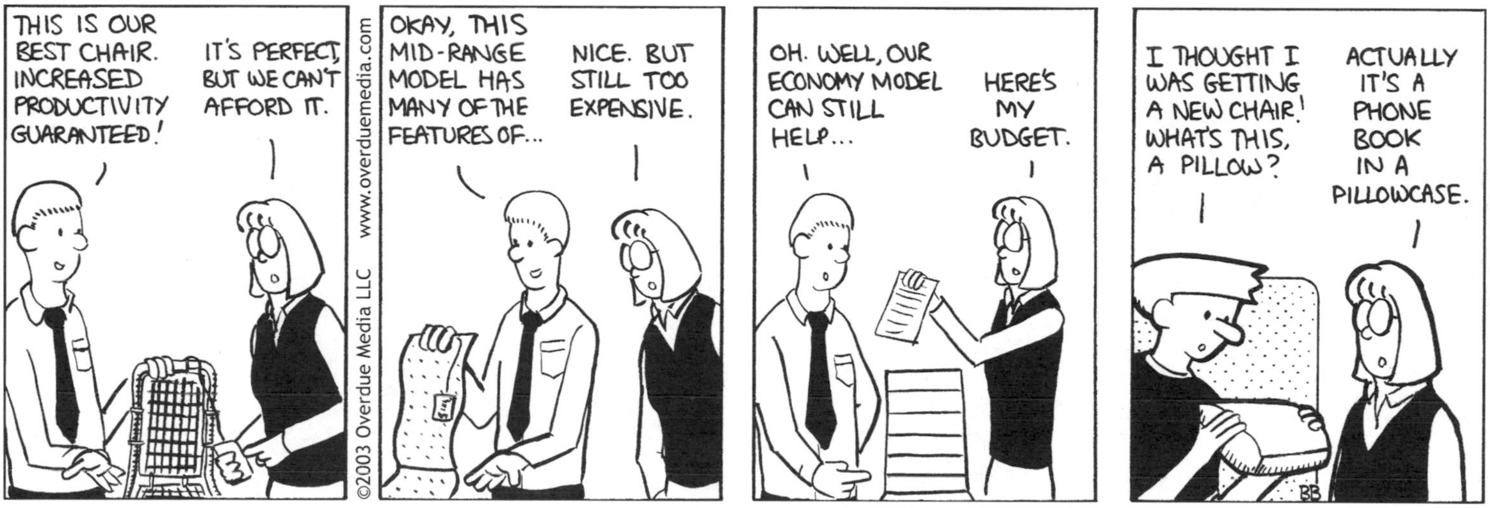
THIS IS OUR BEST CHAIR. INCREASED PRODUCTIVITY GUARANTEED!
IT'S PERFECT, BUT WE CAN'T AFFORD IT.
OKAY, THIS MID-RANGE MODEL HAS MANY OF THE FEATURES OF...
NICE. BUT STILL TOO EXPENSIVE.
OH. WELL, OUR ECONOMY MODEL CAN STILL HELP...
HERE'S MY BUDGET.
I THOUGHT I WAS GETTING A NEW CHAIR! WHAT'S THIS, A PILLOW?
ACTUALLY IT'S A PHONE BOOK IN A PILLOWCASE.
BB


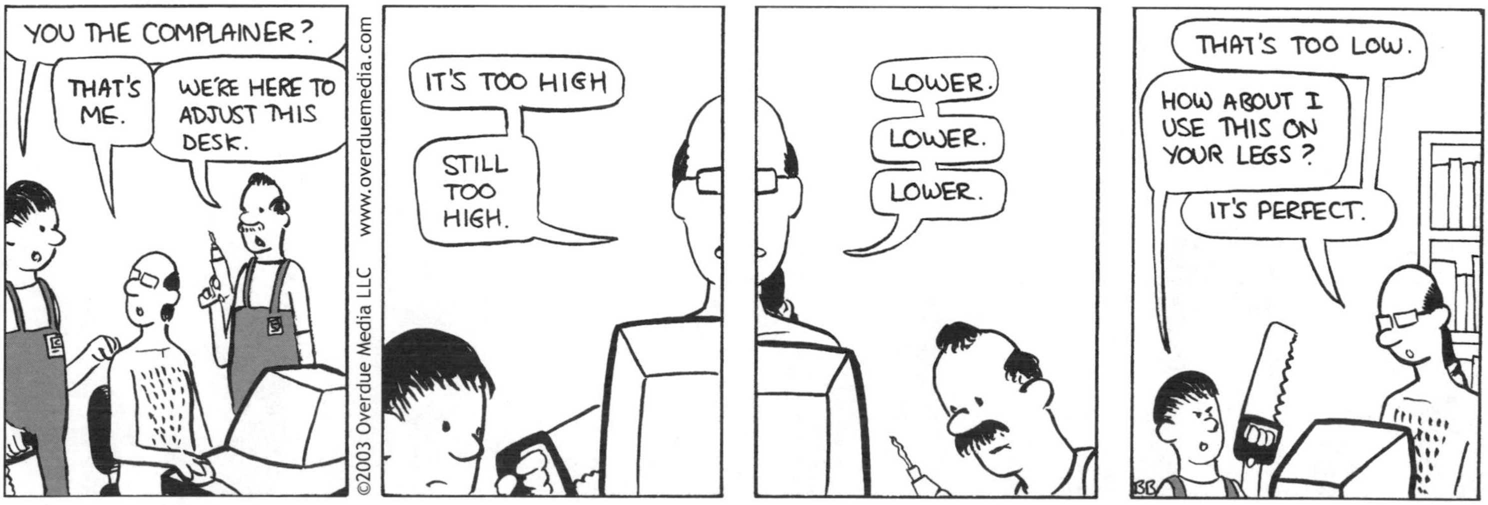
YOU THE COMPLAINER?
THAT'S ME.
WE'RE HERE TO ADJUST THIS DESK.
IT'S TOO HIGH
STILL TOO HIGH.
LOWER.
LOWER.
LOWER.
THAT'S TOO LOW.
HOW ABOUT I USE THIS ON YOUR LEGS?
IT'S PERFECT.
BB

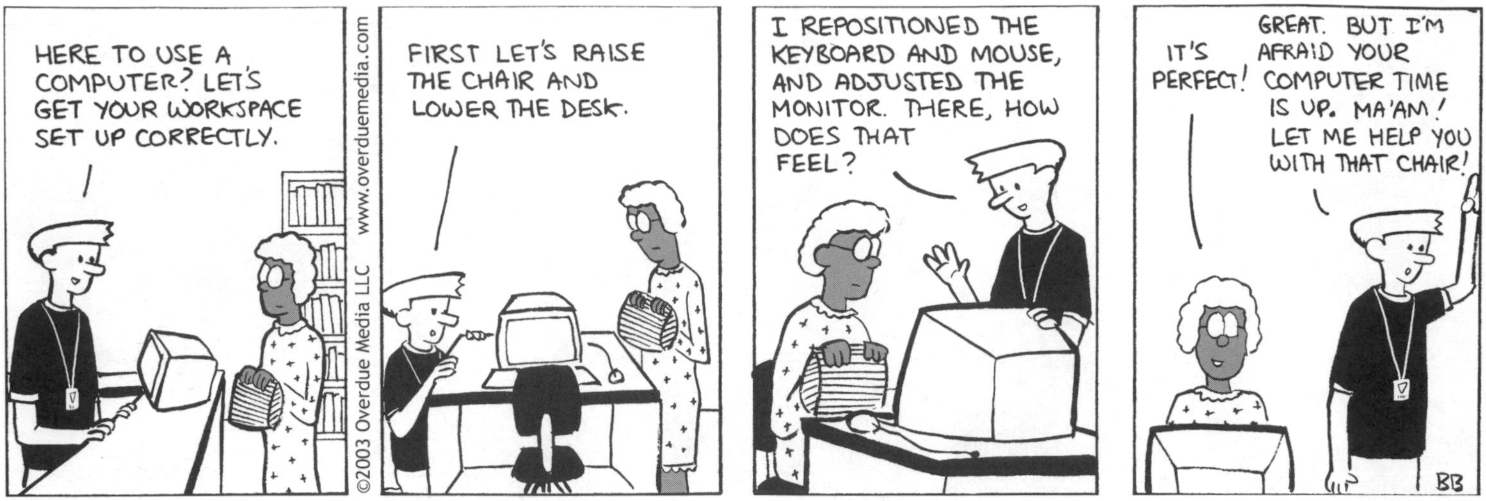
HERE TO USE A COMPUTER? LET'S GET YOUR WORKSPACE SET UP CORRECTLY.
©2003 Overdue Media LLC www.overduemedia.com
FIRST LET'S RAISE THE CHAIR AND LOWER THE DESK.
I REPOSITIONED THE KEYBOARD AND MOUSE, AND ADJUSTED THE MONITOR. THERE, HOW DOES THAT FEEL?
IT'S PERFECT!
GREAT. BUT I'M AFRAID YOUR COMPUTER TIME IS UP. MA'AM! LET ME HELP YOU WITH THAT CHAIR!
BB

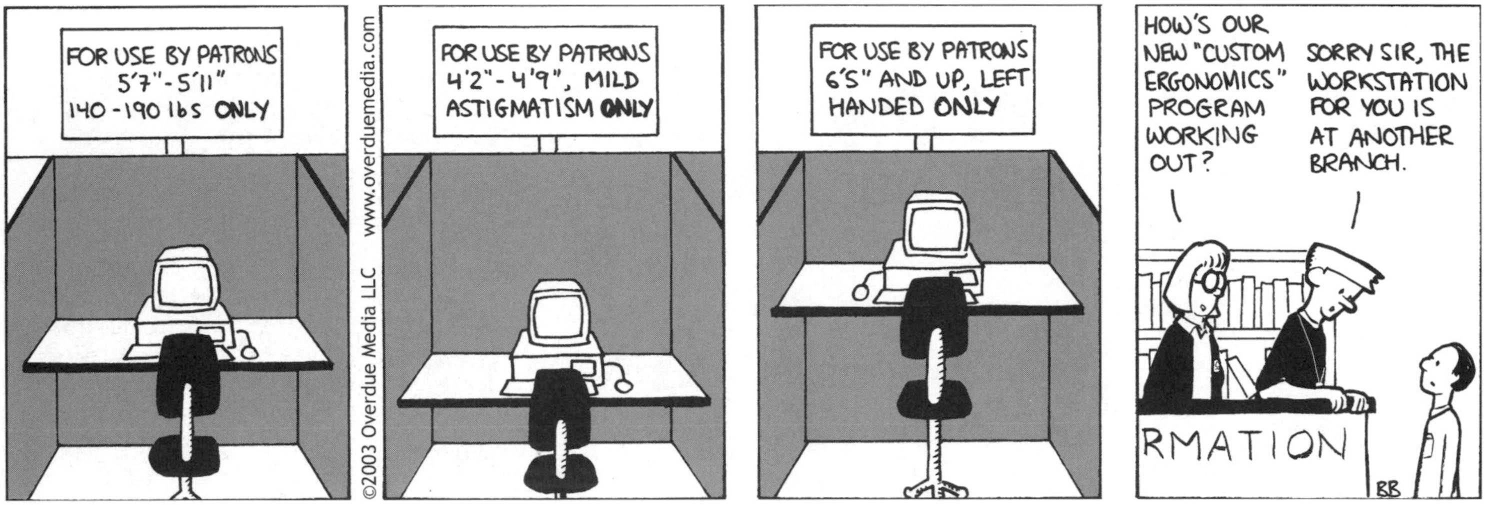
FOR USE BY PATRONS 5'7"-5'11" 140-190 lbs ONLY
©2003 Overdue Media LLC www.overduemedia.com
FOR USE BY PATRONS 4'2"-4'9", MILD ASTIGMATISM ONLY
FOR USE BY PATRONS 6'5" AND UP, LEFT HANDED ONLY
HOW'S OUR NEW "CUSTOM ERGONOMICS" PROGRAM WORKING OUT?
SORRY SIR, THE WORKSTATION FOR YOU IS AT ANOTHER BRANCH.
RMATION
BB

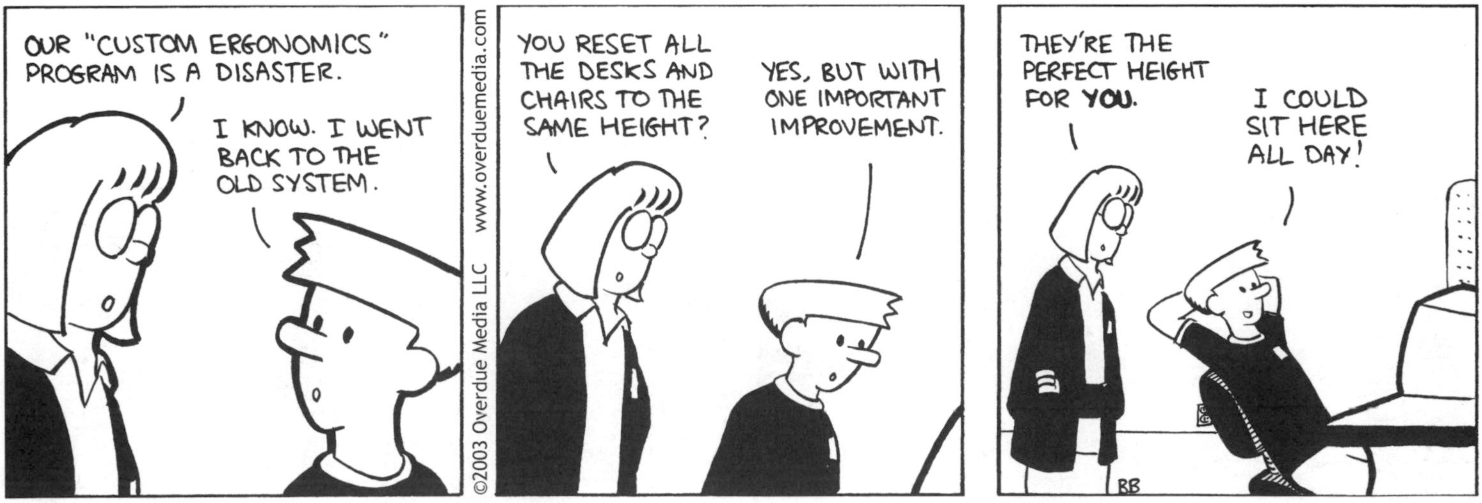
OUR "CUSTOM ERGONOMICS" PROGRAM IS A DISASTER.
I KNOW. I WENT BACK TO THE OLD SYSTEM.
©2003 Overdue Media LLC www.overduemedia.com
YOU RESET ALL THE DESKS AND CHAIRS TO THE SAME HEIGHT?
YES, BUT WITH ONE IMPORTANT IMPROVEMENT.
THEY'RE THE PERFECT HEIGHT FOR YOU.
I COULD SIT HERE ALL DAY!
BB

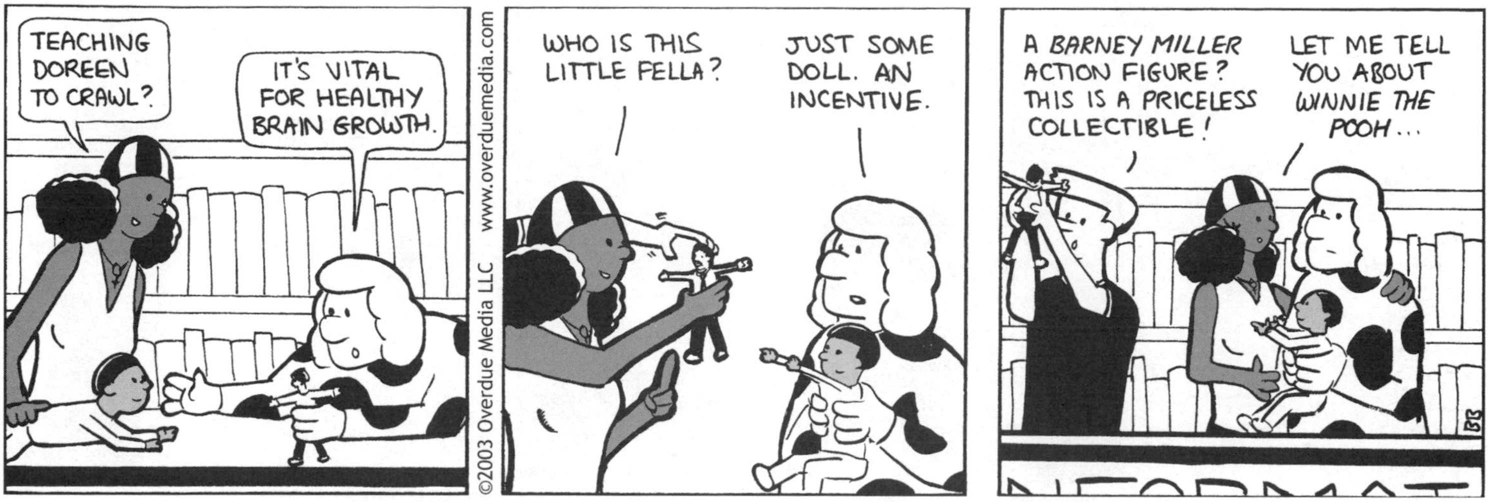
TEACHING DOREEN TO CRAWL?
IT'S VITAL FOR HEALTHY BRAIN GROWTH.
WHO IS THIS LITTLE FELLA?
JUST SOME DOLL. AN INCENTIVE.
A *BARNEY MILLER* ACTION FIGURE? THIS IS A PRICELESS COLLECTIBLE!
LET ME TELL YOU ABOUT *WINNIE THE POOH*...
©2003 Overdue Media LLC www.overduemedia.com
BB

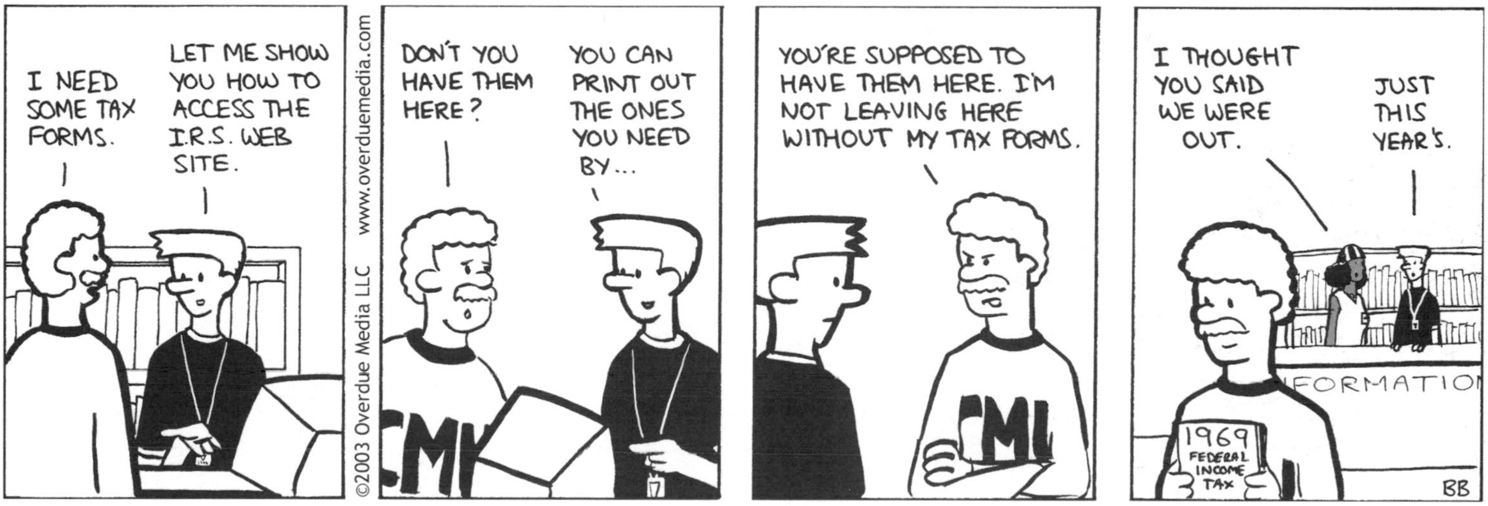
I NEED SOME TAX FORMS.
LET ME SHOW YOU HOW TO ACCESS THE I.R.S. WEB SITE.
DON'T YOU HAVE THEM HERE?
YOU CAN PRINT OUT THE ONES YOU NEED BY...
YOU'RE SUPPOSED TO HAVE THEM HERE. I'M NOT LEAVING HERE WITHOUT MY TAX FORMS.
I THOUGHT YOU SAID WE WERE OUT.
JUST THIS YEAR'S.
1969 FEDERAL INCOME TAX
©2003 Overdue Media LLC www.overduemedia.com
BB

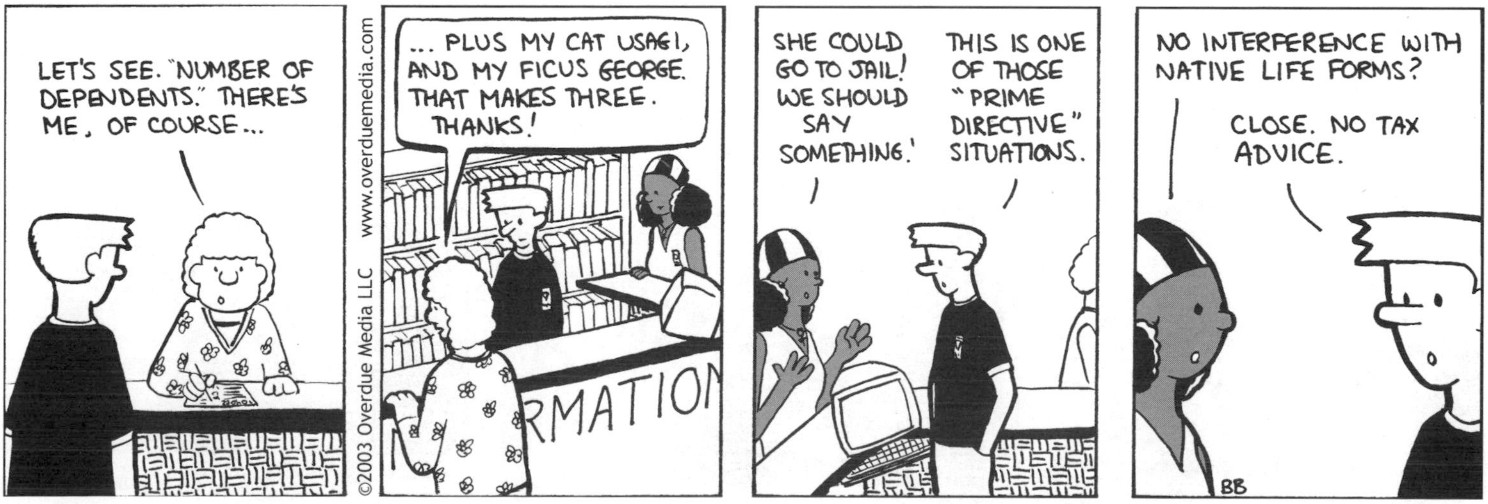
LET'S SEE. "NUMBER OF DEPENDENTS." THERE'S ME, OF COURSE...
... PLUS MY CAT USAGI, AND MY FICUS GEORGE. THAT MAKES THREE. THANKS!
SHE COULD GO TO JAIL! WE SHOULD SAY SOMETHING!
THIS IS ONE OF THOSE "PRIME DIRECTIVE" SITUATIONS.
NO INTERFERENCE WITH NATIVE LIFE FORMS?
CLOSE. NO TAX ADVICE.
©2003 Overdue Media LLC www.overduemedia.com
BB

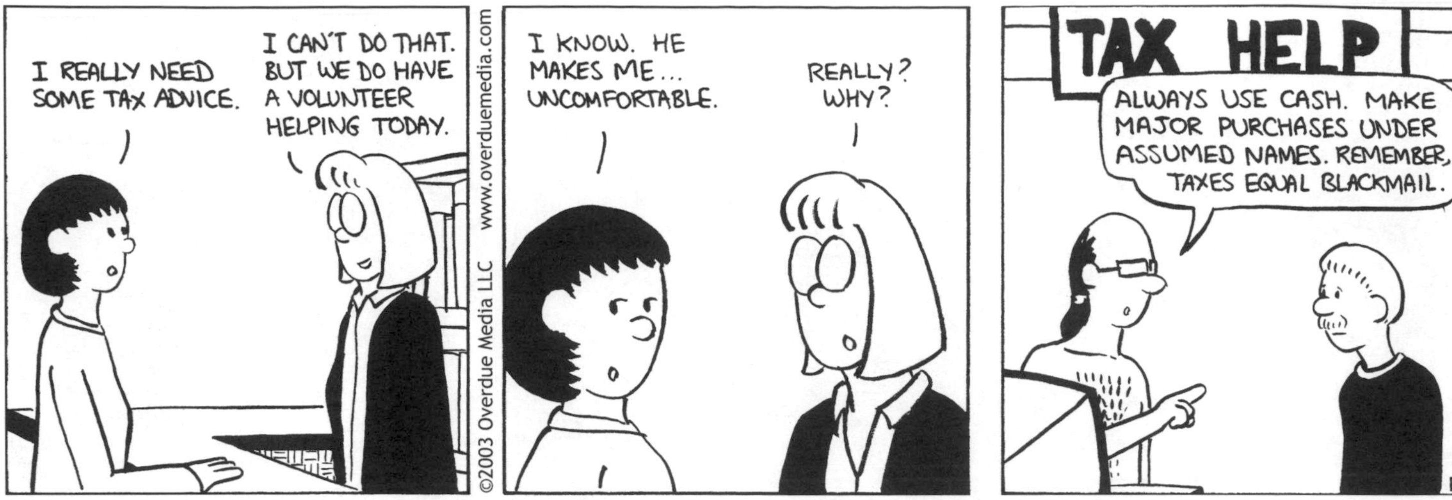
I REALLY NEED SOME TAX ADVICE.
I CAN'T DO THAT. BUT WE DO HAVE A VOLUNTEER HELPING TODAY.
©2003 Overdue Media LLC www.overduemedia.com
I KNOW. HE MAKES ME... UNCOMFORTABLE.
REALLY? WHY?
TAX HELP
ALWAYS USE CASH. MAKE MAJOR PURCHASES UNDER ASSUMED NAMES. REMEMBER, TAXES EQUAL BLACKMAIL.
BB

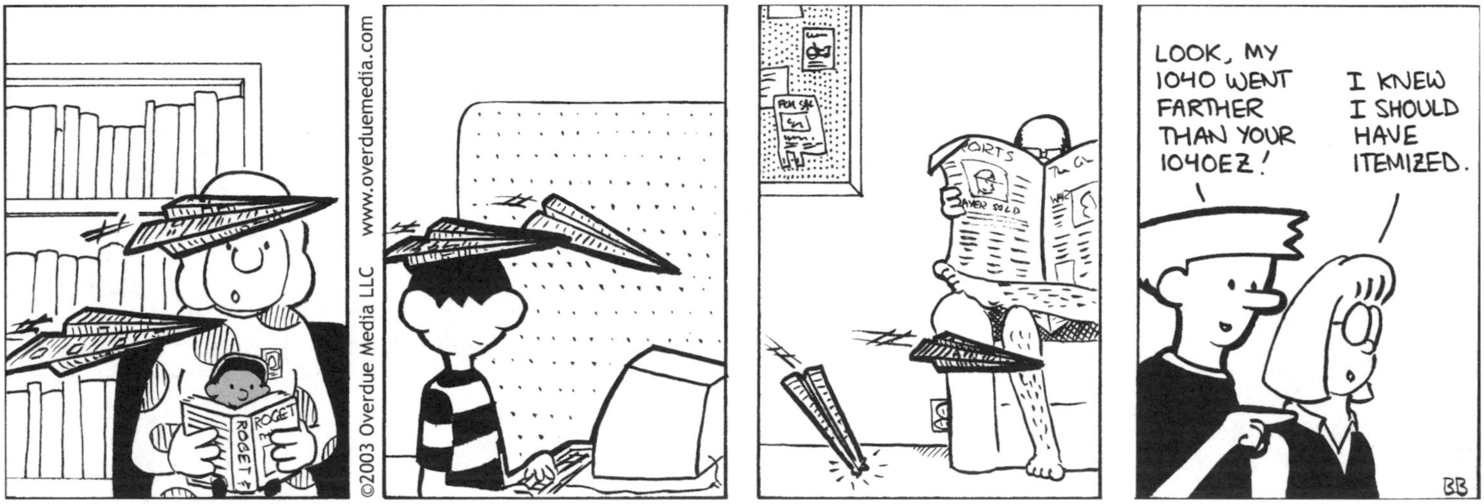
©2003 Overdue Media LLC www.overduemedia.com
LOOK, MY 1040 WENT FARTHER THAN YOUR 1040EZ!
I KNEW I SHOULD HAVE ITEMIZED.
BB

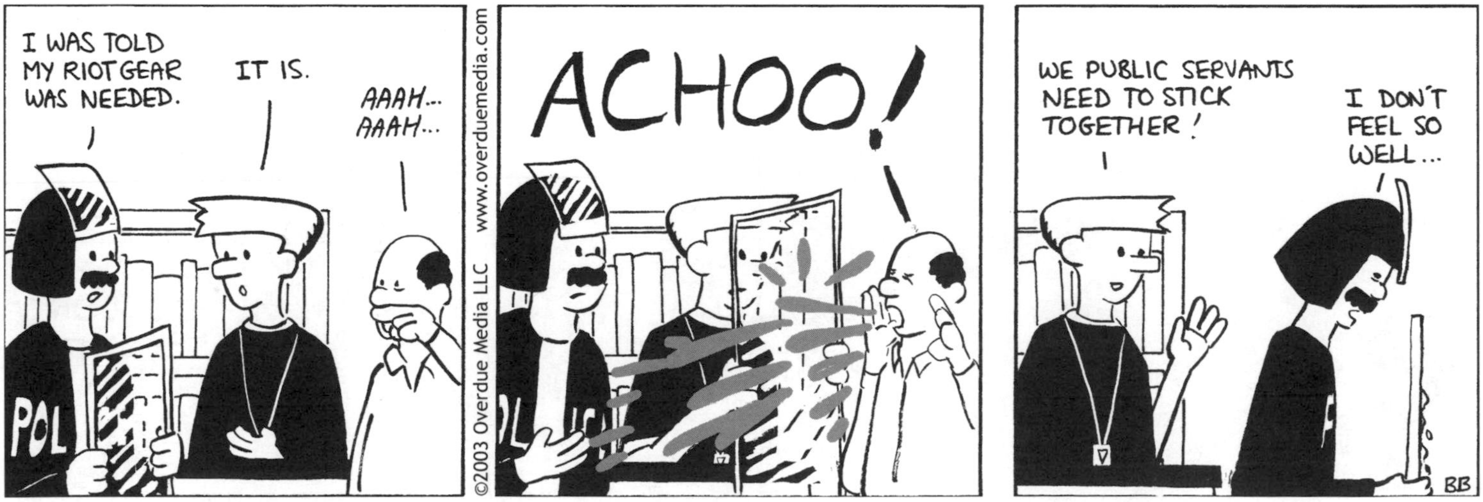
I WAS TOLD MY RIOT GEAR WAS NEEDED.
IT IS.
AAAH... AAAH...
©2003 Overdue Media LLC www.overduemedia.com
ACHOO!
WE PUBLIC SERVANTS NEED TO STICK TOGETHER!
I DON'T FEEL SO WELL...
BB

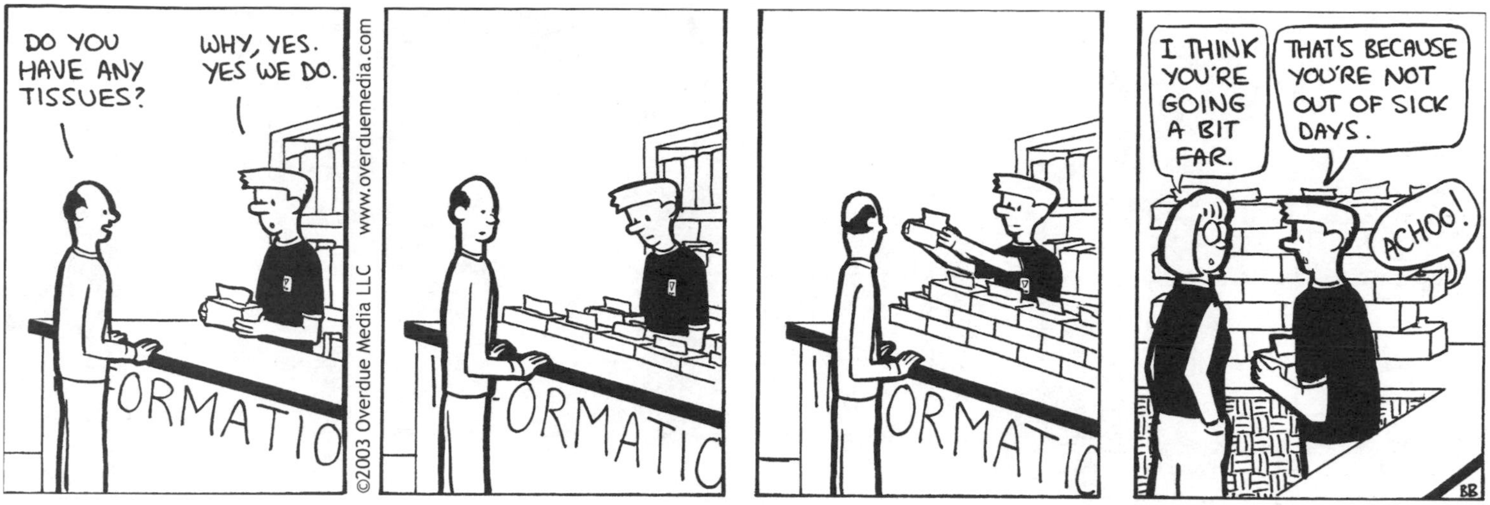
DO YOU HAVE ANY TISSUES?
WHY, YES. YES WE DO.
©2003 Overdue Media LLC www.overduemedia.com
ORMATIO
I THINK YOU'RE GOING A BIT FAR.
THAT'S BECAUSE YOU'RE NOT OUT OF SICK DAYS.
ACHOO!
BB

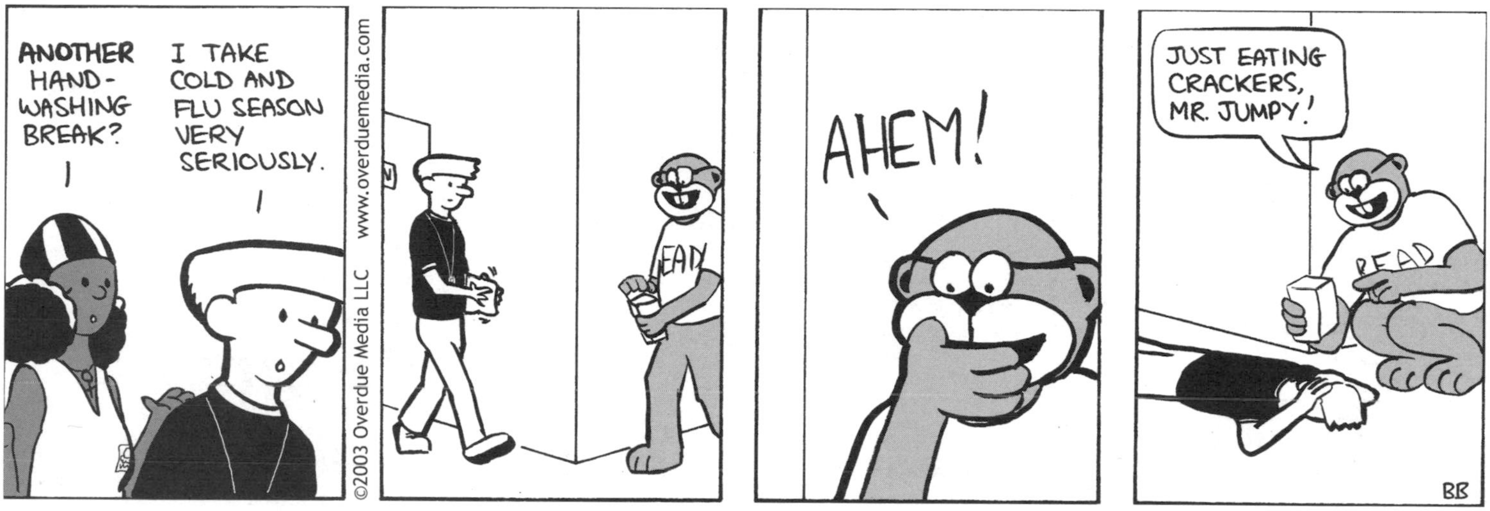
ANOTHER HAND-WASHING BREAK?
I TAKE COLD AND FLU SEASON VERY SERIOUSLY.
©2003 Overdue Media LLC www.overduemedia.com
AHEM!
JUST EATING CRACKERS, MR. JUMPY!
BB

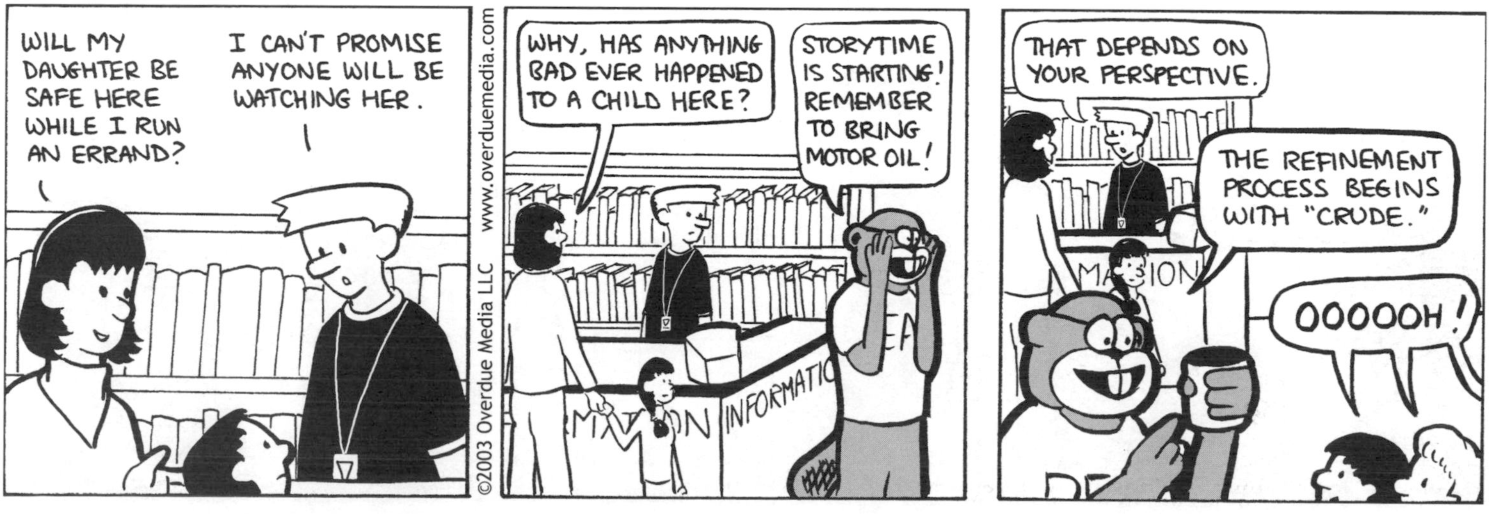
WILL MY DAUGHTER BE SAFE HERE WHILE I RUN AN ERRAND?
I CAN'T PROMISE ANYONE WILL BE WATCHING HER.
©2003 Overdue Media LLC www.overduemedia.com
WHY, HAS ANYTHING BAD EVER HAPPENED TO A CHILD HERE?
STORYTIME IS STARTING! REMEMBER TO BRING MOTOR OIL!
INFORMATIO
THAT DEPENDS ON YOUR PERSPECTIVE.
THE REFINEMENT PROCESS BEGINS WITH "CRUDE."
OOOOOH!

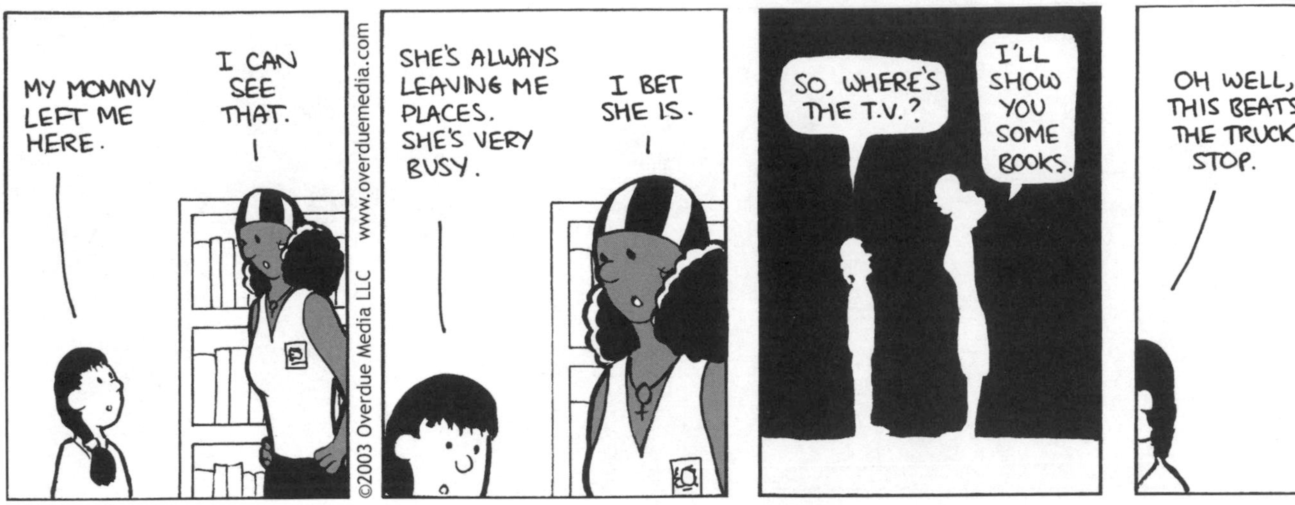
MY MOMMY LEFT ME HERE.
I CAN SEE THAT.
©2003 Overdue Media LLC www.overduemedia.com
SHE'S ALWAYS LEAVING ME PLACES. SHE'S VERY BUSY.
I BET SHE IS.
SO, WHERE'S THE T.V.?
I'LL SHOW YOU SOME BOOKS.
OH WELL, THIS BEATS THE TRUCK STOP.
BB

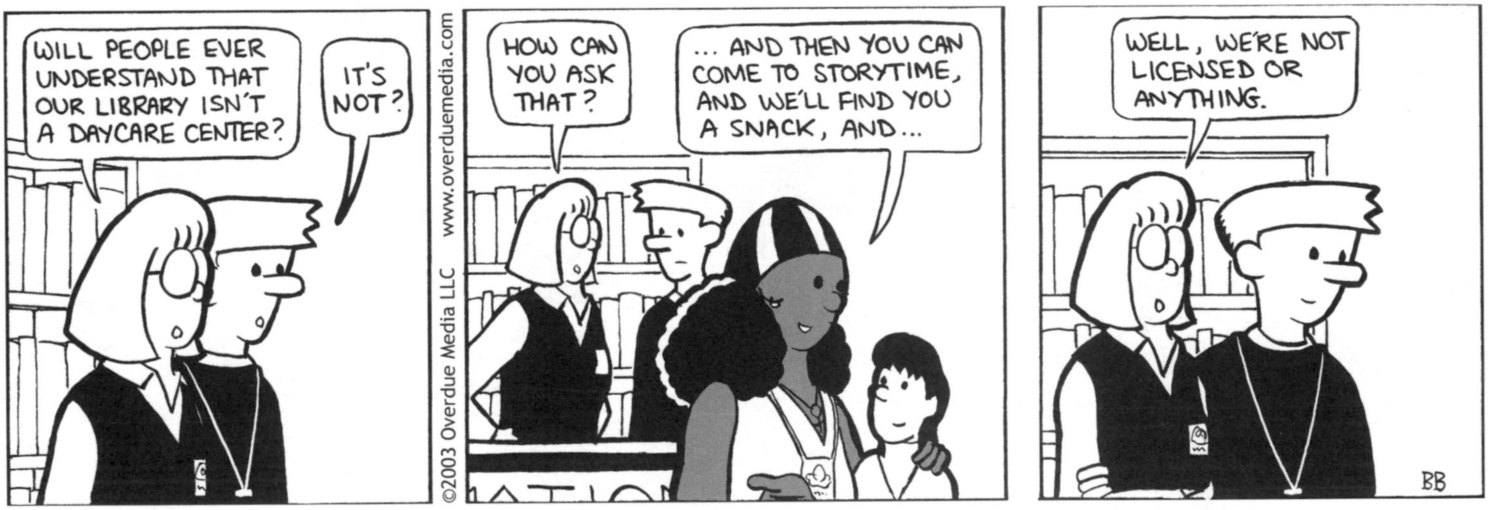
WILL PEOPLE EVER UNDERSTAND THAT OUR LIBRARY ISN'T A DAYCARE CENTER?
IT'S NOT?
©2003 Overdue Media LLC www.overduemedia.com
HOW CAN YOU ASK THAT?
... AND THEN YOU CAN COME TO STORYTIME, AND WE'LL FIND YOU A SNACK, AND...
WELL, WE'RE NOT LICENSED OR ANYTHING.
BB

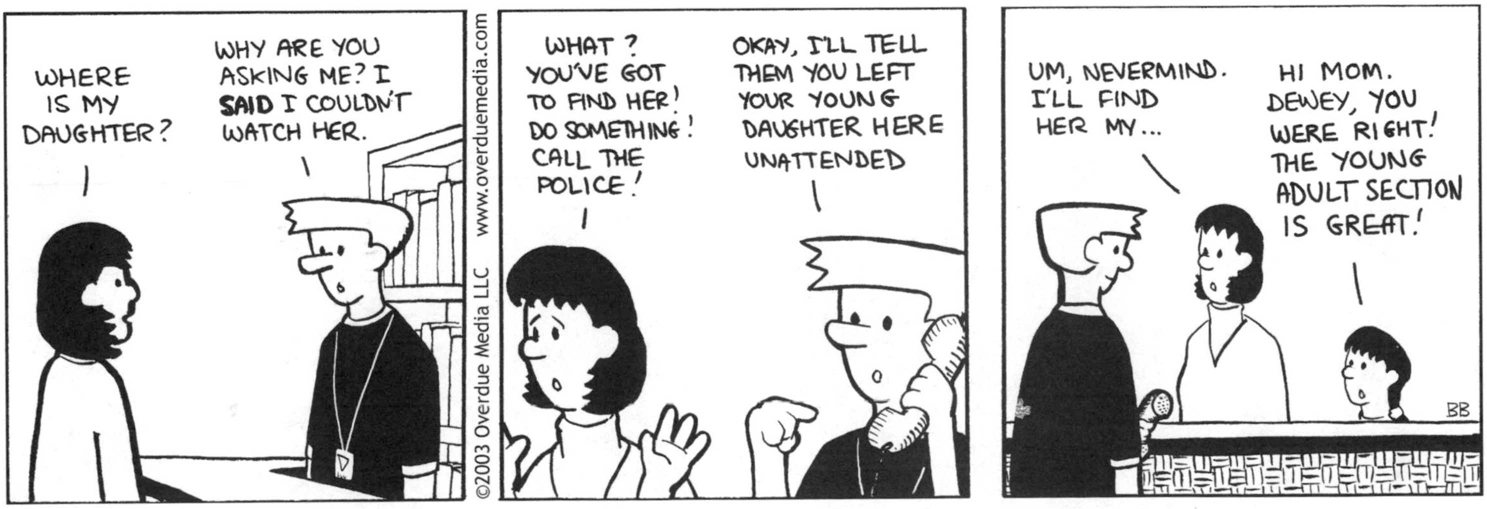
WHERE IS MY DAUGHTER?
WHY ARE YOU ASKING ME? I **SAID** I COULDN'T WATCH HER.
©2003 Overdue Media LLC www.overduemedia.com
WHAT? YOU'VE GOT TO FIND HER! DO SOMETHING! CALL THE POLICE!
OKAY, I'LL TELL THEM YOU LEFT YOUR YOUNG DAUGHTER HERE UNATTENDED
UM, NEVERMIND. I'LL FIND HER MY...
HI MOM. DEWEY, YOU WERE RIGHT! THE YOUNG ADULT SECTION IS GREAT!
BB

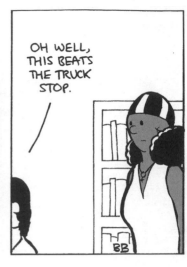

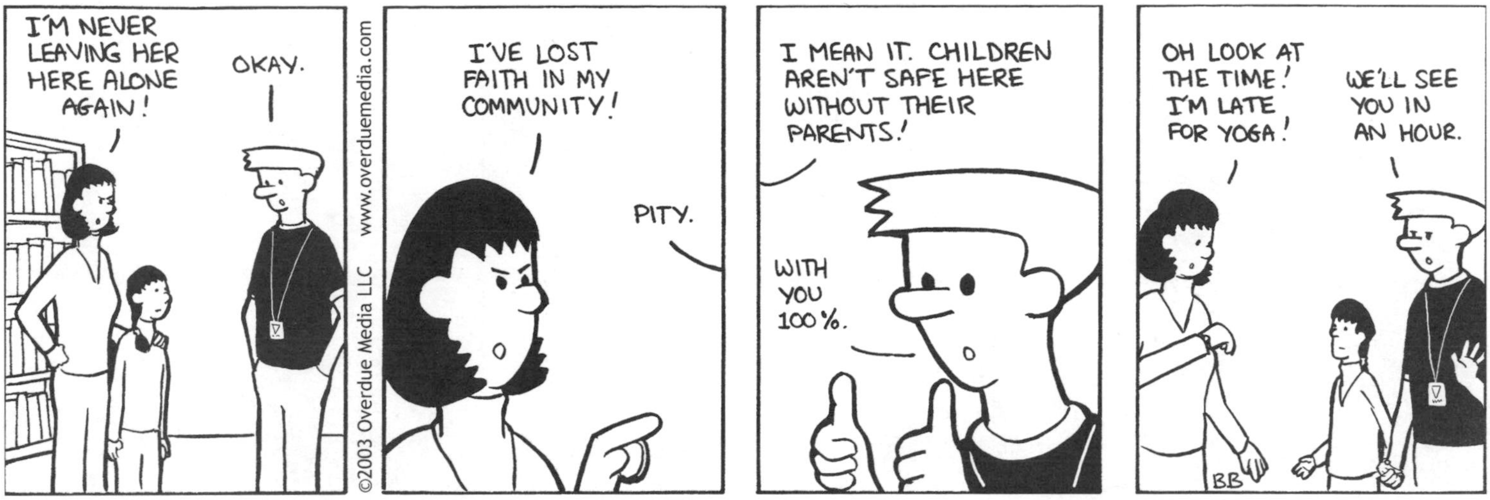
I'M NEVER LEAVING HER HERE ALONE AGAIN!
OKAY.
©2003 Overdue Media LLC www.overduemedia.com
I'VE LOST FAITH IN MY COMMUNITY!
PITY.
I MEAN IT. CHILDREN AREN'T SAFE HERE WITHOUT THEIR PARENTS!
WITH YOU 100%.
OH LOOK AT THE TIME! I'M LATE FOR YOGA!
WE'LL SEE YOU IN AN HOUR.
BB

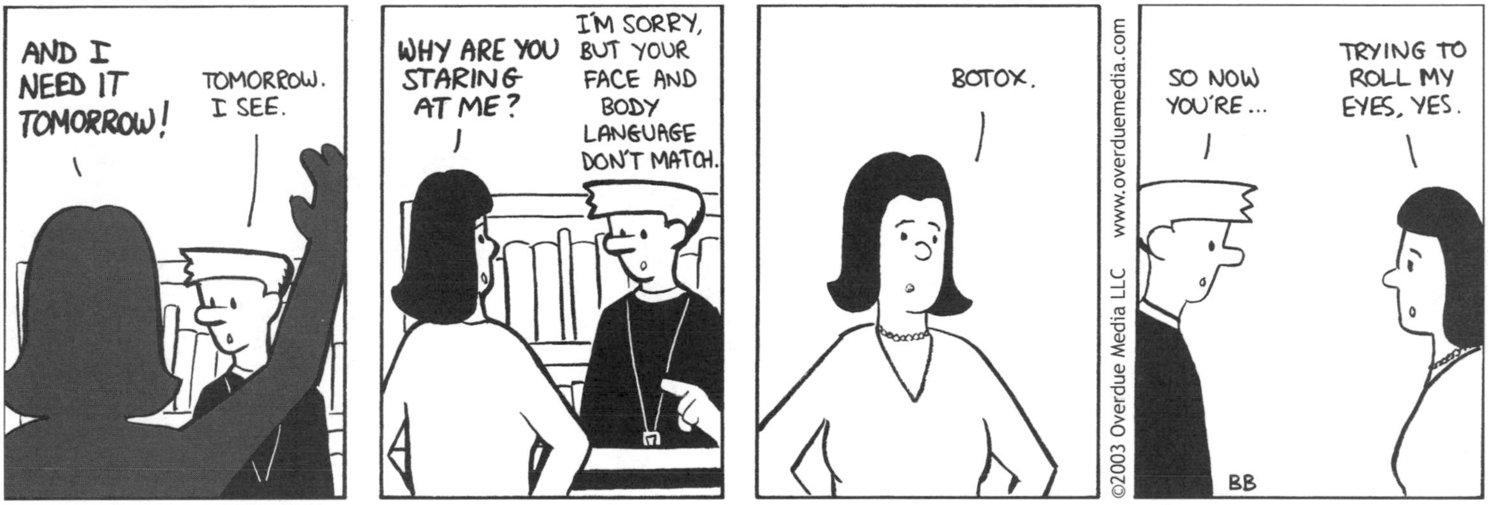
AND I NEED IT TOMORROW!
TOMORROW. I SEE.
WHY ARE YOU STARING AT ME?
I'M SORRY, BUT YOUR FACE AND BODY LANGUAGE DON'T MATCH.
BOTOX.
©2003 Overdue Media LLC www.overduemedia.com
SO NOW YOU'RE...
TRYING TO ROLL MY EYES, YES.
BB

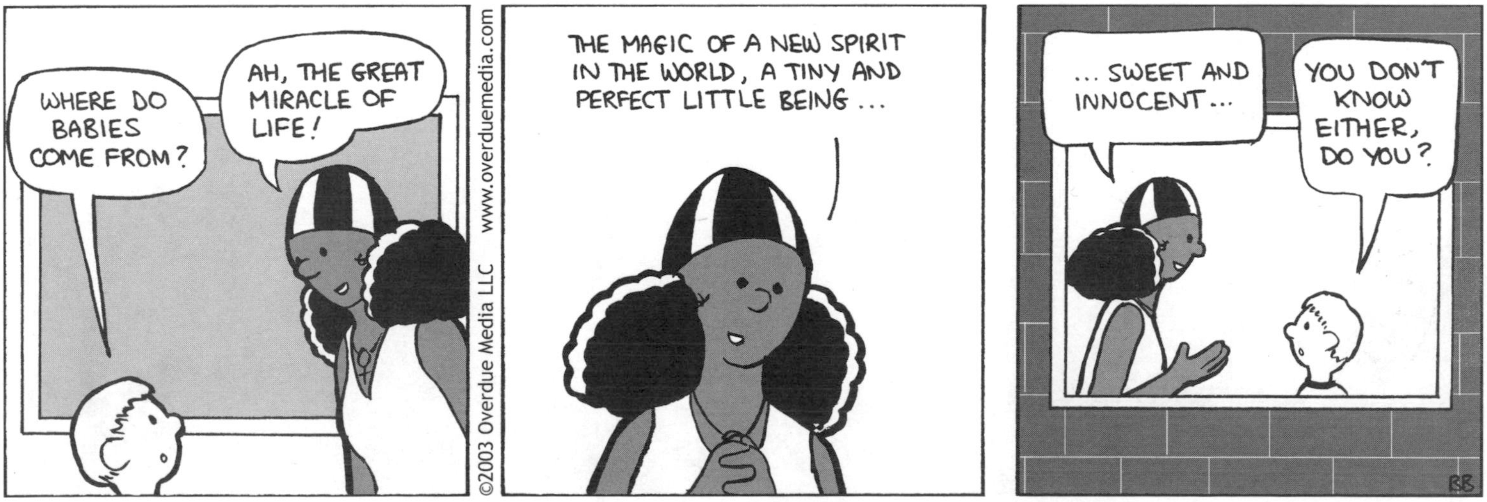
WHERE DO BABIES COME FROM?
AH, THE GREAT MIRACLE OF LIFE!
©2003 Overdue Media LLC www.overduemedia.com
THE MAGIC OF A NEW SPIRIT IN THE WORLD, A TINY AND PERFECT LITTLE BEING...
... SWEET AND INNOCENT...
YOU DON'T KNOW EITHER, DO YOU?
BB

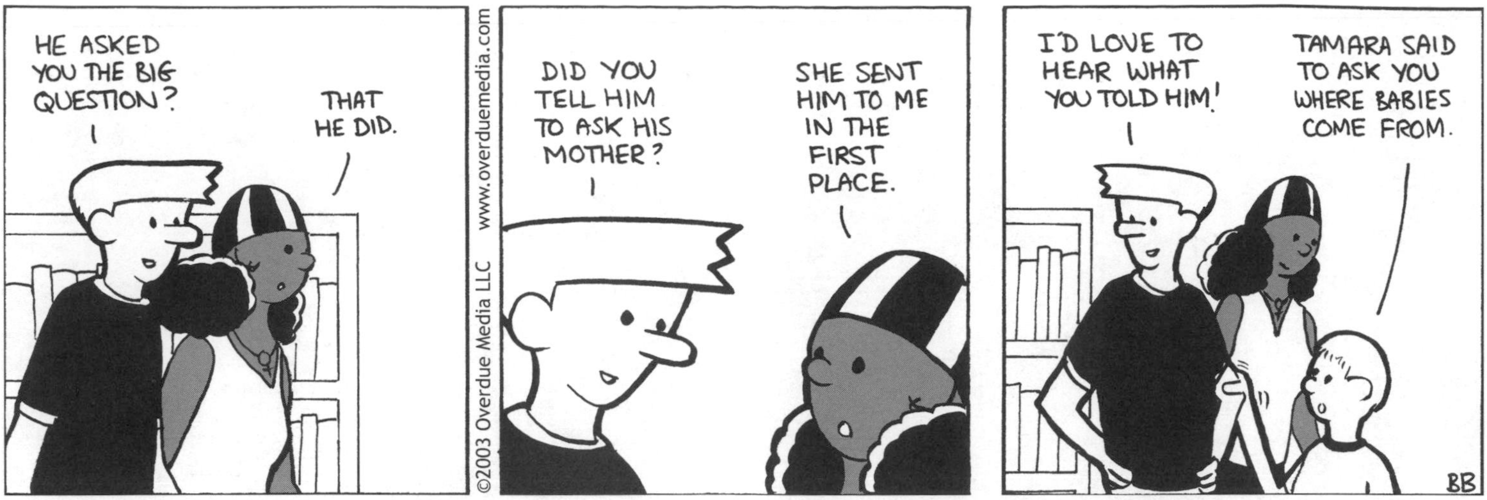
HE ASKED YOU THE BIG QUESTION?
THAT HE DID.
©2003 Overdue Media LLC www.overduemedia.com
DID YOU TELL HIM TO ASK HIS MOTHER?
SHE SENT HIM TO ME IN THE FIRST PLACE.
I'D LOVE TO HEAR WHAT YOU TOLD HIM!
TAMARA SAID TO ASK YOU WHERE BABIES COME FROM.
BB

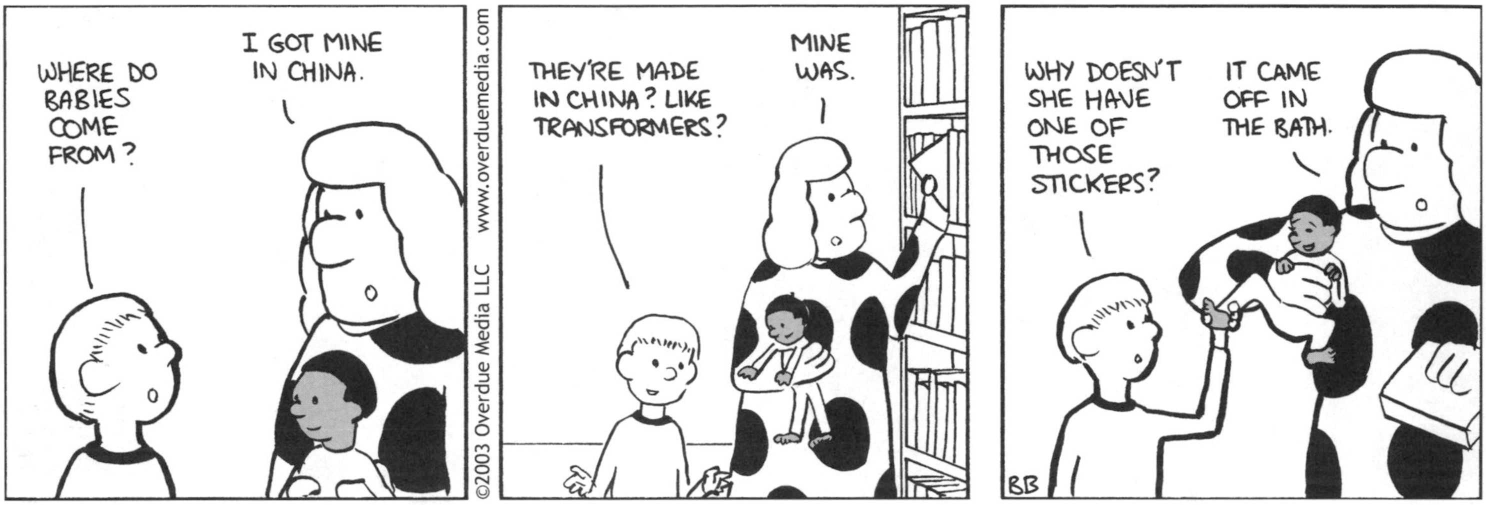
WHERE DO BABIES COME FROM?
I GOT MINE IN CHINA.
©2003 Overdue Media LLC www.overduemedia.com
THEY'RE MADE IN CHINA? LIKE TRANSFORMERS?
MINE WAS.
WHY DOESN'T SHE HAVE ONE OF THOSE STICKERS?
IT CAME OFF IN THE BATH.
BB

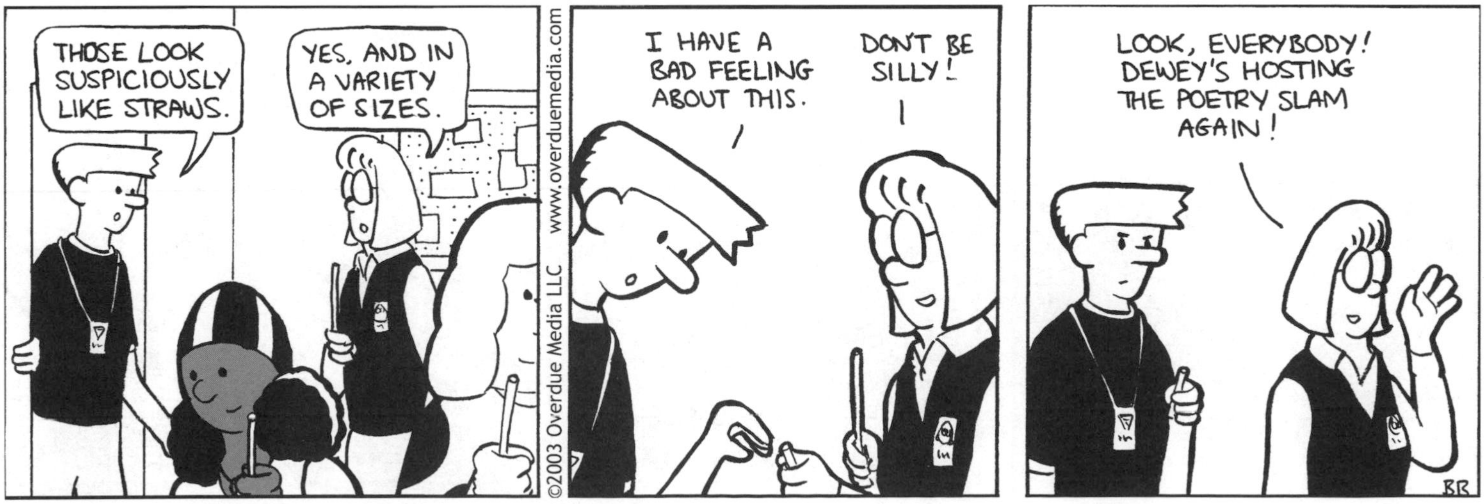
THOSE LOOK SUSPICIOUSLY LIKE STRAWS.
YES, AND IN A VARIETY OF SIZES.
©2003 Overdue Media LLC www.overduemedia.com
I HAVE A BAD FEELING ABOUT THIS.
DON'T BE SILLY!
LOOK, EVERYBODY! DEWEY'S HOSTING THE POETRY SLAM AGAIN!
BB

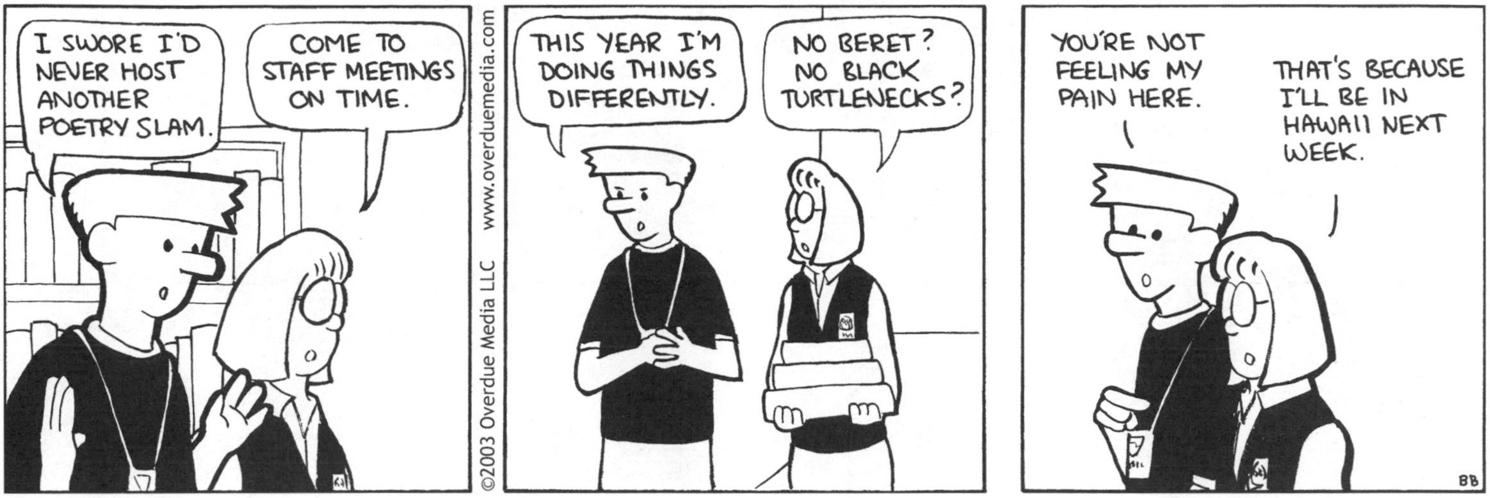
I SWORE I'D NEVER HOST ANOTHER POETRY SLAM.
COME TO STAFF MEETINGS ON TIME.
©2003 Overdue Media LLC www.overduemedia.com
THIS YEAR I'M DOING THINGS DIFFERENTLY.
NO BERET? NO BLACK TURTLENECKS?
YOU'RE NOT FEELING MY PAIN HERE.
THAT'S BECAUSE I'LL BE IN HAWAII NEXT WEEK.
BB

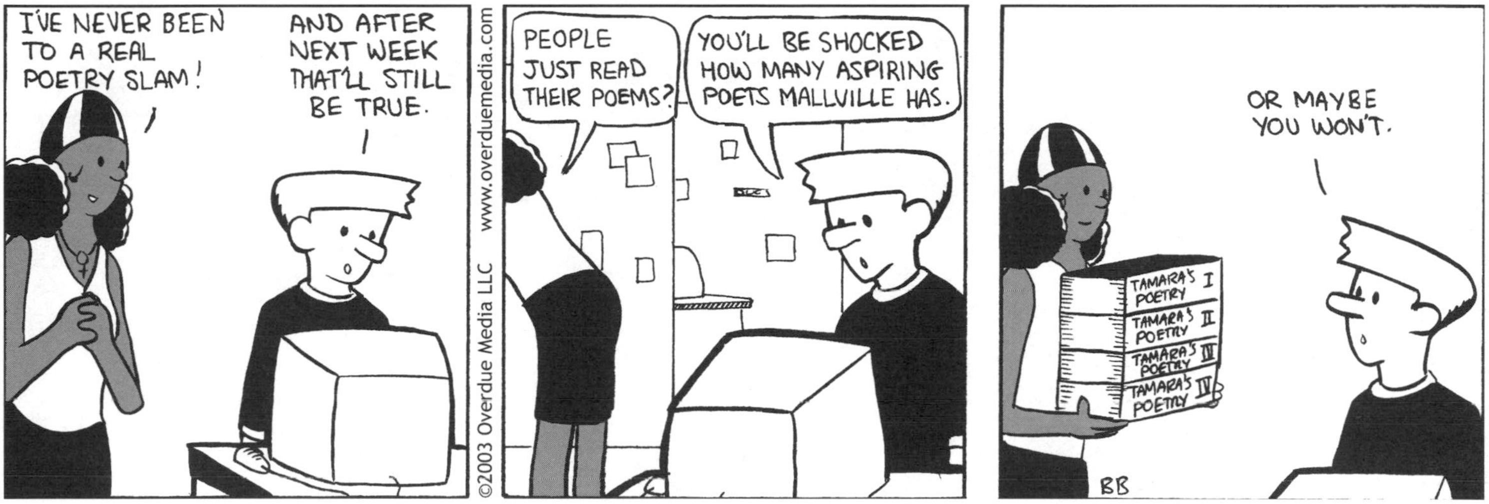
I'VE NEVER BEEN TO A REAL POETRY SLAM!
AND AFTER NEXT WEEK THAT'LL STILL BE TRUE.
©2003 Overdue Media LLC www.overduemedia.com
PEOPLE JUST READ THEIR POEMS?
YOU'LL BE SHOCKED HOW MANY ASPIRING POETS MALLVILLE HAS.
TAMARA'S POETRY I
TAMARA'S POETRY II
TAMARA'S POETRY III
TAMARA'S POETRY IV
OR MAYBE YOU WON'T.
BB

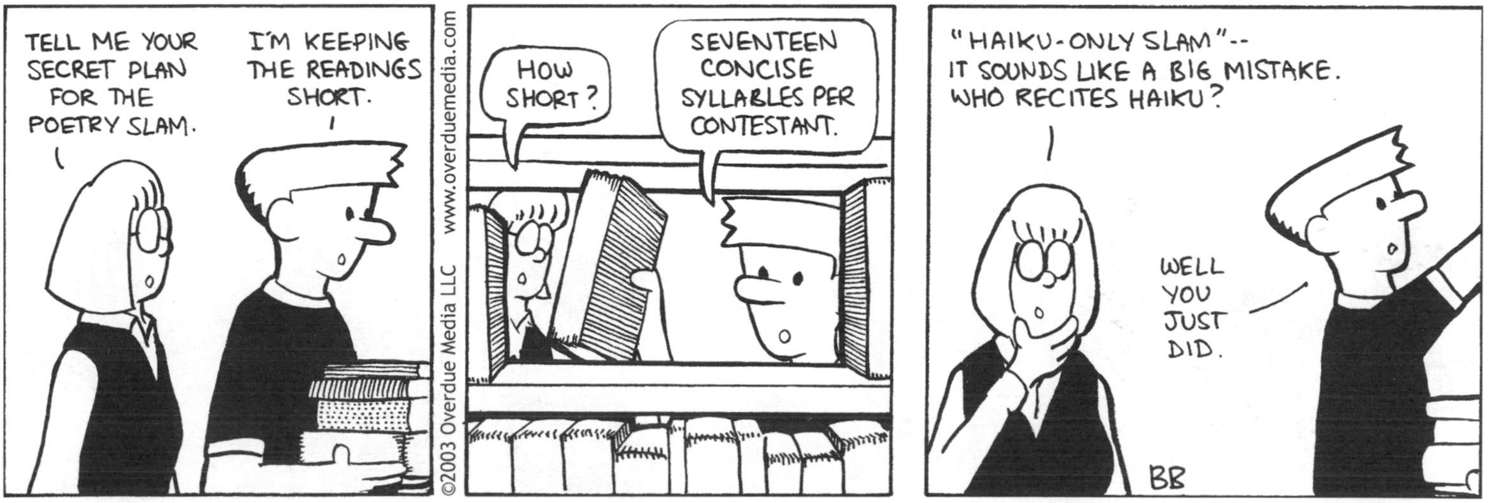
TELL ME YOUR SECRET PLAN FOR THE POETRY SLAM.
I'M KEEPING THE READINGS SHORT.
©2003 Overdue Media LLC www.overduemedia.com
HOW SHORT?
SEVENTEEN CONCISE SYLLABLES PER CONTESTANT.
"HAIKU-ONLY SLAM"-- IT SOUNDS LIKE A BIG MISTAKE. WHO RECITES HAIKU?
WELL YOU JUST DID.
BB

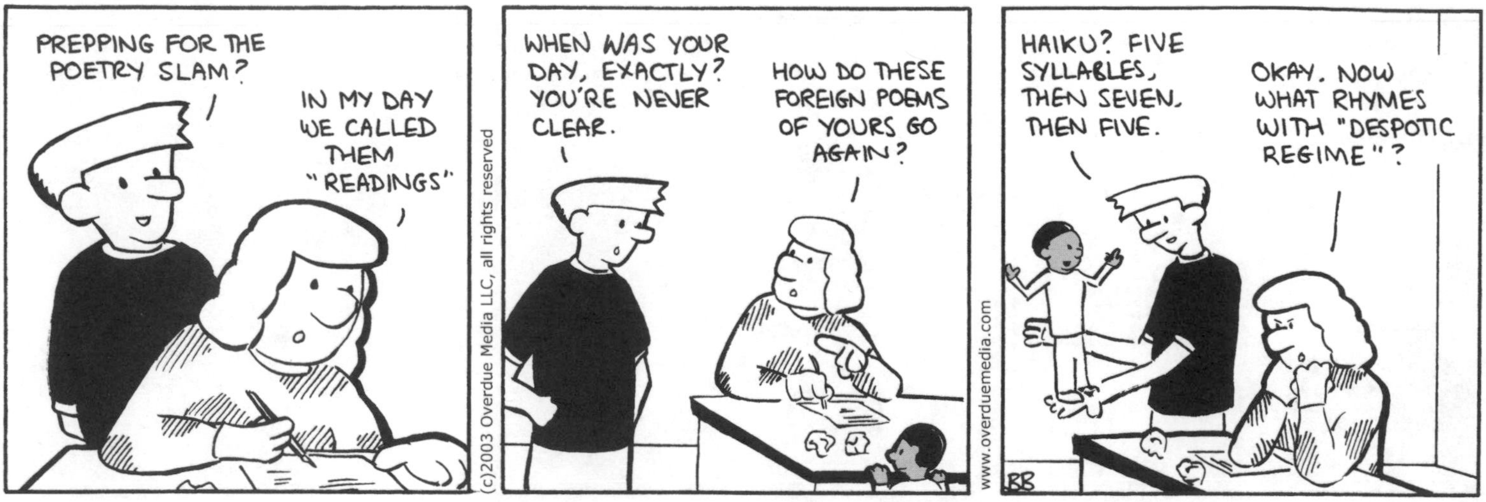
PREPPING FOR THE POETRY SLAM?
IN MY DAY WE CALLED THEM "READINGS"
WHEN WAS YOUR DAY, EXACTLY? YOU'RE NEVER CLEAR.
HOW DO THESE FOREIGN POEMS OF YOURS GO AGAIN?
HAIKU? FIVE SYLLABLES, THEN SEVEN, THEN FIVE.
OKAY. NOW WHAT RHYMES WITH "DESPOTIC REGIME"?
BB
(c)2003 Overdue Media LLC, all rights reserved
www.overduemedia.com

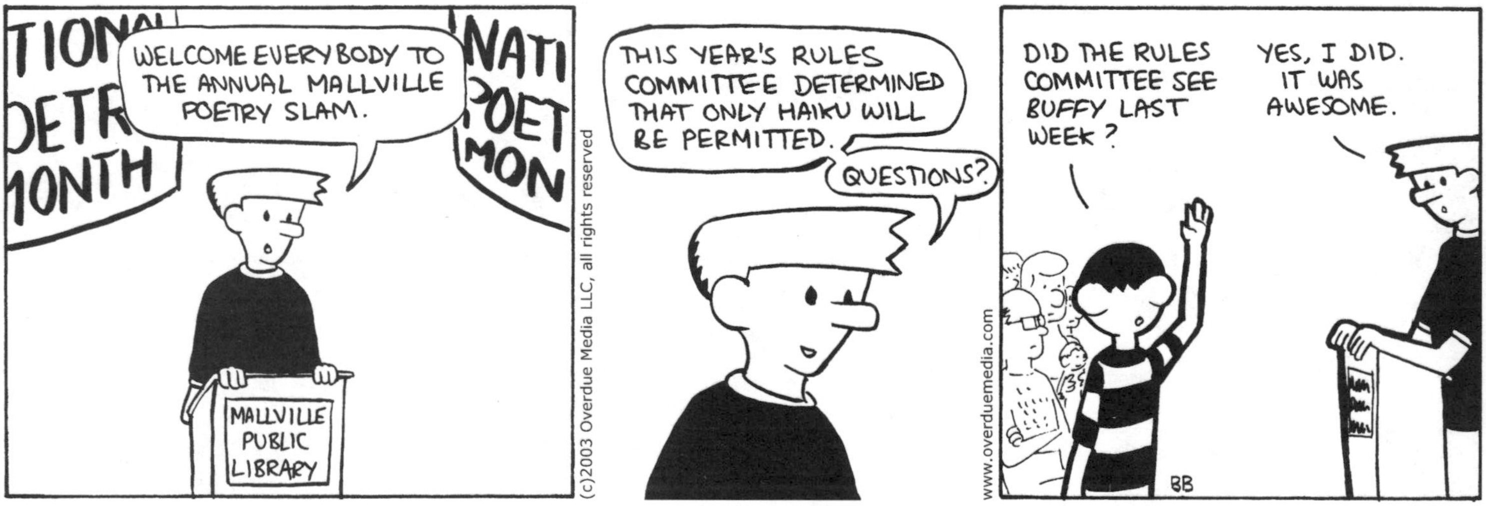
TIONA
OETR
MONTH
NATI
POET
MON
WELCOME EVERYBODY TO THE ANNUAL MALLVILLE POETRY SLAM.
MALLVILLE PUBLIC LIBRARY
THIS YEAR'S RULES COMMITTEE DETERMINED THAT ONLY HAIKU WILL BE PERMITTED.
QUESTIONS?
DID THE RULES COMMITTEE SEE BUFFY LAST WEEK?
YES, I DID. IT WAS AWESOME.
BB
(c)2003 Overdue Media LLC, all rights reserved
www.overduemedia.com

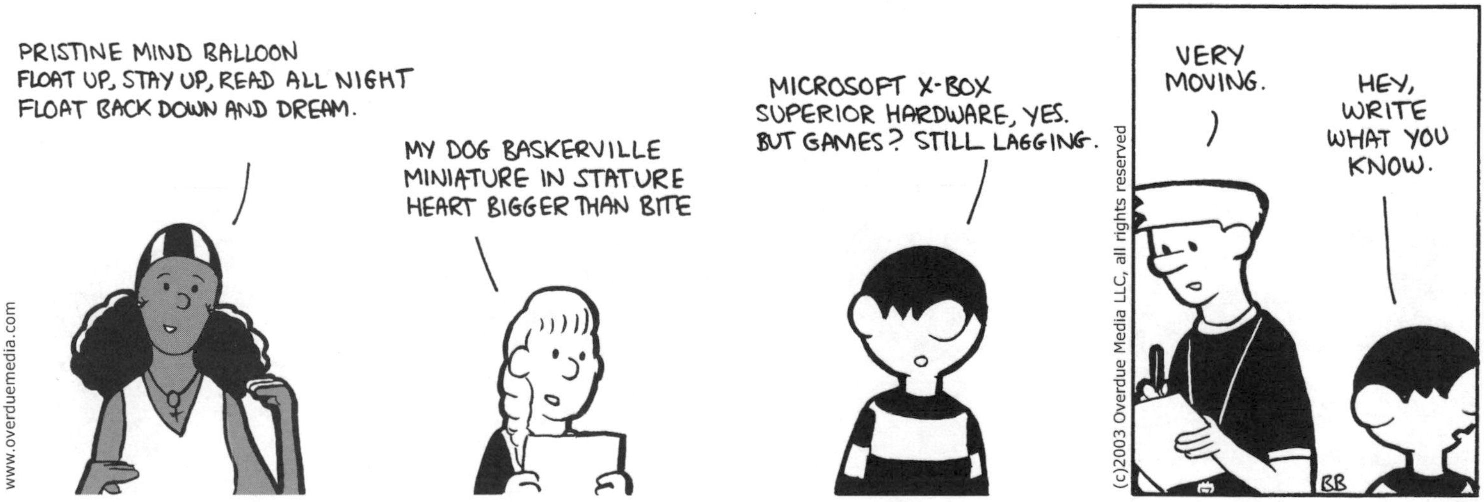
PRISTINE MIND BALLOON
FLOAT UP, STAY UP, READ ALL NIGHT
FLOAT BACK DOWN AND DREAM.
MY DOG BASKERVILLE
MINIATURE IN STATURE
HEART BIGGER THAN BITE
MICROSOFT X-BOX
SUPERIOR HARDWARE, YES.
BUT GAMES? STILL LAGGING.
VERY MOVING.
HEY, WRITE WHAT YOU KNOW.
BB
www.overduemedia.com
(c)2003 Overdue Media LLC, all rights reserved

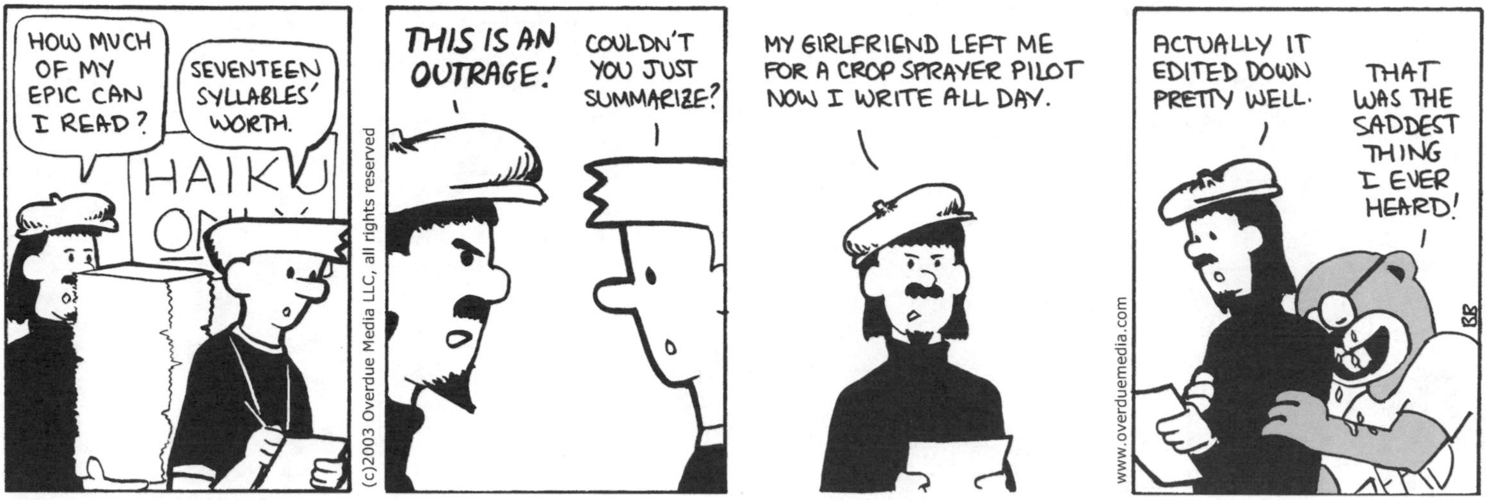
HOW MUCH OF MY EPIC CAN I READ?
SEVENTEEN SYLLABLES' WORTH.
HAIKU
(c)2003 Overdue Media LLC, all rights reserved
THIS IS AN OUTRAGE!
COULDN'T YOU JUST SUMMARIZE?
MY GIRLFRIEND LEFT ME FOR A CROP SPRAYER PILOT NOW I WRITE ALL DAY.
www.overduemedia.com
ACTUALLY IT EDITED DOWN PRETTY WELL.
THAT WAS THE SADDEST THING I EVER HEARD!
BB

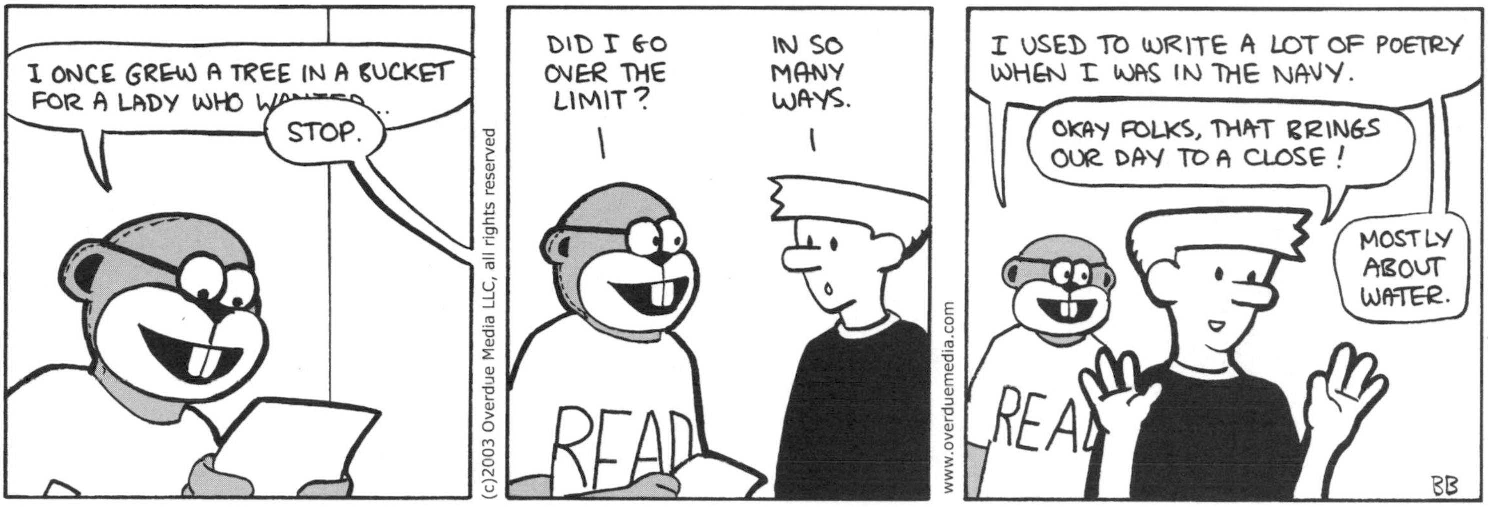
I ONCE GREW A TREE IN A BUCKET FOR A LADY WHO
STOP.
(c)2003 Overdue Media LLC, all rights reserved
DID I GO OVER THE LIMIT?
IN SO MANY WAYS.
READ
www.overduemedia.com
I USED TO WRITE A LOT OF POETRY WHEN I WAS IN THE NAVY.
OKAY FOLKS, THAT BRINGS OUR DAY TO A CLOSE!
MOSTLY ABOUT WATER.
BB

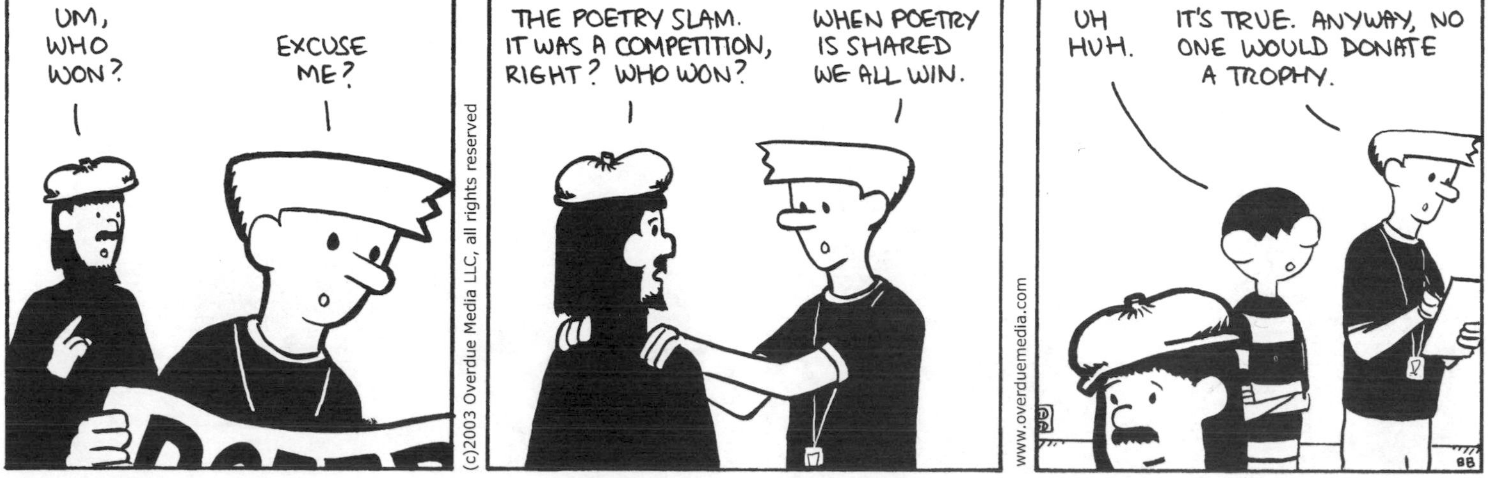
UM, WHO WON?
EXCUSE ME?
(c)2003 Overdue Media LLC, all rights reserved
THE POETRY SLAM. IT WAS A COMPETITION, RIGHT? WHO WON?
WHEN POETRY IS SHARED WE ALL WIN.
www.overduemedia.com
UH HUH.
IT'S TRUE. ANYWAY, NO ONE WOULD DONATE A TROPHY.
BB

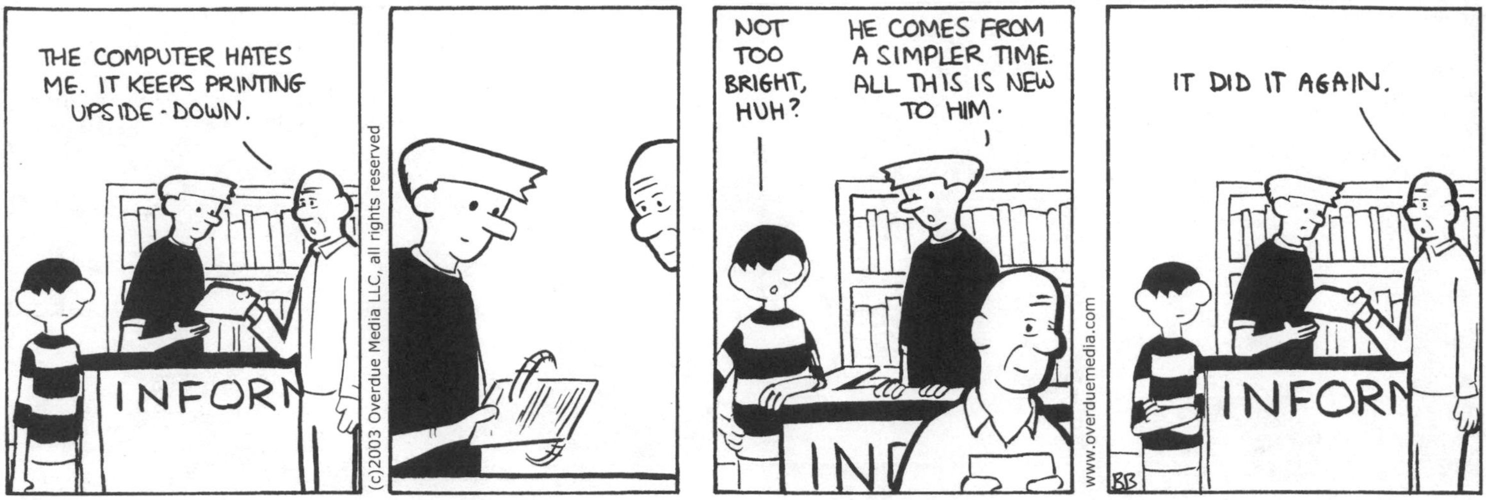
THE COMPUTER HATES ME. IT KEEPS PRINTING UPSIDE-DOWN.
(c)2003 Overdue Media LLC, all rights reserved
NOT TOO BRIGHT, HUH?
HE COMES FROM A SIMPLER TIME. ALL THIS IS NEW TO HIM.
INFOR
www.overduemedia.com
IT DID IT AGAIN.
INFOR
BB

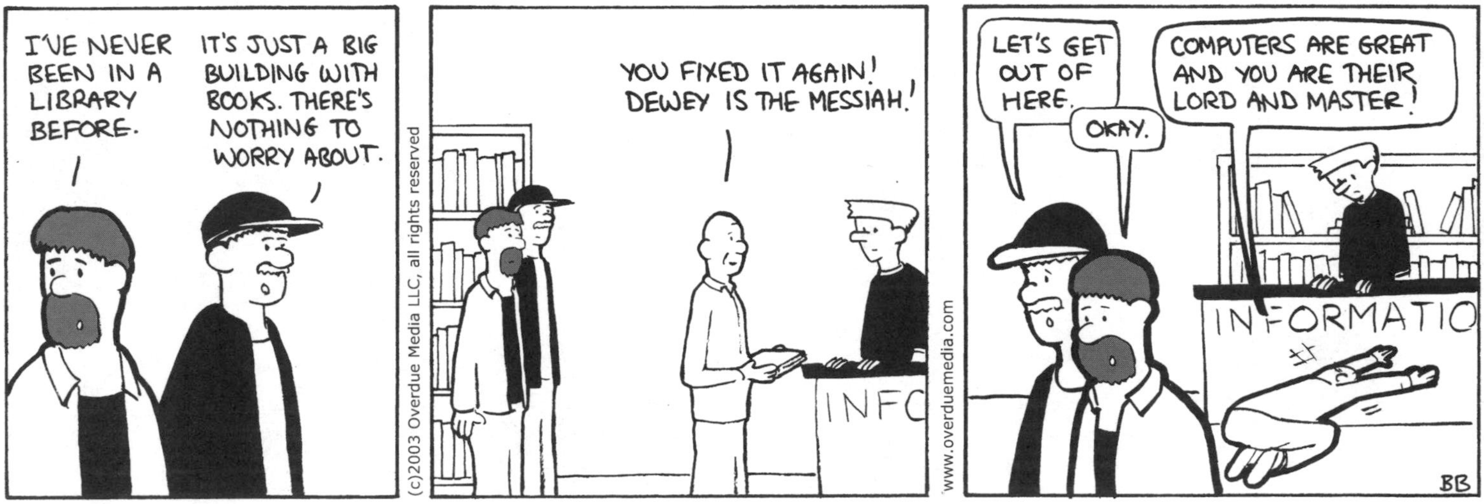
I'VE NEVER BEEN IN A LIBRARY BEFORE.
IT'S JUST A BIG BUILDING WITH BOOKS. THERE'S NOTHING TO WORRY ABOUT.
(c)2003 Overdue Media LLC, all rights reserved
YOU FIXED IT AGAIN! DEWEY IS THE MESSIAH!
INFO
www.overduemedia.com
LET'S GET OUT OF HERE.
OKAY.
COMPUTERS ARE GREAT AND YOU ARE THEIR LORD AND MASTER!
INFORMATIO
BB

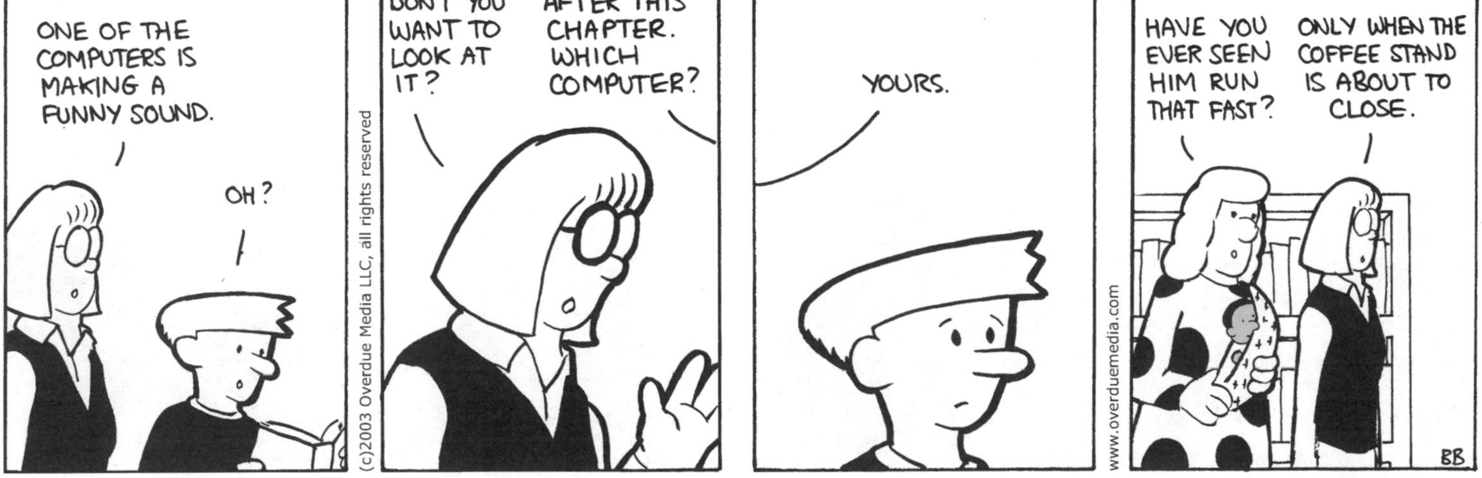
ONE OF THE COMPUTERS IS MAKING A FUNNY SOUND.
OH?
(c)2003 Overdue Media LLC, all rights reserved
DON'T YOU WANT TO LOOK AT IT?
AFTER THIS CHAPTER. WHICH COMPUTER?
YOURS.
www.overduemedia.com
HAVE YOU EVER SEEN HIM RUN THAT FAST?
ONLY WHEN THE COFFEE STAND IS ABOUT TO CLOSE.
BB

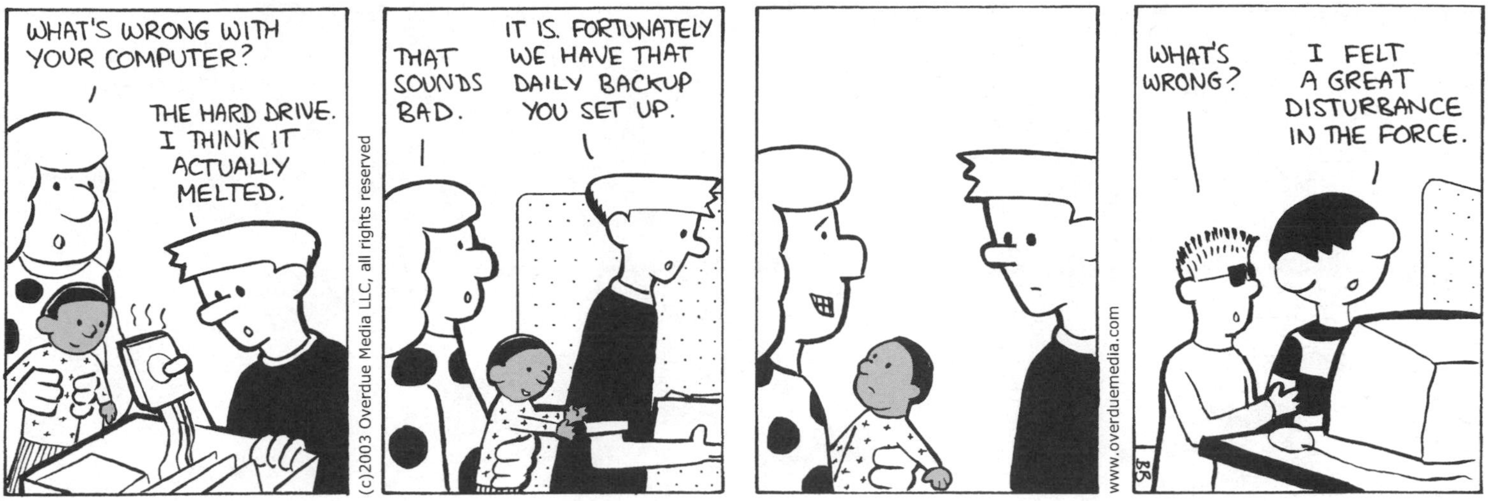
WHAT'S WRONG WITH YOUR COMPUTER?
THE HARD DRIVE. I THINK IT ACTUALLY MELTED.
THAT SOUNDS BAD.
IT IS. FORTUNATELY WE HAVE THAT DAILY BACKUP YOU SET UP.
WHAT'S WRONG?
I FELT A GREAT DISTURBANCE IN THE FORCE.
BB


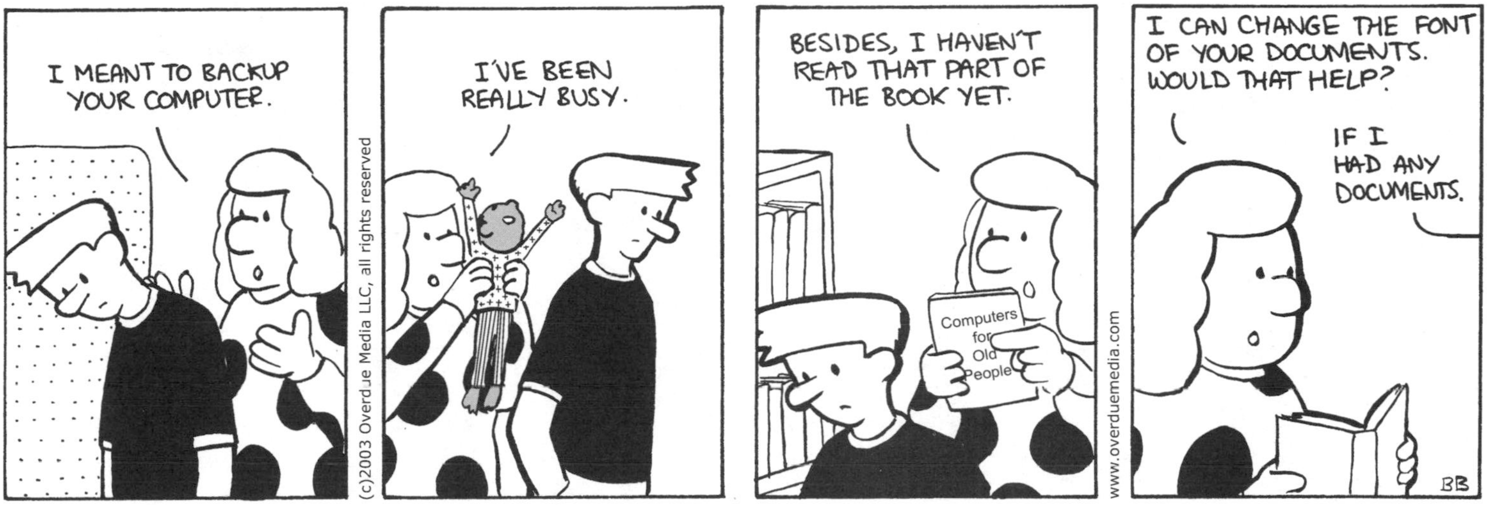
I MEANT TO BACKUP YOUR COMPUTER.
I'VE BEEN REALLY BUSY.
BESIDES, I HAVEN'T READ THAT PART OF THE BOOK YET.
Computers for Old People
I CAN CHANGE THE FONT OF YOUR DOCUMENTS. WOULD THAT HELP?
IF I HAD ANY DOCUMENTS.
BB


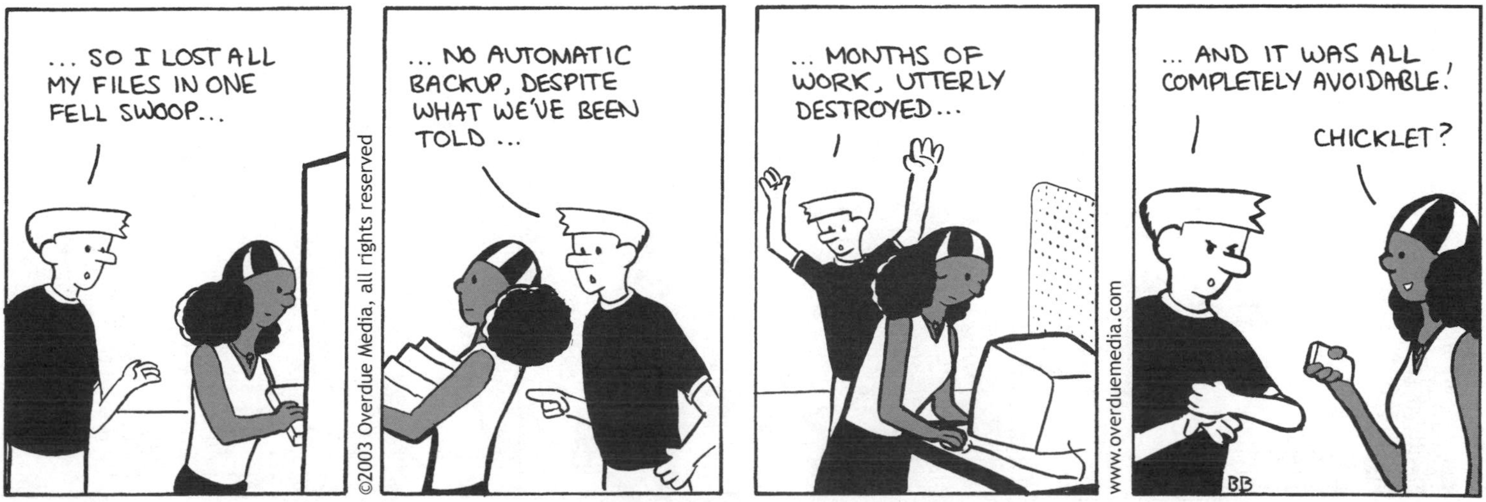
... SO I LOST ALL MY FILES IN ONE FELL SWOOP...
... NO AUTOMATIC BACKUP, DESPITE WHAT WE'VE BEEN TOLD ...
... MONTHS OF WORK, UTTERLY DESTROYED...
... AND IT WAS ALL COMPLETELY AVOIDABLE!
CHICKLET?
BB

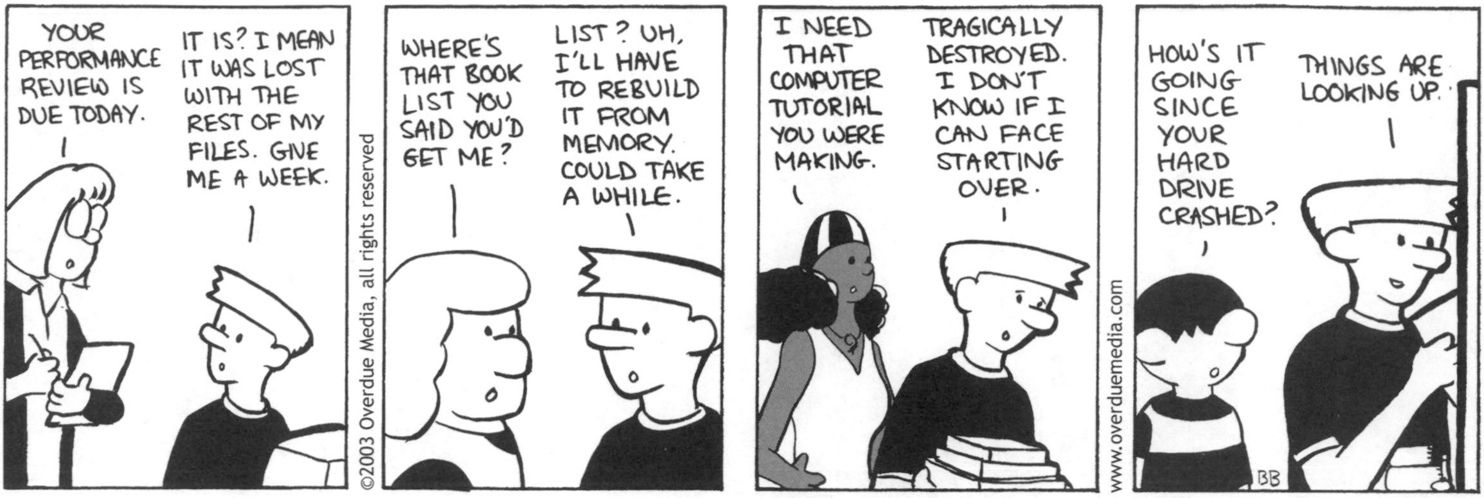
YOUR PERFORMANCE REVIEW IS DUE TODAY.
IT IS? I MEAN IT WAS LOST WITH THE REST OF MY FILES. GIVE ME A WEEK.
©2003 Overdue Media, all rights reserved
WHERE'S THAT BOOK LIST YOU SAID YOU'D GET ME?
LIST? UH, I'LL HAVE TO REBUILD IT FROM MEMORY. COULD TAKE A WHILE.
I NEED THAT COMPUTER TUTORIAL YOU WERE MAKING.
TRAGICALLY DESTROYED. I DON'T KNOW IF I CAN FACE STARTING OVER.
www.overduemedia.com
HOW'S IT GOING SINCE YOUR HARD DRIVE CRASHED?
THINGS ARE LOOKING UP.
BB

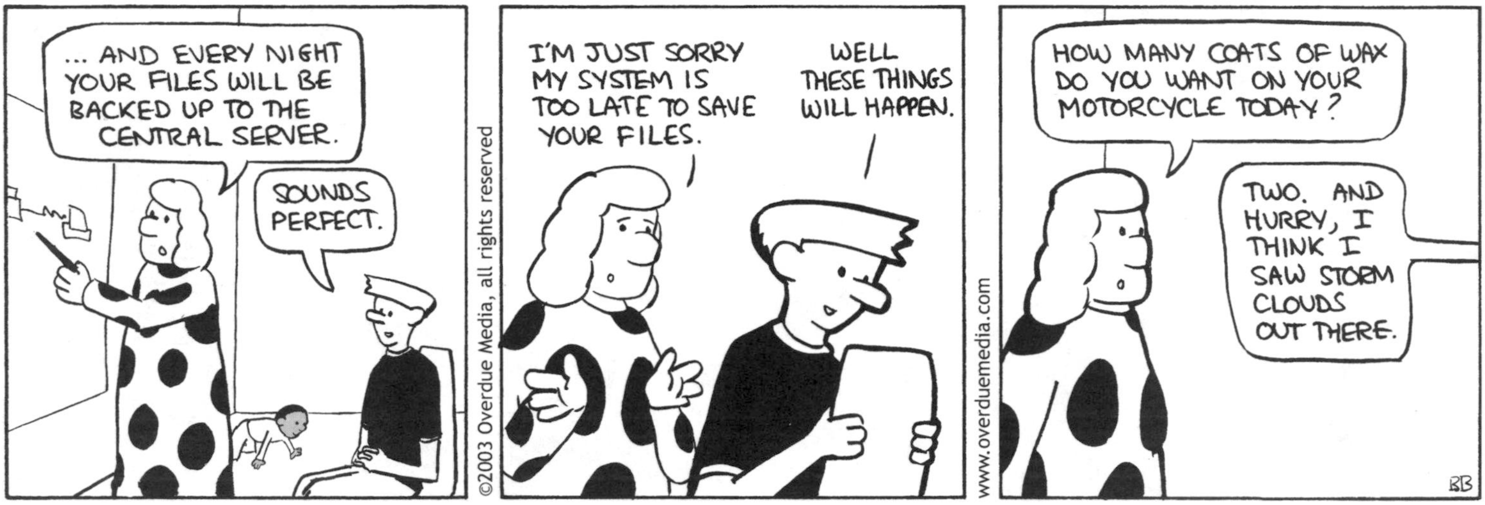
... AND EVERY NIGHT YOUR FILES WILL BE BACKED UP TO THE CENTRAL SERVER.
SOUNDS PERFECT.
©2003 Overdue Media, all rights reserved
I'M JUST SORRY MY SYSTEM IS TOO LATE TO SAVE YOUR FILES.
WELL THESE THINGS WILL HAPPEN.
www.overduemedia.com
HOW MANY COATS OF WAX DO YOU WANT ON YOUR MOTORCYCLE TODAY?
TWO. AND HURRY, I THINK I SAW STORM CLOUDS OUT THERE.
BB

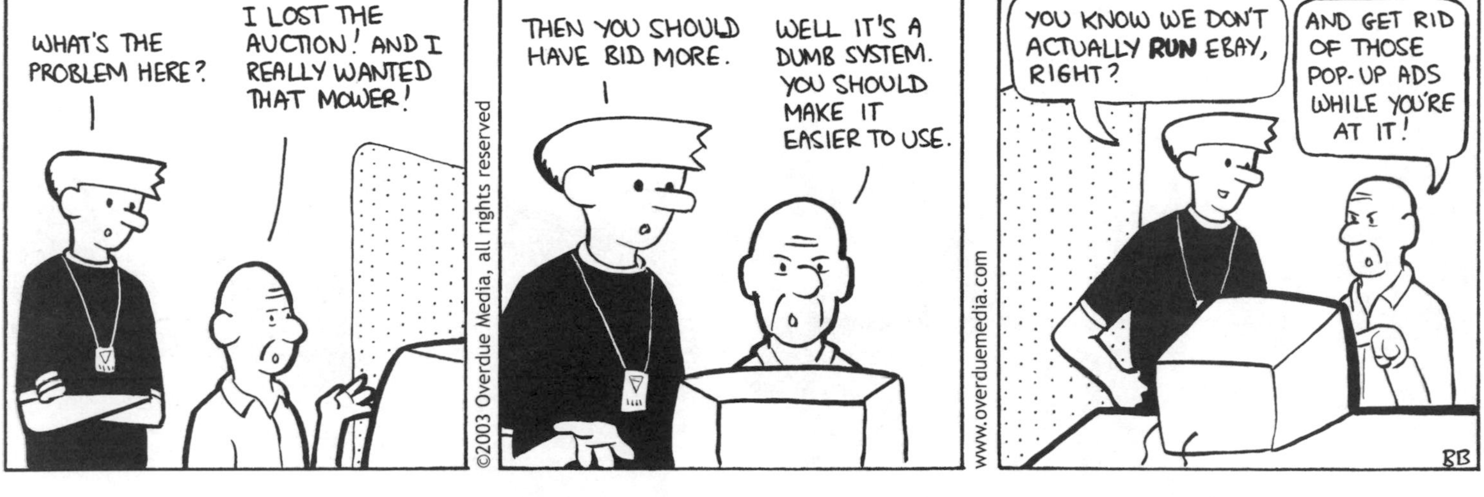
WHAT'S THE PROBLEM HERE?
I LOST THE AUCTION! AND I REALLY WANTED THAT MOWER!
©2003 Overdue Media, all rights reserved
THEN YOU SHOULD HAVE BID MORE.
WELL IT'S A DUMB SYSTEM. YOU SHOULD MAKE IT EASIER TO USE.
www.overduemedia.com
YOU KNOW WE DON'T ACTUALLY **RUN** EBAY, RIGHT?
AND GET RID OF THOSE POP-UP ADS WHILE YOU'RE AT IT!
BB

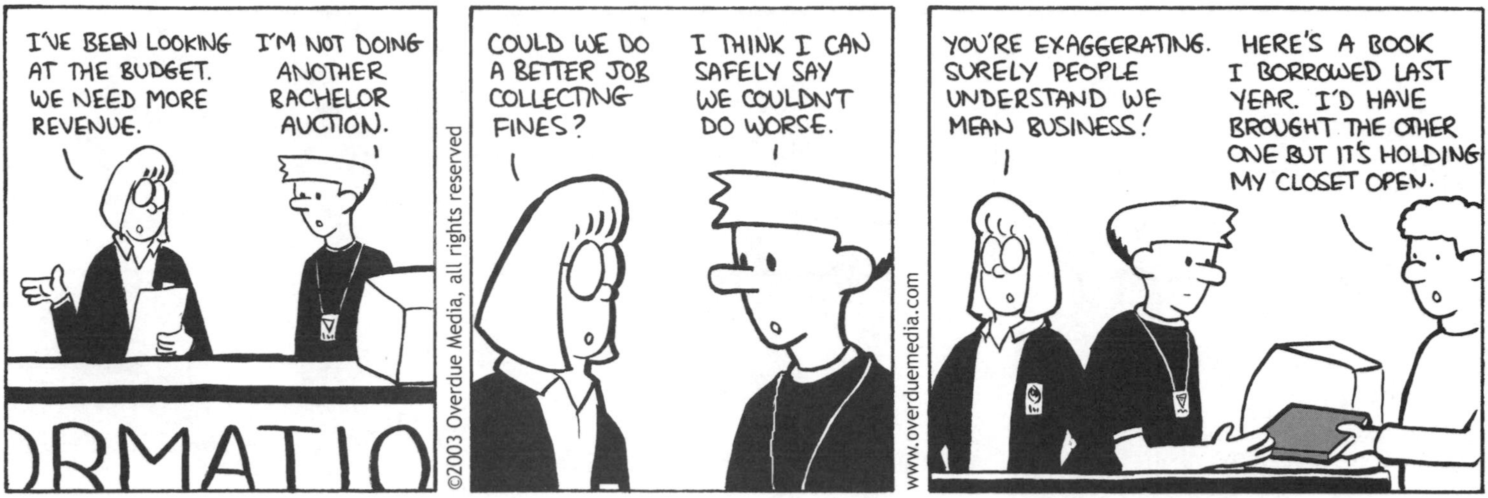
I'VE BEEN LOOKING AT THE BUDGET. WE NEED MORE REVENUE.
I'M NOT DOING ANOTHER BACHELOR AUCTION.
COULD WE DO A BETTER JOB COLLECTING FINES?
I THINK I CAN SAFELY SAY WE COULDN'T DO WORSE.
YOU'RE EXAGGERATING. SURELY PEOPLE UNDERSTAND WE MEAN BUSINESS!
HERE'S A BOOK I BORROWED LAST YEAR. I'D HAVE BROUGHT THE OTHER ONE BUT IT'S HOLDING MY CLOSET OPEN.
©2003 Overdue Media, all rights reserved
www.overduemedia.com

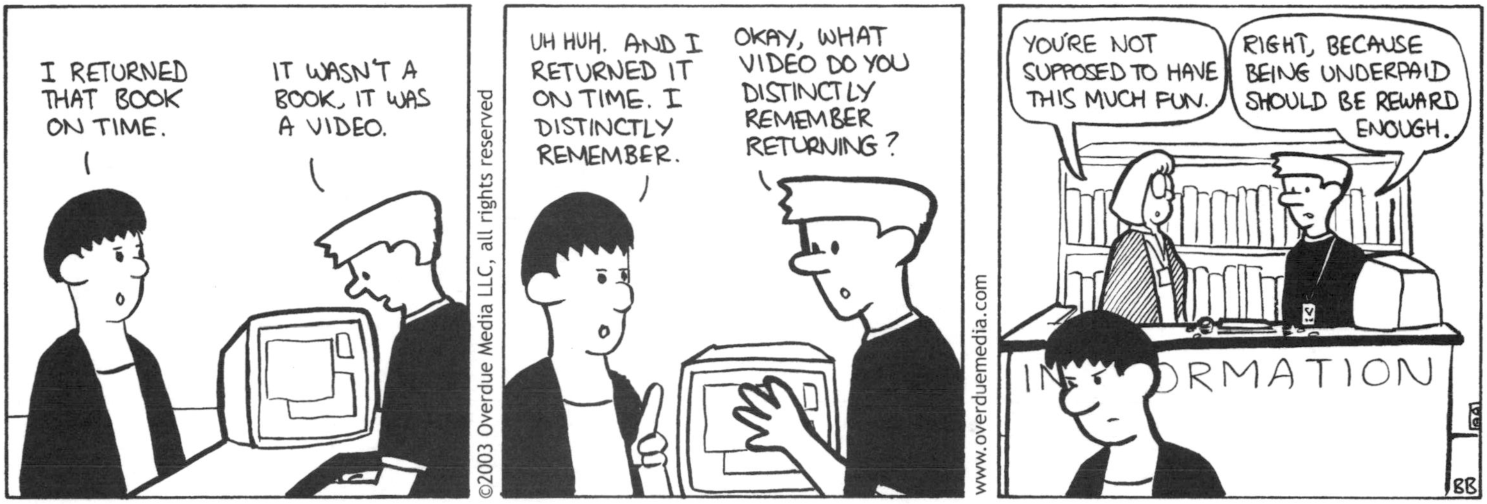
I RETURNED THAT BOOK ON TIME.
IT WASN'T A BOOK, IT WAS A VIDEO.
UH HUH. AND I RETURNED IT ON TIME. I DISTINCTLY REMEMBER.
OKAY, WHAT VIDEO DO YOU DISTINCTLY REMEMBER RETURNING?
YOU'RE NOT SUPPOSED TO HAVE THIS MUCH FUN.
RIGHT, BECAUSE BEING UNDERPAID SHOULD BE REWARD ENOUGH.
©2003 Overdue Media LLC, all rights reserved
www.overduemedia.com

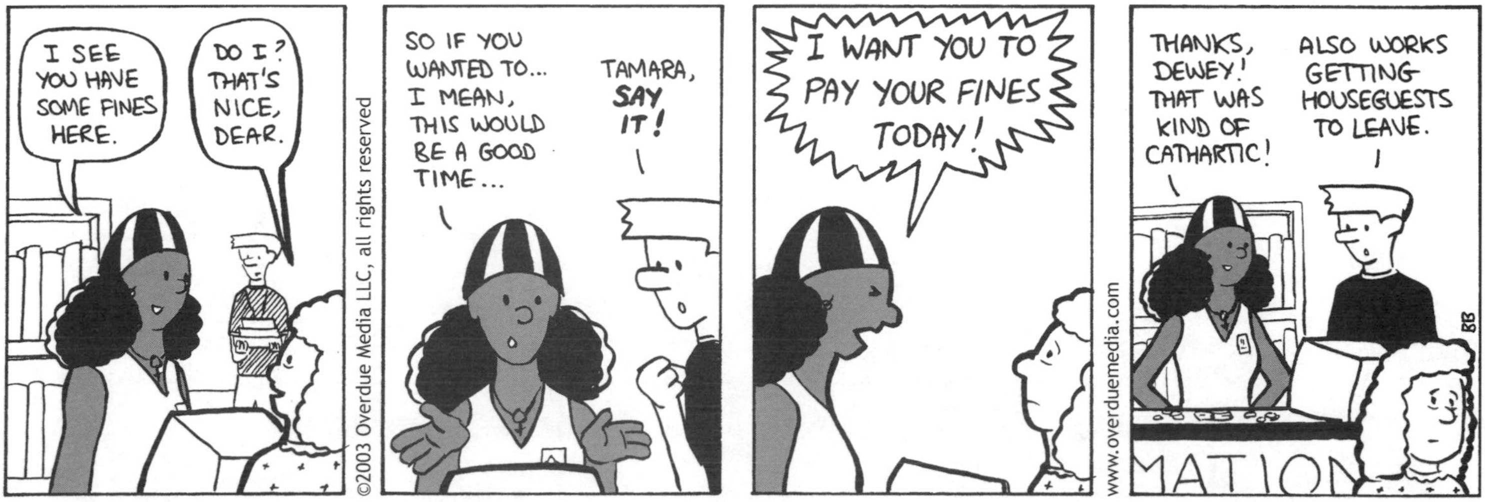
I SEE YOU HAVE SOME FINES HERE.
DO I? THAT'S NICE, DEAR.
SO IF YOU WANTED TO... I MEAN, THIS WOULD BE A GOOD TIME...
TAMARA, **SAY IT!**
I WANT YOU TO PAY YOUR FINES TODAY!
THANKS, DEWEY! THAT WAS KIND OF CATHARTIC!
ALSO WORKS GETTING HOUSEGUESTS TO LEAVE.
©2003 Overdue Media LLC, all rights reserved
www.overduemedia.com

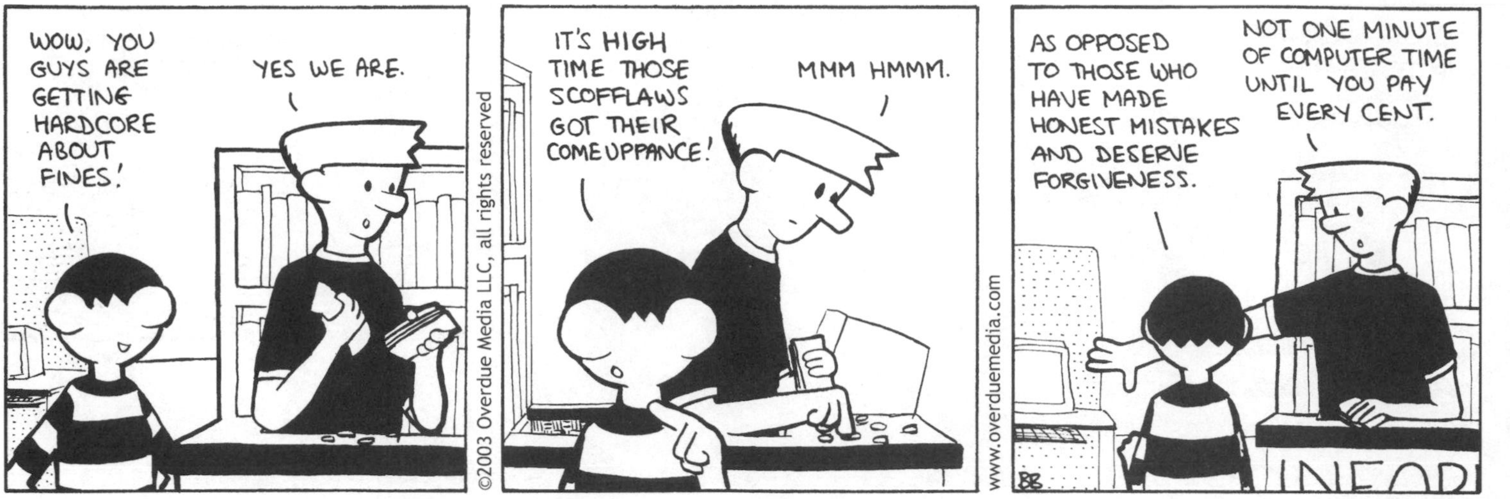
WOW, YOU GUYS ARE GETTING HARDCORE ABOUT FINES!
YES WE ARE.
©2003 Overdue Media LLC, all rights reserved
IT'S HIGH TIME THOSE SCOFFLAWS GOT THEIR COMEUPPANCE!
MMM HMMM.
www.overduemedia.com
AS OPPOSED TO THOSE WHO HAVE MADE HONEST MISTAKES AND DESERVE FORGIVENESS.
NOT ONE MINUTE OF COMPUTER TIME UNTIL YOU PAY EVERY CENT.
BB

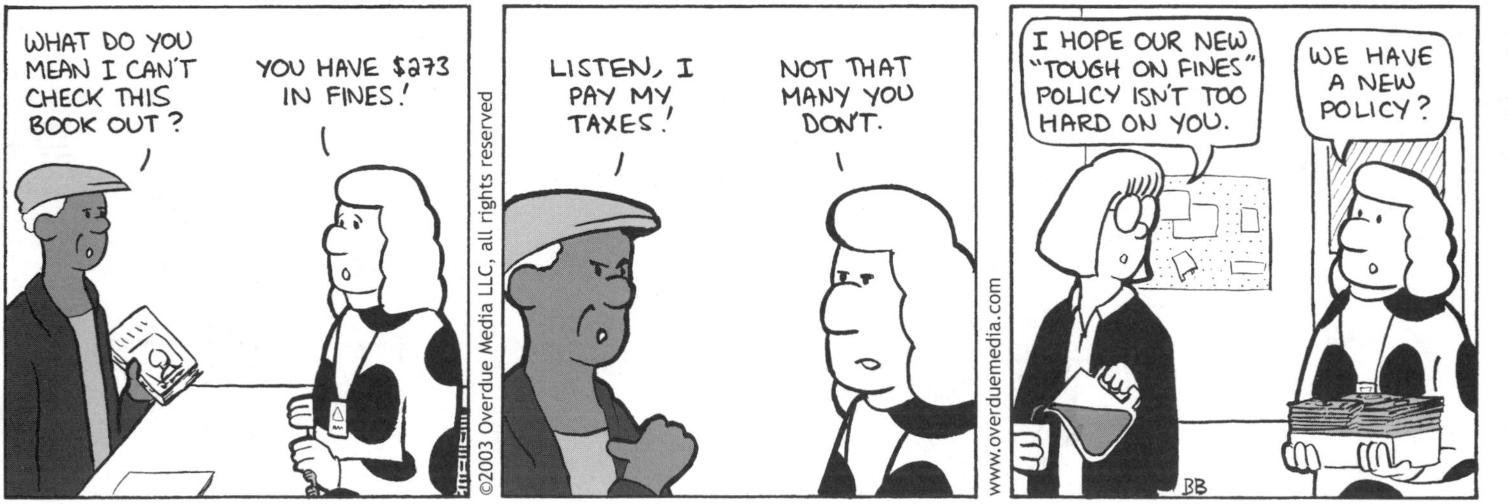
WHAT DO YOU MEAN I CAN'T CHECK THIS BOOK OUT?
YOU HAVE $273 IN FINES!
©2003 Overdue Media LLC, all rights reserved
LISTEN, I PAY MY TAXES!
NOT THAT MANY YOU DON'T.
www.overduemedia.com
I HOPE OUR NEW "TOUGH ON FINES" POLICY ISN'T TOO HARD ON YOU.
WE HAVE A NEW POLICY?
BB

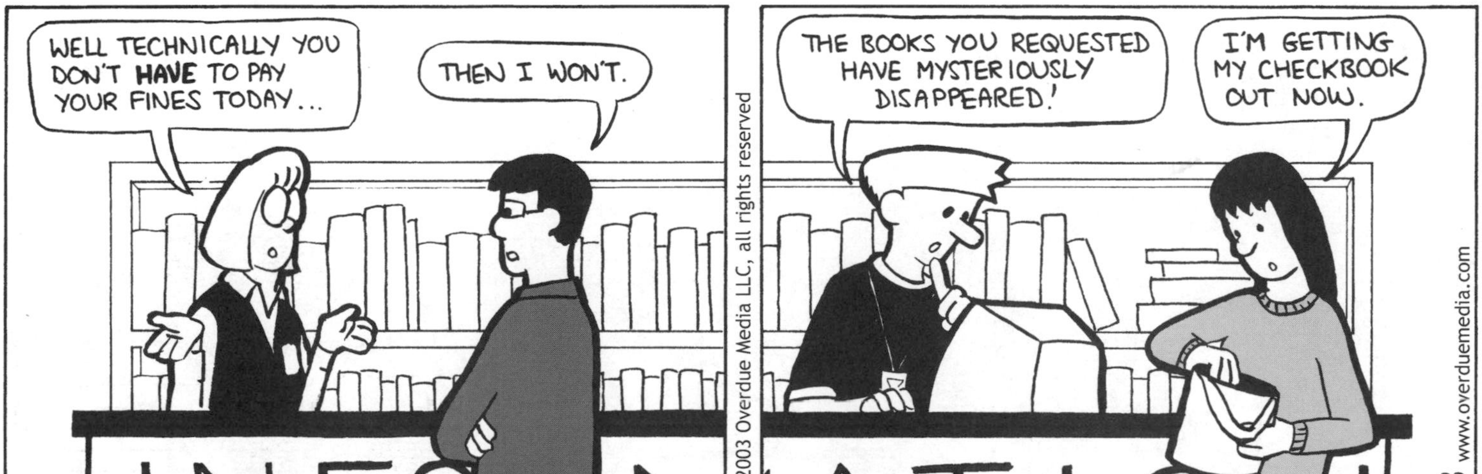
WELL TECHNICALLY YOU DON'T **HAVE** TO PAY YOUR FINES TODAY...
THEN I WON'T.
©2003 Overdue Media LLC, all rights reserved
THE BOOKS YOU REQUESTED HAVE MYSTERIOUSLY DISAPPEARED!
I'M GETTING MY CHECKBOOK OUT NOW.
www.overduemedia.com
BB

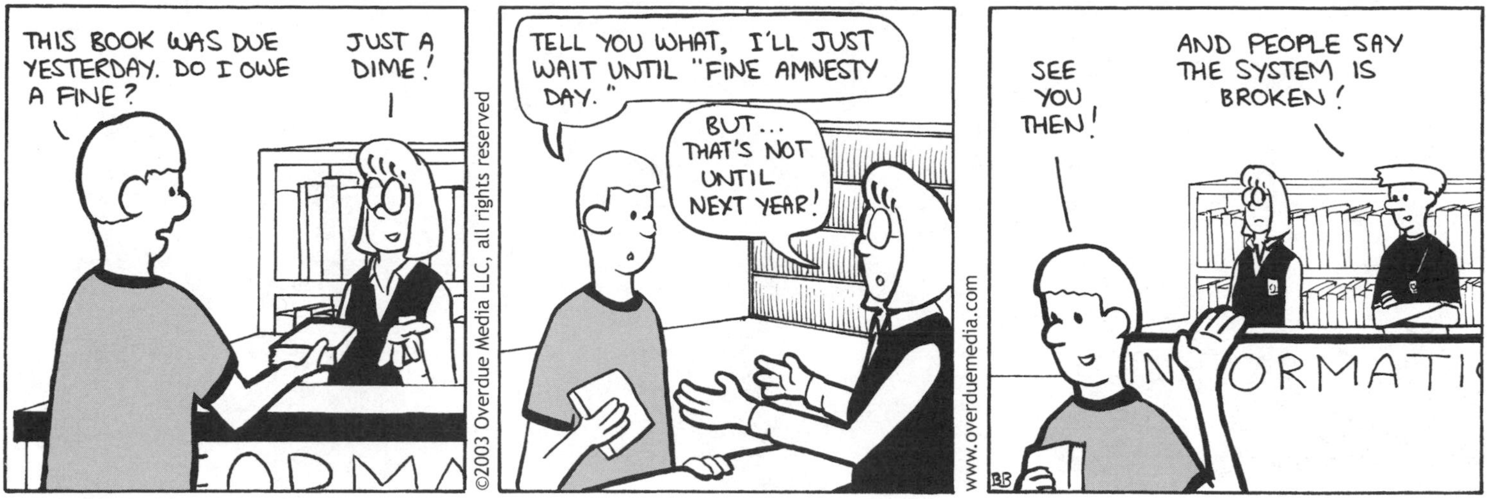
THIS BOOK WAS DUE YESTERDAY. DO I OWE A FINE?
JUST A DIME!
TELL YOU WHAT, I'LL JUST WAIT UNTIL "FINE AMNESTY DAY."
BUT... THAT'S NOT UNTIL NEXT YEAR!
SEE YOU THEN!
AND PEOPLE SAY THE SYSTEM IS BROKEN!
©2003 Overdue Media LLC, all rights reserved
www.overduemedia.com
BB

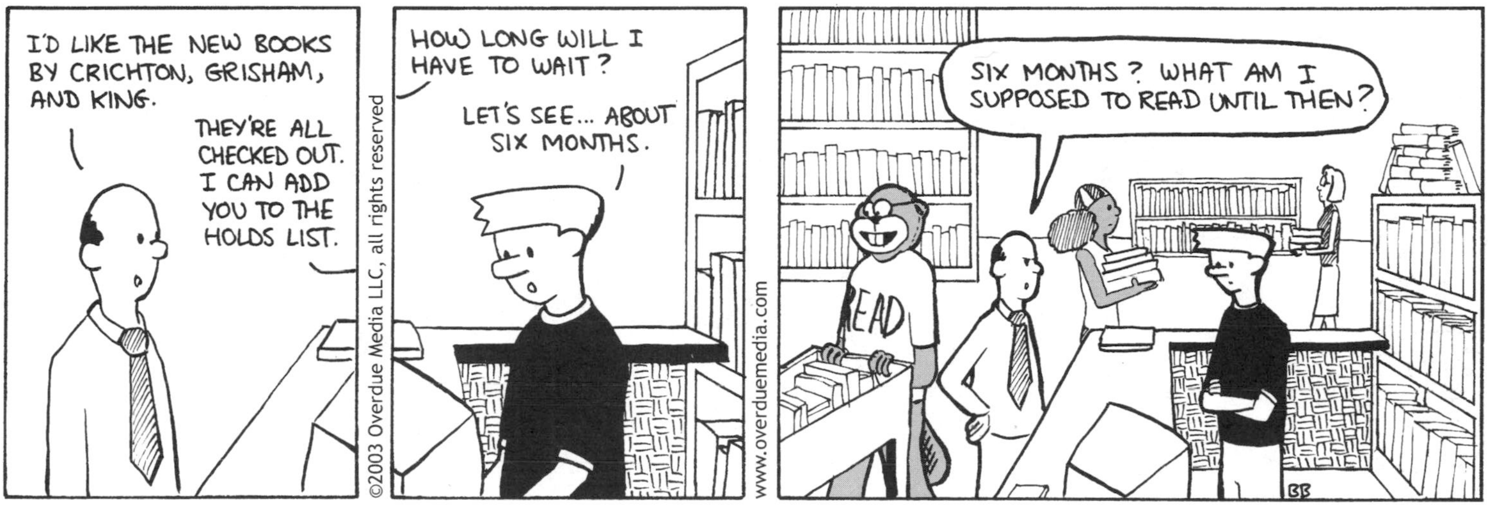
I'D LIKE THE NEW BOOKS BY CRICHTON, GRISHAM, AND KING.
THEY'RE ALL CHECKED OUT. I CAN ADD YOU TO THE HOLDS LIST.
HOW LONG WILL I HAVE TO WAIT?
LET'S SEE... ABOUT SIX MONTHS.
SIX MONTHS? WHAT AM I SUPPOSED TO READ UNTIL THEN?
READ
©2003 Overdue Media LLC, all rights reserved
www.overduemedia.com
BB

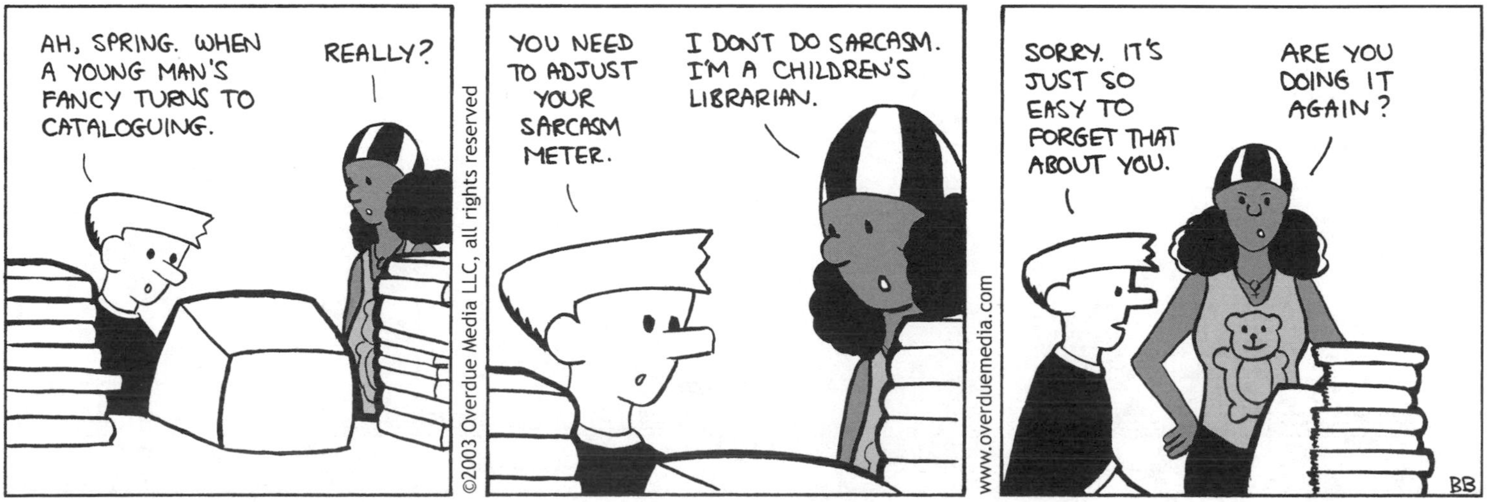
AH, SPRING. WHEN A YOUNG MAN'S FANCY TURNS TO CATALOGUING.
REALLY?
YOU NEED TO ADJUST YOUR SARCASM METER.
I DON'T DO SARCASM. I'M A CHILDREN'S LIBRARIAN.
SORRY. IT'S JUST SO EASY TO FORGET THAT ABOUT YOU.
ARE YOU DOING IT AGAIN?
©2003 Overdue Media LLC, all rights reserved
www.overduemedia.com
BB

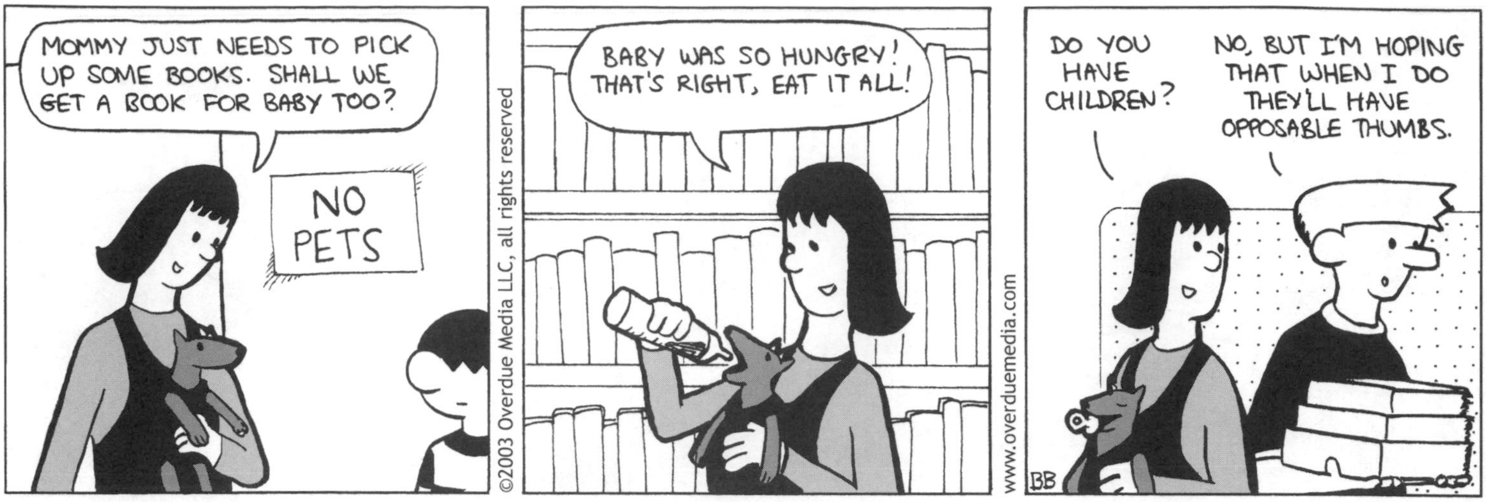
MOMMY JUST NEEDS TO PICK UP SOME BOOKS. SHALL WE GET A BOOK FOR BABY TOO?
NO PETS
BABY WAS SO HUNGRY! THAT'S RIGHT, EAT IT ALL!
DO YOU HAVE CHILDREN?
NO, BUT I'M HOPING THAT WHEN I DO THEY'LL HAVE OPPOSABLE THUMBS.
©2003 Overdue Media LLC, all rights reserved
www.overduemedia.com
BB

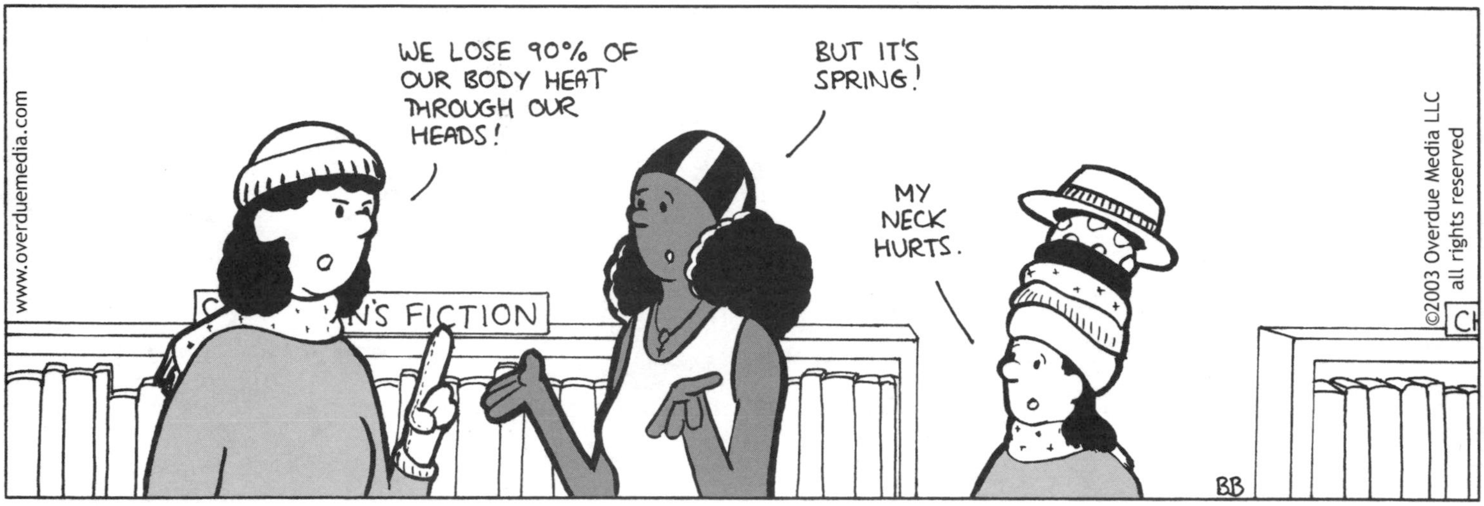
www.overduemedia.com
WE LOSE 90% OF OUR BODY HEAT THROUGH OUR HEADS!
BUT IT'S SPRING!
MY NECK HURTS.
'S FICTION
©2003 Overdue Media LLC all rights reserved
BB

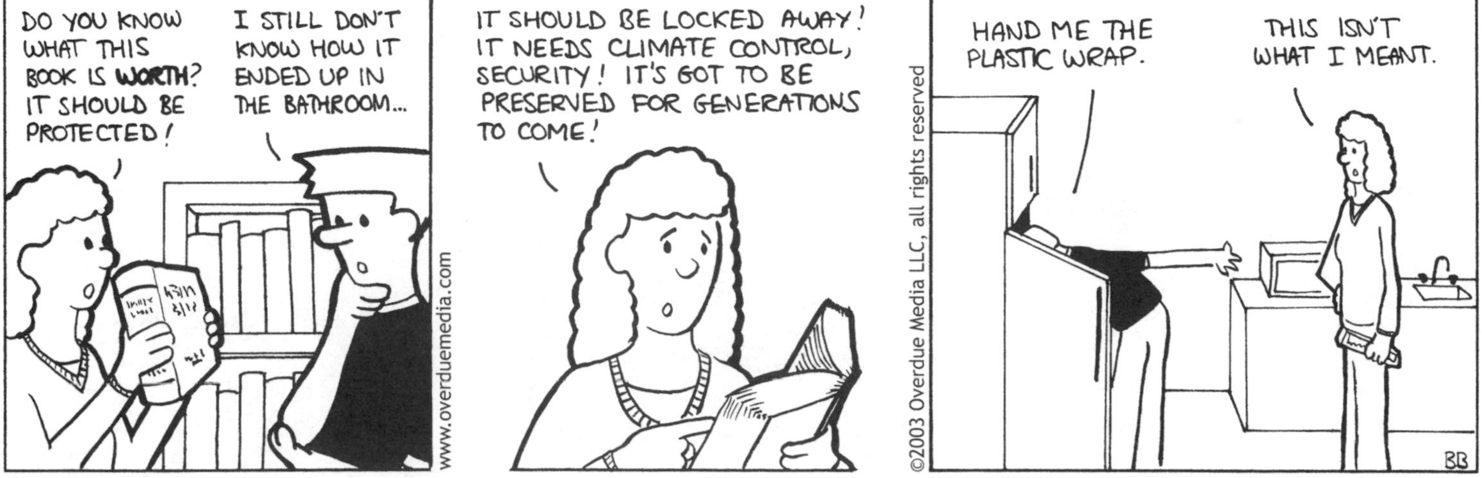
DO YOU KNOW WHAT THIS BOOK IS **WORTH**? IT SHOULD BE PROTECTED!
I STILL DON'T KNOW HOW IT ENDED UP IN THE BATHROOM...
www.overduemedia.com
IT SHOULD BE LOCKED AWAY! IT NEEDS CLIMATE CONTROL, SECURITY! IT'S GOT TO BE PRESERVED FOR GENERATIONS TO COME!
©2003 Overdue Media LLC, all rights reserved
HAND ME THE PLASTIC WRAP.
THIS ISN'T WHAT I MEANT.
BB

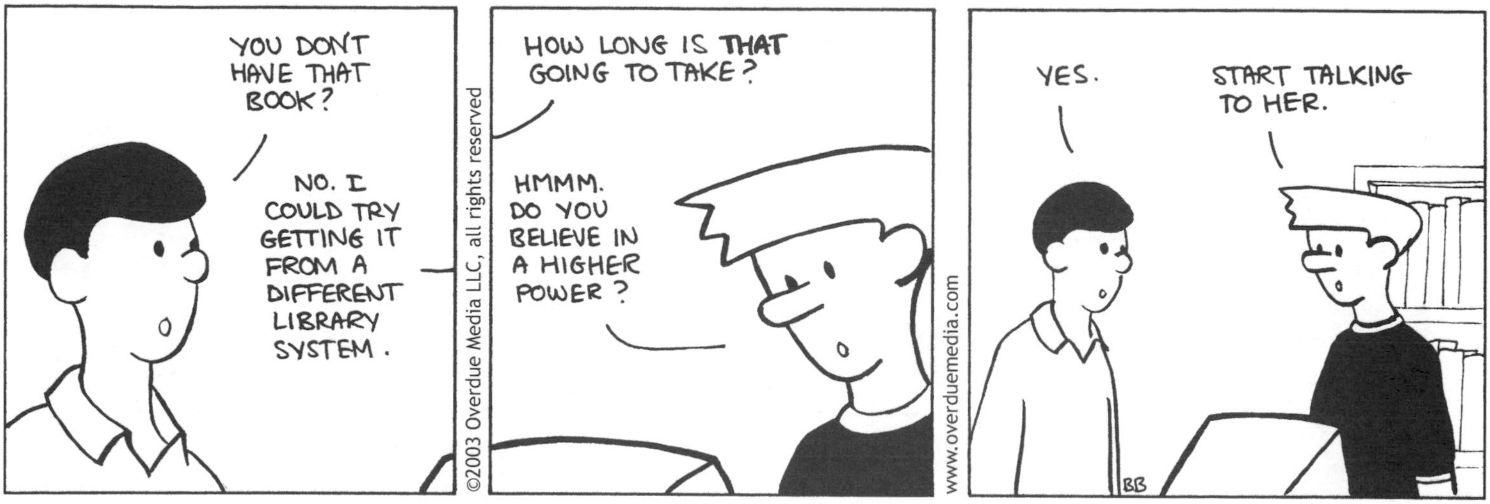
YOU DON'T HAVE THAT BOOK?
NO. I COULD TRY GETTING IT FROM A DIFFERENT LIBRARY SYSTEM.
HOW LONG IS THAT GOING TO TAKE?
HMMM. DO YOU BELIEVE IN A HIGHER POWER?
YES.
START TALKING TO HER.
©2003 Overdue Media LLC, all rights reserved
www.overduemedia.com
BB

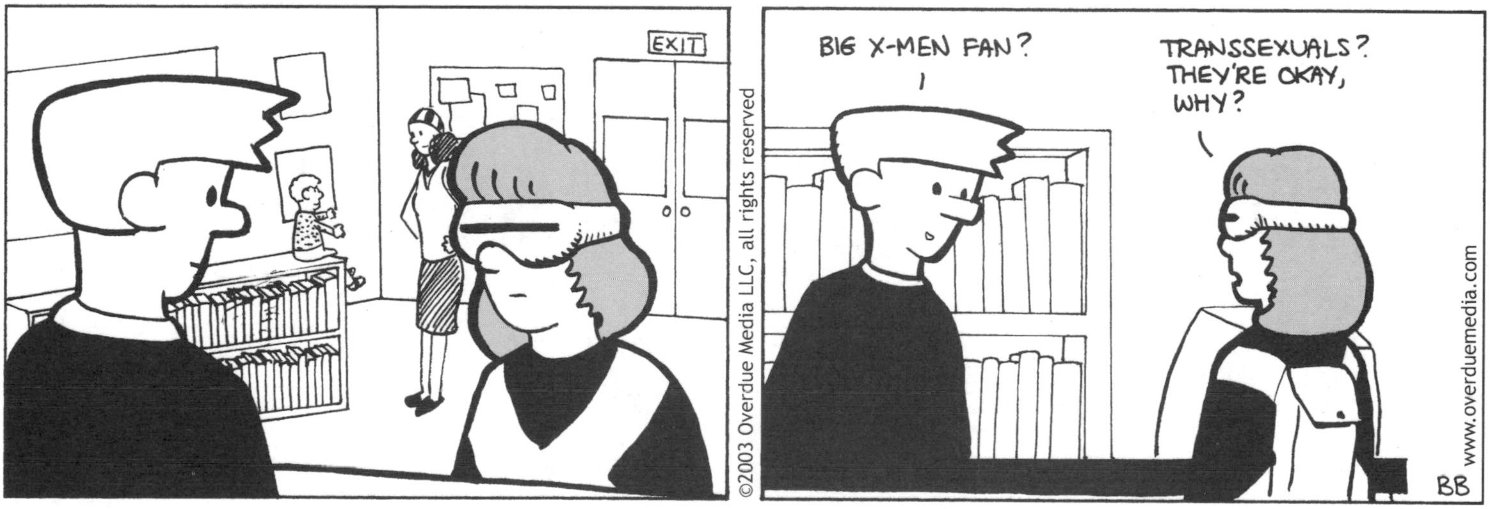
EXIT
BIG X-MEN FAN?
TRANSSEXUALS? THEY'RE OKAY, WHY?
©2003 Overdue Media LLC, all rights reserved
www.overduemedia.com
BB

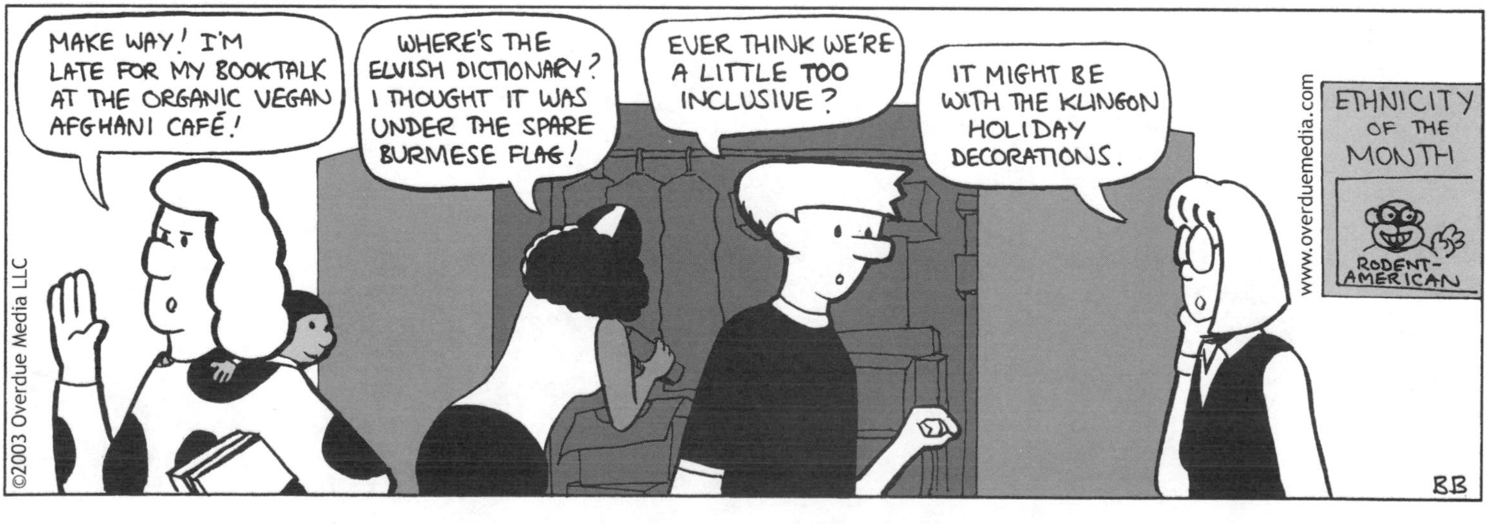
MAKE WAY! I'M LATE FOR MY BOOKTALK AT THE ORGANIC VEGAN AFGHANI CAFÉ!
WHERE'S THE ELVISH DICTIONARY? I THOUGHT IT WAS UNDER THE SPARE BURMESE FLAG!
EVER THINK WE'RE A LITTLE TOO INCLUSIVE?
IT MIGHT BE WITH THE KLINGON HOLIDAY DECORATIONS.
ETHNICITY OF THE MONTH
RODENT-AMERICAN
©2003 Overdue Media LLC
www.overduemedia.com
BB

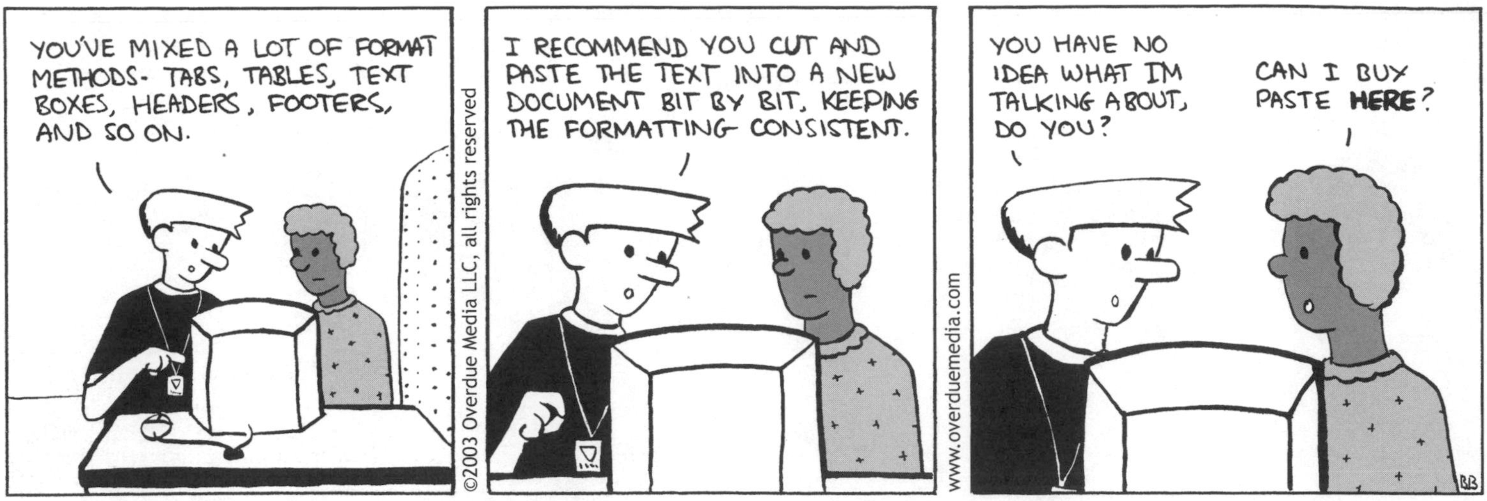
YOU'VE MIXED A LOT OF FORMAT METHODS- TABS, TABLES, TEXT BOXES, HEADERS, FOOTERS, AND SO ON.
©2003 Overdue Media LLC, all rights reserved
I RECOMMEND YOU CUT AND PASTE THE TEXT INTO A NEW DOCUMENT BIT BY BIT, KEEPING THE FORMATTING CONSISTENT.
www.overduemedia.com
YOU HAVE NO IDEA WHAT I'M TALKING ABOUT, DO YOU?
CAN I BUY PASTE **HERE**?
BB

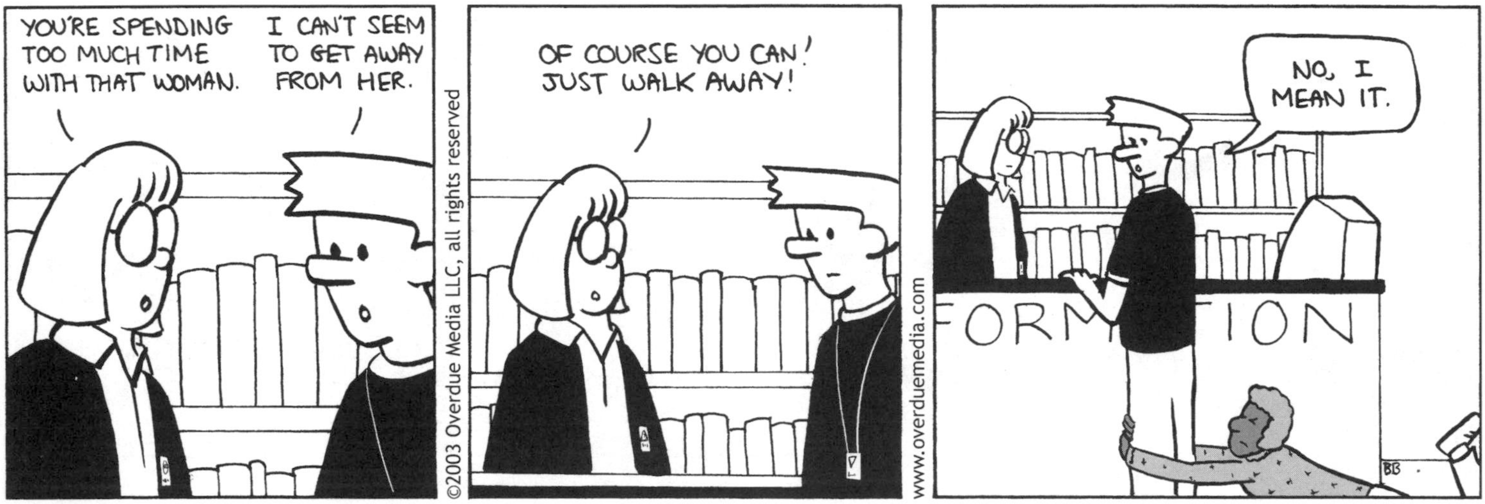
YOU'RE SPENDING TOO MUCH TIME WITH THAT WOMAN.
I CAN'T SEEM TO GET AWAY FROM HER.
©2003 Overdue Media LLC, all rights reserved
OF COURSE YOU CAN! JUST WALK AWAY!
www.overduemedia.com
NO, I MEAN IT.
BB

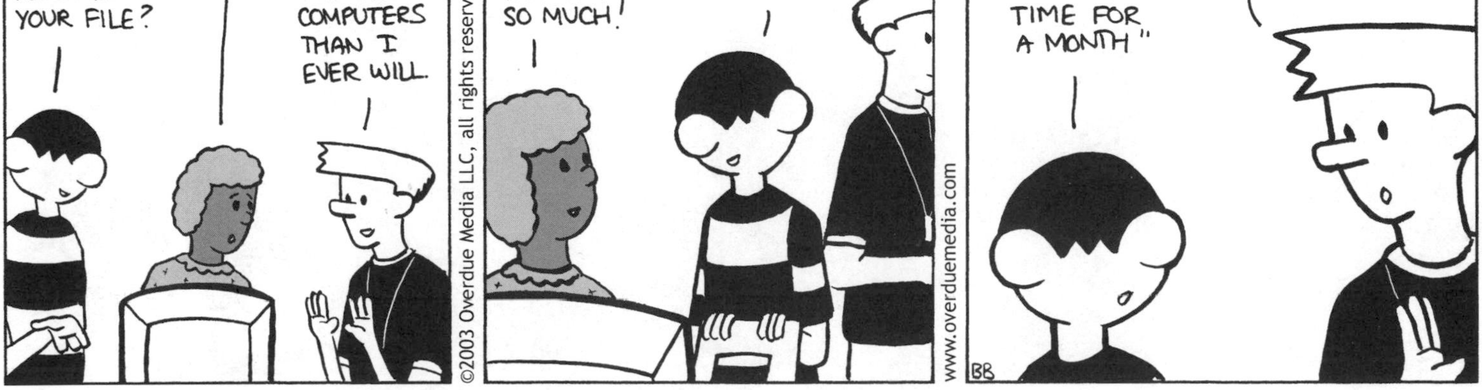
WOULD YOU LIKE HELP REFORMATTING YOUR FILE?
UMM...
GO FOR IT. MERV KNOWS MORE ABOUT COMPUTERS THAN I EVER WILL.
©2003 Overdue Media LLC, all rights reserved
THAT WOULD BE WONDERFUL! THANK YOU SO MUCH!
IT'S MY PLEASURE.
www.overduemedia.com
"UNLIMITED COMPUTER TIME FOR A MONTH"
AND WORTH EVERY MINUTE.
BB

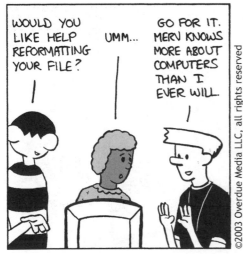

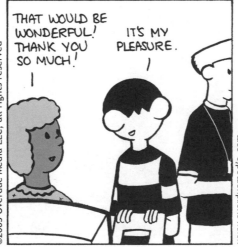

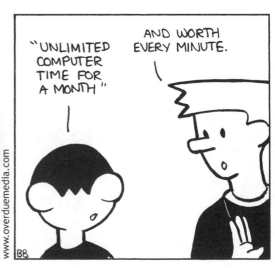

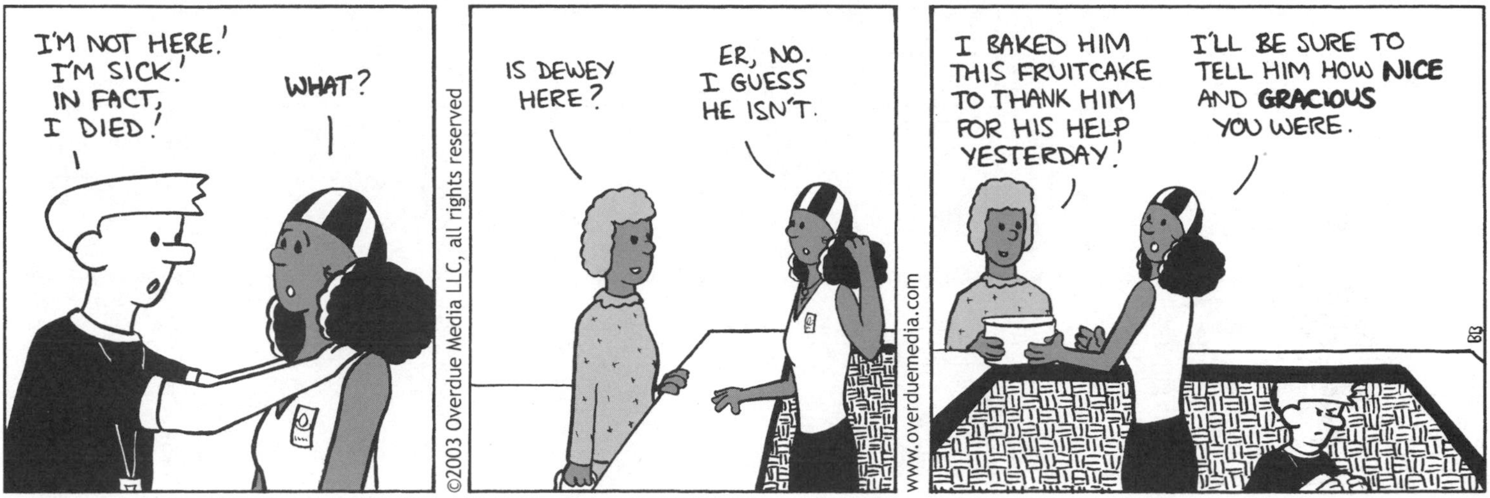
I'M NOT HERE! I'M SICK! IN FACT, I DIED!
WHAT?
IS DEWEY HERE?
ER, NO. I GUESS HE ISN'T.
I BAKED HIM THIS FRUITCAKE TO THANK HIM FOR HIS HELP YESTERDAY!
I'LL BE SURE TO TELL HIM HOW **NICE** AND **GRACIOUS** YOU WERE.
BB
©2003 Overdue Media LLC, all rights reserved
www.overduemedia.com

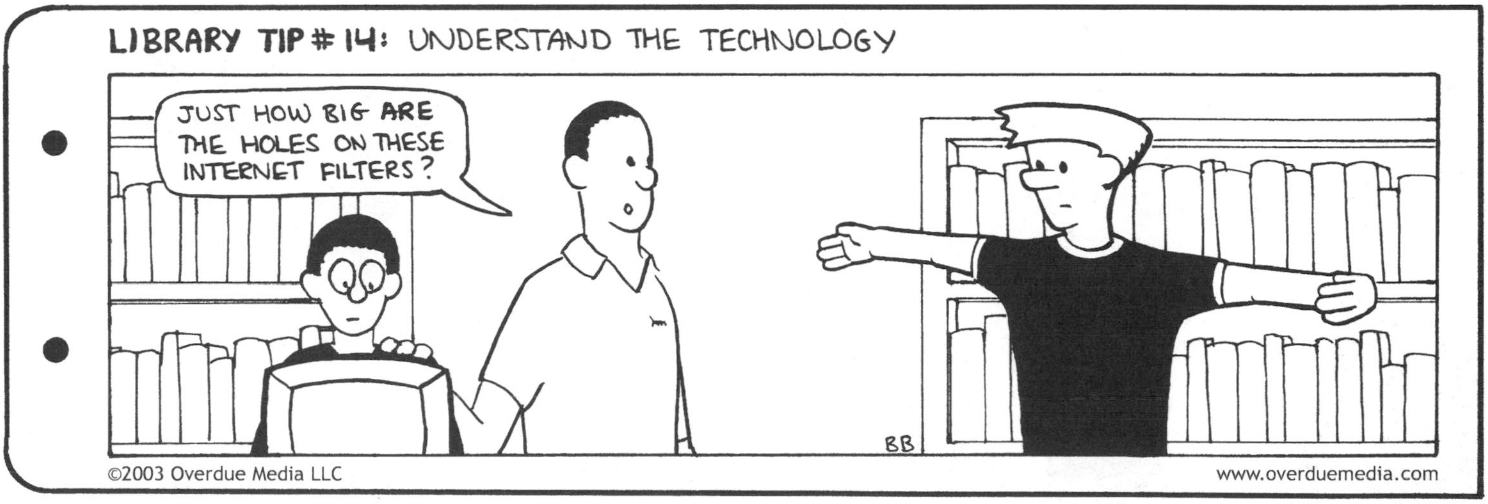
LIBRARY TIP # 14: UNDERSTAND THE TECHNOLOGY
JUST HOW BIG **ARE** THE HOLES ON THESE INTERNET FILTERS?
BB
©2003 Overdue Media LLC
www.overduemedia.com

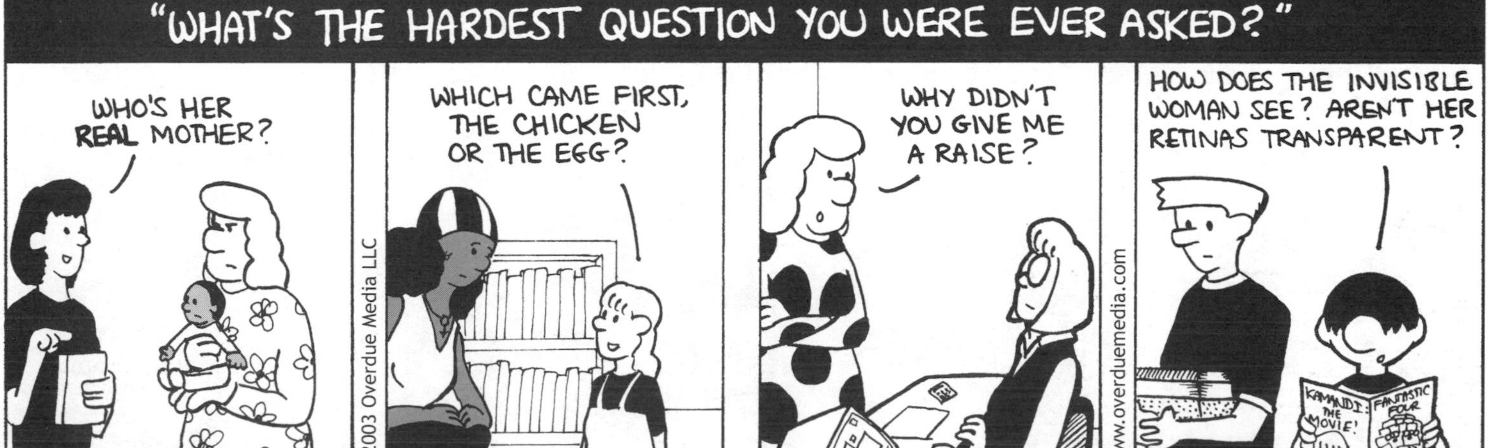
"WHAT'S THE HARDEST QUESTION YOU WERE EVER ASKED?"
WHO'S HER **REAL** MOTHER?
WHICH CAME FIRST, THE CHICKEN OR THE EGG?
WHY DIDN'T YOU GIVE ME A RAISE?
HOW DOES THE INVISIBLE WOMAN SEE? AREN'T HER RETINAS TRANSPARENT?
KAMANDI: THE MOVIE!
FANTASTIC FOUR
BB
©2003 Overdue Media LLC
www.overduemedia.com

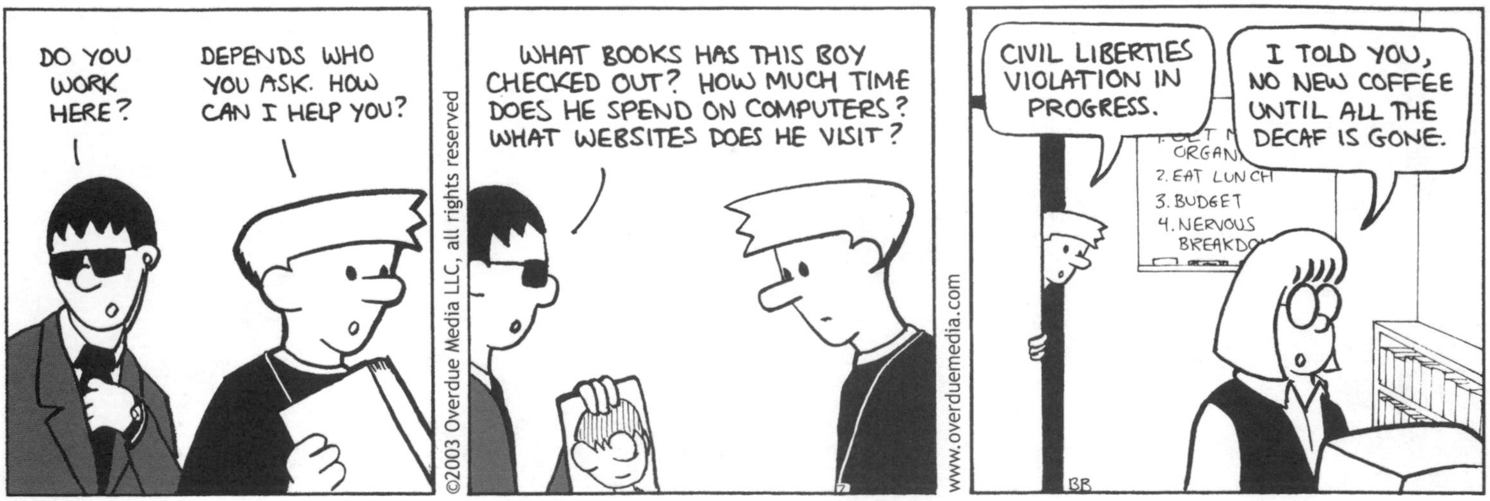

DO YOU WORK HERE?
DEPENDS WHO YOU ASK. HOW CAN I HELP YOU?
©2003 Overdue Media LLC, all rights reserved
WHAT BOOKS HAS THIS BOY CHECKED OUT? HOW MUCH TIME DOES HE SPEND ON COMPUTERS? WHAT WEBSITES DOES HE VISIT?
www.overduemedia.com
CIVIL LIBERTIES VIOLATION IN PROGRESS.
I TOLD YOU, NO NEW COFFEE UNTIL ALL THE DECAF IS GONE.


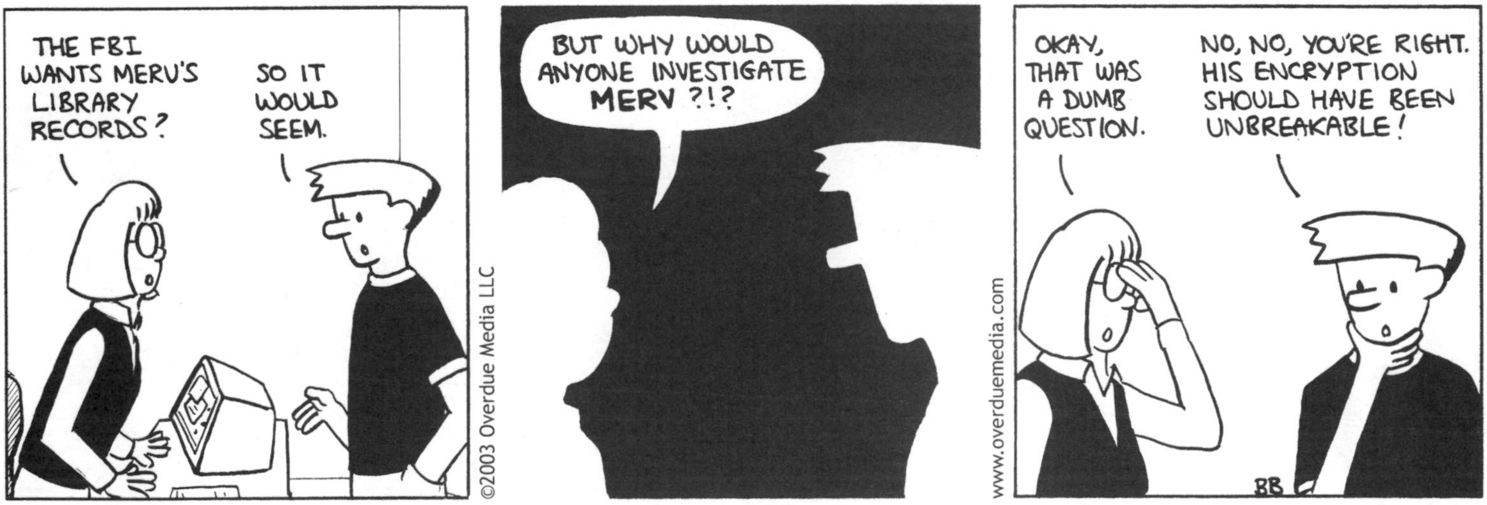

THE FBI WANTS MERV'S LIBRARY RECORDS?
SO IT WOULD SEEM.
©2003 Overdue Media LLC
BUT WHY WOULD ANYONE INVESTIGATE MERV?!?
www.overduemedia.com
OKAY, THAT WAS A DUMB QUESTION.
NO, NO, YOU'RE RIGHT. HIS ENCRYPTION SHOULD HAVE BEEN UNBREAKABLE!


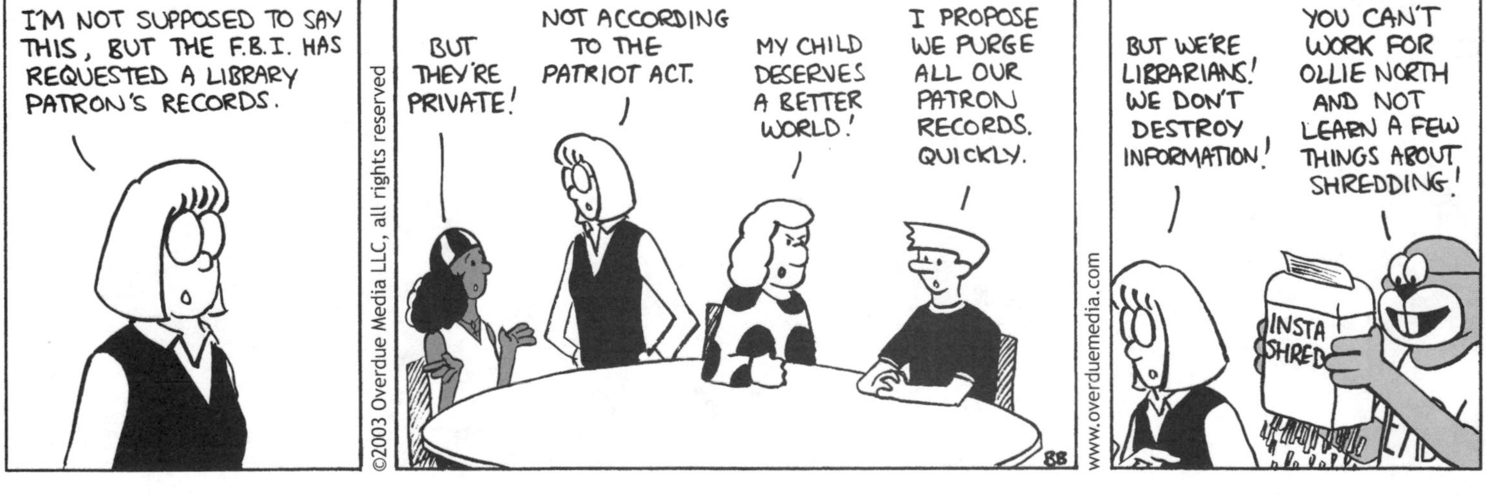

I'M NOT SUPPOSED TO SAY THIS, BUT THE F.B.I. HAS REQUESTED A LIBRARY PATRON'S RECORDS.
©2003 Overdue Media LLC, all rights reserved
BUT THEY'RE PRIVATE!
NOT ACCORDING TO THE PATRIOT ACT.
MY CHILD DESERVES A BETTER WORLD!
I PROPOSE WE PURGE ALL OUR PATRON RECORDS. QUICKLY.
www.overduemedia.com
BUT WE'RE LIBRARIANS! WE DON'T DESTROY INFORMATION!
YOU CAN'T WORK FOR OLLIE NORTH AND NOT LEARN A FEW THINGS ABOUT SHREDDING!
INSTA SHRED

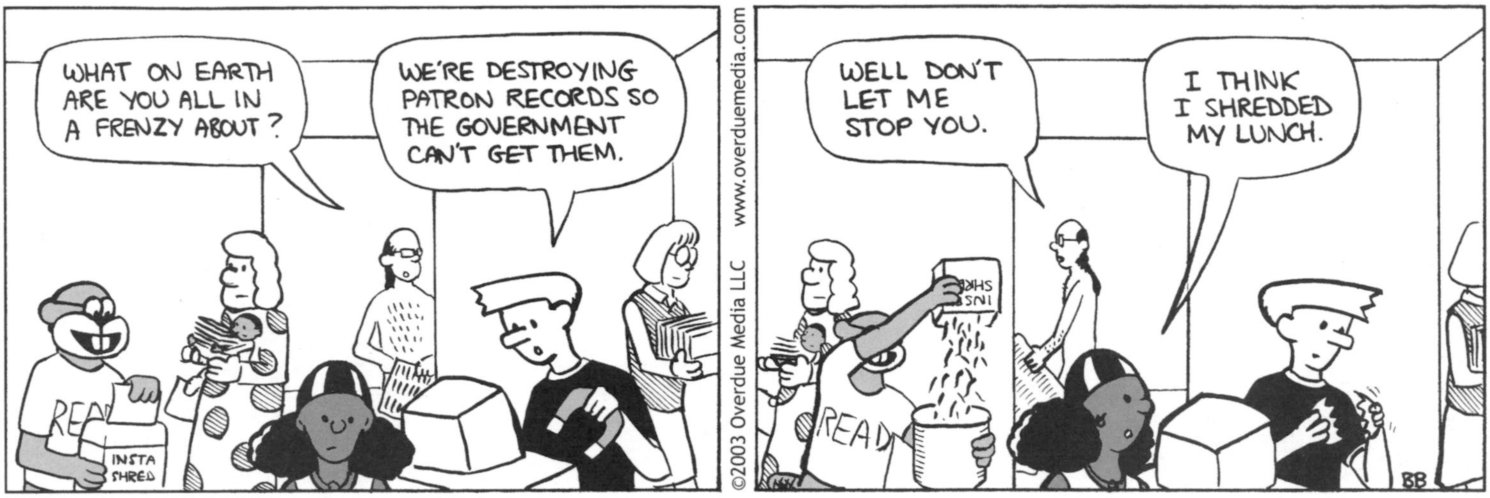
WHAT ON EARTH ARE YOU ALL IN A FRENZY ABOUT?
WE'RE DESTROYING PATRON RECORDS SO THE GOVERNMENT CAN'T GET THEM.
READ
INSTA SHRED
©2003 Overdue Media LLC www.overduemedia.com
WELL DON'T LET ME STOP YOU.
I THINK I SHREDDED MY LUNCH.
READ
BB

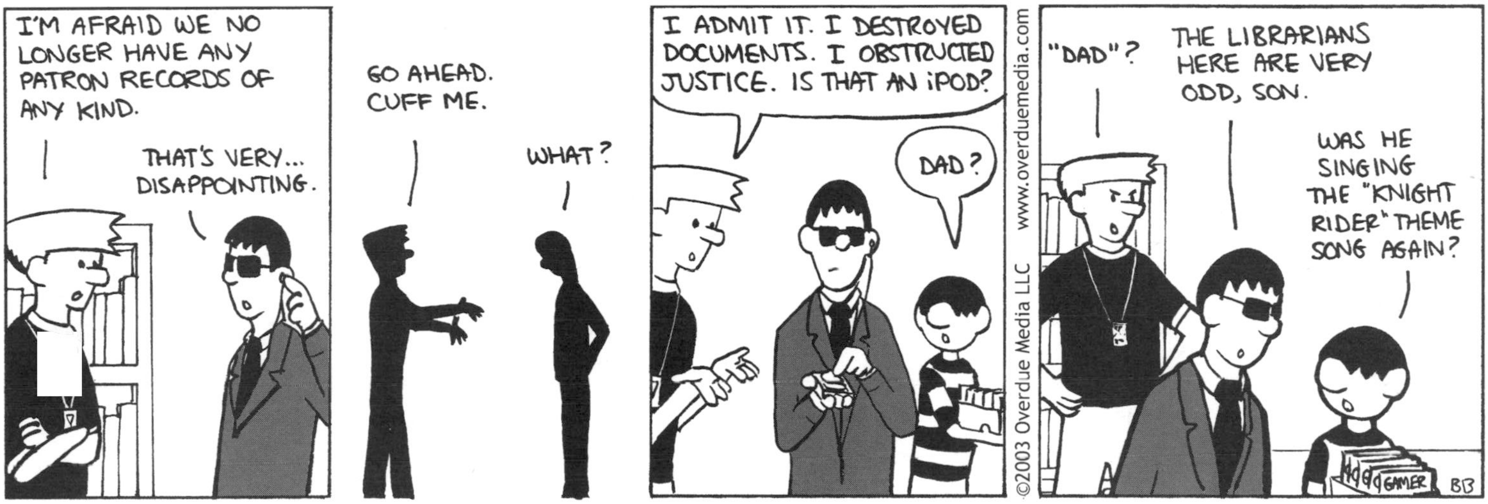
I'M AFRAID WE NO LONGER HAVE ANY PATRON RECORDS OF ANY KIND.
THAT'S VERY... DISAPPOINTING.
GO AHEAD. CUFF ME.
WHAT?
I ADMIT IT. I DESTROYED DOCUMENTS. I OBSTRUCTED JUSTICE. IS THAT AN iPOD?
DAD?
©2003 Overdue Media LLC www.overduemedia.com
"DAD"?
THE LIBRARIANS HERE ARE VERY ODD, SON.
WAS HE SINGING THE "KNIGHT RIDER" THEME SONG AGAIN?
GAMER
BB

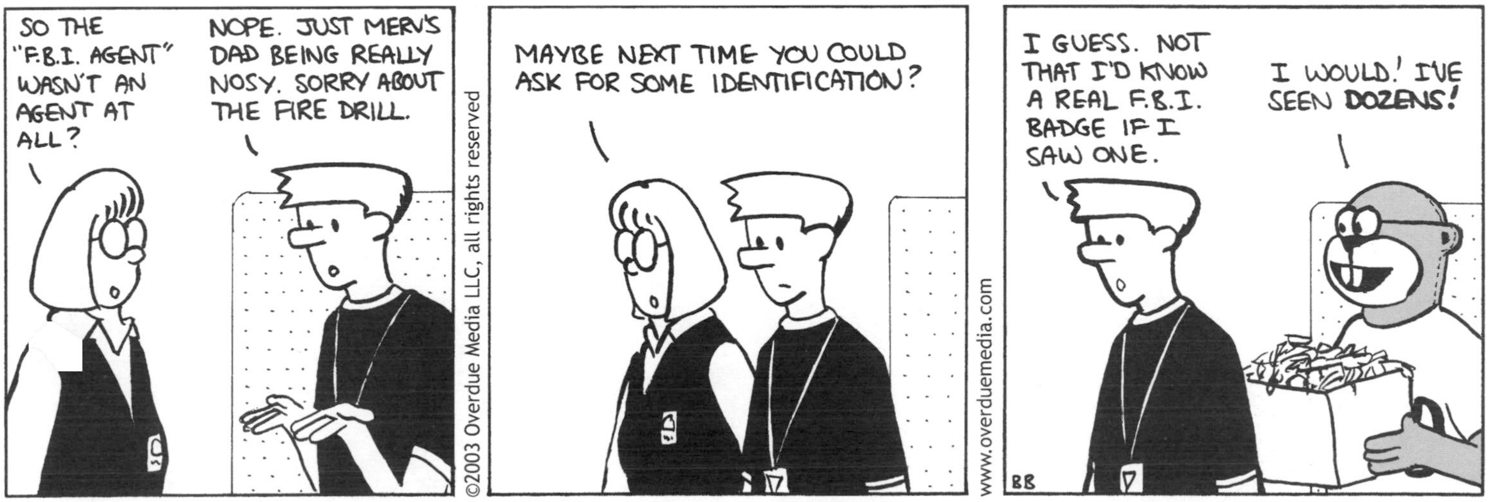
SO THE "F.B.I. AGENT" WASN'T AN AGENT AT ALL?
NOPE. JUST MERV'S DAD BEING REALLY NOSY. SORRY ABOUT THE FIRE DRILL.
©2003 Overdue Media LLC, all rights reserved
MAYBE NEXT TIME YOU COULD ASK FOR SOME IDENTIFICATION?
www.overduemedia.com
I GUESS. NOT THAT I'D KNOW A REAL F.B.I. BADGE IF I SAW ONE.
I WOULD! I'VE SEEN **DOZENS**!
BB

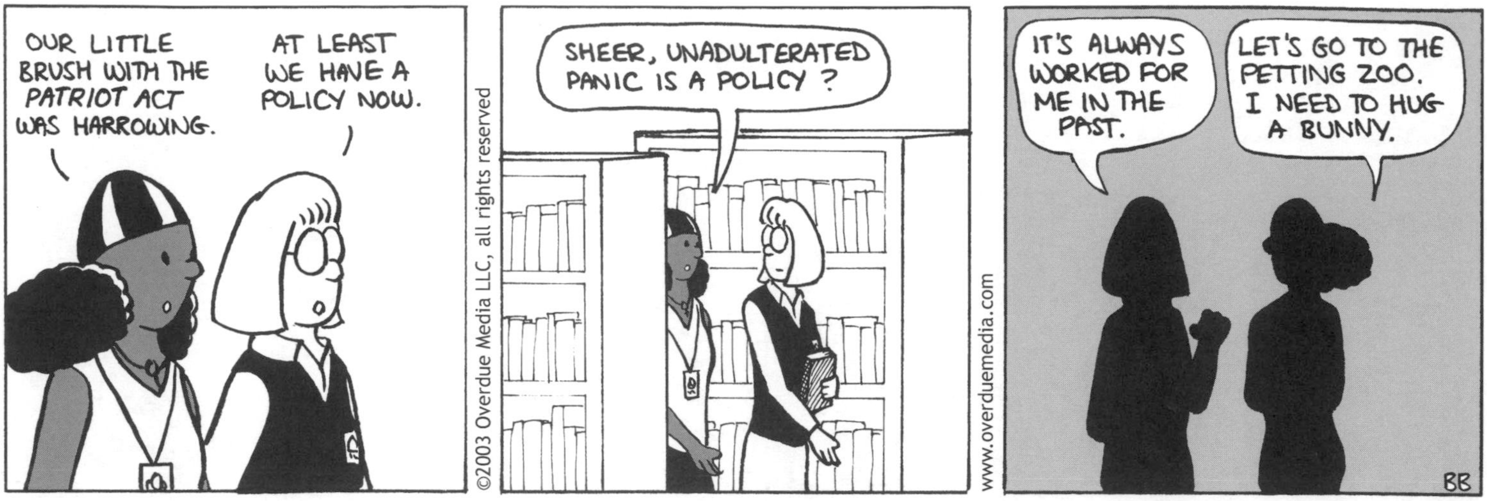
OUR LITTLE BRUSH WITH THE PATRIOT ACT WAS HARROWING.
AT LEAST WE HAVE A POLICY NOW.
©2003 Overdue Media LLC, all rights reserved
SHEER, UNADULTERATED PANIC IS A POLICY ?
www.overduemedia.com
IT'S ALWAYS WORKED FOR ME IN THE PAST.
LET'S GO TO THE PETTING ZOO. I NEED TO HUG A BUNNY.
BB

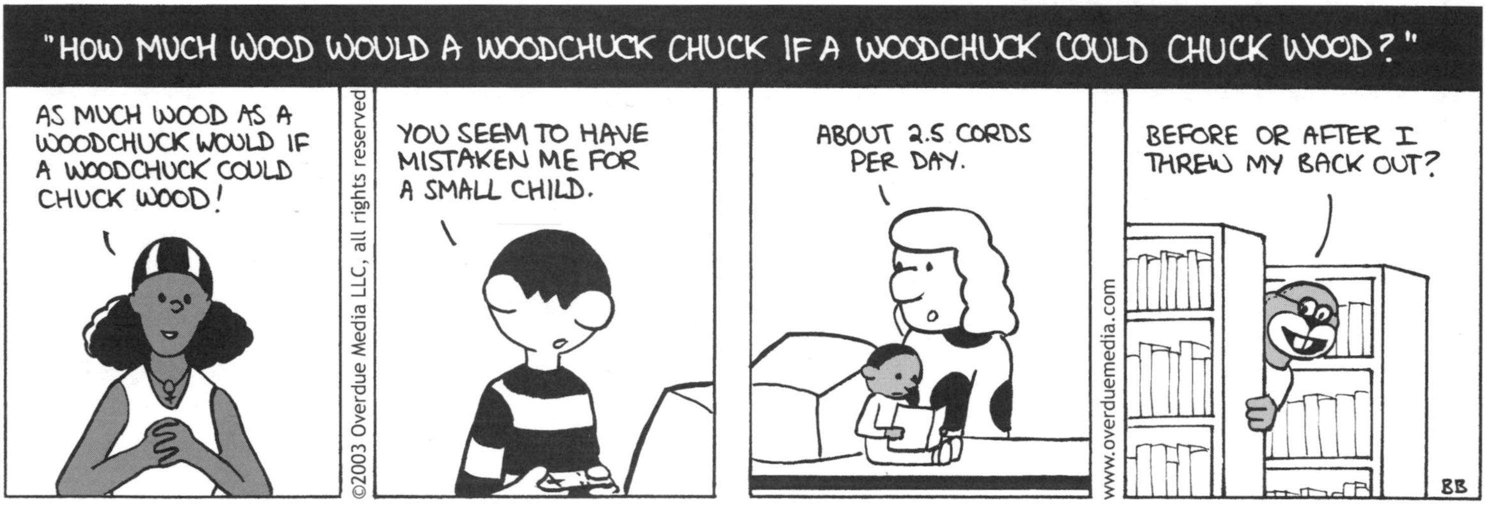
"HOW MUCH WOOD WOULD A WOODCHUCK CHUCK IF A WOODCHUCK COULD CHUCK WOOD?"
AS MUCH WOOD AS A WOODCHUCK WOULD IF A WOODCHUCK COULD CHUCK WOOD!
©2003 Overdue Media LLC, all rights reserved
YOU SEEM TO HAVE MISTAKEN ME FOR A SMALL CHILD.
ABOUT 2.5 CORDS PER DAY.
www.overduemedia.com
BEFORE OR AFTER I THREW MY BACK OUT?
BB

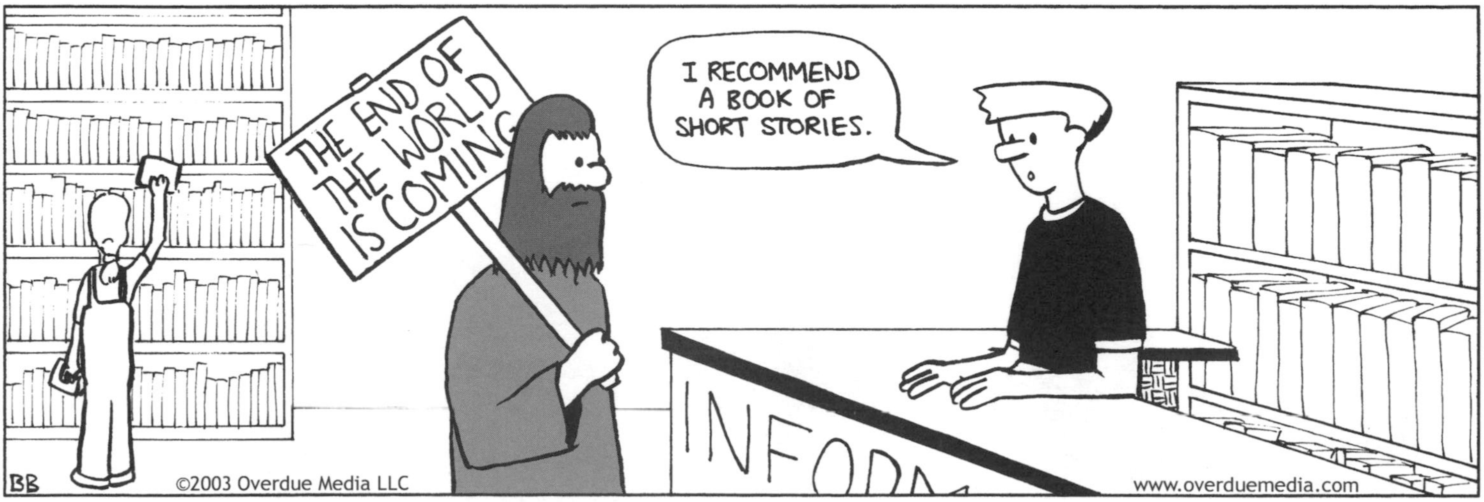
THE END OF THE WORLD IS COMING
I RECOMMEND A BOOK OF SHORT STORIES.
INFORM
BB
©2003 Overdue Media LLC
www.overduemedia.com

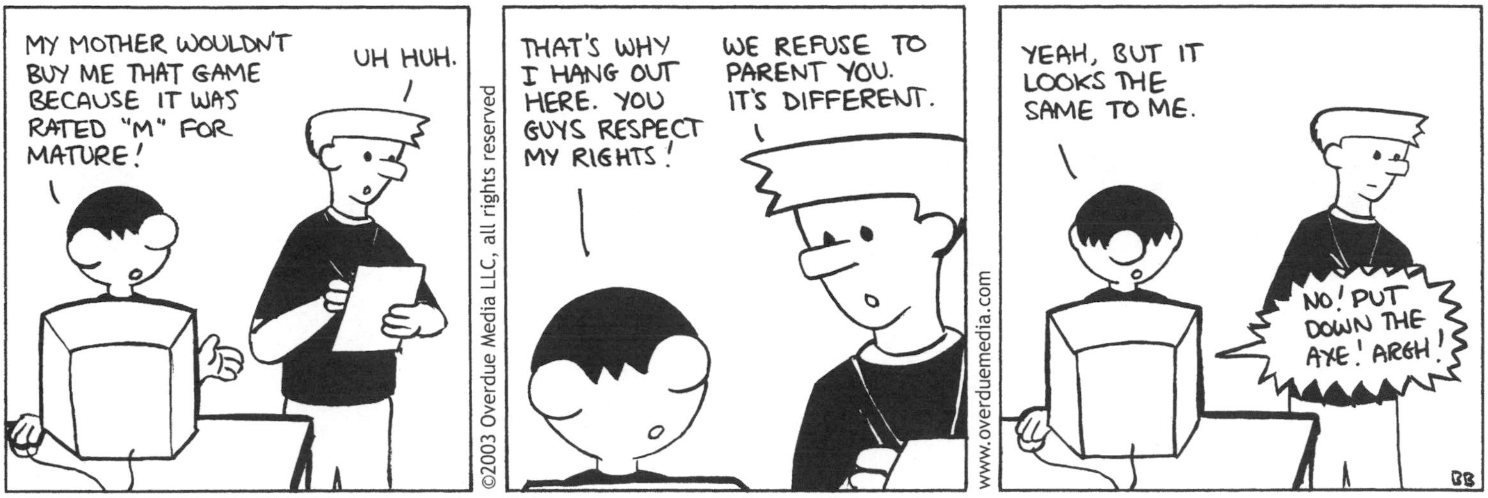
MY MOTHER WOULDN'T BUY ME THAT GAME BECAUSE IT WAS RATED "M" FOR MATURE!
UH HUH.
THAT'S WHY I HANG OUT HERE. YOU GUYS RESPECT MY RIGHTS!
WE REFUSE TO PARENT YOU. IT'S DIFFERENT.
YEAH, BUT IT LOOKS THE SAME TO ME.
NO! PUT DOWN THE AXE! ARGH!
BB
©2003 Overdue Media LLC, all rights reserved
www.overduemedia.com

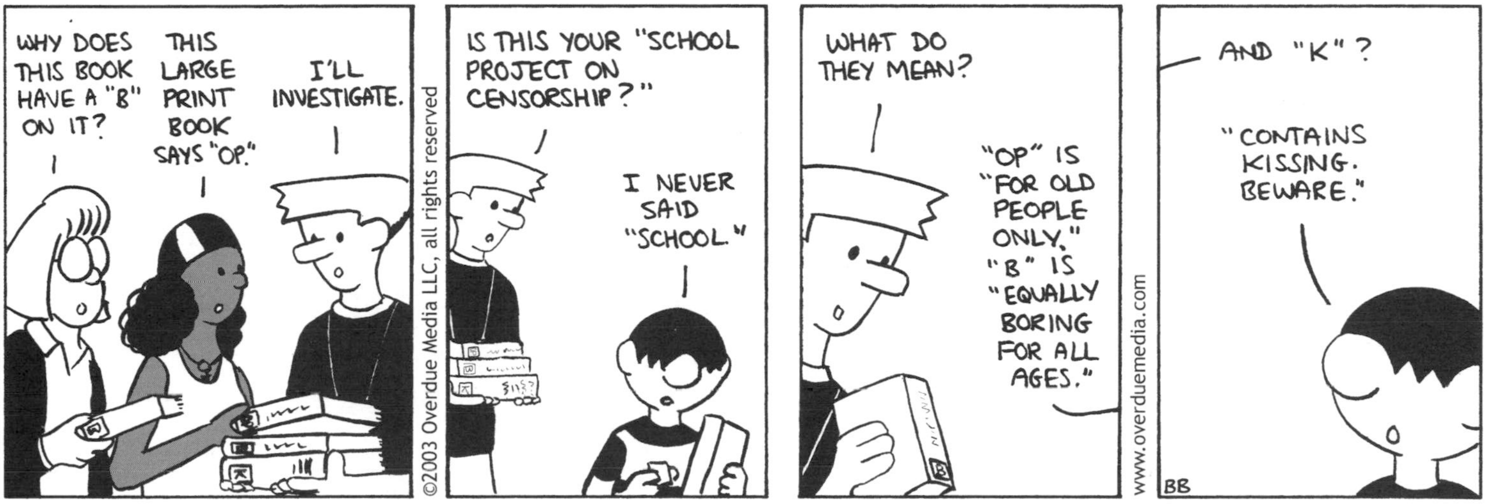
WHY DOES THIS BOOK HAVE A "B" ON IT?
THIS LARGE PRINT BOOK SAYS "OP."
I'LL INVESTIGATE.
IS THIS YOUR "SCHOOL PROJECT ON CENSORSHIP?"
I NEVER SAID "SCHOOL."
WHAT DO THEY MEAN?
"OP" IS "FOR OLD PEOPLE ONLY." "B" IS "EQUALLY BORING FOR ALL AGES."
AND "K"?
"CONTAINS KISSING. BEWARE."
BB
©2003 Overdue Media LLC, all rights reserved
www.overduemedia.com

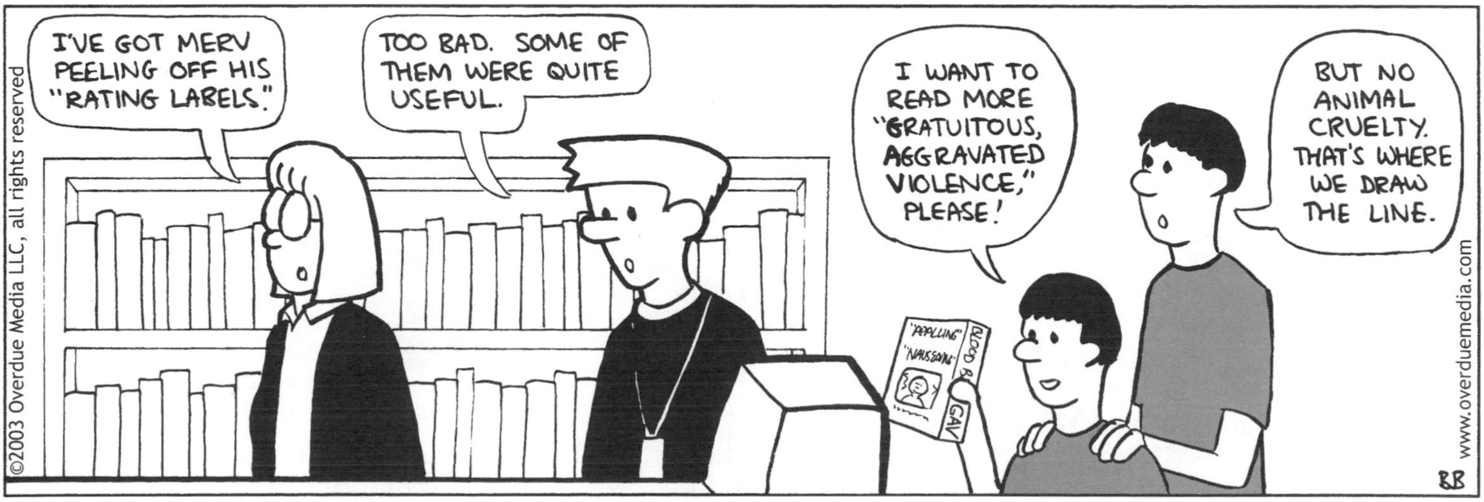
I'VE GOT MERV PEELING OFF HIS "RATING LABELS."
TOO BAD. SOME OF THEM WERE QUITE USEFUL.
I WANT TO READ MORE "GRATUITOUS, AGGRAVATED VIOLENCE," PLEASE!
BUT NO ANIMAL CRUELTY. THAT'S WHERE WE DRAW THE LINE.
BB
©2003 Overdue Media LLC, all rights reserved
www.overduemedia.com

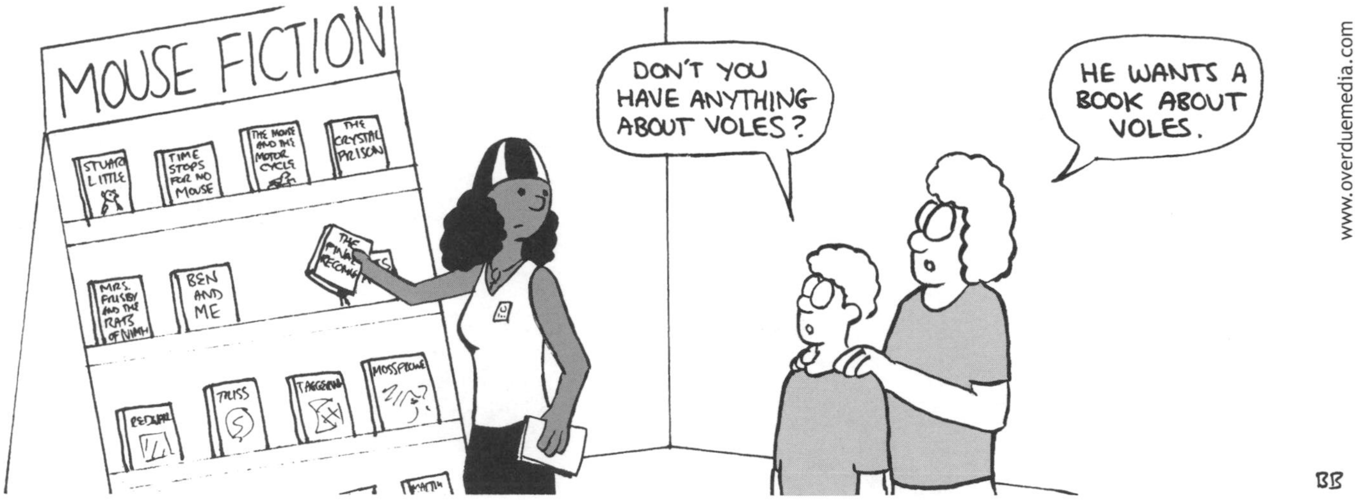
MOUSE FICTION
STUART LITTLE
TIME STOPS FOR NO MOUSE
THE CRYSTAL PRISON
MRS. FRISBY AND THE RATS OF NIMH
BEN AND ME
TRISS
MOSSFLOWER
DON'T YOU HAVE ANYTHING ABOUT VOLES?
HE WANTS A BOOK ABOUT VOLES.
BB



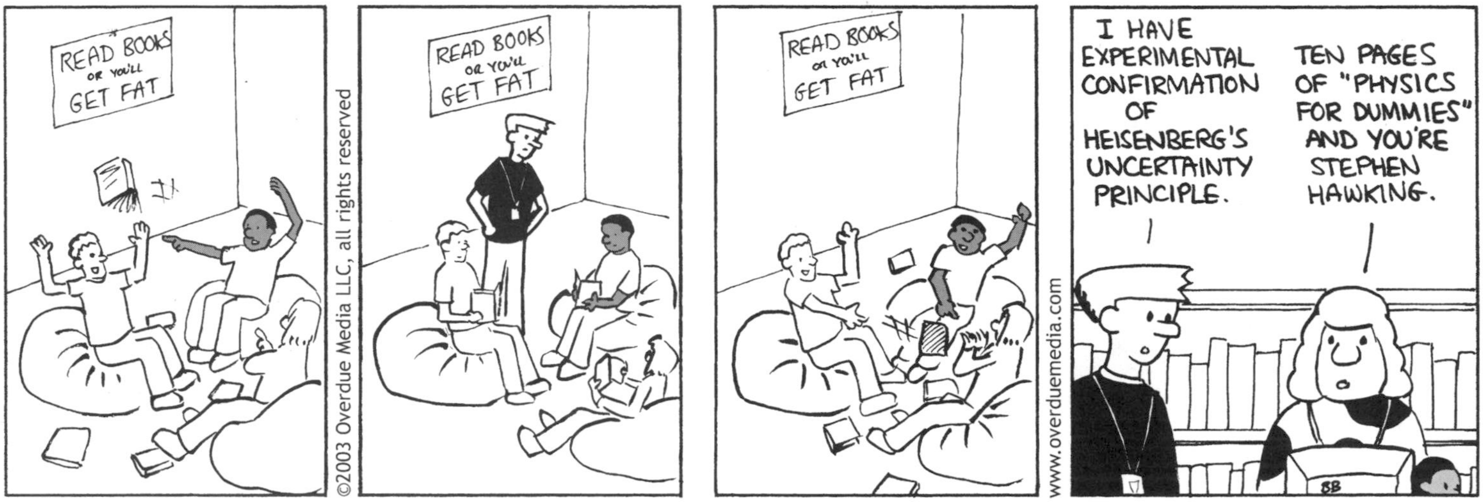
READ BOOKS OR YOU'LL GET FAT
READ BOOKS OR YOU'LL GET FAT
READ BOOKS OR YOU'LL GET FAT
I HAVE EXPERIMENTAL CONFIRMATION OF HEISENBERG'S UNCERTAINTY PRINCIPLE.
TEN PAGES OF "PHYSICS FOR DUMMIES" AND YOU'RE STEPHEN HAWKING.
BB



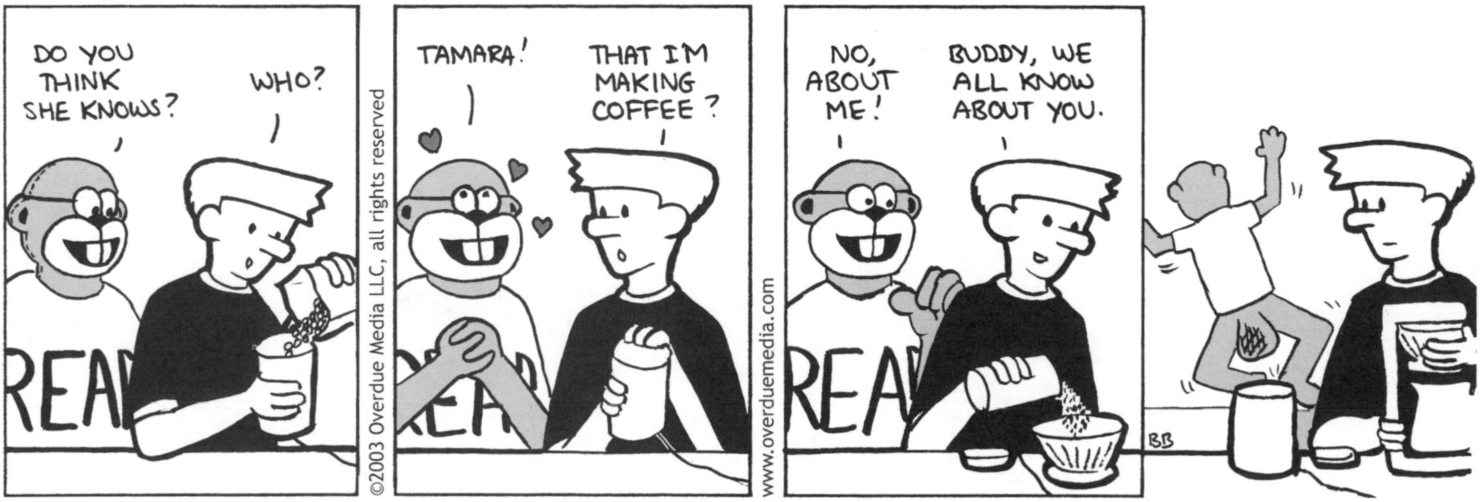
DO YOU THINK SHE KNOWS?
WHO?
READ
TAMARA!
THAT I'M MAKING COFFEE?
NO, ABOUT ME!
BUDDY, WE ALL KNOW ABOUT YOU.
READ
BB

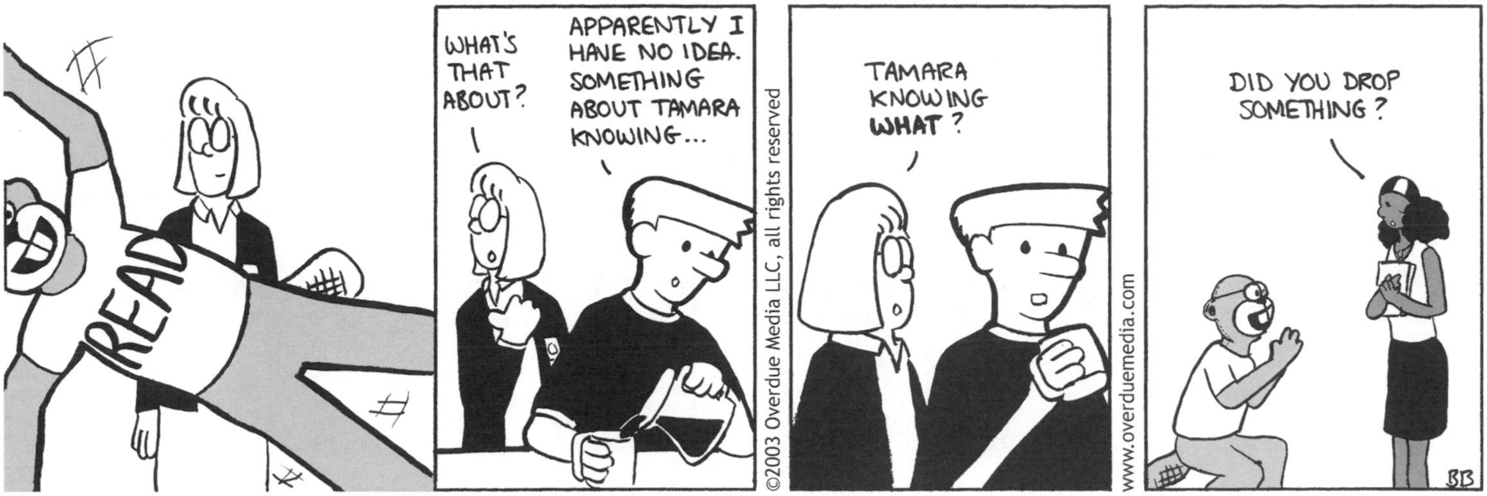
READ
WHAT'S THAT ABOUT?
APPARENTLY I HAVE NO IDEA. SOMETHING ABOUT TAMARA KNOWING...
©2003 Overdue Media LLC, all rights reserved
TAMARA KNOWING **WHAT**?
www.overduemedia.com
DID YOU DROP SOMETHING?
BB

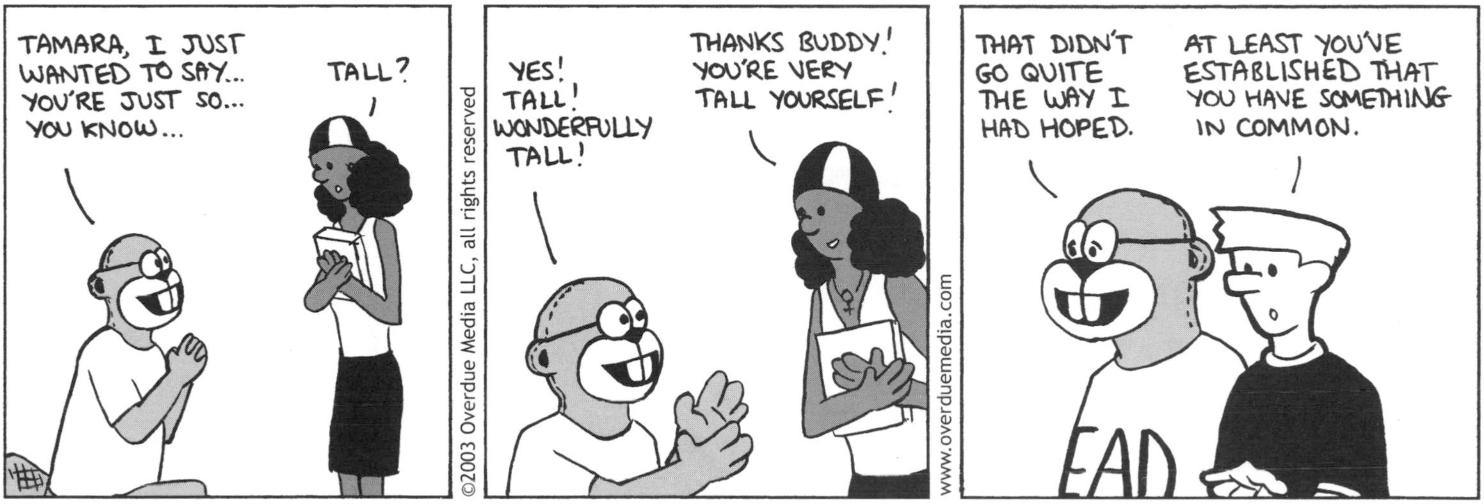
TAMARA, I JUST WANTED TO SAY... YOU'RE JUST SO... YOU KNOW...
TALL?
©2003 Overdue Media LLC, all rights reserved
YES! TALL! WONDERFULLY TALL!
THANKS BUDDY! YOU'RE VERY TALL YOURSELF!
www.overduemedia.com
THAT DIDN'T GO QUITE THE WAY I HAD HOPED.
AT LEAST YOU'VE ESTABLISHED THAT YOU HAVE SOMETHING IN COMMON.
EAD

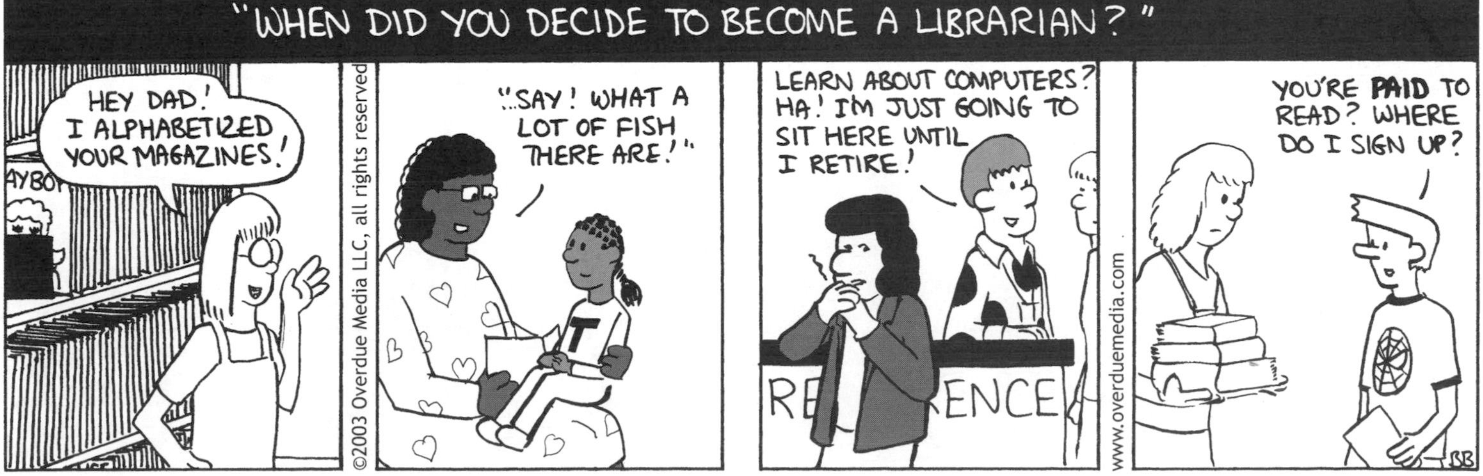
"WHEN DID YOU DECIDE TO BECOME A LIBRARIAN?"
HEY DAD! I ALPHABETIZED YOUR MAGAZINES!
©2003 Overdue Media LLC, all rights reserved
"...SAY! WHAT A LOT OF FISH THERE ARE!"
T
LEARN ABOUT COMPUTERS? HA! I'M JUST GOING TO SIT HERE UNTIL I RETIRE!
RE ENCE
www.overduemedia.com
YOU'RE **PAID** TO READ? WHERE DO I SIGN UP?
BB

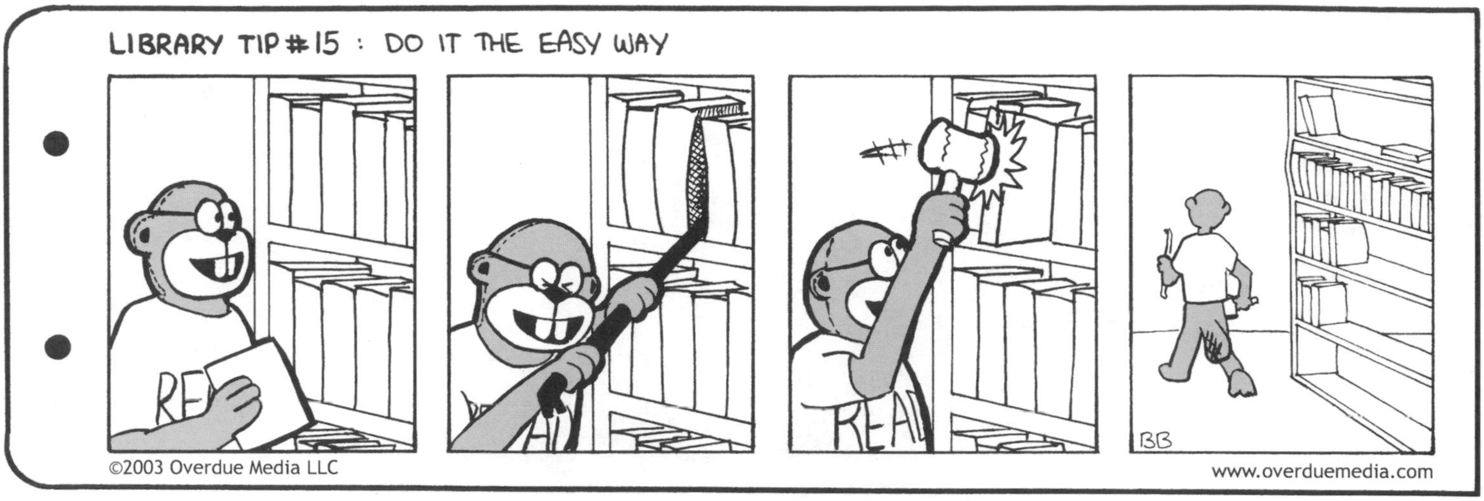
LIBRARY TIP #15 : DO IT THE EASY WAY
READ
BB
©2003 Overdue Media LLC
www.overduemedia.com

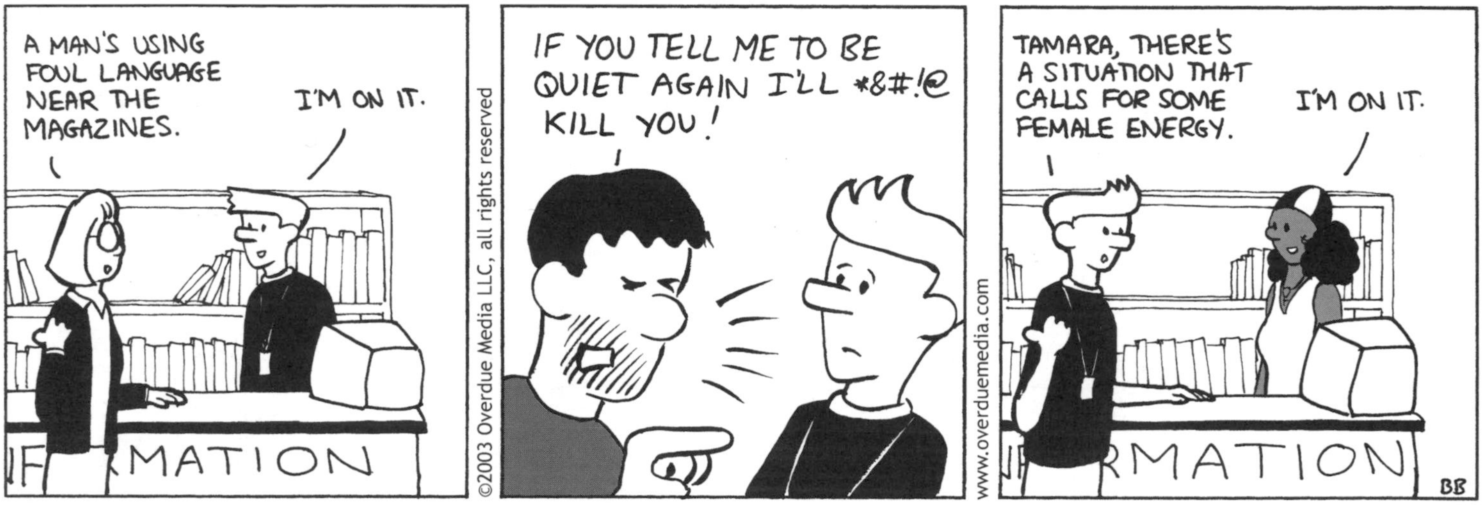
A MAN'S USING FOUL LANGUAGE NEAR THE MAGAZINES.
I'M ON IT.
INFORMATION
©2003 Overdue Media LLC, all rights reserved
IF YOU TELL ME TO BE QUIET AGAIN I'LL *&#!@ KILL YOU!
www.overduemedia.com
TAMARA, THERE'S A SITUATION THAT CALLS FOR SOME FEMALE ENERGY.
I'M ON IT.
INFORMATION
BB

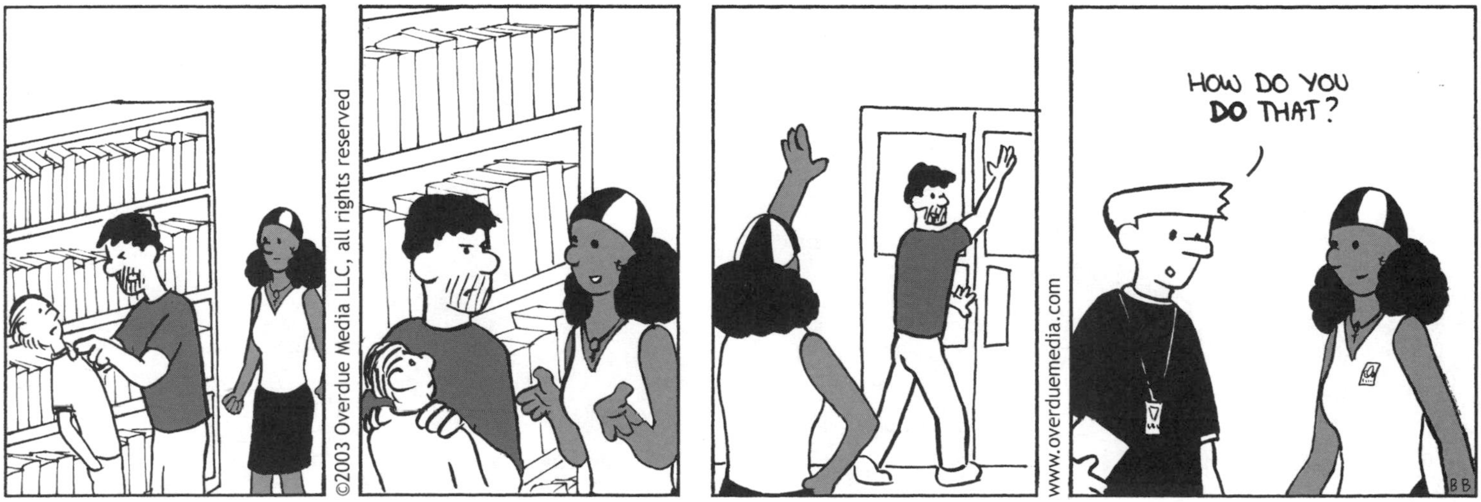
©2003 Overdue Media LLC, all rights reserved
www.overduemedia.com
HOW DO YOU **DO** THAT?
BB

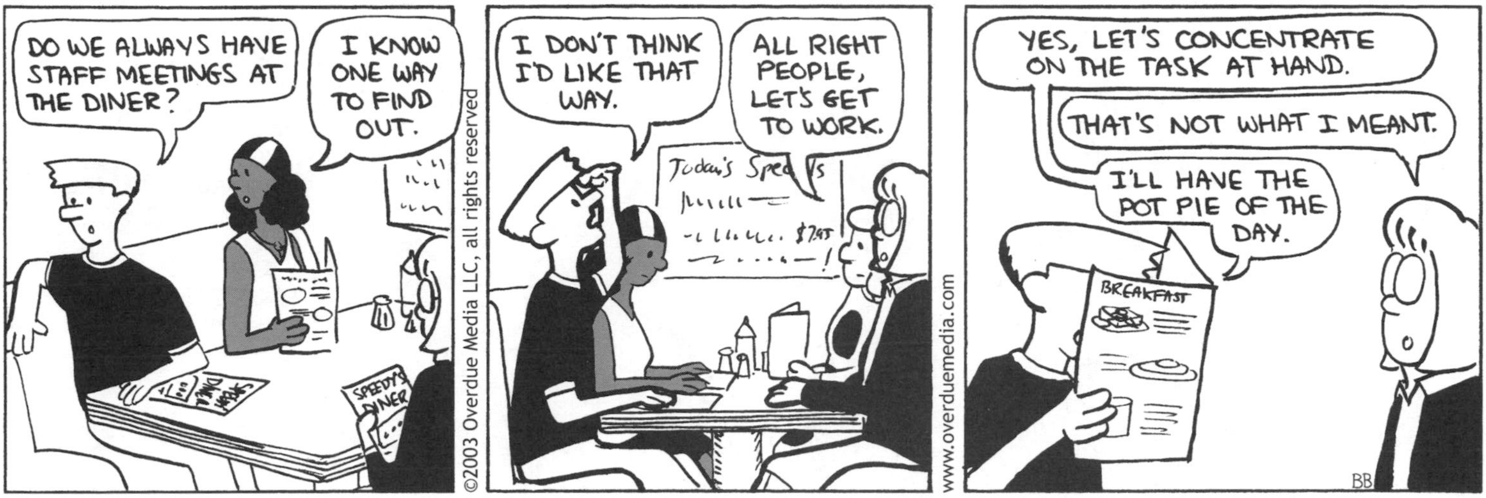
DO WE ALWAYS HAVE STAFF MEETINGS AT THE DINER?
I KNOW ONE WAY TO FIND OUT.
SPEEDY'S DINER
©2003 Overdue Media LLC, all rights reserved
I DON'T THINK I'D LIKE THAT WAY.
ALL RIGHT PEOPLE, LET'S GET TO WORK.
www.overduemedia.com
YES, LET'S CONCENTRATE ON THE TASK AT HAND.
THAT'S NOT WHAT I MEANT.
I'LL HAVE THE POT PIE OF THE DAY.
BREAKFAST
BB

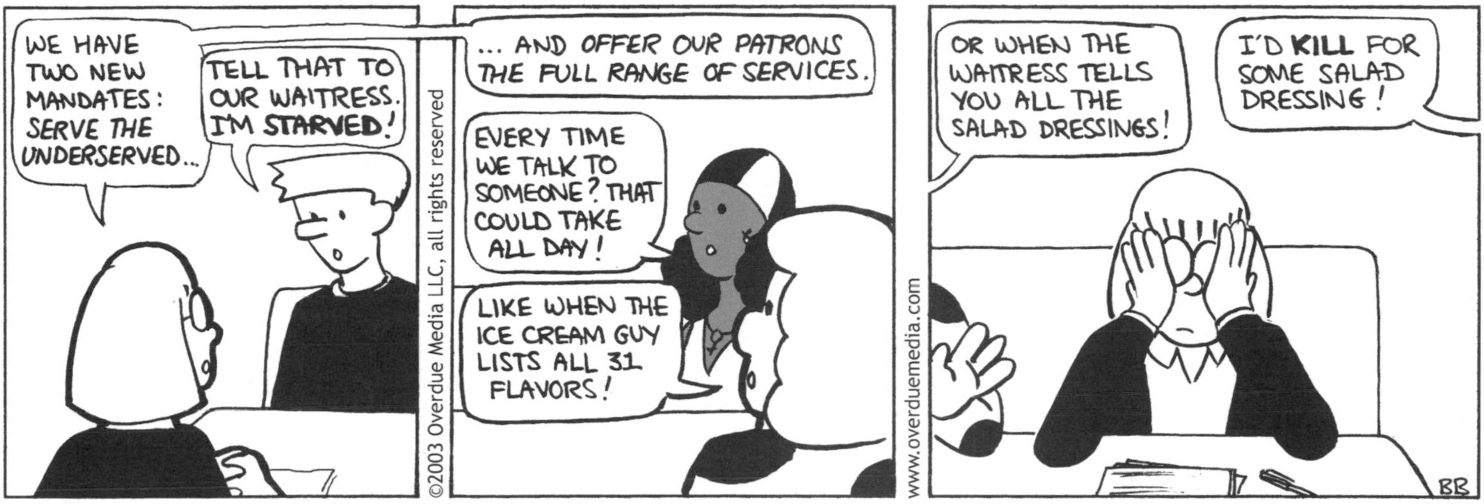
WE HAVE TWO NEW MANDATES: SERVE THE UNDERSERVED...
TELL THAT TO OUR WAITRESS. I'M **STARVED**!
©2003 Overdue Media LLC, all rights reserved
... AND OFFER OUR PATRONS THE FULL RANGE OF SERVICES.
EVERY TIME WE TALK TO SOMEONE? THAT COULD TAKE ALL DAY!
LIKE WHEN THE ICE CREAM GUY LISTS ALL 31 FLAVORS!
www.overduemedia.com
OR WHEN THE WAITRESS TELLS YOU ALL THE SALAD DRESSINGS!
I'D **KILL** FOR SOME SALAD DRESSING!
BB

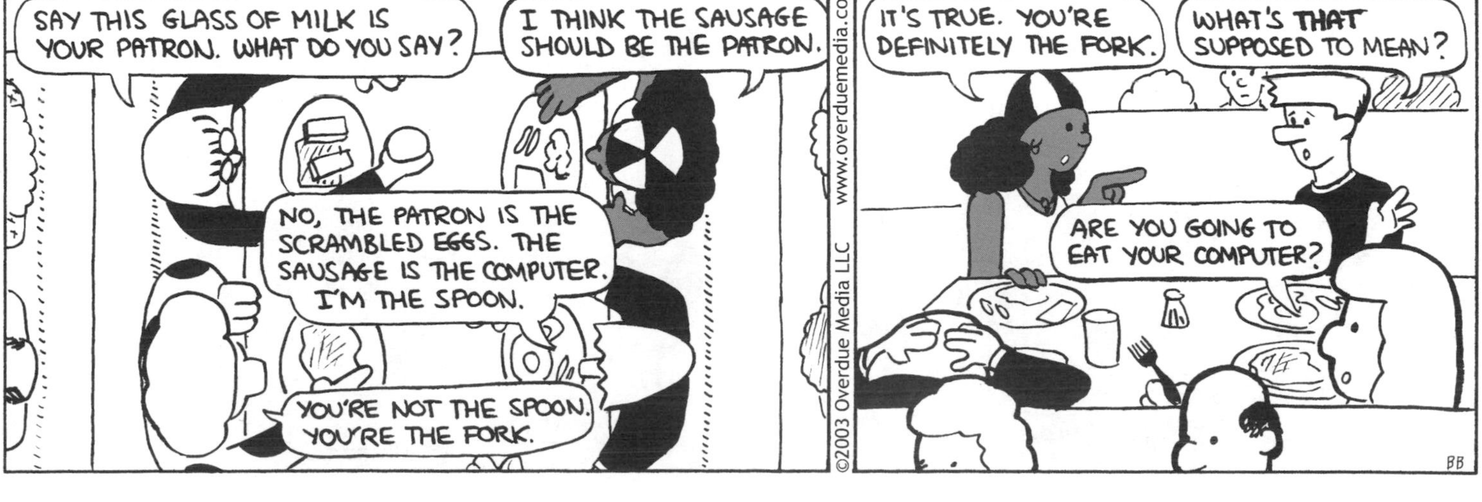
SAY THIS GLASS OF MILK IS YOUR PATRON. WHAT DO YOU SAY?
I THINK THE SAUSAGE SHOULD BE THE PATRON.
NO, THE PATRON IS THE SCRAMBLED EGGS. THE SAUSAGE IS THE COMPUTER. I'M THE SPOON.
YOU'RE NOT THE SPOON. YOU'RE THE FORK.
©2003 Overdue Media LLC www.overduemedia.com
IT'S TRUE. YOU'RE DEFINITELY THE FORK.
WHAT'S **THAT** SUPPOSED TO MEAN?
ARE YOU GOING TO EAT YOUR COMPUTER?
BB

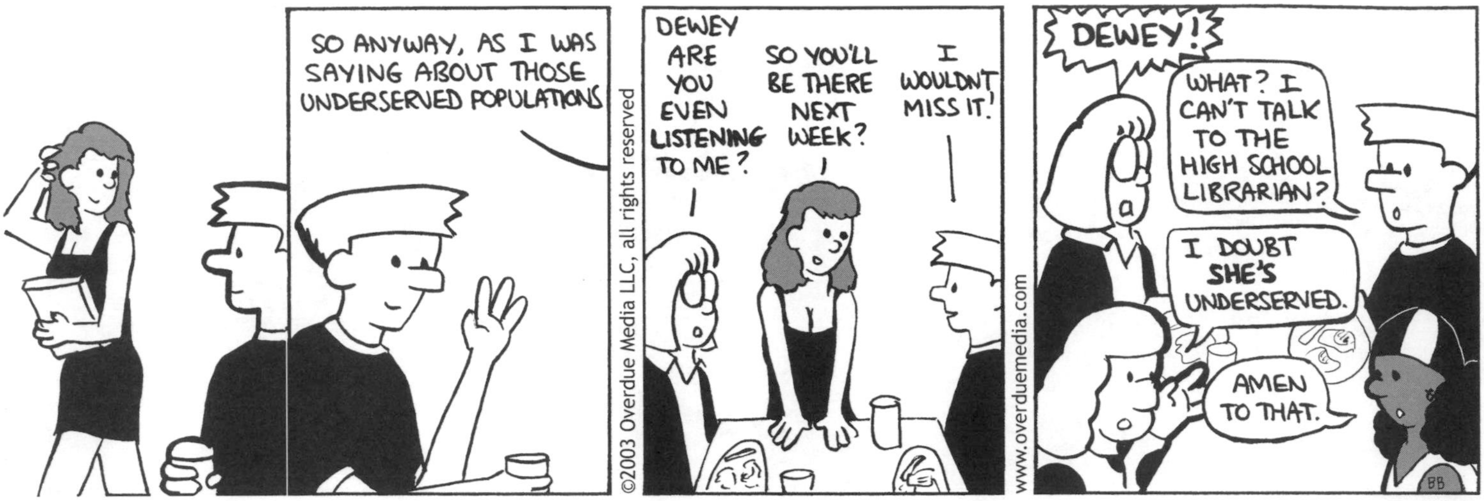
SO ANYWAY, AS I WAS SAYING ABOUT THOSE UNDERSERVED POPULATIONS
©2003 Overdue Media LLC, all rights reserved
DEWEY ARE YOU EVEN LISTENING TO ME?
SO YOU'LL BE THERE NEXT WEEK?
I WOULDN'T MISS IT!
www.overduemedia.com
DEWEY!
WHAT? I CAN'T TALK TO THE HIGH SCHOOL LIBRARIAN?
I DOUBT SHE'S UNDERSERVED.
AMEN TO THAT.
BB

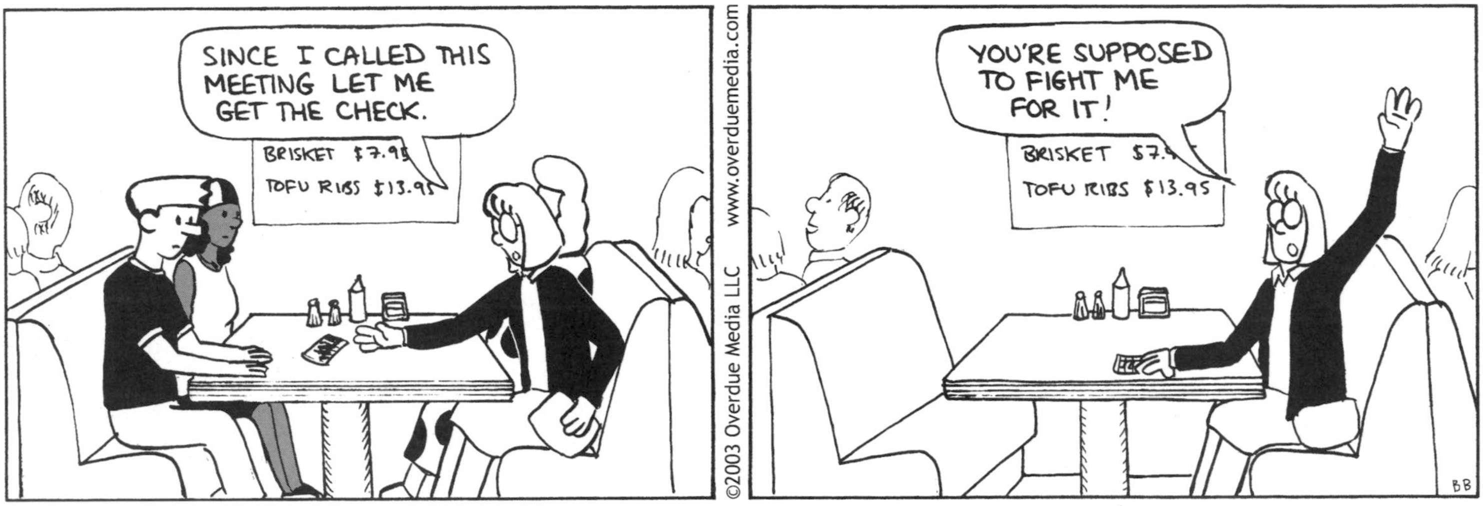
SINCE I CALLED THIS MEETING LET ME GET THE CHECK.
BRISKET $7.95
TOFU RIBS $13.95
www.overduemedia.com
©2003 Overdue Media LLC
YOU'RE SUPPOSED TO FIGHT ME FOR IT!
BRISKET
TOFU RIBS $13.95
BB

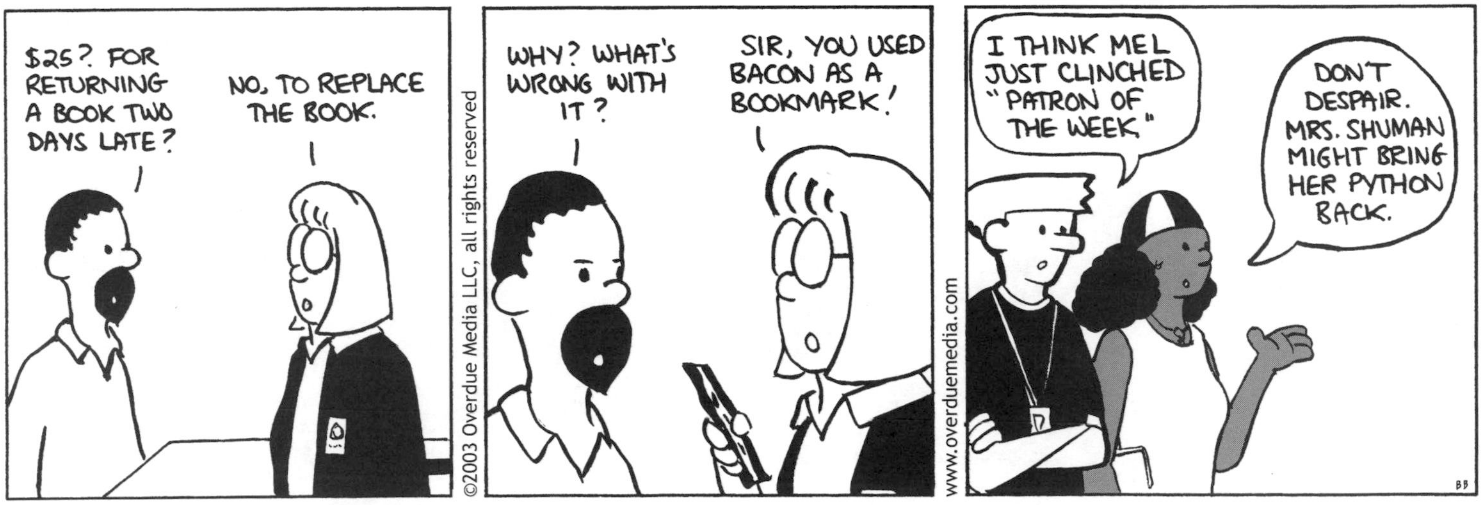
$25? FOR RETURNING A BOOK TWO DAYS LATE?
NO, TO REPLACE THE BOOK.
©2003 Overdue Media LLC, all rights reserved
WHY? WHAT'S WRONG WITH IT?
SIR, YOU USED BACON AS A BOOKMARK!
www.overduemedia.com
I THINK MEL JUST CLINCHED "PATRON OF THE WEEK."
DON'T DESPAIR. MRS. SHUMAN MIGHT BRING HER PYTHON BACK.
BB

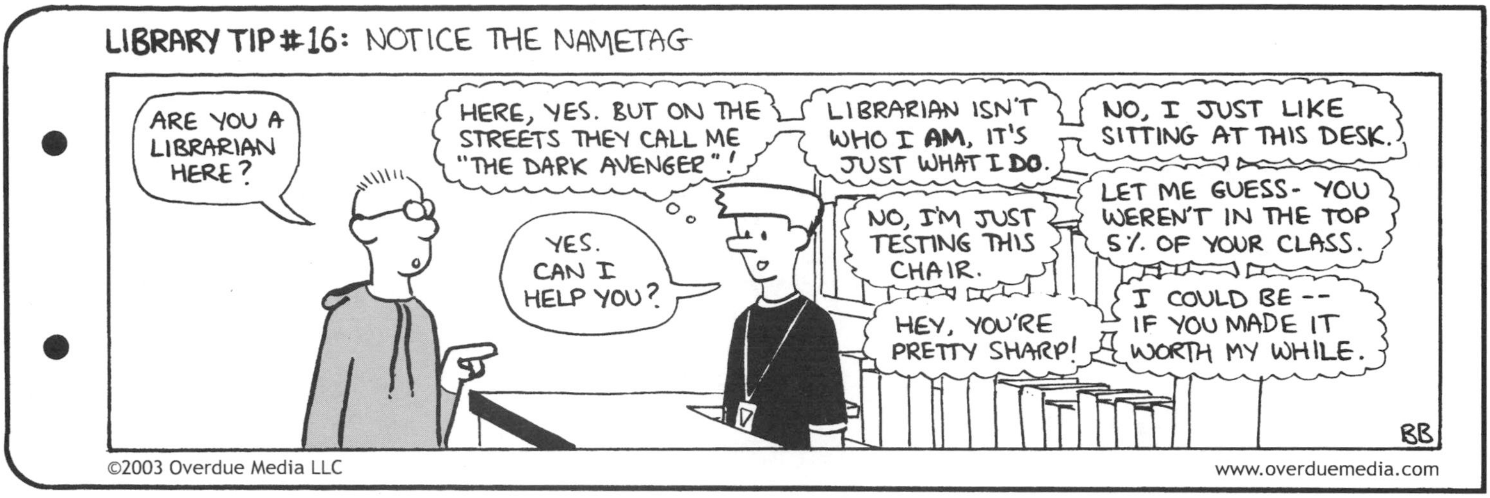
LIBRARY TIP #16: NOTICE THE NAMETAG
ARE YOU A LIBRARIAN HERE?
YES. CAN I HELP YOU?
HERE, YES. BUT ON THE STREETS THEY CALL ME "THE DARK AVENGER"!
LIBRARIAN ISN'T WHO I AM, IT'S JUST WHAT I DO.
NO, I JUST LIKE SITTING AT THIS DESK.
NO, I'M JUST TESTING THIS CHAIR.
LET ME GUESS- YOU WEREN'T IN THE TOP 5% OF YOUR CLASS.
HEY, YOU'RE PRETTY SHARP!
I COULD BE -- IF YOU MADE IT WORTH MY WHILE.
BB


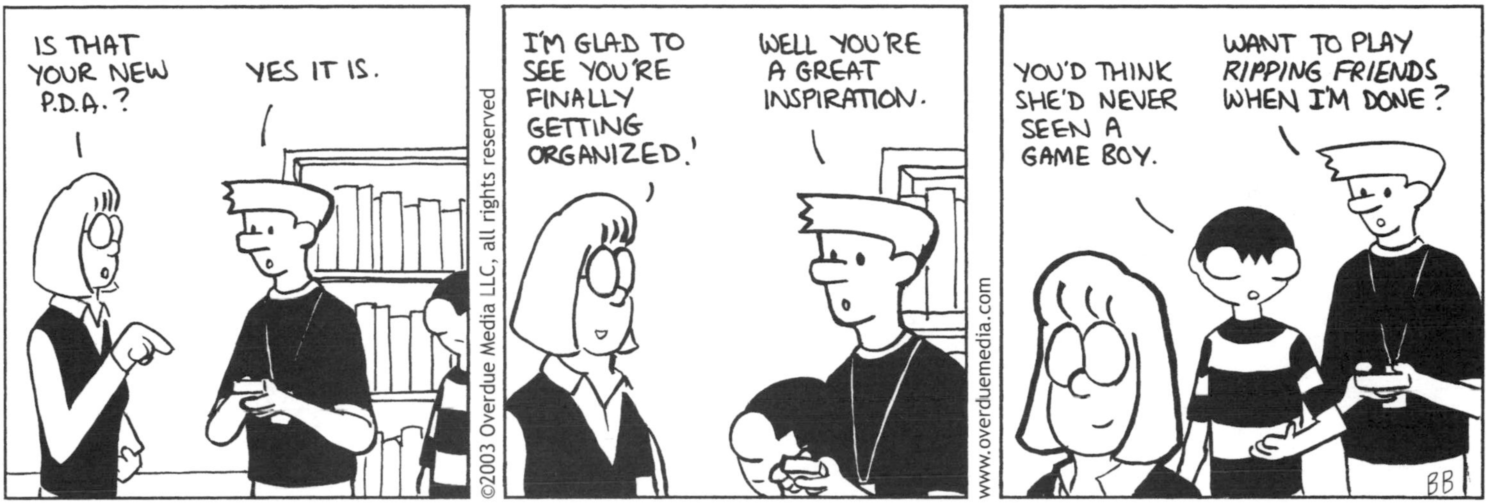
IS THAT YOUR NEW P.D.A.?
YES IT IS.
I'M GLAD TO SEE YOU'RE FINALLY GETTING ORGANIZED!
WELL YOU'RE A GREAT INSPIRATION.
YOU'D THINK SHE'D NEVER SEEN A GAME BOY.
WANT TO PLAY *RIPPING FRIENDS* WHEN I'M DONE?
BB


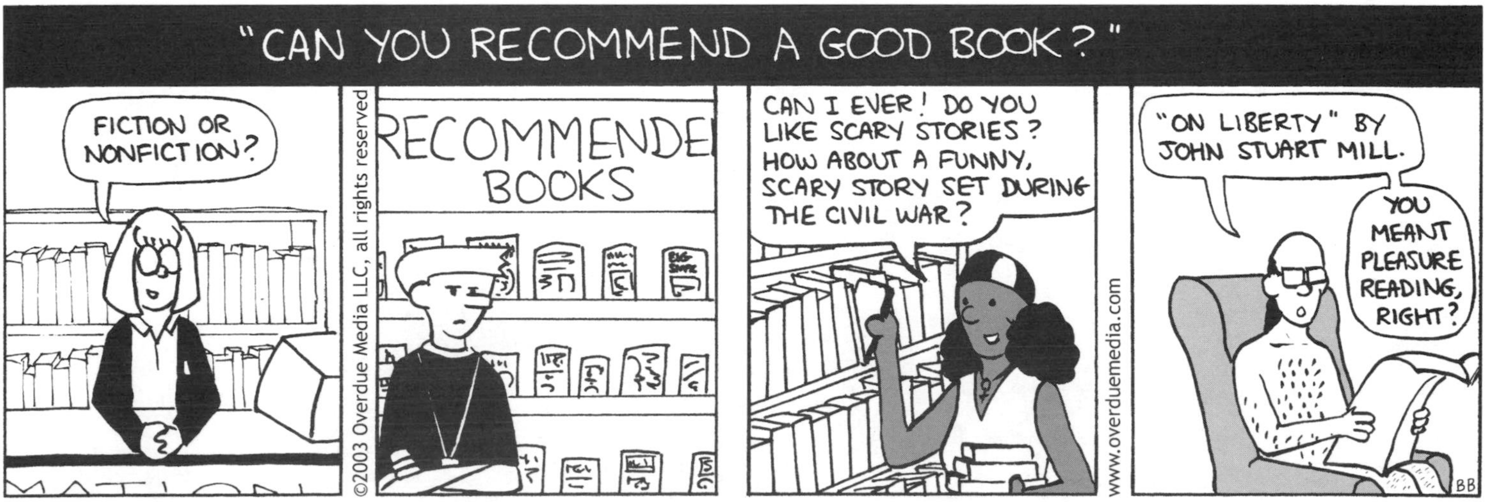
"CAN YOU RECOMMEND A GOOD BOOK?"
FICTION OR NONFICTION?
RECOMMENDE BOOKS
CAN I EVER! DO YOU LIKE SCARY STORIES? HOW ABOUT A FUNNY, SCARY STORY SET DURING THE CIVIL WAR?
"ON LIBERTY" BY JOHN STUART MILL.
YOU MEANT PLEASURE READING, RIGHT?
BB

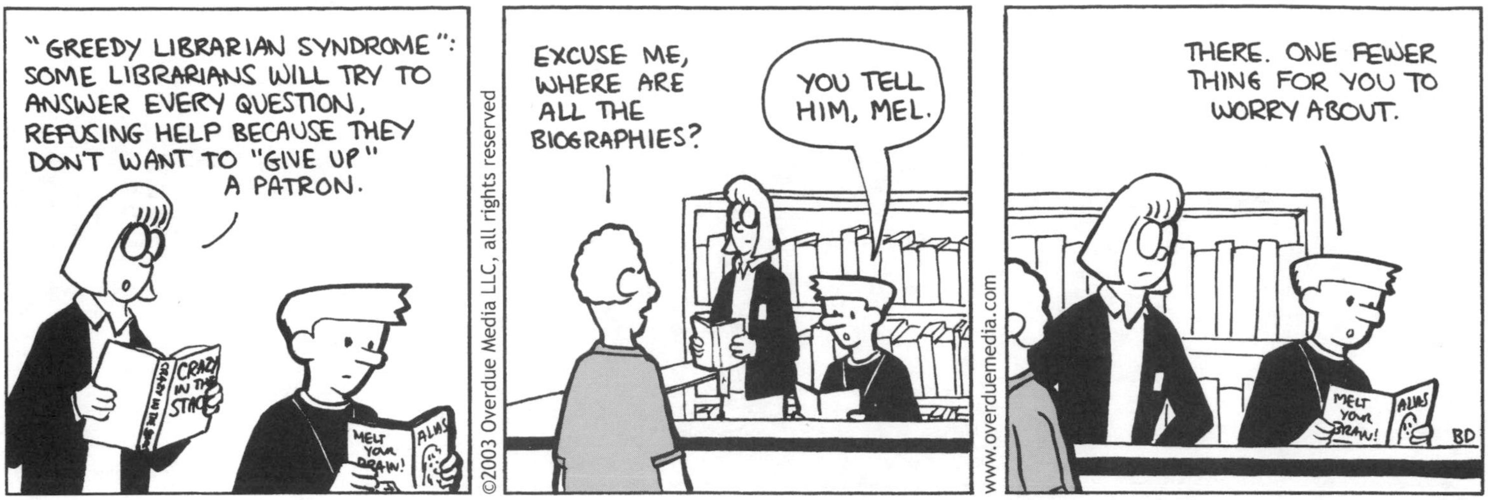
"GREEDY LIBRARIAN SYNDROME": SOME LIBRARIANS WILL TRY TO ANSWER EVERY QUESTION, REFUSING HELP BECAUSE THEY DON'T WANT TO "GIVE UP" A PATRON.
CRAZY IN THE STACKS
MELT YOUR BRAIN!
ALIAS
©2003 Overdue Media LLC, all rights reserved
EXCUSE ME, WHERE ARE ALL THE BIOGRAPHIES?
YOU TELL HIM, MEL.
www.overduemedia.com
THERE. ONE FEWER THING FOR YOU TO WORRY ABOUT.
BD

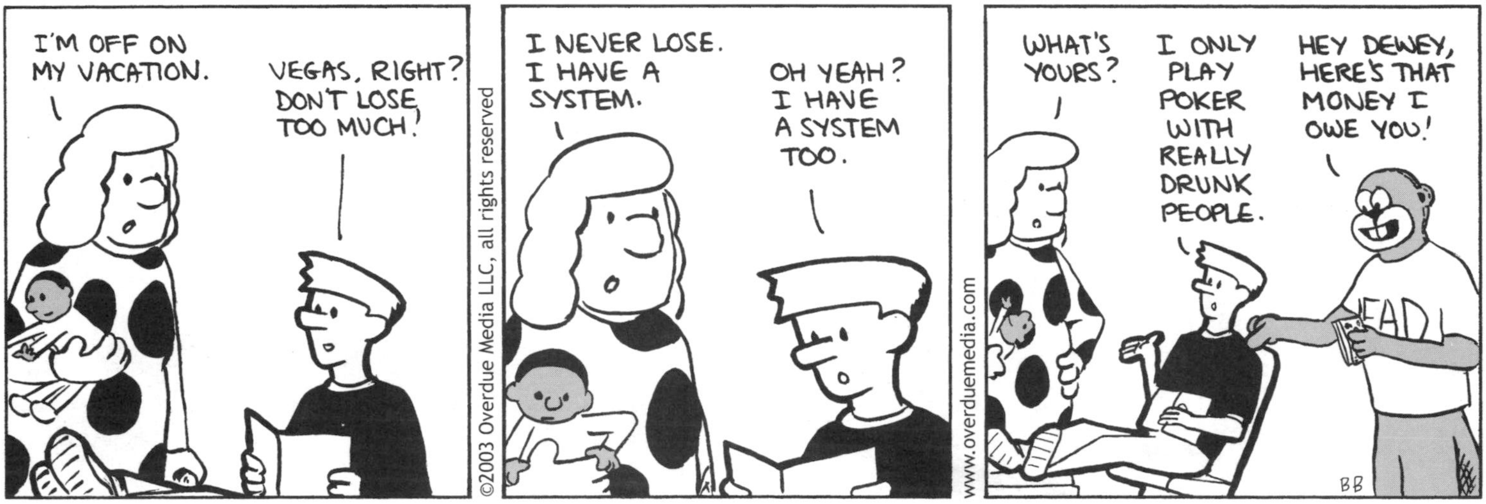
I'M OFF ON MY VACATION.
VEGAS, RIGHT? DON'T LOSE TOO MUCH!
©2003 Overdue Media LLC, all rights reserved
I NEVER LOSE. I HAVE A SYSTEM.
OH YEAH? I HAVE A SYSTEM TOO.
www.overduemedia.com
WHAT'S YOURS?
I ONLY PLAY POKER WITH REALLY DRUNK PEOPLE.
HEY DEWEY, HERE'S THAT MONEY I OWE YOU!
BB

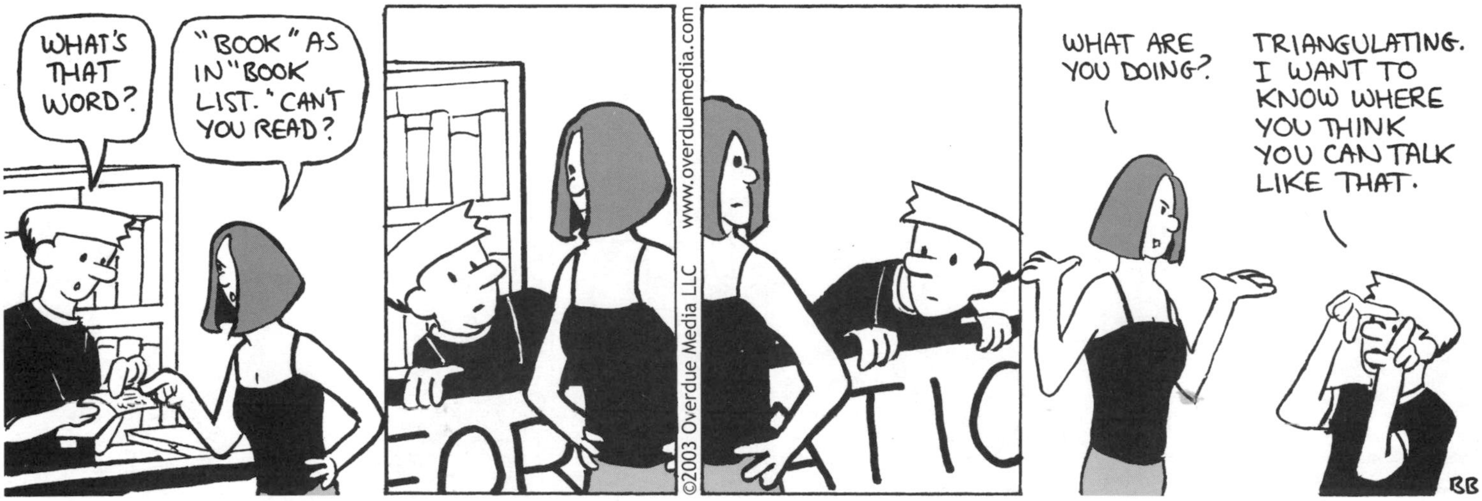
WHAT'S THAT WORD?
"BOOK" AS IN "BOOK LIST." CAN'T YOU READ?
www.overduemedia.com
©2003 Overdue Media LLC
WHAT ARE YOU DOING?
TRIANGULATING. I WANT TO KNOW WHERE YOU THINK YOU CAN TALK LIKE THAT.
BB

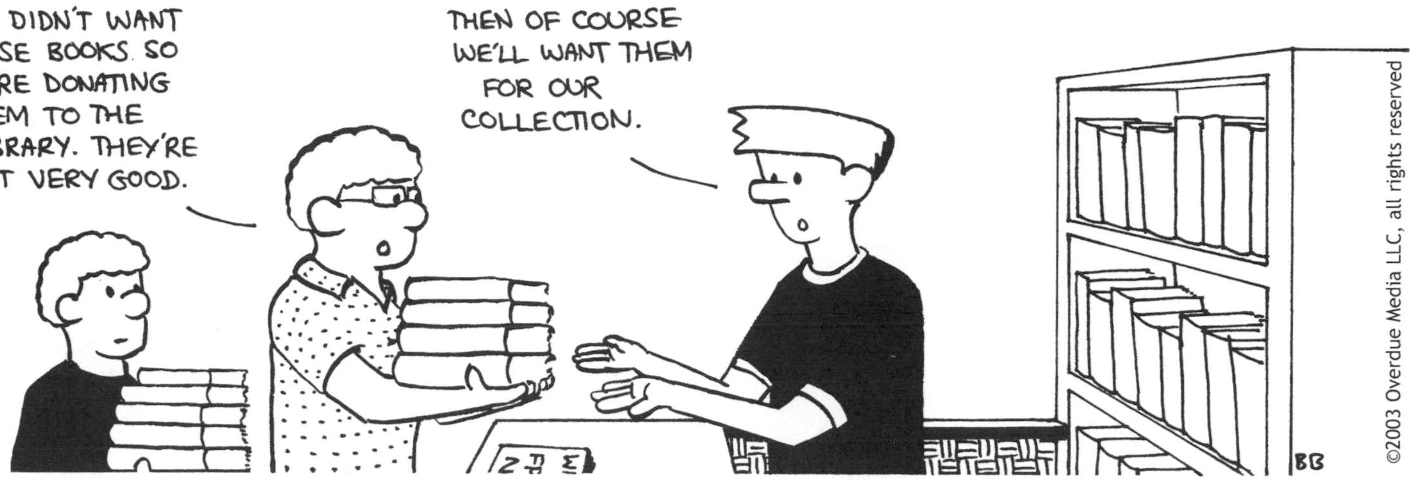
WE DIDN'T WANT THESE BOOKS. SO WE'RE DONATING THEM TO THE LIBRARY. THEY'RE NOT VERY GOOD.
THEN OF COURSE WE'LL WANT THEM FOR OUR COLLECTION.
BB



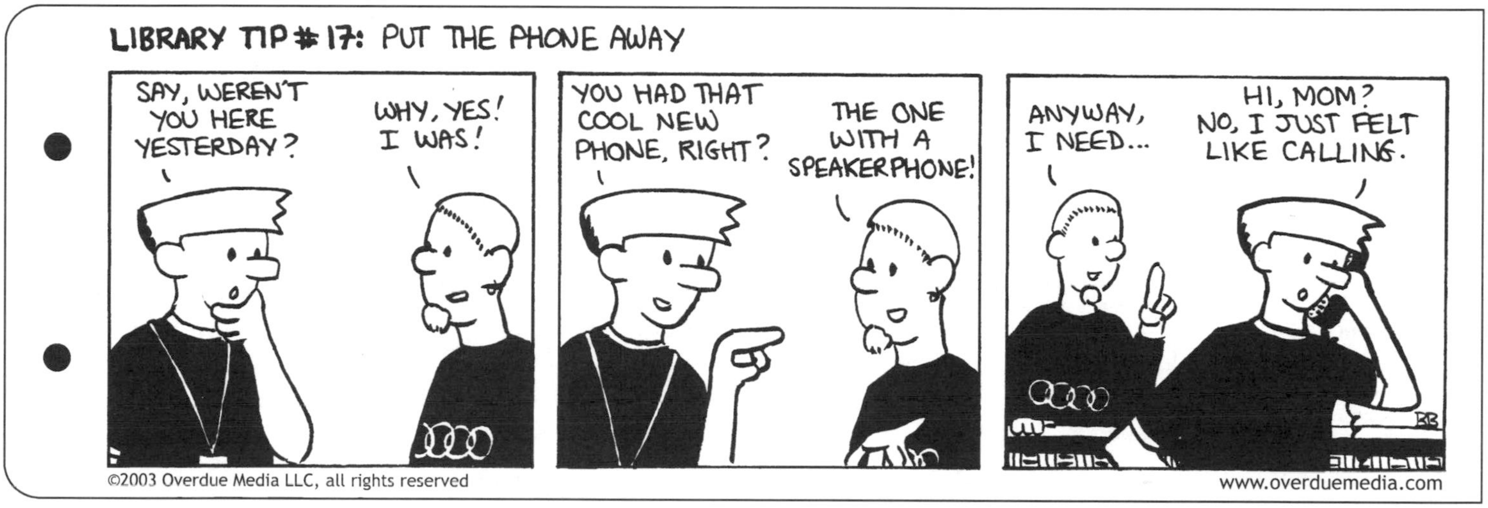
LIBRARY TIP #17: PUT THE PHONE AWAY
SAY, WEREN'T YOU HERE YESTERDAY?
WHY, YES! I WAS!
YOU HAD THAT COOL NEW PHONE, RIGHT?
THE ONE WITH A SPEAKERPHONE!
ANYWAY, I NEED...
HI, MOM? NO, I JUST FELT LIKE CALLING.
BB



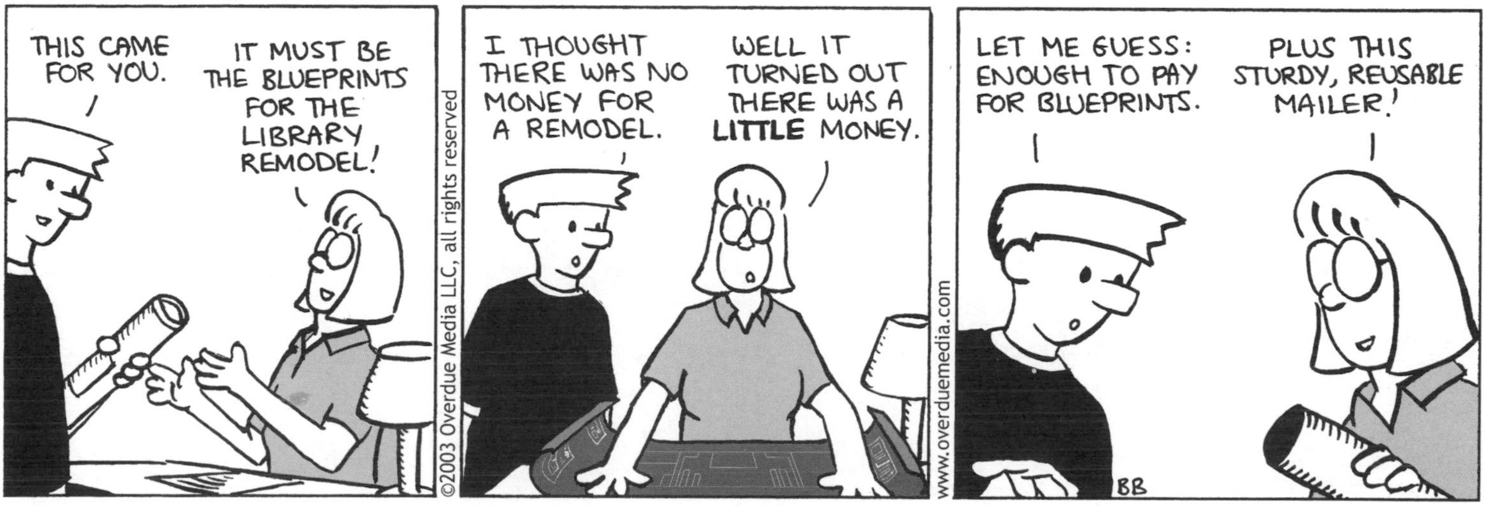
THIS CAME FOR YOU.
IT MUST BE THE BLUEPRINTS FOR THE LIBRARY REMODEL!
I THOUGHT THERE WAS NO MONEY FOR A REMODEL.
WELL IT TURNED OUT THERE WAS A **LITTLE** MONEY.
LET ME GUESS: ENOUGH TO PAY FOR BLUEPRINTS.
PLUS THIS STURDY, REUSABLE MAILER!
BB

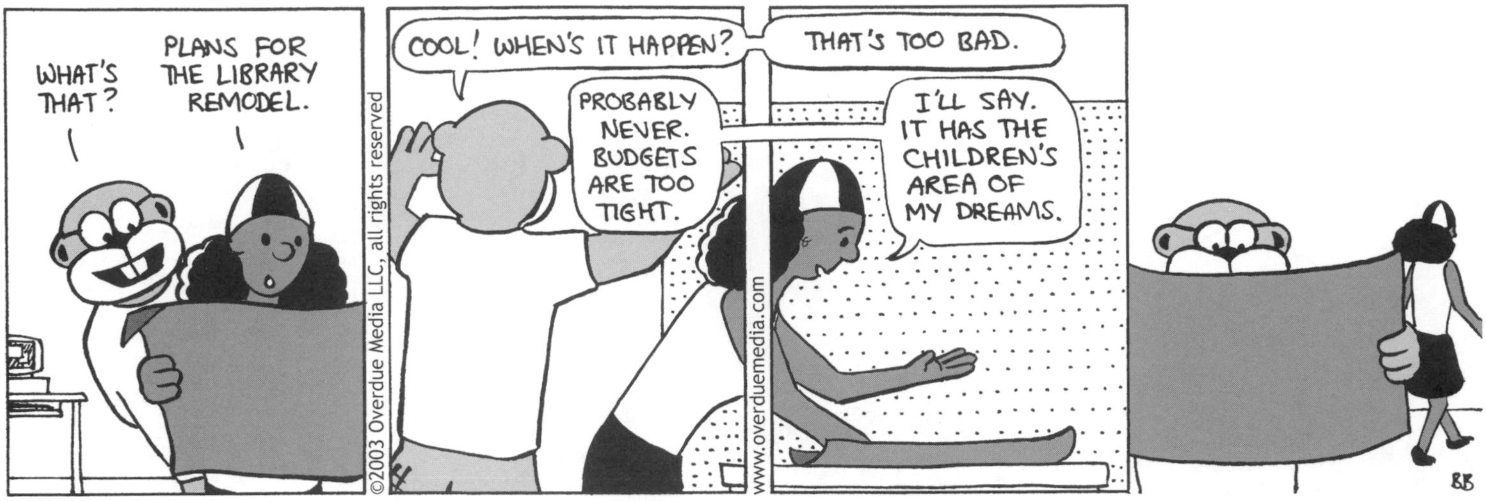
WHAT'S THAT?
PLANS FOR THE LIBRARY REMODEL.
©2003 Overdue Media LLC, all rights reserved
COOL! WHEN'S IT HAPPEN?
PROBABLY NEVER. BUDGETS ARE TOO TIGHT.
www.overduemedia.com
THAT'S TOO BAD.
I'LL SAY. IT HAS THE CHILDREN'S AREA OF MY DREAMS.
BB

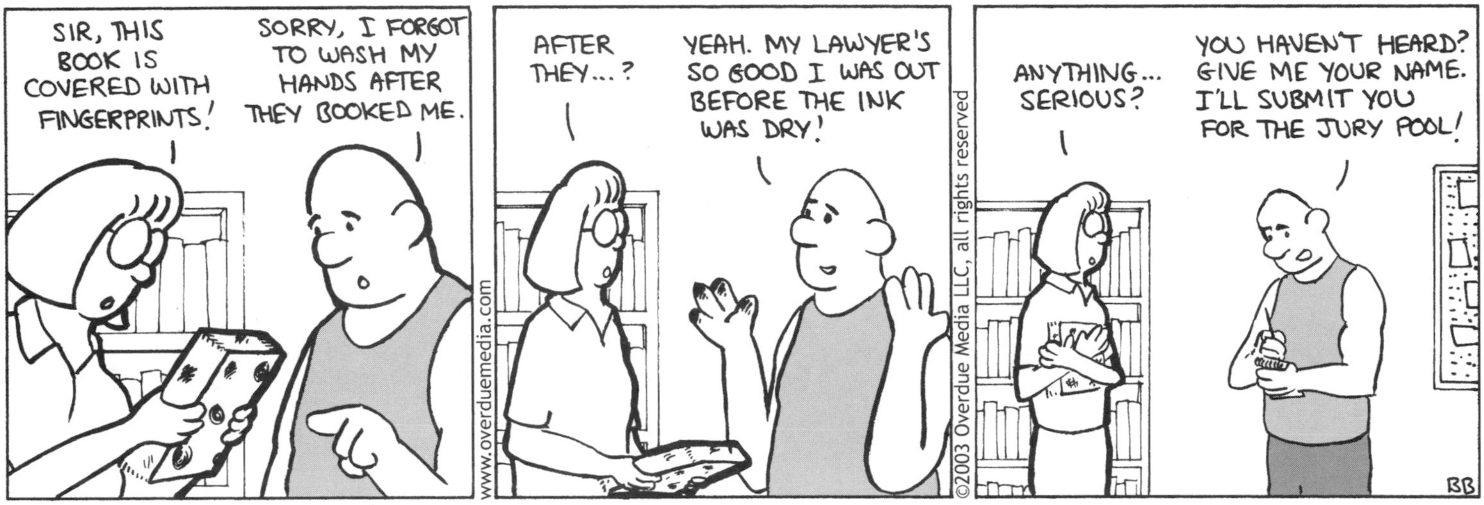
SIR, THIS BOOK IS COVERED WITH FINGERPRINTS!
SORRY, I FORGOT TO WASH MY HANDS AFTER THEY BOOKED ME.
www.overduemedia.com
AFTER THEY...?
YEAH. MY LAWYER'S SO GOOD I WAS OUT BEFORE THE INK WAS DRY!
©2003 Overdue Media LLC, all rights reserved
ANYTHING... SERIOUS?
YOU HAVEN'T HEARD? GIVE ME YOUR NAME. I'LL SUBMIT YOU FOR THE JURY POOL!
BB

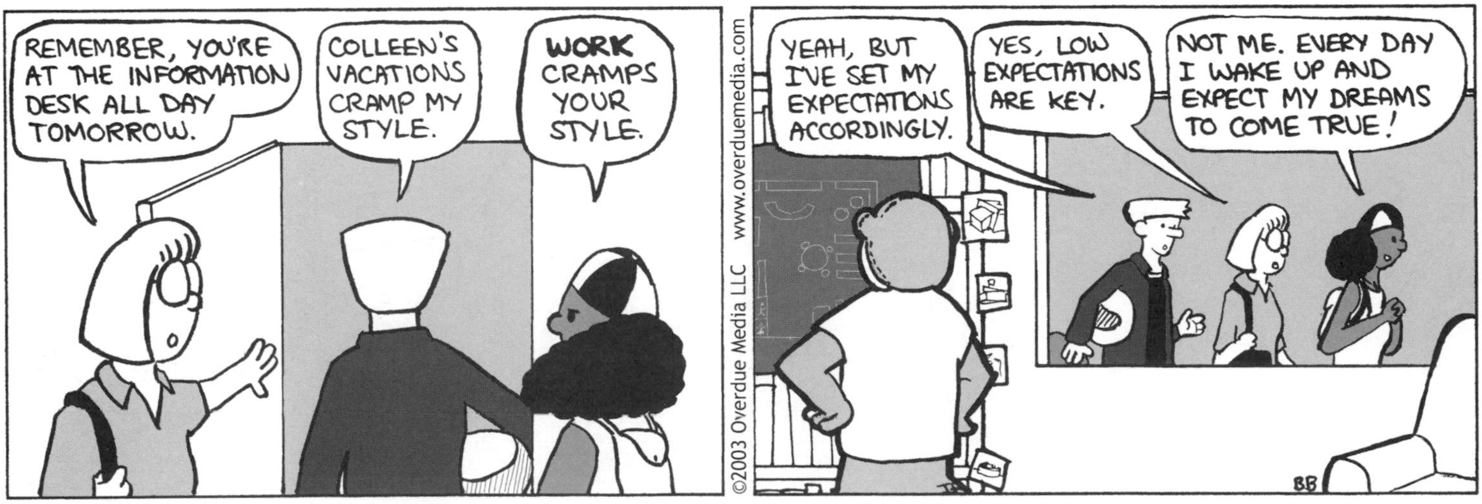
REMEMBER, YOU'RE AT THE INFORMATION DESK ALL DAY TOMORROW.
COLLEEN'S VACATIONS CRAMP MY STYLE.
**WORK** CRAMPS YOUR STYLE.
©2003 Overdue Media LLC www.overduemedia.com
YEAH, BUT I'VE SET MY EXPECTATIONS ACCORDINGLY.
YES, LOW EXPECTATIONS ARE KEY.
NOT ME. EVERY DAY I WAKE UP AND EXPECT MY DREAMS TO COME TRUE!
BB

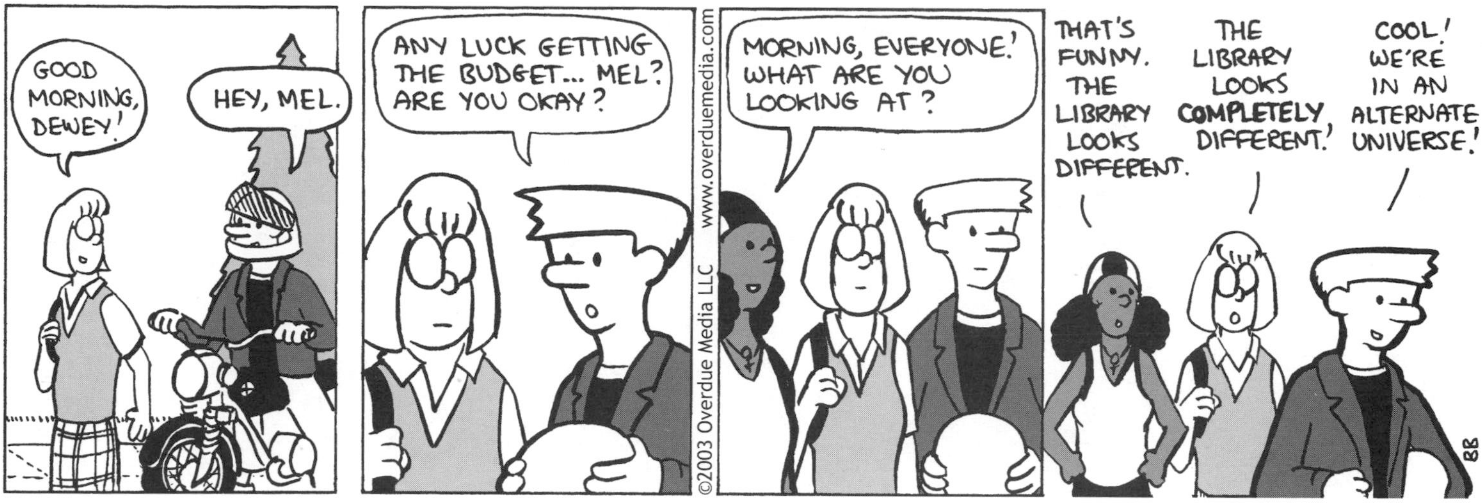
GOOD MORNING, DEWEY!
HEY, MEL.
ANY LUCK GETTING THE BUDGET... MEL? ARE YOU OKAY?
©2003 Overdue Media LLC www.overduemedia.com
MORNING, EVERYONE! WHAT ARE YOU LOOKING AT?
THAT'S FUNNY. THE LIBRARY LOOKS DIFFERENT.
THE LIBRARY LOOKS **COMPLETELY** DIFFERENT!
COOL! WE'RE IN AN ALTERNATE UNIVERSE!
BB

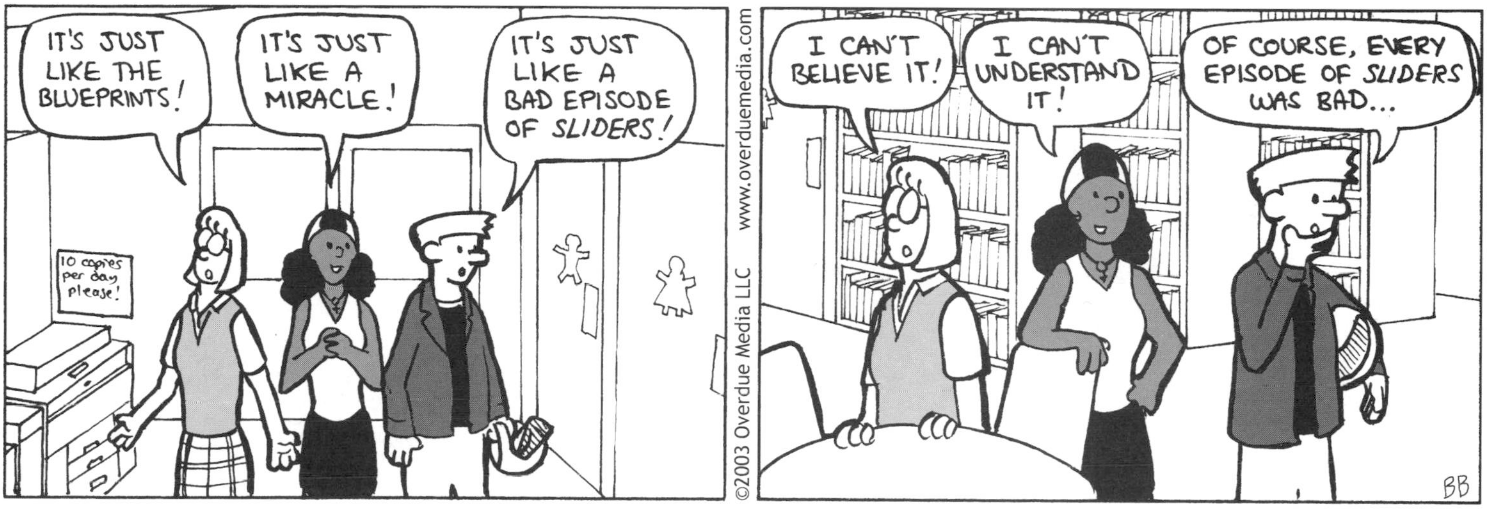
IT'S JUST LIKE THE BLUEPRINTS!
IT'S JUST LIKE A MIRACLE!
IT'S JUST LIKE A BAD EPISODE OF *SLIDERS*!
10 copies per day please!
©2003 Overdue Media LLC www.overduemedia.com
I CAN'T BELIEVE IT!
I CAN'T UNDERSTAND IT!
OF COURSE, **EVERY** EPISODE OF *SLIDERS* WAS BAD...
BB

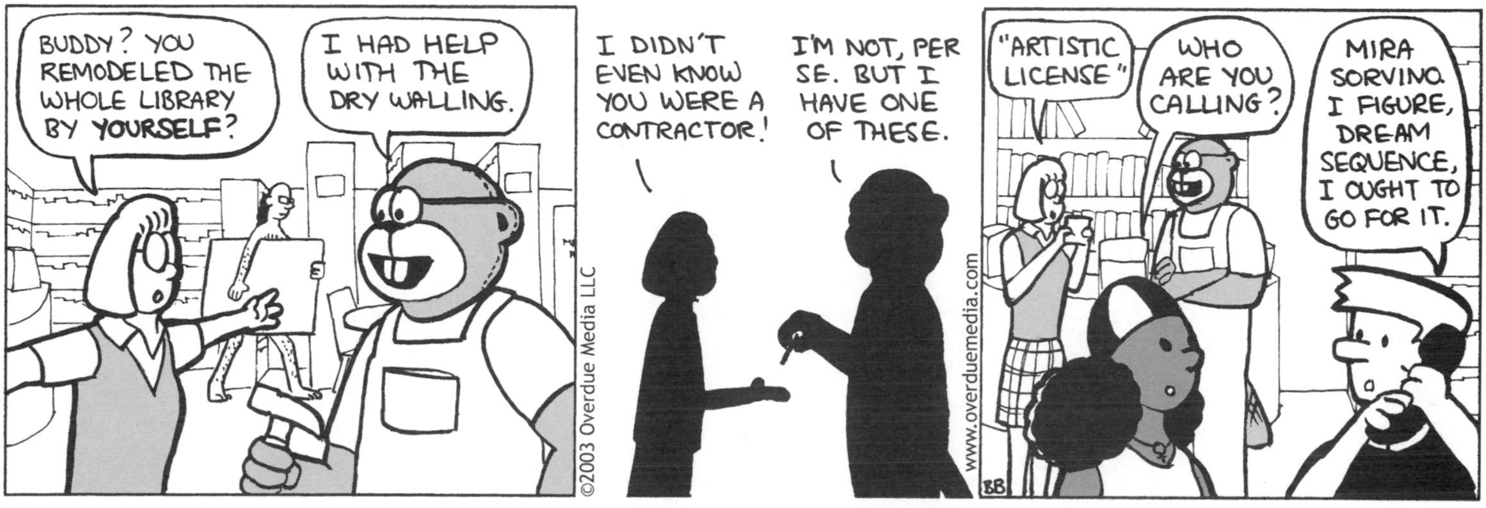
BUDDY? YOU REMODELED THE WHOLE LIBRARY BY **YOURSELF**?
I HAD HELP WITH THE DRY WALLING.
©2003 Overdue Media LLC
I DIDN'T EVEN KNOW YOU WERE A CONTRACTOR!
I'M NOT, PER SE. BUT I HAVE ONE OF THESE.
www.overduemedia.com
"ARTISTIC LICENSE"
WHO ARE YOU CALLING?
MIRA SORVINO. I FIGURE, DREAM SEQUENCE, I OUGHT TO GO FOR IT.
BB

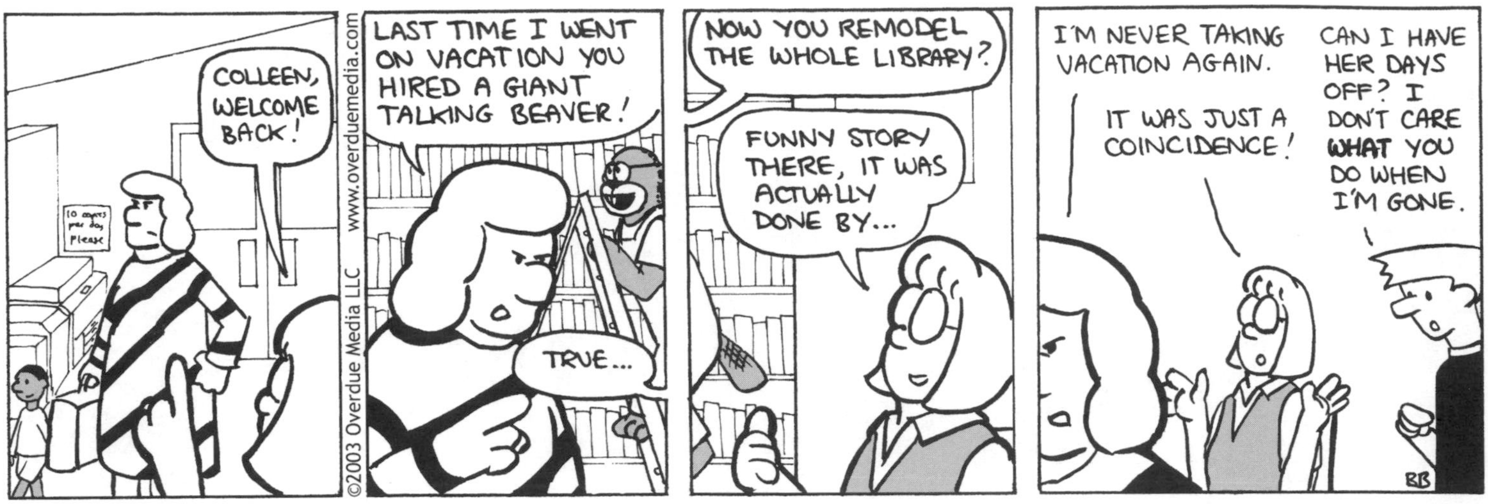
COLLEEN, WELCOME BACK!
LAST TIME I WENT ON VACATION YOU HIRED A GIANT TALKING BEAVER!
TRUE...
NOW YOU REMODEL THE WHOLE LIBRARY?
FUNNY STORY THERE, IT WAS ACTUALLY DONE BY...
I'M NEVER TAKING VACATION AGAIN.
IT WAS JUST A COINCIDENCE!
CAN I HAVE HER DAYS OFF? I DON'T CARE **WHAT** YOU DO WHEN I'M GONE.
©2003 Overdue Media LLC www.overduemedia.com

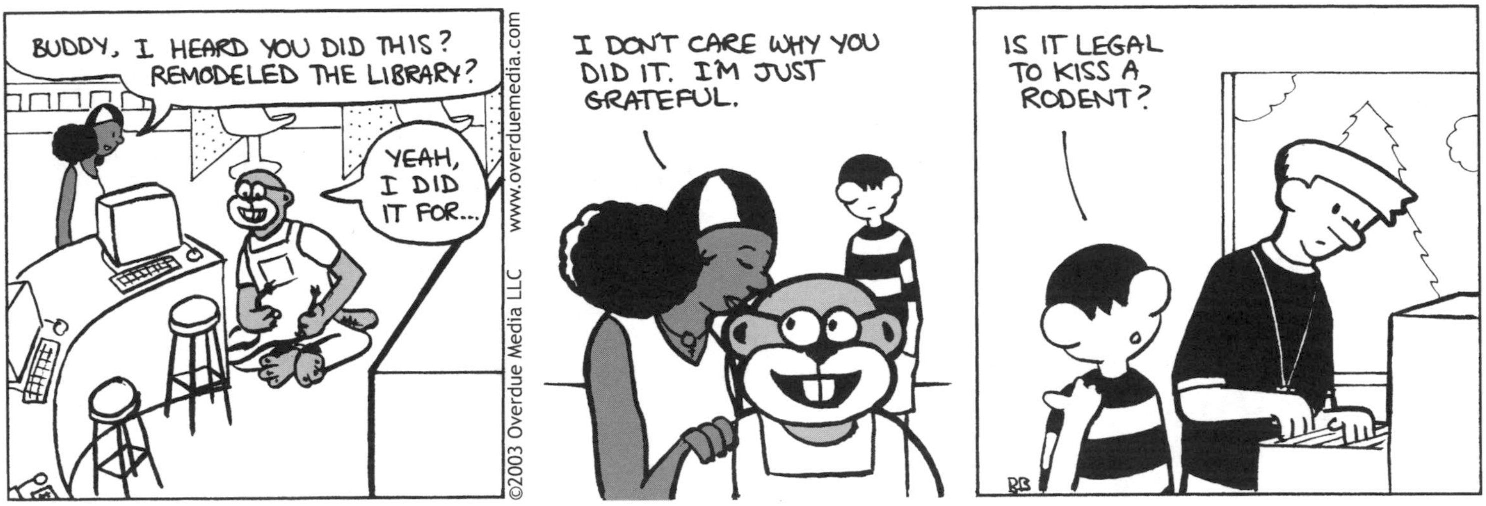
BUDDY, I HEARD YOU DID THIS? REMODELED THE LIBRARY?
YEAH, I DID IT FOR...
I DON'T CARE WHY YOU DID IT. I'M JUST GRATEFUL.
IS IT LEGAL TO KISS A RODENT?
©2003 Overdue Media LLC www.overduemedia.com

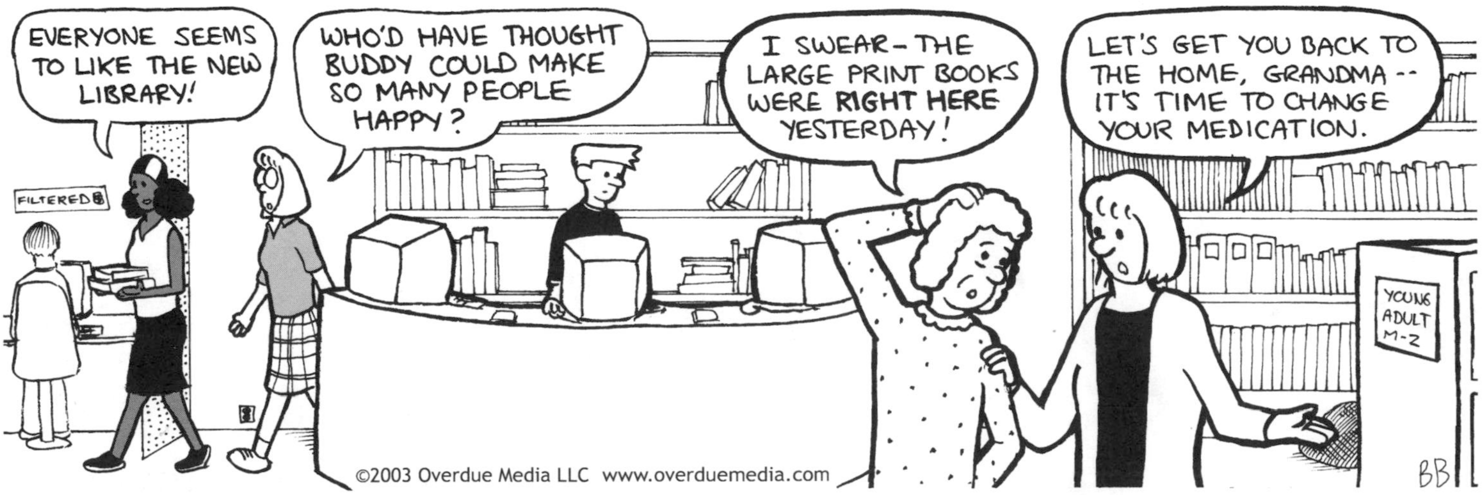
EVERYONE SEEMS TO LIKE THE NEW LIBRARY!
WHO'D HAVE THOUGHT BUDDY COULD MAKE SO MANY PEOPLE HAPPY?
I SWEAR– THE LARGE PRINT BOOKS WERE **RIGHT HERE** YESTERDAY!
LET'S GET YOU BACK TO THE HOME, GRANDMA -- IT'S TIME TO CHANGE YOUR MEDICATION.
FILTERED
YOUNG ADULT M-Z
©2003 Overdue Media LLC www.overduemedia.com

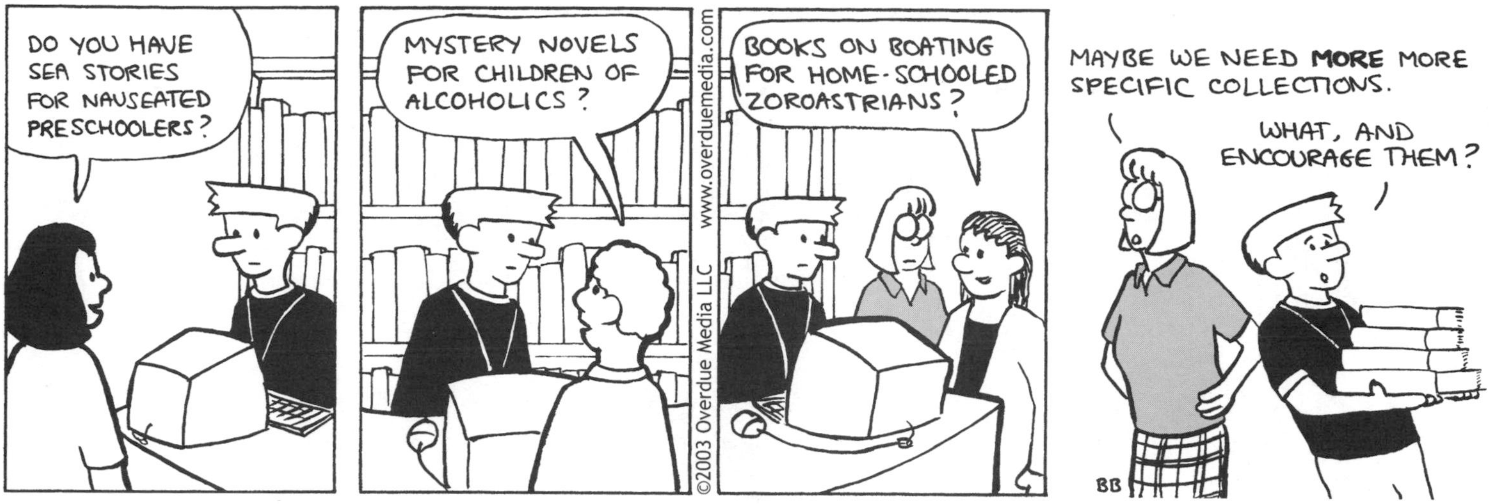
DO YOU HAVE SEA STORIES FOR NAUSEATED PRESCHOOLERS?
MYSTERY NOVELS FOR CHILDREN OF ALCOHOLICS?
BOOKS ON BOATING FOR HOME-SCHOOLED ZOROASTRIANS?
MAYBE WE NEED **MORE** MORE SPECIFIC COLLECTIONS.
WHAT, AND ENCOURAGE THEM?
BB
©2003 Overdue Media LLC www.overduemedia.com

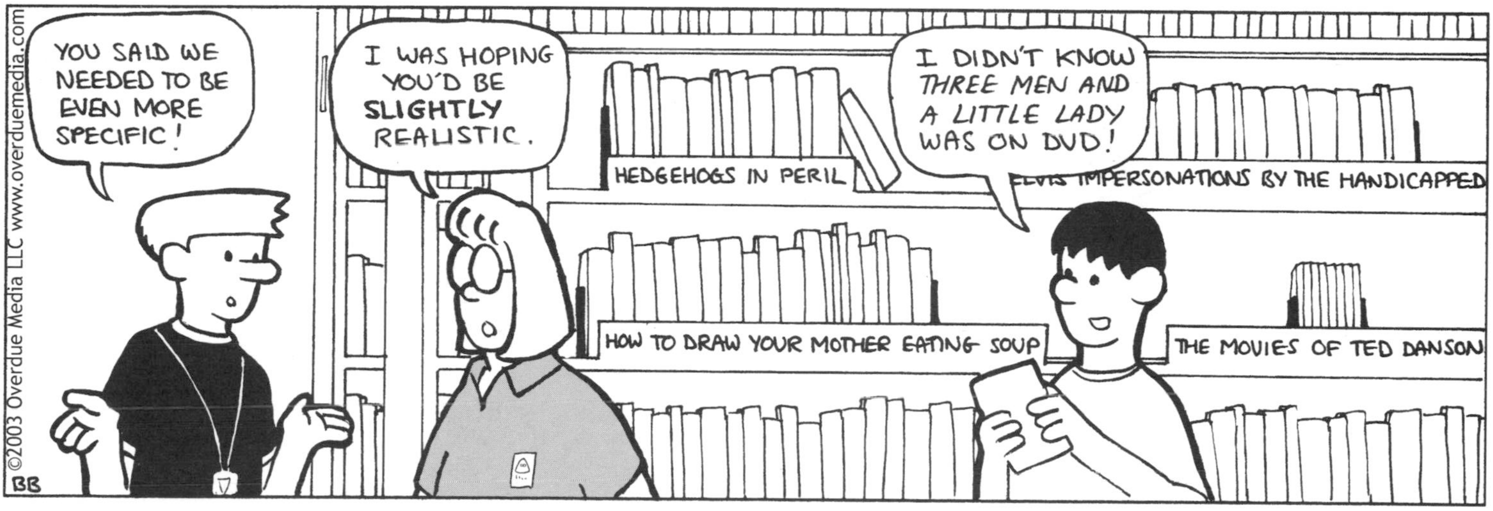
YOU SAID WE NEEDED TO BE EVEN MORE SPECIFIC!
I WAS HOPING YOU'D BE **SLIGHTLY** REALISTIC.
I DIDN'T KNOW *THREE MEN AND A LITTLE LADY* WAS ON DVD!
HEDGEHOGS IN PERIL
ELVIS IMPERSONATIONS BY THE HANDICAPPED
HOW TO DRAW YOUR MOTHER EATING SOUP
THE MOVIES OF TED DANSON
BB
©2003 Overdue Media LLC www.overduemedia.com

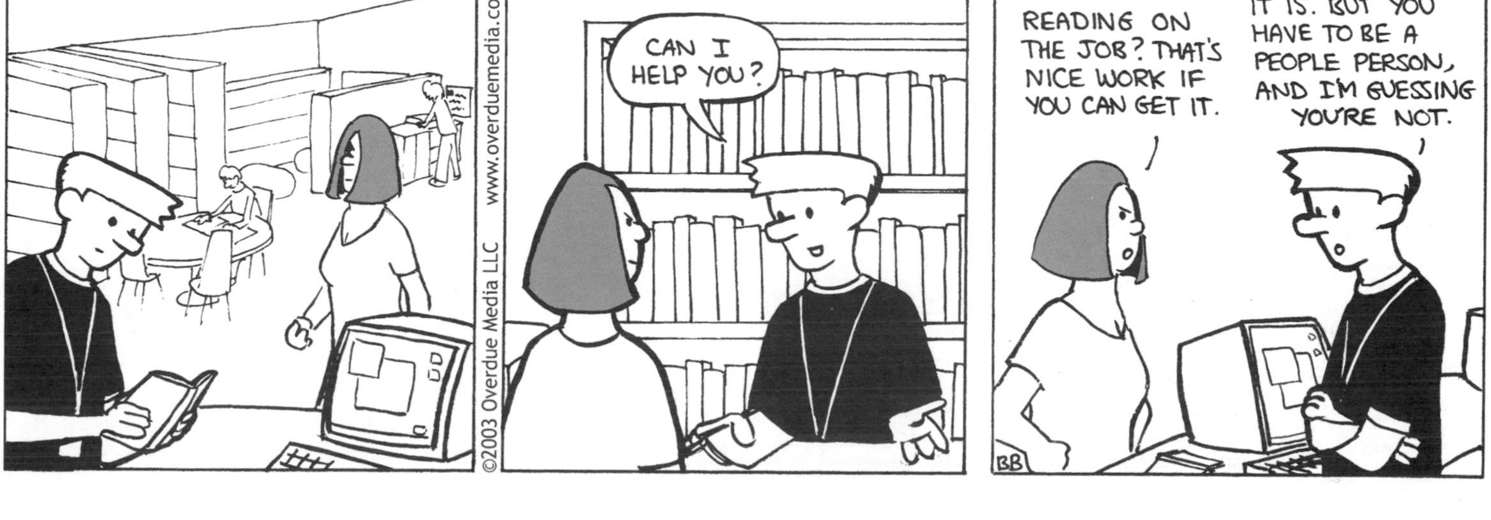
CAN I HELP YOU?
READING ON THE JOB? THAT'S NICE WORK IF YOU CAN GET IT.
IT IS. BUT YOU HAVE TO BE A PEOPLE PERSON, AND I'M GUESSING YOU'RE NOT.
BB
©2003 Overdue Media LLC www.overduemedia.com

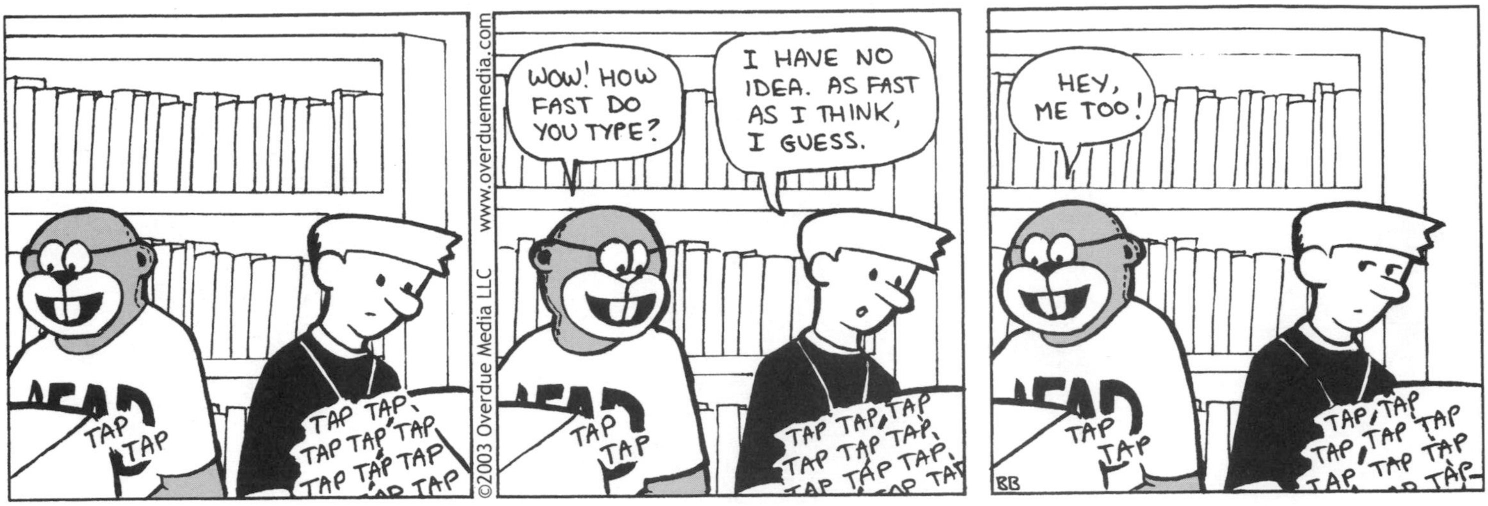
TAP TAP
TAP TAP TAP TAP TAP TAP TAP TAP TAP
©2003 Overdue Media LLC www.overduemedia.com
WOW! HOW FAST DO YOU TYPE?
I HAVE NO IDEA. AS FAST AS I THINK, I GUESS.
TAP TAP
TAP TAP TAP TAP TAP TAP TAP TAP
HEY, ME TOO!
TAP TAP
TAP TAP TAP TAP TAP TAP TAP TAP TAP
BB

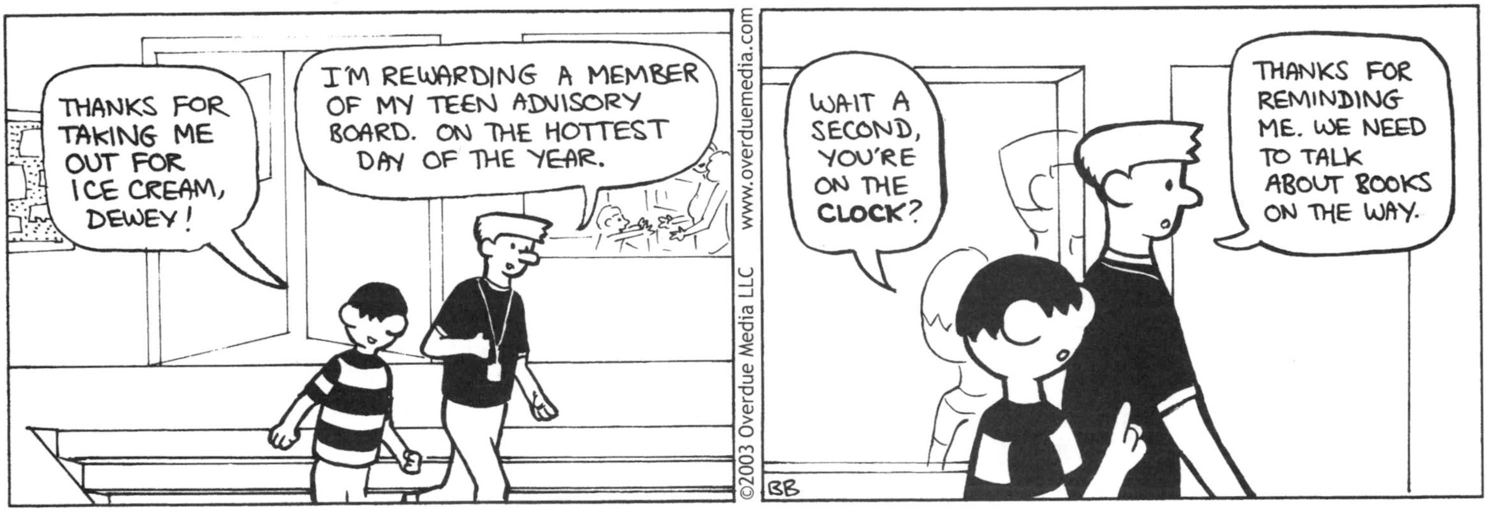
THANKS FOR TAKING ME OUT FOR ICE CREAM, DEWEY!
I'M REWARDING A MEMBER OF MY TEEN ADVISORY BOARD. ON THE HOTTEST DAY OF THE YEAR.
©2003 Overdue Media LLC www.overduemedia.com
WAIT A SECOND, YOU'RE ON THE **CLOCK**?
THANKS FOR REMINDING ME. WE NEED TO TALK ABOUT BOOKS ON THE WAY.
BB

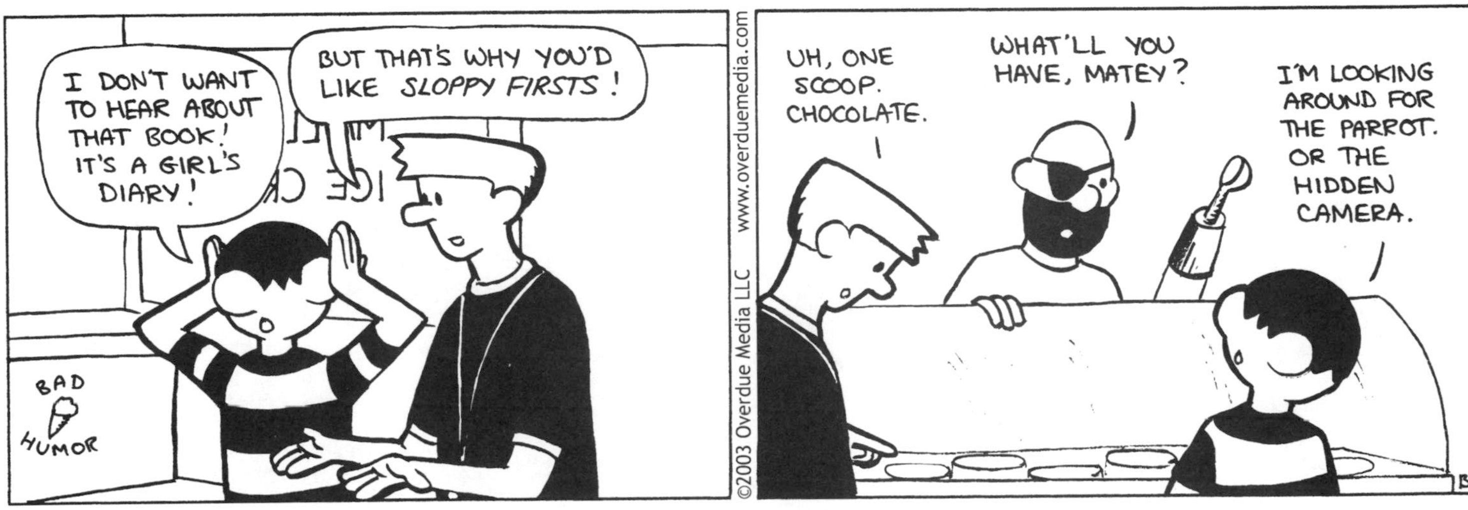
I DON'T WANT TO HEAR ABOUT THAT BOOK! IT'S A GIRL'S DIARY!
BUT THAT'S WHY YOU'D LIKE *SLOPPY FIRSTS*!
BAD HUMOR
©2003 Overdue Media LLC www.overduemedia.com
UH, ONE SCOOP. CHOCOLATE.
WHAT'LL YOU HAVE, MATEY?
I'M LOOKING AROUND FOR THE PARROT. OR THE HIDDEN CAMERA.
BB

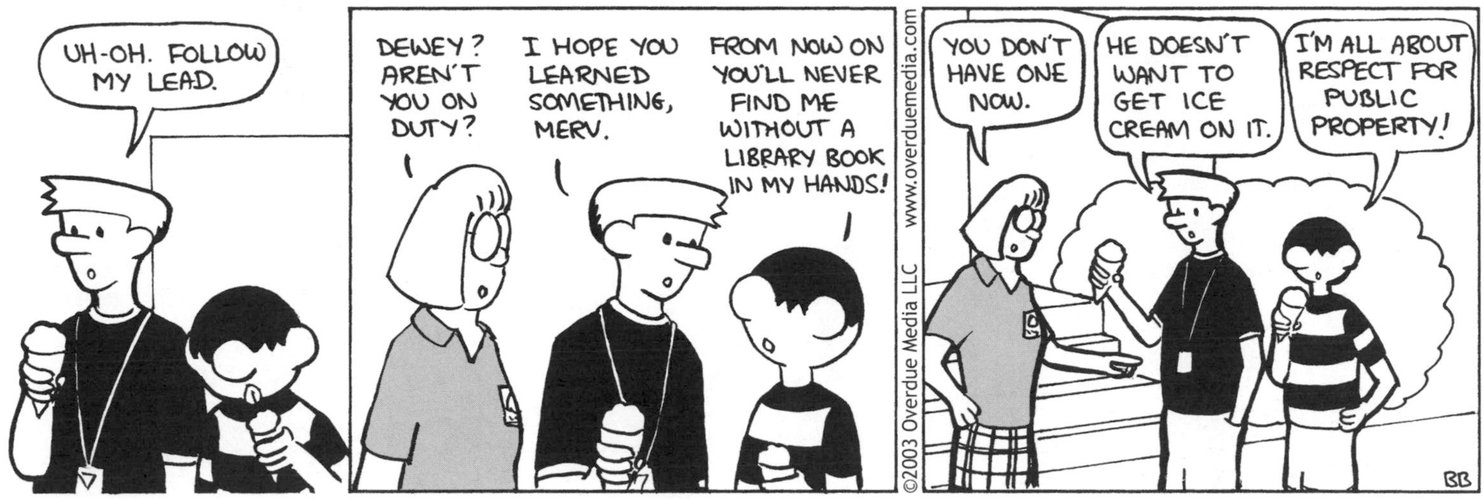
UH-OH. FOLLOW MY LEAD.
DEWEY? AREN'T YOU ON DUTY?
I HOPE YOU LEARNED SOMETHING, MERV.
FROM NOW ON YOU'LL NEVER FIND ME WITHOUT A LIBRARY BOOK IN MY HANDS!
©2003 Overdue Media LLC www.overduemedia.com
YOU DON'T HAVE ONE NOW.
HE DOESN'T WANT TO GET ICE CREAM ON IT.
I'M ALL ABOUT RESPECT FOR PUBLIC PROPERTY!
BB

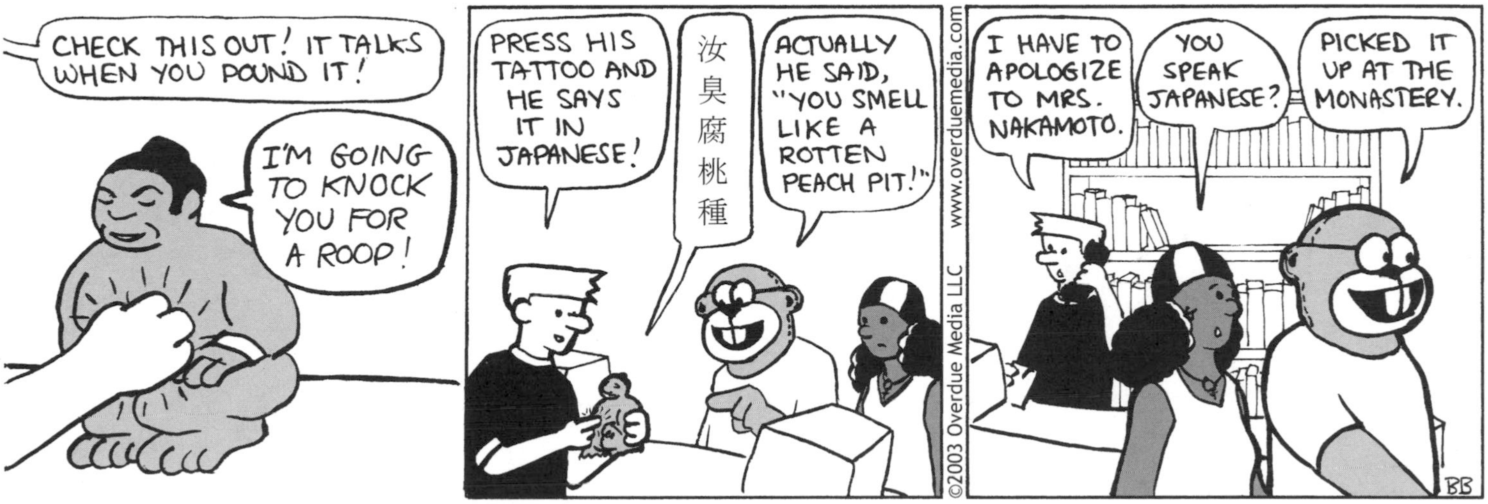
CHECK THIS OUT! IT TALKS WHEN YOU POUND IT!
I'M GOING TO KNOCK YOU FOR A ROOP!
PRESS HIS TATTOO AND HE SAYS IT IN JAPANESE!
汝臭腐桃種
ACTUALLY HE SAID, "YOU SMELL LIKE A ROTTEN PEACH PIT!"
©2003 Overdue Media LLC www.overduemedia.com
I HAVE TO APOLOGIZE TO MRS. NAKAMOTO.
YOU SPEAK JAPANESE?
PICKED IT UP AT THE MONASTERY.
BB

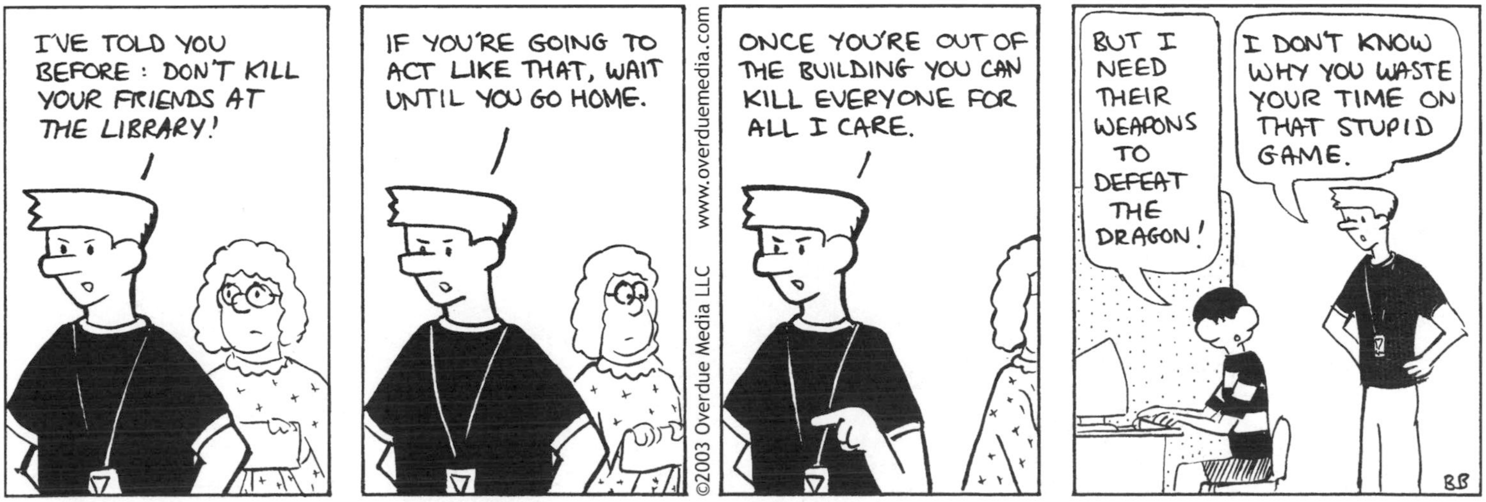
I'VE TOLD YOU BEFORE: DON'T KILL YOUR FRIENDS AT THE LIBRARY!
IF YOU'RE GOING TO ACT LIKE THAT, WAIT UNTIL YOU GO HOME.
©2003 Overdue Media LLC www.overduemedia.com
ONCE YOU'RE OUT OF THE BUILDING YOU CAN KILL EVERYONE FOR ALL I CARE.
BUT I NEED THEIR WEAPONS TO DEFEAT THE DRAGON!
I DON'T KNOW WHY YOU WASTE YOUR TIME ON THAT STUPID GAME.
BB

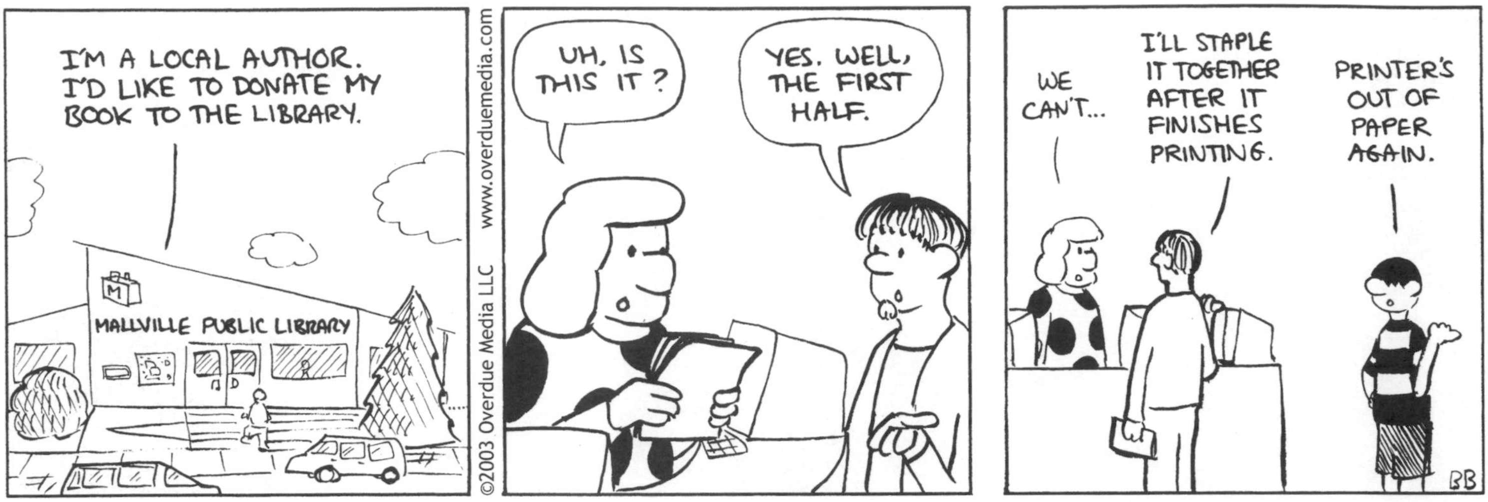
I'M A LOCAL AUTHOR. I'D LIKE TO DONATE MY BOOK TO THE LIBRARY.
MALLVILLE PUBLIC LIBRARY
UH, IS THIS IT?
YES. WELL, THE FIRST HALF.
WE CAN'T...
I'LL STAPLE IT TOGETHER AFTER IT FINISHES PRINTING.
PRINTER'S OUT OF PAPER AGAIN.
BB
©2003 Overdue Media LLC www.overduemedia.com

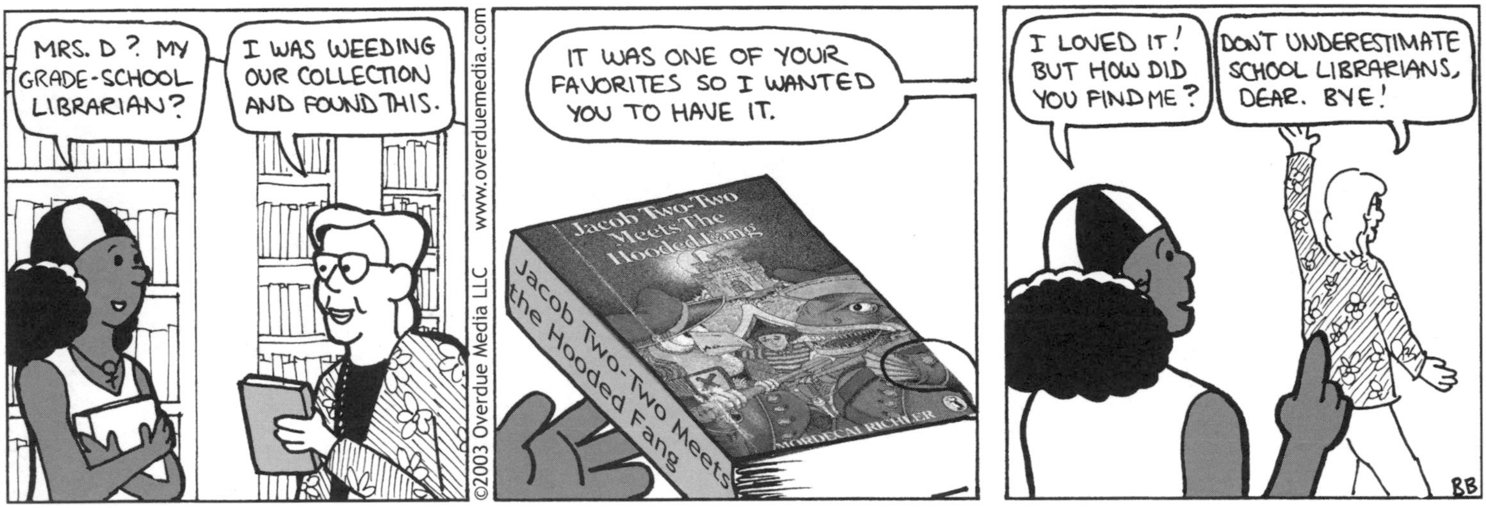
MRS. D? MY GRADE-SCHOOL LIBRARIAN?
I WAS WEEDING OUR COLLECTION AND FOUND THIS.
IT WAS ONE OF YOUR FAVORITES SO I WANTED YOU TO HAVE IT.
Jacob Two-Two Meets The Hooded Fang
MORDECAI RICHLER
Jacob Two-Two Meets the Hooded Fang
I LOVED IT! BUT HOW DID YOU FIND ME?
DON'T UNDERESTIMATE SCHOOL LIBRARIANS, DEAR. BYE!
BB
©2003 Overdue Media LLC www.overduemedia.com

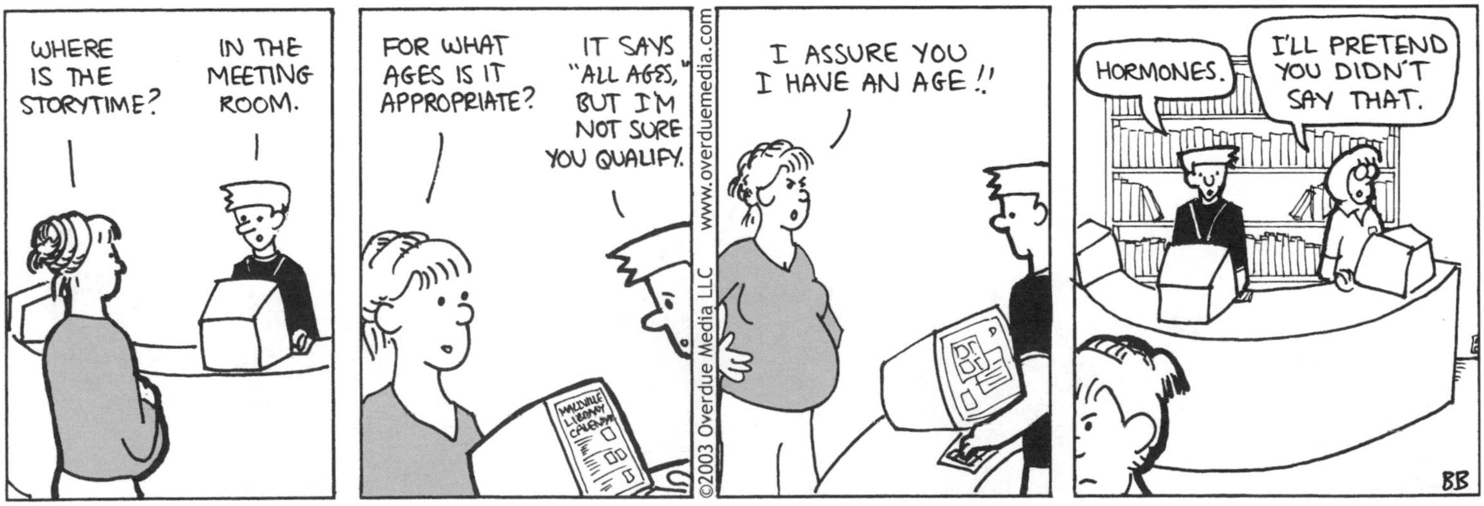
WHERE IS THE STORYTIME?
IN THE MEETING ROOM.
FOR WHAT AGES IS IT APPROPRIATE?
IT SAYS "ALL AGES," BUT I'M NOT SURE YOU QUALIFY.
MALLVILLE LIBRARY CALENDAR
I ASSURE YOU I HAVE AN AGE!!
HORMONES.
I'LL PRETEND YOU DIDN'T SAY THAT.
BB
©2003 Overdue Media LLC www.overduemedia.com

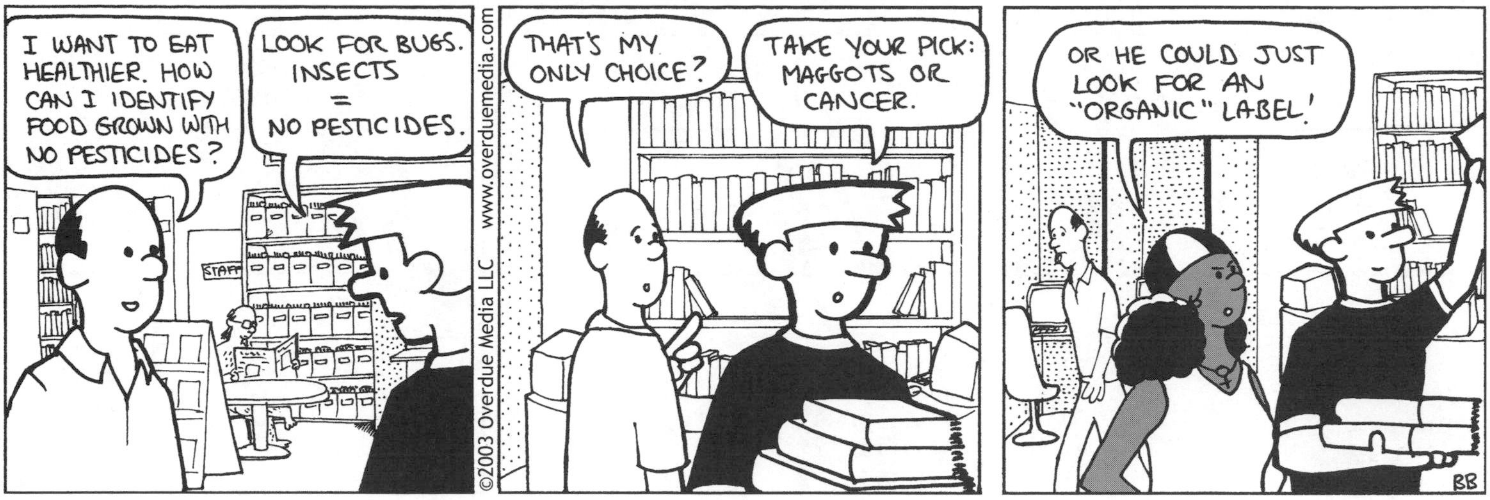
I WANT TO EAT HEALTHIER. HOW CAN I IDENTIFY FOOD GROWN WITH NO PESTICIDES?
LOOK FOR BUGS. INSECTS = NO PESTICIDES.
STAFF
©2003 Overdue Media LLC www.overduemedia.com
THAT'S MY ONLY CHOICE?
TAKE YOUR PICK: MAGGOTS OR CANCER.
OR HE COULD JUST LOOK FOR AN "ORGANIC" LABEL!
BB

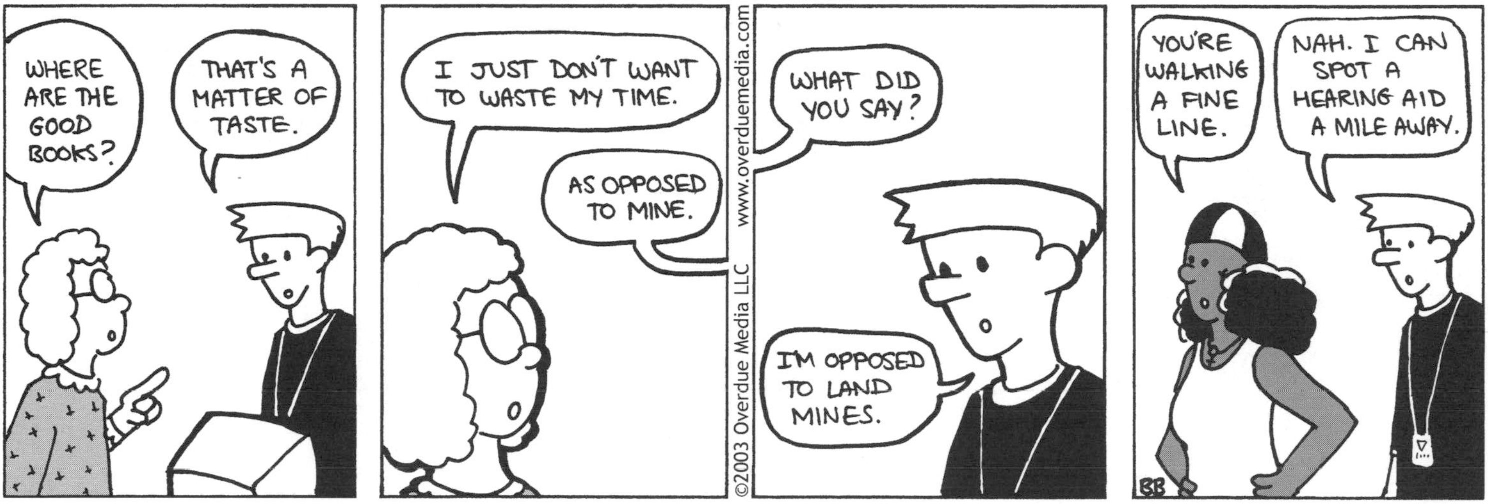
WHERE ARE THE GOOD BOOKS?
THAT'S A MATTER OF TASTE.
I JUST DON'T WANT TO WASTE MY TIME.
AS OPPOSED TO MINE.
©2003 Overdue Media LLC www.overduemedia.com
WHAT DID YOU SAY?
I'M OPPOSED TO LAND MINES.
YOU'RE WALKING A FINE LINE.
NAH. I CAN SPOT A HEARING AID A MILE AWAY.
BB

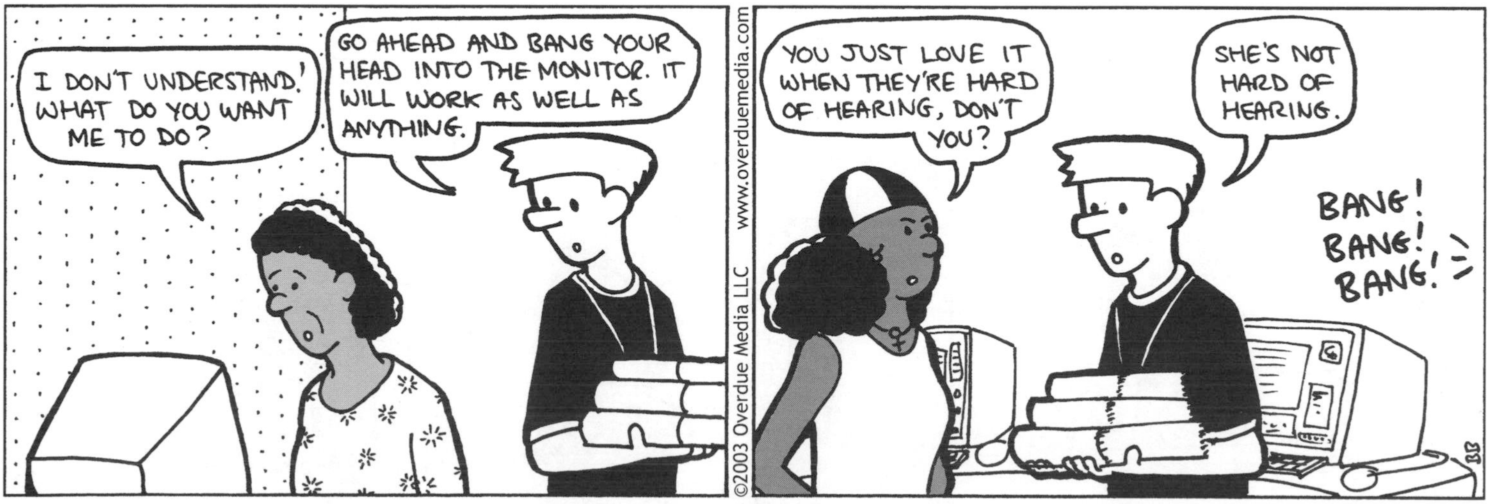
I DON'T UNDERSTAND! WHAT DO YOU WANT ME TO DO?
GO AHEAD AND BANG YOUR HEAD INTO THE MONITOR. IT WILL WORK AS WELL AS ANYTHING.
©2003 Overdue Media LLC www.overduemedia.com
YOU JUST LOVE IT WHEN THEY'RE HARD OF HEARING, DON'T YOU?
SHE'S NOT HARD OF HEARING.
BANG! BANG! BANG!
BB

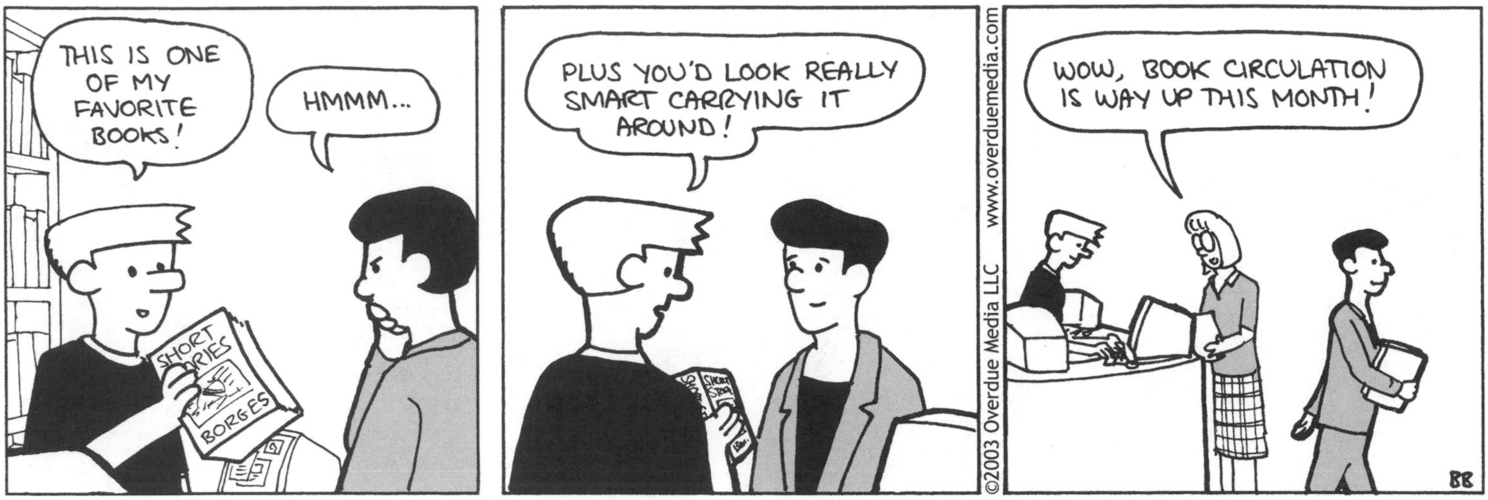
THIS IS ONE OF MY FAVORITE BOOKS!
HMMM...
PLUS YOU'D LOOK REALLY SMART CARRYING IT AROUND!
WOW, BOOK CIRCULATION IS WAY UP THIS MONTH!
©2003 Overdue Media LLC www.overduemedia.com
BB

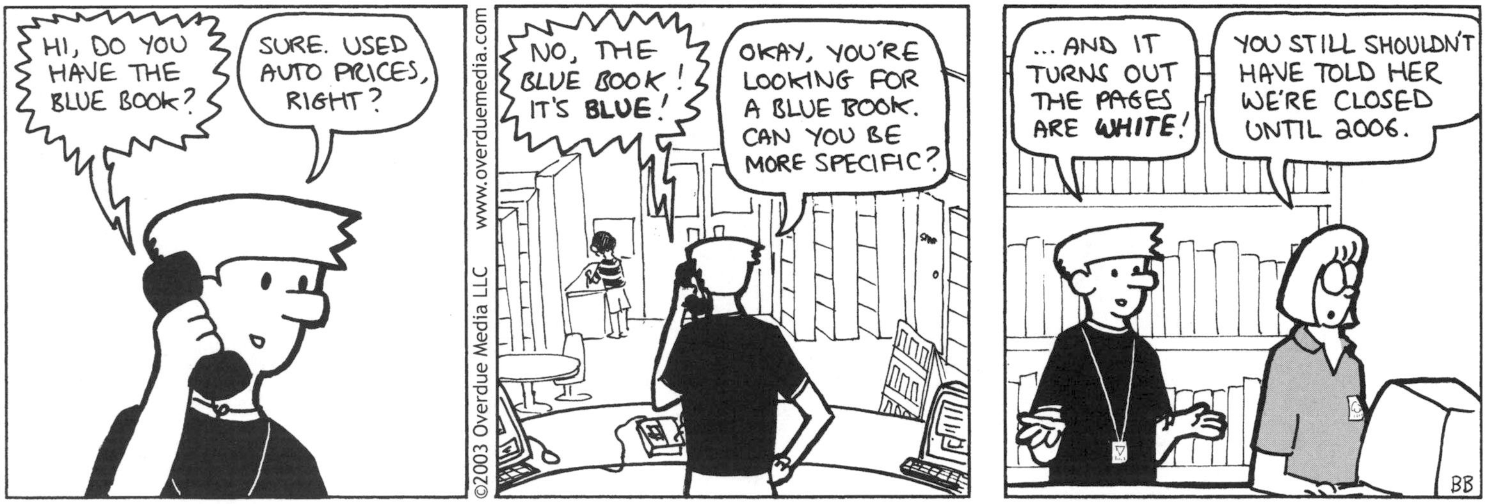
HI, DO YOU HAVE THE BLUE BOOK?
SURE. USED AUTO PRICES, RIGHT?
©2003 Overdue Media LLC www.overduemedia.com
NO, THE BLUE BOOK! IT'S **BLUE**!
OKAY, YOU'RE LOOKING FOR A BLUE BOOK. CAN YOU BE MORE SPECIFIC?
...AND IT TURNS OUT THE PAGES ARE ***WHITE***!
YOU STILL SHOULDN'T HAVE TOLD HER WE'RE CLOSED UNTIL 2006.
BB

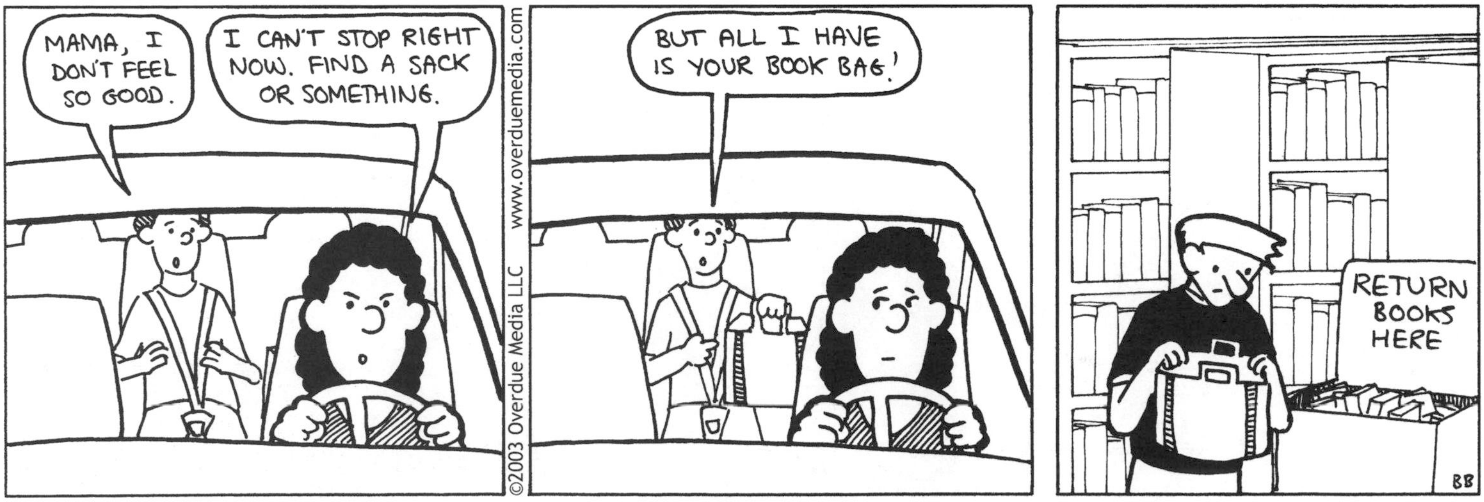
MAMA, I DON'T FEEL SO GOOD.
I CAN'T STOP RIGHT NOW. FIND A SACK OR SOMETHING.
©2003 Overdue Media LLC www.overduemedia.com
BUT ALL I HAVE IS YOUR BOOK BAG!
RETURN BOOKS HERE
BB

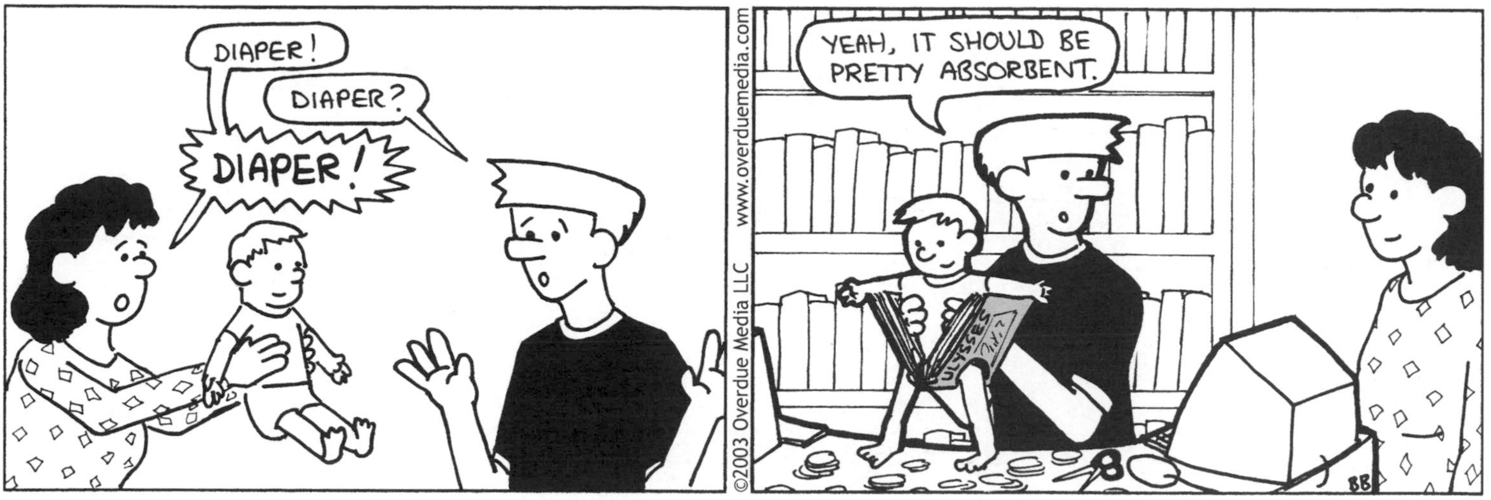
DIAPER!
DIAPER?
DIAPER!
YEAH, IT SHOULD BE PRETTY ABSORBENT.
ULYSSES
BB
©2003 Overdue Media LLC www.overduemedia.com

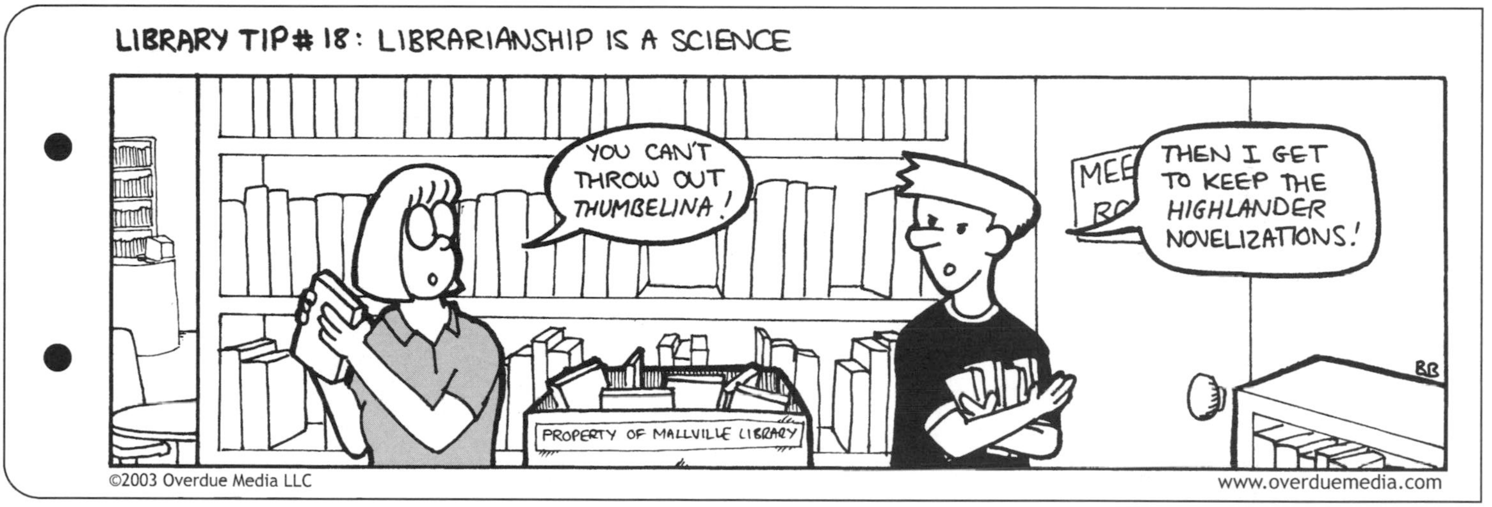
LIBRARY TIP # 18: LIBRARIANSHIP IS A SCIENCE
YOU CAN'T THROW OUT THUMBELINA!
THEN I GET TO KEEP THE HIGHLANDER NOVELIZATIONS!
PROPERTY OF MALLVILLE LIBRARY
BB
©2003 Overdue Media LLC
www.overduemedia.com

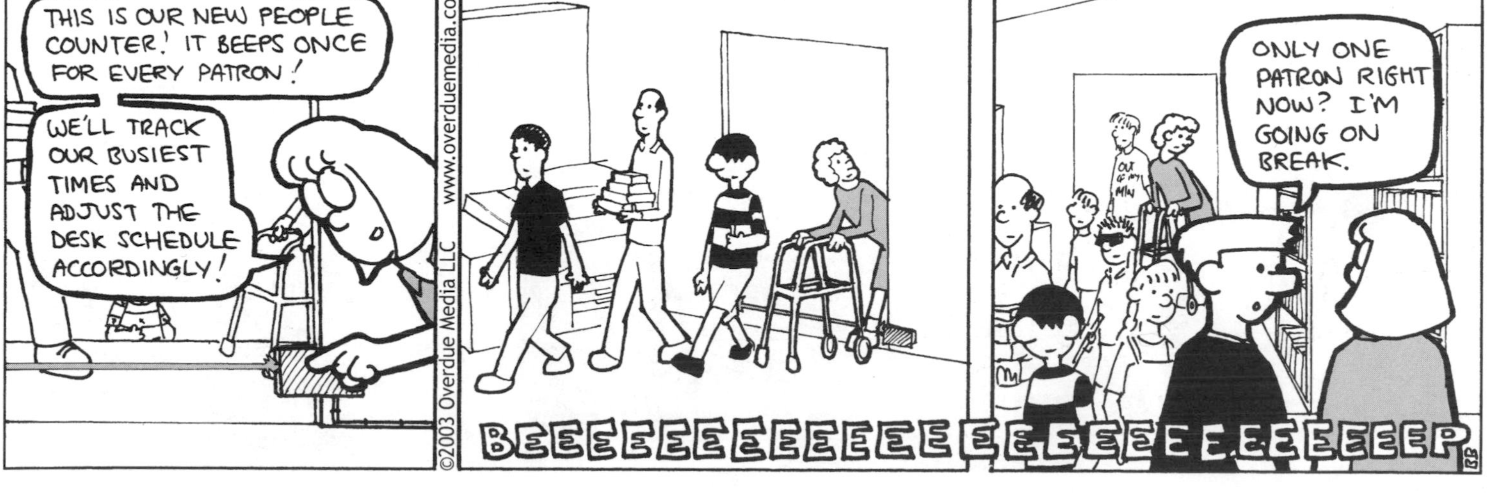
THIS IS OUR NEW PEOPLE COUNTER! IT BEEPS ONCE FOR EVERY PATRON!
WE'LL TRACK OUR BUSIEST TIMES AND ADJUST THE DESK SCHEDULE ACCORDINGLY!
©2003 Overdue Media LLC www.overduemedia.com
ONLY ONE PATRON RIGHT NOW? I'M GOING ON BREAK.
BEEEEEEEEEEEEEEEEEEEEEEEEEEEP
BB

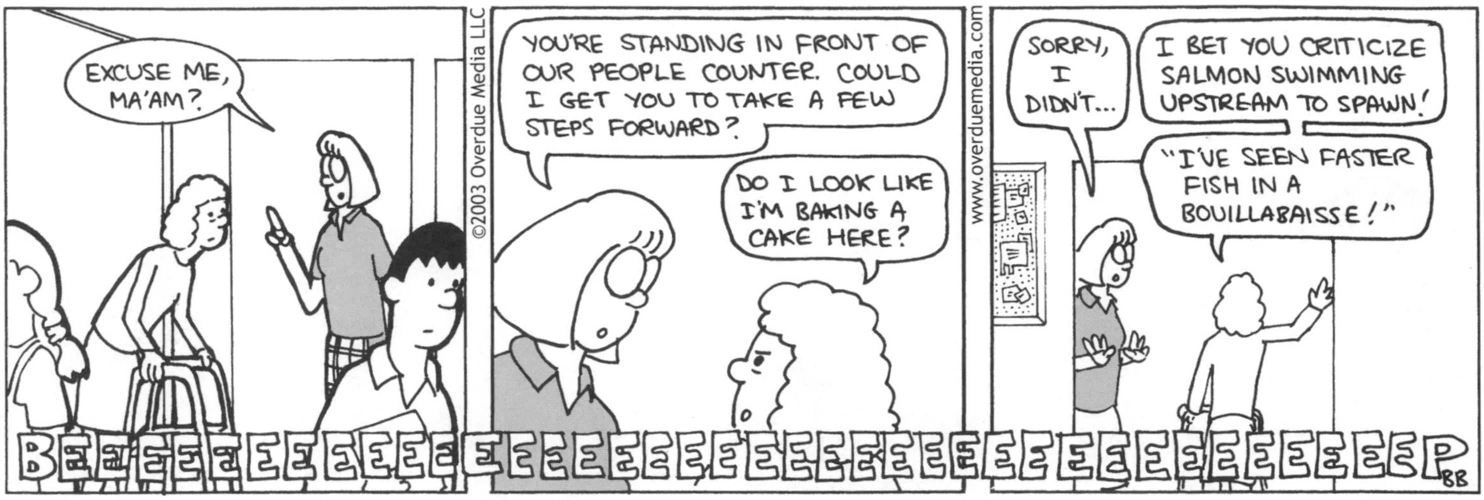
EXCUSE ME, MA'AM?
YOU'RE STANDING IN FRONT OF OUR PEOPLE COUNTER. COULD I GET YOU TO TAKE A FEW STEPS FORWARD?
DO I LOOK LIKE I'M BAKING A CAKE HERE?
SORRY, I DIDN'T...
I BET YOU CRITICIZE SALMON SWIMMING UPSTREAM TO SPAWN!
"I'VE SEEN FASTER FISH IN A BOUILLABAISSE!"
BEEEEEEEEEEEEEEEEEEEEEEEEEEEEEEEEEEEEEEEEEEEEP
©2003 Overdue Media LLC
www.overduemedia.com

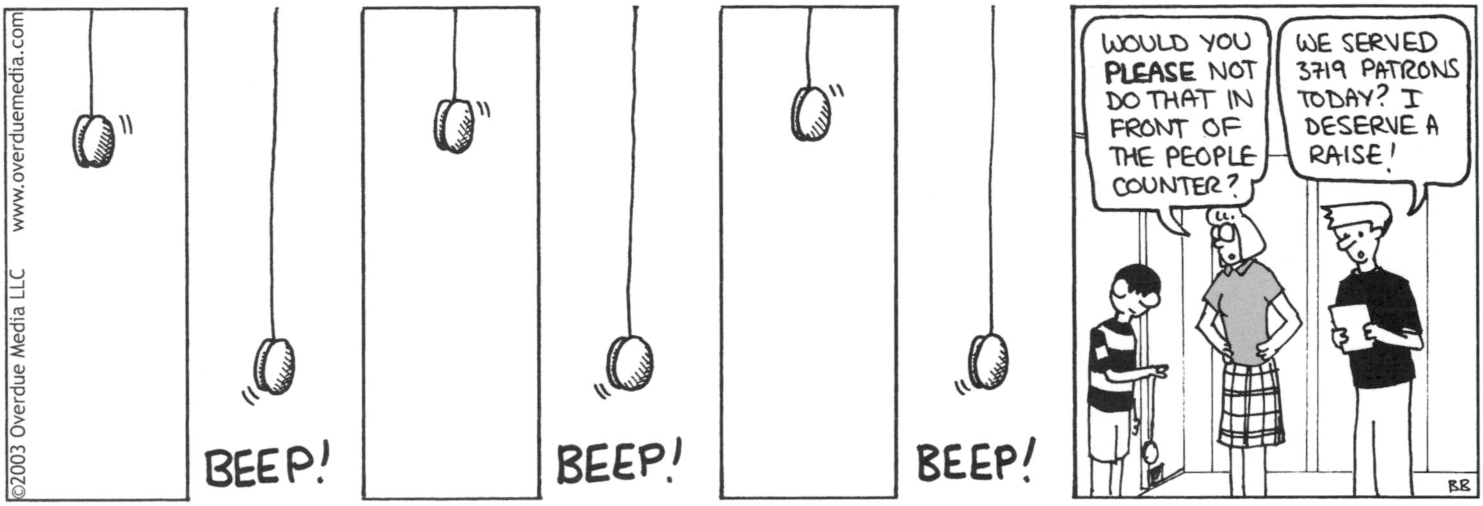
BEEP!
BEEP!
BEEP!
WOULD YOU **PLEASE** NOT DO THAT IN FRONT OF THE PEOPLE COUNTER?
WE SERVED 3719 PATRONS TODAY? I DESERVE A RAISE!
©2003 Overdue Media LLC www.overduemedia.com

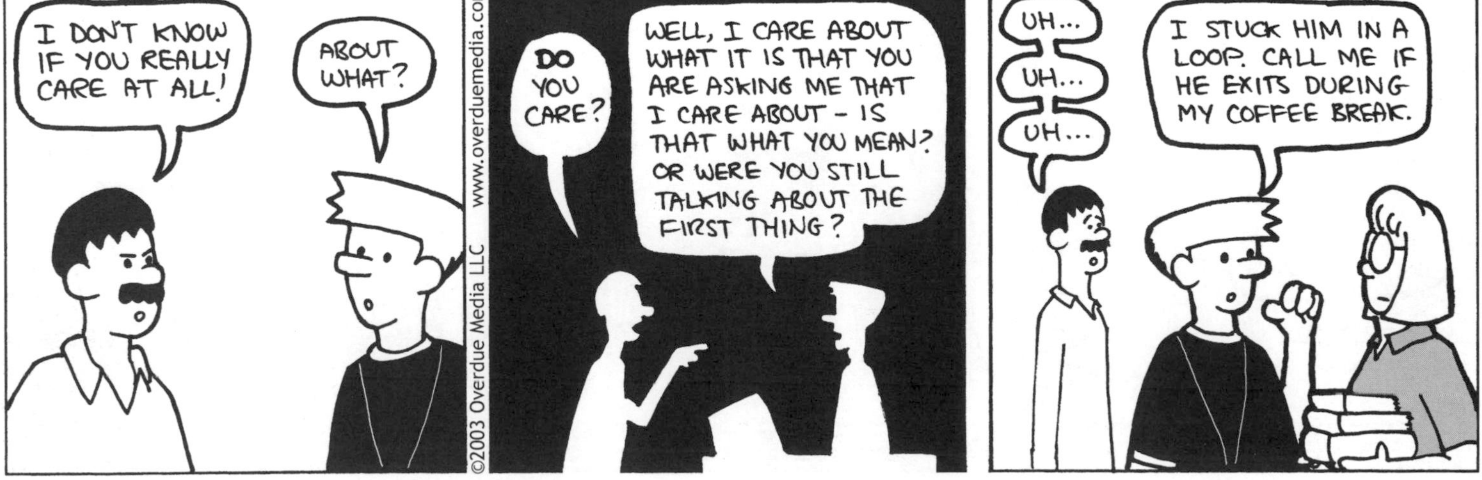
I DON'T KNOW IF YOU REALLY CARE AT ALL!
ABOUT WHAT?
**DO** YOU CARE?
WELL, I CARE ABOUT WHAT IT IS THAT YOU ARE ASKING ME THAT I CARE ABOUT - IS THAT WHAT YOU MEAN? OR WERE YOU STILL TALKING ABOUT THE FIRST THING?
UH...
UH...
UH...
I STUCK HIM IN A LOOP. CALL ME IF HE EXITS DURING MY COFFEE BREAK.
©2003 Overdue Media LLC
www.overduemedia.com

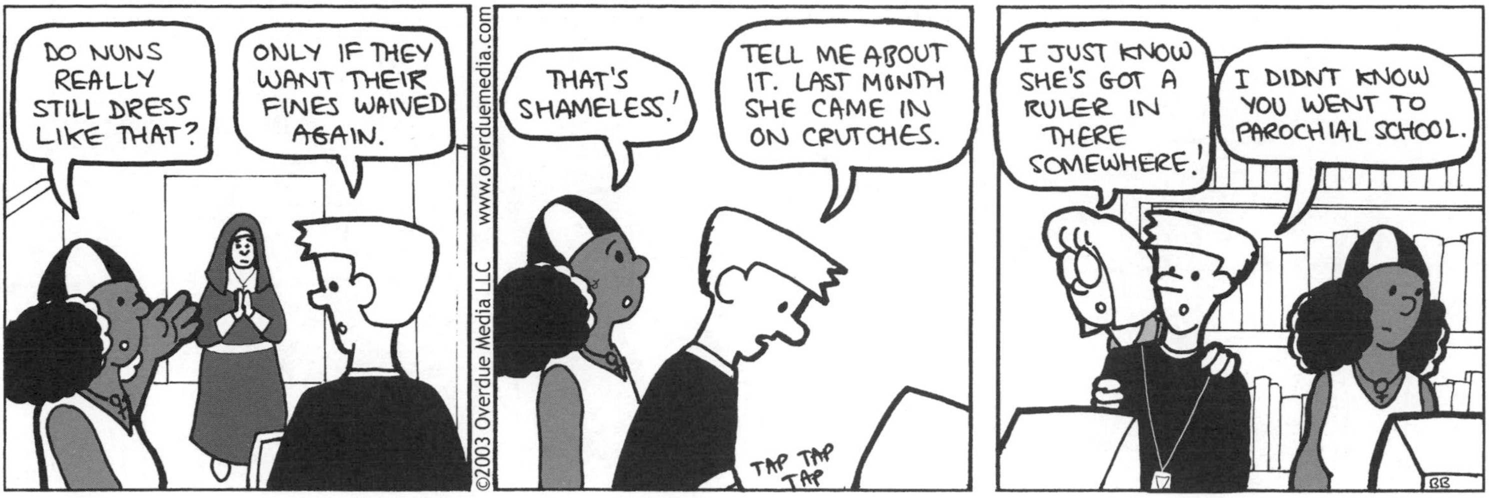
DO NUNS REALLY STILL DRESS LIKE THAT?
ONLY IF THEY WANT THEIR FINES WAIVED AGAIN.
©2003 Overdue Media LLC www.overduemedia.com
THAT'S SHAMELESS!
TELL ME ABOUT IT. LAST MONTH SHE CAME IN ON CRUTCHES.
TAP TAP TAP
I JUST KNOW SHE'S GOT A RULER IN THERE SOMEWHERE!
I DIDN'T KNOW YOU WENT TO PAROCHIAL SCHOOL.
BB

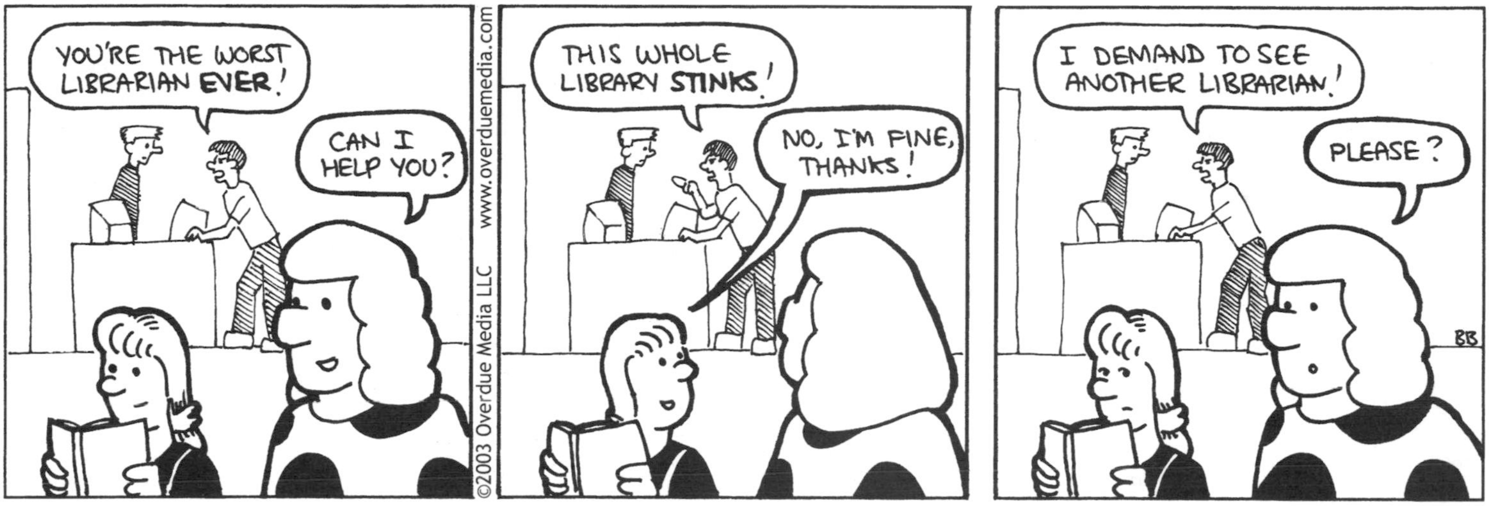
YOU'RE THE WORST LIBRARIAN **EVER**!
CAN I HELP YOU?
©2003 Overdue Media LLC www.overduemedia.com
THIS WHOLE LIBRARY **STINKS**!
NO, I'M FINE, THANKS!
I DEMAND TO SEE ANOTHER LIBRARIAN!
PLEASE?
BB

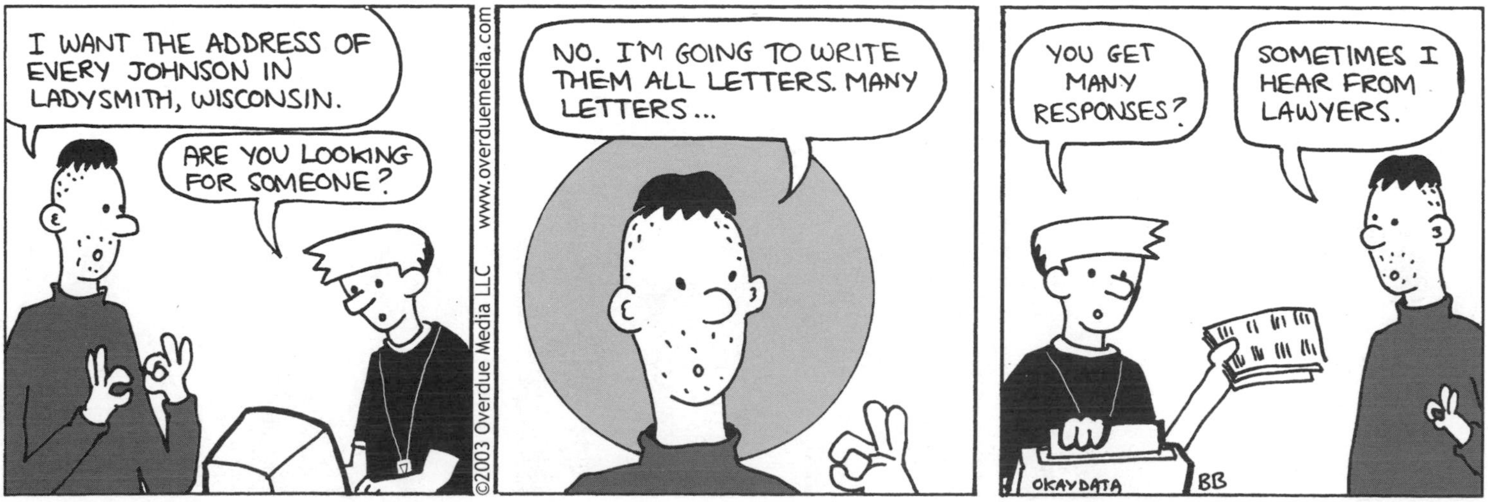
I WANT THE ADDRESS OF EVERY JOHNSON IN LADYSMITH, WISCONSIN.
ARE YOU LOOKING FOR SOMEONE?
©2003 Overdue Media LLC www.overduemedia.com
NO. I'M GOING TO WRITE THEM ALL LETTERS. MANY LETTERS...
YOU GET MANY RESPONSES?
SOMETIMES I HEAR FROM LAWYERS.
OKAYDATA
BB

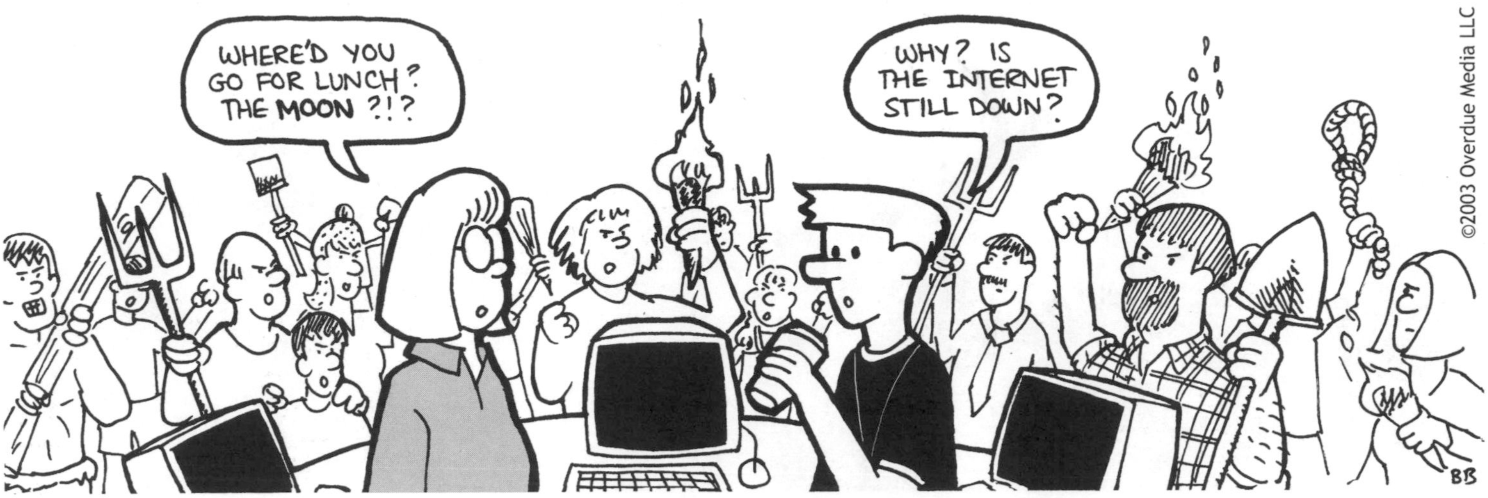
WHERE'D YOU GO FOR LUNCH? THE MOON?!?
WHY? IS THE INTERNET STILL DOWN?
©2003 Overdue Media LLC
BB

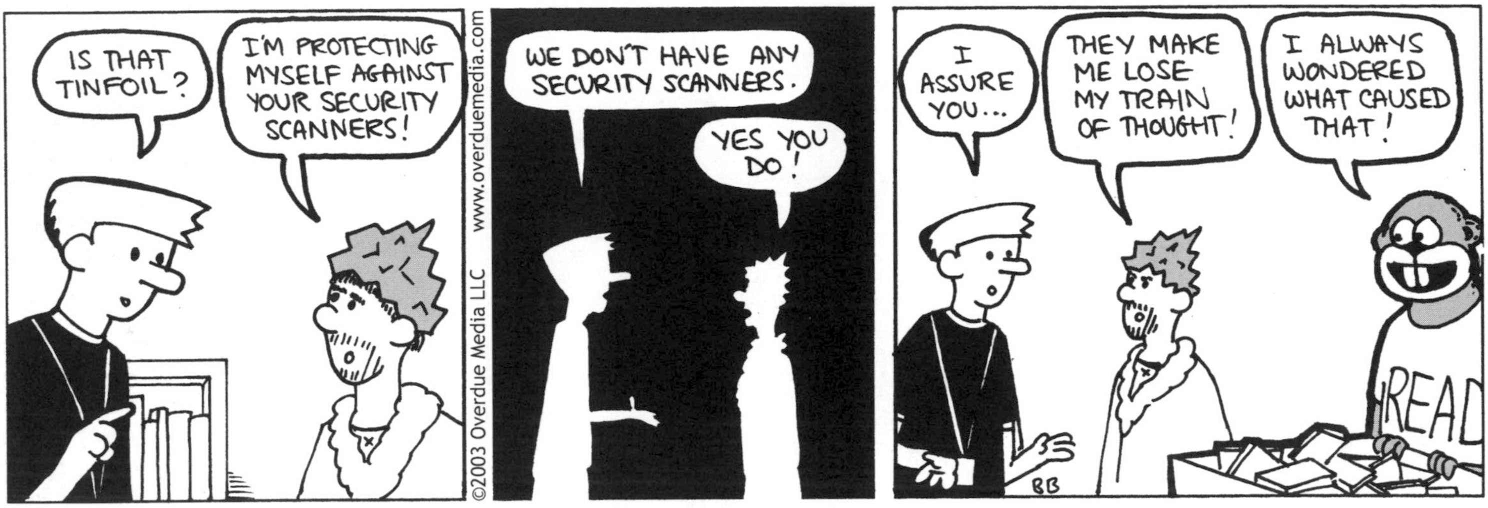
IS THAT TINFOIL?
I'M PROTECTING MYSELF AGAINST YOUR SECURITY SCANNERS!
©2003 Overdue Media LLC www.overduemedia.com
WE DON'T HAVE ANY SECURITY SCANNERS.
YES YOU DO!
I ASSURE YOU...
THEY MAKE ME LOSE MY TRAIN OF THOUGHT!
I ALWAYS WONDERED WHAT CAUSED THAT!
READ
BB

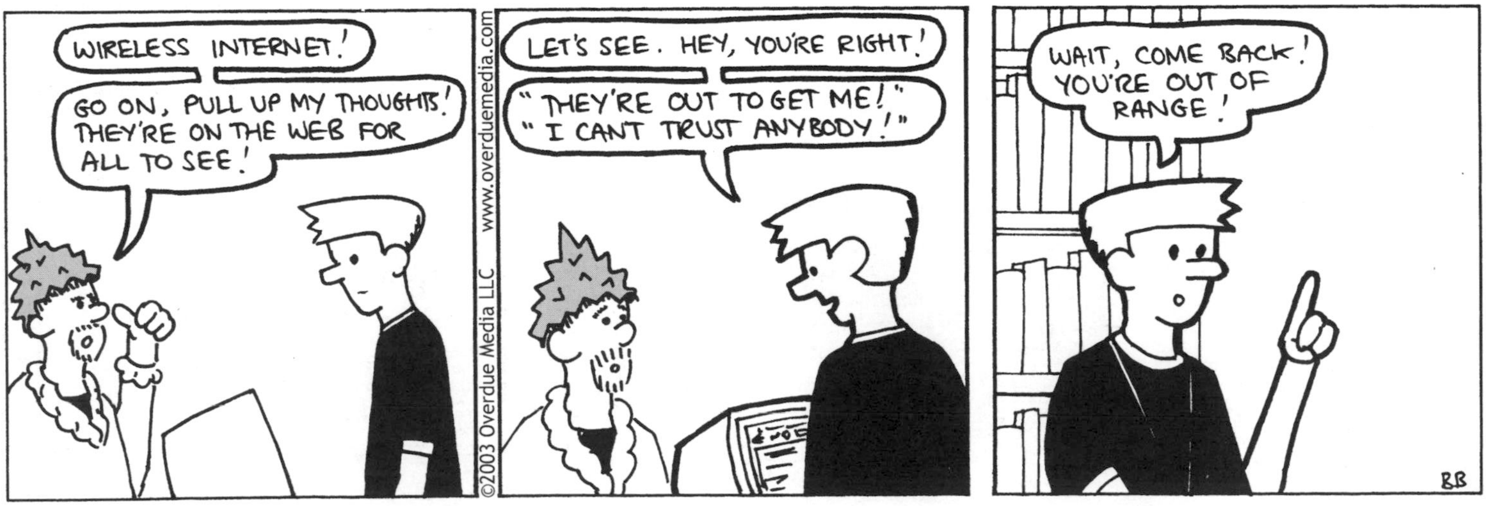
WIRELESS INTERNET!
GO ON, PULL UP MY THOUGHTS! THEY'RE ON THE WEB FOR ALL TO SEE!
©2003 Overdue Media LLC www.overduemedia.com
LET'S SEE. HEY, YOU'RE RIGHT!
"THEY'RE OUT TO GET ME!" "I CANT TRUST ANYBODY!"
WAIT, COME BACK! YOU'RE OUT OF RANGE!
BB

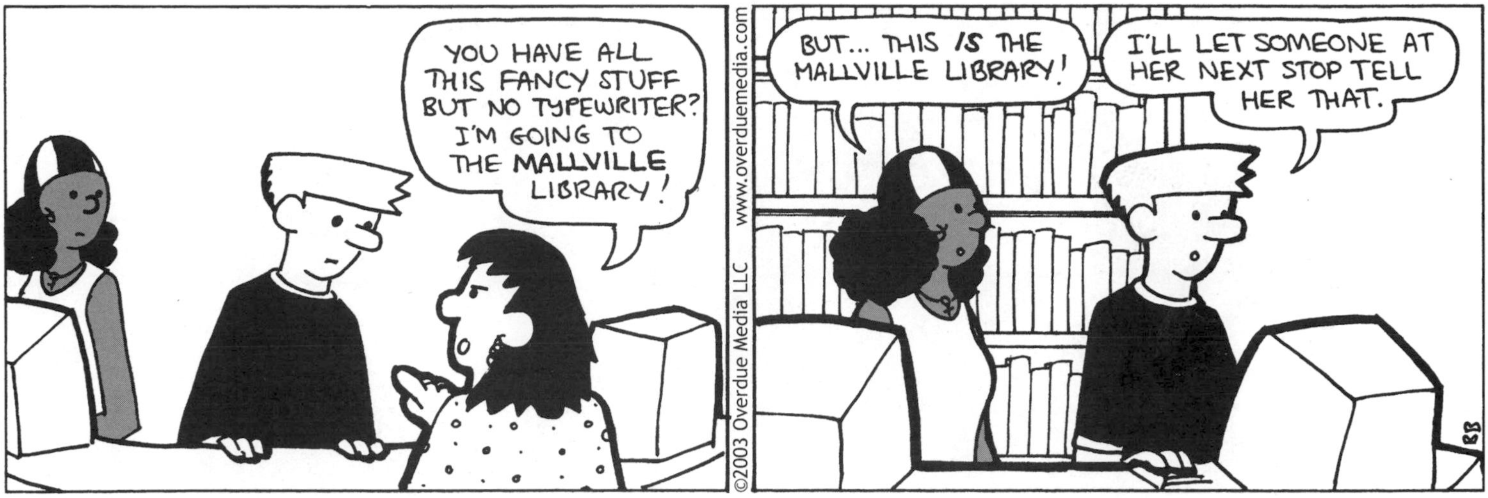
YOU HAVE ALL THIS FANCY STUFF BUT NO TYPEWRITER? I'M GOING TO THE MALLVILLE LIBRARY!
BUT... THIS IS THE MALLVILLE LIBRARY!
I'LL LET SOMEONE AT HER NEXT STOP TELL HER THAT.
©2003 Overdue Media LLC www.overduemedia.com
BB

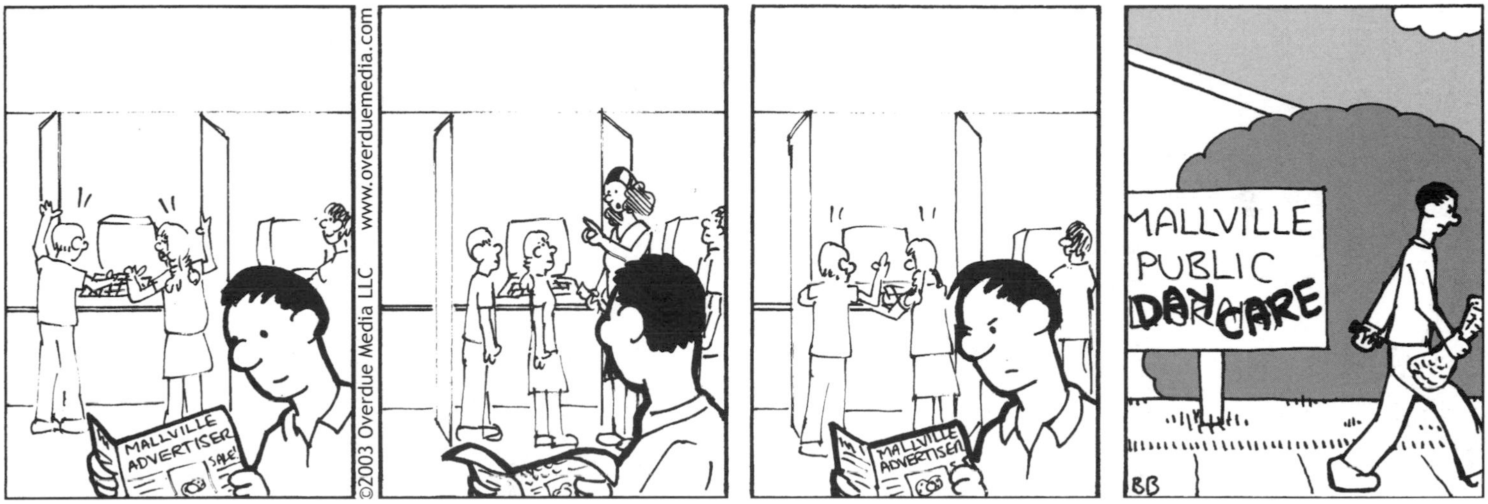
MALLVILLE ADVERTISER
SALE!
MALLVILLE PUBLIC DAY CARE
©2003 Overdue Media LLC www.overduemedia.com
BB

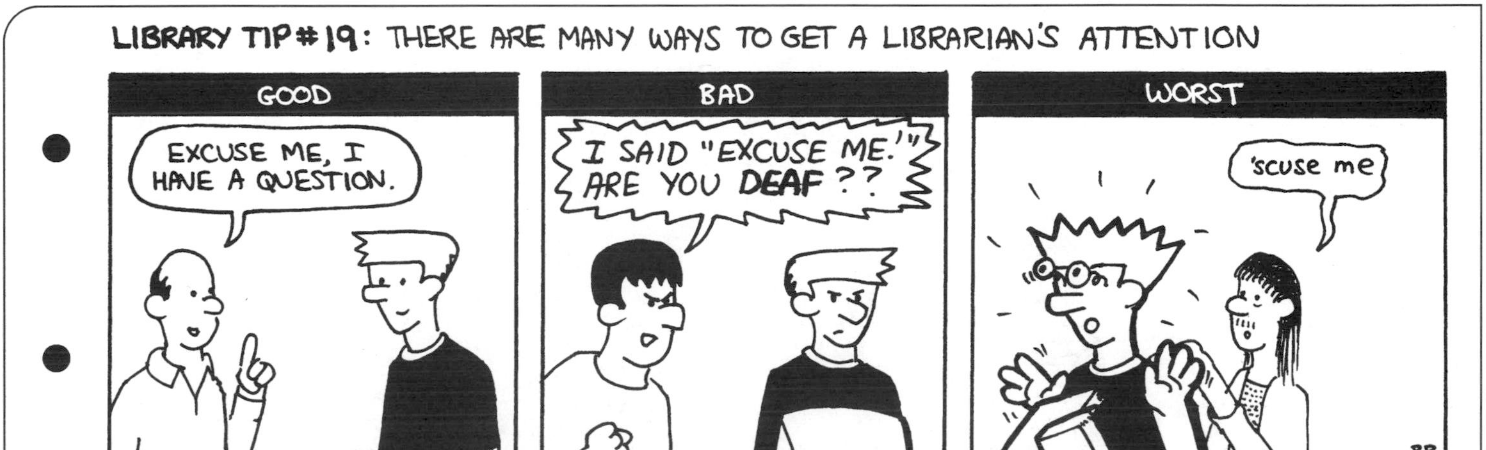
LIBRARY TIP #19: THERE ARE MANY WAYS TO GET A LIBRARIAN'S ATTENTION
GOOD
EXCUSE ME, I HAVE A QUESTION.
BAD
I SAID "EXCUSE ME!" ARE YOU DEAF??
WORST
'scuse me
BB
©2003 Overdue Media LLC
www.overduemedia.com

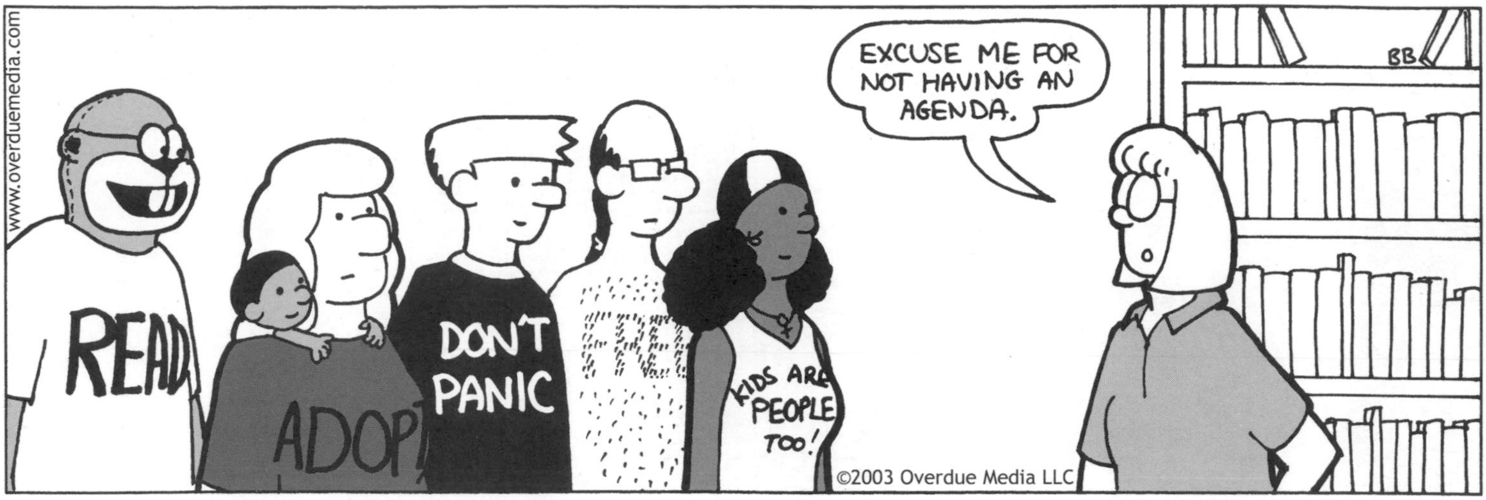

www.overduemedia.com
READ
ADOPT
DON'T PANIC
KIDS ARE PEOPLE TOO!
EXCUSE ME FOR NOT HAVING AN AGENDA.
BB
©2003 Overdue Media LLC


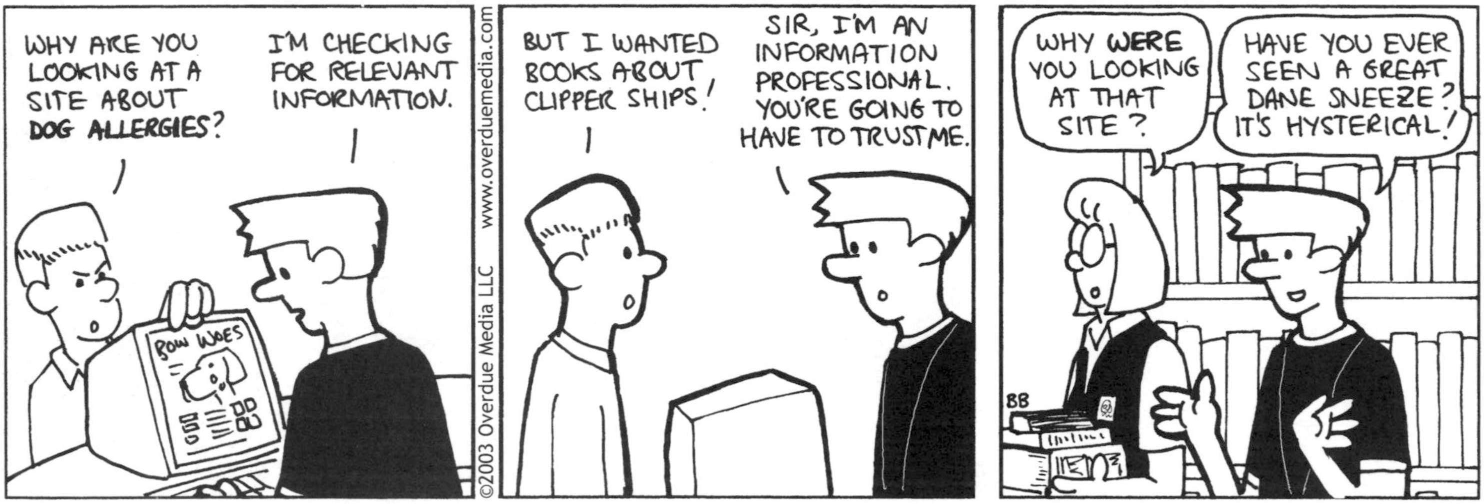

WHY ARE YOU LOOKING AT A SITE ABOUT DOG ALLERGIES?
I'M CHECKING FOR RELEVANT INFORMATION.
BOW WOES
www.overduemedia.com
©2003 Overdue Media LLC
BUT I WANTED BOOKS ABOUT CLIPPER SHIPS!
SIR, I'M AN INFORMATION PROFESSIONAL. YOU'RE GOING TO HAVE TO TRUST ME.
WHY WERE YOU LOOKING AT THAT SITE?
HAVE YOU EVER SEEN A GREAT DANE SNEEZE? IT'S HYSTERICAL!
BB


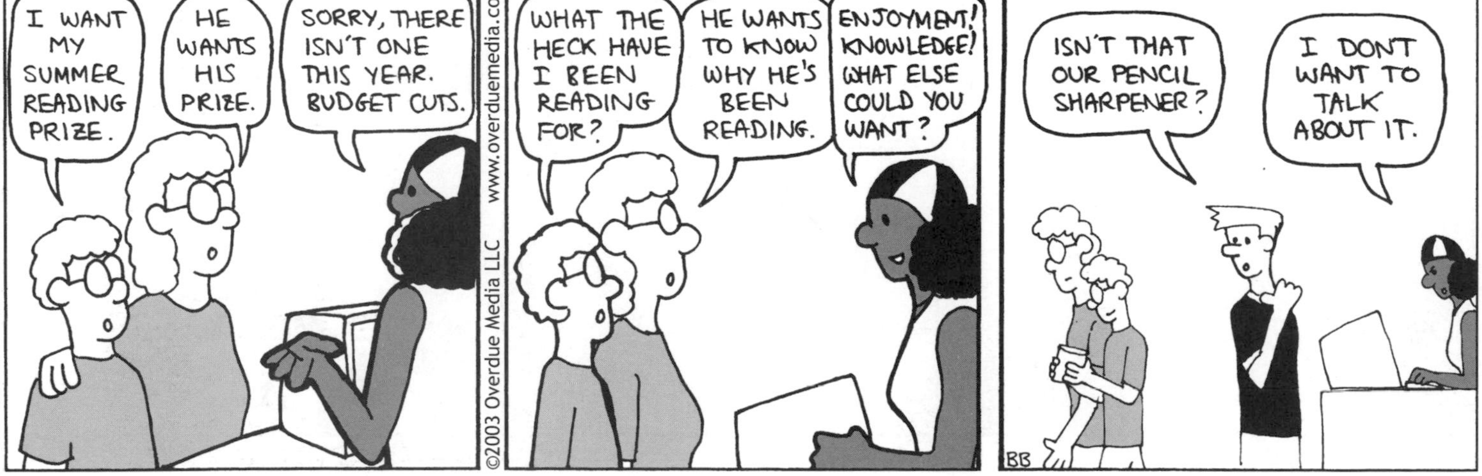

I WANT MY SUMMER READING PRIZE.
HE WANTS HIS PRIZE.
SORRY, THERE ISN'T ONE THIS YEAR. BUDGET CUTS.
www.overduemedia.com
©2003 Overdue Media LLC
WHAT THE HECK HAVE I BEEN READING FOR?
HE WANTS TO KNOW WHY HE'S BEEN READING.
ENJOYMENT! KNOWLEDGE! WHAT ELSE COULD YOU WANT?
ISN'T THAT OUR PENCIL SHARPENER?
I DONT WANT TO TALK ABOUT IT.
BB

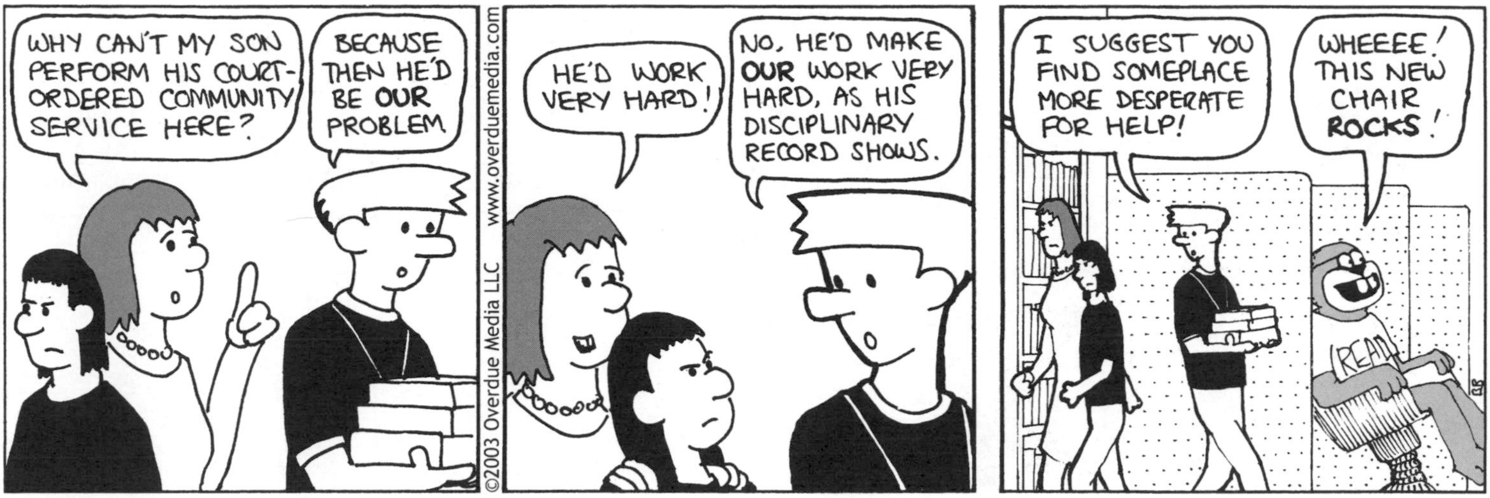
WHY CAN'T MY SON PERFORM HIS COURT-ORDERED COMMUNITY SERVICE HERE?
BECAUSE THEN HE'D BE **OUR** PROBLEM.
©2003 Overdue Media LLC www.overduemedia.com
HE'D WORK VERY HARD!
NO, HE'D MAKE **OUR** WORK VERY HARD, AS HIS DISCIPLINARY RECORD SHOWS.
I SUGGEST YOU FIND SOMEPLACE MORE DESPERATE FOR HELP!
WHEEEE! THIS NEW CHAIR **ROCKS**!

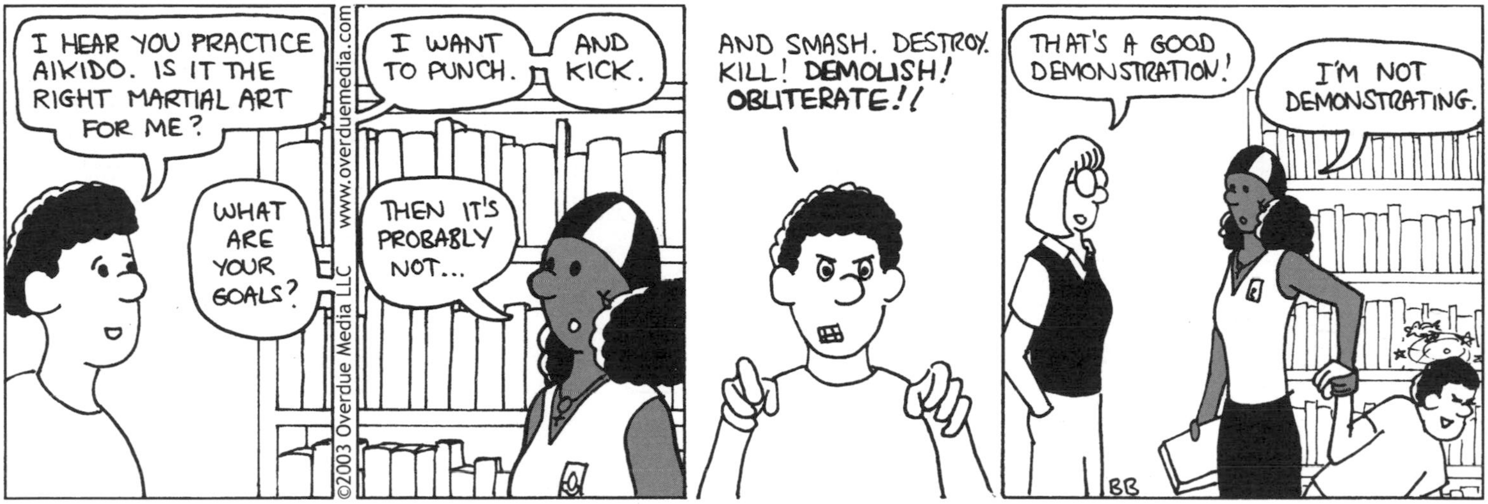
I HEAR YOU PRACTICE AIKIDO. IS IT THE RIGHT MARTIAL ART FOR ME?
WHAT ARE YOUR GOALS?
©2003 Overdue Media LLC www.overduemedia.com
I WANT TO PUNCH.
AND KICK.
THEN IT'S PROBABLY NOT...
AND SMASH. DESTROY. KILL! **DEMOLISH**! **OBLITERATE**!!
THAT'S A GOOD DEMONSTRATION!
I'M NOT DEMONSTRATING.
BB

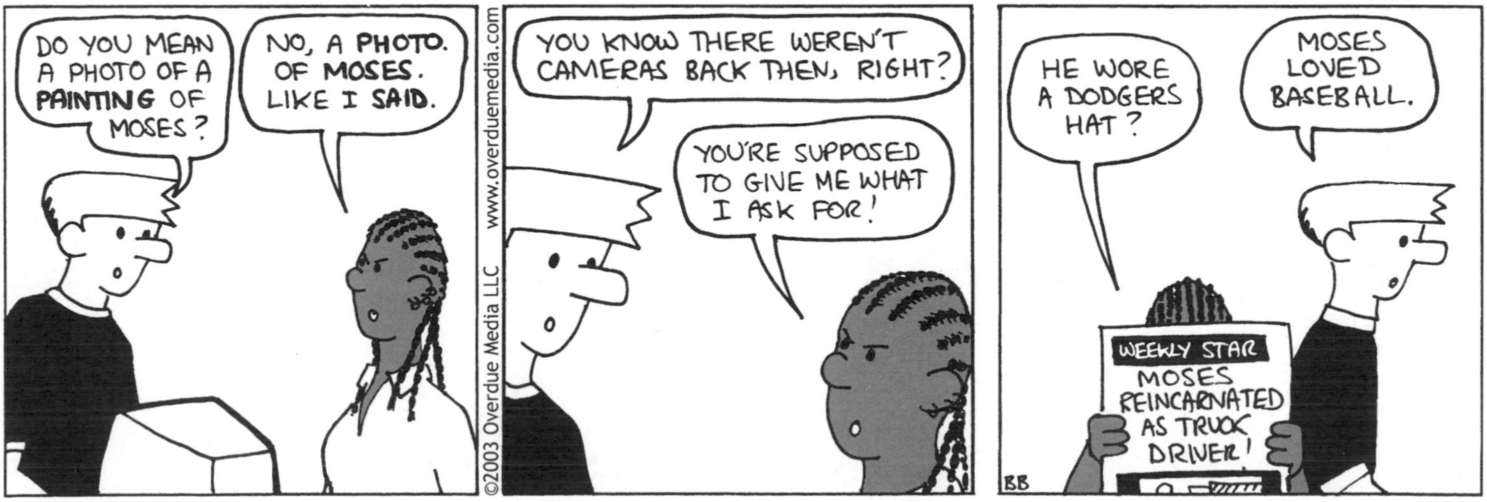
DO YOU MEAN A PHOTO OF A **PAINTING** OF MOSES?
NO, A **PHOTO**. OF **MOSES**. LIKE I **SAID**.
©2003 Overdue Media LLC www.overduemedia.com
YOU KNOW THERE WEREN'T CAMERAS BACK THEN, RIGHT?
YOU'RE SUPPOSED TO GIVE ME WHAT I ASK FOR!
HE WORE A DODGERS HAT?
MOSES LOVED BASEBALL.
WEEKLY STAR
MOSES REINCARNATED AS TRUCK DRIVER!
BB

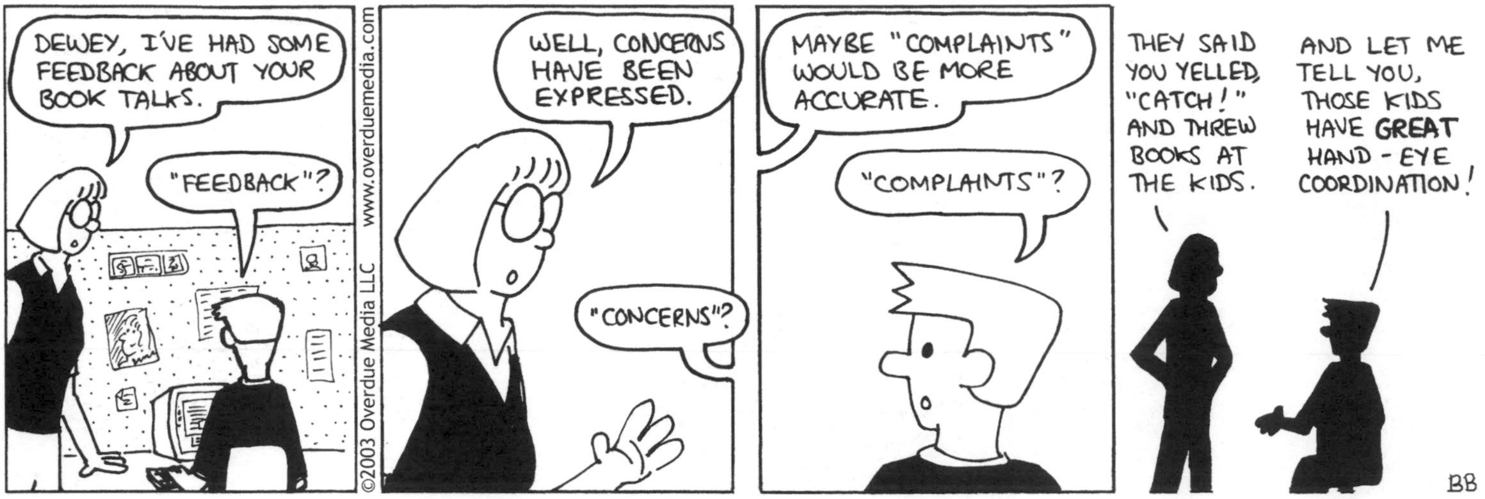
DEWEY, I'VE HAD SOME FEEDBACK ABOUT YOUR BOOK TALKS.
"FEEDBACK"?
www.overduemedia.com
©2003 Overdue Media LLC
WELL, CONCERNS HAVE BEEN EXPRESSED.
"CONCERNS"?
MAYBE "COMPLAINTS" WOULD BE MORE ACCURATE.
"COMPLAINTS"?
THEY SAID YOU YELLED, "CATCH!" AND THREW BOOKS AT THE KIDS.
AND LET ME TELL YOU, THOSE KIDS HAVE **GREAT** HAND-EYE COORDINATION!
BB

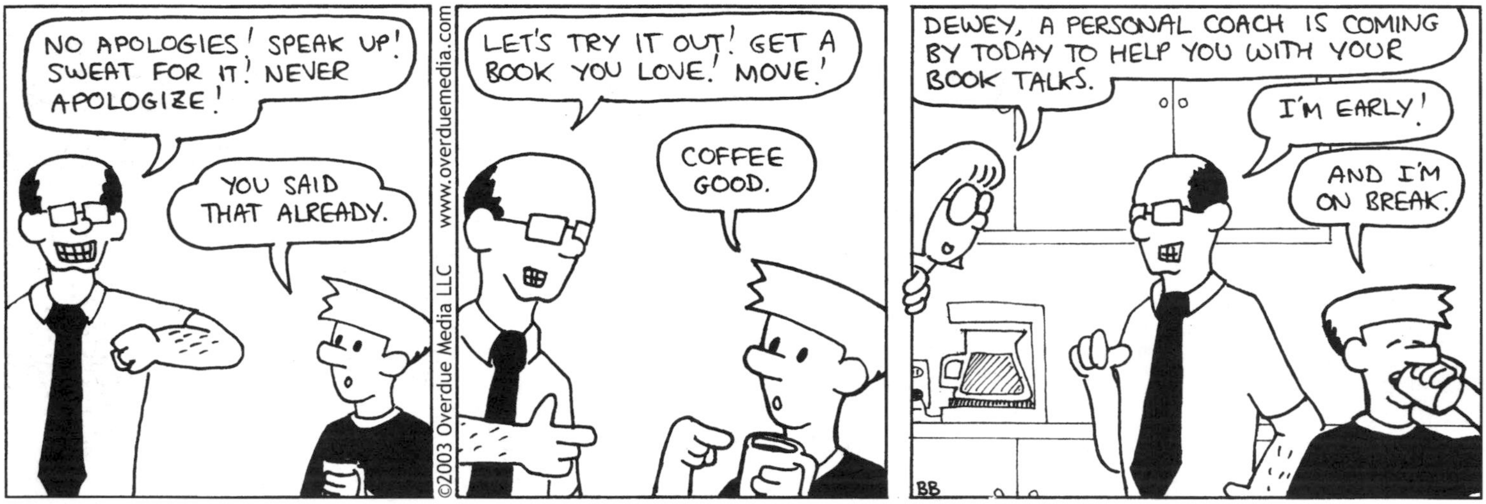
NO APOLOGIES! SPEAK UP! SWEAT FOR IT! NEVER APOLOGIZE!
YOU SAID THAT ALREADY.
www.overduemedia.com
©2003 Overdue Media LLC
LET'S TRY IT OUT! GET A BOOK YOU LOVE! MOVE!
COFFEE GOOD.
DEWEY, A PERSONAL COACH IS COMING BY TODAY TO HELP YOU WITH YOUR BOOK TALKS.
I'M EARLY!
AND I'M ON BREAK.
BB

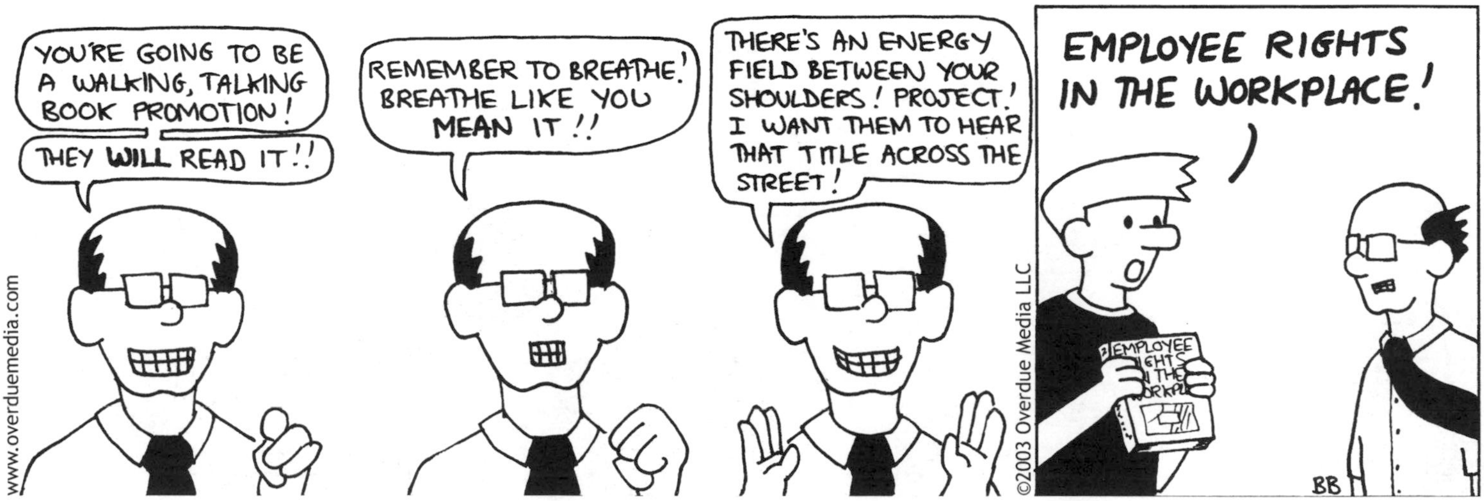
www.overduemedia.com
YOU'RE GOING TO BE A WALKING, TALKING BOOK PROMOTION!
THEY **WILL** READ IT!!
REMEMBER TO BREATHE! BREATHE LIKE YOU **MEAN** IT!!
THERE'S AN ENERGY FIELD BETWEEN YOUR SHOULDERS! PROJECT! I WANT THEM TO HEAR THAT TITLE ACROSS THE STREET!
©2003 Overdue Media LLC
**EMPLOYEE RIGHTS IN THE WORKPLACE!**
BB

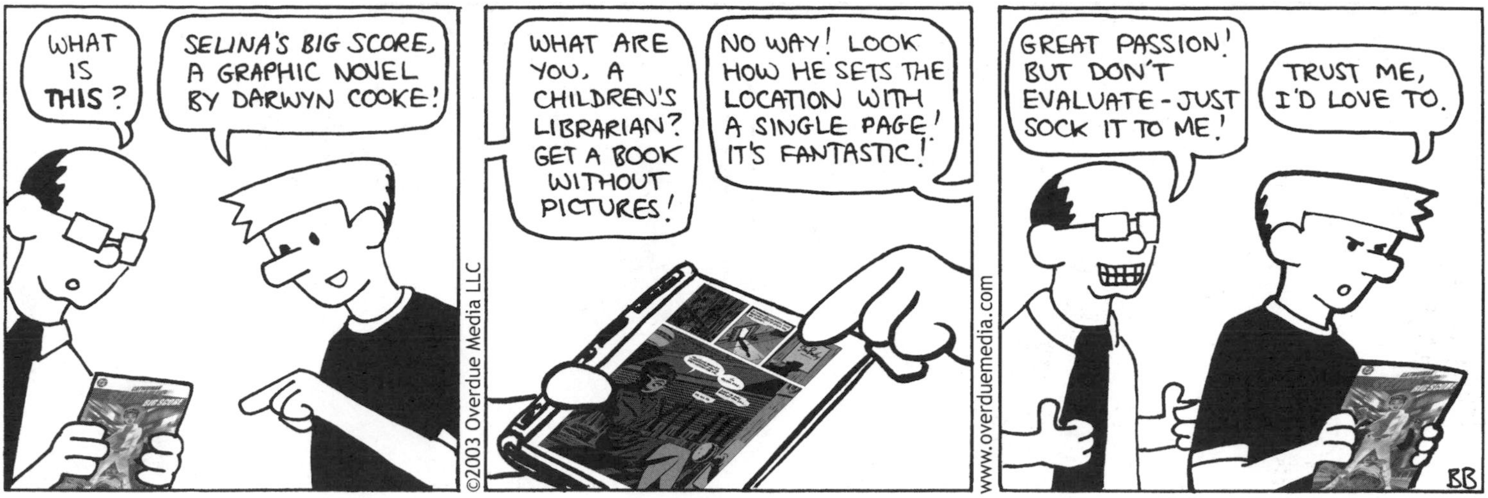
WHAT IS THIS?
SELINA'S BIG SCORE, A GRAPHIC NOVEL BY DARWYN COOKE!
©2003 Overdue Media LLC
WHAT ARE YOU, A CHILDREN'S LIBRARIAN? GET A BOOK WITHOUT PICTURES!
NO WAY! LOOK HOW HE SETS THE LOCATION WITH A SINGLE PAGE! IT'S FANTASTIC!
www.overduemedia.com
GREAT PASSION! BUT DON'T EVALUATE - JUST SOCK IT TO ME!
TRUST ME, I'D LOVE TO.
BB

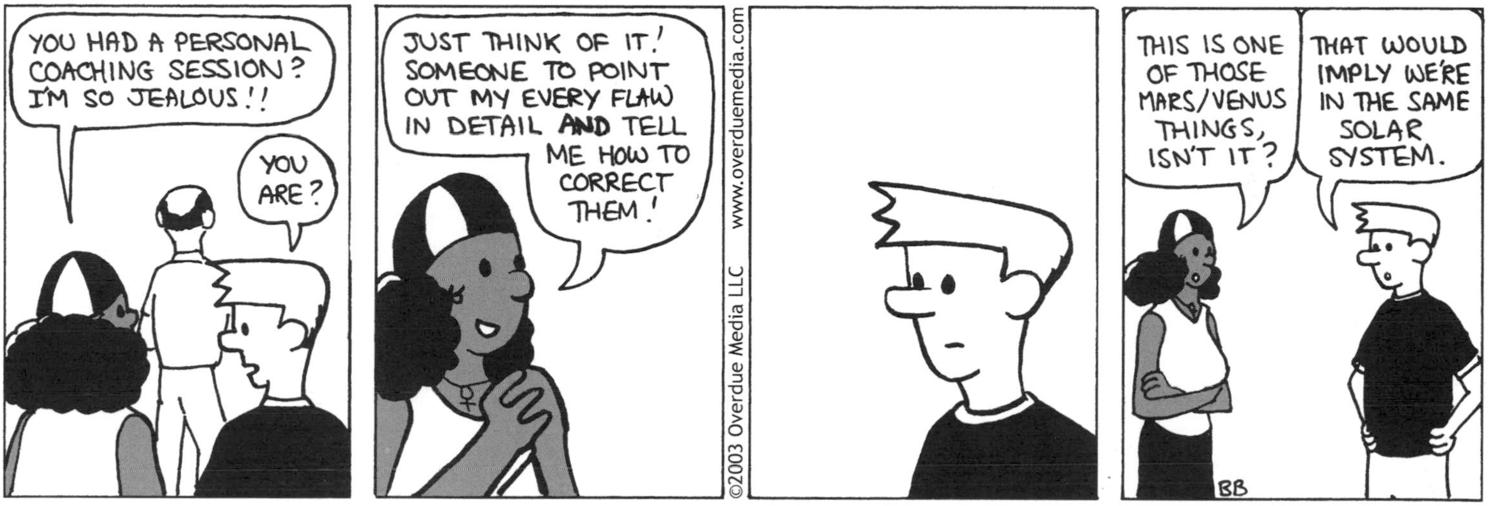
YOU HAD A PERSONAL COACHING SESSION? I'M SO JEALOUS!!
YOU ARE?
JUST THINK OF IT! SOMEONE TO POINT OUT MY EVERY FLAW IN DETAIL AND TELL ME HOW TO CORRECT THEM!
©2003 Overdue Media LLC
www.overduemedia.com
THIS IS ONE OF THOSE MARS/VENUS THINGS, ISN'T IT?
THAT WOULD IMPLY WE'RE IN THE SAME SOLAR SYSTEM.
BB

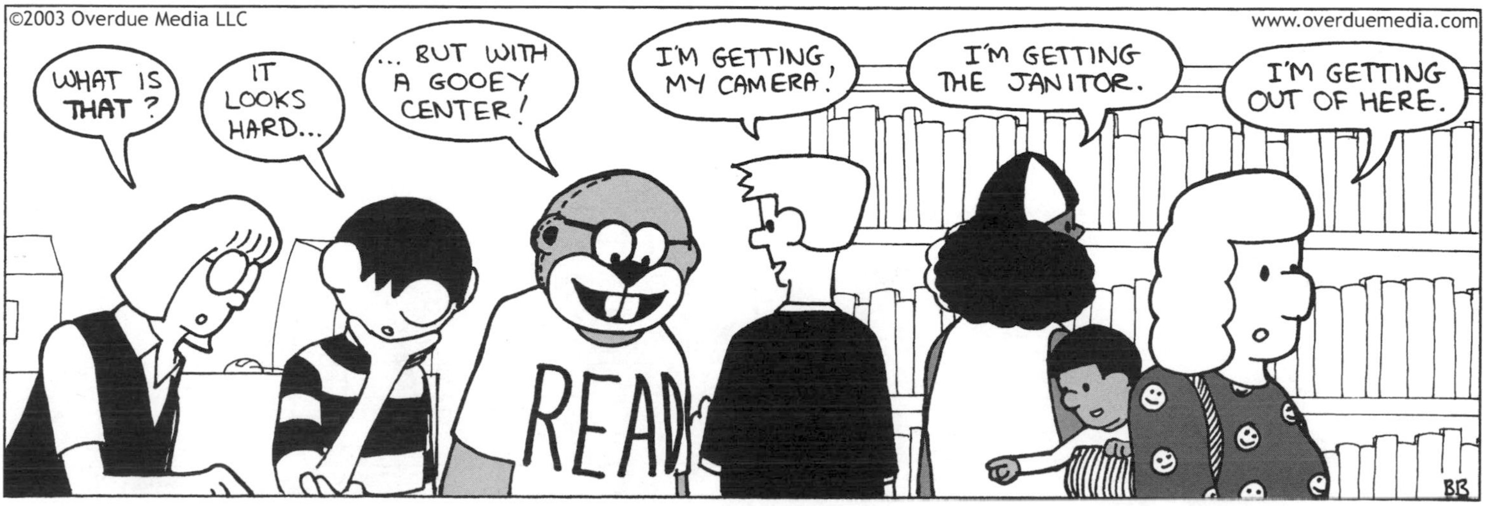
©2003 Overdue Media LLC
www.overduemedia.com
WHAT IS THAT?
IT LOOKS HARD...
...BUT WITH A GOOEY CENTER!
I'M GETTING MY CAMERA!
I'M GETTING THE JANITOR.
I'M GETTING OUT OF HERE.
READ
BB

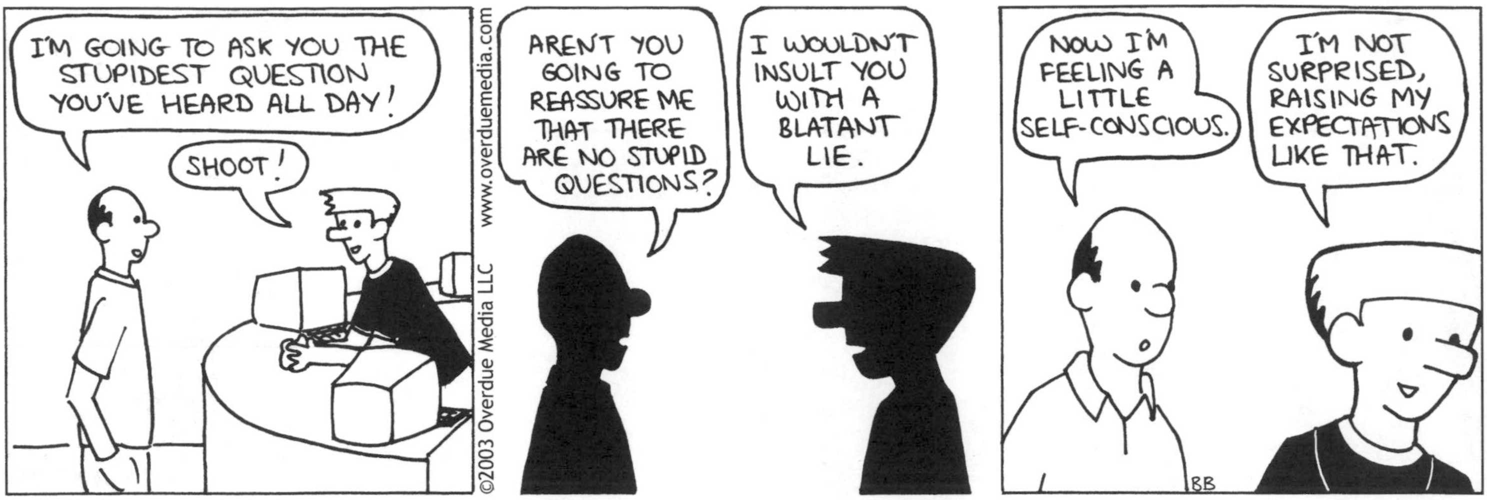
I'M GOING TO ASK YOU THE STUPIDEST QUESTION YOU'VE HEARD ALL DAY!
SHOOT!
©2003 Overdue Media LLC www.overduemedia.com
AREN'T YOU GOING TO REASSURE ME THAT THERE ARE NO STUPID QUESTIONS?
I WOULDN'T INSULT YOU WITH A BLATANT LIE.
NOW I'M FEELING A LITTLE SELF-CONSCIOUS.
I'M NOT SURPRISED, RAISING MY EXPECTATIONS LIKE THAT.
BB

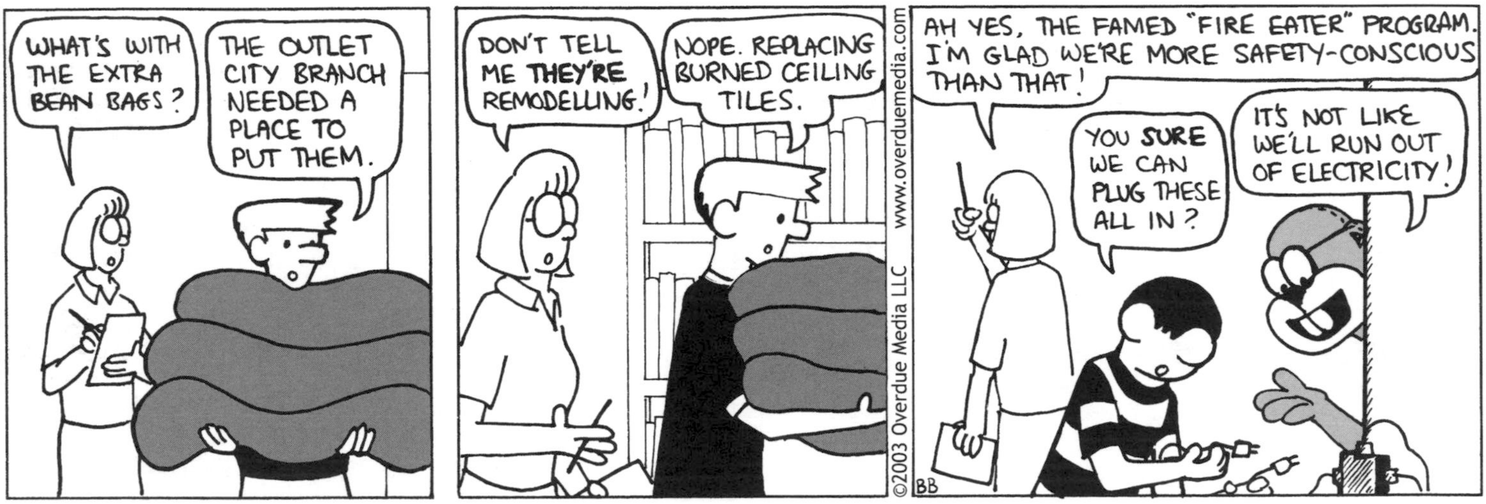
WHAT'S WITH THE EXTRA BEAN BAGS?
THE OUTLET CITY BRANCH NEEDED A PLACE TO PUT THEM.
DON'T TELL ME **THEY'RE** REMODELLING!
NOPE. REPLACING BURNED CEILING TILES.
©2003 Overdue Media LLC www.overduemedia.com
AH YES, THE FAMED "FIRE EATER" PROGRAM. I'M GLAD WE'RE MORE SAFETY-CONSCIOUS THAN THAT!
YOU **SURE** WE CAN PLUG THESE ALL IN?
IT'S NOT LIKE WE'LL RUN OUT OF ELECTRICITY!
BB

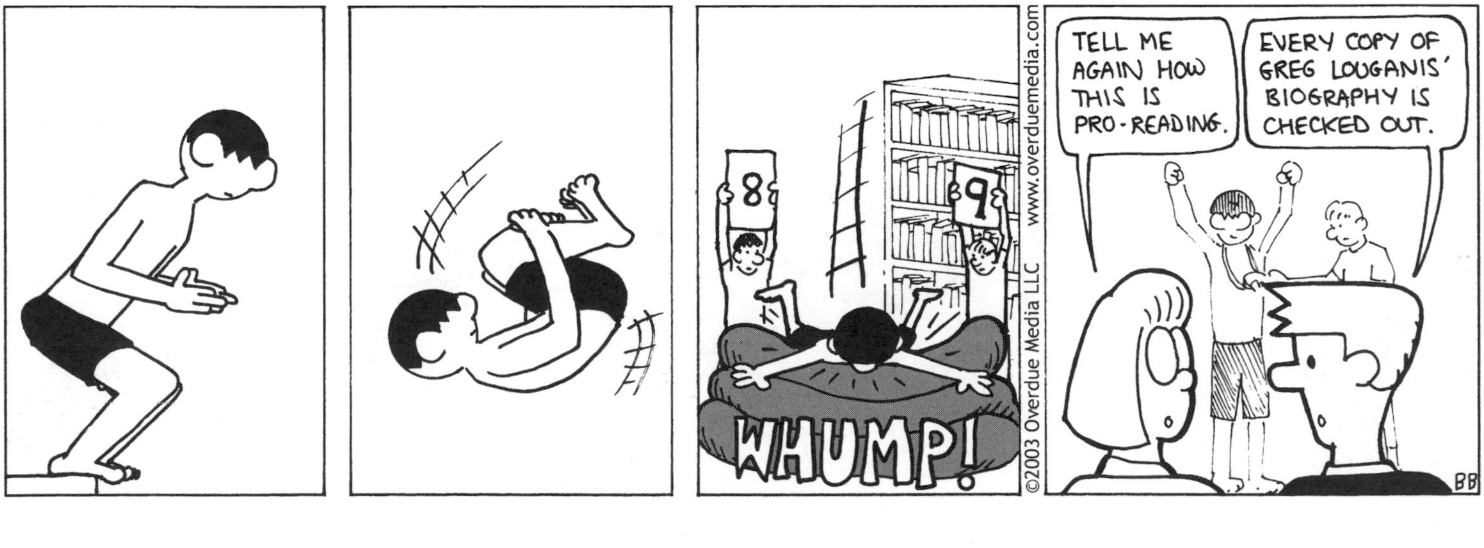
8
9
WHUMP!
©2003 Overdue Media LLC www.overduemedia.com
TELL ME AGAIN HOW THIS IS PRO-READING.
EVERY COPY OF GREG LOUGANIS' BIOGRAPHY IS CHECKED OUT.
BB

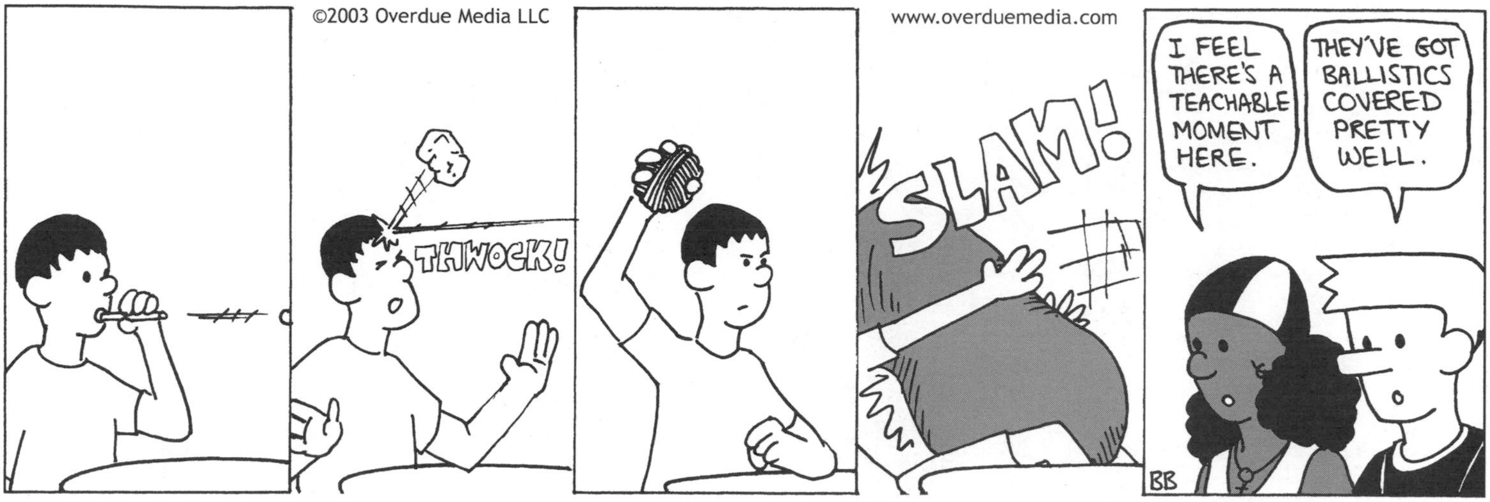
©2003 Overdue Media LLC
www.overduemedia.com
THWOCK!
SLAM!
I FEEL THERE'S A TEACHABLE MOMENT HERE.
THEY'VE GOT BALLISTICS COVERED PRETTY WELL.
BB

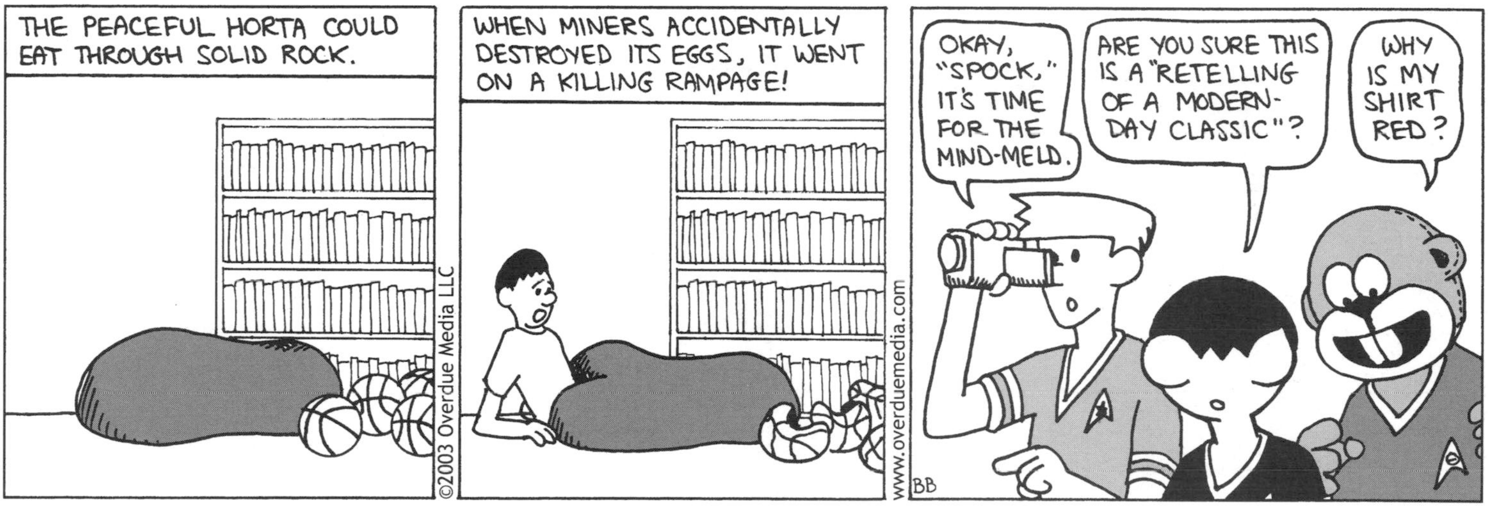
THE PEACEFUL HORTA COULD EAT THROUGH SOLID ROCK.
©2003 Overdue Media LLC
WHEN MINERS ACCIDENTALLY DESTROYED ITS EGGS, IT WENT ON A KILLING RAMPAGE!
www.overduemedia.com
OKAY, "SPOCK," IT'S TIME FOR THE MIND-MELD.
ARE YOU SURE THIS IS A "RETELLING OF A MODERN-DAY CLASSIC"?
WHY IS MY SHIRT RED?
BB

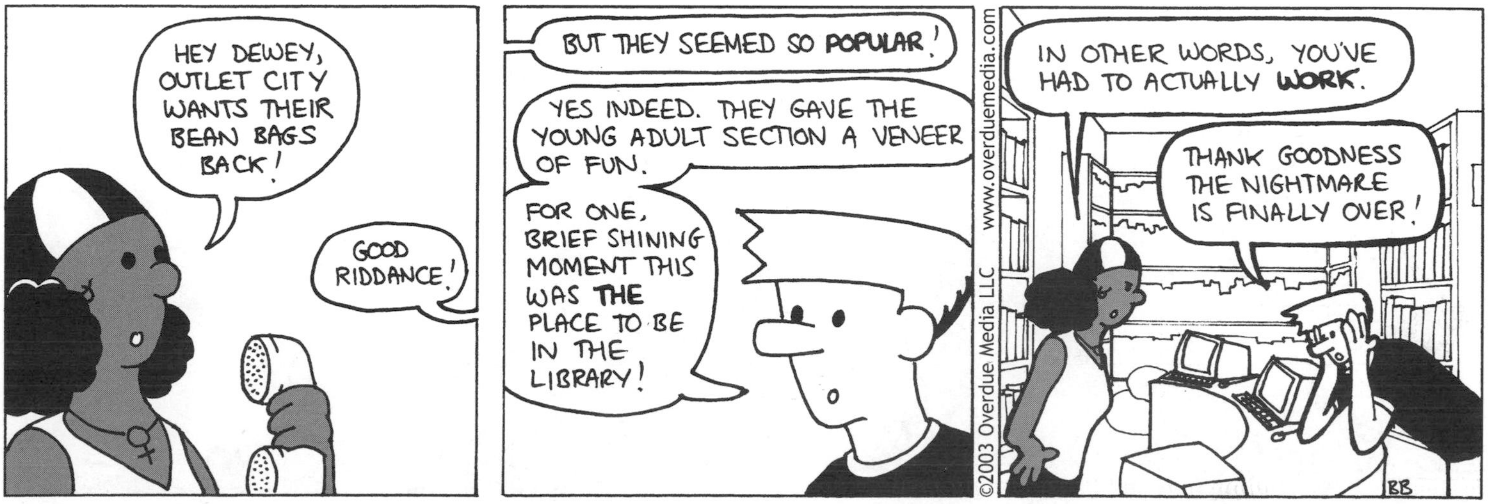
HEY DEWEY, OUTLET CITY WANTS THEIR BEAN BAGS BACK!
GOOD RIDDANCE!
BUT THEY SEEMED SO **POPULAR**!
YES INDEED. THEY GAVE THE YOUNG ADULT SECTION A VENEER OF FUN.
FOR ONE, BRIEF SHINING MOMENT THIS WAS **THE** PLACE TO BE IN THE LIBRARY!
©2003 Overdue Media LLC www.overduemedia.com
IN OTHER WORDS, YOU'VE HAD TO ACTUALLY **WORK**.
THANK GOODNESS THE NIGHTMARE IS FINALLY OVER!
BB

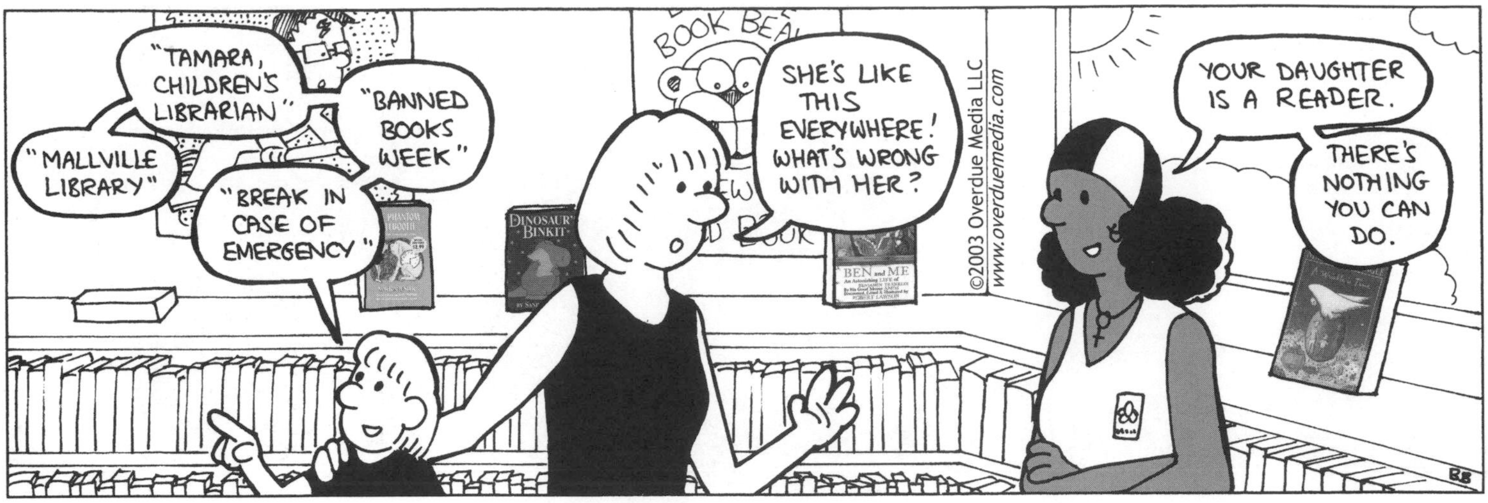
"MALLVILLE LIBRARY"
"TAMARA, CHILDREN'S LIBRARIAN"
"BANNED BOOKS WEEK"
"BREAK IN CASE OF EMERGENCY"
SHE'S LIKE THIS EVERYWHERE! WHAT'S WRONG WITH HER?
YOUR DAUGHTER IS A READER.
THERE'S NOTHING YOU CAN DO.
©2003 Overdue Media LLC
www.overduemedia.com
BB

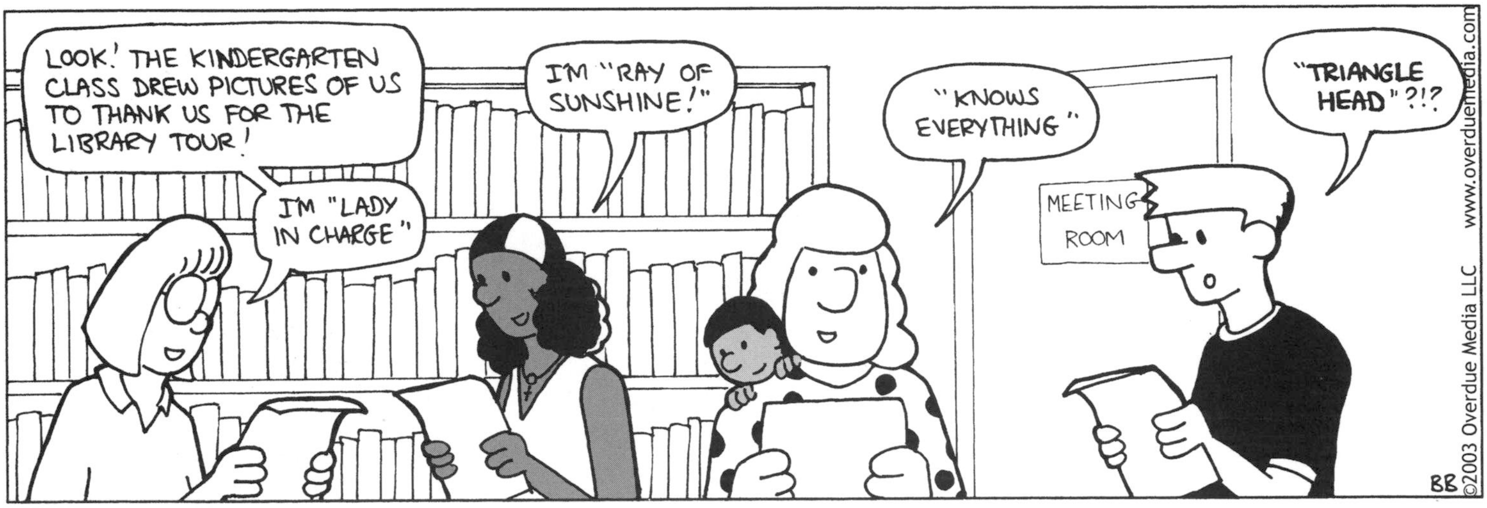
LOOK! THE KINDERGARTEN CLASS DREW PICTURES OF US TO THANK US FOR THE LIBRARY TOUR!
I'M "LADY IN CHARGE"
I'M "RAY OF SUNSHINE!"
"KNOWS EVERYTHING"
"TRIANGLE HEAD"?!?
MEETING ROOM
BB
©2003 Overdue Media LLC
www.overduemedia.com

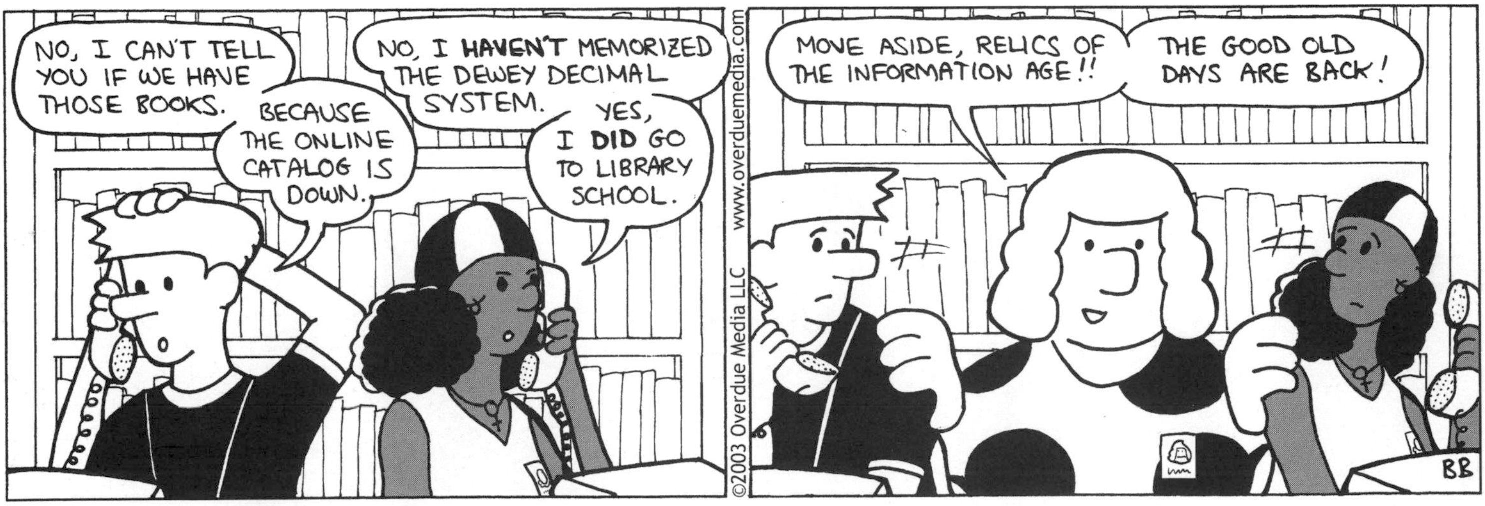
NO, I CAN'T TELL YOU IF WE HAVE THOSE BOOKS.
BECAUSE THE ONLINE CATALOG IS DOWN.
NO, I **HAVEN'T** MEMORIZED THE DEWEY DECIMAL SYSTEM.
YES, I **DID** GO TO LIBRARY SCHOOL.
©2003 Overdue Media LLC
www.overduemedia.com
MOVE ASIDE, RELICS OF THE INFORMATION AGE!!
THE GOOD OLD DAYS ARE BACK!
BB

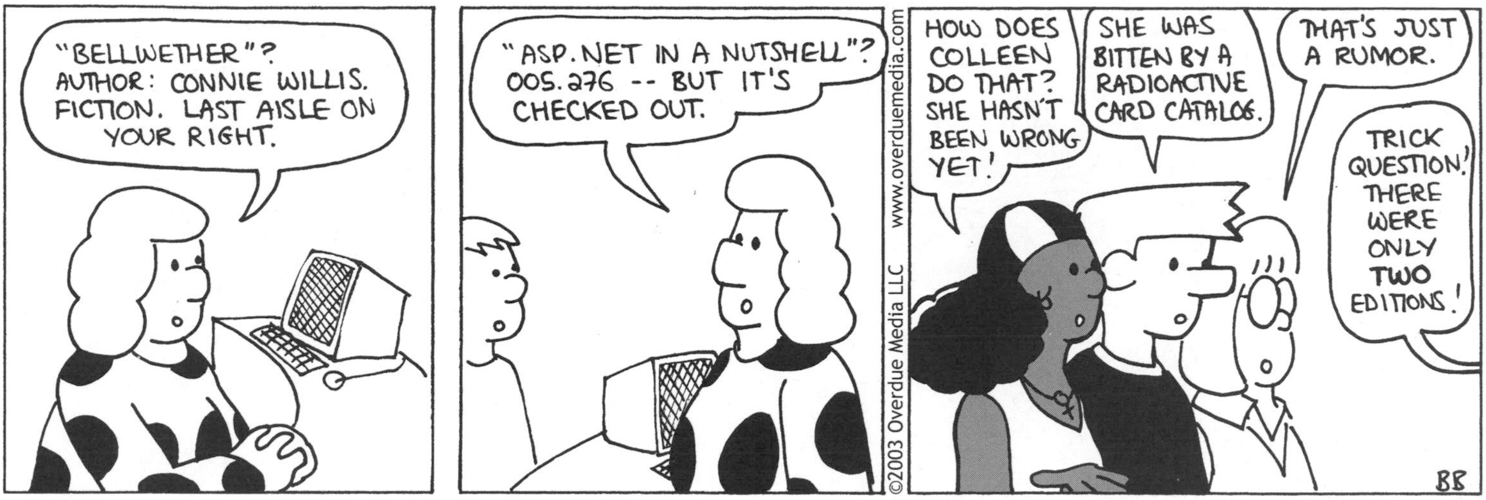
"BELLWETHER"? AUTHOR: CONNIE WILLIS. FICTION. LAST AISLE ON YOUR RIGHT.
"ASP.NET IN A NUTSHELL"? 005.276 -- BUT IT'S CHECKED OUT.
©2003 Overdue Media LLC www.overduemedia.com
HOW DOES COLLEEN DO THAT? SHE HASN'T BEEN WRONG YET!
SHE WAS BITTEN BY A RADIOACTIVE CARD CATALOG.
THAT'S JUST A RUMOR.
TRICK QUESTION! THERE WERE ONLY **TWO** EDITIONS!
BB

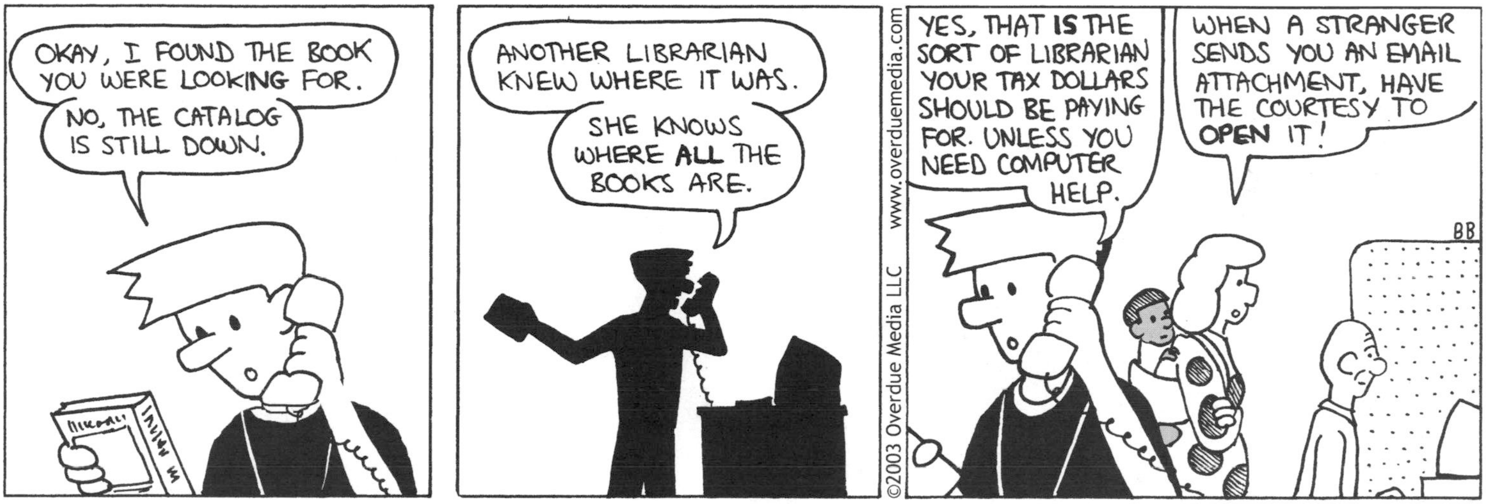
OKAY, I FOUND THE BOOK YOU WERE LOOKING FOR.
NO, THE CATALOG IS STILL DOWN.
ANOTHER LIBRARIAN KNEW WHERE IT WAS.
SHE KNOWS WHERE **ALL** THE BOOKS ARE.
©2003 Overdue Media LLC www.overduemedia.com
YES, THAT **IS** THE SORT OF LIBRARIAN YOUR TAX DOLLARS SHOULD BE PAYING FOR. UNLESS YOU NEED COMPUTER HELP.
WHEN A STRANGER SENDS YOU AN EMAIL ATTACHMENT, HAVE THE COURTESY TO **OPEN** IT!
BB

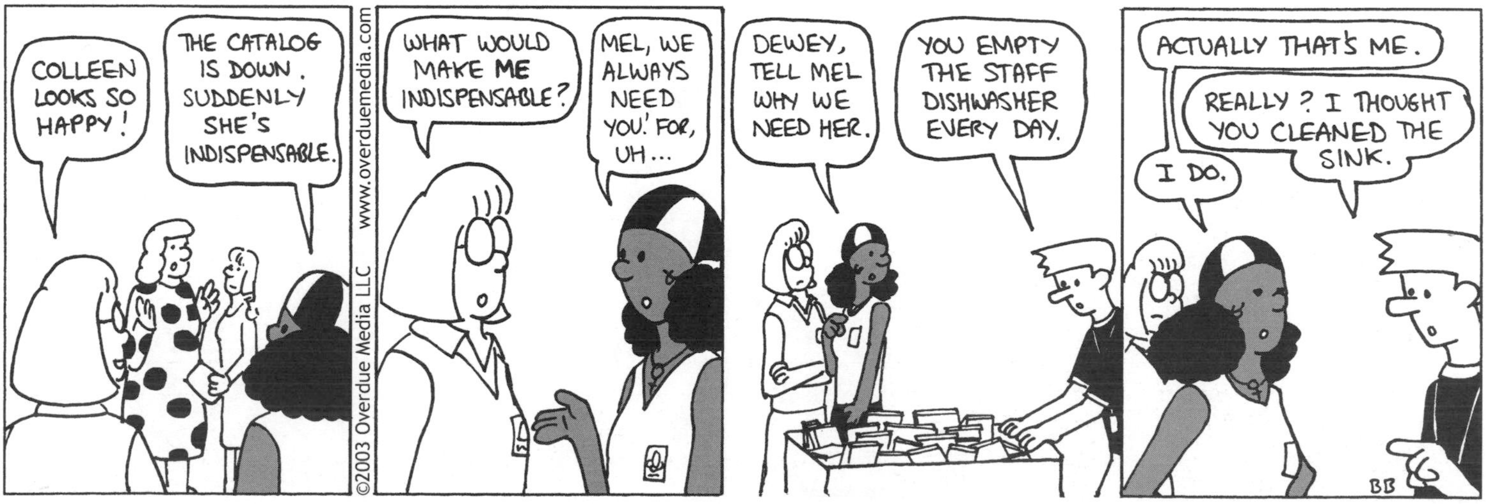
COLLEEN LOOKS SO HAPPY!
THE CATALOG IS DOWN. SUDDENLY SHE'S INDISPENSABLE.
©2003 Overdue Media LLC www.overduemedia.com
WHAT WOULD MAKE **ME** INDISPENSABLE?
MEL, WE ALWAYS NEED YOU! FOR, UH...
DEWEY, TELL MEL WHY WE NEED HER.
YOU EMPTY THE STAFF DISHWASHER EVERY DAY.
ACTUALLY THAT'S ME.
REALLY? I THOUGHT YOU CLEANED THE SINK.
I DO.
BB

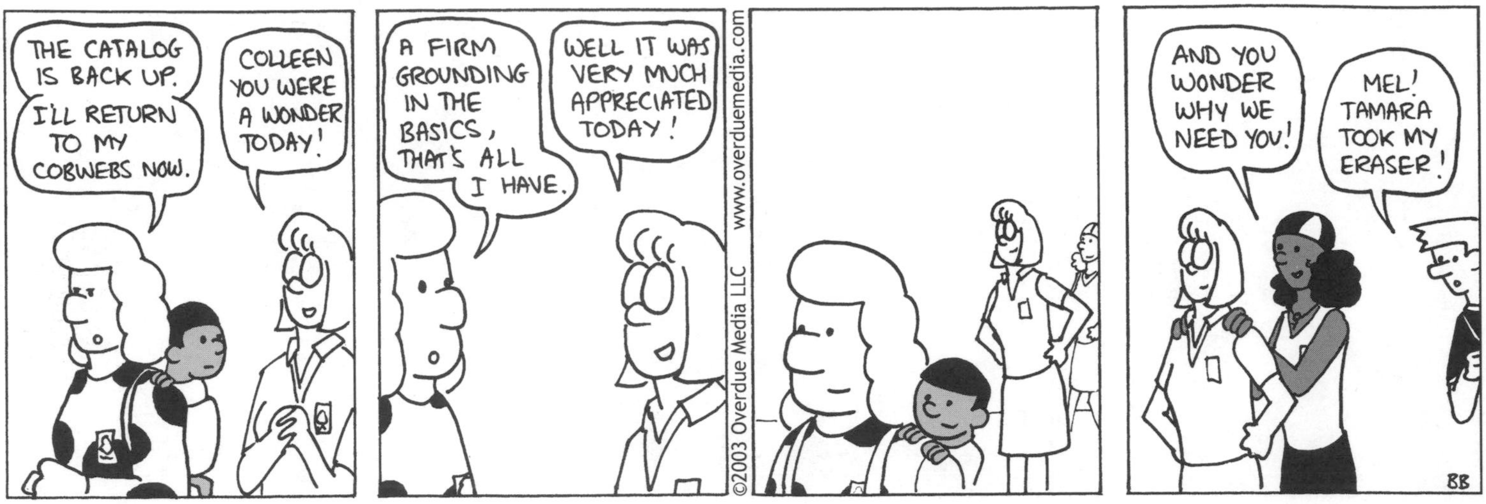
THE CATALOG IS BACK UP.
I'LL RETURN TO MY COBWEBS NOW.
COLLEEN YOU WERE A WONDER TODAY!
A FIRM GROUNDING IN THE BASICS, THAT'S ALL I HAVE.
WELL IT WAS VERY MUCH APPRECIATED TODAY!
©2003 Overdue Media LLC www.overduemedia.com
AND YOU WONDER WHY WE NEED YOU!
MEL! TAMARA TOOK MY ERASER!
BB

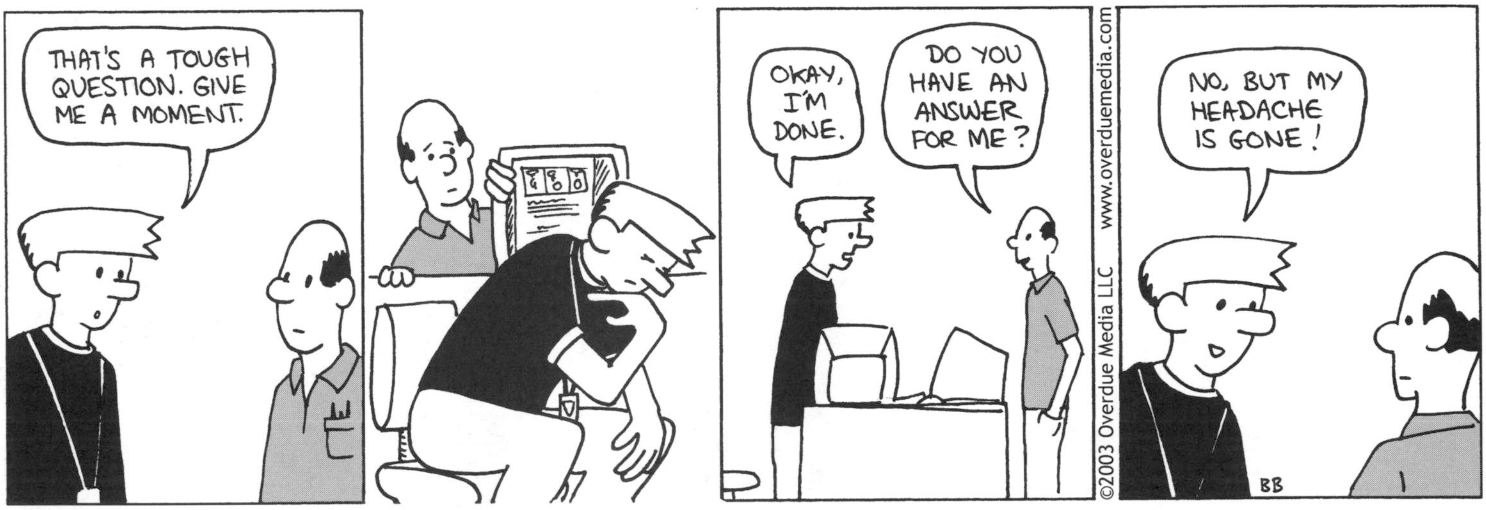
THAT'S A TOUGH QUESTION. GIVE ME A MOMENT.
OKAY, I'M DONE.
DO YOU HAVE AN ANSWER FOR ME?
©2003 Overdue Media LLC www.overduemedia.com
NO, BUT MY HEADACHE IS GONE!
BB

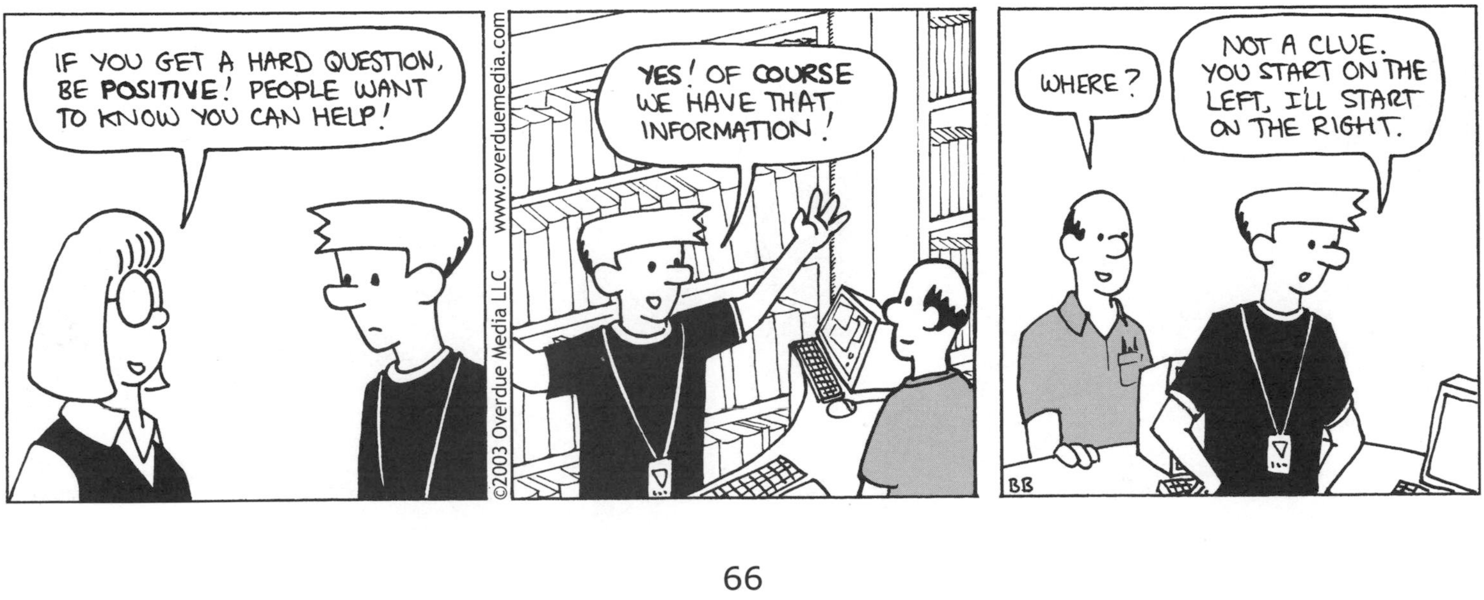
IF YOU GET A HARD QUESTION, BE POSITIVE! PEOPLE WANT TO KNOW YOU CAN HELP!
©2003 Overdue Media LLC www.overduemedia.com
YES! OF COURSE WE HAVE THAT INFORMATION!
WHERE?
NOT A CLUE. YOU START ON THE LEFT, I'LL START ON THE RIGHT.
BB

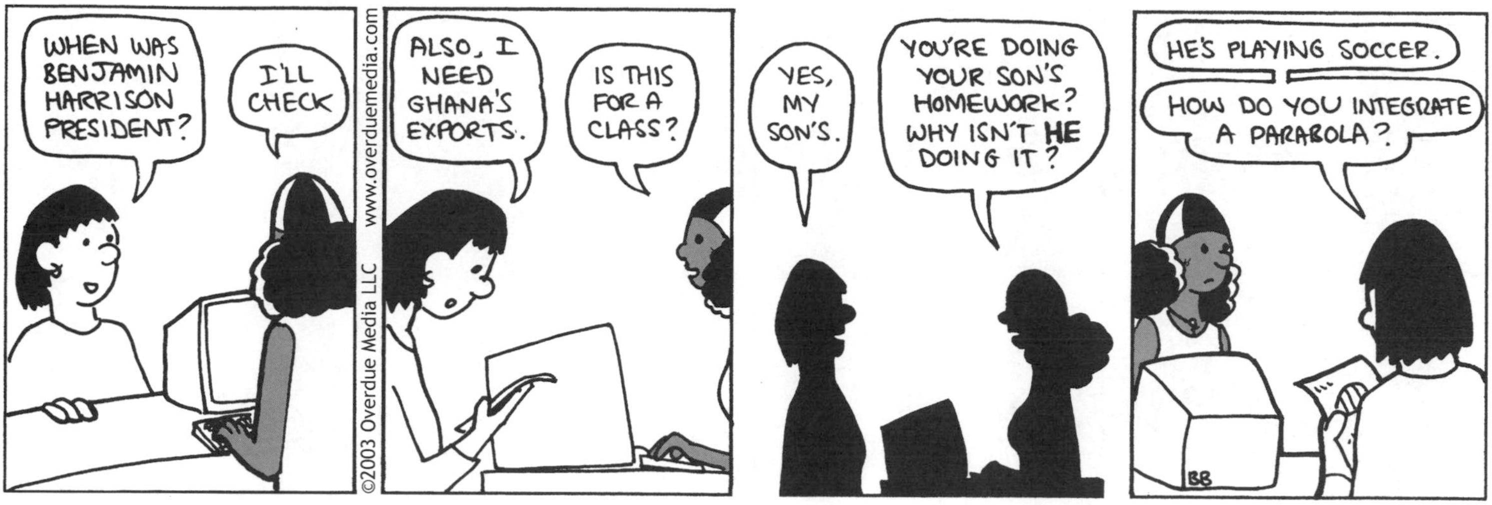
WHEN WAS BENJAMIN HARRISON PRESIDENT?
I'LL CHECK
©2003 Overdue Media LLC www.overduemedia.com
ALSO, I NEED GHANA'S EXPORTS.
IS THIS FOR A CLASS?
YES, MY SON'S.
YOU'RE DOING YOUR SON'S HOMEWORK? WHY ISN'T HE DOING IT?
HE'S PLAYING SOCCER.
HOW DO YOU INTEGRATE A PARABOLA?
BB

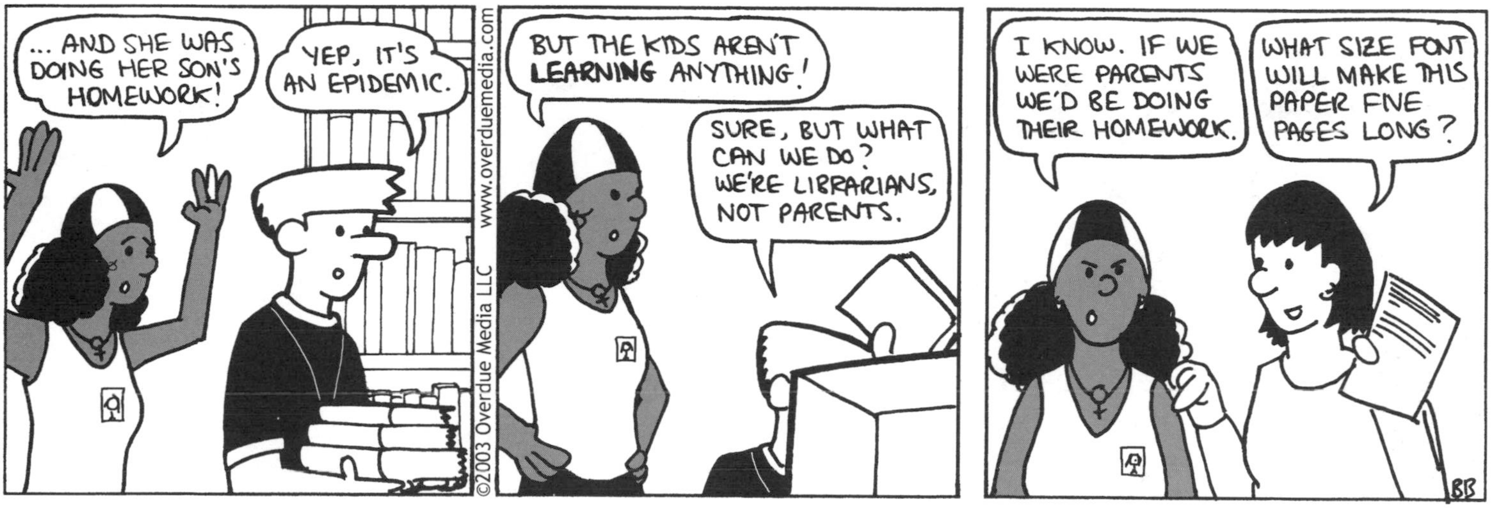
... AND SHE WAS DOING HER SON'S HOMEWORK!
YEP, IT'S AN EPIDEMIC.
©2003 Overdue Media LLC www.overduemedia.com
BUT THE KIDS AREN'T LEARNING ANYTHING!
SURE, BUT WHAT CAN WE DO? WE'RE LIBRARIANS, NOT PARENTS.
I KNOW. IF WE WERE PARENTS WE'D BE DOING THEIR HOMEWORK.
WHAT SIZE FONT WILL MAKE THIS PAPER FIVE PAGES LONG?
BB

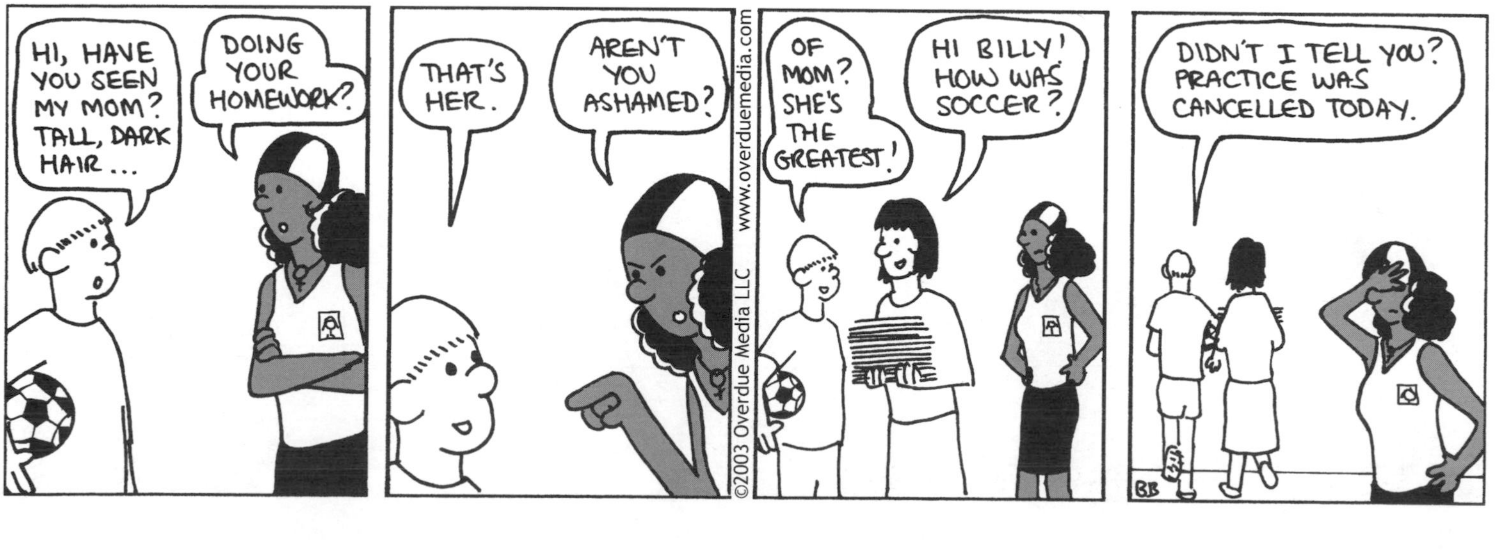
HI, HAVE YOU SEEN MY MOM? TALL, DARK HAIR...
DOING YOUR HOMEWORK?
THAT'S HER.
AREN'T YOU ASHAMED?
©2003 Overdue Media LLC www.overduemedia.com
OF MOM? SHE'S THE GREATEST!
HI BILLY! HOW WAS SOCCER?
DIDN'T I TELL YOU? PRACTICE WAS CANCELLED TODAY.
BB

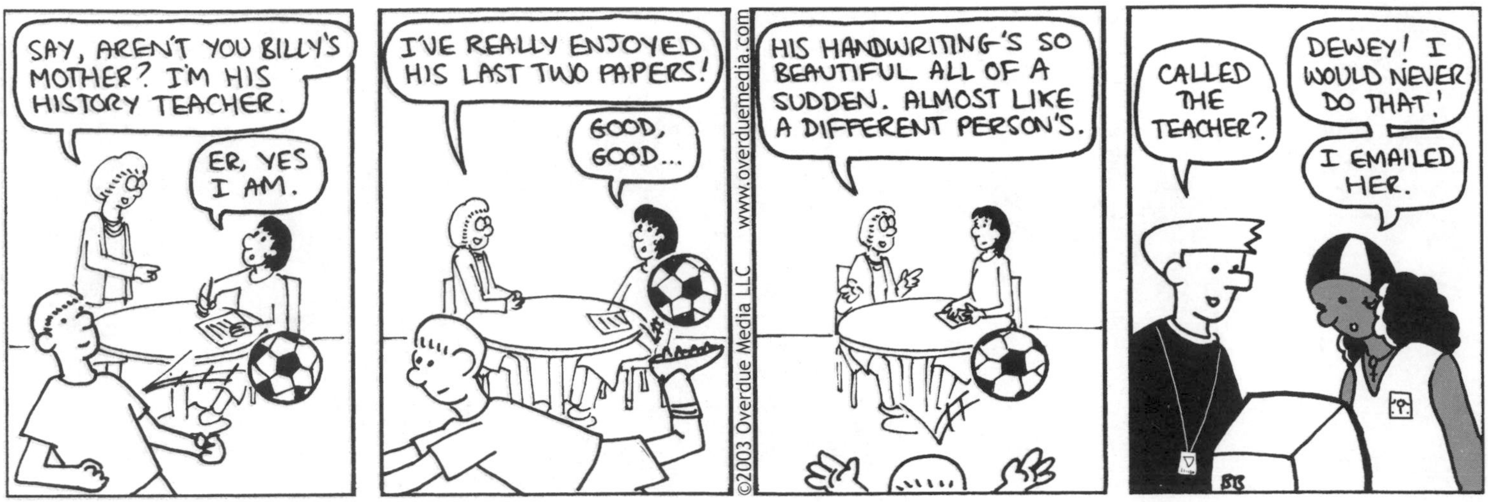
SAY, AREN'T YOU BILLY'S MOTHER? I'M HIS HISTORY TEACHER.
ER, YES I AM.
I'VE REALLY ENJOYED HIS LAST TWO PAPERS!
GOOD, GOOD...
HIS HANDWRITING'S SO BEAUTIFUL ALL OF A SUDDEN. ALMOST LIKE A DIFFERENT PERSON'S.
CALLED THE TEACHER?
DEWEY! I WOULD NEVER DO THAT!
I EMAILED HER.
©2003 Overdue Media LLC
www.overduemedia.com

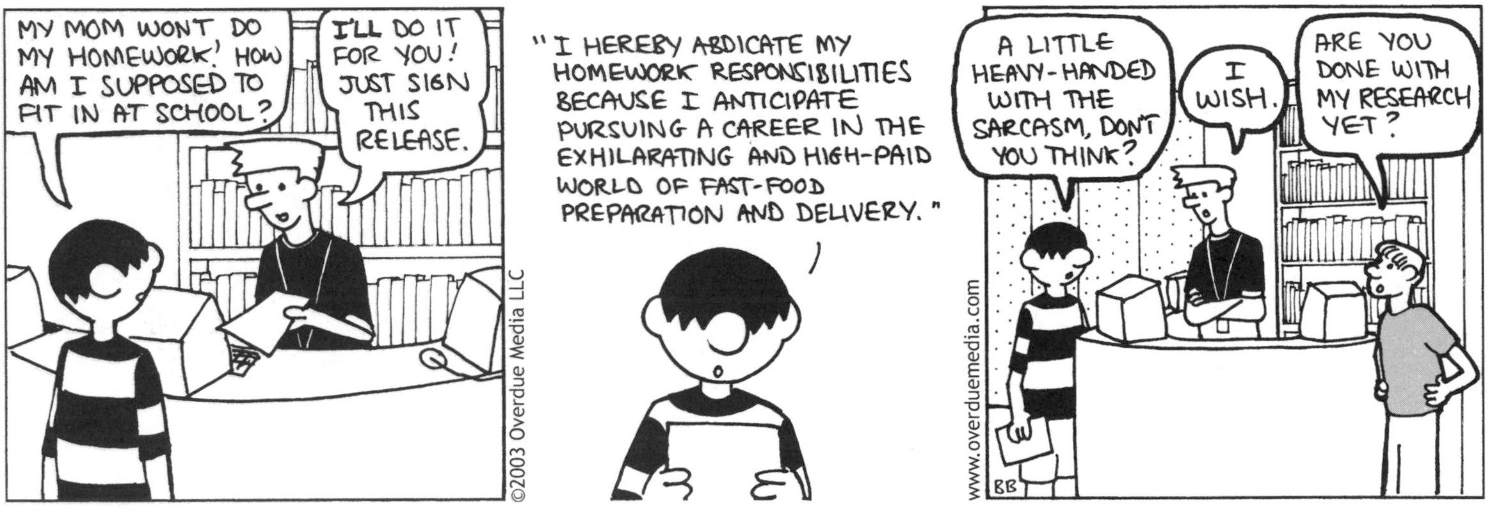
MY MOM WON'T DO MY HOMEWORK! HOW AM I SUPPOSED TO FIT IN AT SCHOOL?
I'LL DO IT FOR YOU! JUST SIGN THIS RELEASE.
"I HEREBY ABDICATE MY HOMEWORK RESPONSIBILITIES BECAUSE I ANTICIPATE PURSUING A CAREER IN THE EXHILARATING AND HIGH-PAID WORLD OF FAST-FOOD PREPARATION AND DELIVERY."
A LITTLE HEAVY-HANDED WITH THE SARCASM, DON'T YOU THINK?
I WISH.
ARE YOU DONE WITH MY RESEARCH YET?
©2003 Overdue Media LLC
www.overduemedia.com

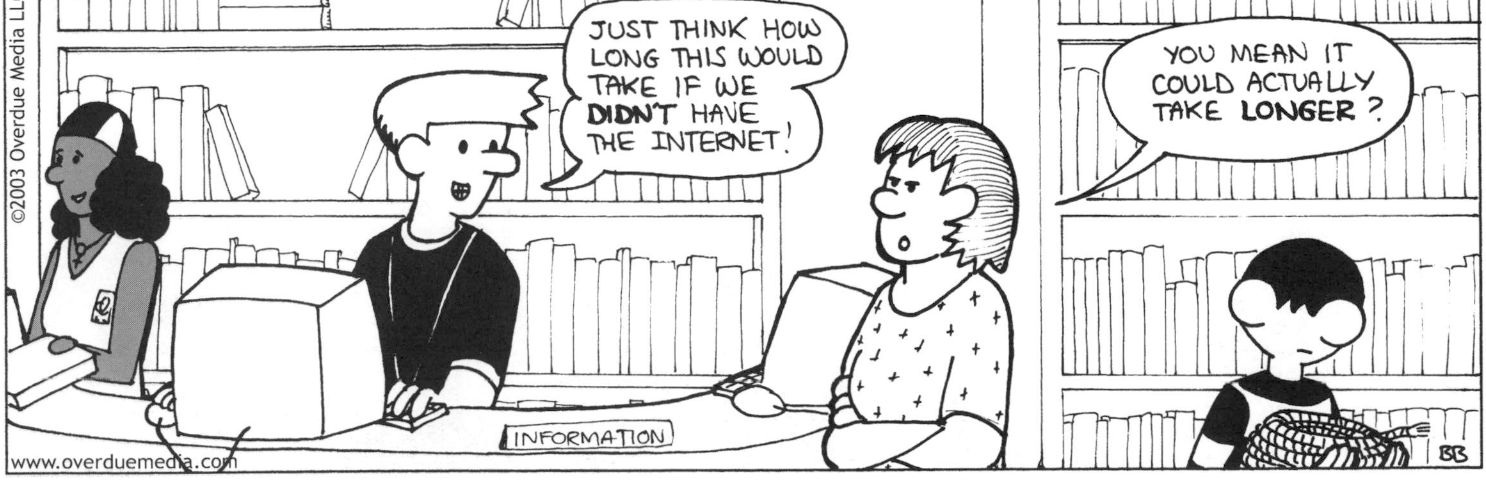
JUST THINK HOW LONG THIS WOULD TAKE IF WE **DIDN'T** HAVE THE INTERNET!
YOU MEAN IT COULD ACTUALLY TAKE **LONGER**?
INFORMATION
©2003 Overdue Media LLC
www.overduemedia.com

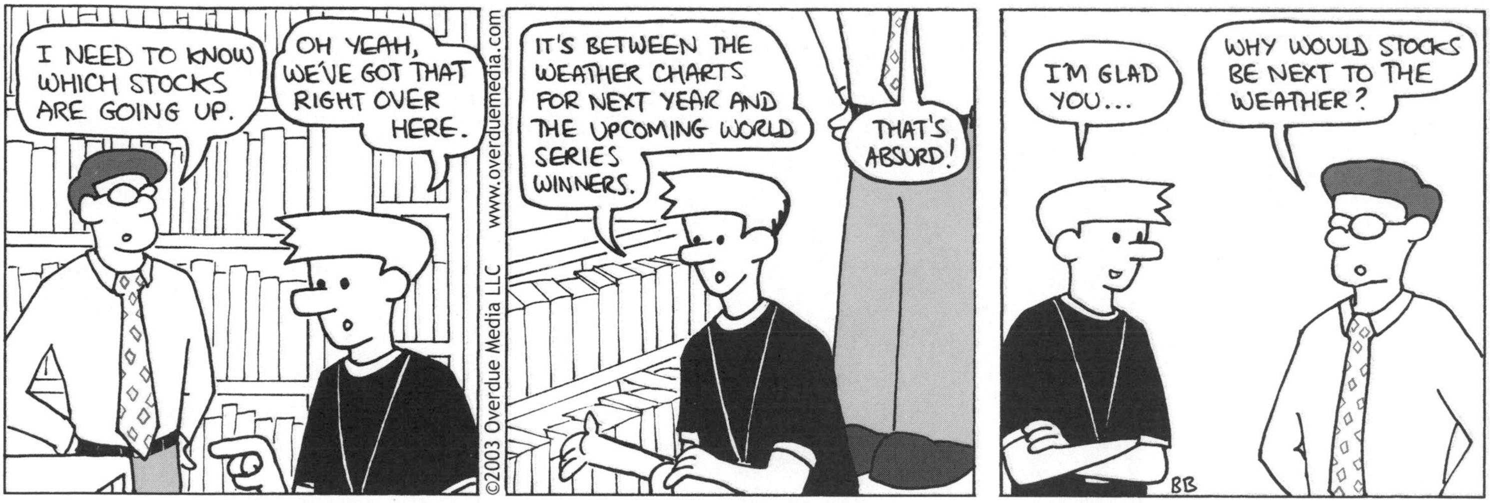

I NEED TO KNOW WHICH STOCKS ARE GOING UP.
OH YEAH, WE'VE GOT THAT RIGHT OVER HERE.
©2003 Overdue Media LLC www.overduemedia.com
IT'S BETWEEN THE WEATHER CHARTS FOR NEXT YEAR AND THE UPCOMING WORLD SERIES WINNERS.
THAT'S ABSURD!
I'M GLAD YOU...
WHY WOULD STOCKS BE NEXT TO THE WEATHER?
BB


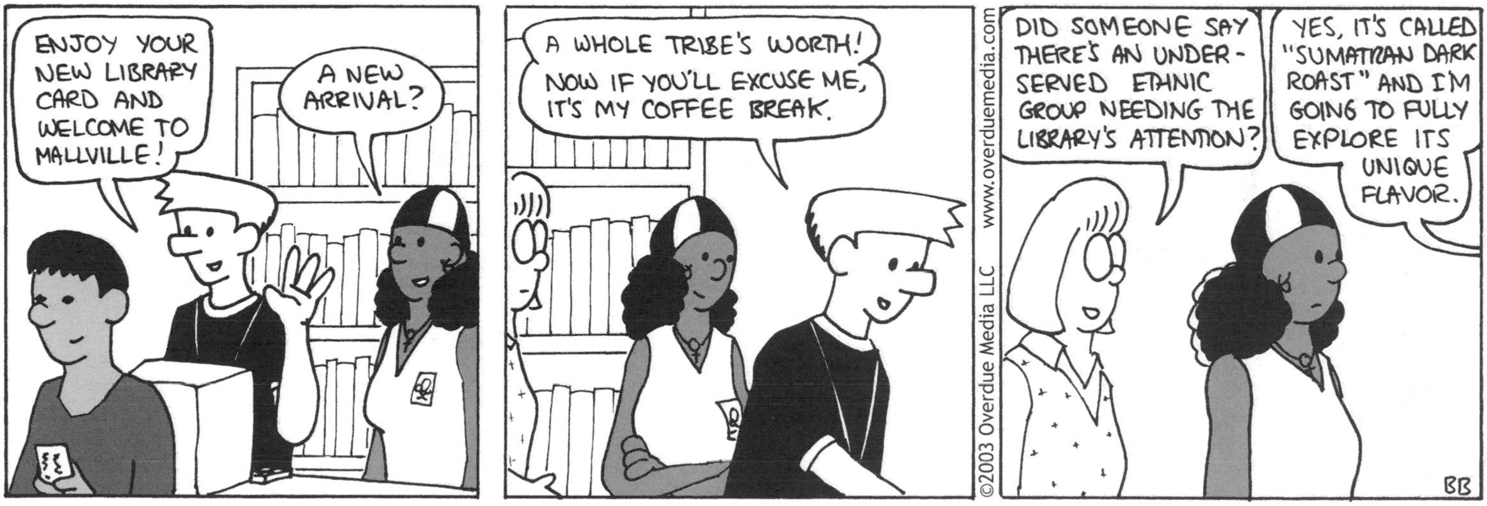

ENJOY YOUR NEW LIBRARY CARD AND WELCOME TO MALLVILLE!
A NEW ARRIVAL?
A WHOLE TRIBE'S WORTH!
NOW IF YOU'LL EXCUSE ME, IT'S MY COFFEE BREAK.
©2003 Overdue Media LLC www.overduemedia.com
DID SOMEONE SAY THERE'S AN UNDER-SERVED ETHNIC GROUP NEEDING THE LIBRARY'S ATTENTION?
YES, IT'S CALLED "SUMATRAN DARK ROAST" AND I'M GOING TO FULLY EXPLORE ITS UNIQUE FLAVOR.
BB


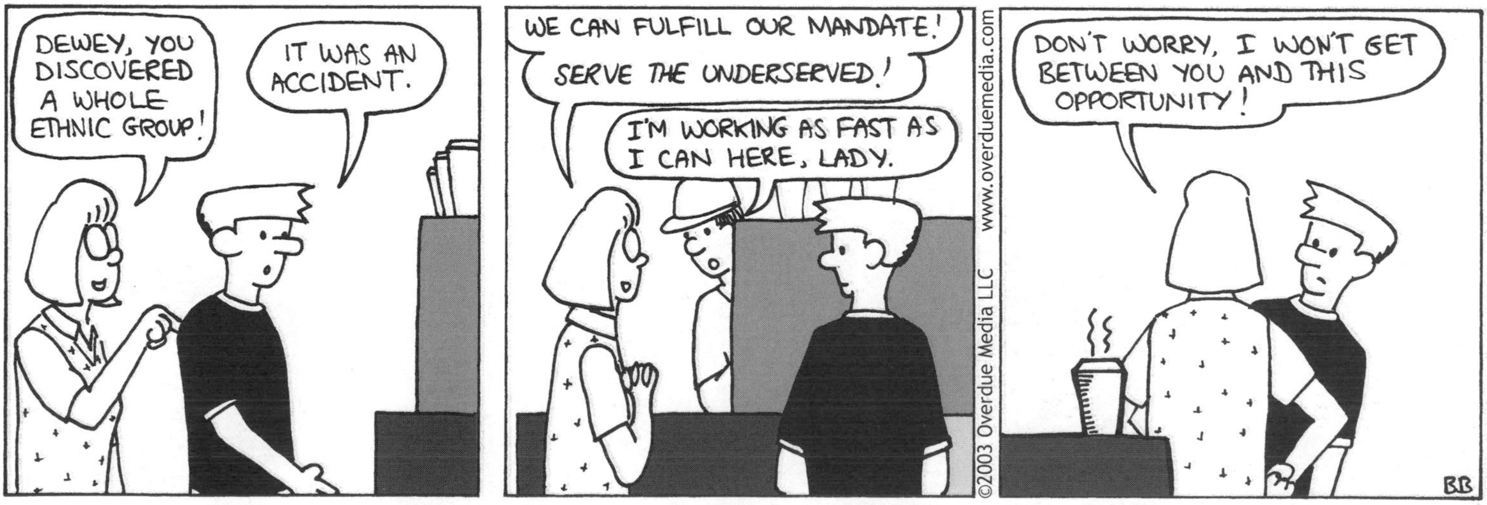

DEWEY, YOU DISCOVERED A WHOLE ETHNIC GROUP!
IT WAS AN ACCIDENT.
WE CAN FULFILL OUR MANDATE!
SERVE THE UNDERSERVED!
I'M WORKING AS FAST AS I CAN HERE, LADY.
©2003 Overdue Media LLC www.overduemedia.com
DON'T WORRY, I WON'T GET BETWEEN YOU AND THIS OPPORTUNITY!
BB

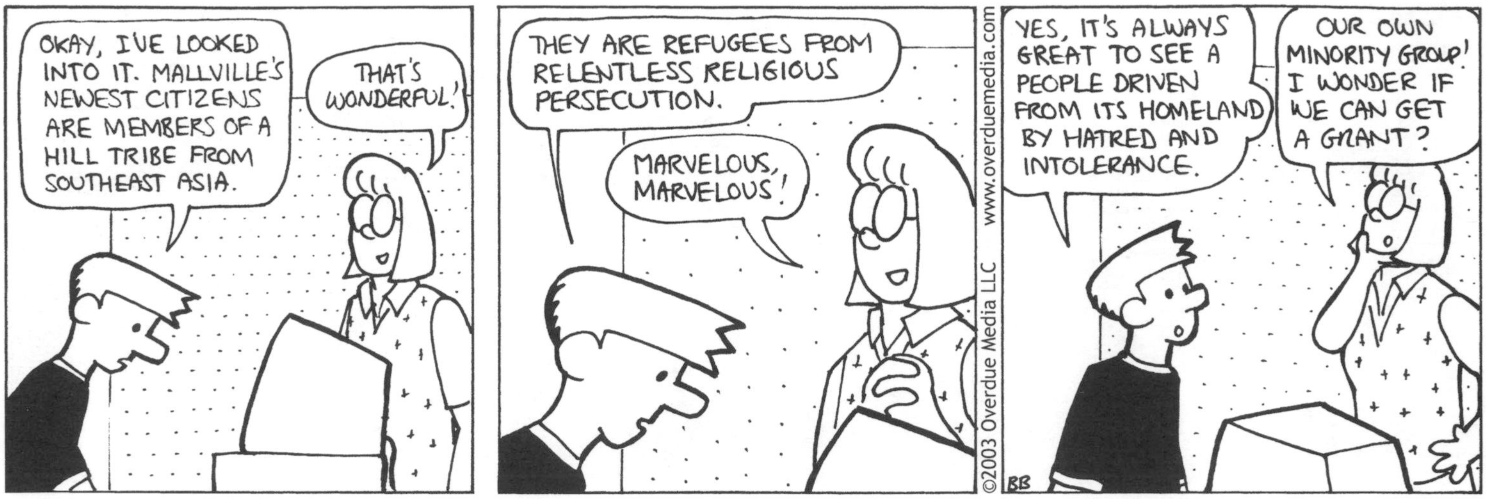
OKAY, I'VE LOOKED INTO IT. MALLVILLE'S NEWEST CITIZENS ARE MEMBERS OF A HILL TRIBE FROM SOUTHEAST ASIA.
THAT'S WONDERFUL!
THEY ARE REFUGEES FROM RELENTLESS RELIGIOUS PERSECUTION.
MARVELOUS, MARVELOUS!
©2003 Overdue Media LLC www.overduemedia.com
YES, IT'S ALWAYS GREAT TO SEE A PEOPLE DRIVEN FROM ITS HOMELAND BY HATRED AND INTOLERANCE.
OUR OWN MINORITY GROUP! I WONDER IF WE CAN GET A GRANT?
BB

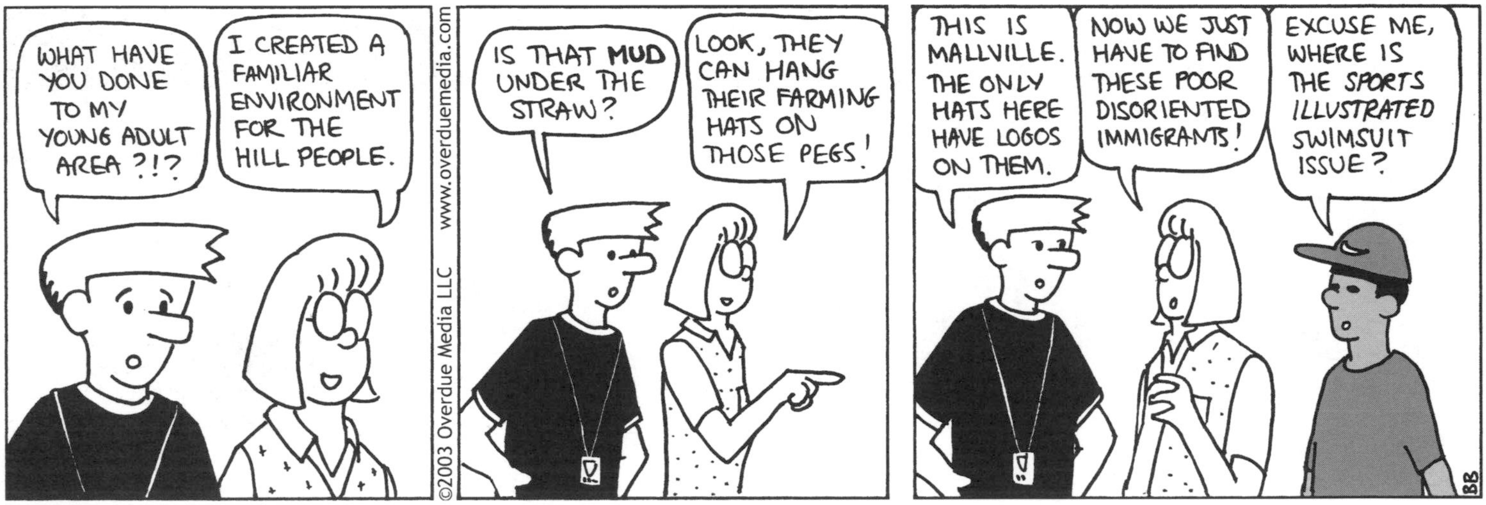
WHAT HAVE YOU DONE TO MY YOUNG ADULT AREA?!?
I CREATED A FAMILIAR ENVIRONMENT FOR THE HILL PEOPLE.
©2003 Overdue Media LLC www.overduemedia.com
IS THAT **MUD** UNDER THE STRAW?
LOOK, THEY CAN HANG THEIR FARMING HATS ON THOSE PEGS!
THIS IS MALLVILLE. THE ONLY HATS HERE HAVE LOGOS ON THEM.
NOW WE JUST HAVE TO FIND THESE POOR DISORIENTED IMMIGRANTS!
EXCUSE ME, WHERE IS THE *SPORTS ILLUSTRATED* SWIMSUIT ISSUE?
BB

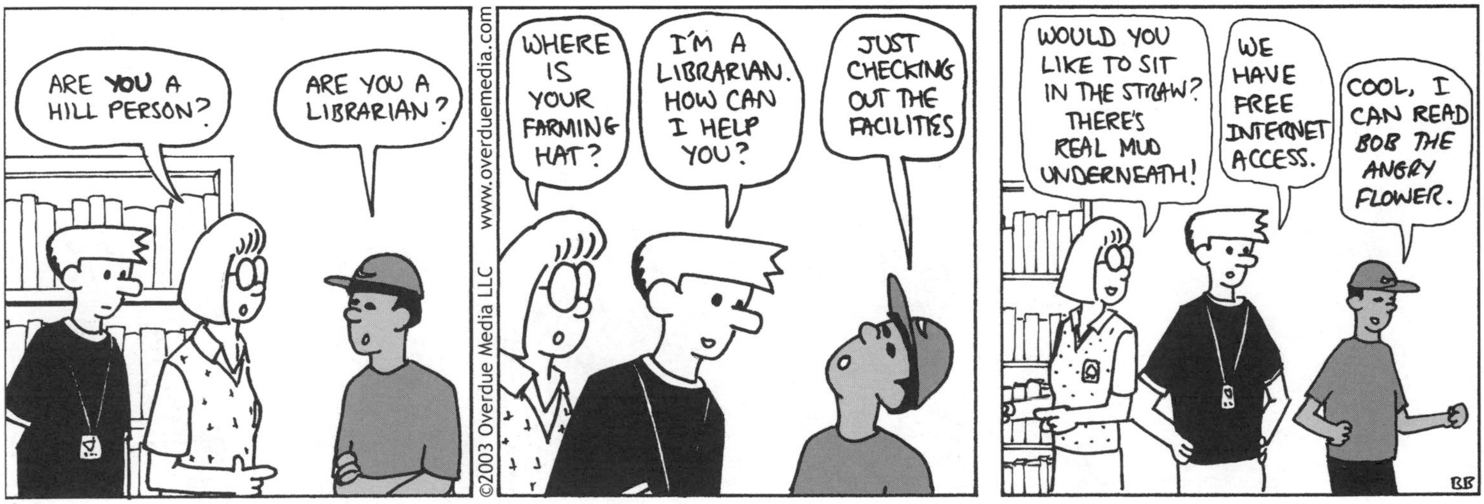
ARE **YOU** A HILL PERSON?
ARE YOU A LIBRARIAN?
©2003 Overdue Media LLC www.overduemedia.com
WHERE IS YOUR FARMING HAT?
I'M A LIBRARIAN. HOW CAN I HELP YOU?
JUST CHECKING OUT THE FACILITIES
WOULD YOU LIKE TO SIT IN THE STRAW? THERE'S REAL MUD UNDERNEATH!
WE HAVE FREE INTERNET ACCESS.
COOL, I CAN READ *BOB THE ANGRY FLOWER*.
BB

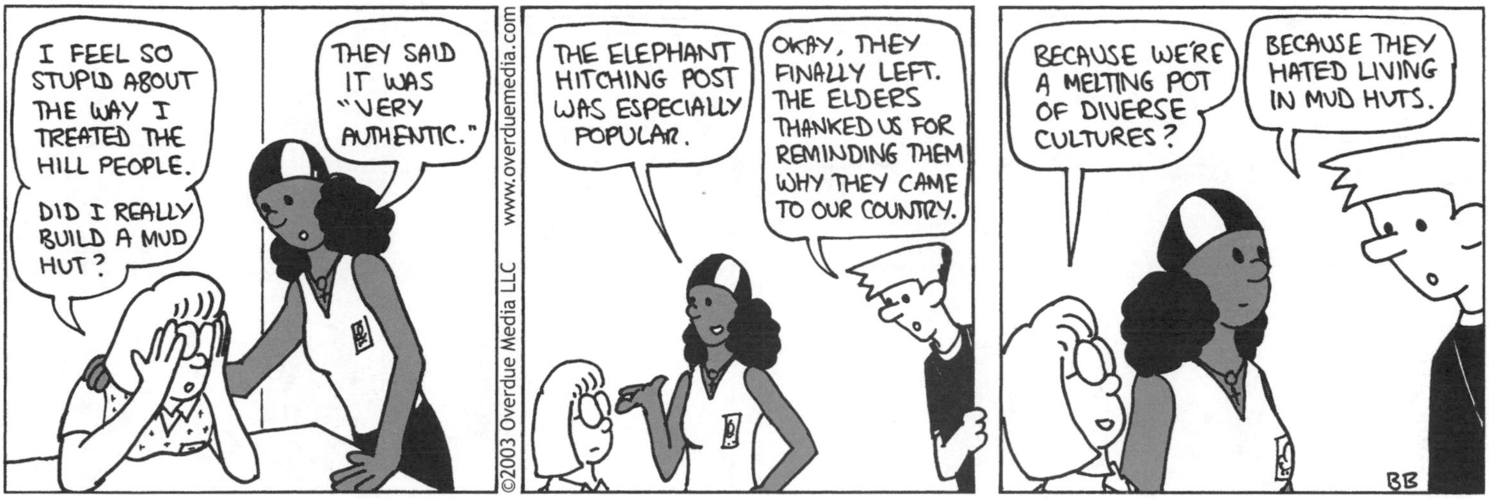
I FEEL SO STUPID ABOUT THE WAY I TREATED THE HILL PEOPLE.
DID I REALLY BUILD A MUD HUT?
THEY SAID IT WAS "VERY AUTHENTIC."
©2003 Overdue Media LLC www.overduemedia.com
THE ELEPHANT HITCHING POST WAS ESPECIALLY POPULAR.
OKAY, THEY FINALLY LEFT. THE ELDERS THANKED US FOR REMINDING THEM WHY THEY CAME TO OUR COUNTRY.
BECAUSE WE'RE A MELTING POT OF DIVERSE CULTURES?
BECAUSE THEY HATED LIVING IN MUD HUTS.
BB

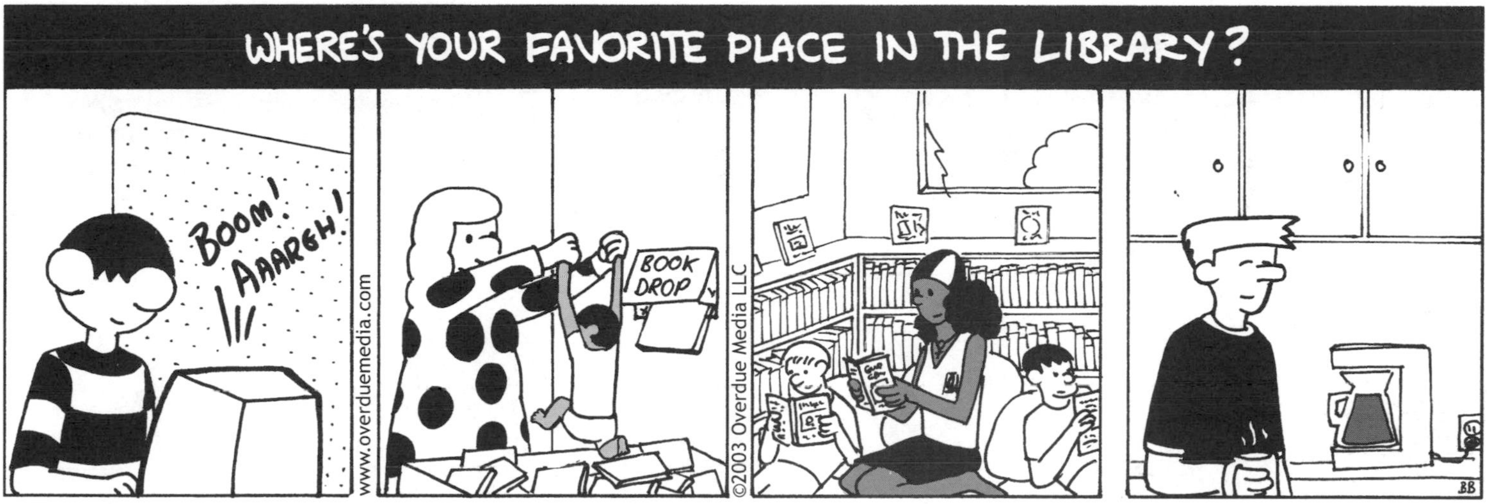
WHERE'S YOUR FAVORITE PLACE IN THE LIBRARY?
BOOM! AAARGH!
www.overduemedia.com
BOOK DROP
©2003 Overdue Media LLC
BB

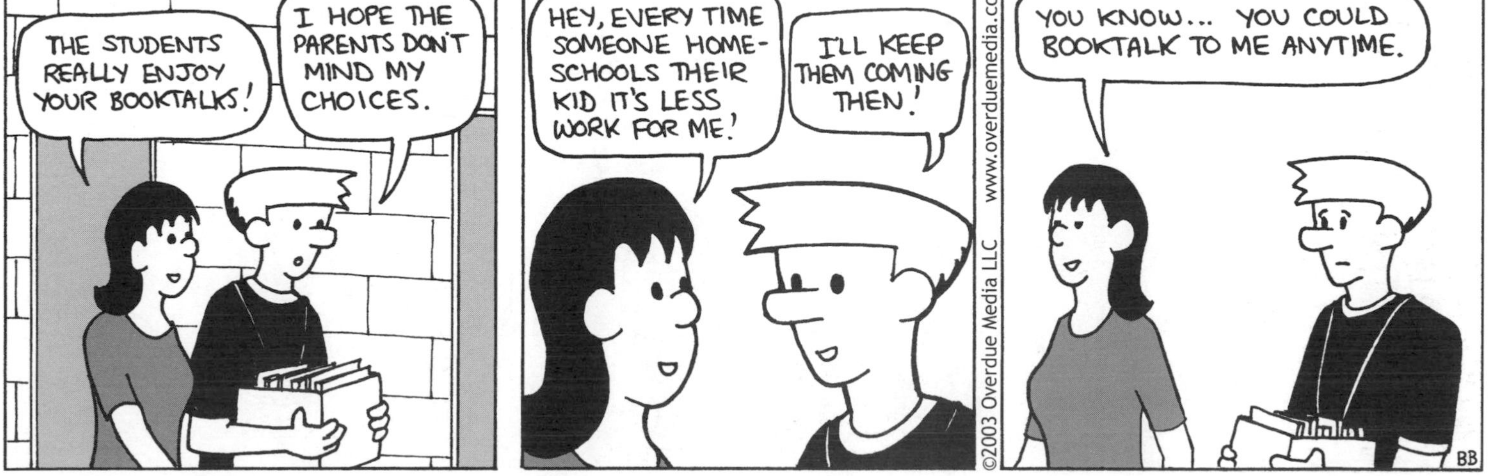
THE STUDENTS REALLY ENJOY YOUR BOOKTALKS!
I HOPE THE PARENTS DON'T MIND MY CHOICES.
HEY, EVERY TIME SOMEONE HOME-SCHOOLS THEIR KID IT'S LESS WORK FOR ME!
I'LL KEEP THEM COMING THEN!
©2003 Overdue Media LLC www.overduemedia.com
YOU KNOW... YOU COULD BOOKTALK TO ME ANYTIME.
BB

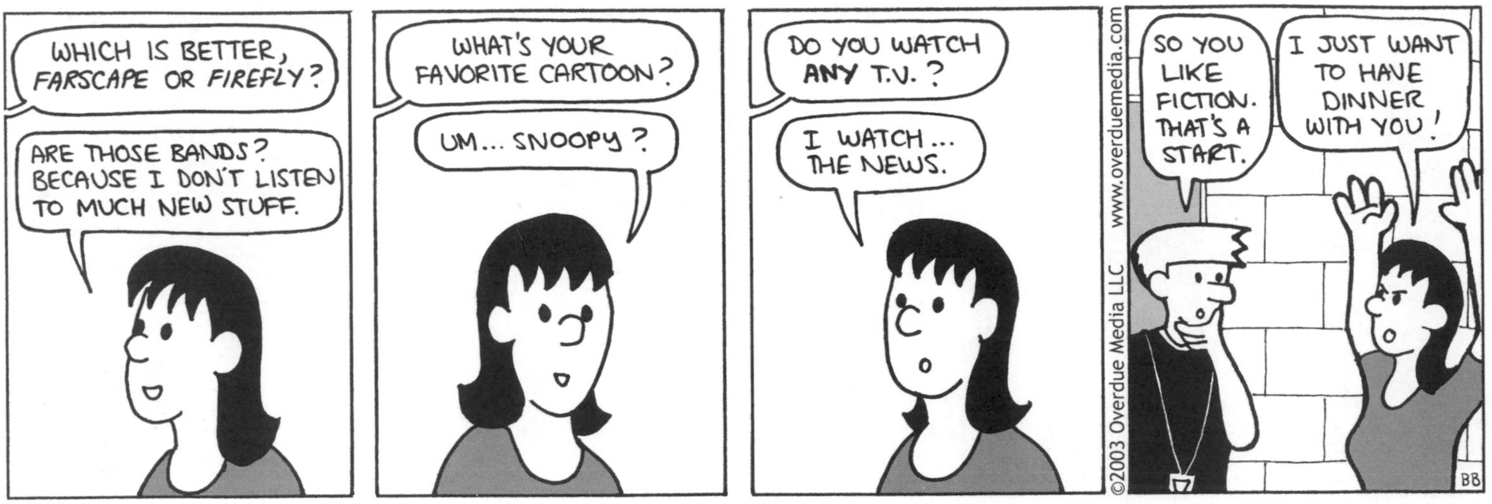

WHICH IS BETTER, *FARSCAPE* OR *FIREFLY*?
ARE THOSE BANDS? BECAUSE I DON'T LISTEN TO MUCH NEW STUFF.
WHAT'S YOUR FAVORITE CARTOON?
UM... SNOOPY?
DO YOU WATCH **ANY** T.V.?
I WATCH... THE NEWS.
©2003 Overdue Media LLC www.overduemedia.com
SO YOU LIKE FICTION. THAT'S A START.
I JUST WANT TO HAVE DINNER WITH YOU!
BB


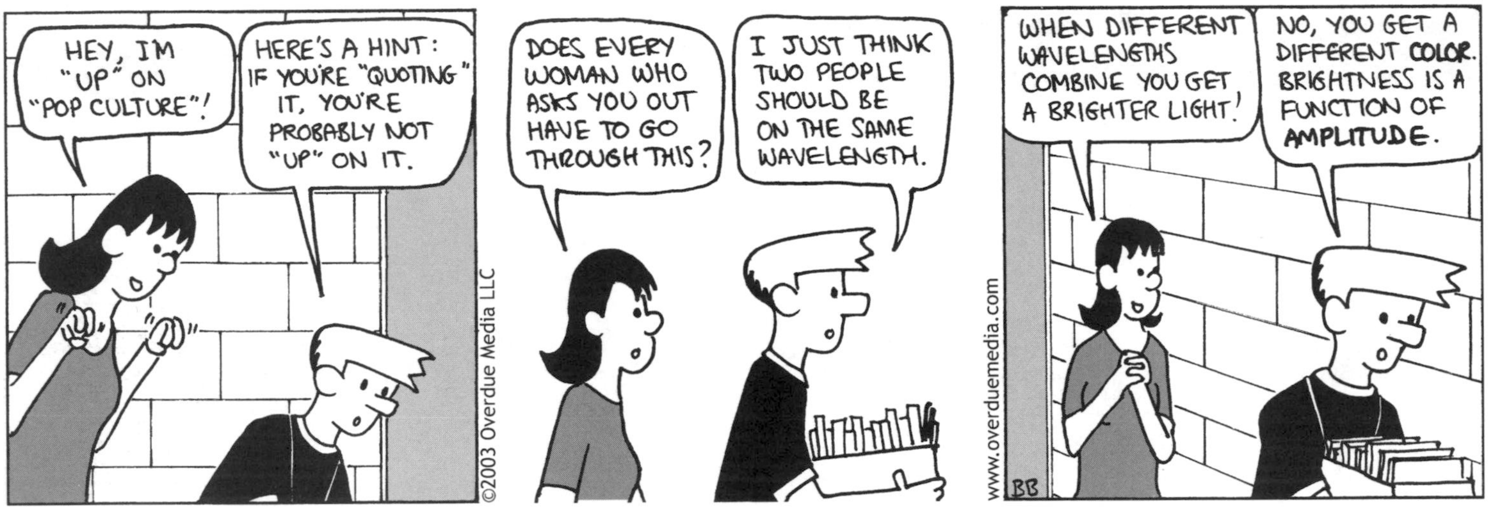

HEY, I'M "UP" ON "POP CULTURE"!
HERE'S A HINT: IF YOU'RE "QUOTING" IT, YOU'RE PROBABLY NOT "UP" ON IT.
©2003 Overdue Media LLC
DOES EVERY WOMAN WHO ASKS YOU OUT HAVE TO GO THROUGH THIS?
I JUST THINK TWO PEOPLE SHOULD BE ON THE SAME WAVELENGTH.
www.overduemedia.com
WHEN DIFFERENT WAVELENGTHS COMBINE YOU GET A BRIGHTER LIGHT!
NO, YOU GET A DIFFERENT **COLOR**. BRIGHTNESS IS A FUNCTION OF **AMPLITUDE**.
BB


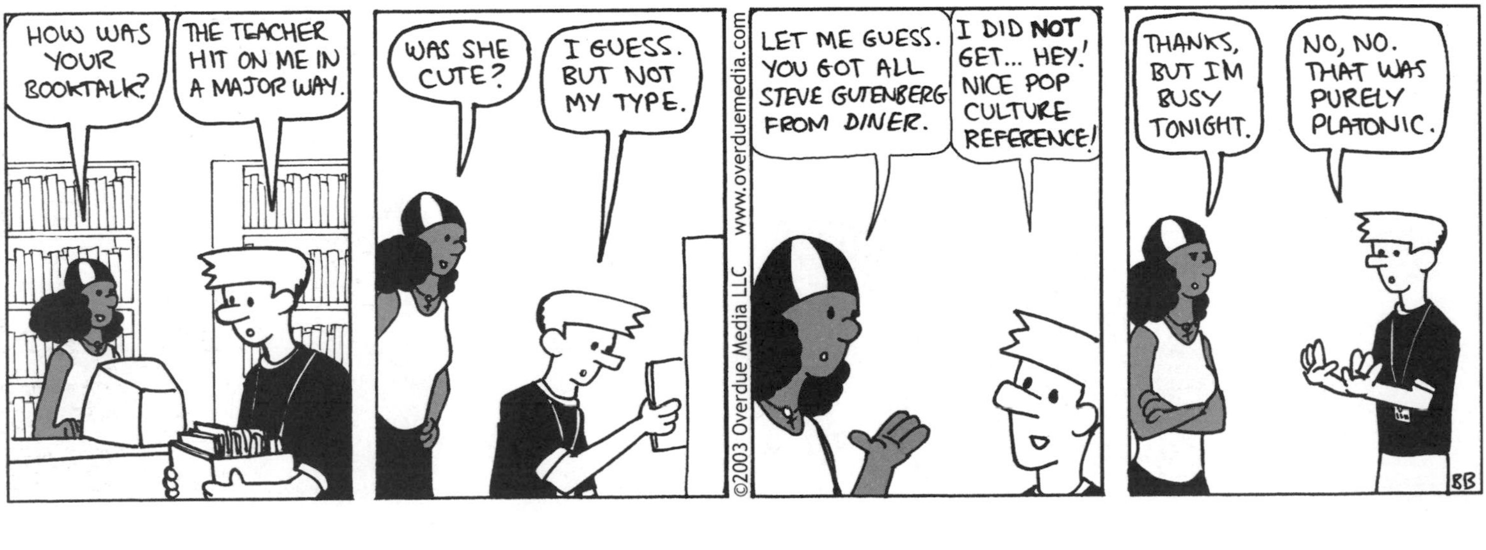

HOW WAS YOUR BOOKTALK?
THE TEACHER HIT ON ME IN A MAJOR WAY.
WAS SHE CUTE?
I GUESS. BUT NOT MY TYPE.
©2003 Overdue Media LLC www.overduemedia.com
LET ME GUESS. YOU GOT ALL STEVE GUTENBERG FROM *DINER*.
I DID **NOT** GET... HEY! NICE POP CULTURE REFERENCE!
THANKS, BUT I'M BUSY TONIGHT.
NO, NO. THAT WAS PURELY PLATONIC.
BB

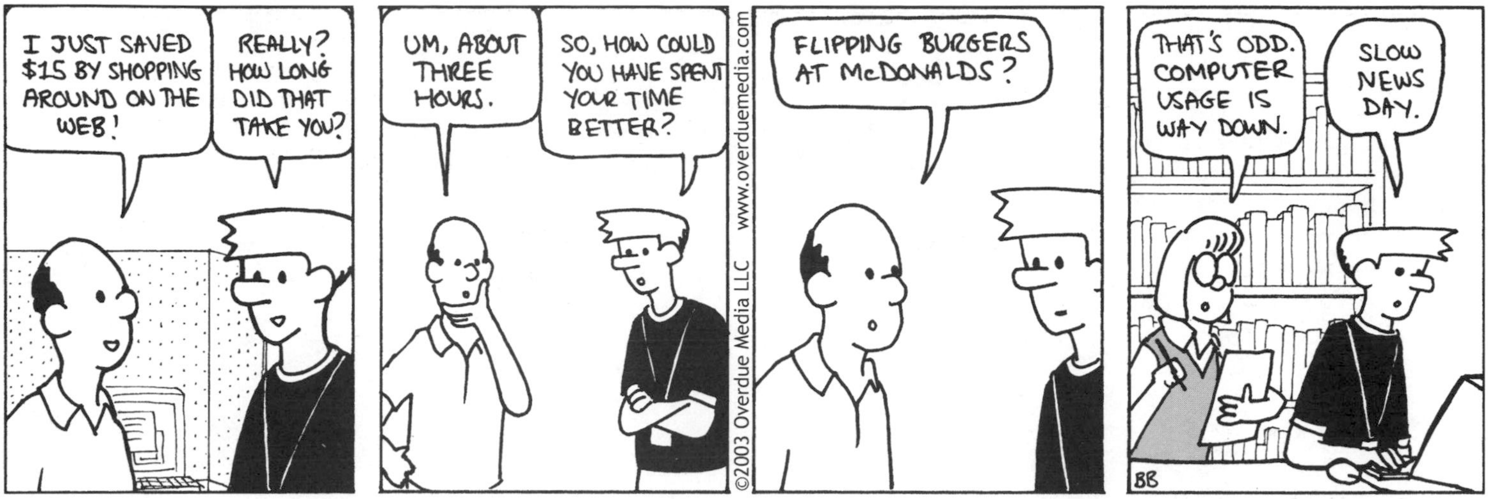
I JUST SAVED $15 BY SHOPPING AROUND ON THE WEB!
REALLY? HOW LONG DID THAT TAKE YOU?
UM, ABOUT THREE HOURS.
SO, HOW COULD YOU HAVE SPENT YOUR TIME BETTER?
FLIPPING BURGERS AT McDONALDS?
©2003 Overdue Media LLC www.overduemedia.com
THAT'S ODD. COMPUTER USAGE IS WAY DOWN.
SLOW NEWS DAY.
BB

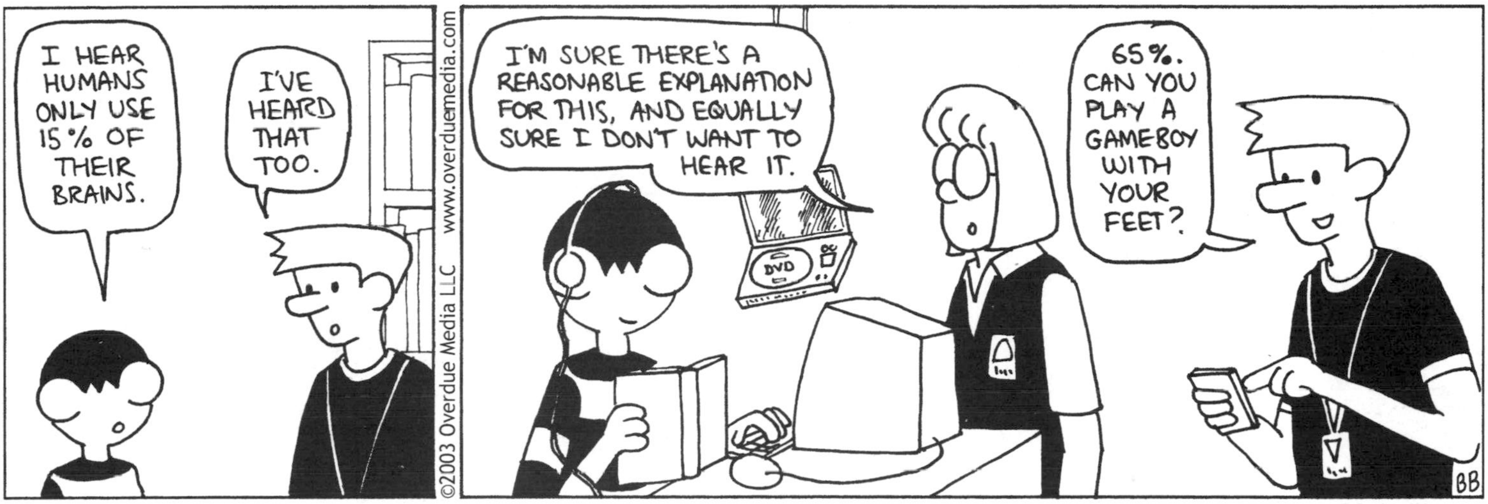
I HEAR HUMANS ONLY USE 15% OF THEIR BRAINS.
I'VE HEARD THAT TOO.
©2003 Overdue Media LLC www.overduemedia.com
I'M SURE THERE'S A REASONABLE EXPLANATION FOR THIS, AND EQUALLY SURE I DON'T WANT TO HEAR IT.
65%. CAN YOU PLAY A GAMEBOY WITH YOUR FEET?
DVD
BB

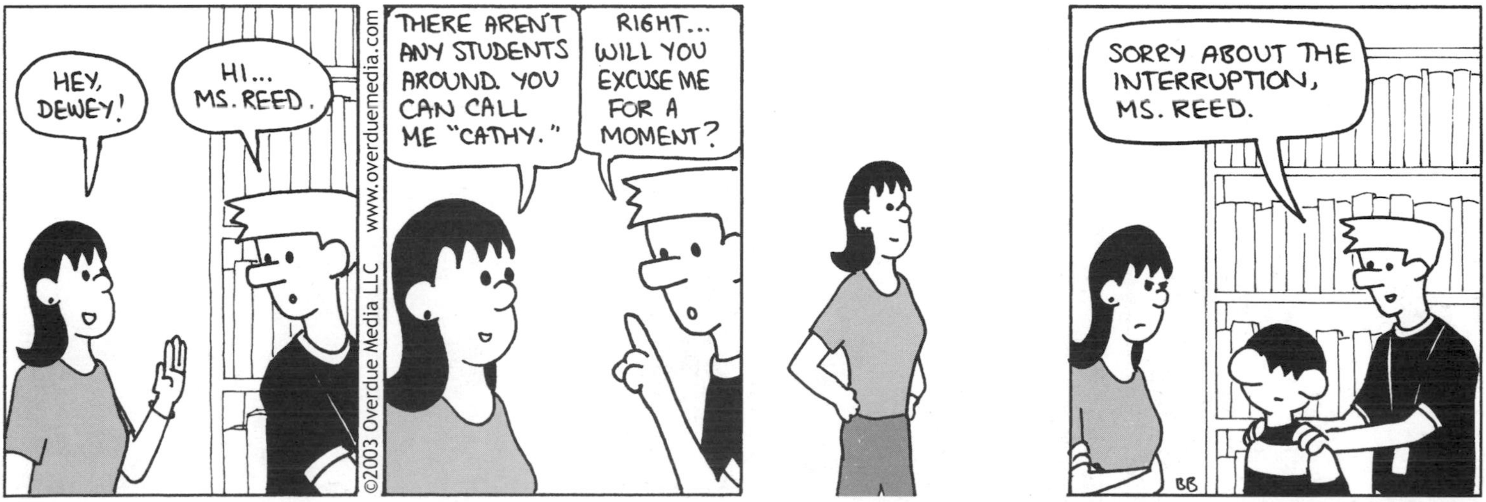
HEY, DEWEY!
HI... MS. REED.
©2003 Overdue Media LLC www.overduemedia.com
THERE AREN'T ANY STUDENTS AROUND. YOU CAN CALL ME "CATHY."
RIGHT... WILL YOU EXCUSE ME FOR A MOMENT?
SORRY ABOUT THE INTERRUPTION, MS. REED.
BB

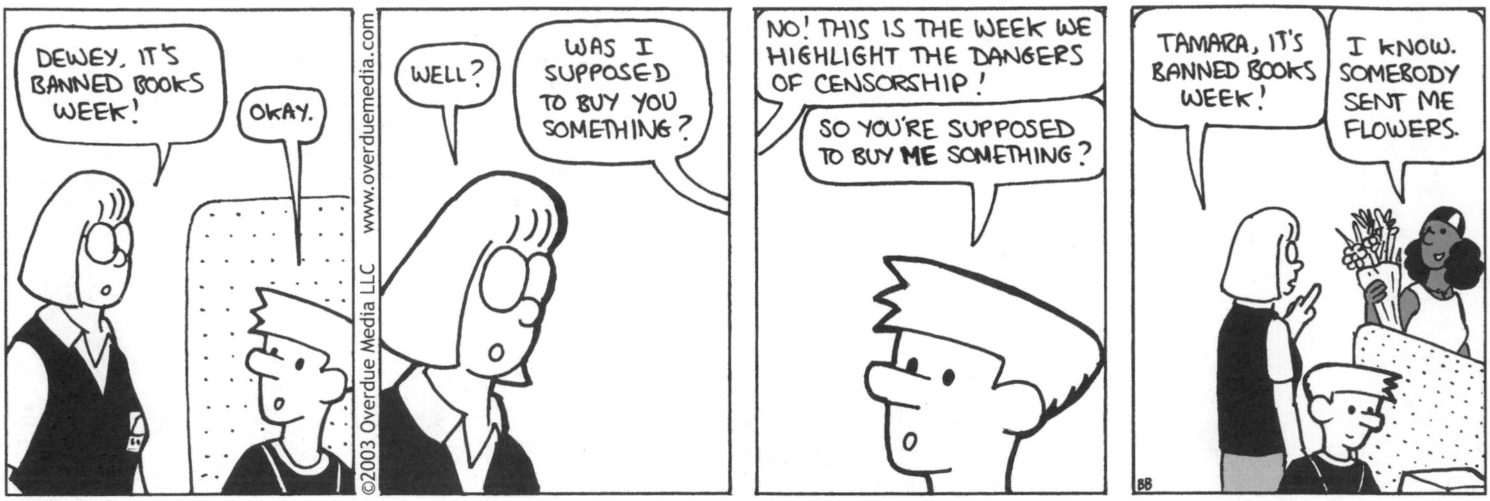
DEWEY, IT'S BANNED BOOKS WEEK!
OKAY.
©2003 Overdue Media LLC www.overduemedia.com
WELL?
WAS I SUPPOSED TO BUY YOU SOMETHING?
NO! THIS IS THE WEEK WE HIGHLIGHT THE DANGERS OF CENSORSHIP!
SO YOU'RE SUPPOSED TO BUY **ME** SOMETHING?
TAMARA, IT'S BANNED BOOKS WEEK!
I KNOW. SOMEBODY SENT ME FLOWERS.
BB

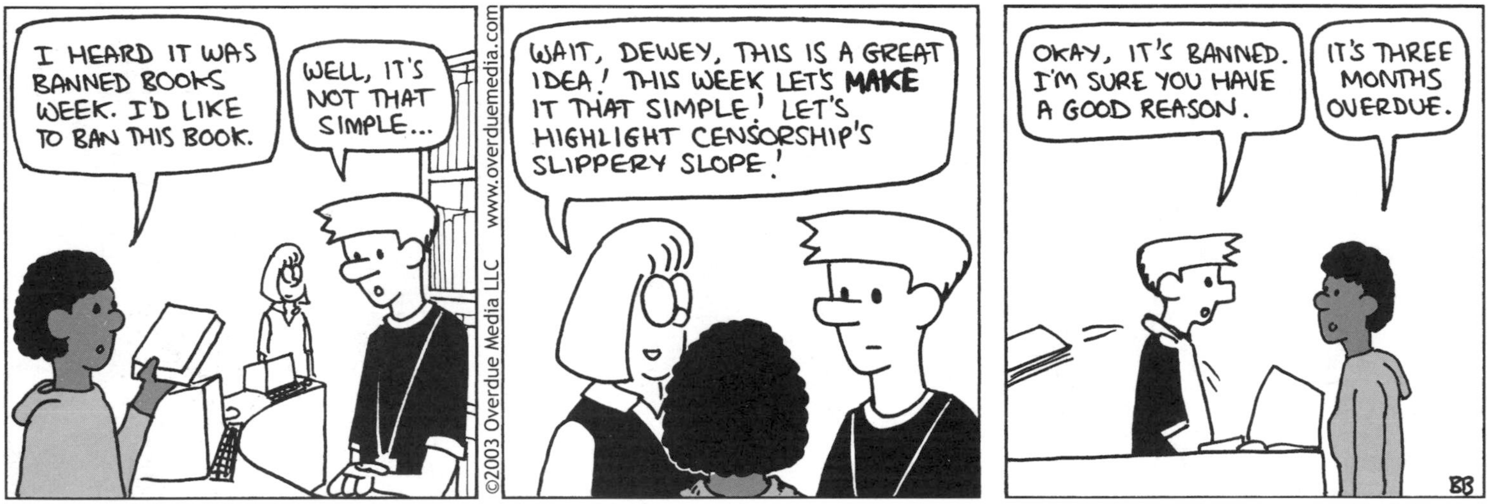
I HEARD IT WAS BANNED BOOKS WEEK. I'D LIKE TO BAN THIS BOOK.
WELL, IT'S NOT THAT SIMPLE...
©2003 Overdue Media LLC www.overduemedia.com
WAIT, DEWEY, THIS IS A GREAT IDEA! THIS WEEK LET'S **MAKE** IT THAT SIMPLE! LET'S HIGHLIGHT CENSORSHIP'S SLIPPERY SLOPE!
OKAY, IT'S BANNED. I'M SURE YOU HAVE A GOOD REASON.
IT'S THREE MONTHS OVERDUE.
BB

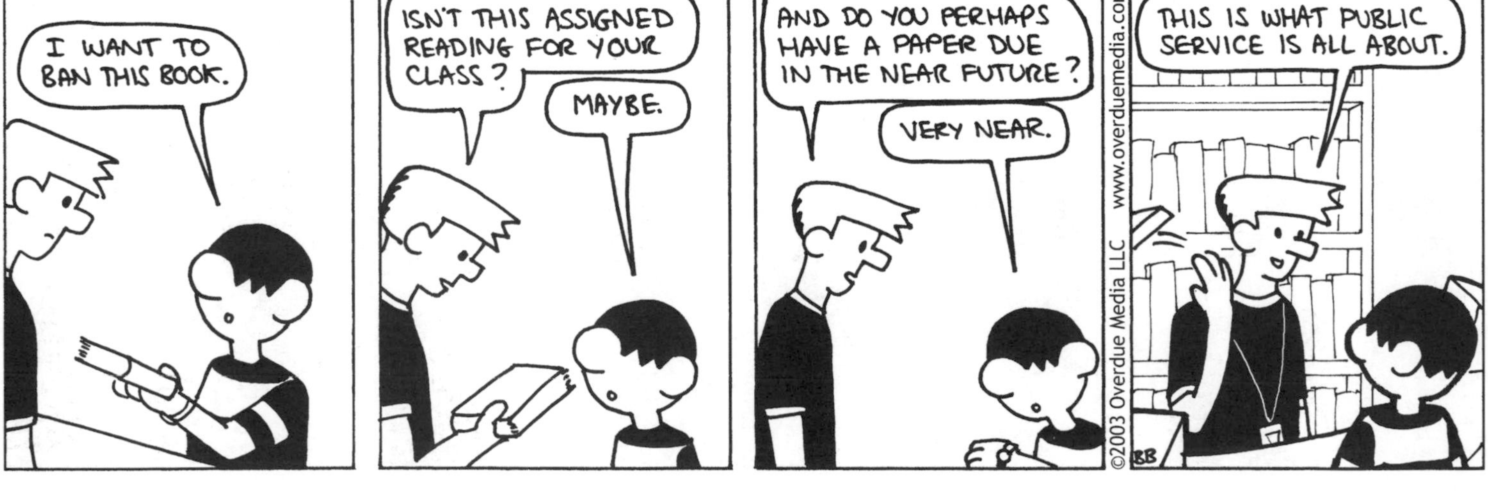
I WANT TO BAN THIS BOOK.
ISN'T THIS ASSIGNED READING FOR YOUR CLASS?
MAYBE.
AND DO YOU PERHAPS HAVE A PAPER DUE IN THE NEAR FUTURE?
VERY NEAR.
©2003 Overdue Media LLC www.overduemedia.com
THIS IS WHAT PUBLIC SERVICE IS ALL ABOUT.
BB

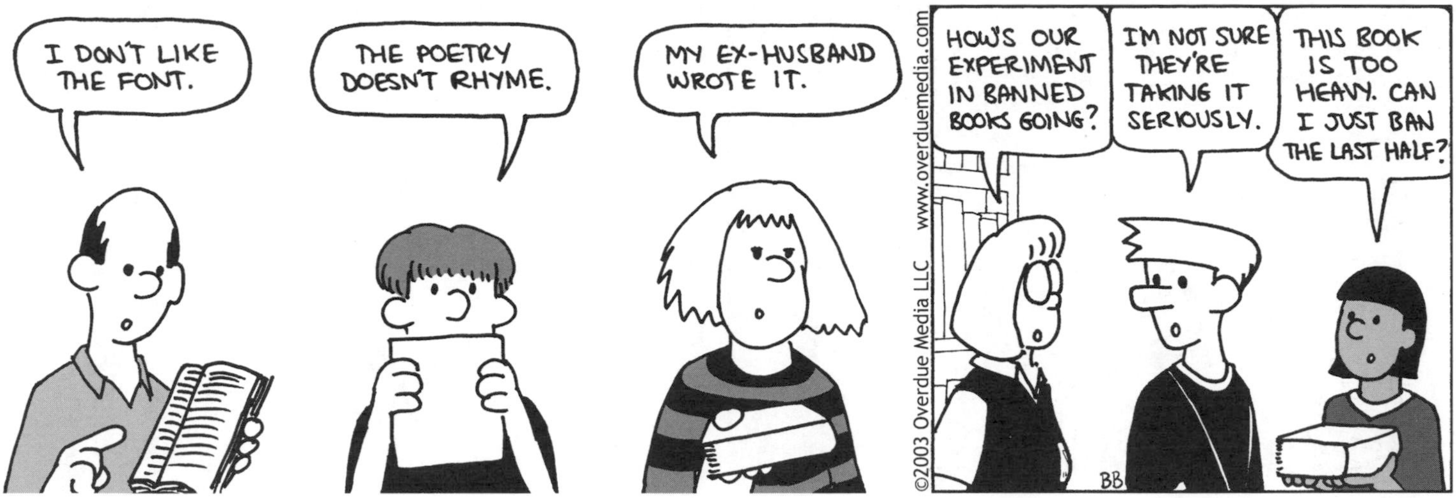
I DON'T LIKE THE FONT.
THE POETRY DOESN'T RHYME.
MY EX-HUSBAND WROTE IT.
HOW'S OUR EXPERIMENT IN BANNED BOOKS GOING?
I'M NOT SURE THEY'RE TAKING IT SERIOUSLY.
THIS BOOK IS TOO HEAVY. CAN I JUST BAN THE LAST HALF?
©2003 Overdue Media LLC www.overduemedia.com
BB

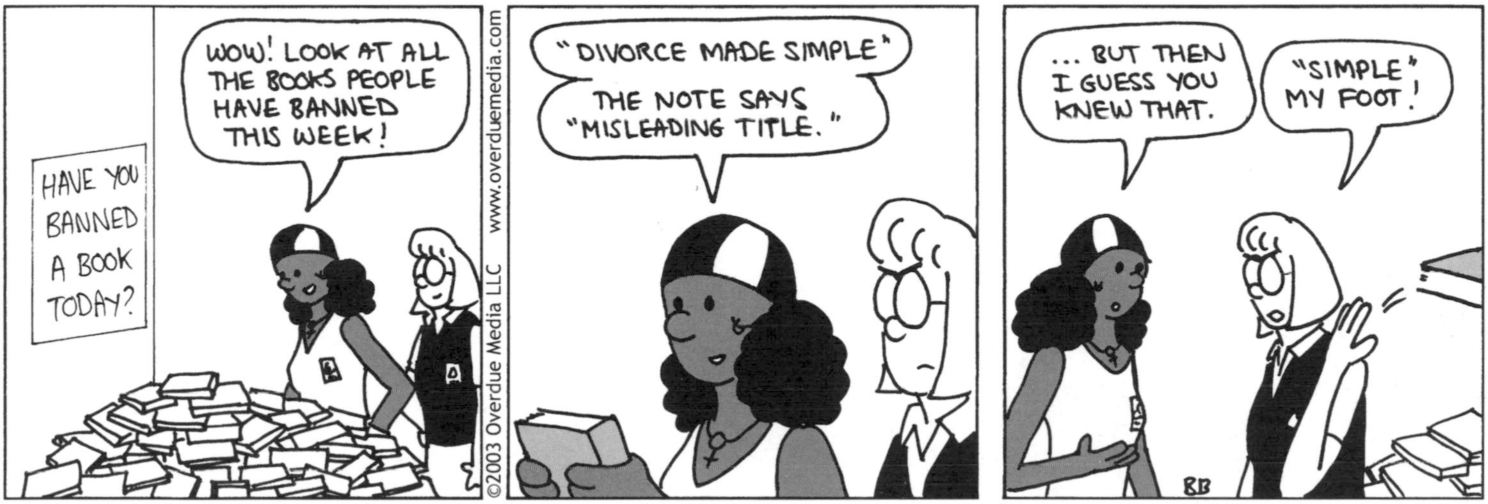
HAVE YOU BANNED A BOOK TODAY?
WOW! LOOK AT ALL THE BOOKS PEOPLE HAVE BANNED THIS WEEK!
©2003 Overdue Media LLC www.overduemedia.com
"DIVORCE MADE SIMPLE" THE NOTE SAYS "MISLEADING TITLE."
... BUT THEN I GUESS YOU KNEW THAT.
"SIMPLE" MY FOOT!
BB

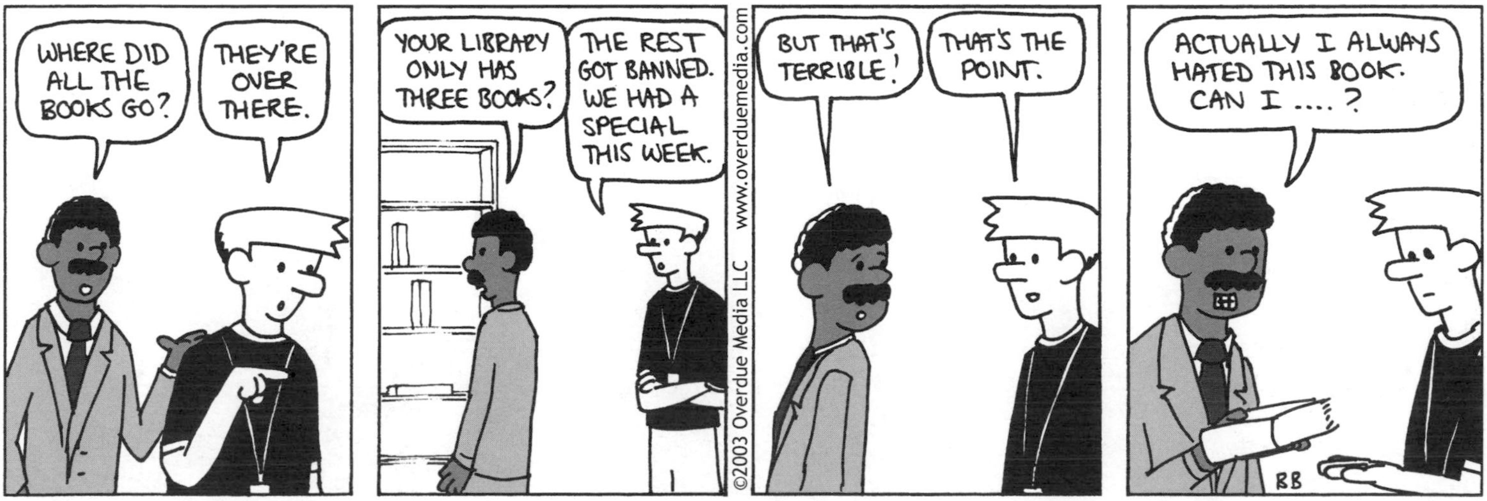
WHERE DID ALL THE BOOKS GO?
THEY'RE OVER THERE.
YOUR LIBRARY ONLY HAS THREE BOOKS?
THE REST GOT BANNED. WE HAD A SPECIAL THIS WEEK.
©2003 Overdue Media LLC www.overduemedia.com
BUT THAT'S TERRIBLE!
THAT'S THE POINT.
ACTUALLY I ALWAYS HATED THIS BOOK. CAN I .... ?
BB

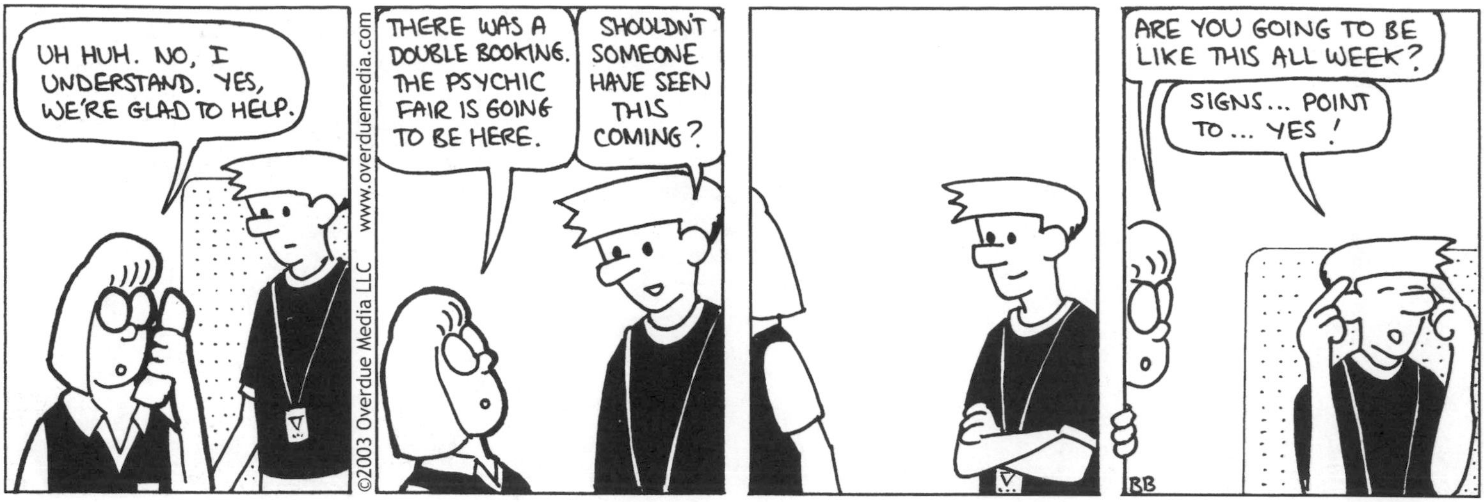
UH HUH. NO, I UNDERSTAND. YES, WE'RE GLAD TO HELP.
©2003 Overdue Media LLC www.overduemedia.com
THERE WAS A DOUBLE BOOKING. THE PSYCHIC FAIR IS GOING TO BE HERE.
SHOULDN'T SOMEONE HAVE SEEN THIS COMING?
ARE YOU GOING TO BE LIKE THIS ALL WEEK?
SIGNS... POINT TO... YES!
BB

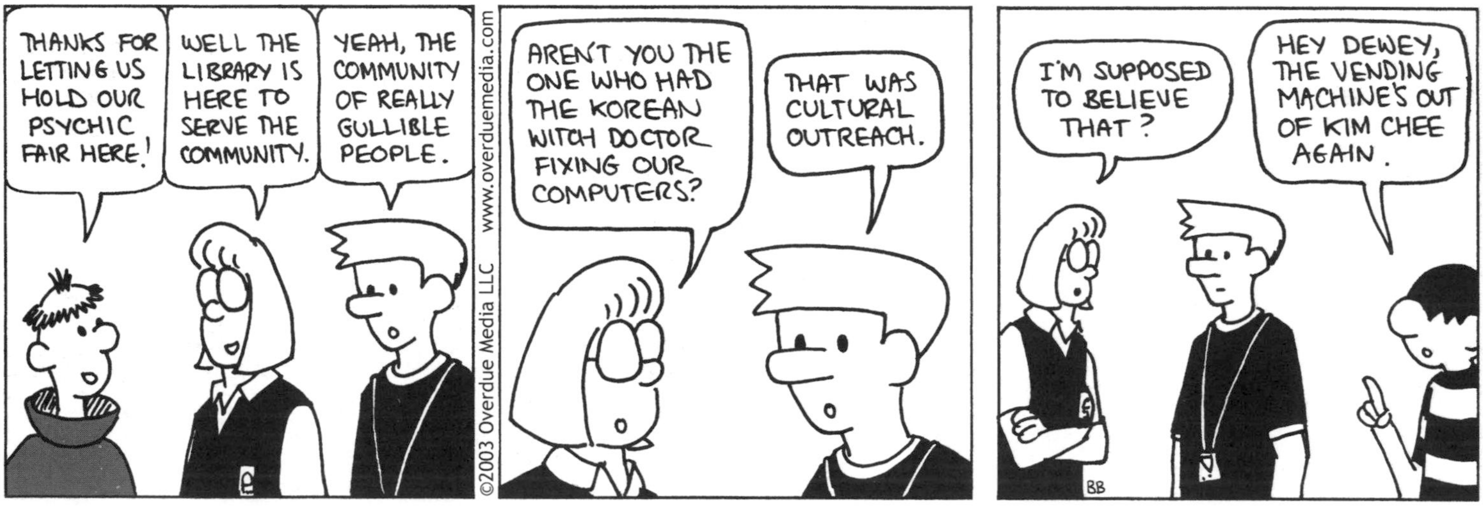
THANKS FOR LETTING US HOLD OUR PSYCHIC FAIR HERE!
WELL THE LIBRARY IS HERE TO SERVE THE COMMUNITY.
YEAH, THE COMMUNITY OF REALLY GULLIBLE PEOPLE.
©2003 Overdue Media LLC www.overduemedia.com
AREN'T YOU THE ONE WHO HAD THE KOREAN WITCH DOCTOR FIXING OUR COMPUTERS?
THAT WAS CULTURAL OUTREACH.
I'M SUPPOSED TO BELIEVE THAT?
HEY DEWEY, THE VENDING MACHINE'S OUT OF KIM CHEE AGAIN.
BB

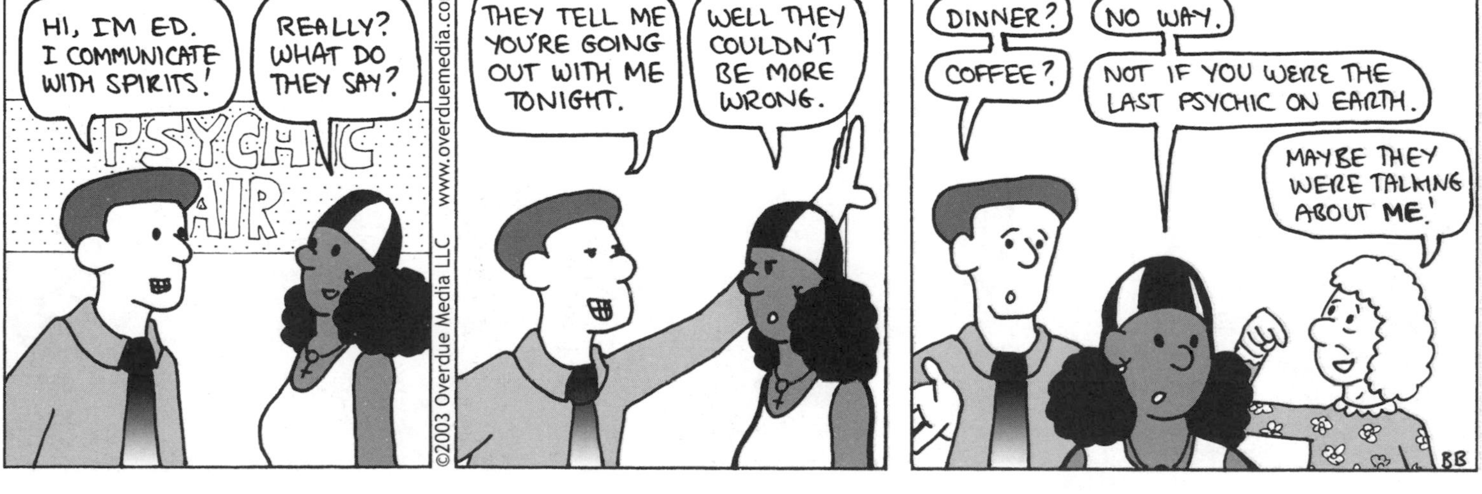
HI, I'M ED. I COMMUNICATE WITH SPIRITS!
REALLY? WHAT DO THEY SAY?
PSYCHIC FAIR
©2003 Overdue Media LLC www.overduemedia.com
THEY TELL ME YOU'RE GOING OUT WITH ME TONIGHT.
WELL THEY COULDN'T BE MORE WRONG.
DINNER?
NO WAY.
COFFEE?
NOT IF YOU WERE THE LAST PSYCHIC ON EARTH.
MAYBE THEY WERE TALKING ABOUT ME!
BB

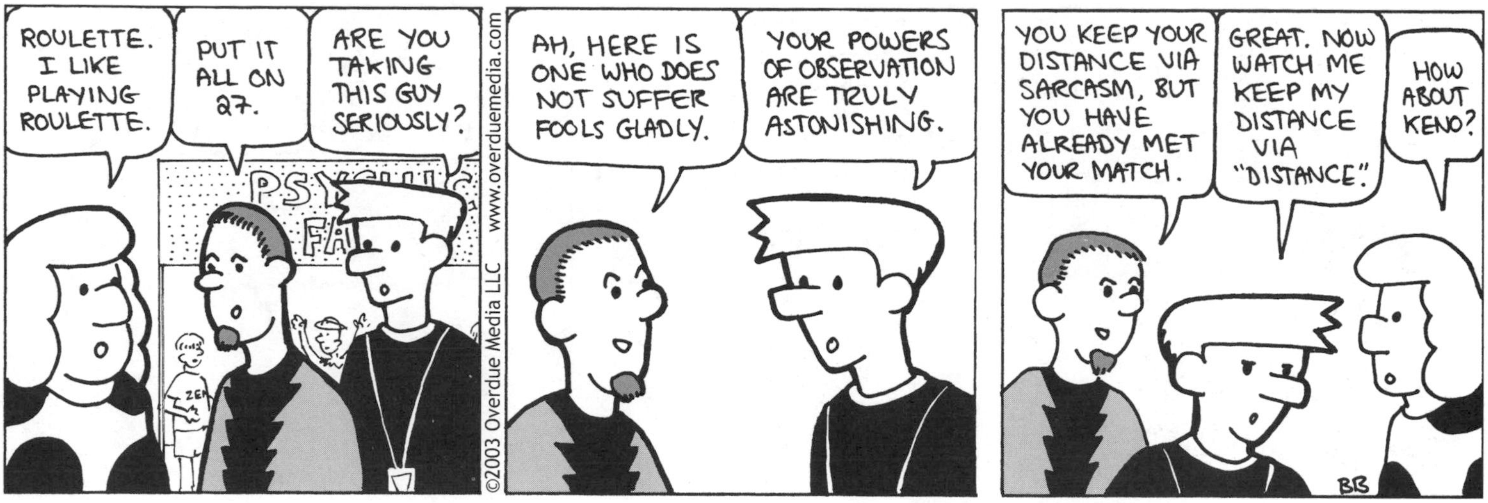
ROULETTE. I LIKE PLAYING ROULETTE.
PUT IT ALL ON 27.
ARE YOU TAKING THIS GUY SERIOUSLY?
©2003 Overdue Media LLC www.overduemedia.com
AH, HERE IS ONE WHO DOES NOT SUFFER FOOLS GLADLY.
YOUR POWERS OF OBSERVATION ARE TRULY ASTONISHING.
YOU KEEP YOUR DISTANCE VIA SARCASM, BUT YOU HAVE ALREADY MET YOUR MATCH.
GREAT. NOW WATCH ME KEEP MY DISTANCE VIA "DISTANCE."
HOW ABOUT KENO?
BB

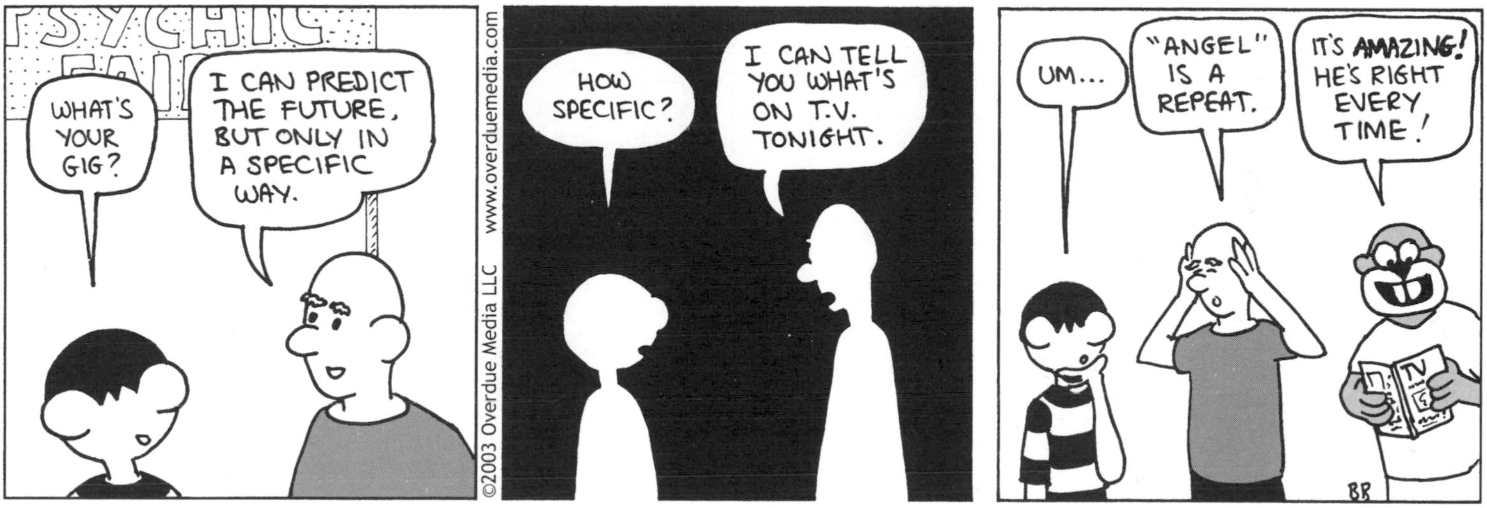
WHAT'S YOUR GIG?
I CAN PREDICT THE FUTURE, BUT ONLY IN A SPECIFIC WAY.
©2003 Overdue Media LLC www.overduemedia.com
HOW SPECIFIC?
I CAN TELL YOU WHAT'S ON T.V. TONIGHT.
UM...
"ANGEL" IS A REPEAT.
IT'S AMAZING! HE'S RIGHT EVERY TIME!
BB

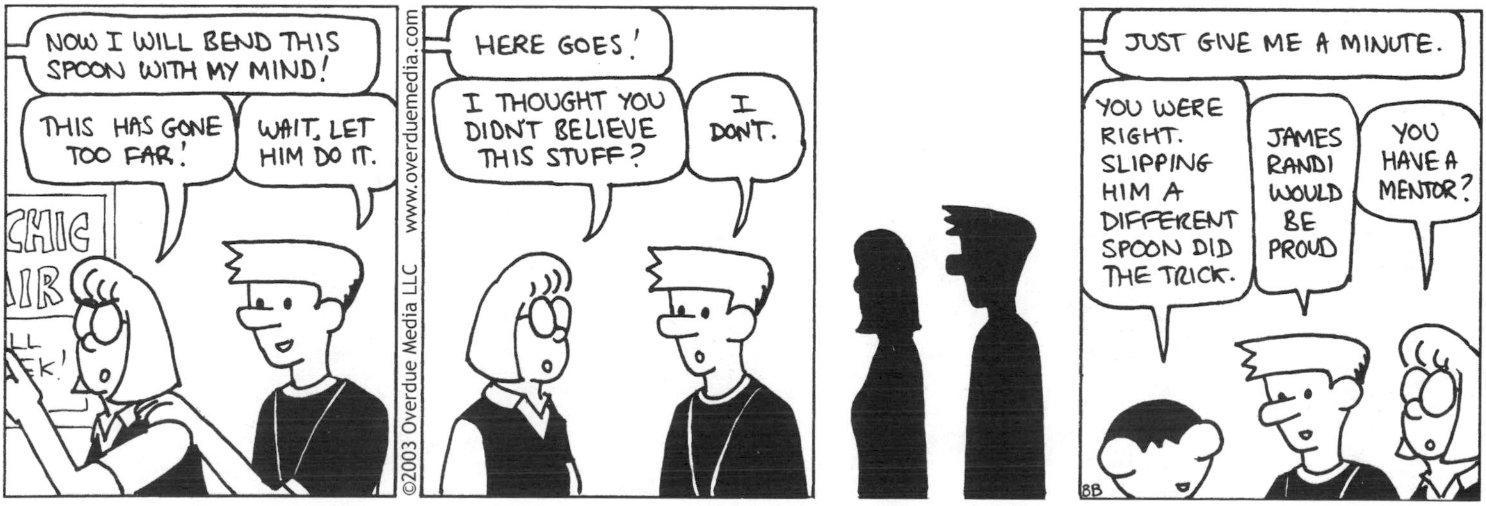
NOW I WILL BEND THIS SPOON WITH MY MIND!
THIS HAS GONE TOO FAR!
WAIT, LET HIM DO IT.
©2003 Overdue Media LLC www.overduemedia.com
HERE GOES!
I THOUGHT YOU DIDN'T BELIEVE THIS STUFF?
I DON'T.
JUST GIVE ME A MINUTE.
YOU WERE RIGHT. SLIPPING HIM A DIFFERENT SPOON DID THE TRICK.
JAMES RANDI WOULD BE PROUD
YOU HAVE A MENTOR?
BB

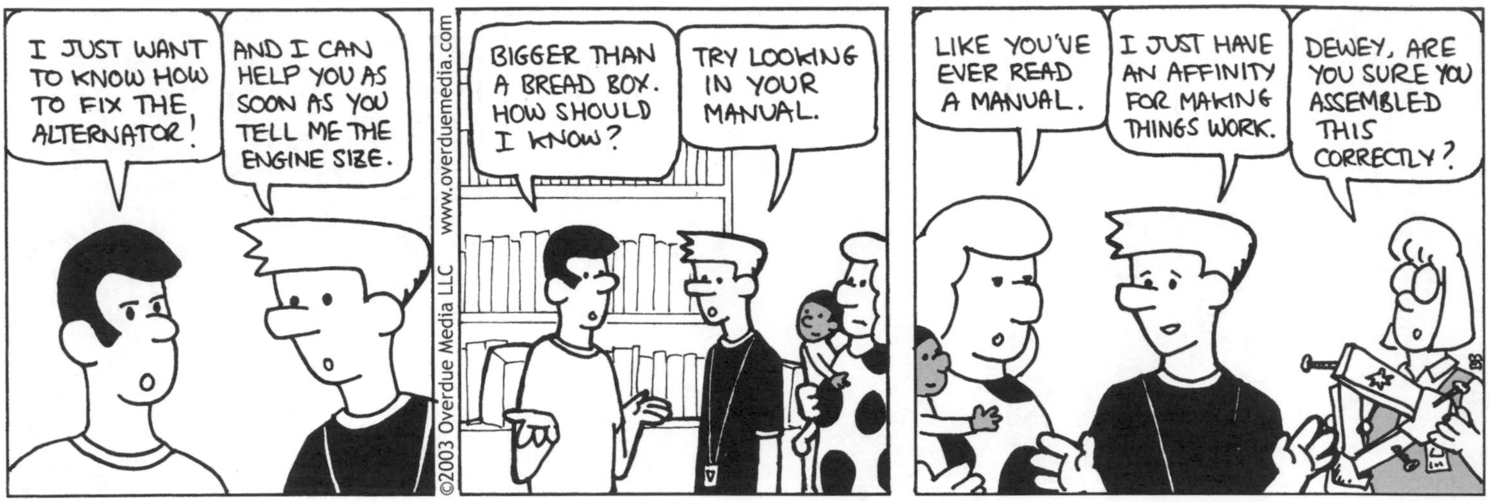
I JUST WANT TO KNOW HOW TO FIX THE ALTERNATOR!
AND I CAN HELP YOU AS SOON AS YOU TELL ME THE ENGINE SIZE.
©2003 Overdue Media LLC www.overduemedia.com
BIGGER THAN A BREAD BOX. HOW SHOULD I KNOW?
TRY LOOKING IN YOUR MANUAL.
LIKE YOU'VE EVER READ A MANUAL.
I JUST HAVE AN AFFINITY FOR MAKING THINGS WORK.
DEWEY, ARE YOU SURE YOU ASSEMBLED THIS CORRECTLY?
BB

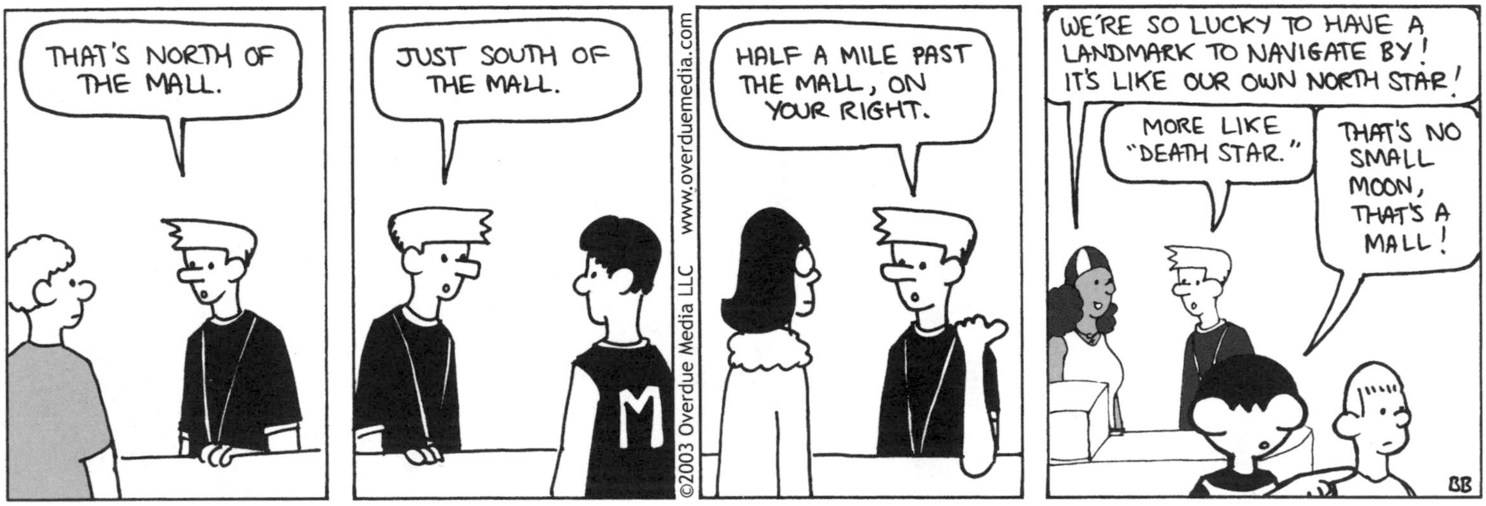
THAT'S NORTH OF THE MALL.
JUST SOUTH OF THE MALL.
©2003 Overdue Media LLC www.overduemedia.com
HALF A MILE PAST THE MALL, ON YOUR RIGHT.
WE'RE SO LUCKY TO HAVE A LANDMARK TO NAVIGATE BY! IT'S LIKE OUR OWN NORTH STAR!
MORE LIKE "DEATH STAR."
THAT'S NO SMALL MOON, THAT'S A MALL!
BB

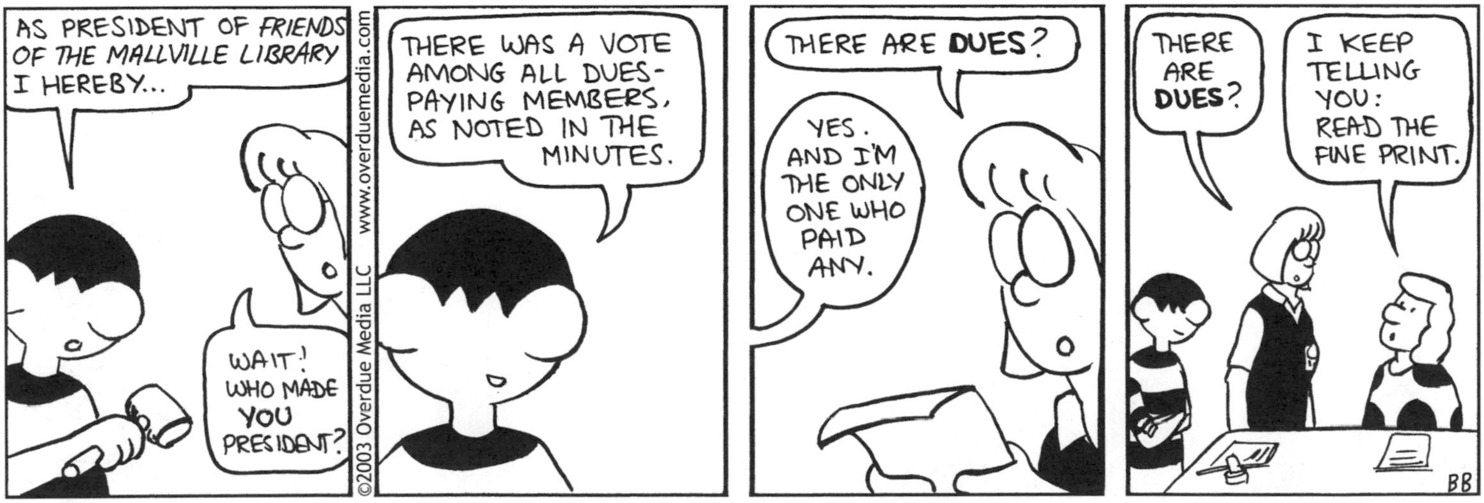
AS PRESIDENT OF *FRIENDS OF THE MALLVILLE LIBRARY* I HEREBY...
WAIT! WHO MADE **YOU** PRESIDENT?
©2003 Overdue Media LLC www.overduemedia.com
THERE WAS A VOTE AMONG ALL DUES-PAYING MEMBERS, AS NOTED IN THE MINUTES.
THERE ARE **DUES**?
YES. AND I'M THE ONLY ONE WHO PAID ANY.
THERE ARE **DUES**?
I KEEP TELLING YOU: READ THE FINE PRINT.
BB

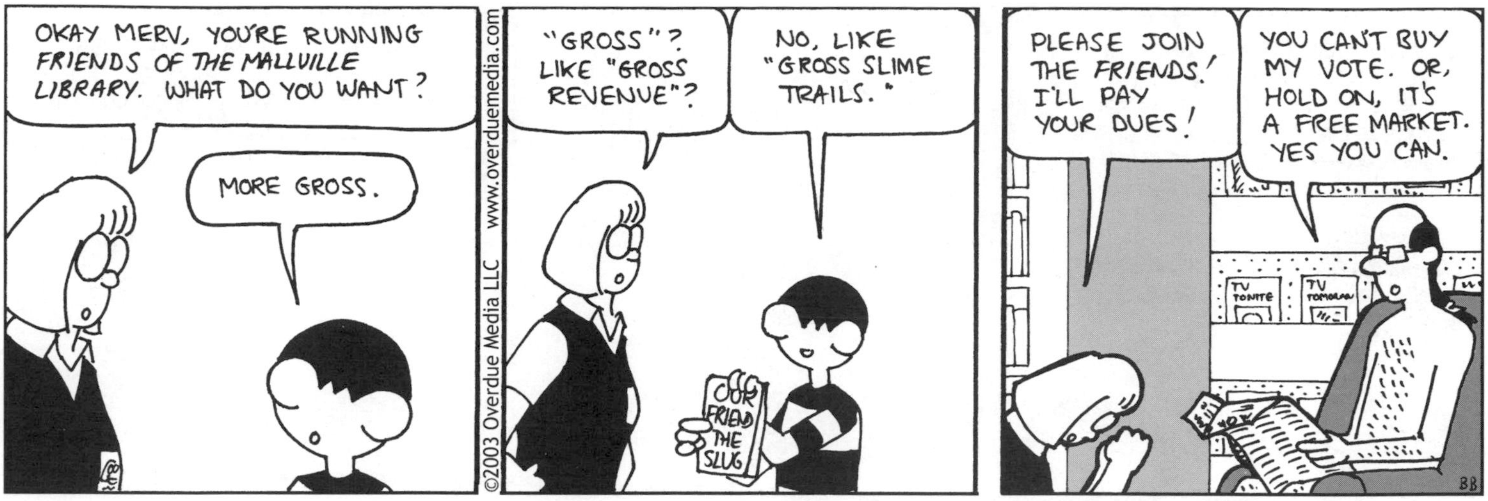
OKAY MERV, YOU'RE RUNNING *FRIENDS OF THE MALLVILLE LIBRARY*. WHAT DO YOU WANT?
MORE GROSS.
©2003 Overdue Media LLC www.overduemedia.com
"GROSS"? LIKE "GROSS REVENUE"?
NO, LIKE "GROSS SLIME TRAILS."
OUR FRIEND THE SLUG
PLEASE JOIN THE *FRIENDS*! I'LL PAY YOUR DUES!
YOU CAN'T BUY MY VOTE. OR, HOLD ON, IT'S A FREE MARKET. YES YOU CAN.
TV TONITE
TV TOMORROW
BB

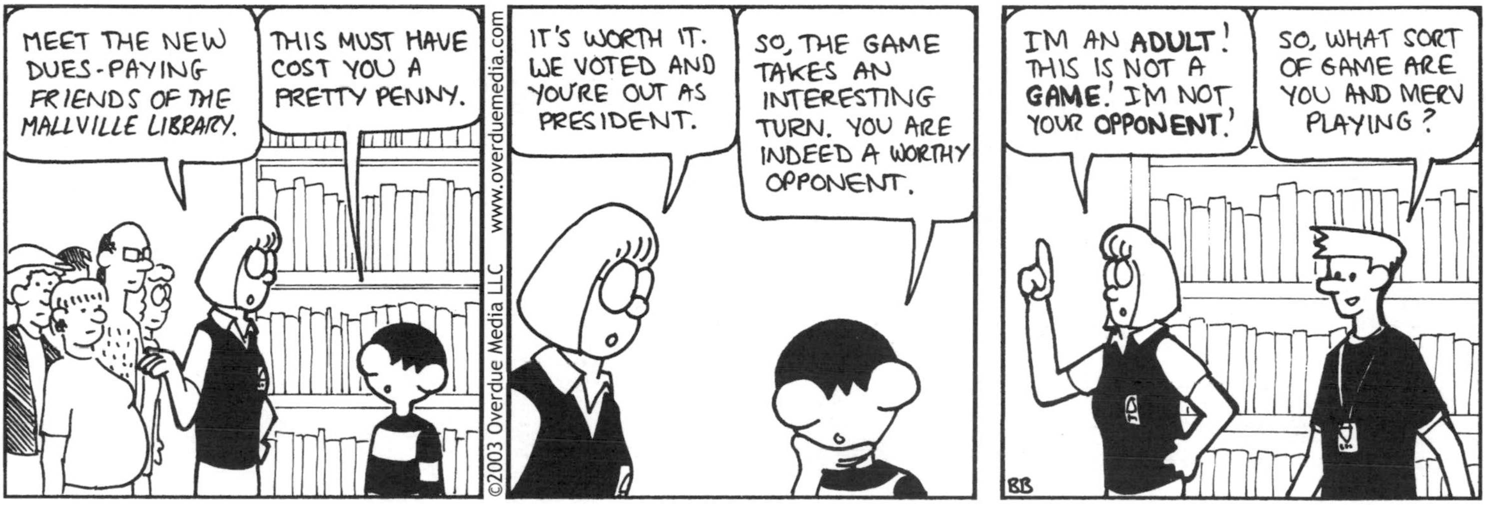
MEET THE NEW DUES-PAYING FRIENDS OF THE MALLVILLE LIBRARY.
THIS MUST HAVE COST YOU A PRETTY PENNY.
©2003 Overdue Media LLC www.overduemedia.com
IT'S WORTH IT. WE VOTED AND YOU'RE OUT AS PRESIDENT.
SO, THE GAME TAKES AN INTERESTING TURN. YOU ARE INDEED A WORTHY OPPONENT.
I'M AN **ADULT**! THIS IS NOT A **GAME**! I'M NOT YOUR **OPPONENT**!
SO, WHAT SORT OF GAME ARE YOU AND MERV PLAYING?
BB

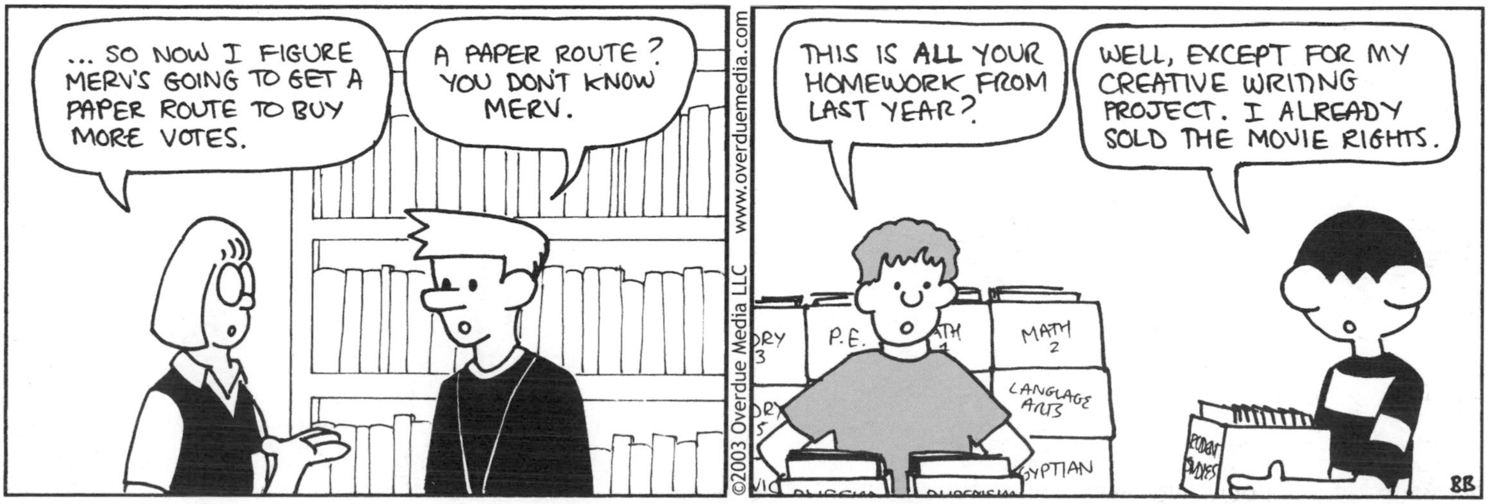
...SO NOW I FIGURE MERV'S GOING TO GET A PAPER ROUTE TO BUY MORE VOTES.
A PAPER ROUTE? YOU DON'T KNOW MERV.
©2003 Overdue Media LLC www.overduemedia.com
THIS IS **ALL** YOUR HOMEWORK FROM LAST YEAR?
WELL, EXCEPT FOR MY CREATIVE WRITING PROJECT. I ALREADY SOLD THE MOVIE RIGHTS.
P.E.
MATH 2
BB

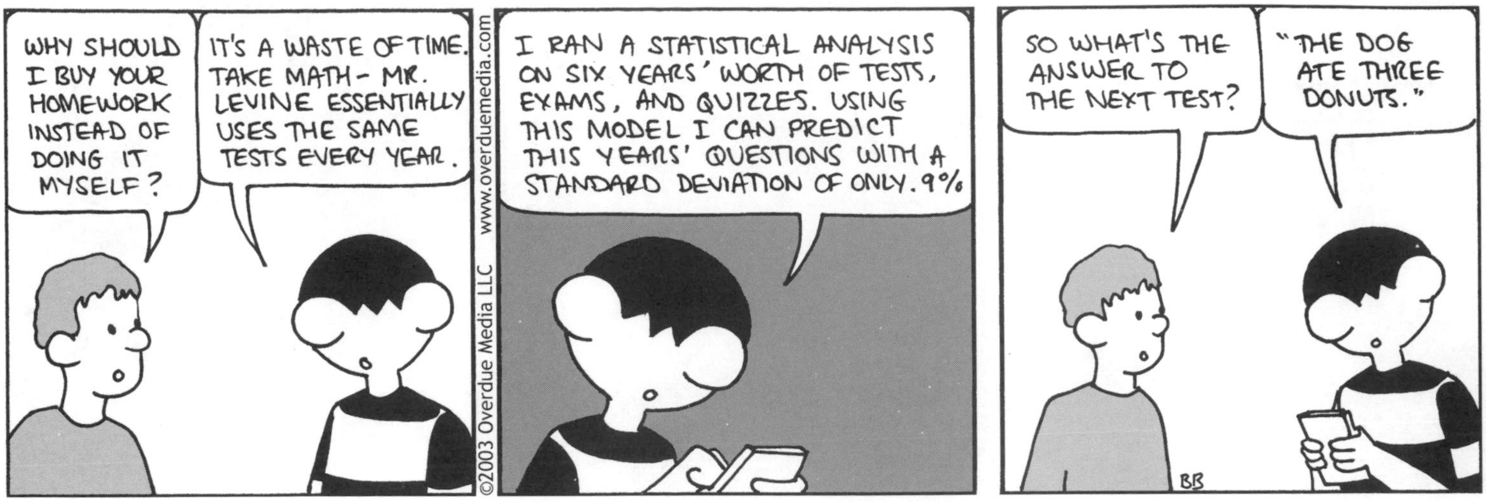
WHY SHOULD I BUY YOUR HOMEWORK INSTEAD OF DOING IT MYSELF?
IT'S A WASTE OF TIME. TAKE MATH - MR. LEVINE ESSENTIALLY USES THE SAME TESTS EVERY YEAR.
©2003 Overdue Media LLC www.overduemedia.com
I RAN A STATISTICAL ANALYSIS ON SIX YEARS' WORTH OF TESTS, EXAMS, AND QUIZZES. USING THIS MODEL I CAN PREDICT THIS YEARS' QUESTIONS WITH A STANDARD DEVIATION OF ONLY .9%
SO WHAT'S THE ANSWER TO THE NEXT TEST?
"THE DOG ATE THREE DONUTS."
BB

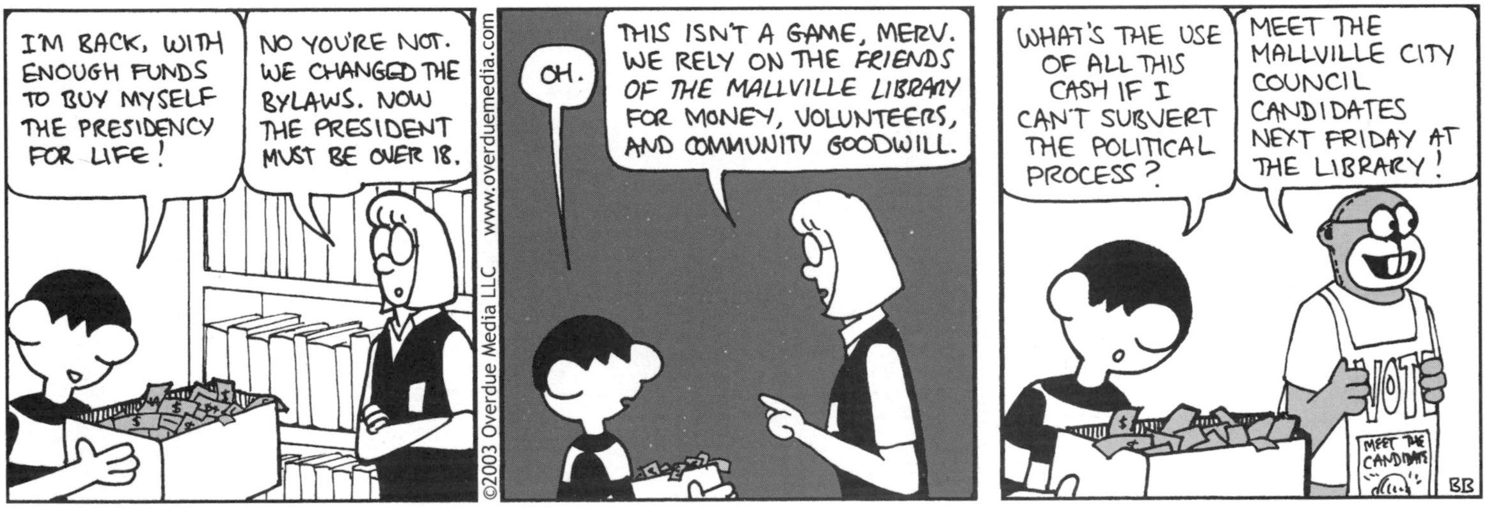
I'M BACK, WITH ENOUGH FUNDS TO BUY MYSELF THE PRESIDENCY FOR LIFE!
NO YOU'RE NOT. WE CHANGED THE BYLAWS. NOW THE PRESIDENT MUST BE OVER 18.
©2003 Overdue Media LLC www.overduemedia.com
OH.
THIS ISN'T A GAME, MERV. WE RELY ON THE FRIENDS OF THE MALLVILLE LIBRARY FOR MONEY, VOLUNTEERS, AND COMMUNITY GOODWILL.
WHAT'S THE USE OF ALL THIS CASH IF I CAN'T SUBVERT THE POLITICAL PROCESS?
MEET THE MALLVILLE CITY COUNCIL CANDIDATES NEXT FRIDAY AT THE LIBRARY!
VOTE
MEET THE CANDIDATES
BB

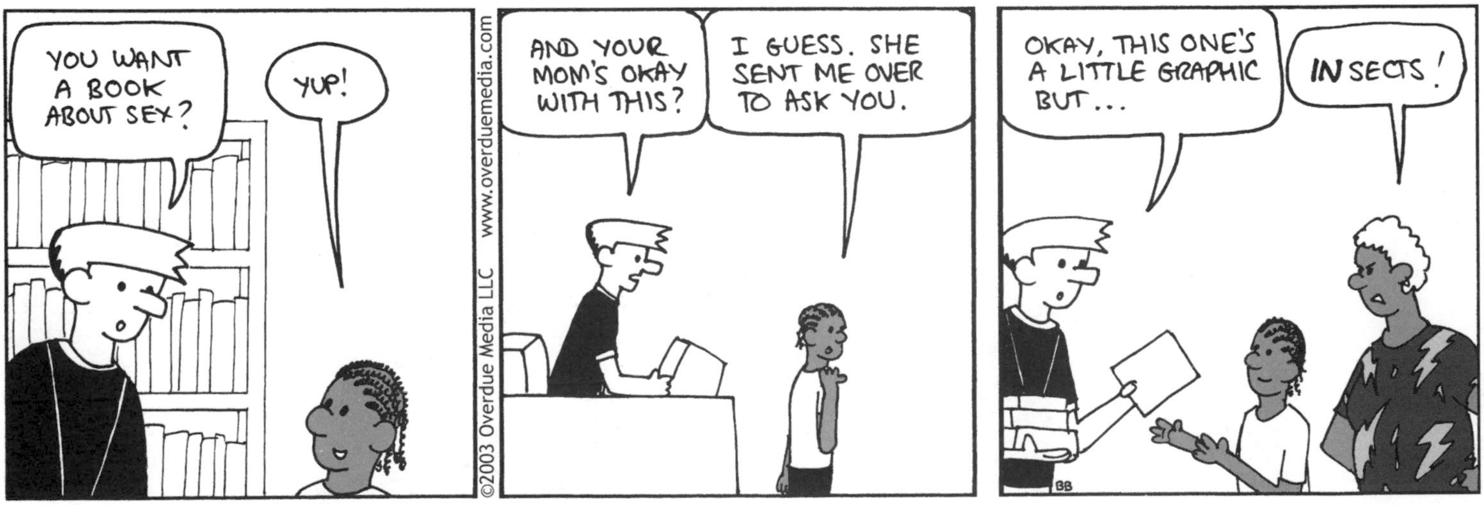
YOU WANT A BOOK ABOUT SEX?
YUP!
©2003 Overdue Media LLC www.overduemedia.com
AND YOUR MOM'S OKAY WITH THIS?
I GUESS. SHE SENT ME OVER TO ASK YOU.
OKAY, THIS ONE'S A LITTLE GRAPHIC BUT...
INSECTS!
BB

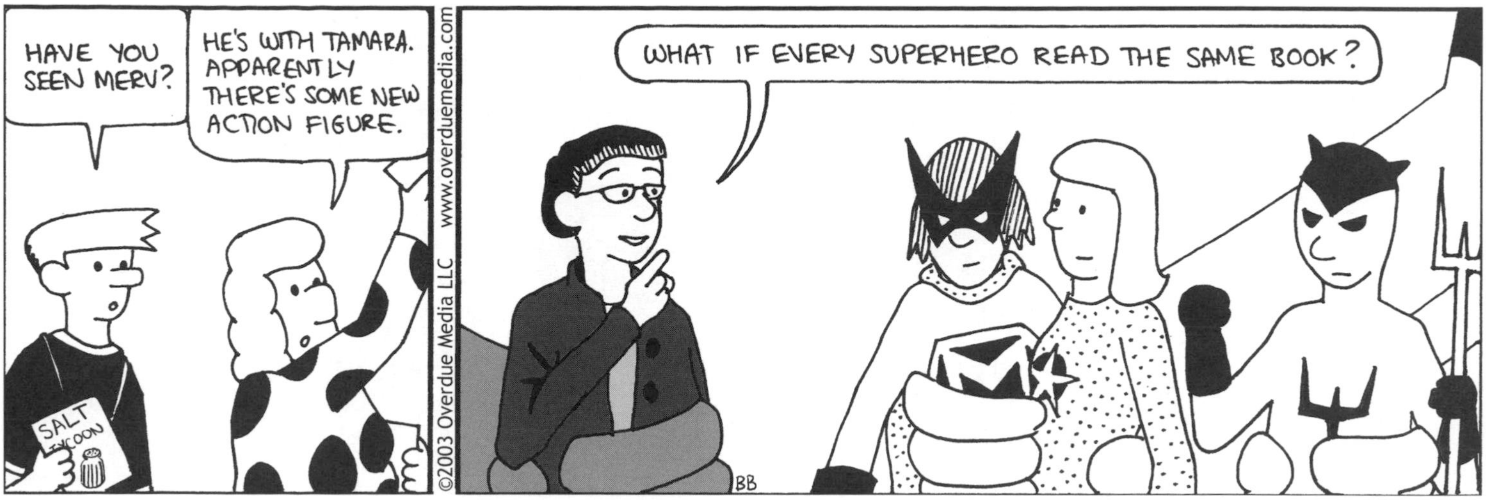
HAVE YOU SEEN MERV?
HE'S WITH TAMARA. APPARENTLY THERE'S SOME NEW ACTION FIGURE.
WHAT IF EVERY SUPERHERO READ THE SAME BOOK?
SALT TYCOON
www.overduemedia.com
©2003 Overdue Media LLC
BB

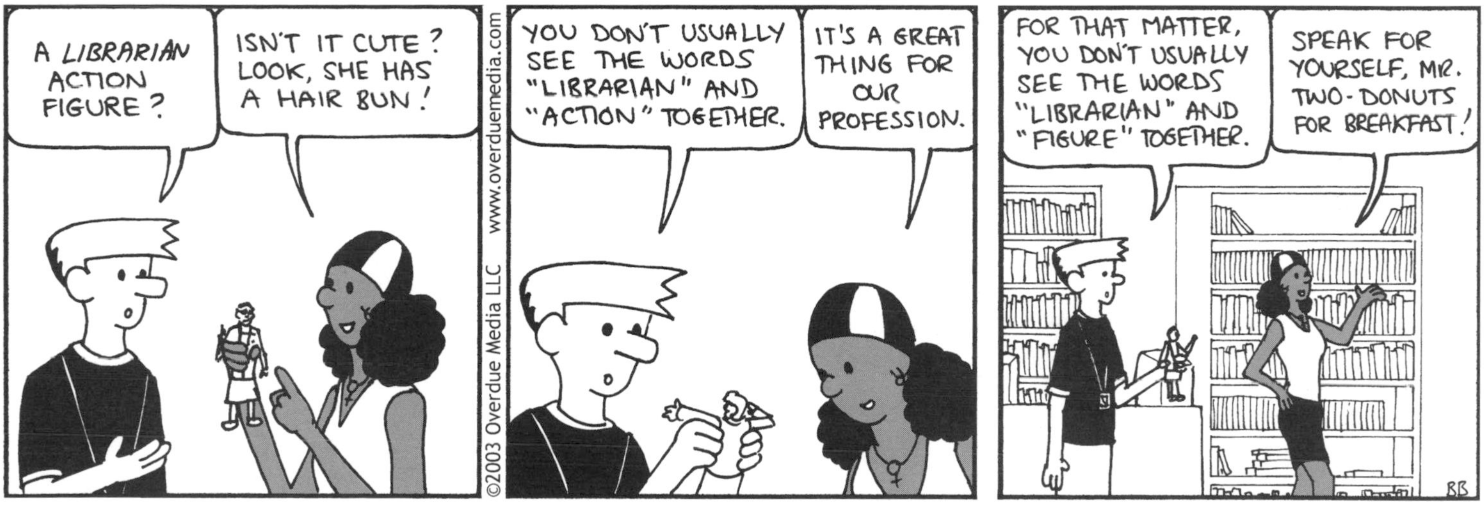
A *LIBRARIAN* ACTION FIGURE?
ISN'T IT CUTE? LOOK, SHE HAS A HAIR BUN!
YOU DON'T USUALLY SEE THE WORDS "LIBRARIAN" AND "ACTION" TOGETHER.
IT'S A GREAT THING FOR OUR PROFESSION.
FOR THAT MATTER, YOU DON'T USUALLY SEE THE WORDS "LIBRARIAN" AND "FIGURE" TOGETHER.
SPEAK FOR YOURSELF, MR. TWO-DONUTS FOR BREAKFAST!
www.overduemedia.com
©2003 Overdue Media LLC
BB

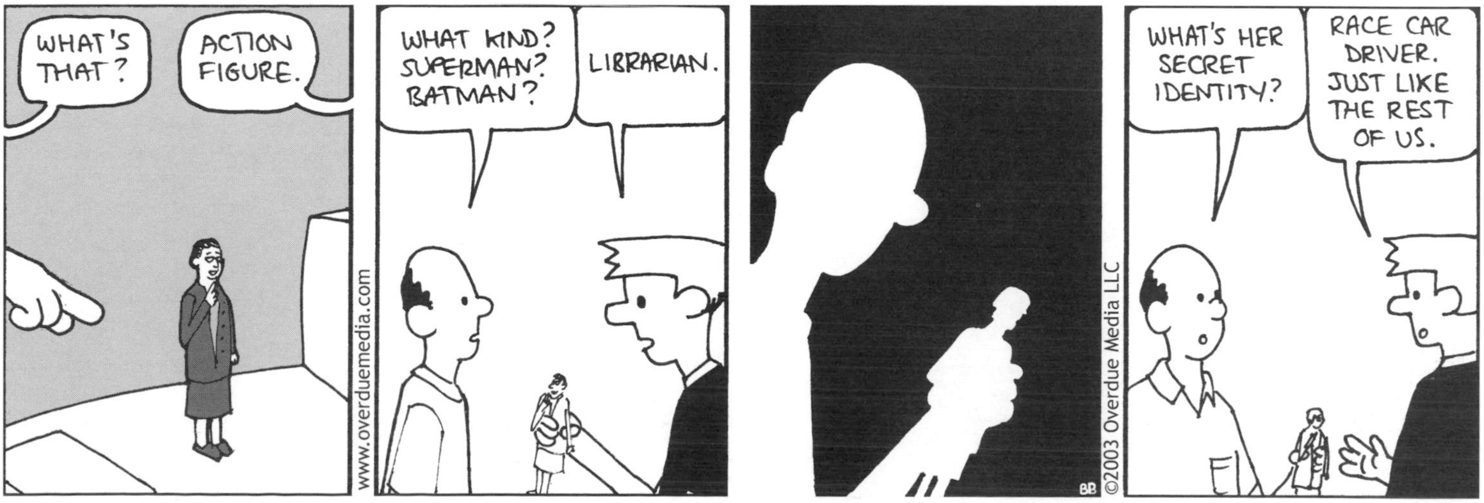
WHAT'S THAT?
ACTION FIGURE.
WHAT KIND? SUPERMAN? BATMAN?
LIBRARIAN.
WHAT'S HER SECRET IDENTITY?
RACE CAR DRIVER. JUST LIKE THE REST OF US.
www.overduemedia.com
©2003 Overdue Media LLC
BB

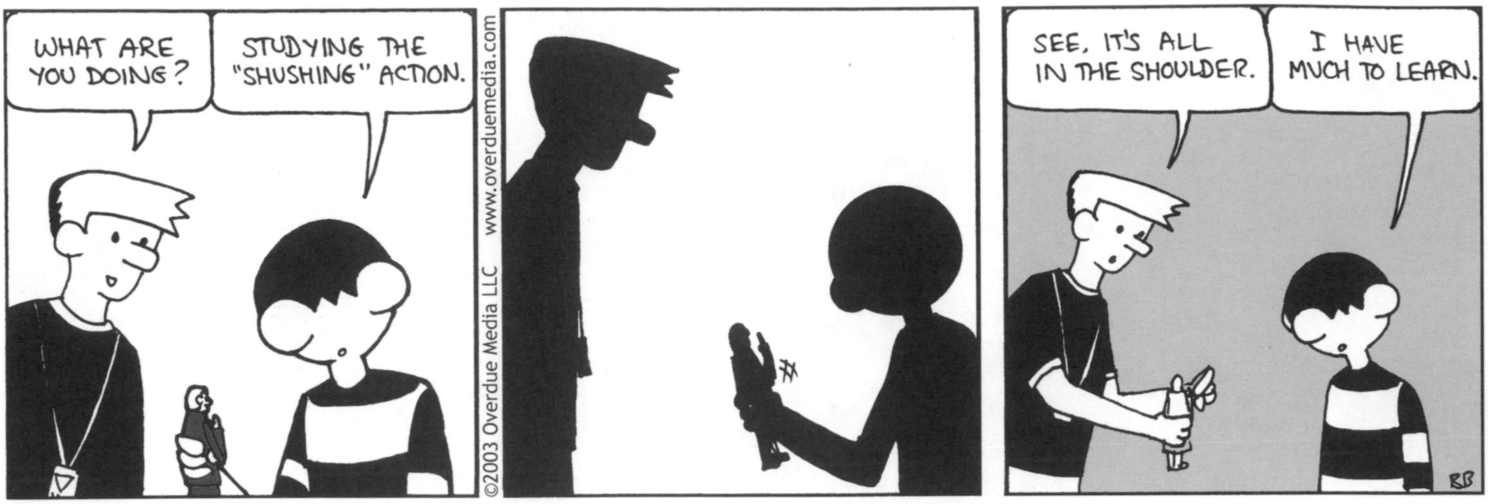
WHAT ARE YOU DOING?
STUDYING THE "SHUSHING" ACTION.
©2003 Overdue Media LLC www.overduemedia.com
SEE, IT'S ALL IN THE SHOULDER.
I HAVE MUCH TO LEARN.
BB

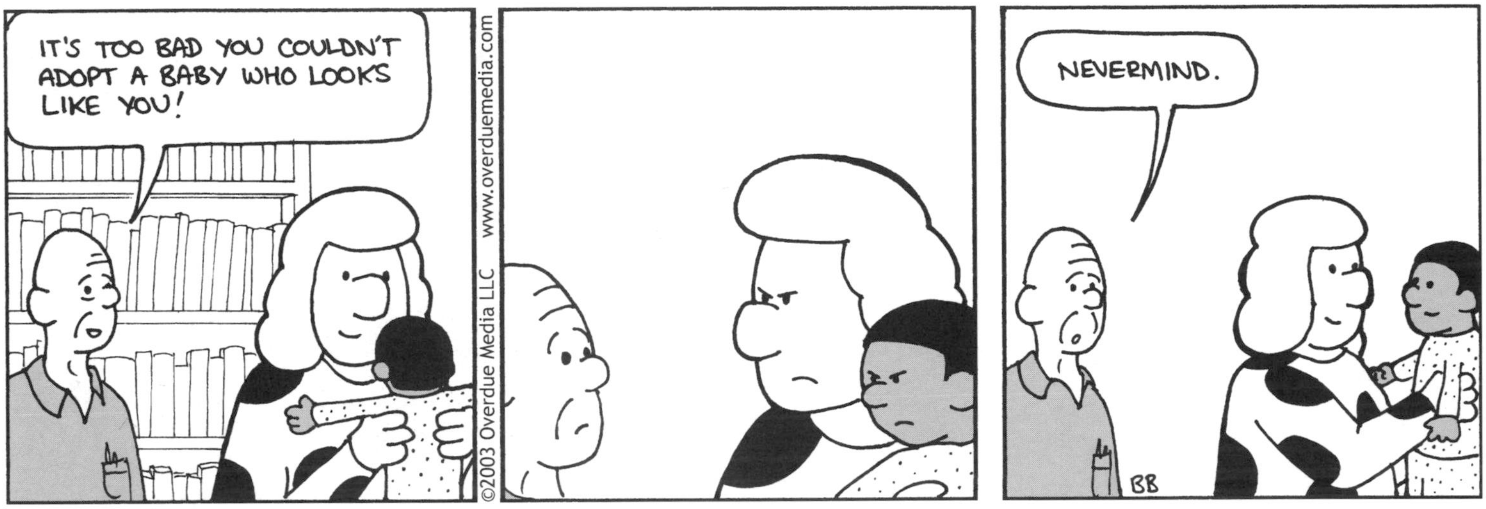
IT'S TOO BAD YOU COULDN'T ADOPT A BABY WHO LOOKS LIKE YOU!
©2003 Overdue Media LLC www.overduemedia.com
NEVERMIND.
BB

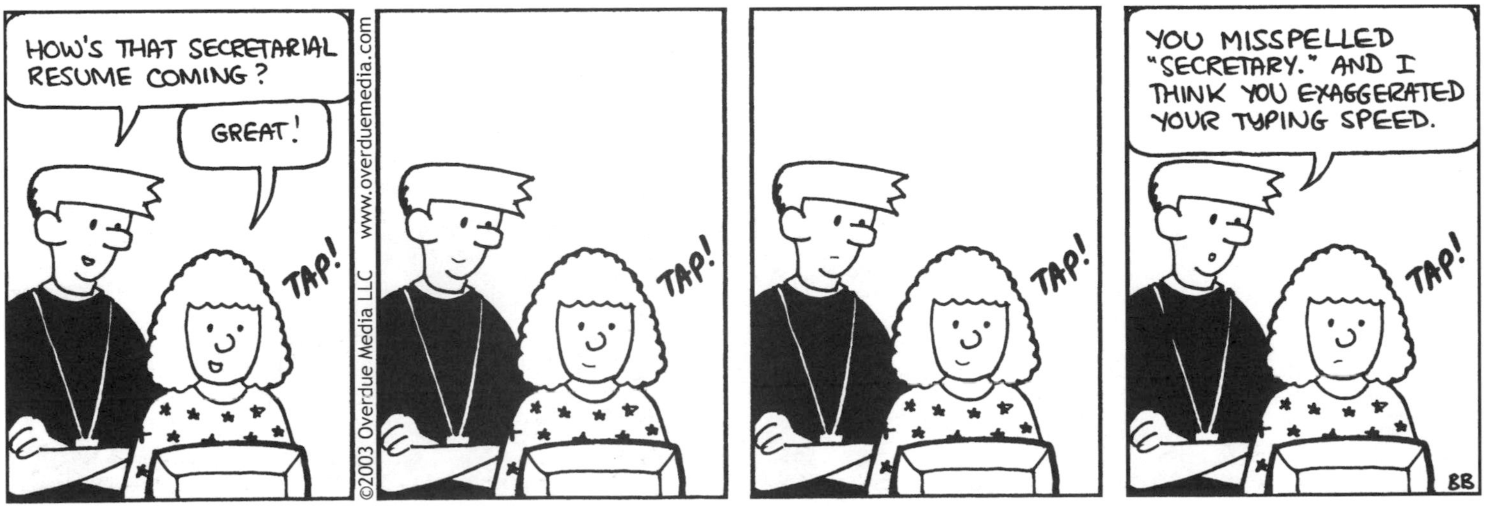
HOW'S THAT SECRETARIAL RESUME COMING?
GREAT!
TAP!
©2003 Overdue Media LLC www.overduemedia.com
TAP!
TAP!
YOU MISSPELLED "SECRETARY." AND I THINK YOU EXAGGERATED YOUR TYPING SPEED.
TAP!
BB

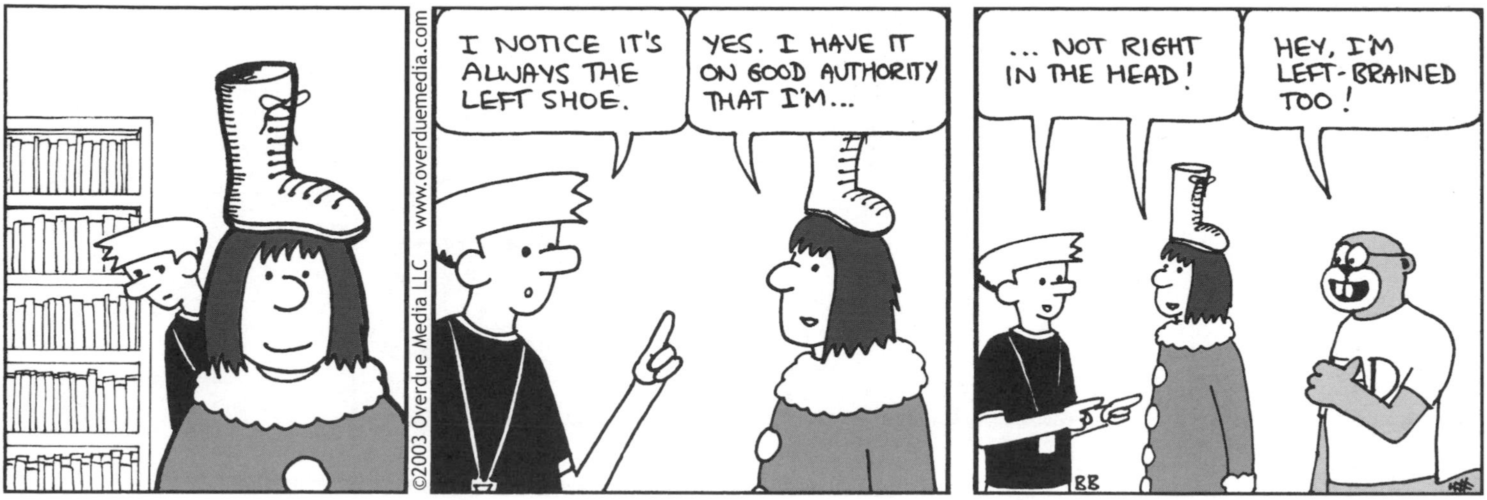
©2003 Overdue Media LLC www.overduemedia.com
I NOTICE IT'S ALWAYS THE LEFT SHOE.
YES. I HAVE IT ON GOOD AUTHORITY THAT I'M...
... NOT RIGHT IN THE HEAD!
HEY, I'M LEFT-BRAINED TOO!

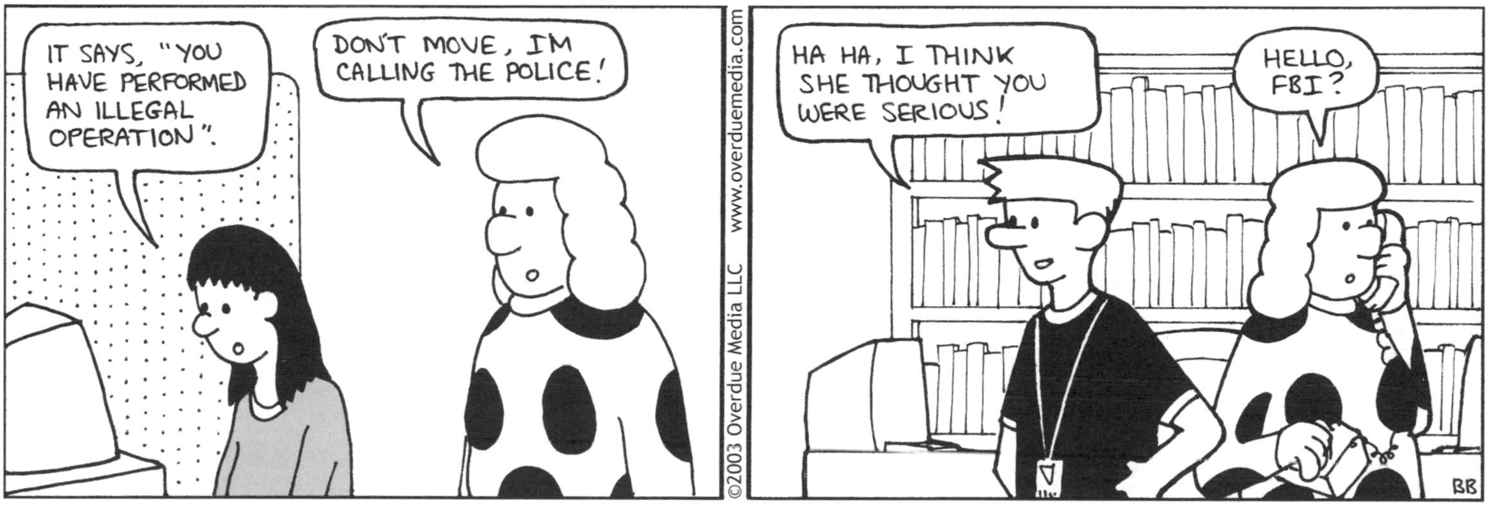
IT SAYS, "YOU HAVE PERFORMED AN ILLEGAL OPERATION".
DON'T MOVE, I'M CALLING THE POLICE!
©2003 Overdue Media LLC www.overduemedia.com
HA HA, I THINK SHE THOUGHT YOU WERE SERIOUS!
HELLO, FBI?

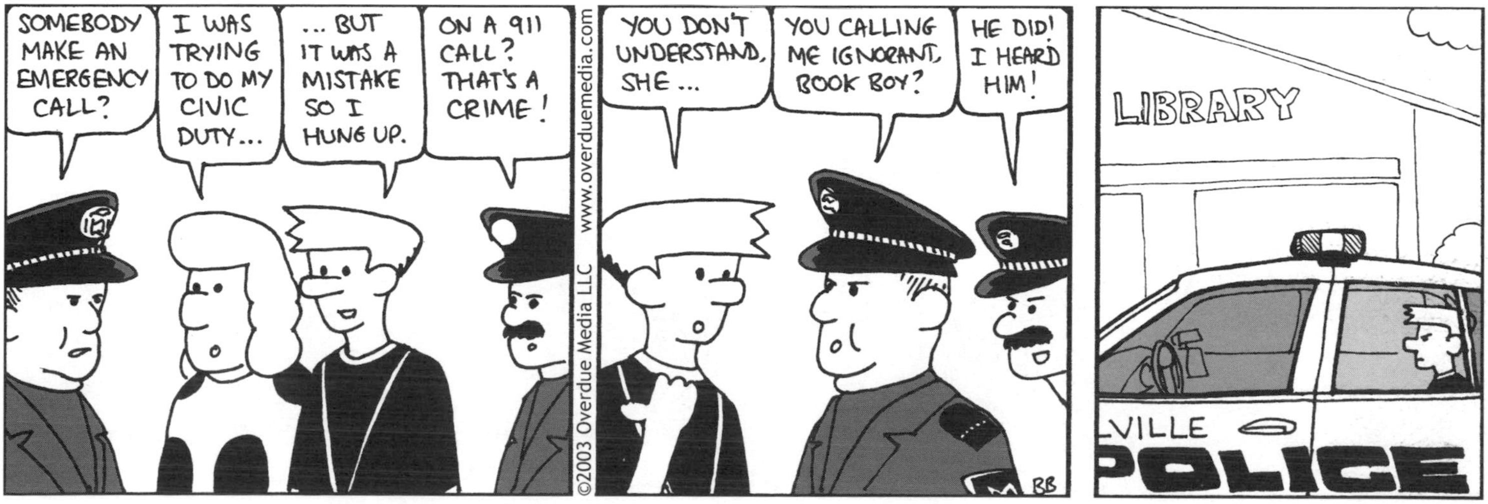
SOMEBODY MAKE AN EMERGENCY CALL?
I WAS TRYING TO DO MY CIVIC DUTY...
... BUT IT WAS A MISTAKE SO I HUNG UP.
ON A 911 CALL? THAT'S A CRIME!
©2003 Overdue Media LLC www.overduemedia.com
YOU DON'T UNDERSTAND, SHE...
YOU CALLING ME IGNORANT, BOOK BOY?
HE DID! I HEARD HIM!
LIBRARY
VILLE
POLICE

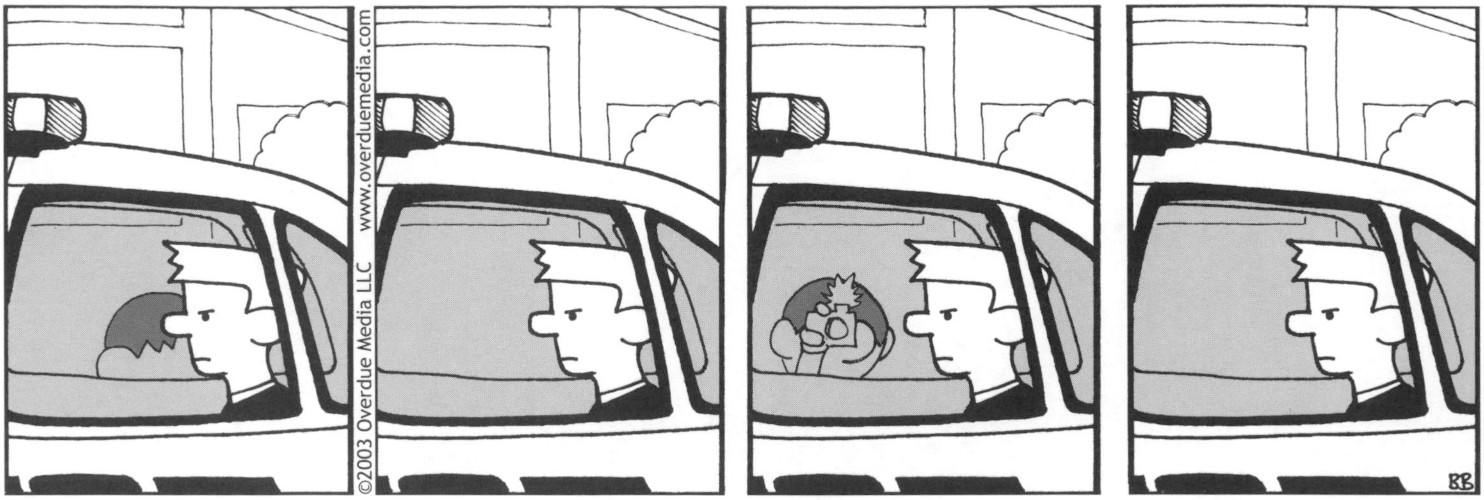
©2003 Overdue Media LLC www.overduemedia.com
BB

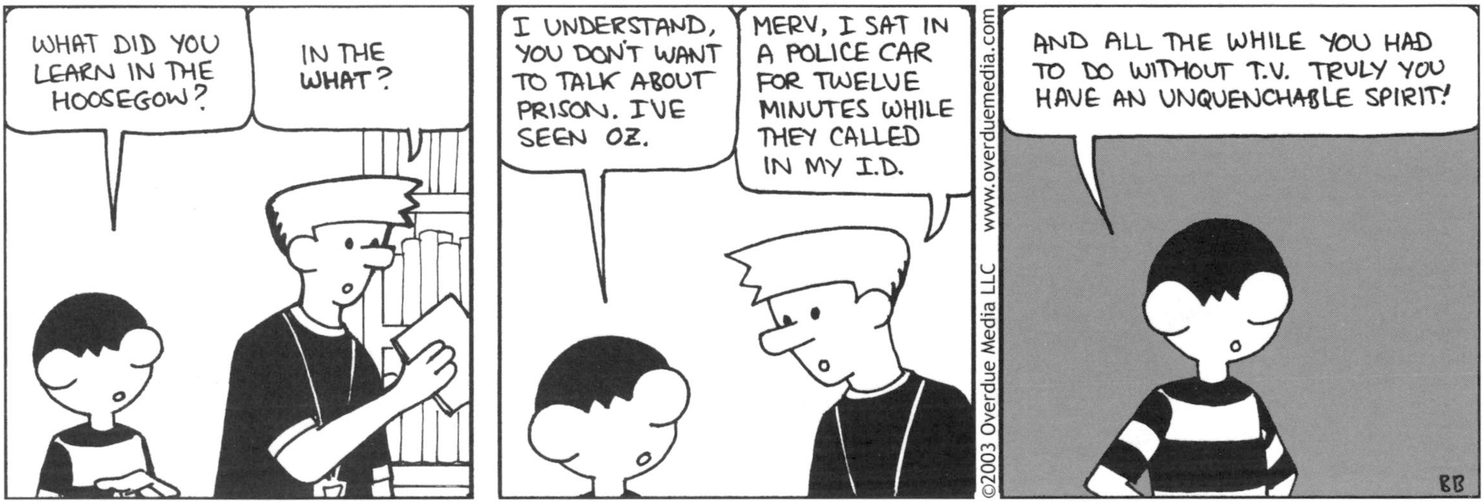
WHAT DID YOU LEARN IN THE HOOSEGOW?
IN THE WHAT?
I UNDERSTAND, YOU DON'T WANT TO TALK ABOUT PRISON. I'VE SEEN OZ.
MERV, I SAT IN A POLICE CAR FOR TWELVE MINUTES WHILE THEY CALLED IN MY I.D.
©2003 Overdue Media LLC www.overduemedia.com
AND ALL THE WHILE YOU HAD TO DO WITHOUT T.V. TRULY YOU HAVE AN UNQUENCHABLE SPIRIT!
BB

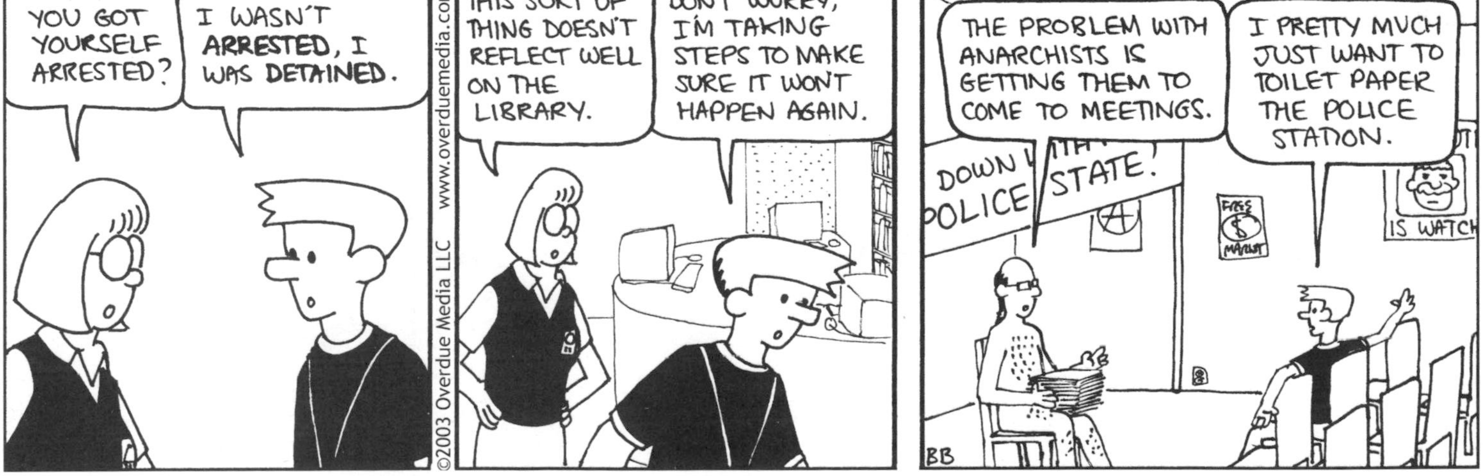
YOU GOT YOURSELF ARRESTED?
I WASN'T ARRESTED, I WAS DETAINED.
©2003 Overdue Media LLC www.overduemedia.com
THIS SORT OF THING DOESN'T REFLECT WELL ON THE LIBRARY.
DON'T WORRY, I'M TAKING STEPS TO MAKE SURE IT WON'T HAPPEN AGAIN.
THE PROBLEM WITH ANARCHISTS IS GETTING THEM TO COME TO MEETINGS.
I PRETTY MUCH JUST WANT TO TOILET PAPER THE POLICE STATION.
DOWN
POLICE STATE!
IS WATCH
BB

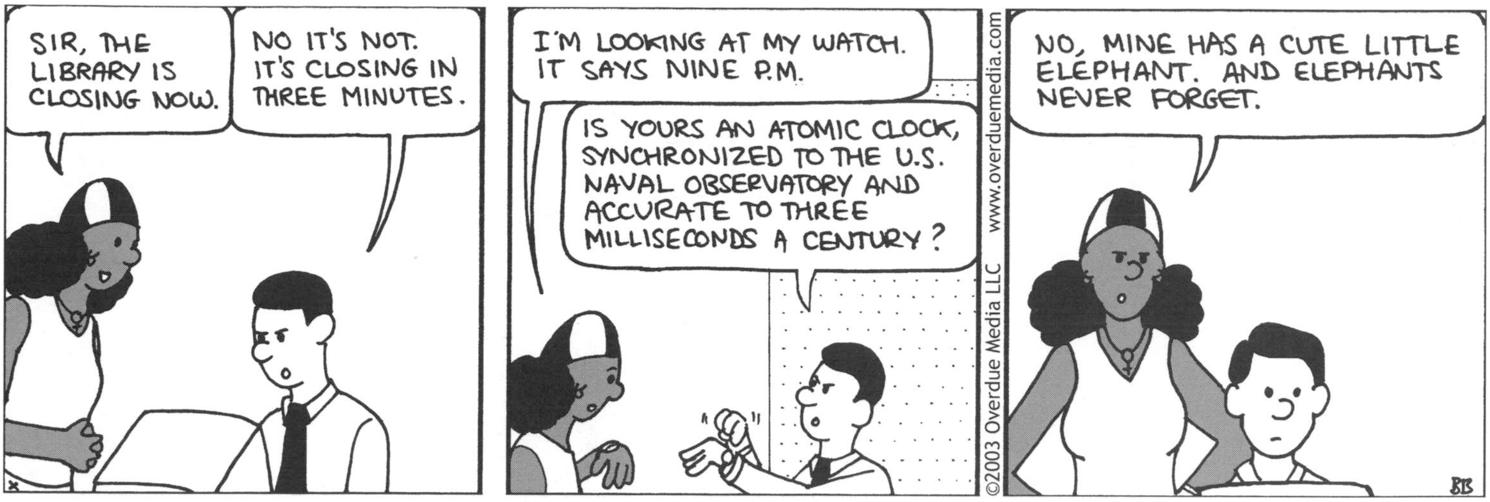
SIR, THE LIBRARY IS CLOSING NOW.
NO IT'S NOT. IT'S CLOSING IN THREE MINUTES.
I'M LOOKING AT MY WATCH. IT SAYS NINE P.M.
IS YOURS AN ATOMIC CLOCK, SYNCHRONIZED TO THE U.S. NAVAL OBSERVATORY AND ACCURATE TO THREE MILLISECONDS A CENTURY?
NO, MINE HAS A CUTE LITTLE ELEPHANT. AND ELEPHANTS NEVER FORGET.
©2003 Overdue Media LLC www.overduemedia.com
BB

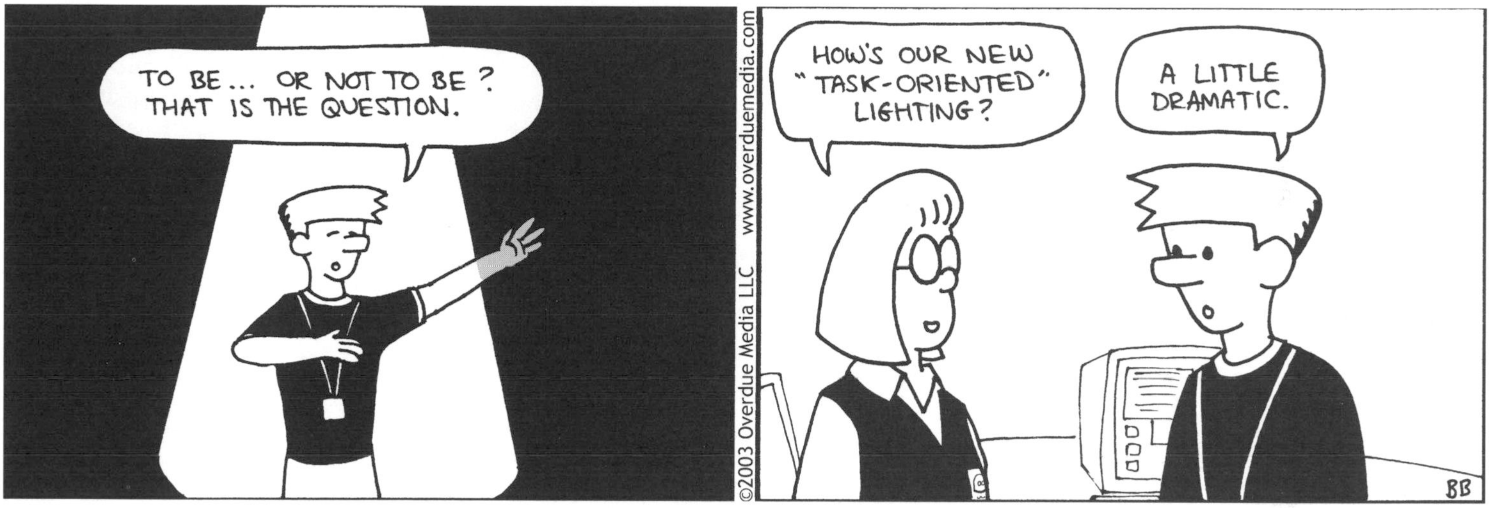
TO BE... OR NOT TO BE? THAT IS THE QUESTION.
©2003 Overdue Media LLC www.overduemedia.com
HOW'S OUR NEW "TASK-ORIENTED" LIGHTING?
A LITTLE DRAMATIC.
BB

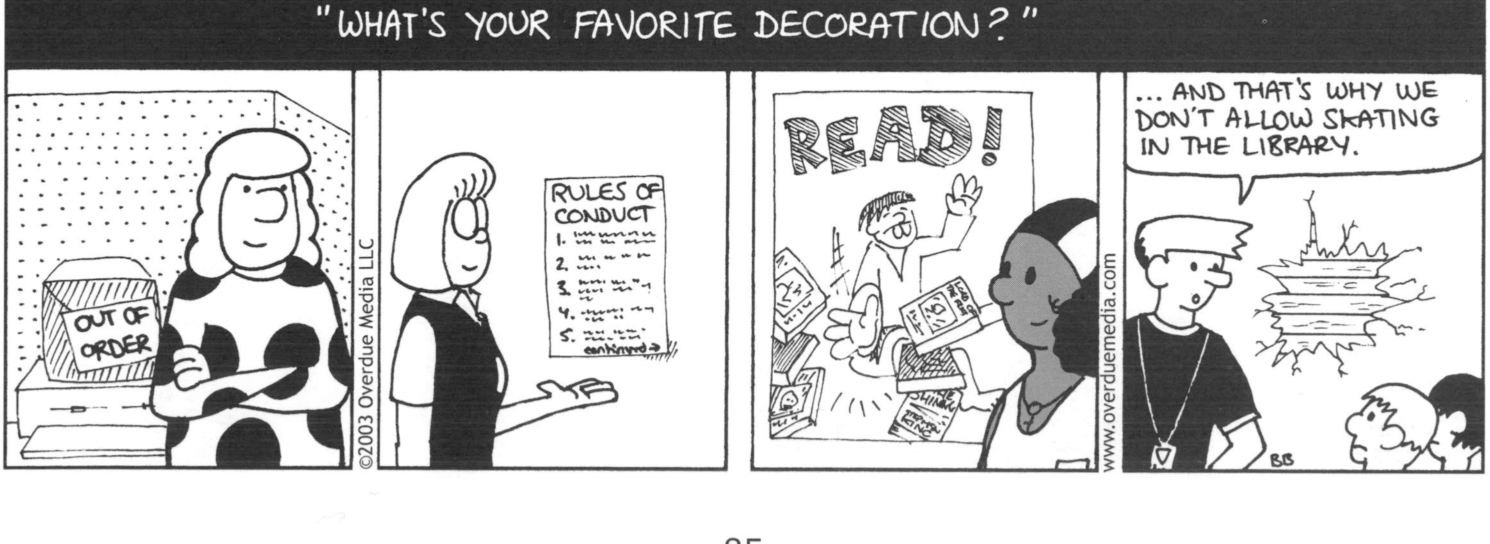
"WHAT'S YOUR FAVORITE DECORATION?"
OUT OF ORDER
©2003 Overdue Media LLC
RULES OF CONDUCT
1.
2.
3.
4.
5.
continued
READ!
www.overduemedia.com
... AND THAT'S WHY WE DON'T ALLOW SKATING IN THE LIBRARY.
BB

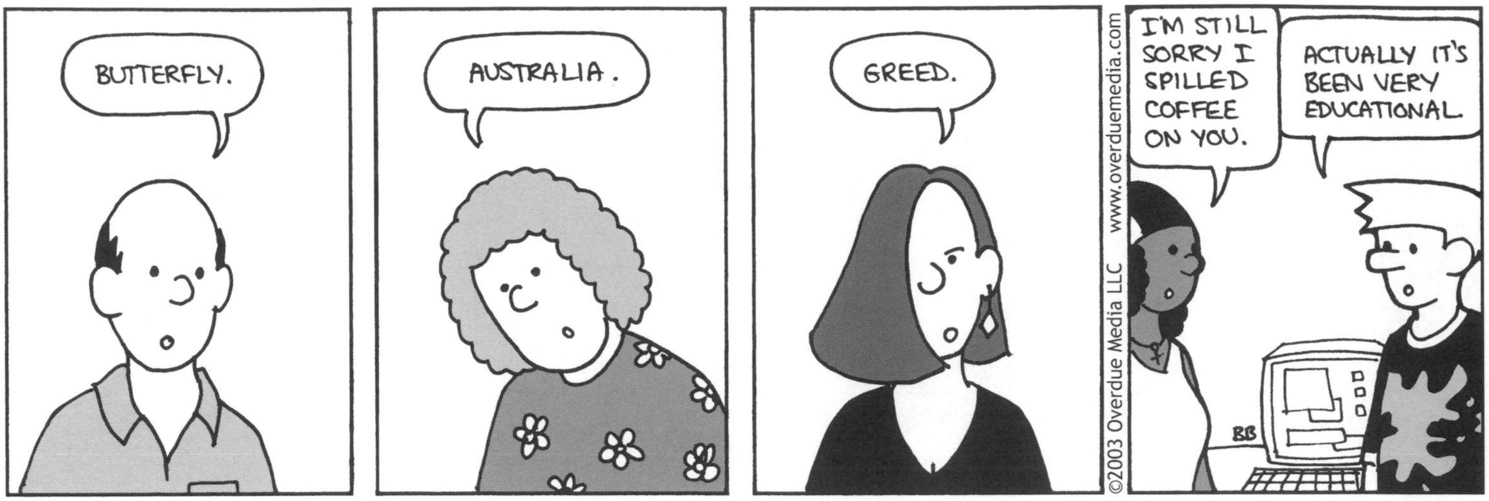
BUTTERFLY.
AUSTRALIA.
GREED.
I'M STILL SORRY I SPILLED COFFEE ON YOU.
ACTUALLY IT'S BEEN VERY EDUCATIONAL.
©2003 Overdue Media LLC www.overduemedia.com

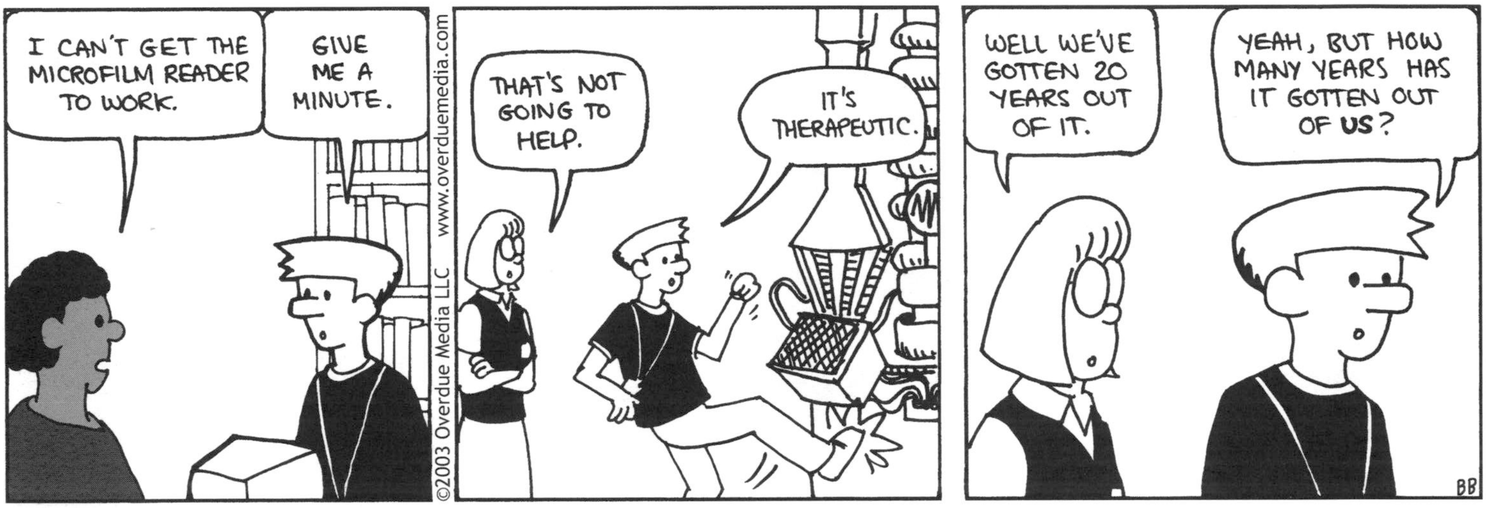
I CAN'T GET THE MICROFILM READER TO WORK.
GIVE ME A MINUTE.
©2003 Overdue Media LLC www.overduemedia.com
THAT'S NOT GOING TO HELP.
IT'S THERAPEUTIC.
WELL WE'VE GOTTEN 20 YEARS OUT OF IT.
YEAH, BUT HOW MANY YEARS HAS IT GOTTEN OUT OF **US**?

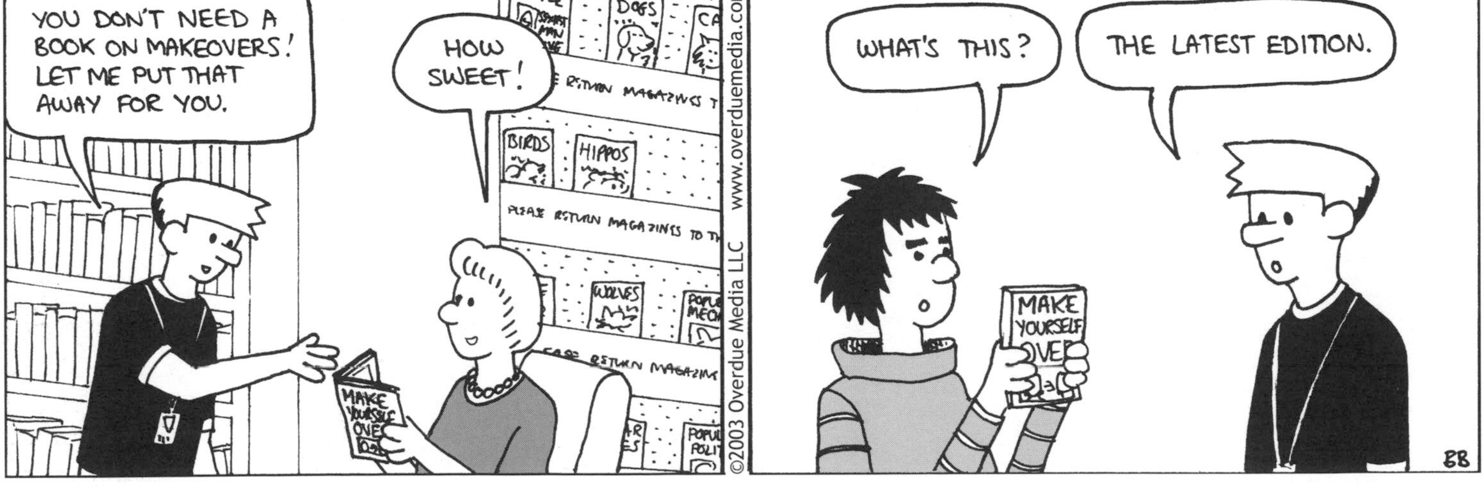
YOU DON'T NEED A BOOK ON MAKEOVERS! LET ME PUT THAT AWAY FOR YOU.
HOW SWEET!
PEOPLE
DOGS
BIRDS
HIPPOS
PLEASE RETURN MAGAZINES TO THE
WOLVES
MAKE YOURSELF OVER
©2003 Overdue Media LLC www.overduemedia.com
WHAT'S THIS?
THE LATEST EDITION.

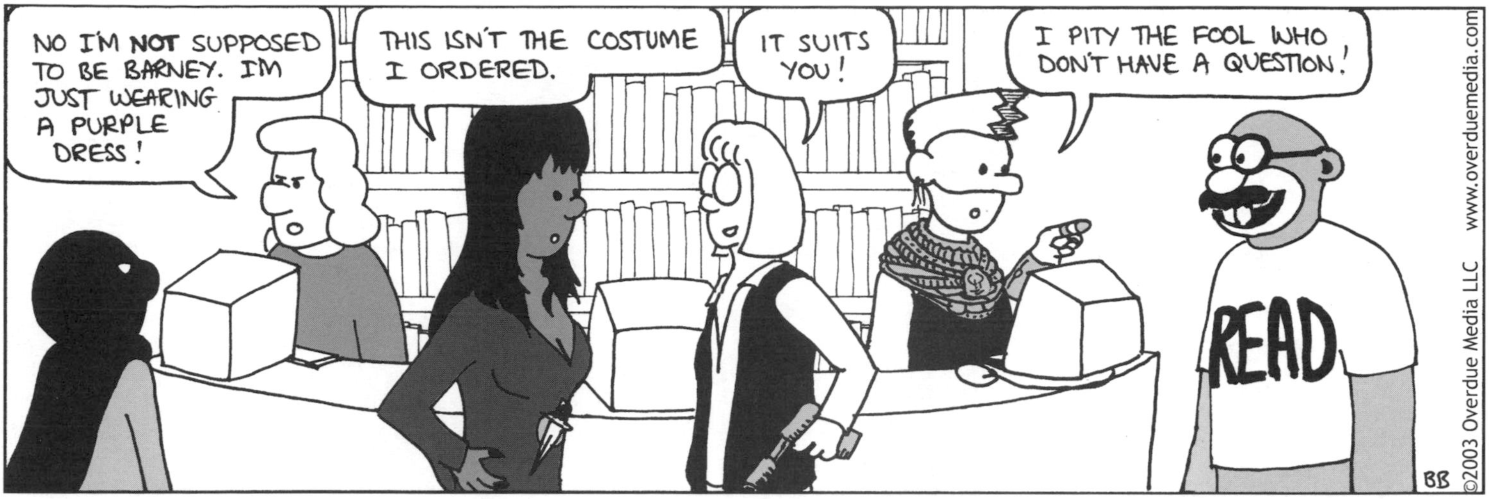
NO I'M NOT SUPPOSED TO BE BARNEY. I'M JUST WEARING A PURPLE DRESS!
THIS ISN'T THE COSTUME I ORDERED.
IT SUITS YOU!
I PITY THE FOOL WHO DON'T HAVE A QUESTION!
READ
BB
©2003 Overdue Media LLC www.overduemedia.com

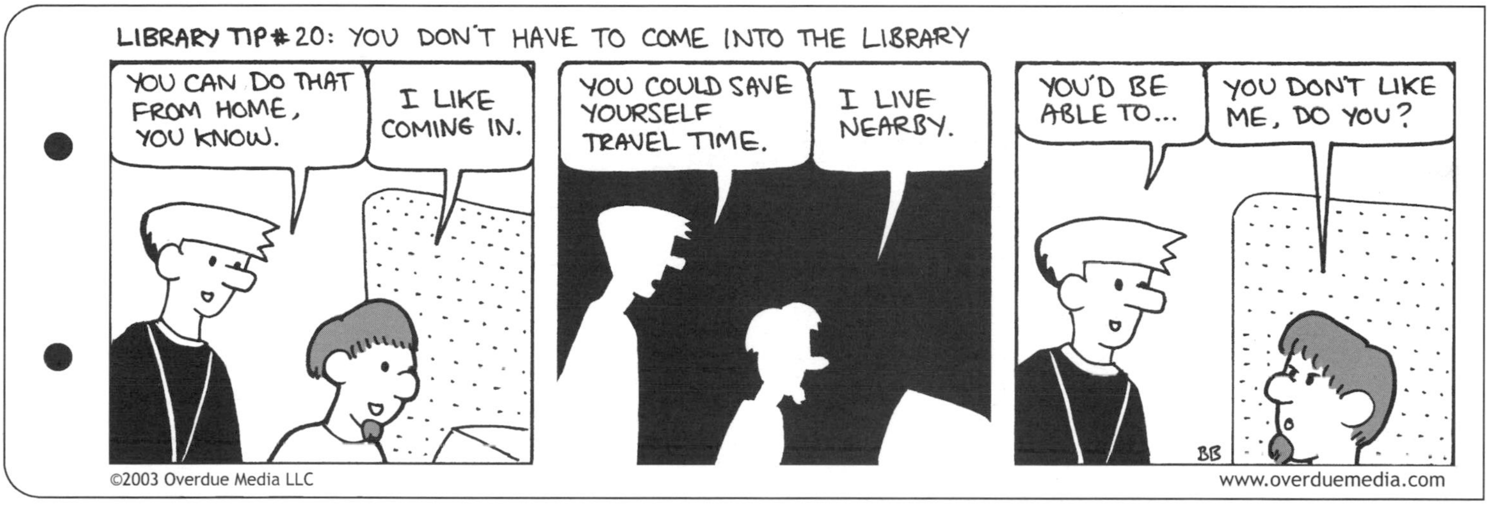
LIBRARY TIP #20: YOU DON'T HAVE TO COME INTO THE LIBRARY
YOU CAN DO THAT FROM HOME, YOU KNOW.
I LIKE COMING IN.
YOU COULD SAVE YOURSELF TRAVEL TIME.
I LIVE NEARBY.
YOU'D BE ABLE TO...
YOU DON'T LIKE ME, DO YOU?
BB
©2003 Overdue Media LLC
www.overduemedia.com

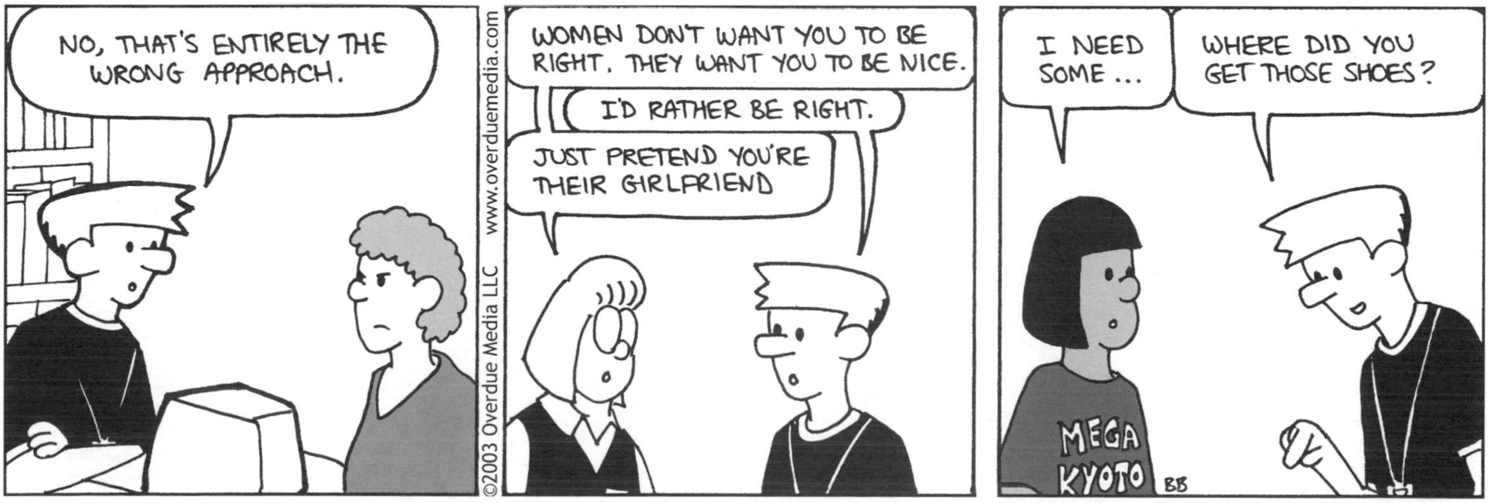
NO, THAT'S ENTIRELY THE WRONG APPROACH.
©2003 Overdue Media LLC www.overduemedia.com
WOMEN DON'T WANT YOU TO BE RIGHT. THEY WANT YOU TO BE NICE.
I'D RATHER BE RIGHT.
JUST PRETEND YOU'RE THEIR GIRLFRIEND
I NEED SOME ...
WHERE DID YOU GET THOSE SHOES?
MEGA KYOTO
BB

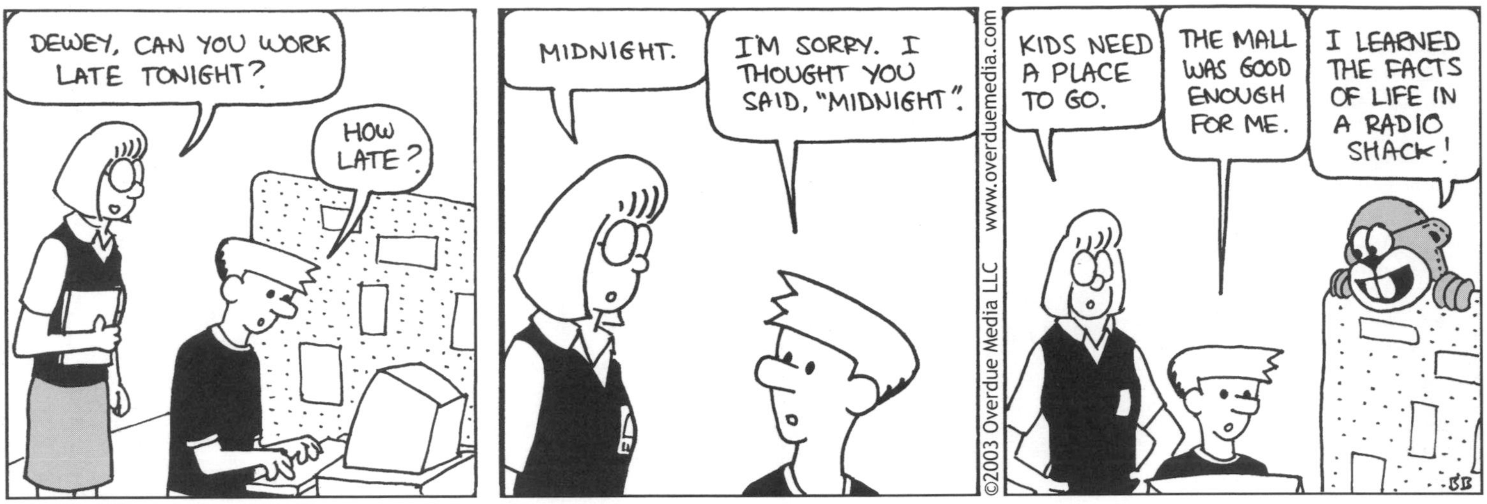
DEWEY, CAN YOU WORK LATE TONIGHT?
HOW LATE?
MIDNIGHT.
I'M SORRY. I THOUGHT YOU SAID, "MIDNIGHT".
©2003 Overdue Media LLC www.overduemedia.com
KIDS NEED A PLACE TO GO.
THE MALL WAS GOOD ENOUGH FOR ME.
I LEARNED THE FACTS OF LIFE IN A RADIO SHACK!
BB

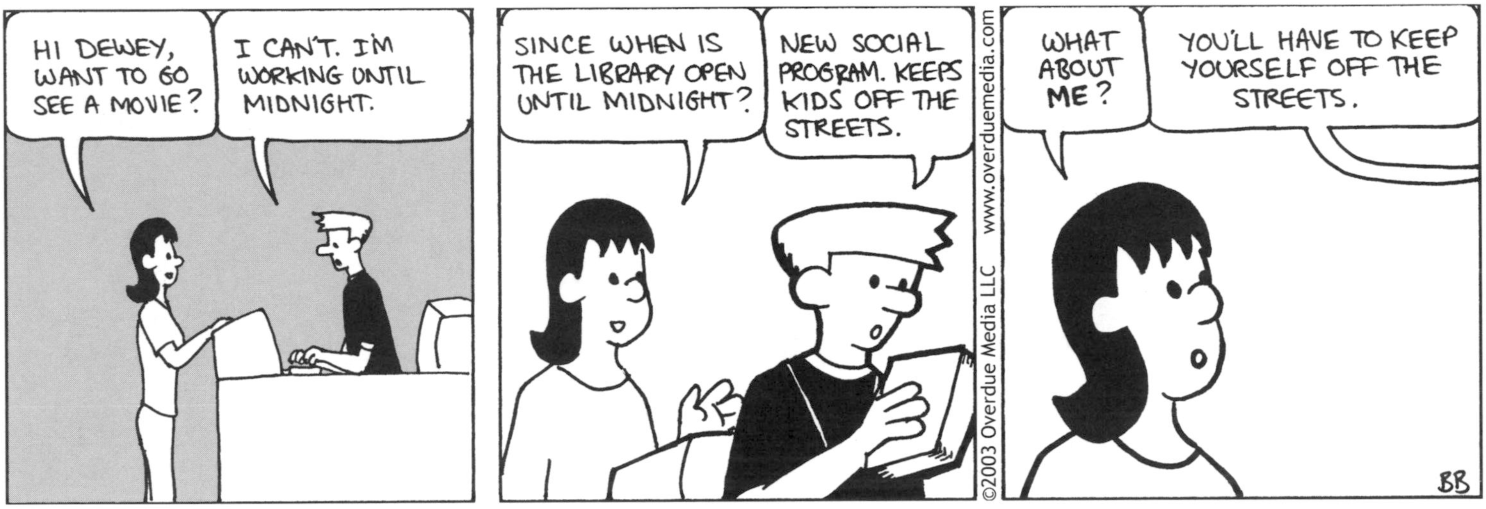
HI DEWEY, WANT TO GO SEE A MOVIE?
I CAN'T. I'M WORKING UNTIL MIDNIGHT.
SINCE WHEN IS THE LIBRARY OPEN UNTIL MIDNIGHT?
NEW SOCIAL PROGRAM. KEEPS KIDS OFF THE STREETS.
©2003 Overdue Media LLC www.overduemedia.com
WHAT ABOUT ME?
YOU'LL HAVE TO KEEP YOURSELF OFF THE STREETS.
BB

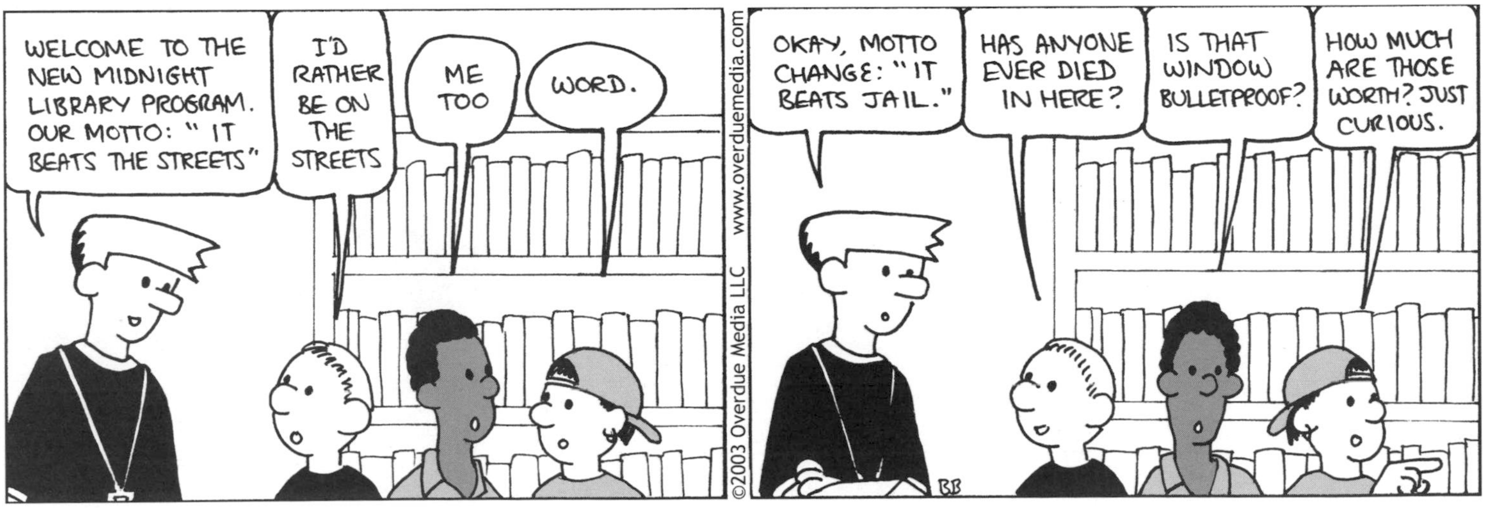
WELCOME TO THE NEW MIDNIGHT LIBRARY PROGRAM. OUR MOTTO: "IT BEATS THE STREETS"
I'D RATHER BE ON THE STREETS
ME TOO
WORD.
©2003 Overdue Media LLC www.overduemedia.com
OKAY, MOTTO CHANGE: "IT BEATS JAIL."
HAS ANYONE EVER DIED IN HERE?
IS THAT WINDOW BULLETPROOF?
HOW MUCH ARE THOSE WORTH? JUST CURIOUS.
BB

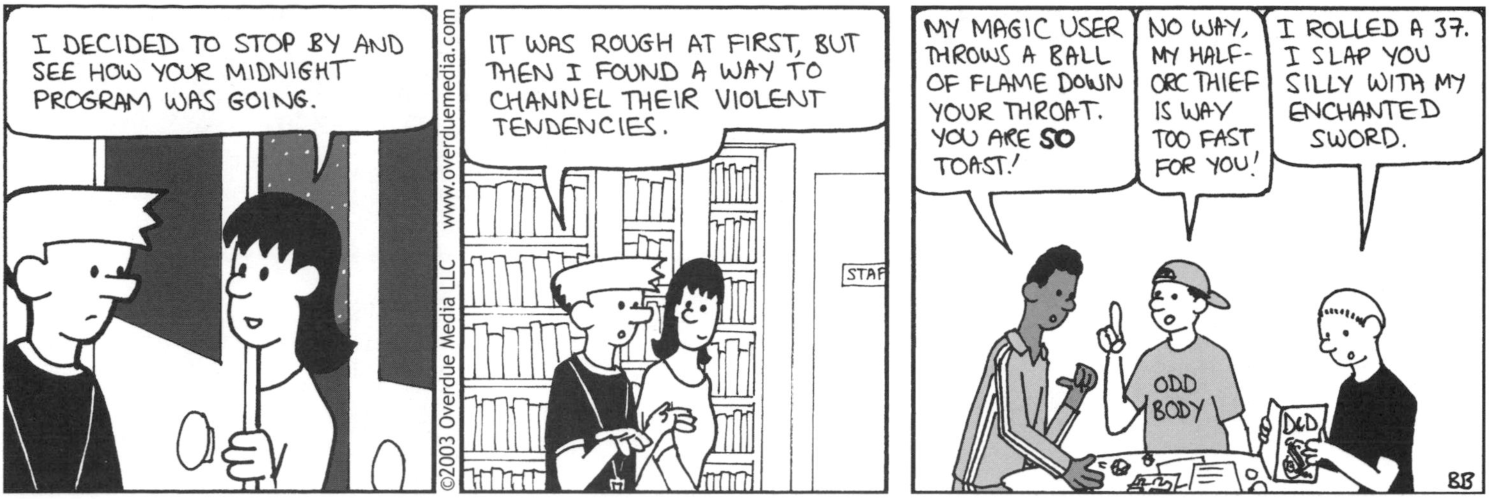
I DECIDED TO STOP BY AND SEE HOW YOUR MIDNIGHT PROGRAM WAS GOING.
©2003 Overdue Media LLC www.overduemedia.com
IT WAS ROUGH AT FIRST, BUT THEN I FOUND A WAY TO CHANNEL THEIR VIOLENT TENDENCIES.
MY MAGIC USER THROWS A BALL OF FLAME DOWN YOUR THROAT. YOU ARE **SO** TOAST!
NO WAY, MY HALF-ORC THIEF IS WAY TOO FAST FOR YOU!
I ROLLED A 37. I SLAP YOU SILLY WITH MY ENCHANTED SWORD.
ODD BODY
D&D
BB

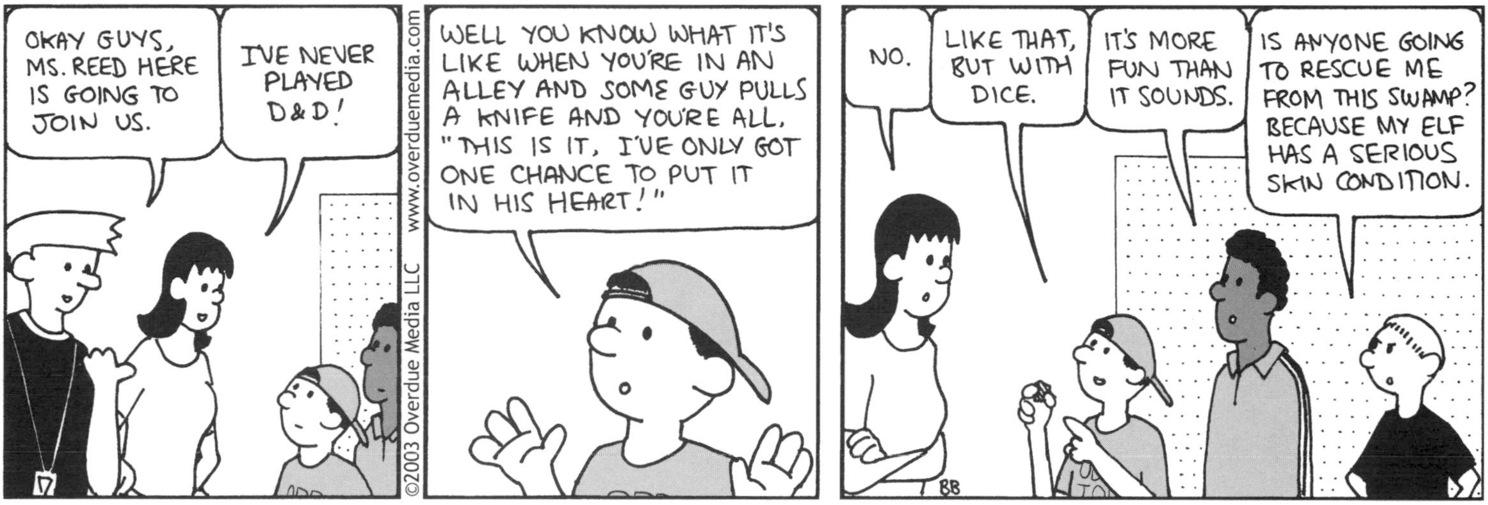
OKAY GUYS, MS. REED HERE IS GOING TO JOIN US.
I'VE NEVER PLAYED D&D!
©2003 Overdue Media LLC www.overduemedia.com
WELL YOU KNOW WHAT IT'S LIKE WHEN YOU'RE IN AN ALLEY AND SOME GUY PULLS A KNIFE AND YOU'RE ALL, "THIS IS IT, I'VE ONLY GOT ONE CHANCE TO PUT IT IN HIS HEART!"
NO.
LIKE THAT, BUT WITH DICE.
IT'S MORE FUN THAN IT SOUNDS.
IS ANYONE GOING TO RESCUE ME FROM THIS SWAMP? BECAUSE MY ELF HAS A SERIOUS SKIN CONDITION.
BB

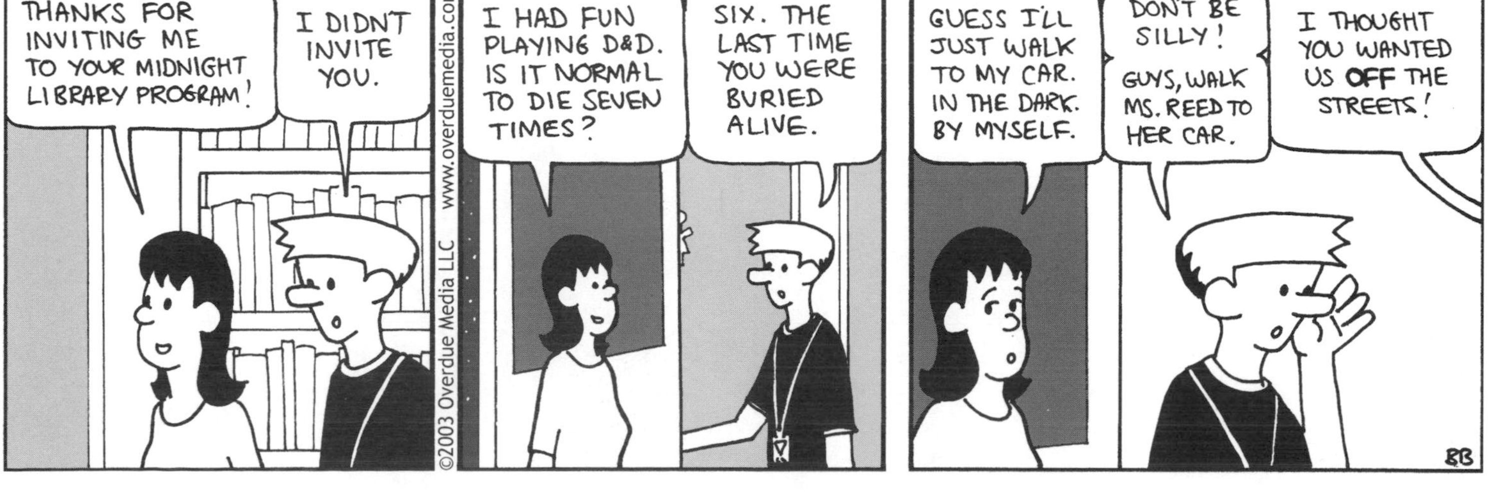
THANKS FOR INVITING ME TO YOUR MIDNIGHT LIBRARY PROGRAM!
I DIDN'T INVITE YOU.
©2003 Overdue Media LLC www.overduemedia.com
I HAD FUN PLAYING D&D. IS IT NORMAL TO DIE SEVEN TIMES?
SIX. THE LAST TIME YOU WERE BURIED ALIVE.
GUESS I'LL JUST WALK TO MY CAR. IN THE DARK. BY MYSELF.
DON'T BE SILLY!
GUYS, WALK MS. REED TO HER CAR.
I THOUGHT YOU WANTED US **OFF** THE STREETS!
BB

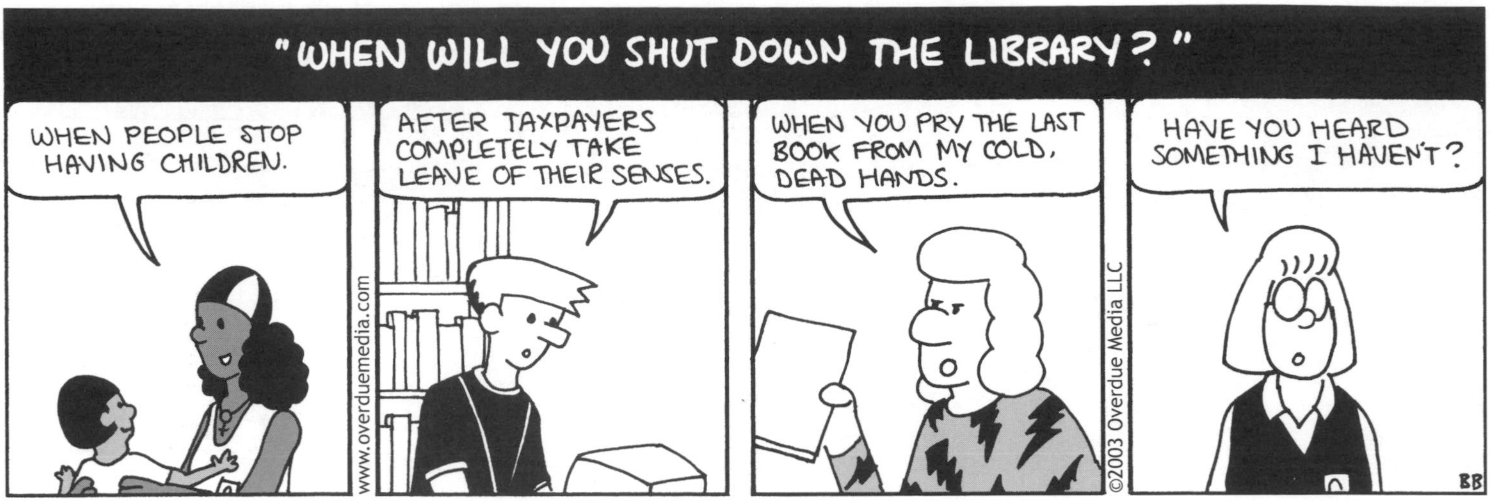
"WHEN WILL YOU SHUT DOWN THE LIBRARY?"
WHEN PEOPLE STOP HAVING CHILDREN.
www.overduemedia.com
AFTER TAXPAYERS COMPLETELY TAKE LEAVE OF THEIR SENSES.
WHEN YOU PRY THE LAST BOOK FROM MY COLD, DEAD HANDS.
©2003 Overdue Media LLC
HAVE YOU HEARD SOMETHING I HAVEN'T?
BB

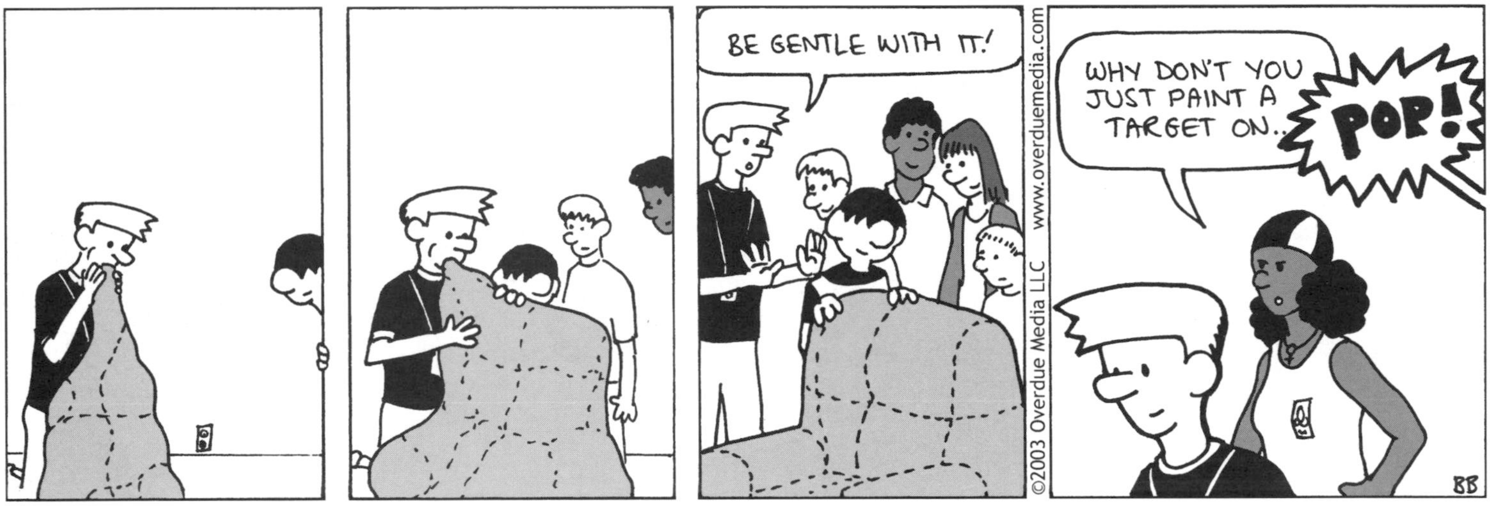
BE GENTLE WITH IT!
©2003 Overdue Media LLC www.overduemedia.com
WHY DON'T YOU JUST PAINT A TARGET ON..
POP!
BB

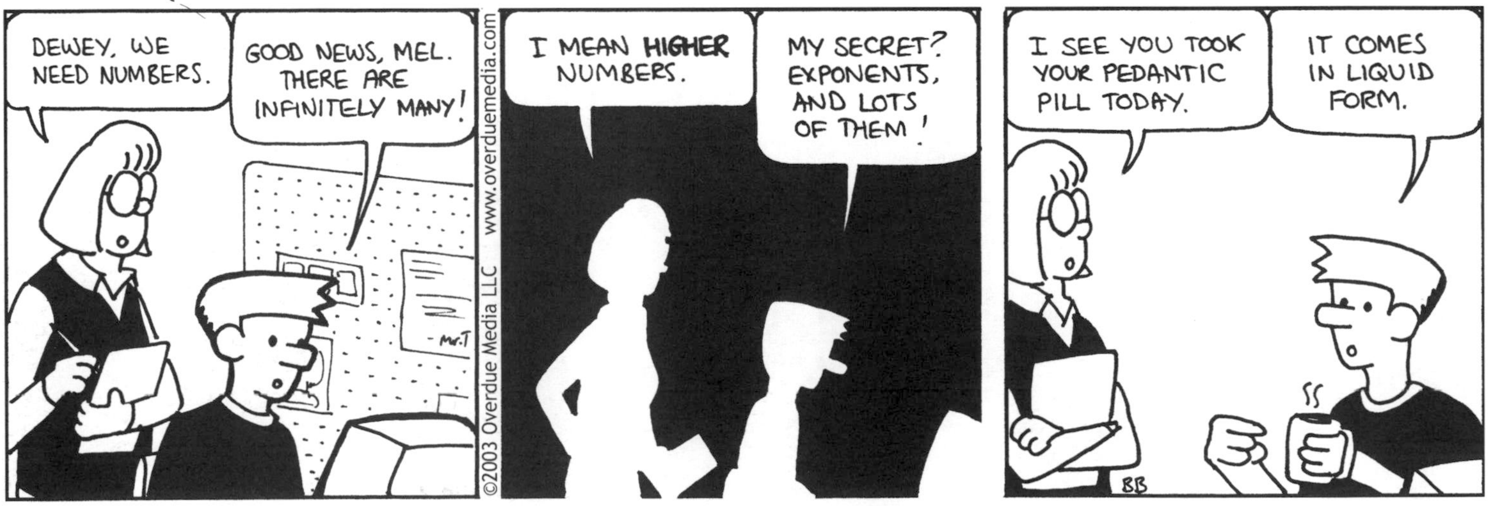
DEWEY, WE NEED NUMBERS.
GOOD NEWS, MEL. THERE ARE INFINITELY MANY!
©2003 Overdue Media LLC www.overduemedia.com
I MEAN HIGHER NUMBERS.
MY SECRET? EXPONENTS, AND LOTS OF THEM!
I SEE YOU TOOK YOUR PEDANTIC PILL TODAY.
IT COMES IN LIQUID FORM.
BB

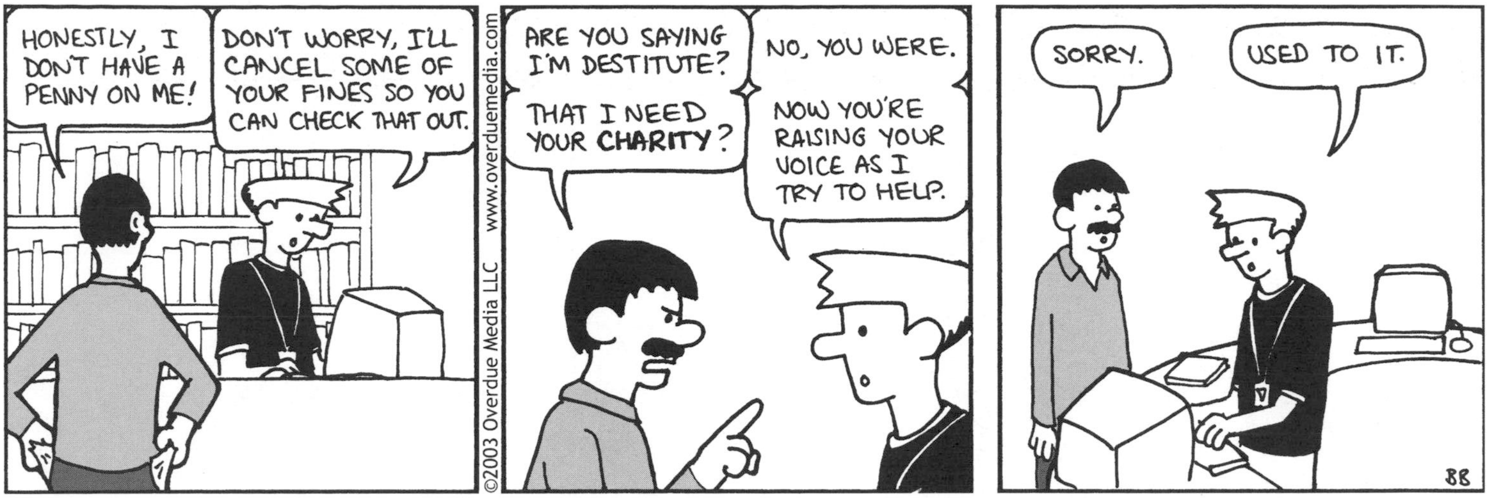
HONESTLY, I DON'T HAVE A PENNY ON ME!
DON'T WORRY, I'LL CANCEL SOME OF YOUR FINES SO YOU CAN CHECK THAT OUT.
©2003 Overdue Media LLC www.overduemedia.com
ARE YOU SAYING I'M DESTITUTE?
THAT I NEED YOUR CHARITY?
NO, YOU WERE.
NOW YOU'RE RAISING YOUR VOICE AS I TRY TO HELP.
SORRY.
USED TO IT.
BB

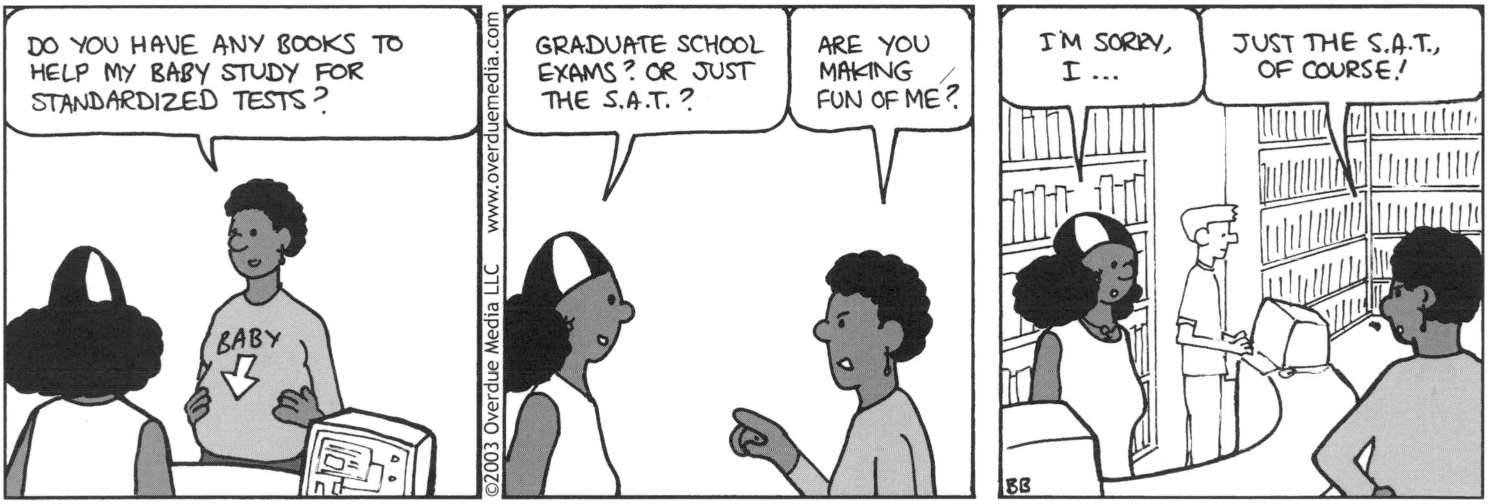
DO YOU HAVE ANY BOOKS TO HELP MY BABY STUDY FOR STANDARDIZED TESTS?
BABY
©2003 Overdue Media LLC www.overduemedia.com
GRADUATE SCHOOL EXAMS? OR JUST THE S.A.T.?
ARE YOU MAKING FUN OF ME?
I'M SORRY, I...
JUST THE S.A.T., OF COURSE!
BB

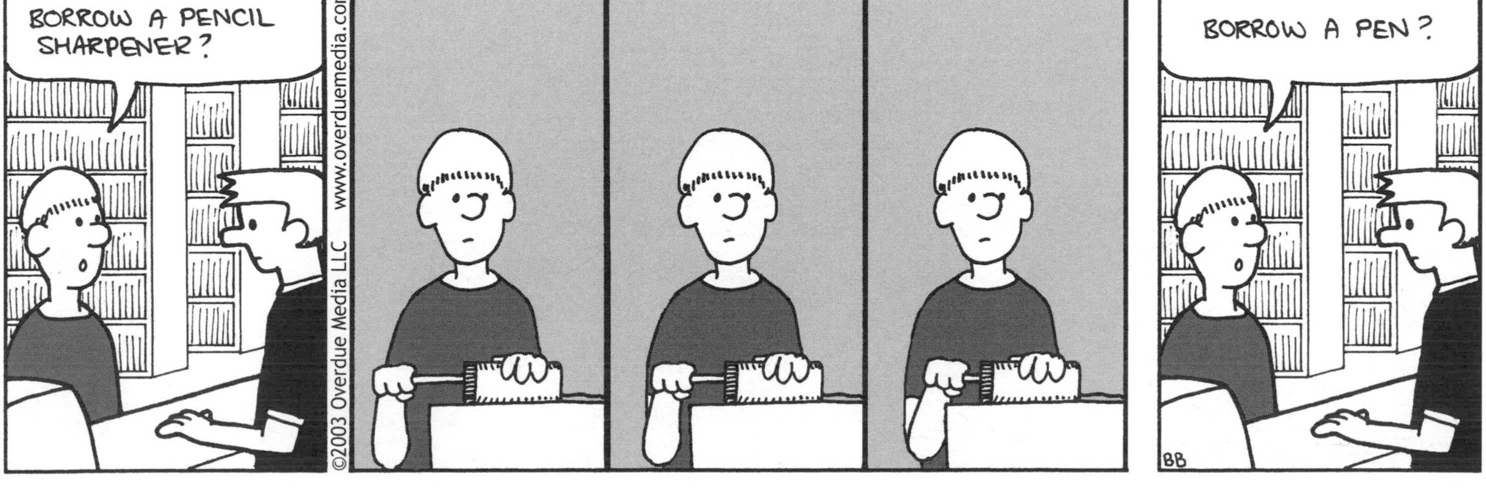
BORROW A PENCIL SHARPENER?
©2003 Overdue Media LLC www.overduemedia.com
BORROW A PEN?
BB

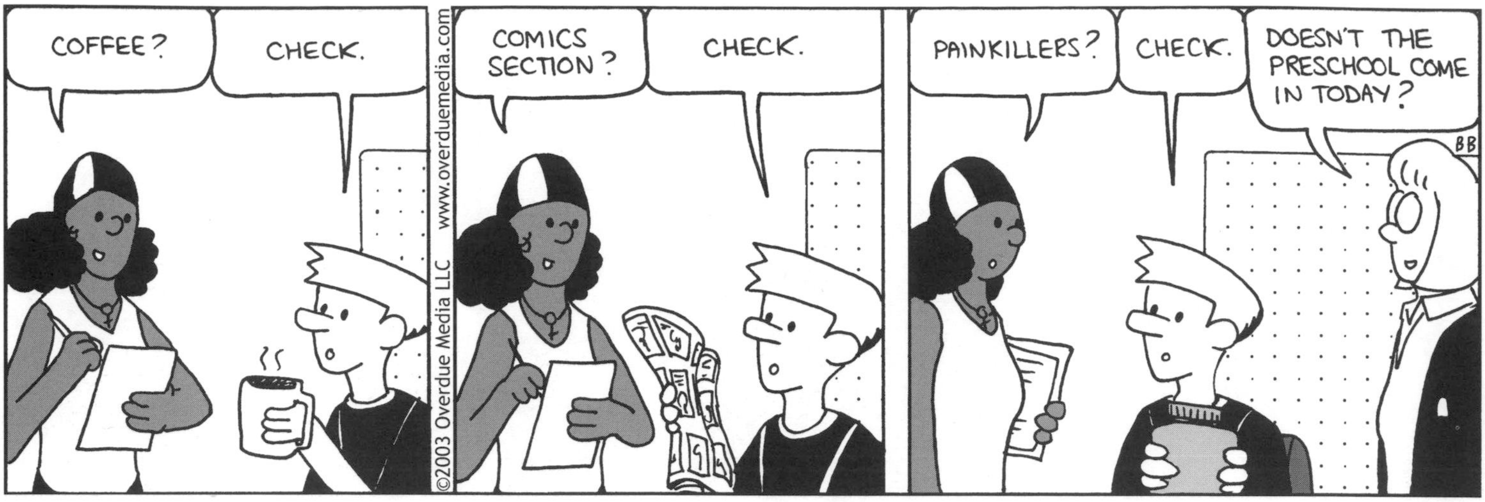
COFFEE?
CHECK.
©2003 Overdue Media LLC www.overduemedia.com
COMICS SECTION?
CHECK.
PAINKILLERS?
CHECK.
DOESN'T THE PRESCHOOL COME IN TODAY?
BB

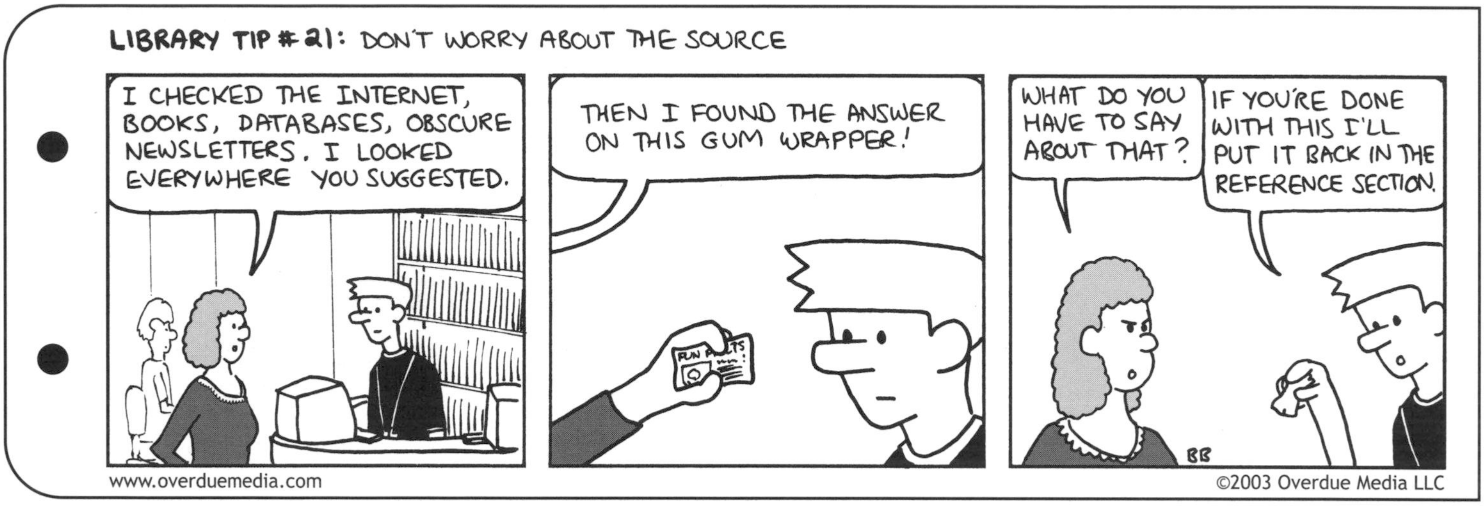
LIBRARY TIP #21: DON'T WORRY ABOUT THE SOURCE
I CHECKED THE INTERNET, BOOKS, DATABASES, OBSCURE NEWSLETTERS. I LOOKED EVERYWHERE YOU SUGGESTED.
THEN I FOUND THE ANSWER ON THIS GUM WRAPPER!
WHAT DO YOU HAVE TO SAY ABOUT THAT?
IF YOU'RE DONE WITH THIS I'LL PUT IT BACK IN THE REFERENCE SECTION.
BB
www.overduemedia.com
©2003 Overdue Media LLC

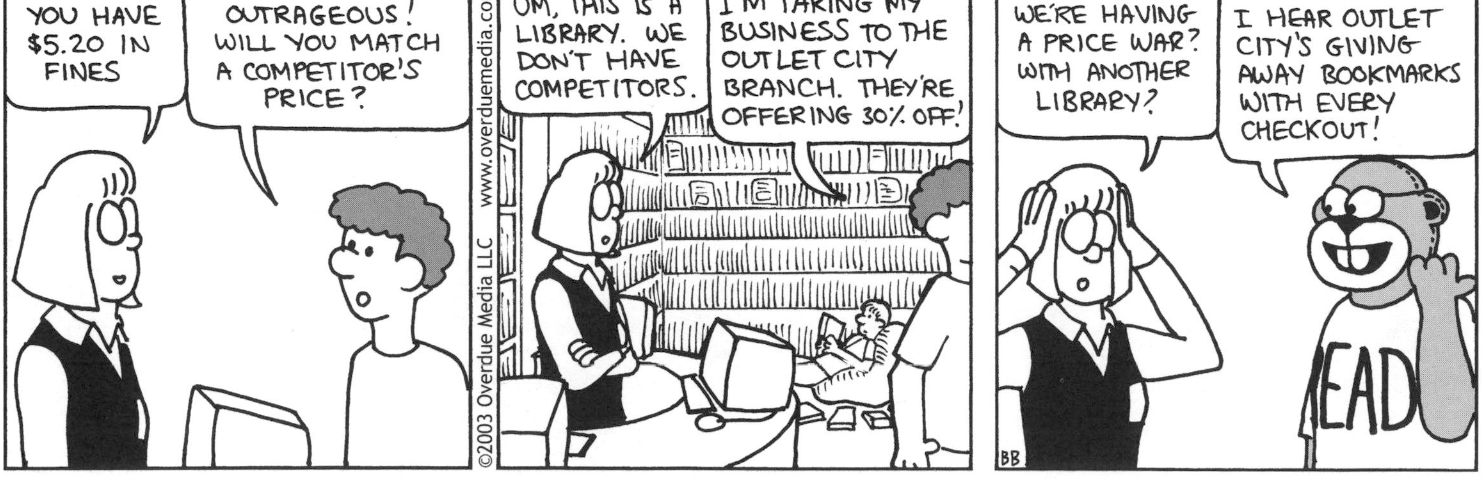
YOU HAVE $5.20 IN FINES
OUTRAGEOUS! WILL YOU MATCH A COMPETITOR'S PRICE?
©2003 Overdue Media LLC www.overduemedia.com
UM, THIS IS A LIBRARY. WE DON'T HAVE COMPETITORS.
I'M TAKING MY BUSINESS TO THE OUTLET CITY BRANCH. THEY'RE OFFERING 30% OFF!
WE'RE HAVING A PRICE WAR? WITH ANOTHER LIBRARY?
I HEAR OUTLET CITY'S GIVING AWAY BOOKMARKS WITH EVERY CHECKOUT!
EAD
BB

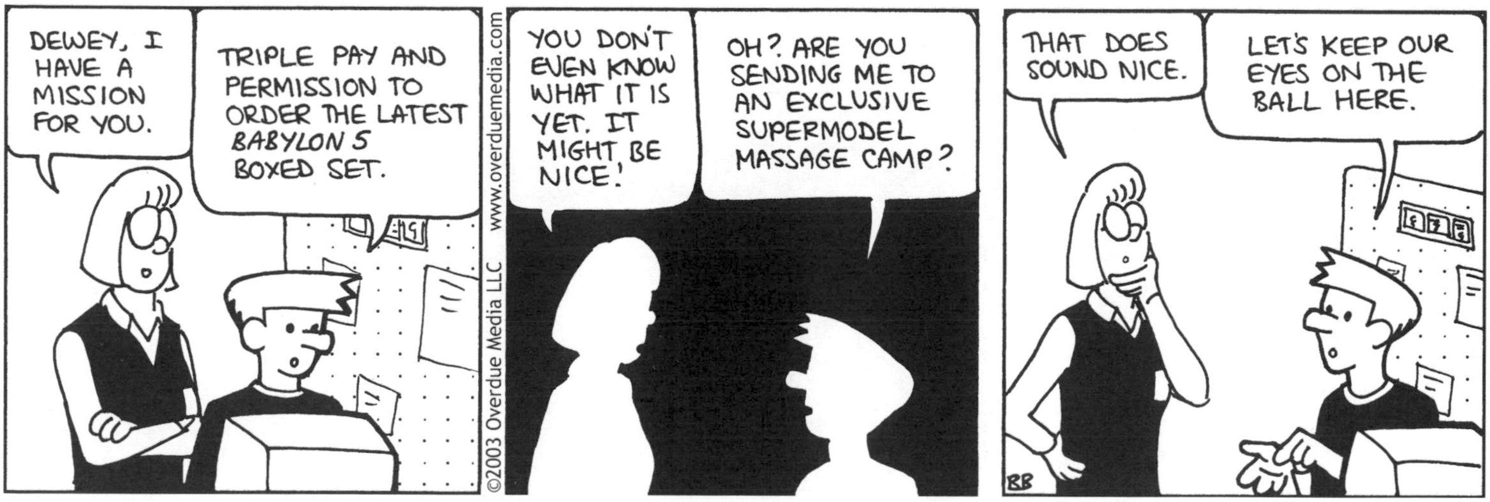
DEWEY, I HAVE A MISSION FOR YOU.
TRIPLE PAY AND PERMISSION TO ORDER THE LATEST *BABYLON 5* BOXED SET.
www.overduemedia.com
©2003 Overdue Media LLC
YOU DON'T EVEN KNOW WHAT IT IS YET. IT MIGHT BE NICE!
OH? ARE YOU SENDING ME TO AN EXCLUSIVE SUPERMODEL MASSAGE CAMP?
THAT DOES SOUND NICE.
LET'S KEEP OUR EYES ON THE BALL HERE.
BB

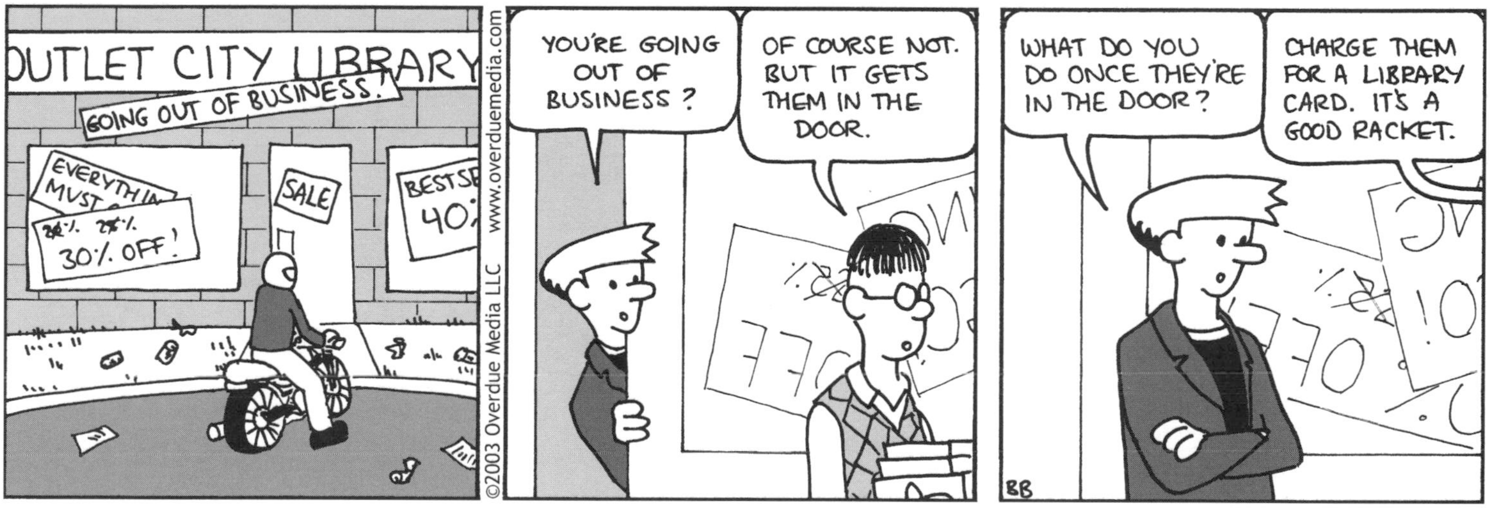
OUTLET CITY LIBRARY
GOING OUT OF BUSINESS!
SALE
30% OFF!
www.overduemedia.com
©2003 Overdue Media LLC
YOU'RE GOING OUT OF BUSINESS?
OF COURSE NOT. BUT IT GETS THEM IN THE DOOR.
WHAT DO YOU DO ONCE THEY'RE IN THE DOOR?
CHARGE THEM FOR A LIBRARY CARD. IT'S A GOOD RACKET.
BB

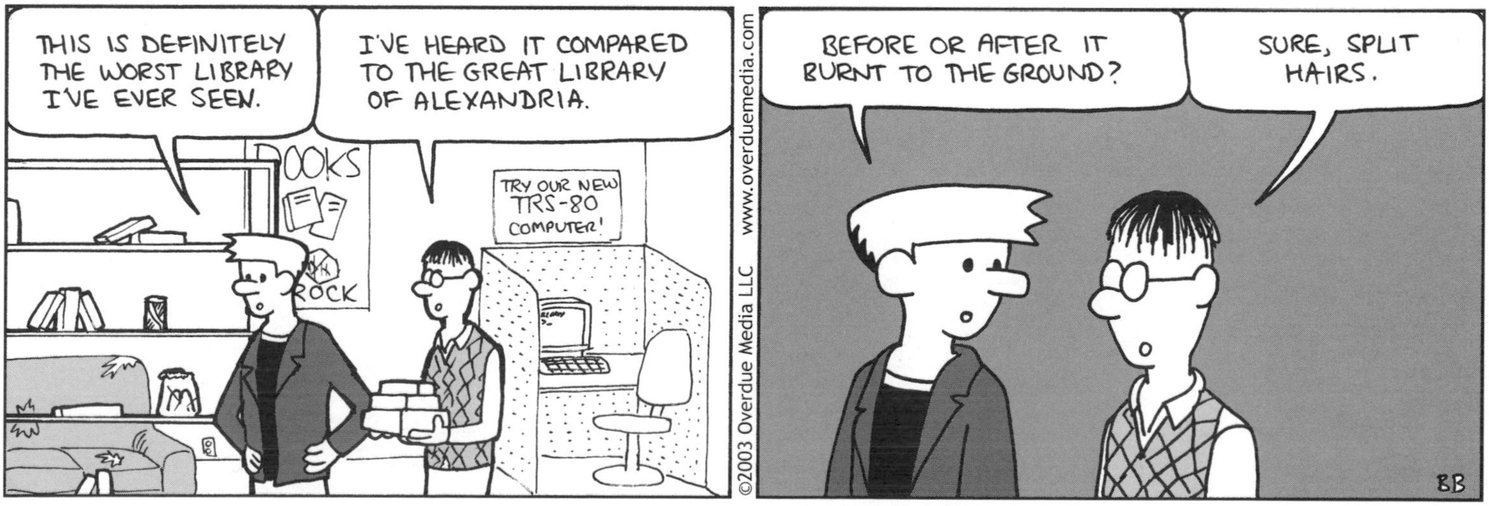
THIS IS DEFINITELY THE WORST LIBRARY I'VE EVER SEEN.
I'VE HEARD IT COMPARED TO THE GREAT LIBRARY OF ALEXANDRIA.
TRY OUR NEW TRS-80 COMPUTER!
www.overduemedia.com
©2003 Overdue Media LLC
BEFORE OR AFTER IT BURNT TO THE GROUND?
SURE, SPLIT HAIRS.
BB

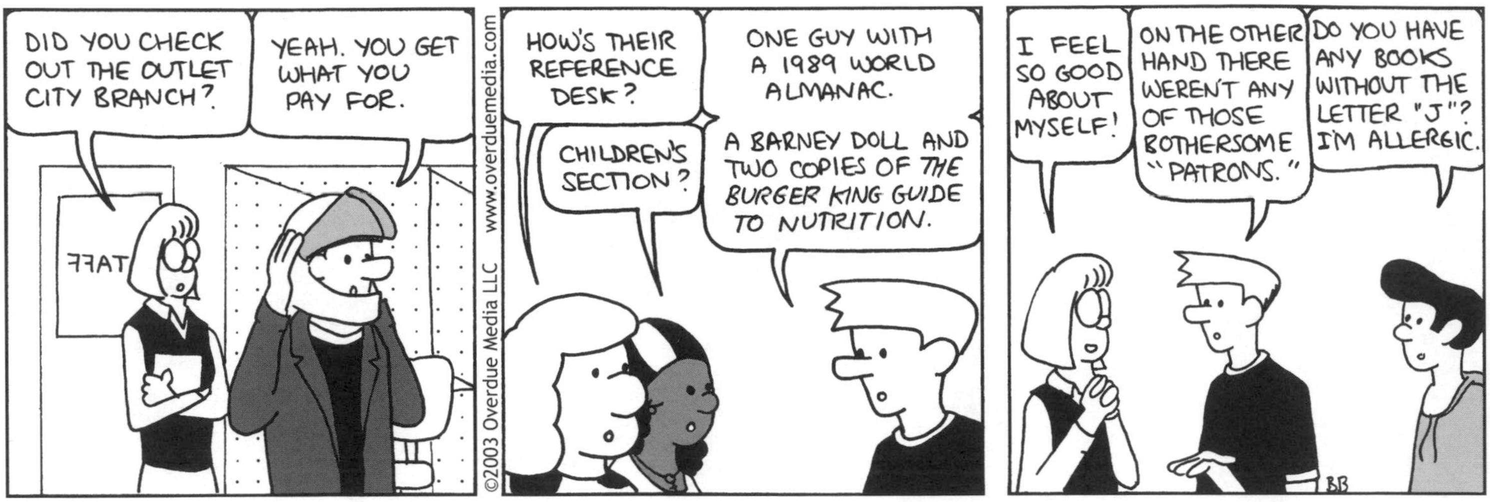
DID YOU CHECK OUT THE OUTLET CITY BRANCH?
YEAH. YOU GET WHAT YOU PAY FOR.
©2003 Overdue Media LLC www.overduemedia.com
HOW'S THEIR REFERENCE DESK?
ONE GUY WITH A 1989 WORLD ALMANAC.
CHILDREN'S SECTION?
A BARNEY DOLL AND TWO COPIES OF *THE BURGER KING GUIDE TO NUTRITION*.
I FEEL SO GOOD ABOUT MYSELF!
ON THE OTHER HAND THERE WEREN'T ANY OF THOSE BOTHERSOME "PATRONS."
DO YOU HAVE ANY BOOKS WITHOUT THE LETTER "J"? I'M ALLERGIC.
BB

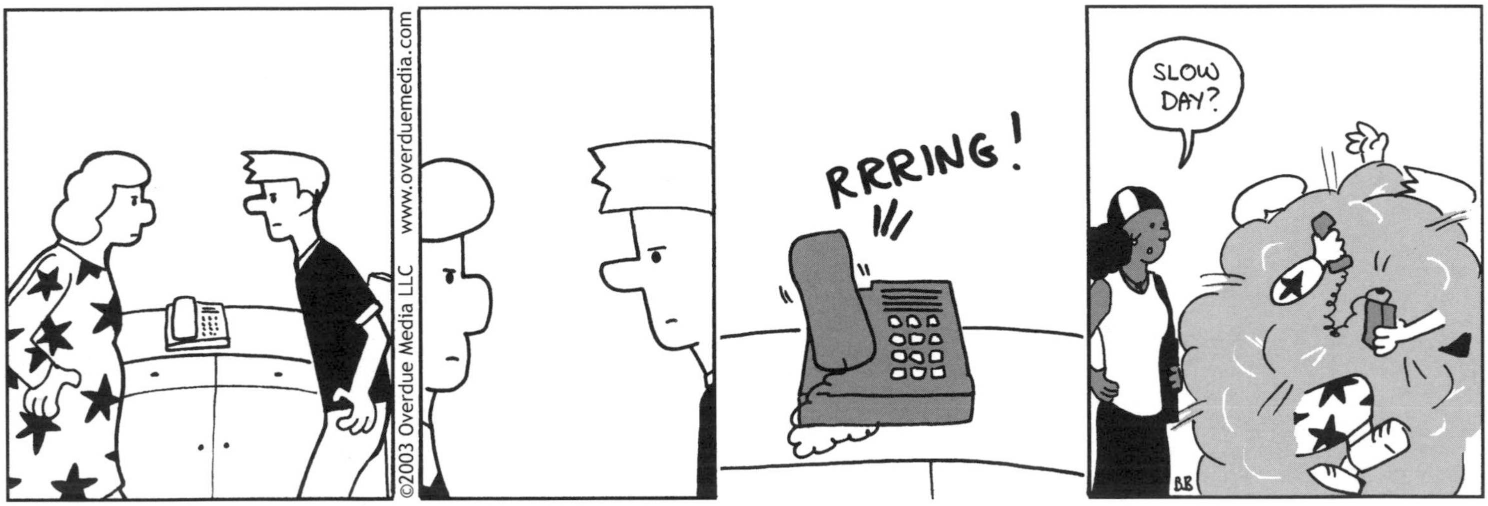
©2003 Overdue Media LLC www.overduemedia.com
RRRING!
SLOW DAY?
BB

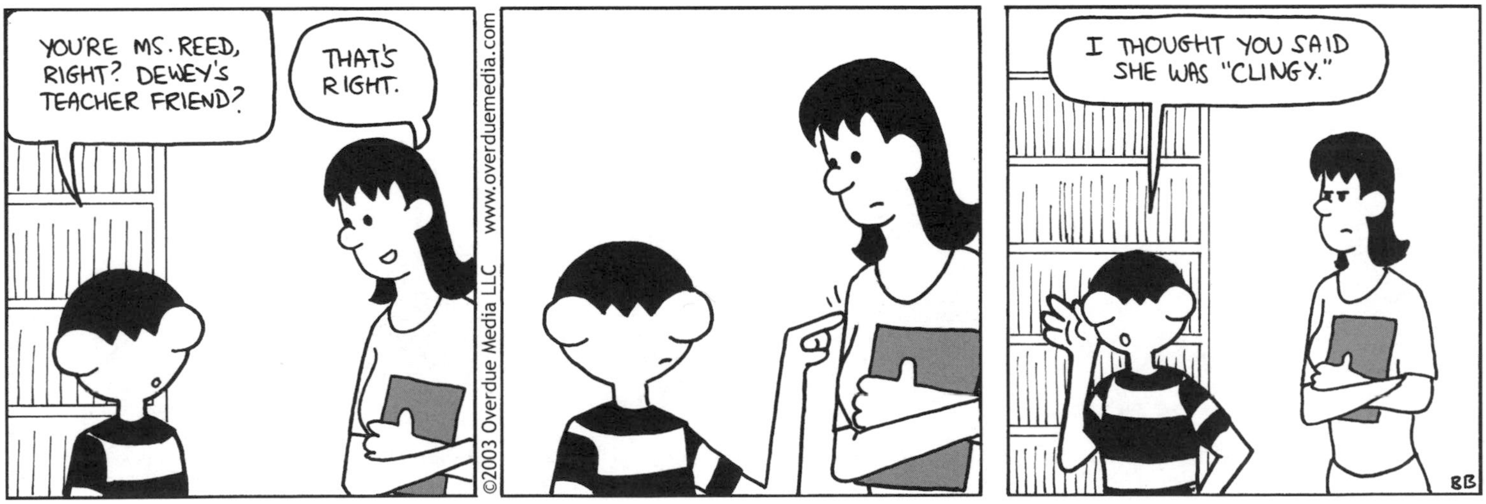
YOU'RE MS. REED, RIGHT? DEWEY'S TEACHER FRIEND?
THAT'S RIGHT.
©2003 Overdue Media LLC www.overduemedia.com
I THOUGHT YOU SAID SHE WAS "CLINGY."
BB

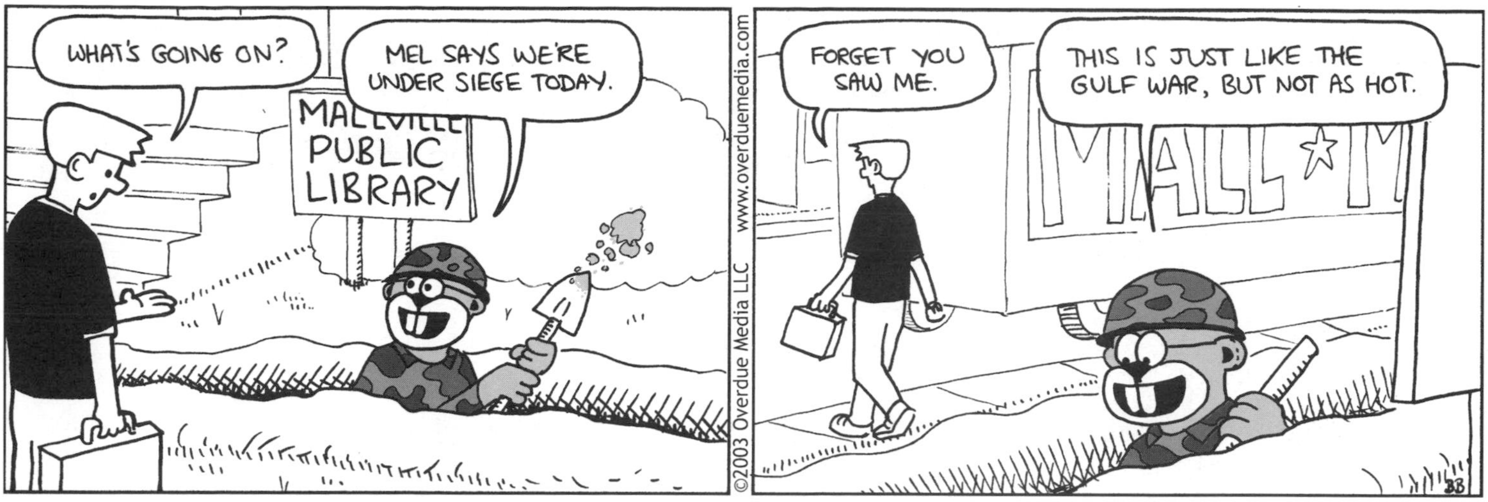
WHAT'S GOING ON?
MEL SAYS WE'RE UNDER SIEGE TODAY.
MALLVILLE PUBLIC LIBRARY
©2003 Overdue Media LLC www.overduemedia.com
FORGET YOU SAW ME.
THIS IS JUST LIKE THE GULF WAR, BUT NOT AS HOT.
BB

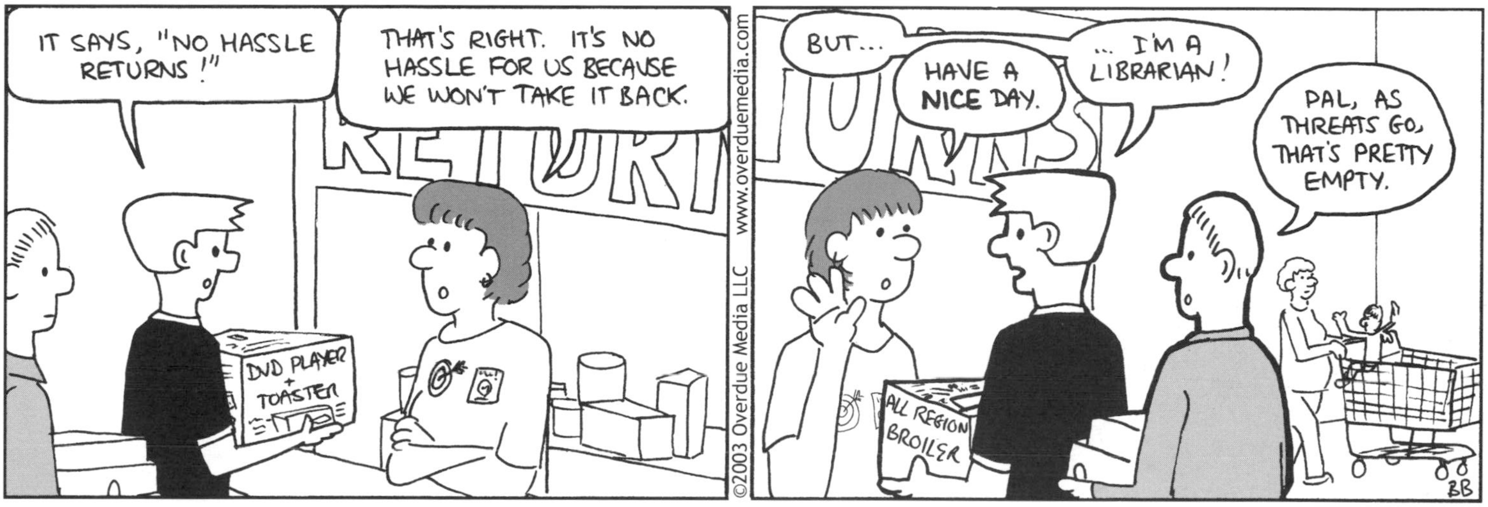
IT SAYS, "NO HASSLE RETURNS!"
THAT'S RIGHT. IT'S NO HASSLE FOR US BECAUSE WE WON'T TAKE IT BACK.
DVD PLAYER + TOASTER
©2003 Overdue Media LLC www.overduemedia.com
BUT...
HAVE A NICE DAY.
... I'M A LIBRARIAN!
PAL, AS THREATS GO, THAT'S PRETTY EMPTY.
ALL REGION BROILER
BB

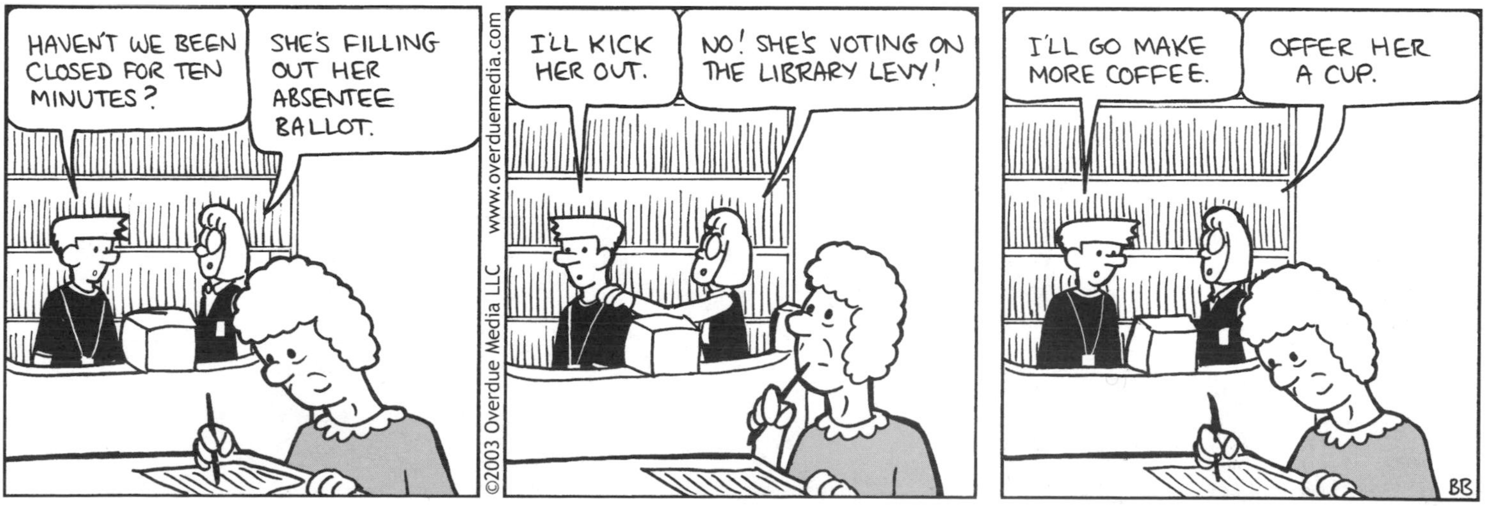
HAVEN'T WE BEEN CLOSED FOR TEN MINUTES?
SHE'S FILLING OUT HER ABSENTEE BALLOT.
©2003 Overdue Media LLC www.overduemedia.com
I'LL KICK HER OUT.
NO! SHE'S VOTING ON THE LIBRARY LEVY!
I'LL GO MAKE MORE COFFEE.
OFFER HER A CUP.
BB

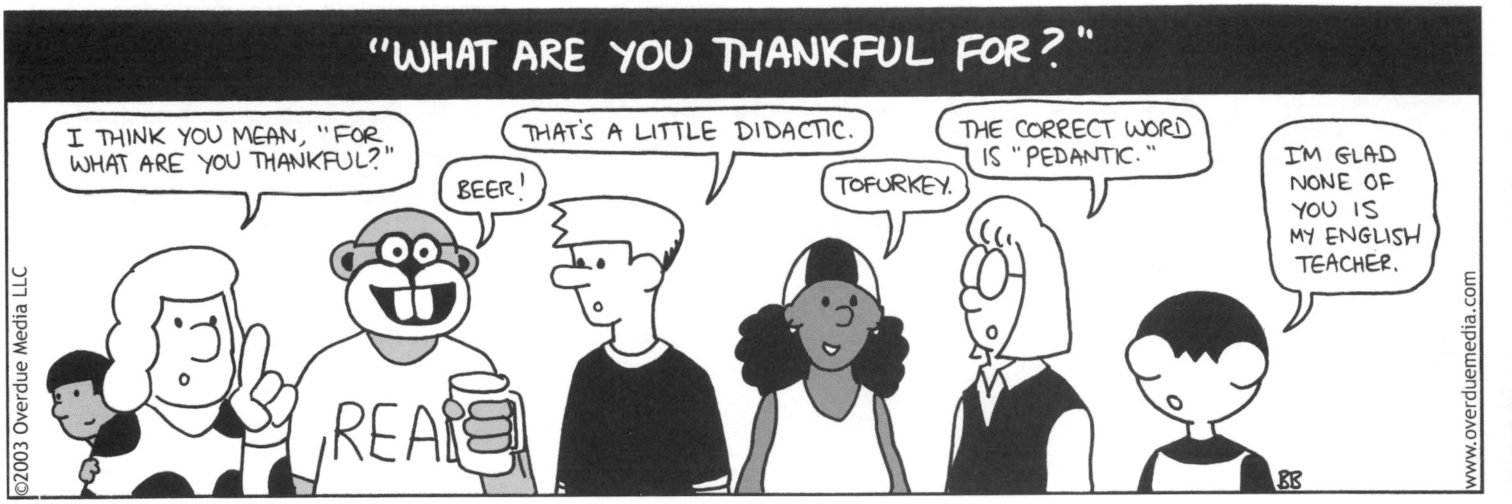
"WHAT ARE YOU THANKFUL FOR?"
I THINK YOU MEAN, "FOR WHAT ARE YOU THANKFUL?"
BEER!
THAT'S A LITTLE DIDACTIC.
TOFURKEY.
THE CORRECT WORD IS "PEDANTIC."
I'M GLAD NONE OF YOU IS MY ENGLISH TEACHER.
REAL
©2003 Overdue Media LLC
www.overduemedia.com

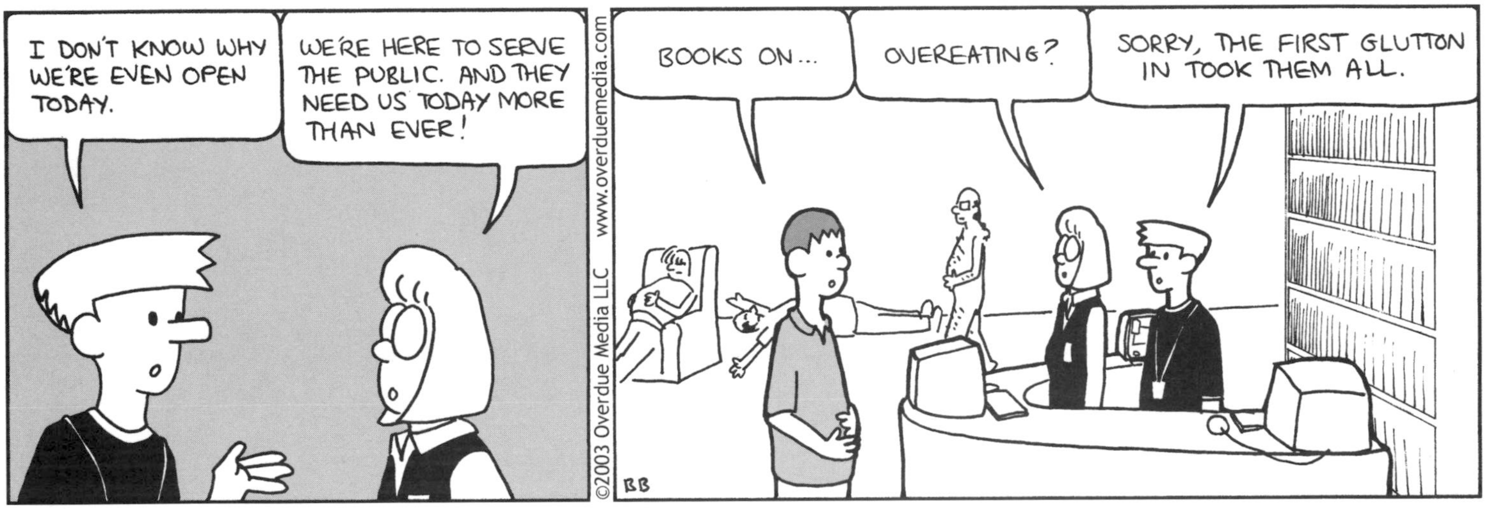
I DON'T KNOW WHY WE'RE EVEN OPEN TODAY.
WE'RE HERE TO SERVE THE PUBLIC. AND THEY NEED US TODAY MORE THAN EVER!
©2003 Overdue Media LLC
www.overduemedia.com
BOOKS ON...
OVEREATING?
SORRY, THE FIRST GLUTTON IN TOOK THEM ALL.

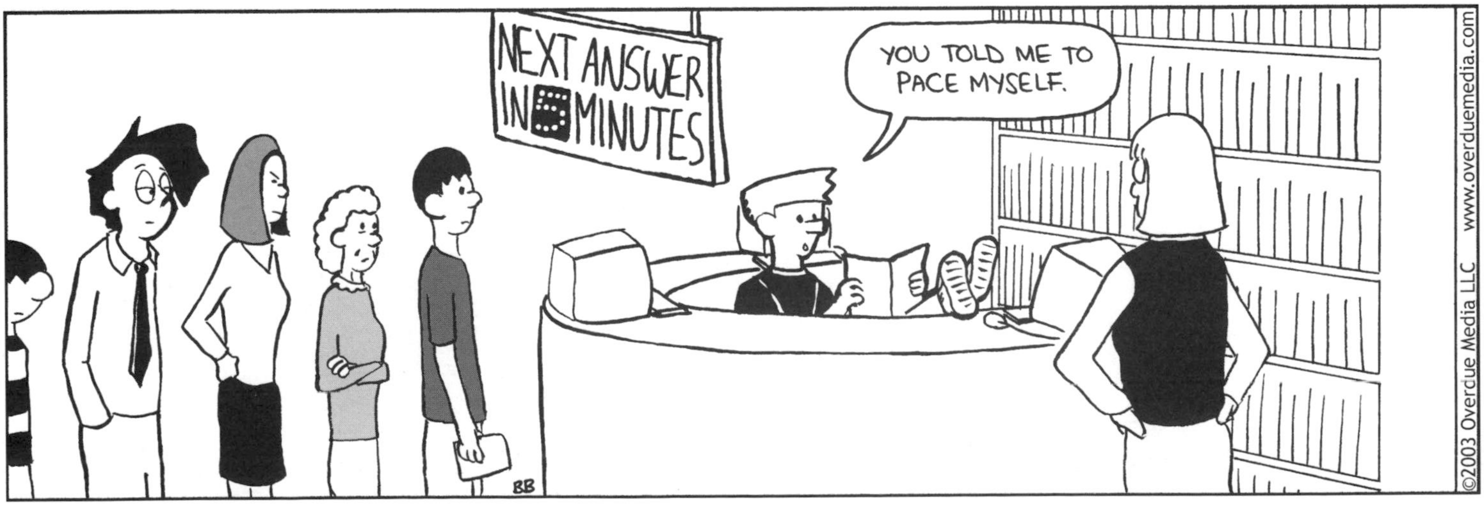
NEXT ANSWER IN 5 MINUTES
YOU TOLD ME TO PACE MYSELF.
©2003 Overdue Media LLC
www.overduemedia.com

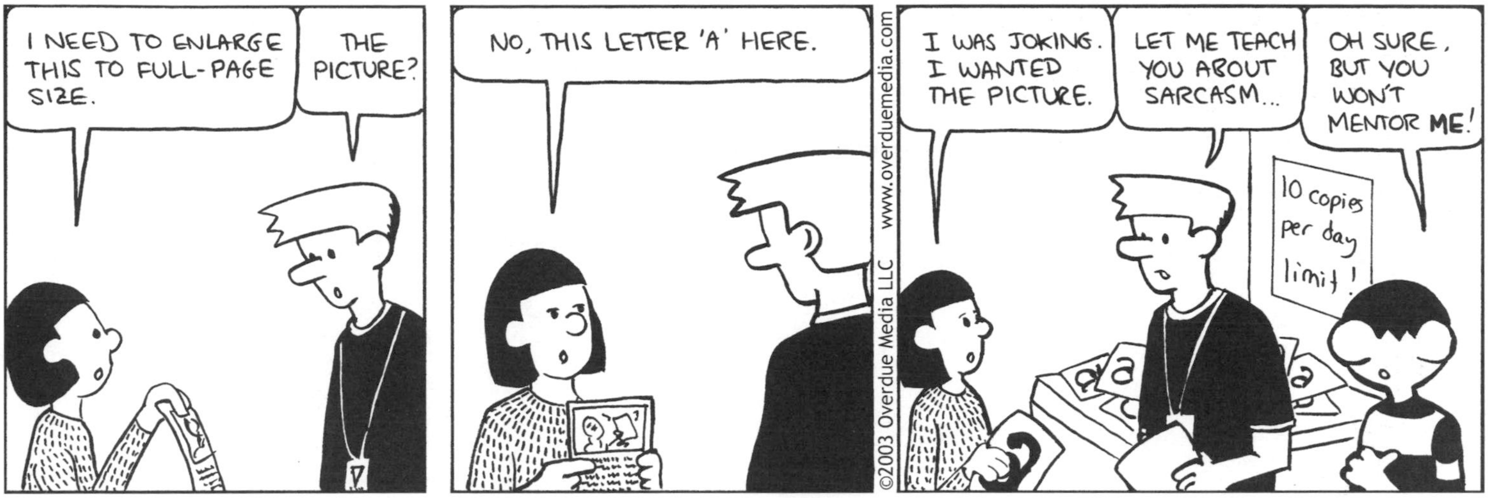
I NEED TO ENLARGE THIS TO FULL-PAGE SIZE.
THE PICTURE?
NO, THIS LETTER 'A' HERE.
I WAS JOKING. I WANTED THE PICTURE.
LET ME TEACH YOU ABOUT SARCASM...
OH SURE, BUT YOU WON'T MENTOR ME!
10 copies per day limit!
©2003 Overdue Media LLC www.overduemedia.com

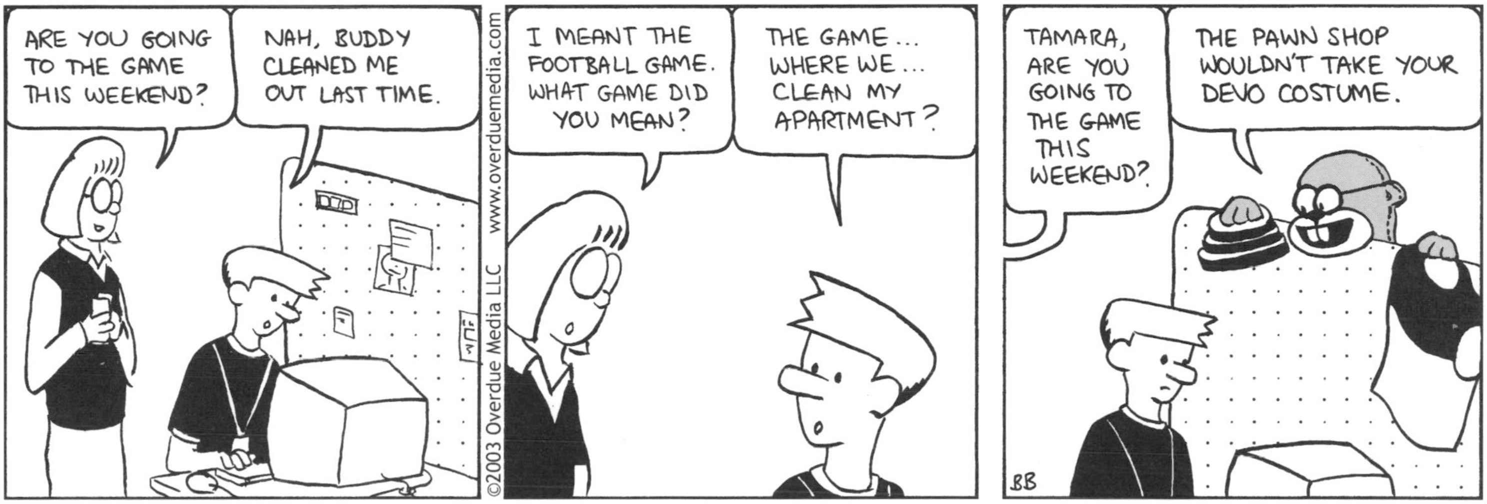
ARE YOU GOING TO THE GAME THIS WEEKEND?
NAH, BUDDY CLEANED ME OUT LAST TIME.
I MEANT THE FOOTBALL GAME. WHAT GAME DID YOU MEAN?
THE GAME... WHERE WE... CLEAN MY APARTMENT?
TAMARA, ARE YOU GOING TO THE GAME THIS WEEKEND?
THE PAWN SHOP WOULDN'T TAKE YOUR DEVO COSTUME.
BB
©2003 Overdue Media LLC www.overduemedia.com

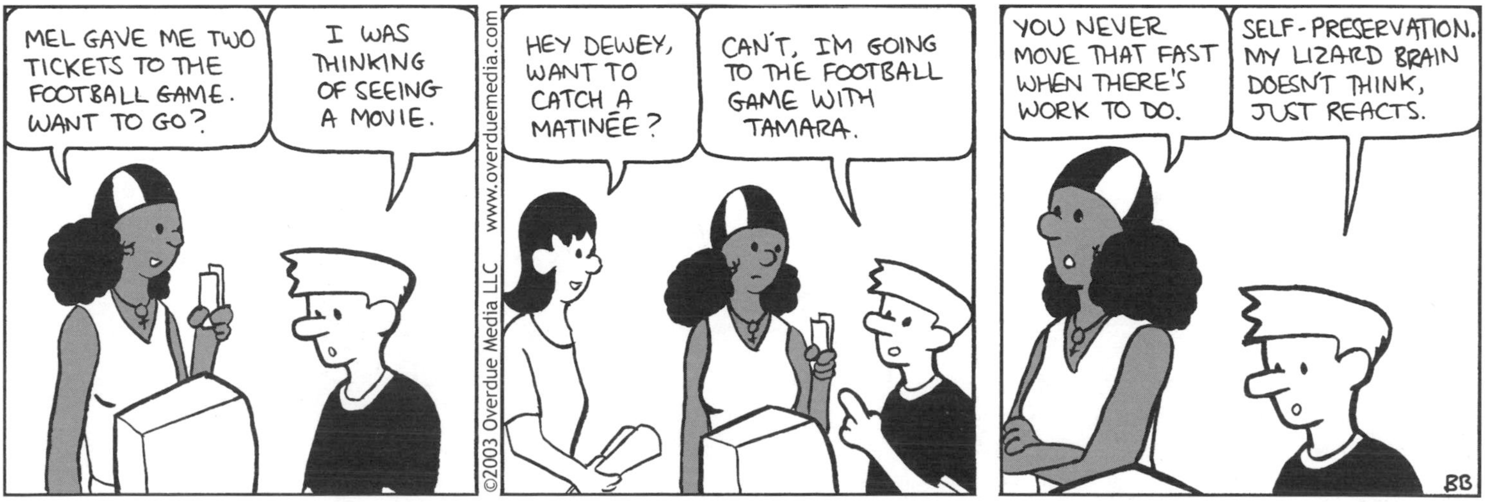
MEL GAVE ME TWO TICKETS TO THE FOOTBALL GAME. WANT TO GO?
I WAS THINKING OF SEEING A MOVIE.
HEY DEWEY, WANT TO CATCH A MATINÉE?
CAN'T, I'M GOING TO THE FOOTBALL GAME WITH TAMARA.
YOU NEVER MOVE THAT FAST WHEN THERE'S WORK TO DO.
SELF-PRESERVATION. MY LIZARD BRAIN DOESN'T THINK, JUST REACTS.
BB
©2003 Overdue Media LLC www.overduemedia.com

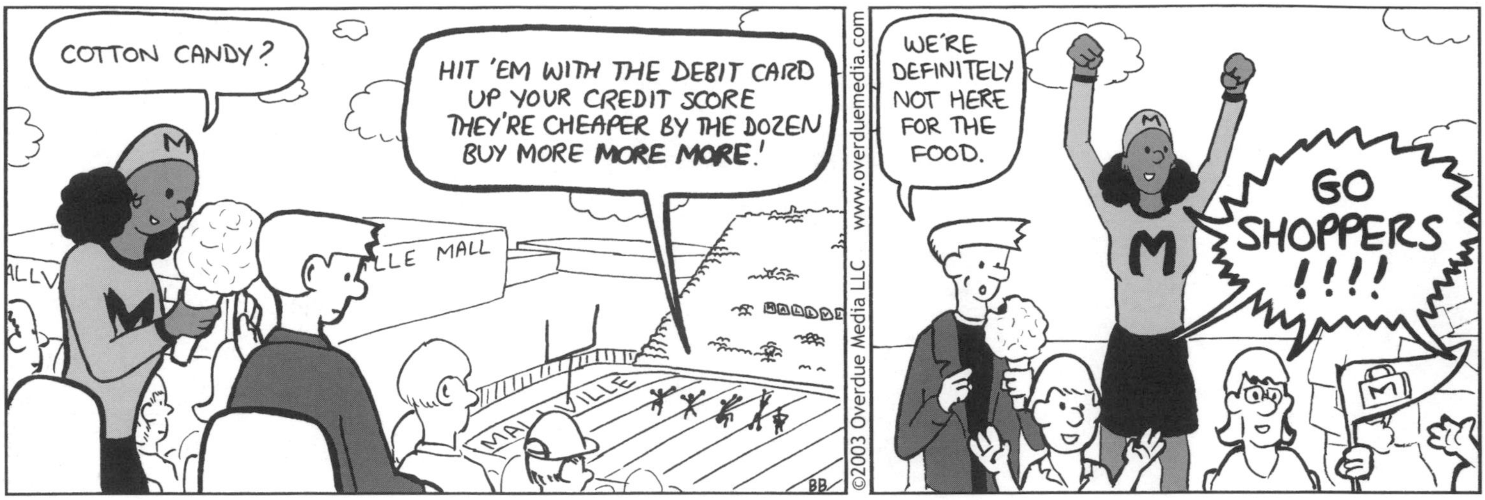
COTTON CANDY?
HIT 'EM WITH THE DEBIT CARD UP YOUR CREDIT SCORE THEY'RE CHEAPER BY THE DOZEN BUY MORE **MORE MORE**!
LLE MALL
WE'RE DEFINITELY NOT HERE FOR THE FOOD.
GO SHOPPERS !!!!
©2003 Overdue Media LLC www.overduemedia.com

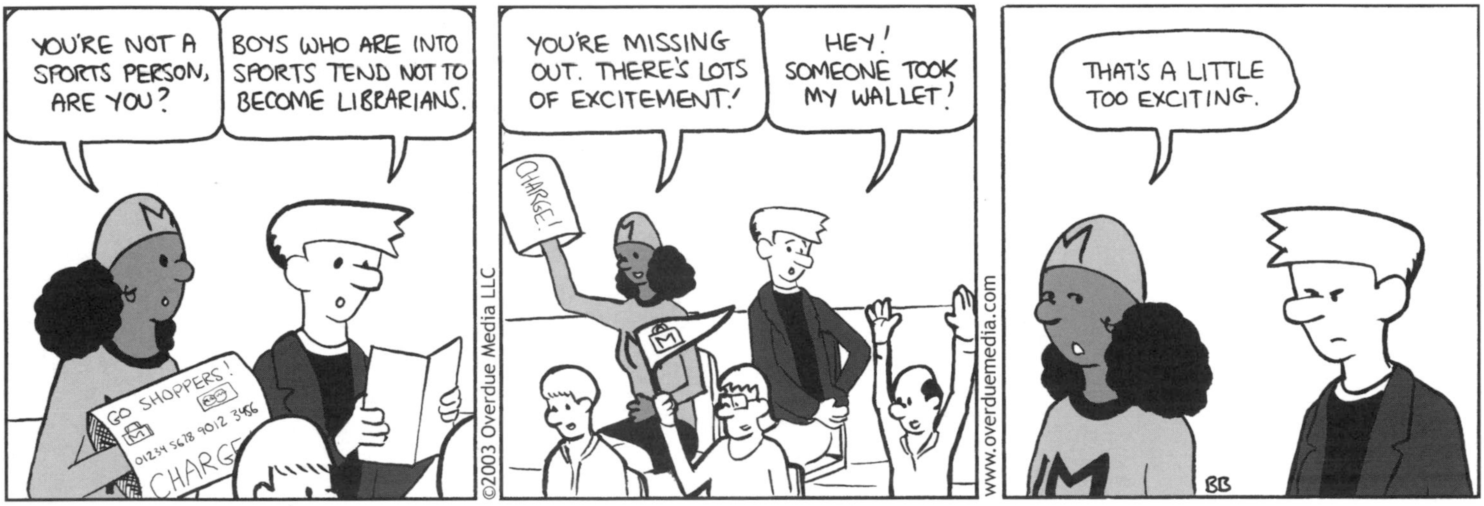
YOU'RE NOT A SPORTS PERSON, ARE YOU?
BOYS WHO ARE INTO SPORTS TEND NOT TO BECOME LIBRARIANS.
GO SHOPPERS!
CHARGE
YOU'RE MISSING OUT. THERE'S LOTS OF EXCITEMENT!
HEY! SOMEONE TOOK MY WALLET!
CHARGE!
THAT'S A LITTLE TOO EXCITING.
©2003 Overdue Media LLC www.overduemedia.com

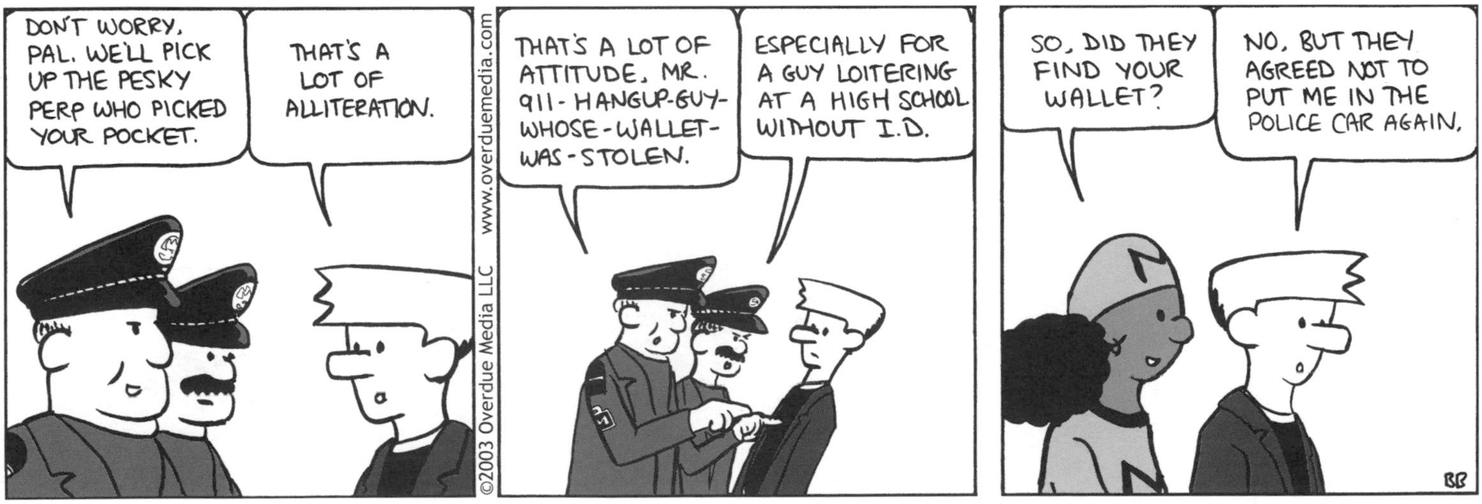
DON'T WORRY, PAL. WE'LL PICK UP THE PESKY PERP WHO PICKED YOUR POCKET.
THAT'S A LOT OF ALLITERATION.
THAT'S A LOT OF ATTITUDE, MR. 911-HANGUP-GUY-WHOSE-WALLET-WAS-STOLEN.
ESPECIALLY FOR A GUY LOITERING AT A HIGH SCHOOL WITHOUT I.D.
SO, DID THEY FIND YOUR WALLET?
NO, BUT THEY AGREED NOT TO PUT ME IN THE POLICE CAR AGAIN.
©2003 Overdue Media LLC www.overduemedia.com

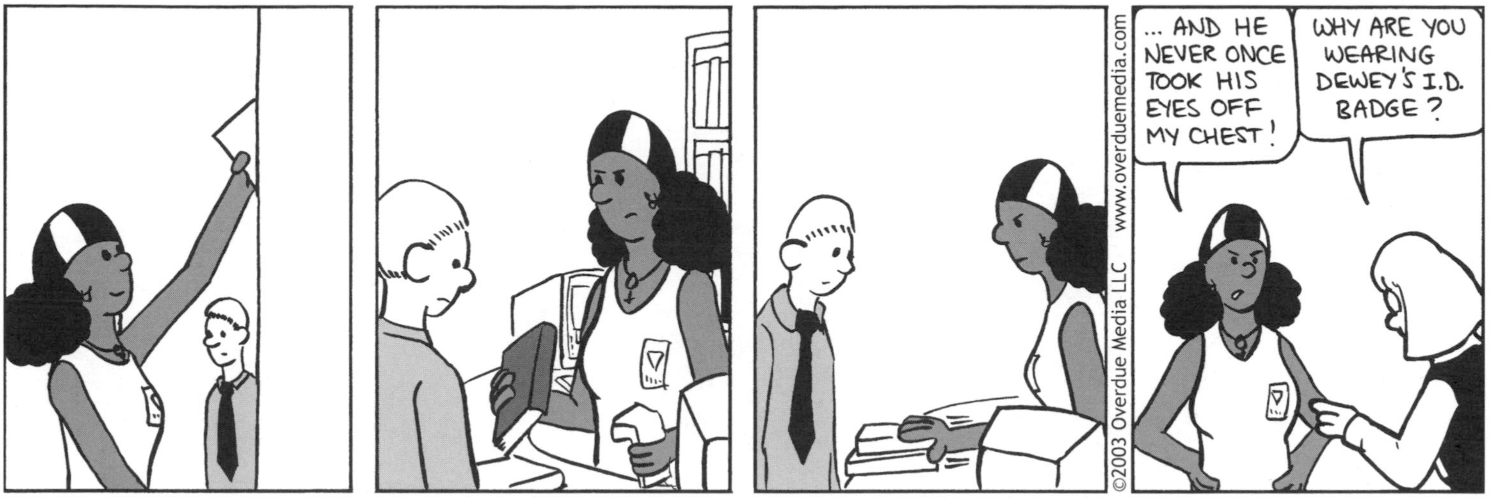
... AND HE NEVER ONCE TOOK HIS EYES OFF MY CHEST!
WHY ARE YOU WEARING DEWEY'S I.D. BADGE?
©2003 Overdue Media LLC www.overduemedia.com

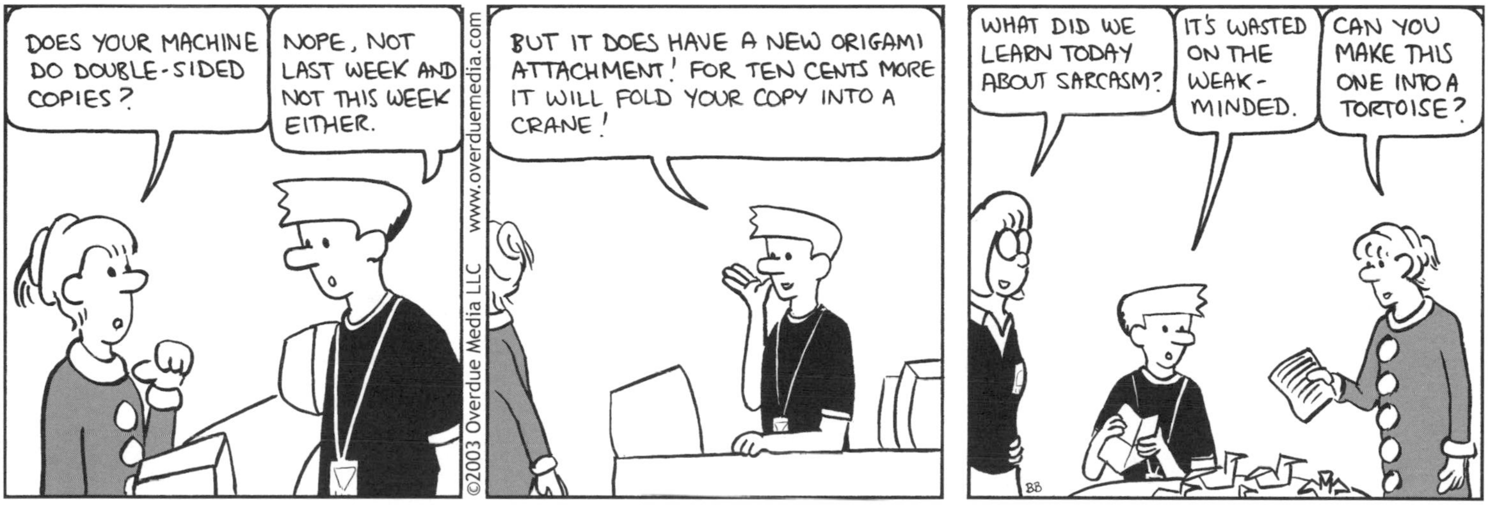
DOES YOUR MACHINE DO DOUBLE-SIDED COPIES?
NOPE, NOT LAST WEEK AND NOT THIS WEEK EITHER.
BUT IT DOES HAVE A NEW ORIGAMI ATTACHMENT! FOR TEN CENTS MORE IT WILL FOLD YOUR COPY INTO A CRANE!
WHAT DID WE LEARN TODAY ABOUT SARCASM?
IT'S WASTED ON THE WEAK-MINDED.
CAN YOU MAKE THIS ONE INTO A TORTOISE?
©2003 Overdue Media LLC www.overduemedia.com
BB

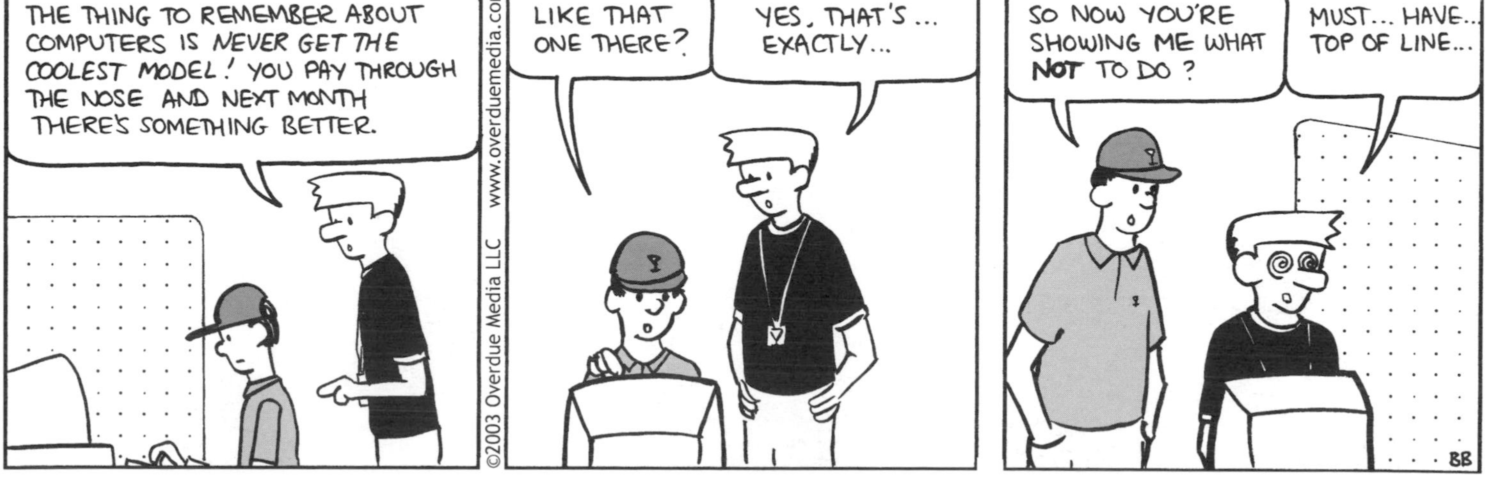
THE THING TO REMEMBER ABOUT COMPUTERS IS NEVER GET THE COOLEST MODEL! YOU PAY THROUGH THE NOSE AND NEXT MONTH THERE'S SOMETHING BETTER.
LIKE THAT ONE THERE?
YES, THAT'S... EXACTLY...
SO NOW YOU'RE SHOWING ME WHAT NOT TO DO?
MUST... HAVE... TOP OF LINE...
©2003 Overdue Media LLC www.overduemedia.com
BB

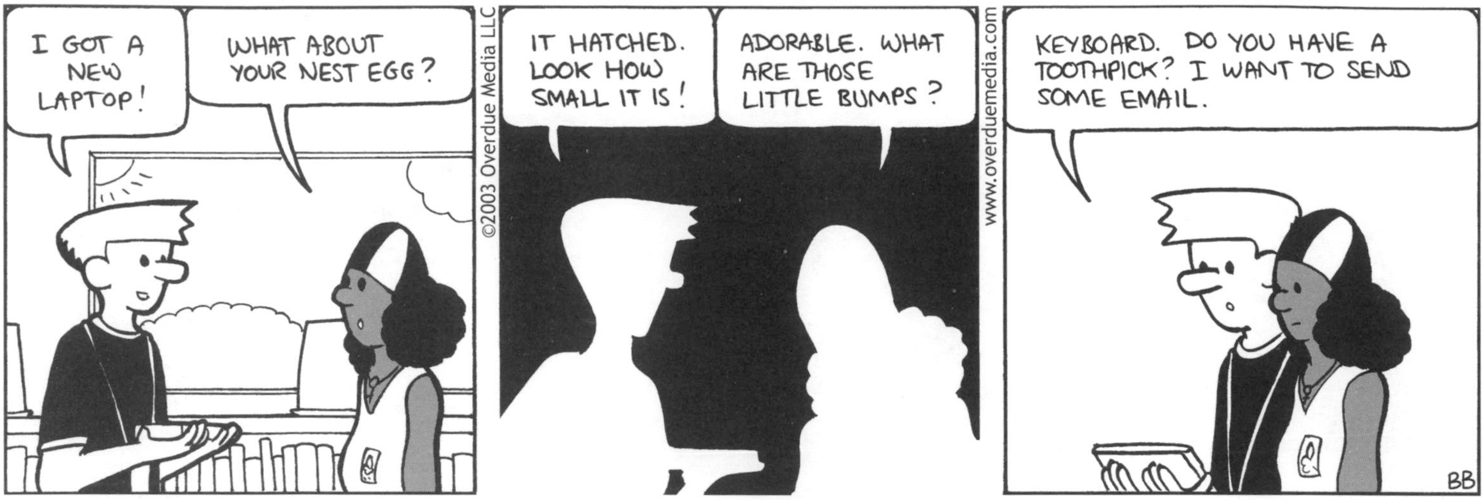
I GOT A NEW LAPTOP!
WHAT ABOUT YOUR NEST EGG?
©2003 Overdue Media LLC
IT HATCHED. LOOK HOW SMALL IT IS!
ADORABLE. WHAT ARE THOSE LITTLE BUMPS?
www.overduemedia.com
KEYBOARD. DO YOU HAVE A TOOTHPICK? I WANT TO SEND SOME EMAIL.
BB

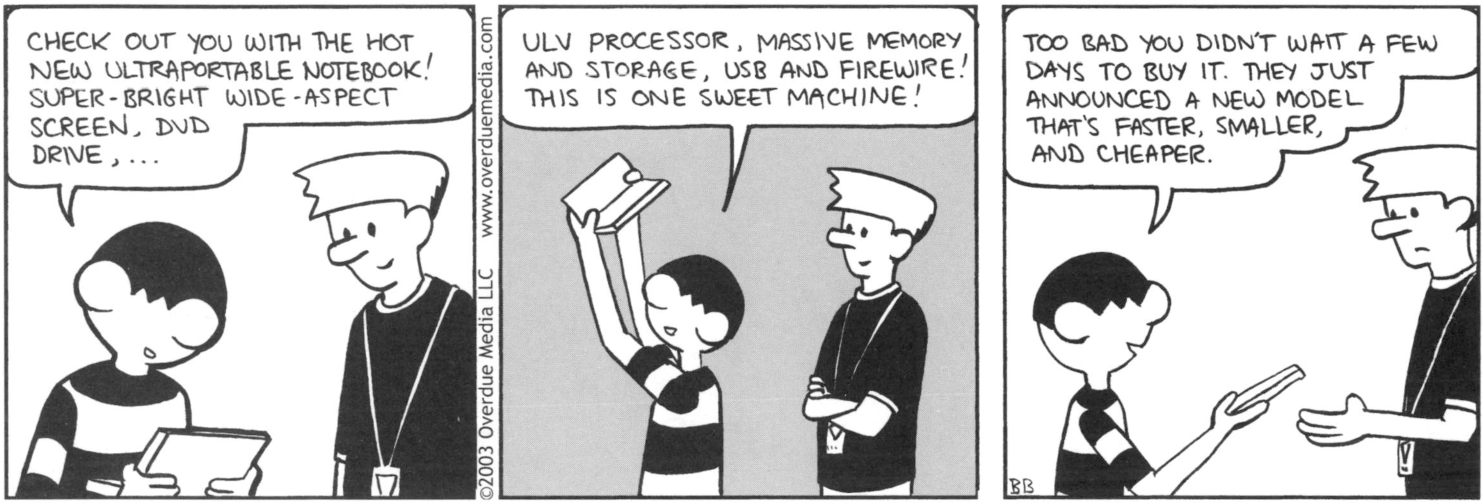
CHECK OUT YOU WITH THE HOT NEW ULTRAPORTABLE NOTEBOOK! SUPER-BRIGHT WIDE-ASPECT SCREEN, DVD DRIVE, ...
©2003 Overdue Media LLC www.overduemedia.com
ULV PROCESSOR, MASSIVE MEMORY AND STORAGE, USB AND FIREWIRE! THIS IS ONE SWEET MACHINE!
TOO BAD YOU DIDN'T WAIT A FEW DAYS TO BUY IT. THEY JUST ANNOUNCED A NEW MODEL THAT'S FASTER, SMALLER, AND CHEAPER.
BB

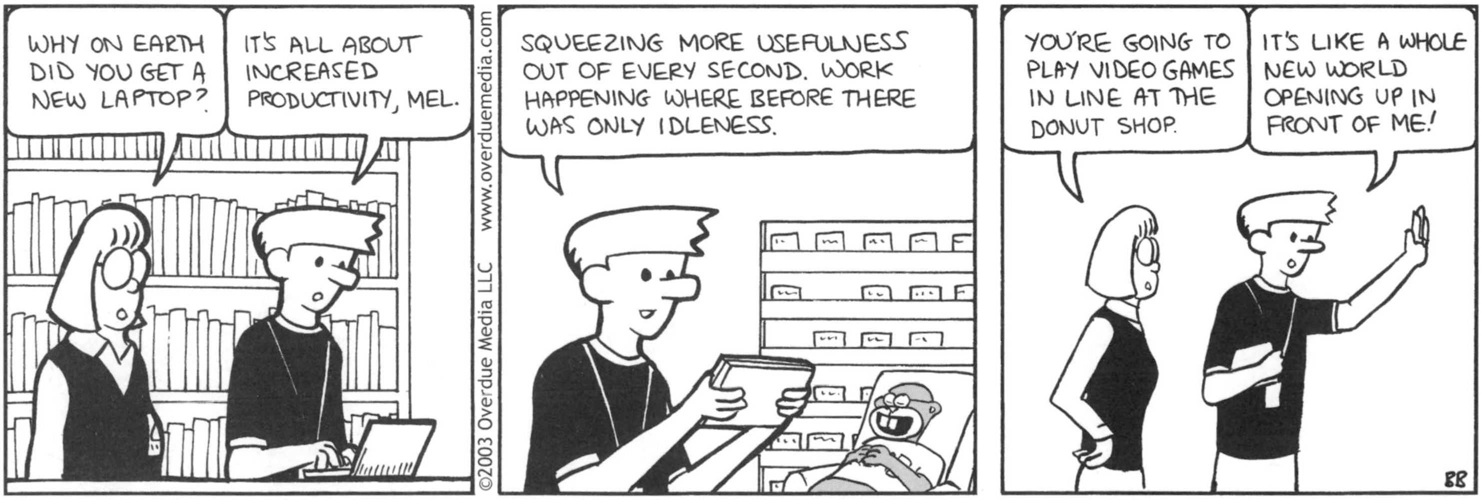
WHY ON EARTH DID YOU GET A NEW LAPTOP?
IT'S ALL ABOUT INCREASED PRODUCTIVITY, MEL.
©2003 Overdue Media LLC www.overduemedia.com
SQUEEZING MORE USEFULNESS OUT OF EVERY SECOND. WORK HAPPENING WHERE BEFORE THERE WAS ONLY IDLENESS.
YOU'RE GOING TO PLAY VIDEO GAMES IN LINE AT THE DONUT SHOP.
IT'S LIKE A WHOLE NEW WORLD OPENING UP IN FRONT OF ME!
BB

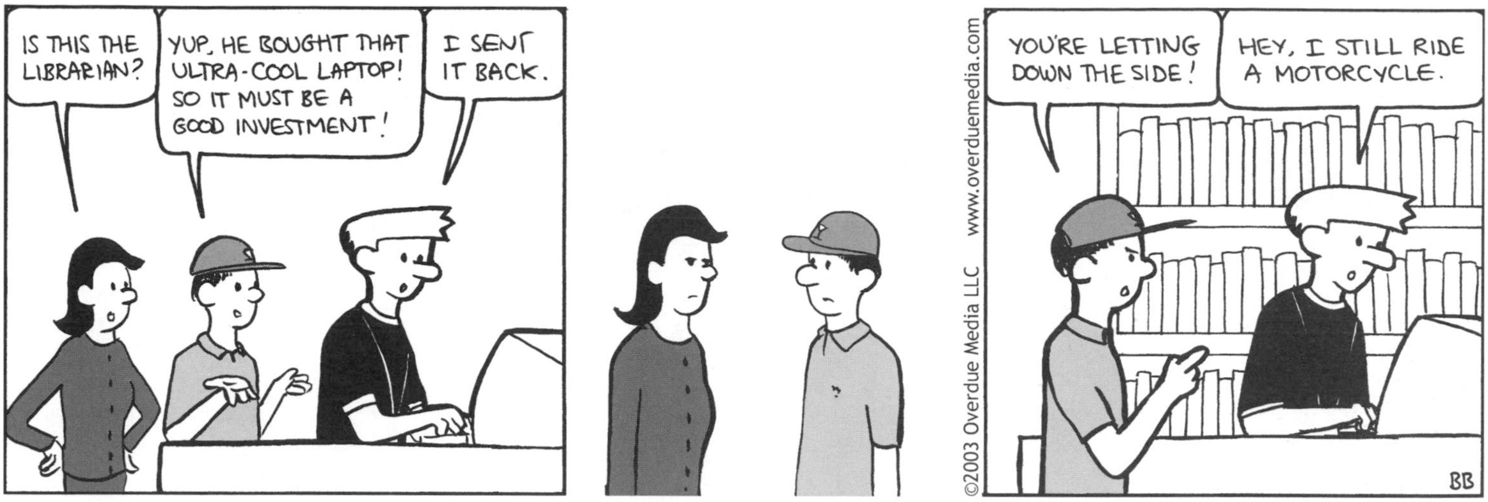
IS THIS THE LIBRARIAN?
YUP, HE BOUGHT THAT ULTRA-COOL LAPTOP! SO IT MUST BE A GOOD INVESTMENT!
I SENT IT BACK.
YOU'RE LETTING DOWN THE SIDE!
HEY, I STILL RIDE A MOTORCYCLE.
©2003 Overdue Media LLC www.overduemedia.com
BB

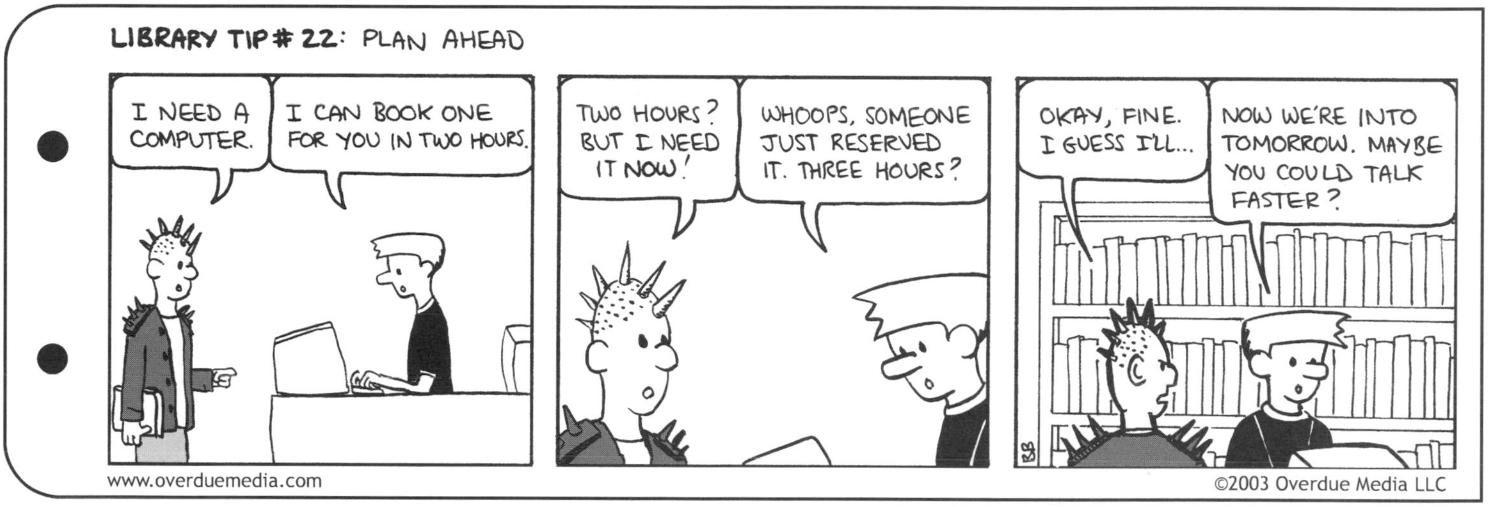
LIBRARY TIP # 22: PLAN AHEAD
I NEED A COMPUTER.
I CAN BOOK ONE FOR YOU IN TWO HOURS.
TWO HOURS? BUT I NEED IT NOW!
WHOOPS, SOMEONE JUST RESERVED IT. THREE HOURS?
OKAY, FINE. I GUESS I'LL...
NOW WE'RE INTO TOMORROW. MAYBE YOU COULD TALK FASTER?
BB
www.overduemedia.com
©2003 Overdue Media LLC

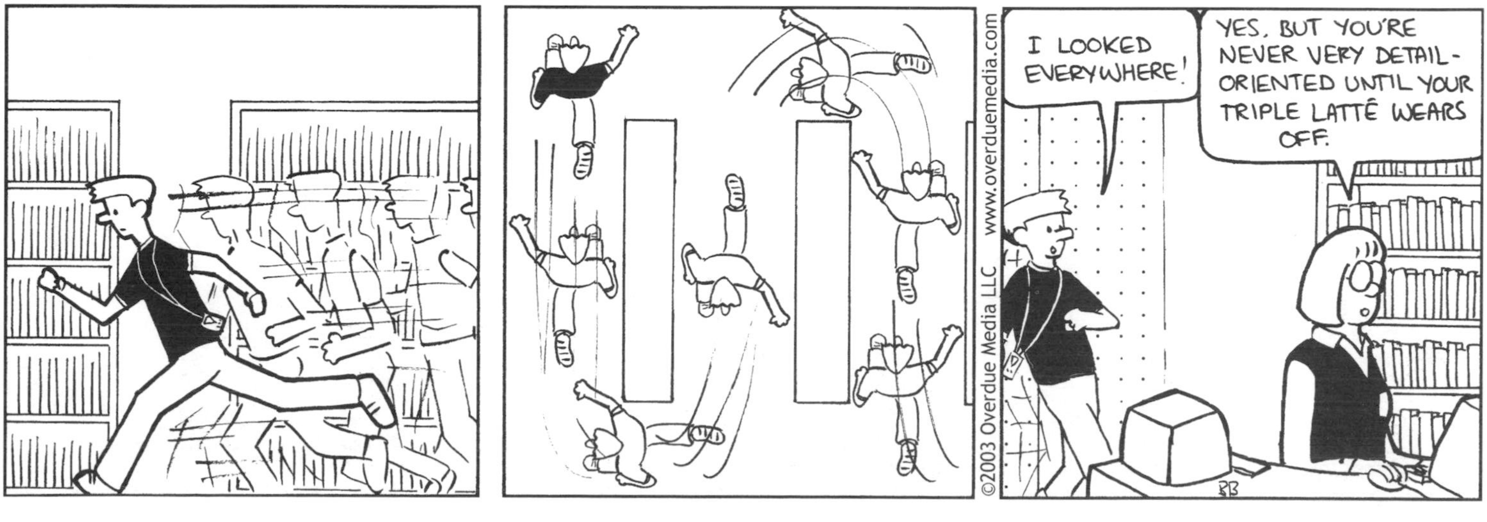
©2003 Overdue Media LLC www.overduemedia.com
I LOOKED EVERYWHERE!
YES, BUT YOU'RE NEVER VERY DETAIL-ORIENTED UNTIL YOUR TRIPLE LATTÊ WEARS OFF.
BB

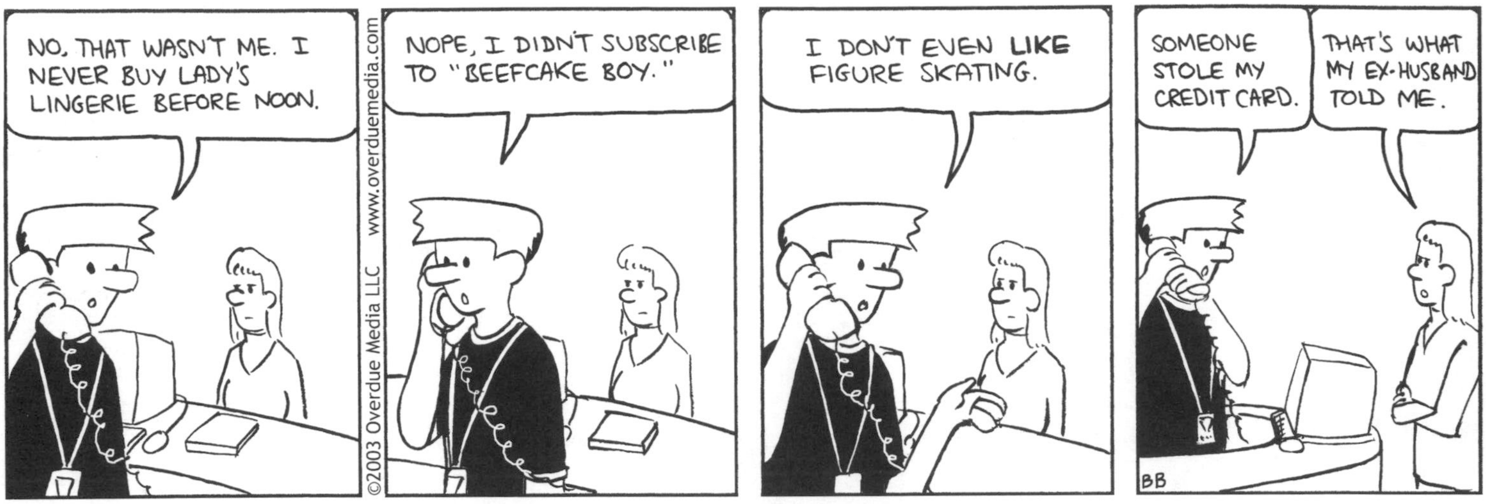
NO, THAT WASN'T ME. I NEVER BUY LADY'S LINGERIE BEFORE NOON.
©2003 Overdue Media LLC www.overduemedia.com
NOPE, I DIDN'T SUBSCRIBE TO "BEEFCAKE BOY."
I DON'T EVEN LIKE FIGURE SKATING.
SOMEONE STOLE MY CREDIT CARD.
THAT'S WHAT MY EX-HUSBAND TOLD ME.
BB

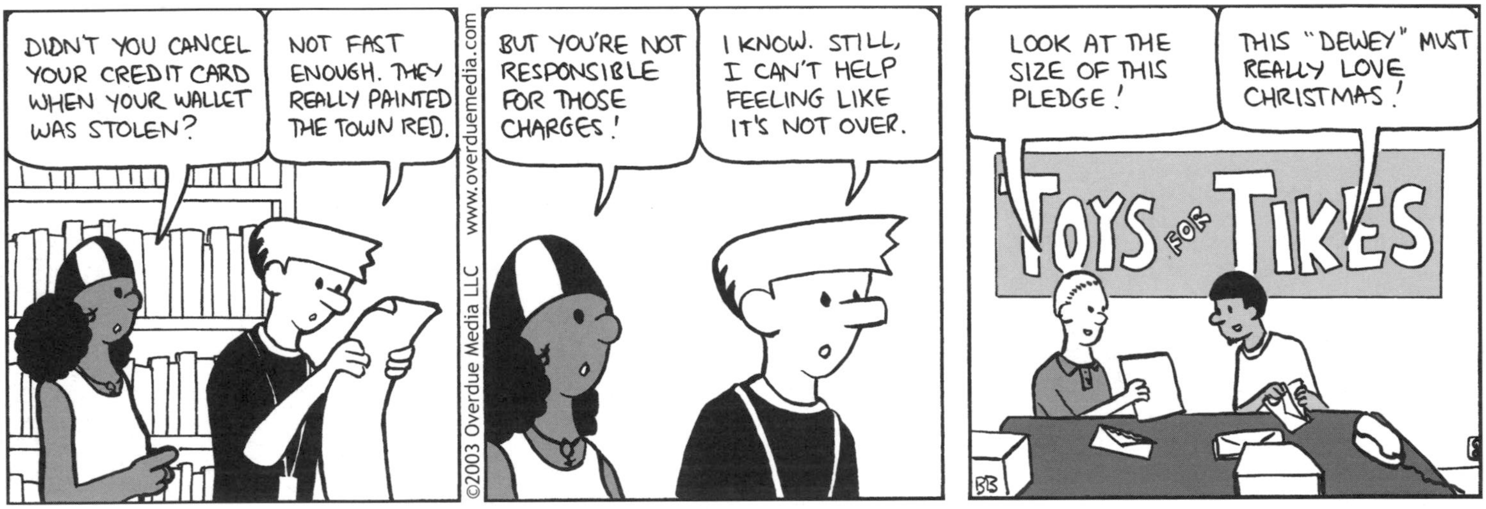
DIDN'T YOU CANCEL YOUR CREDIT CARD WHEN YOUR WALLET WAS STOLEN?
NOT FAST ENOUGH. THEY REALLY PAINTED THE TOWN RED.
©2003 Overdue Media LLC www.overduemedia.com
BUT YOU'RE NOT RESPONSIBLE FOR THOSE CHARGES!
I KNOW. STILL, I CAN'T HELP FEELING LIKE IT'S NOT OVER.
LOOK AT THE SIZE OF THIS PLEDGE!
THIS "DEWEY" MUST REALLY LOVE CHRISTMAS!
TOYS FOR TIKES
BB

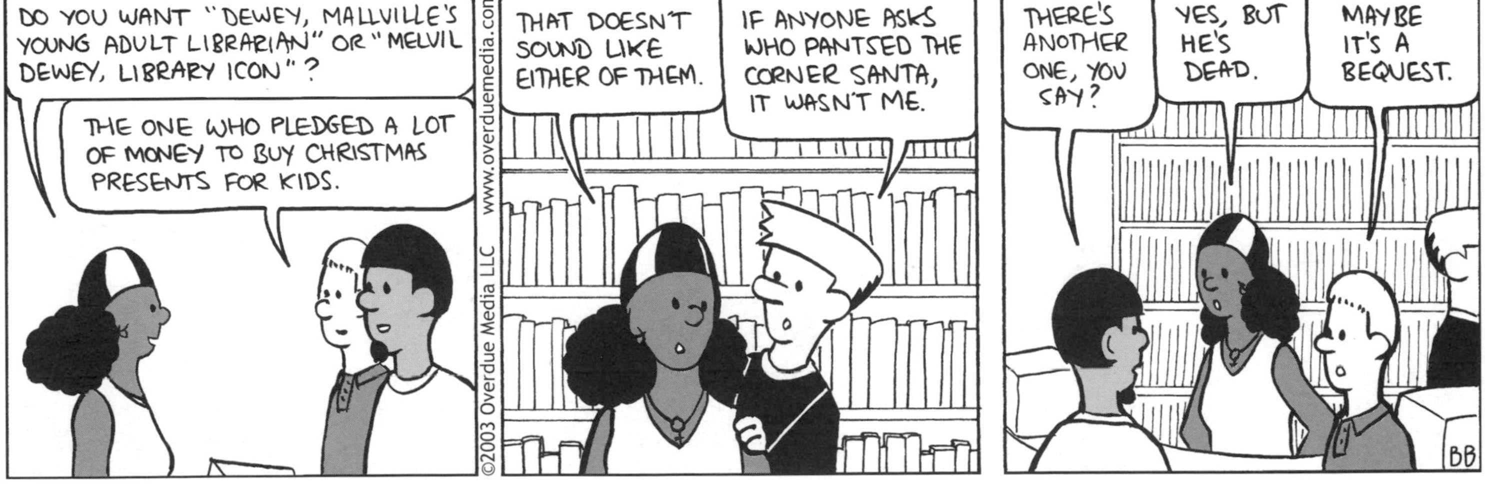
DO YOU WANT "DEWEY, MALLVILLE'S YOUNG ADULT LIBRARIAN" OR "MELVIL DEWEY, LIBRARY ICON"?
THE ONE WHO PLEDGED A LOT OF MONEY TO BUY CHRISTMAS PRESENTS FOR KIDS.
©2003 Overdue Media LLC www.overduemedia.com
THAT DOESN'T SOUND LIKE EITHER OF THEM.
IF ANYONE ASKS WHO PANTSED THE CORNER SANTA, IT WASN'T ME.
THERE'S ANOTHER ONE, YOU SAY?
YES, BUT HE'S DEAD.
MAYBE IT'S A BEQUEST.
BB

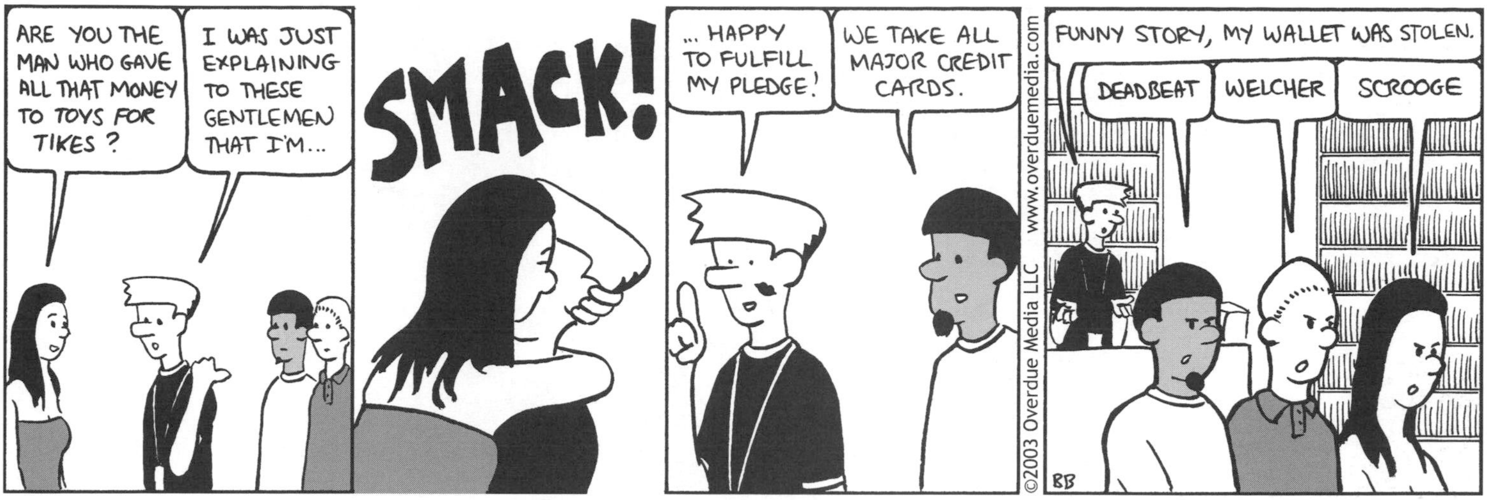
ARE YOU THE MAN WHO GAVE ALL THAT MONEY TO TOYS FOR TIKES?
I WAS JUST EXPLAINING TO THESE GENTLEMEN THAT I'M...
SMACK!
... HAPPY TO FULFILL MY PLEDGE!
WE TAKE ALL MAJOR CREDIT CARDS.
FUNNY STORY, MY WALLET WAS STOLEN.
DEADBEAT
WELCHER
SCROOGE
©2003 Overdue Media LLC www.overduemedia.com
BB

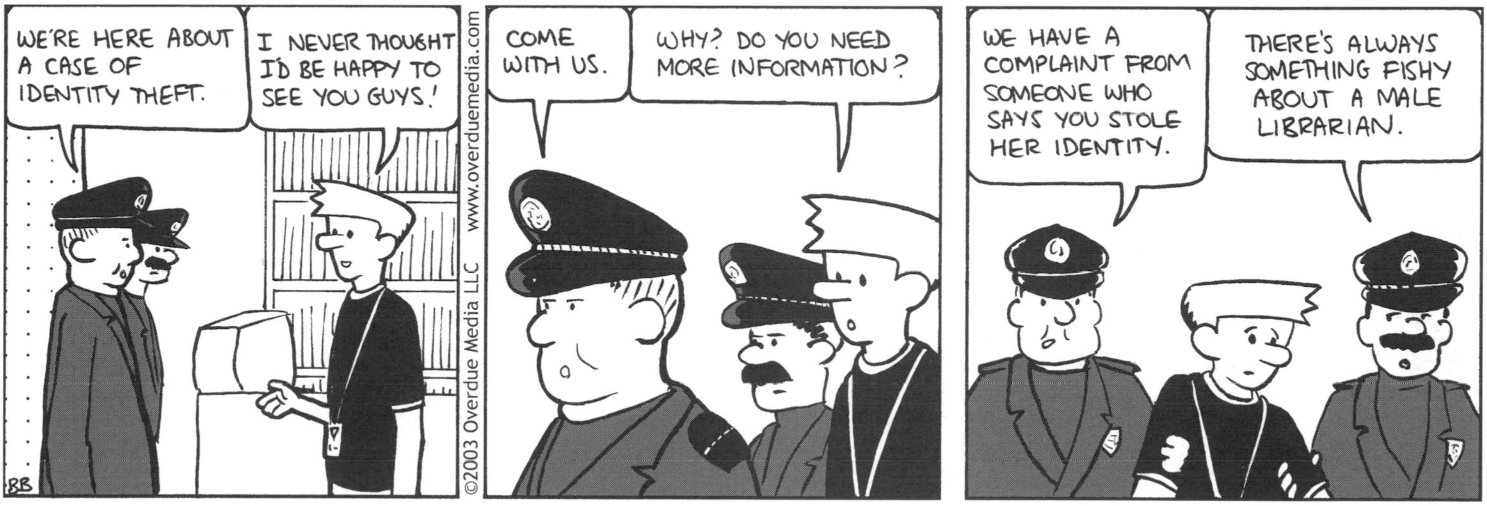
WE'RE HERE ABOUT A CASE OF IDENTITY THEFT.
I NEVER THOUGHT I'D BE HAPPY TO SEE YOU GUYS!
BB
©2003 Overdue Media LLC www.overduemedia.com
COME WITH US.
WHY? DO YOU NEED MORE INFORMATION?
WE HAVE A COMPLAINT FROM SOMEONE WHO SAYS YOU STOLE HER IDENTITY.
THERE'S ALWAYS SOMETHING FISHY ABOUT A MALE LIBRARIAN.

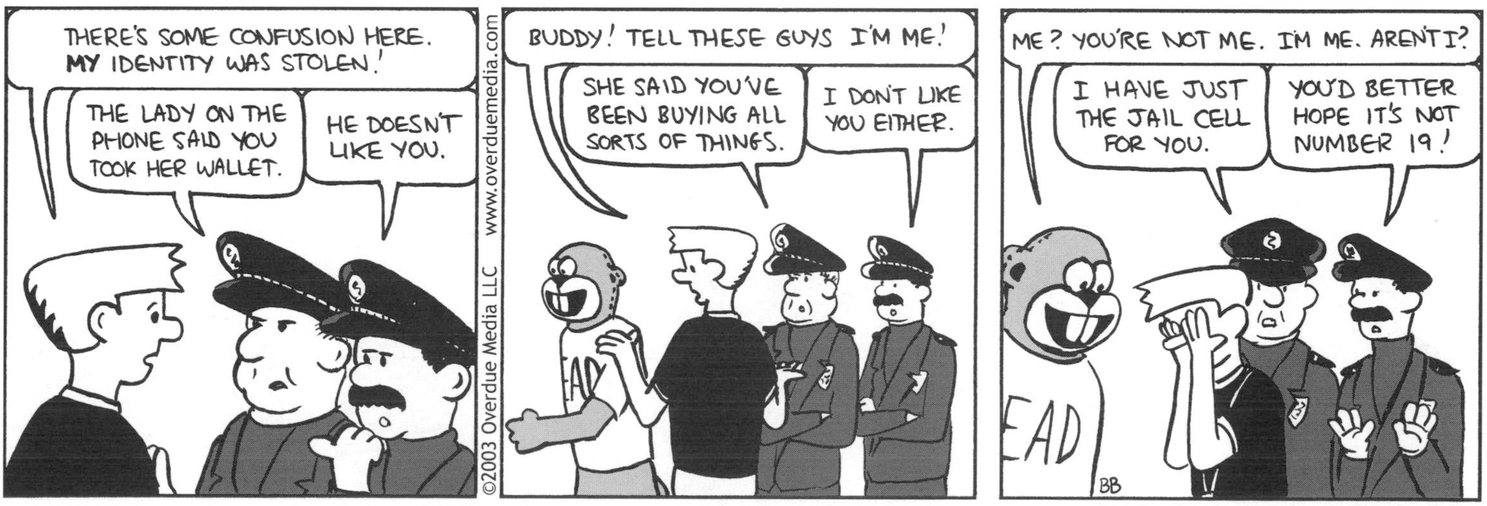
THERE'S SOME CONFUSION HERE. MY IDENTITY WAS STOLEN!
THE LADY ON THE PHONE SAID YOU TOOK HER WALLET.
HE DOESN'T LIKE YOU.
©2003 Overdue Media LLC www.overduemedia.com
BUDDY! TELL THESE GUYS I'M ME!
SHE SAID YOU'VE BEEN BUYING ALL SORTS OF THINGS.
I DON'T LIKE YOU EITHER.
ME? YOU'RE NOT ME. I'M ME. AREN'T I?
I HAVE JUST THE JAIL CELL FOR YOU.
YOU'D BETTER HOPE IT'S NOT NUMBER 19!
BB

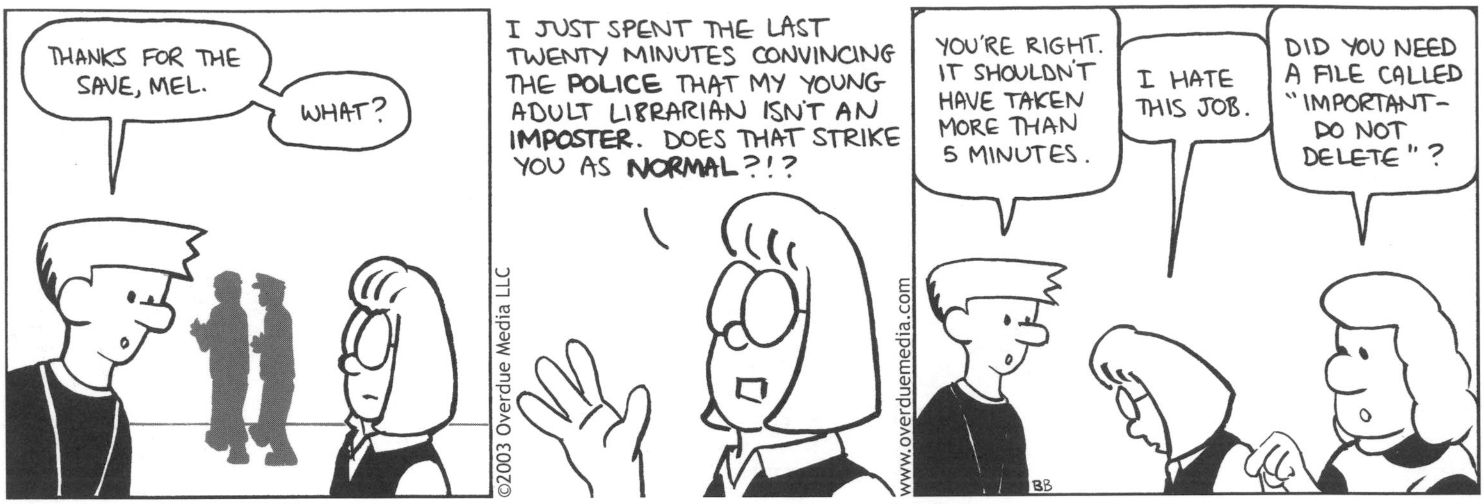
THANKS FOR THE SAVE, MEL.
WHAT?
I JUST SPENT THE LAST TWENTY MINUTES CONVINCING THE **POLICE** THAT MY YOUNG ADULT LIBRARIAN ISN'T AN **IMPOSTER**. DOES THAT STRIKE YOU AS **NORMAL**?!?
YOU'RE RIGHT. IT SHOULDN'T HAVE TAKEN MORE THAN 5 MINUTES.
I HATE THIS JOB.
DID YOU NEED A FILE CALLED "IMPORTANT- DO NOT DELETE"?
©2003 Overdue Media LLC
www.overduemedia.com
BB

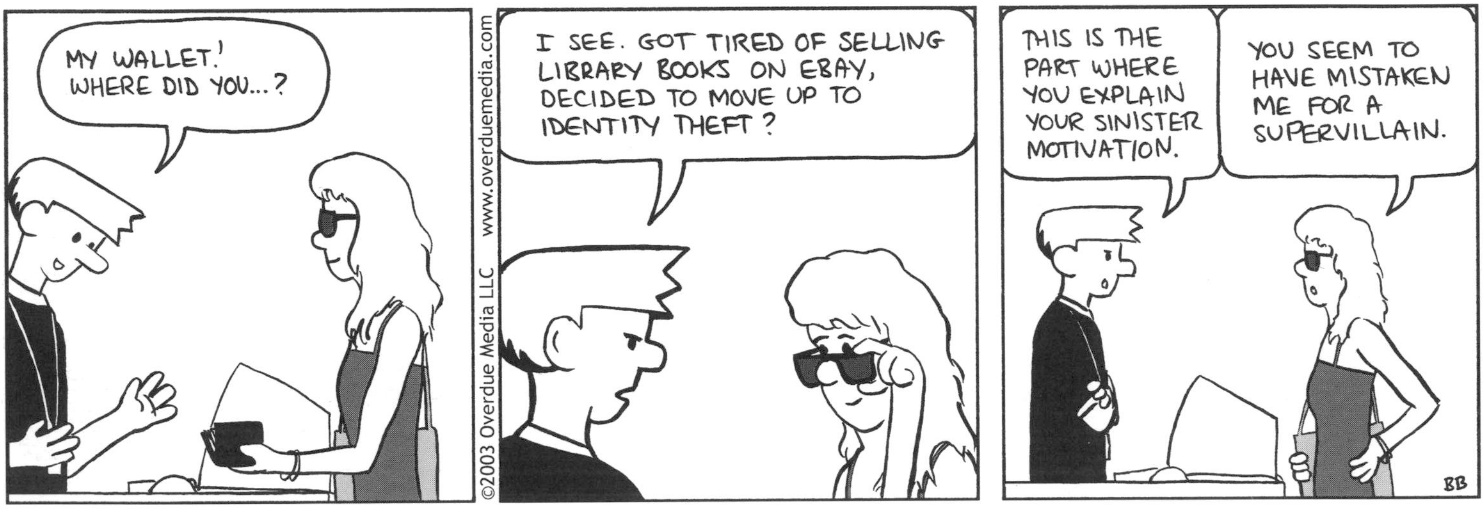
MY WALLET! WHERE DID YOU...?
I SEE. GOT TIRED OF SELLING LIBRARY BOOKS ON EBAY, DECIDED TO MOVE UP TO IDENTITY THEFT?
THIS IS THE PART WHERE YOU EXPLAIN YOUR SINISTER MOTIVATION.
YOU SEEM TO HAVE MISTAKEN ME FOR A SUPERVILLAIN.
©2003 Overdue Media LLC
www.overduemedia.com
BB

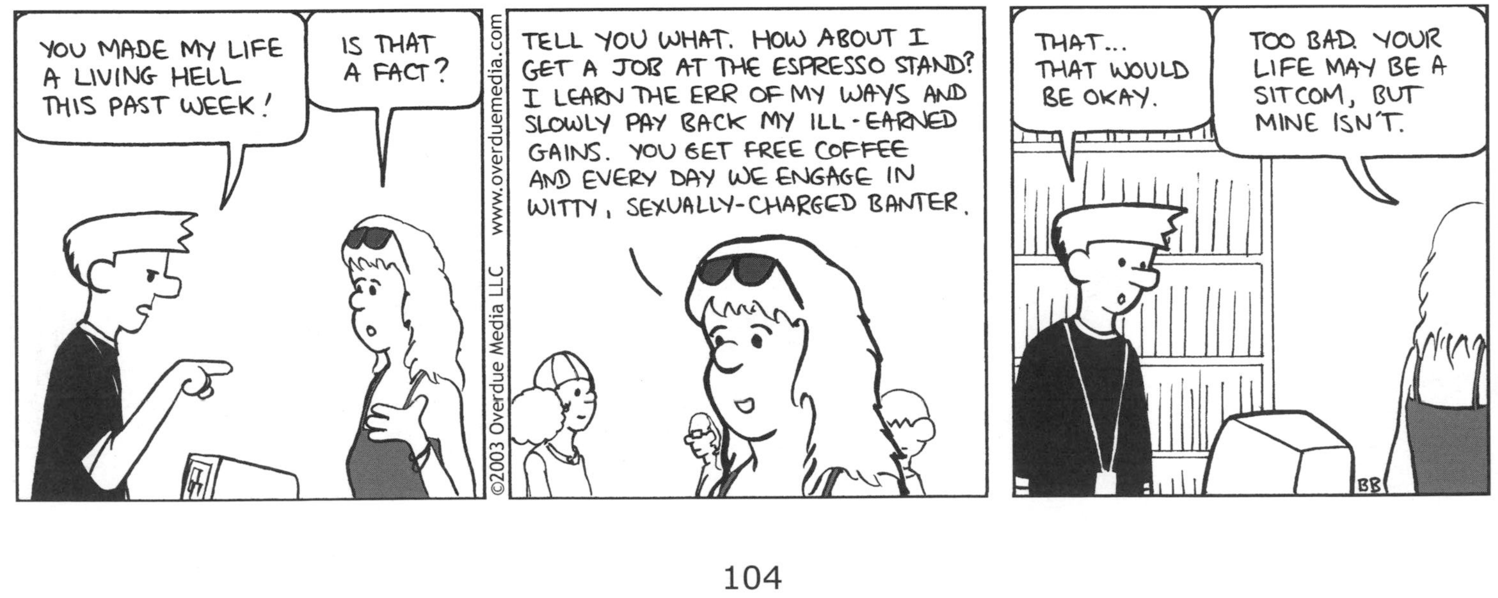
YOU MADE MY LIFE A LIVING HELL THIS PAST WEEK!
IS THAT A FACT?
TELL YOU WHAT. HOW ABOUT I GET A JOB AT THE ESPRESSO STAND? I LEARN THE ERR OF MY WAYS AND SLOWLY PAY BACK MY ILL-EARNED GAINS. YOU GET FREE COFFEE AND EVERY DAY WE ENGAGE IN WITTY, SEXUALLY-CHARGED BANTER.
THAT... THAT WOULD BE OKAY.
TOO BAD. YOUR LIFE MAY BE A SITCOM, BUT MINE ISN'T.
©2003 Overdue Media LLC
www.overduemedia.com
BB

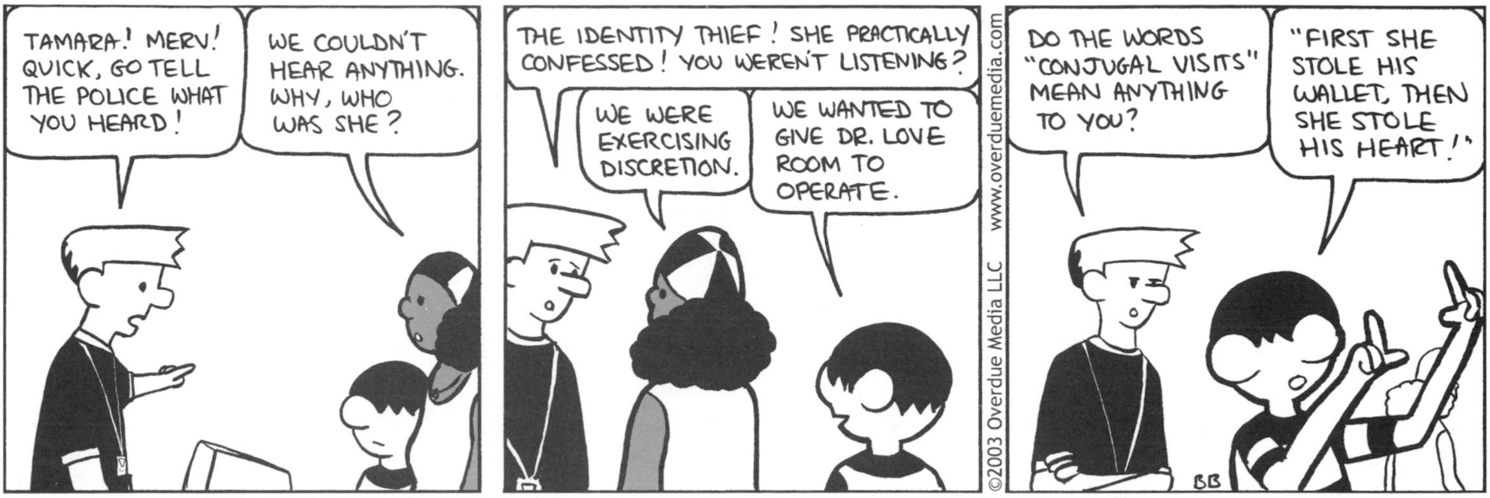
TAMARA! MERV! QUICK, GO TELL THE POLICE WHAT YOU HEARD!
WE COULDN'T HEAR ANYTHING. WHY, WHO WAS SHE?
THE IDENTITY THIEF! SHE PRACTICALLY CONFESSED! YOU WEREN'T LISTENING?
WE WERE EXERCISING DISCRETION.
WE WANTED TO GIVE DR. LOVE ROOM TO OPERATE.
©2003 Overdue Media LLC www.overduemedia.com
DO THE WORDS "CONJUGAL VISITS" MEAN ANYTHING TO YOU?
"FIRST SHE STOLE HIS WALLET, THEN SHE STOLE HIS HEART!"
BB

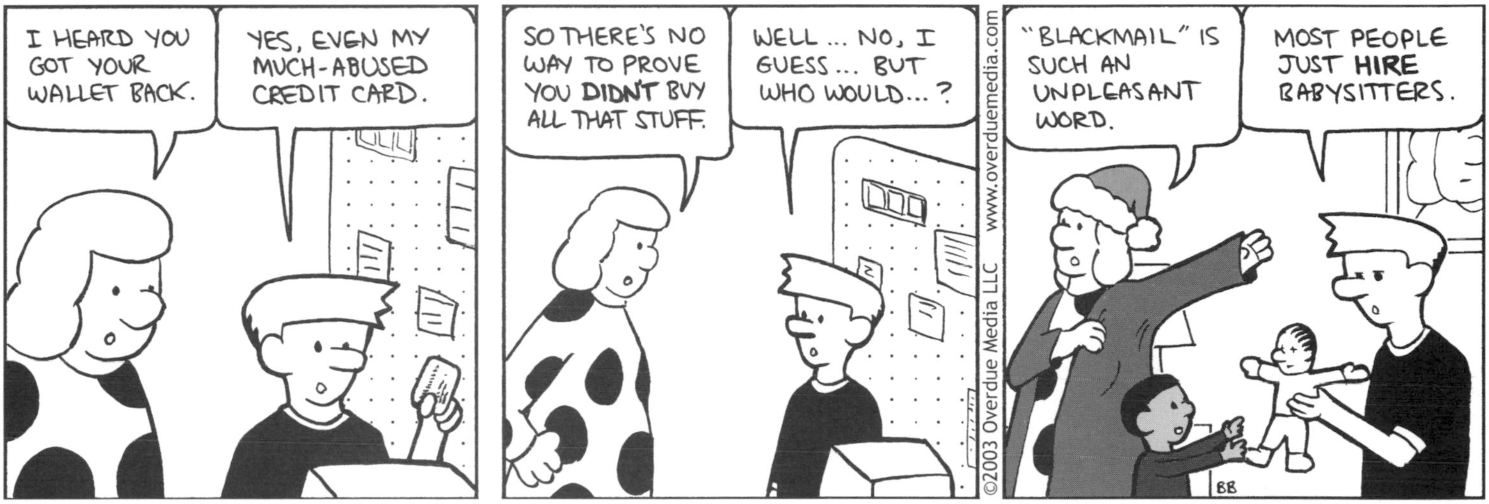
I HEARD YOU GOT YOUR WALLET BACK.
YES, EVEN MY MUCH-ABUSED CREDIT CARD.
SO THERE'S NO WAY TO PROVE YOU DIDN'T BUY ALL THAT STUFF.
WELL ... NO, I GUESS ... BUT WHO WOULD ... ?
©2003 Overdue Media LLC www.overduemedia.com
"BLACKMAIL" IS SUCH AN UNPLEASANT WORD.
MOST PEOPLE JUST HIRE BABYSITTERS.
BB

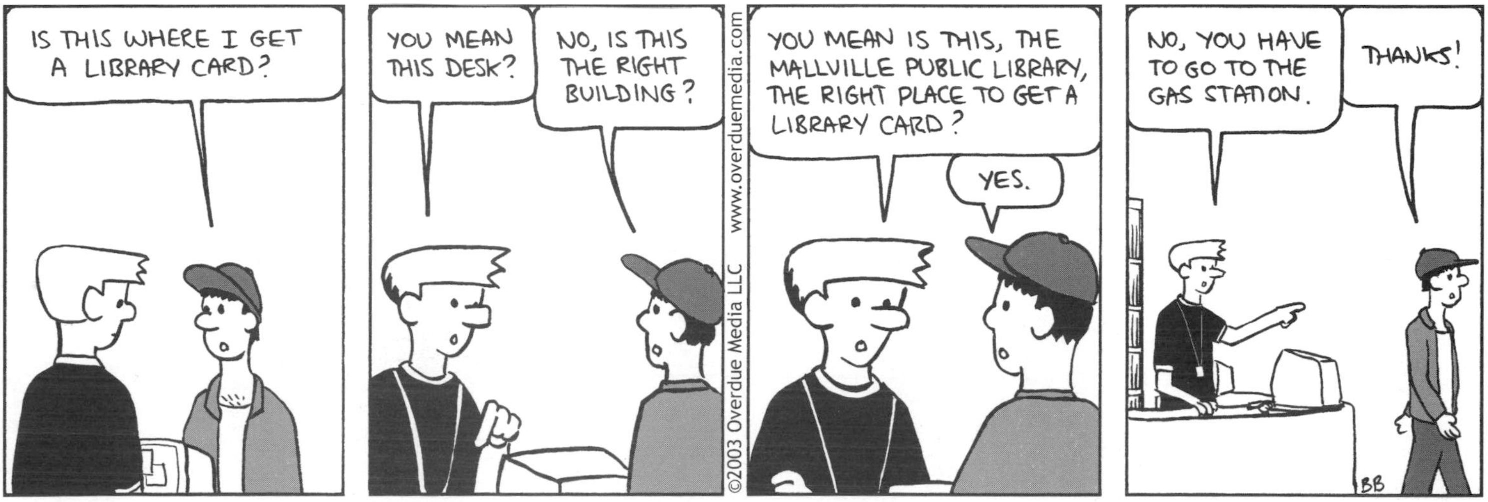
IS THIS WHERE I GET A LIBRARY CARD?
YOU MEAN THIS DESK?
NO, IS THIS THE RIGHT BUILDING?
©2003 Overdue Media LLC www.overduemedia.com
YOU MEAN IS THIS, THE MALLVILLE PUBLIC LIBRARY, THE RIGHT PLACE TO GET A LIBRARY CARD?
YES.
NO, YOU HAVE TO GO TO THE GAS STATION.
THANKS!
BB

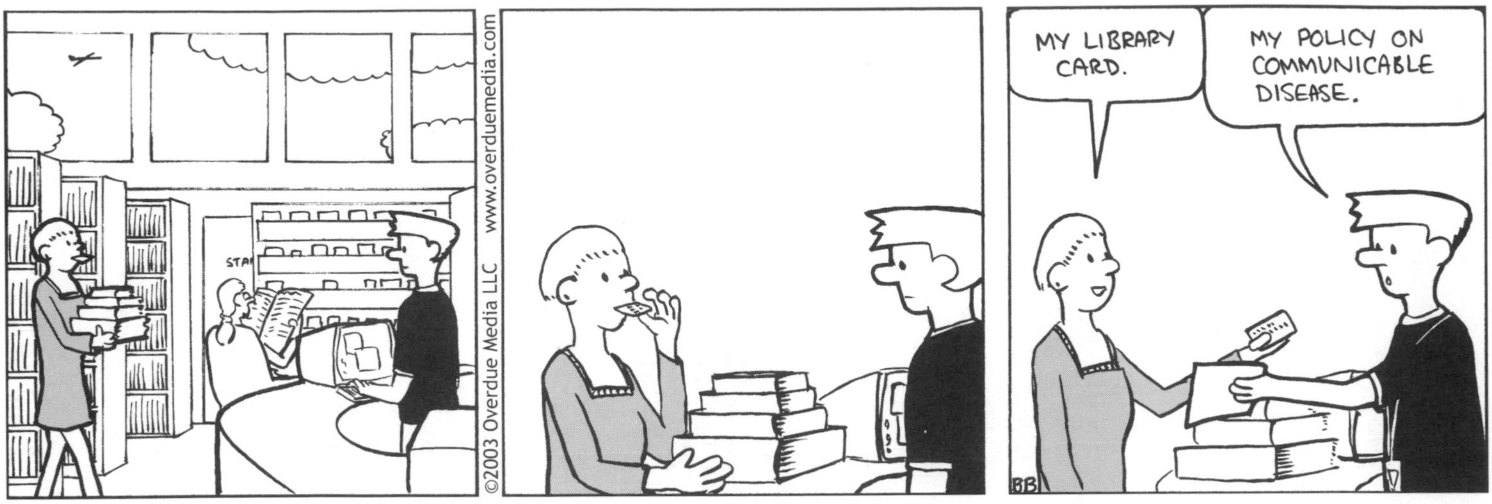
www.overduemedia.com
©2003 Overdue Media LLC
MY LIBRARY CARD.
MY POLICY ON COMMUNICABLE DISEASE.
BB

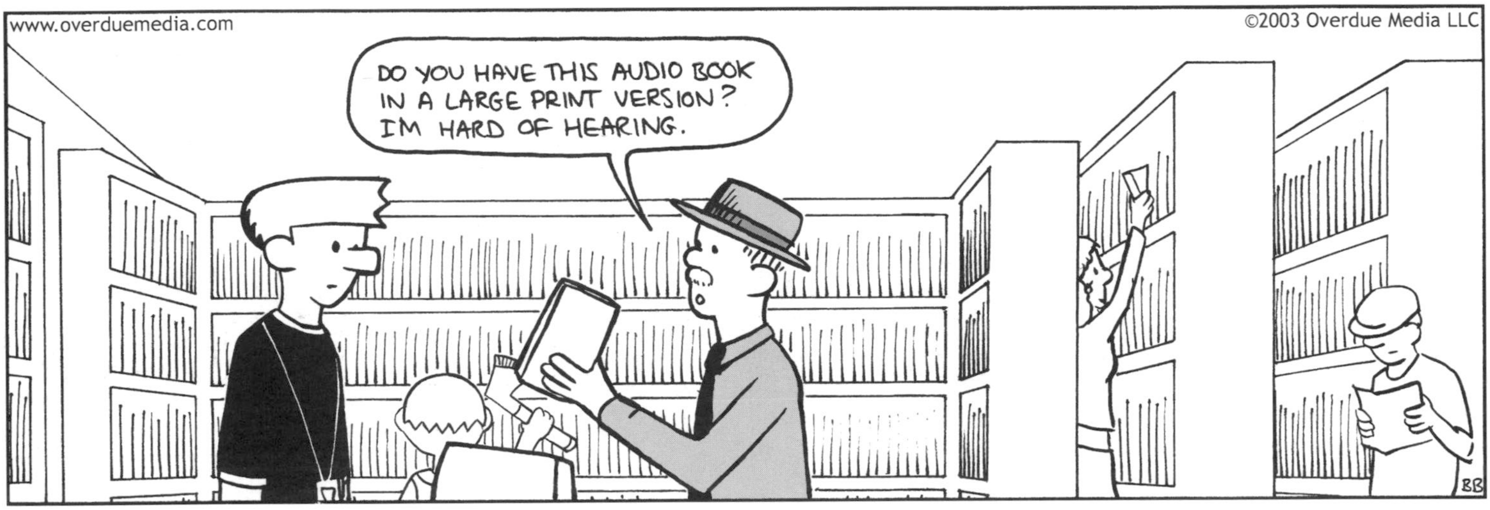
www.overduemedia.com
©2003 Overdue Media LLC
DO YOU HAVE THIS AUDIO BOOK IN A LARGE PRINT VERSION? I'M HARD OF HEARING.
BB

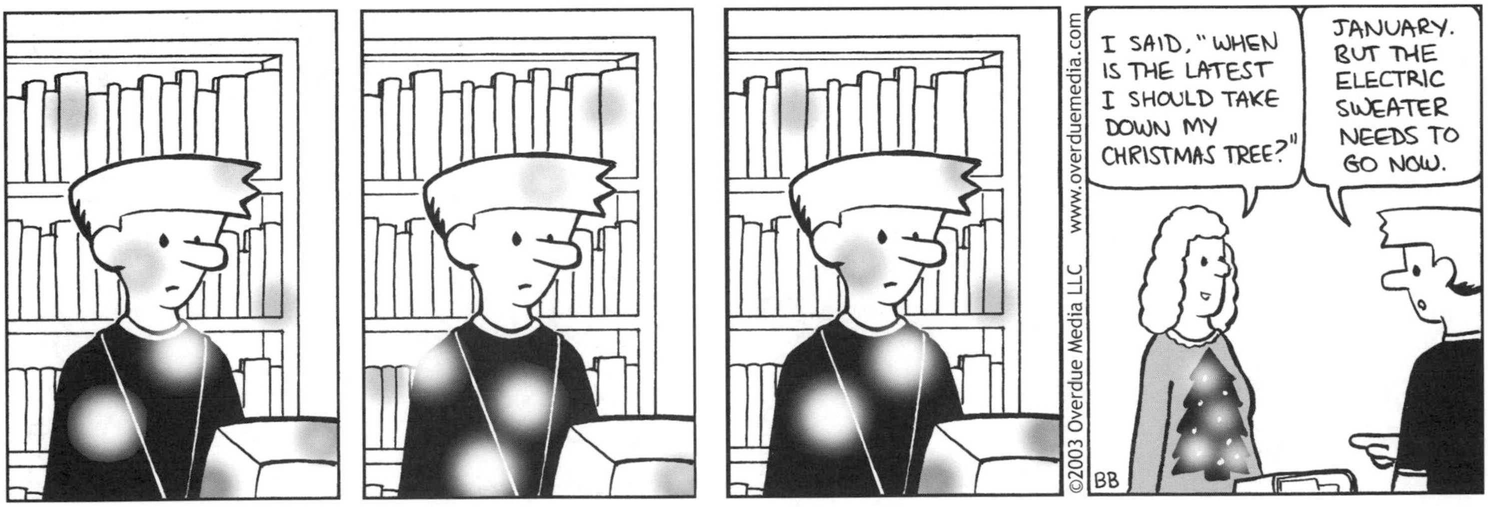
www.overduemedia.com
©2003 Overdue Media LLC
I SAID, "WHEN IS THE LATEST I SHOULD TAKE DOWN MY CHRISTMAS TREE?"
JANUARY. BUT THE ELECTRIC SWEATER NEEDS TO GO NOW.
BB

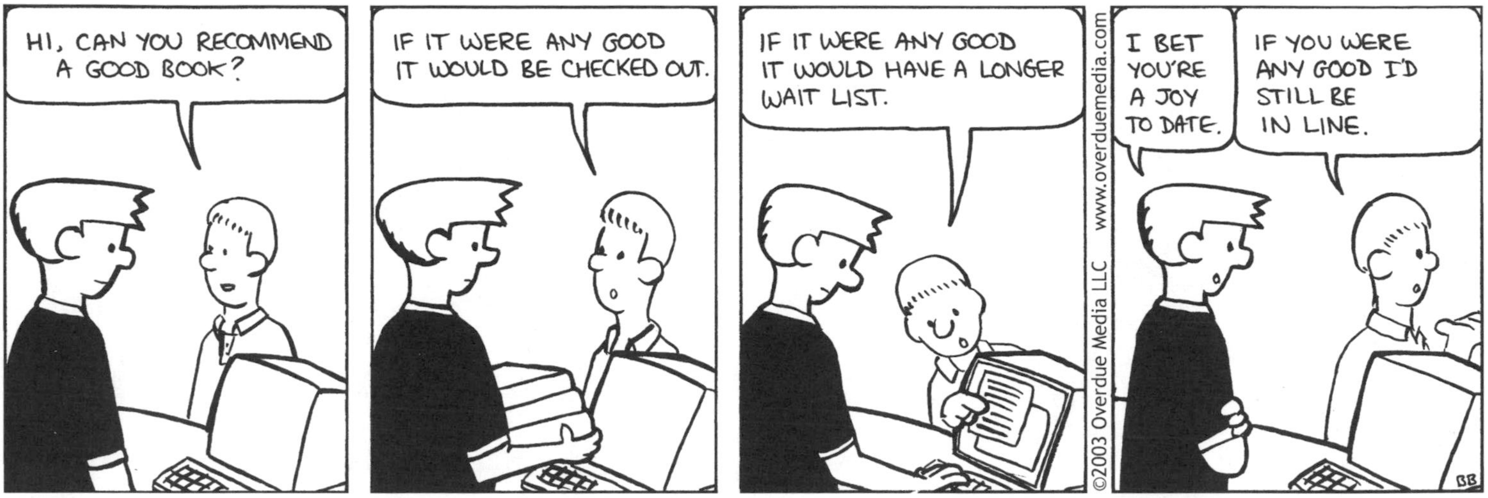
HI, CAN YOU RECOMMEND A GOOD BOOK?
IF IT WERE ANY GOOD IT WOULD BE CHECKED OUT.
IF IT WERE ANY GOOD IT WOULD HAVE A LONGER WAIT LIST.
©2003 Overdue Media LLC www.overduemedia.com
I BET YOU'RE A JOY TO DATE.
IF YOU WERE ANY GOOD I'D STILL BE IN LINE.
BB

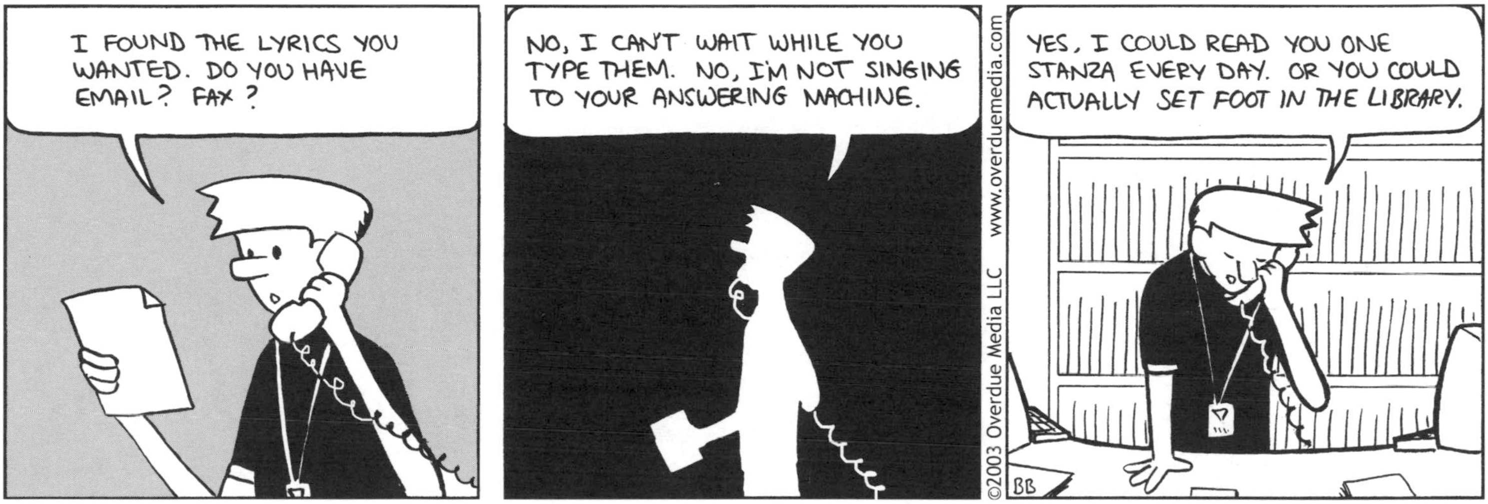
I FOUND THE LYRICS YOU WANTED. DO YOU HAVE EMAIL? FAX?
NO, I CAN'T WAIT WHILE YOU TYPE THEM. NO, I'M NOT SINGING TO YOUR ANSWERING MACHINE.
©2003 Overdue Media LLC www.overduemedia.com
YES, I COULD READ YOU ONE STANZA EVERY DAY. OR YOU COULD ACTUALLY *SET FOOT IN THE LIBRARY.*
BB

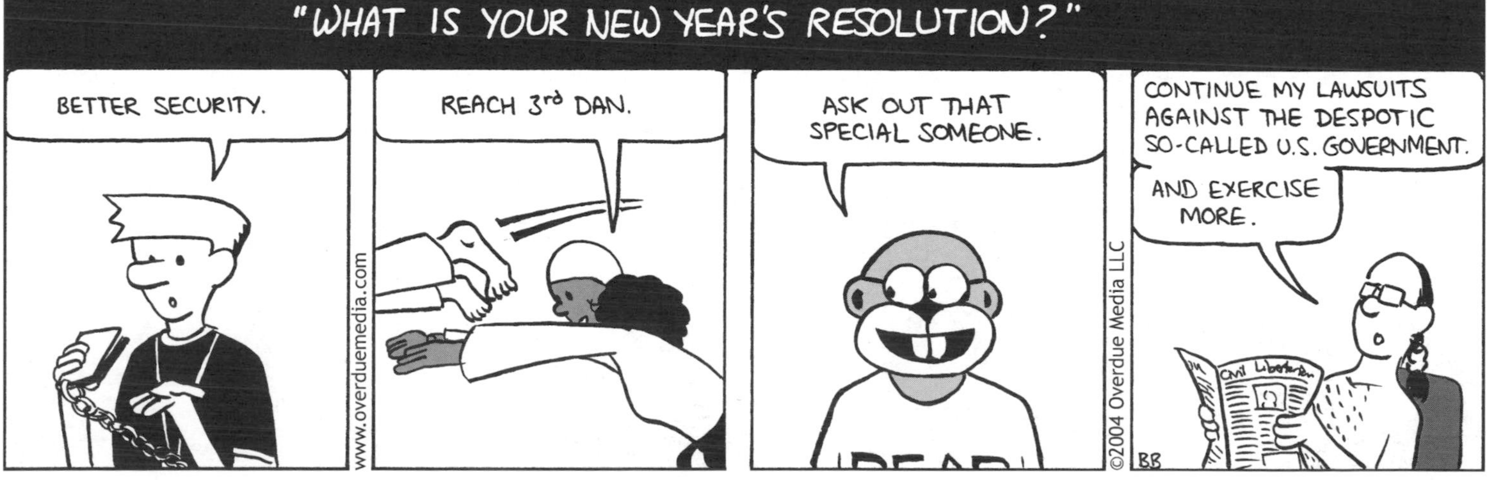
"WHAT IS YOUR NEW YEAR'S RESOLUTION?"
BETTER SECURITY.
www.overduemedia.com
REACH 3rd DAN.
ASK OUT THAT SPECIAL SOMEONE.
©2004 Overdue Media LLC
CONTINUE MY LAWSUITS AGAINST THE DESPOTIC SO-CALLED U.S. GOVERNMENT.
AND EXERCISE MORE.
BB

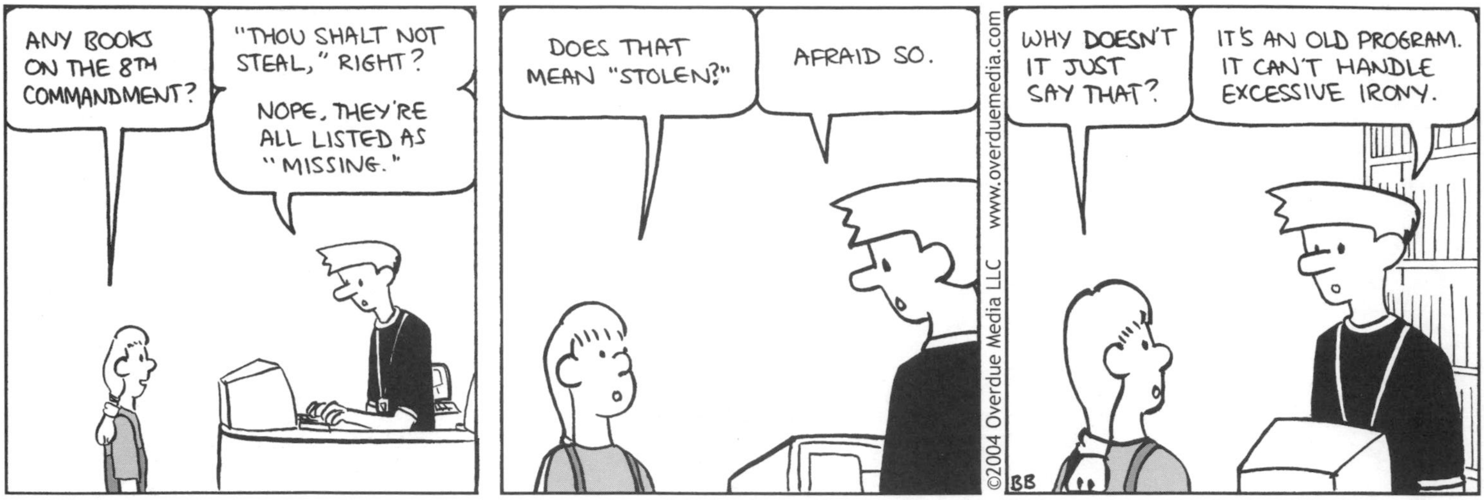
ANY BOOKS ON THE 8TH COMMANDMENT?
"THOU SHALT NOT STEAL," RIGHT?
NOPE. THEY'RE ALL LISTED AS "MISSING."
DOES THAT MEAN "STOLEN?"
AFRAID SO.
WHY DOESN'T IT JUST SAY THAT?
IT'S AN OLD PROGRAM. IT CAN'T HANDLE EXCESSIVE IRONY.
©2004 Overdue Media LLC www.overduemedia.com

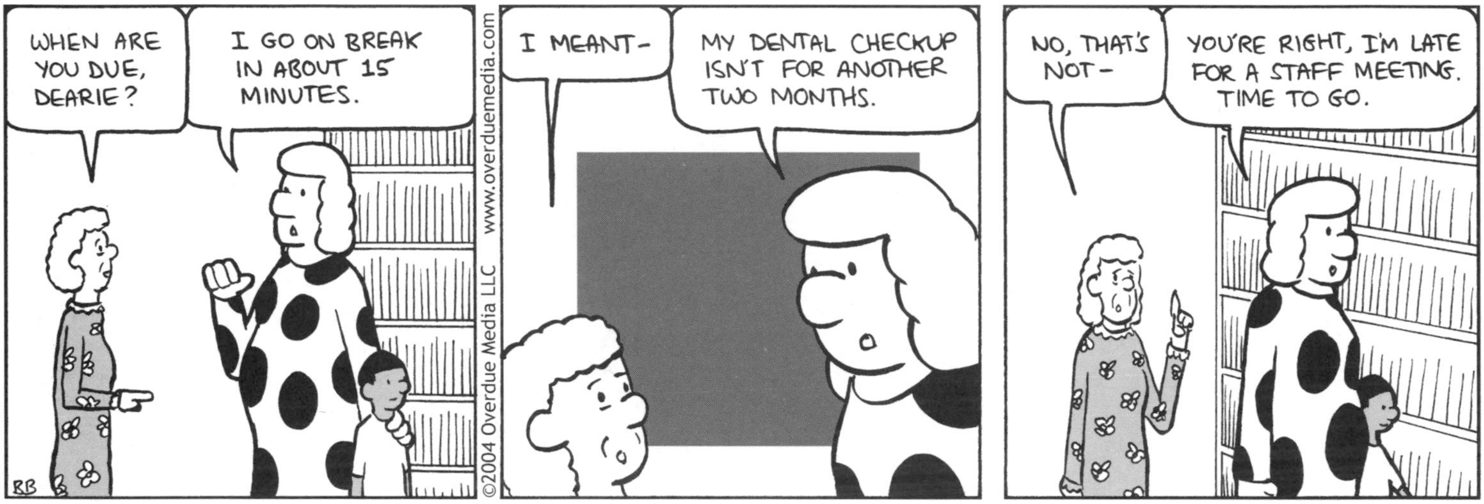
WHEN ARE YOU DUE, DEARIE?
I GO ON BREAK IN ABOUT 15 MINUTES.
I MEANT-
MY DENTAL CHECKUP ISN'T FOR ANOTHER TWO MONTHS.
NO, THAT'S NOT-
YOU'RE RIGHT, I'M LATE FOR A STAFF MEETING. TIME TO GO.
©2004 Overdue Media LLC www.overduemedia.com

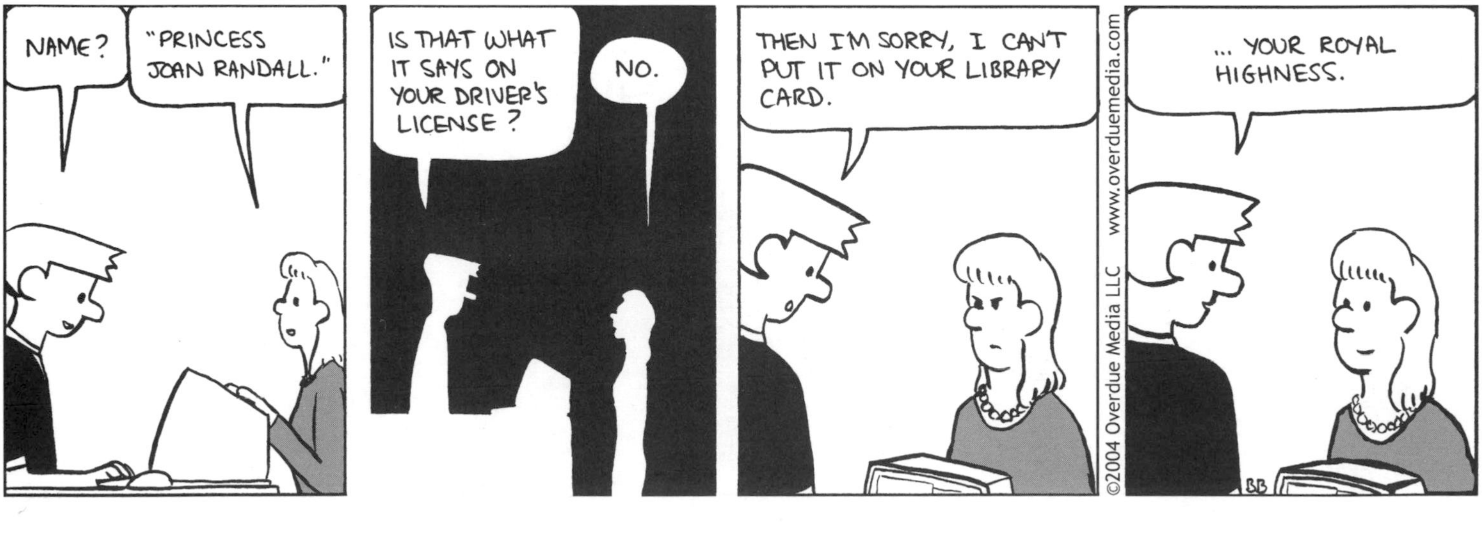
NAME?
"PRINCESS JOAN RANDALL."
IS THAT WHAT IT SAYS ON YOUR DRIVER'S LICENSE?
NO.
THEN I'M SORRY, I CAN'T PUT IT ON YOUR LIBRARY CARD.
... YOUR ROYAL HIGHNESS.
©2004 Overdue Media LLC www.overduemedia.com

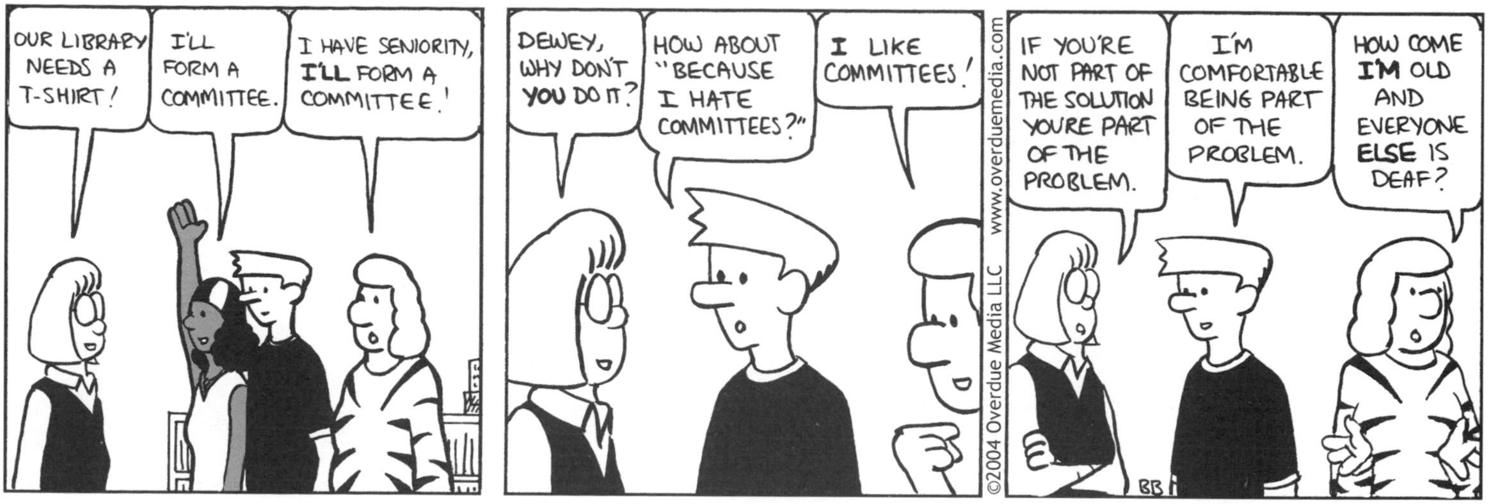
OUR LIBRARY NEEDS A T-SHIRT!
I'LL FORM A COMMITTEE.
I HAVE SENIORITY, I'LL FORM A COMMITTEE!
DEWEY, WHY DON'T YOU DO IT?
HOW ABOUT "BECAUSE I HATE COMMITTEES?"
I LIKE COMMITTEES!
©2004 Overdue Media LLC www.overduemedia.com
IF YOU'RE NOT PART OF THE SOLUTION YOU'RE PART OF THE PROBLEM.
I'M COMFORTABLE BEING PART OF THE PROBLEM.
HOW COME I'M OLD AND EVERYONE ELSE IS DEAF?
BB

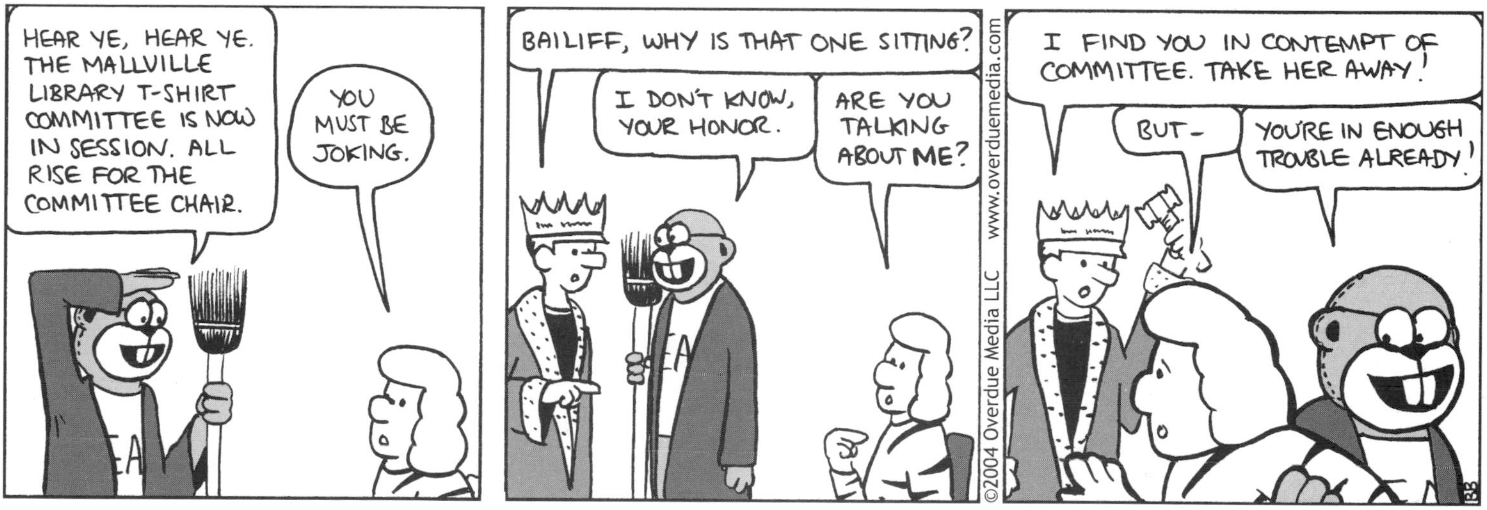
HEAR YE, HEAR YE. THE MALLVILLE LIBRARY T-SHIRT COMMITTEE IS NOW IN SESSION. ALL RISE FOR THE COMMITTEE CHAIR.
YOU MUST BE JOKING.
BAILIFF, WHY IS THAT ONE SITTING?
I DON'T KNOW, YOUR HONOR.
ARE YOU TALKING ABOUT ME?
©2004 Overdue Media LLC www.overduemedia.com
I FIND YOU IN CONTEMPT OF COMMITTEE. TAKE HER AWAY!
BUT-
YOU'RE IN ENOUGH TROUBLE ALREADY!
BB

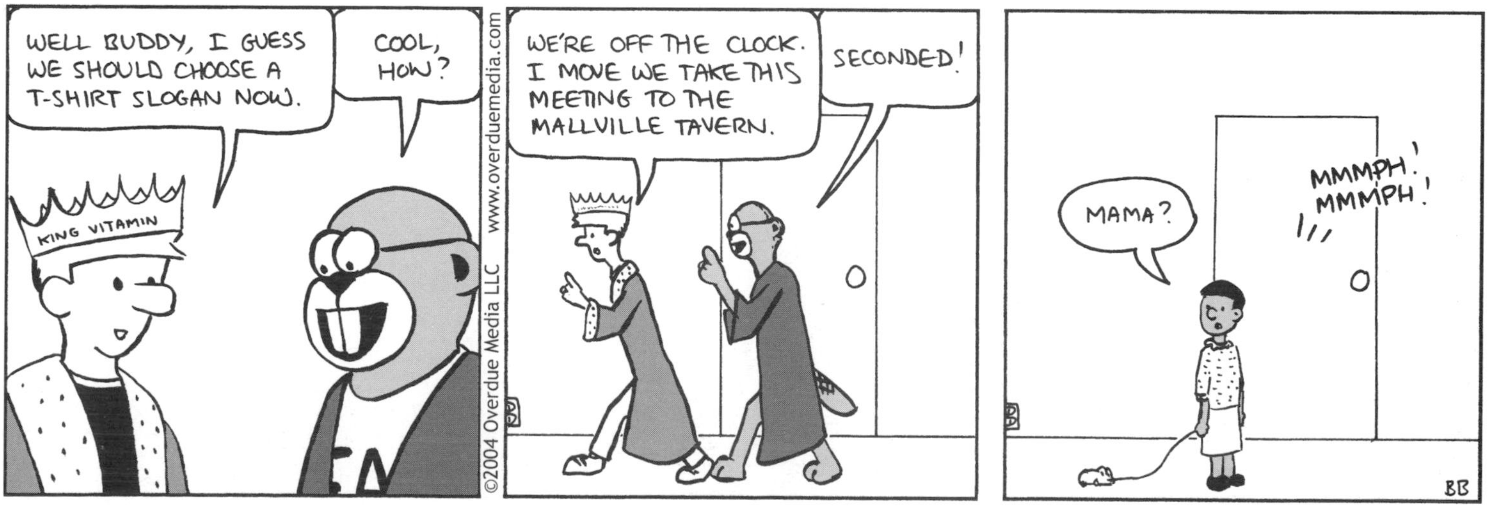
WELL BUDDY, I GUESS WE SHOULD CHOOSE A T-SHIRT SLOGAN NOW.
COOL, HOW?
KING VITAMIN
©2004 Overdue Media LLC www.overduemedia.com
WE'RE OFF THE CLOCK. I MOVE WE TAKE THIS MEETING TO THE MALLVILLE TAVERN.
SECONDED!
MAMA?
MMMPH! MMMPH!
BB

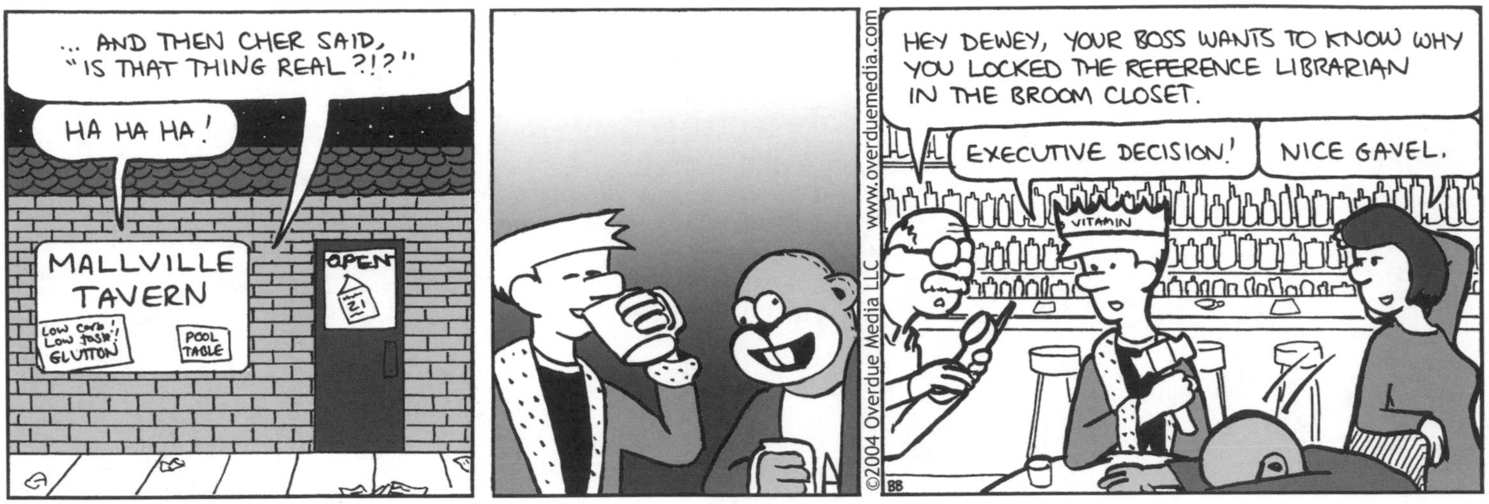
MALLVILLE TAVERN
OPEN
POOL TABLE
... AND THEN CHER SAID, "IS THAT THING REAL?!?"
HA HA HA!
HEY DEWEY, YOUR BOSS WANTS TO KNOW WHY YOU LOCKED THE REFERENCE LIBRARIAN IN THE BROOM CLOSET.
EXECUTIVE DECISION!
NICE GAVEL.
VITAMIN
©2004 Overdue Media LLC www.overduemedia.com

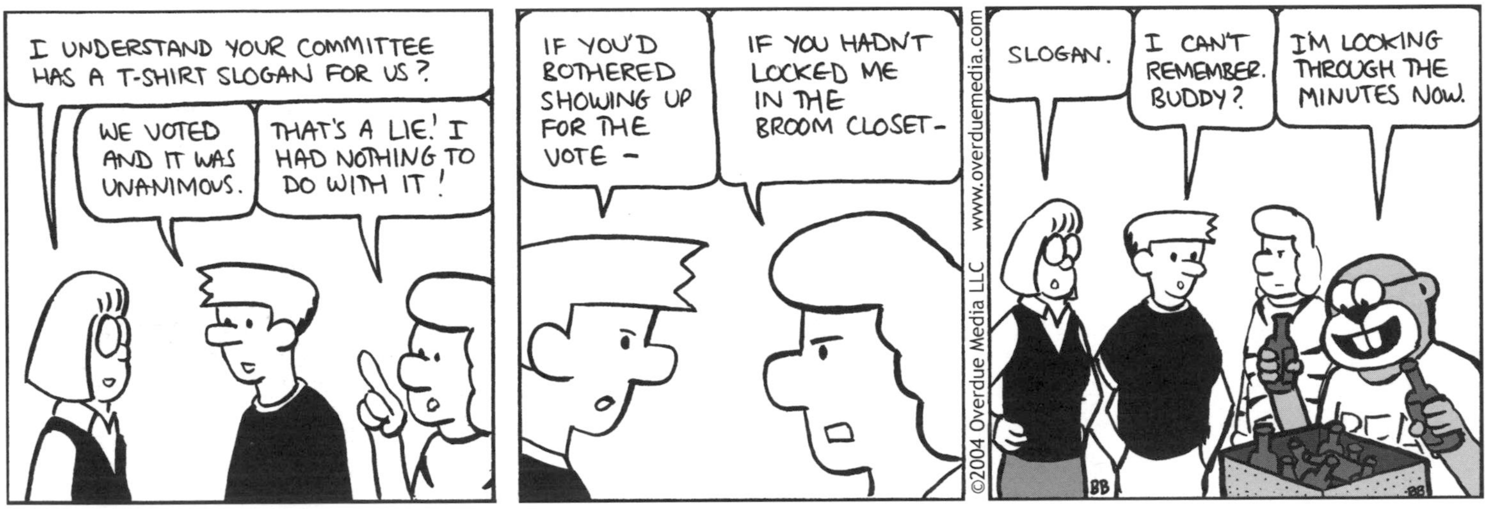
I UNDERSTAND YOUR COMMITTEE HAS A T-SHIRT SLOGAN FOR US?
WE VOTED AND IT WAS UNANIMOUS.
THAT'S A LIE! I HAD NOTHING TO DO WITH IT!
IF YOU'D BOTHERED SHOWING UP FOR THE VOTE -
IF YOU HADN'T LOCKED ME IN THE BROOM CLOSET-
SLOGAN.
I CAN'T REMEMBER. BUDDY?
I'M LOOKING THROUGH THE MINUTES NOW.
©2004 Overdue Media LLC www.overduemedia.com

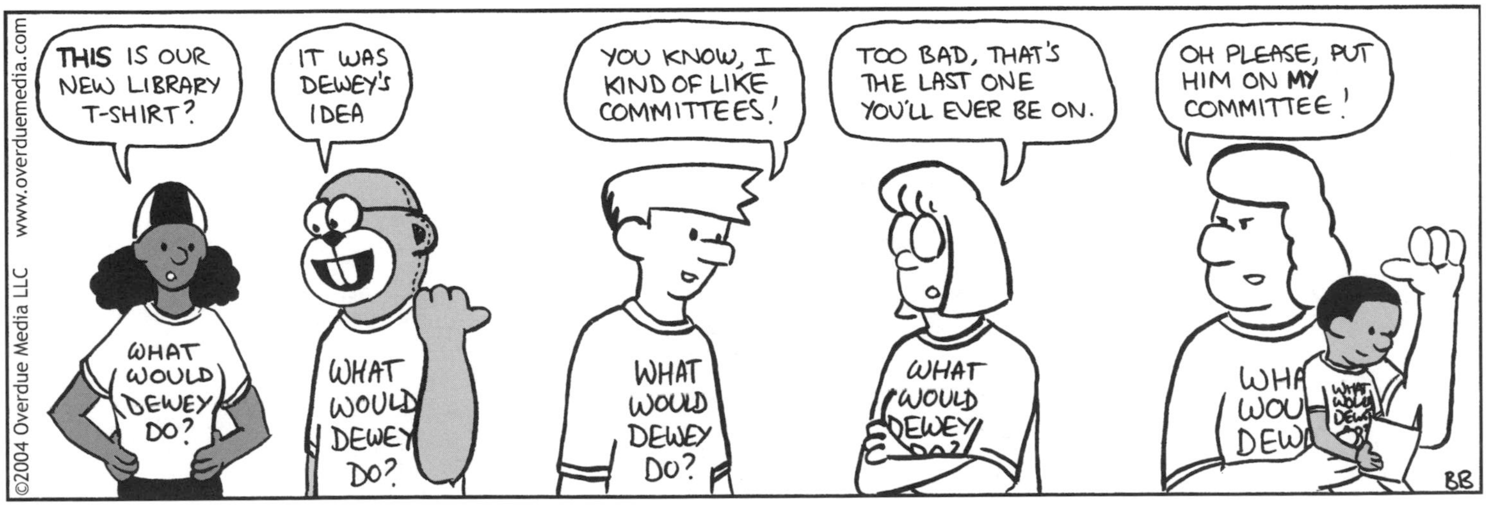
THIS IS OUR NEW LIBRARY T-SHIRT?
IT WAS DEWEY'S IDEA
WHAT WOULD DEWEY DO?
YOU KNOW, I KIND OF LIKE COMMITTEES!
TOO BAD, THAT'S THE LAST ONE YOU'LL EVER BE ON.
OH PLEASE, PUT HIM ON MY COMMITTEE!
©2004 Overdue Media LLC www.overduemedia.com

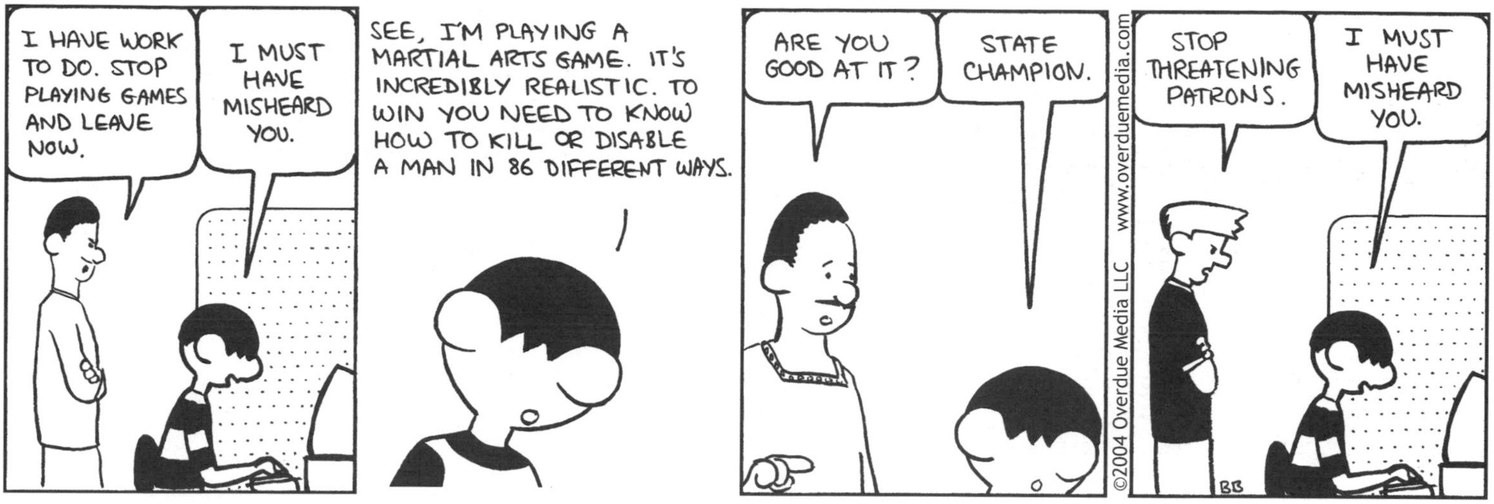
I HAVE WORK TO DO. STOP PLAYING GAMES AND LEAVE NOW.
I MUST HAVE MISHEARD YOU.
SEE, I'M PLAYING A MARTIAL ARTS GAME. IT'S INCREDIBLY REALISTIC. TO WIN YOU NEED TO KNOW HOW TO KILL OR DISABLE A MAN IN 86 DIFFERENT WAYS.
ARE YOU GOOD AT IT?
STATE CHAMPION.
STOP THREATENING PATRONS.
I MUST HAVE MISHEARD YOU.
©2004 Overdue Media LLC www.overduemedia.com
BB

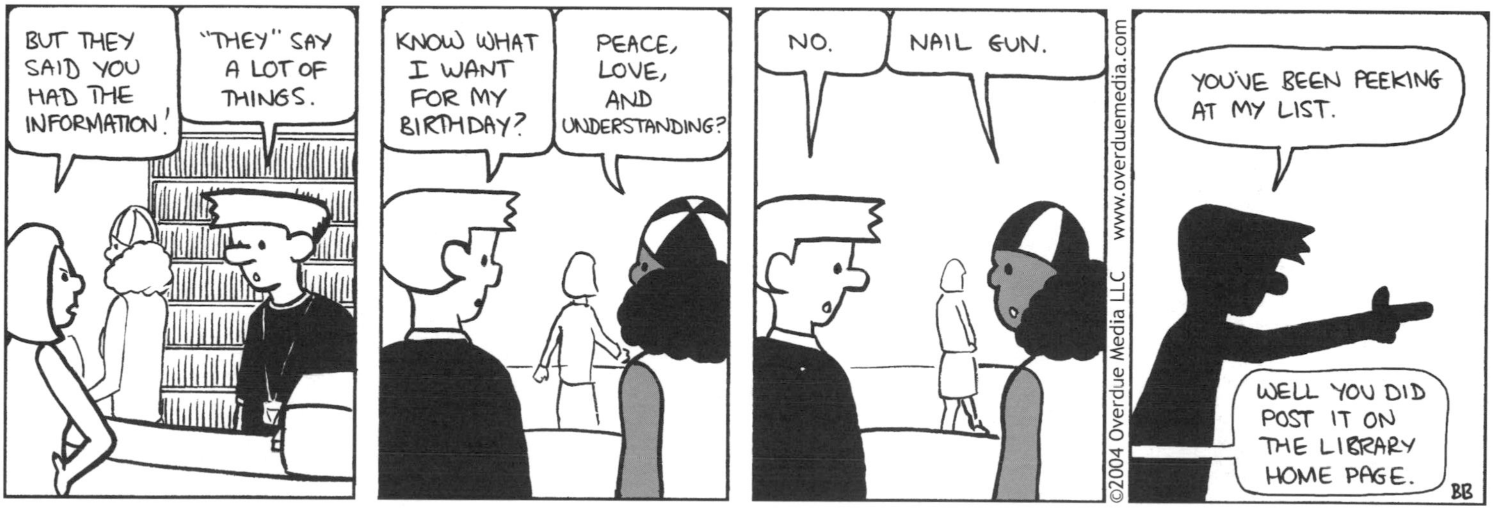
BUT THEY SAID YOU HAD THE INFORMATION!
"THEY" SAY A LOT OF THINGS.
KNOW WHAT I WANT FOR MY BIRTHDAY?
PEACE, LOVE, AND UNDERSTANDING?
NO.
NAIL GUN.
YOU'VE BEEN PEEKING AT MY LIST.
WELL YOU DID POST IT ON THE LIBRARY HOME PAGE.
©2004 Overdue Media LLC www.overduemedia.com
BB

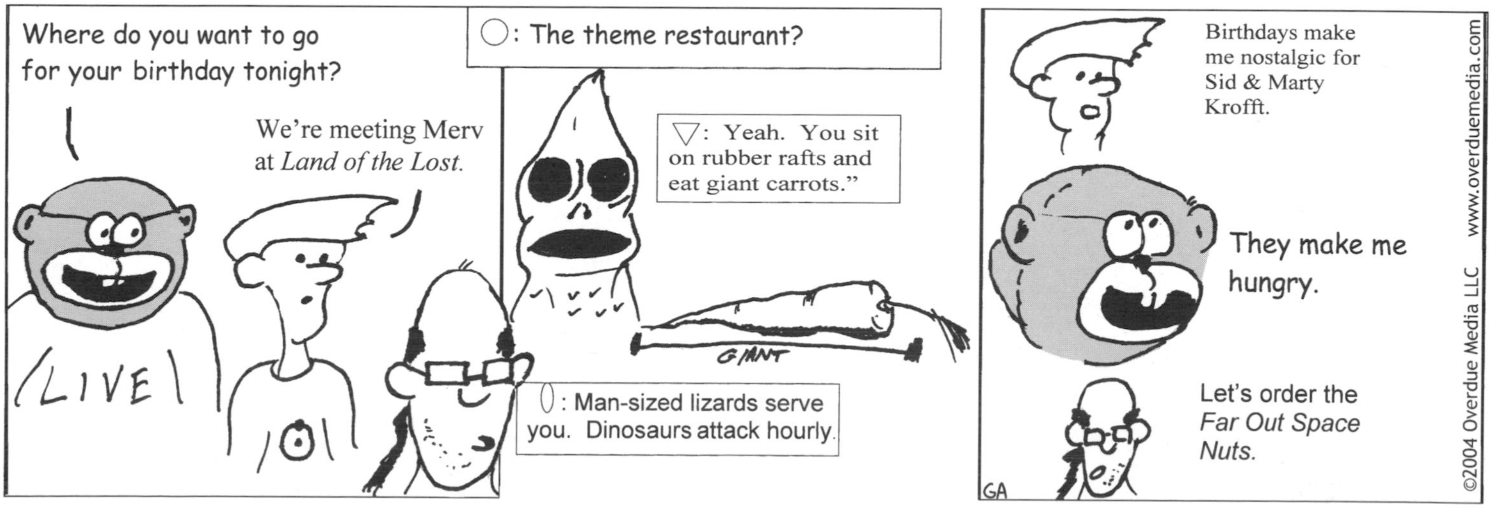
Where do you want to go for your birthday tonight?
We're meeting Merv at *Land of the Lost*.
LIVE
○: The theme restaurant?
▽: Yeah. You sit on rubber rafts and eat giant carrots."
GIANT
⬯ : Man-sized lizards serve you. Dinosaurs attack hourly.
Birthdays make me nostalgic for Sid & Marty Krofft.
They make me hungry.
Let's order the *Far Out Space Nuts.*
GA
©2004 Overdue Media LLC www.overduemedia.com

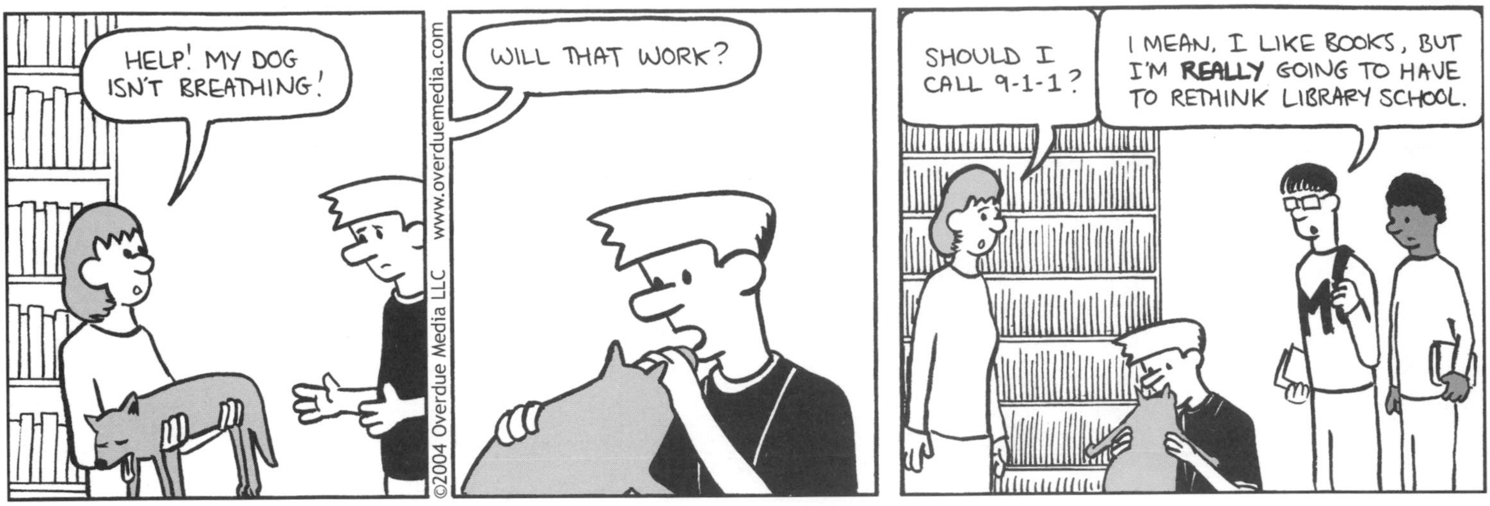
HELP! MY DOG ISN'T BREATHING!
©2004 Overdue Media LLC www.overduemedia.com
WILL THAT WORK?
SHOULD I CALL 9-1-1?
I MEAN, I LIKE BOOKS, BUT I'M **REALLY** GOING TO HAVE TO RETHINK LIBRARY SCHOOL.

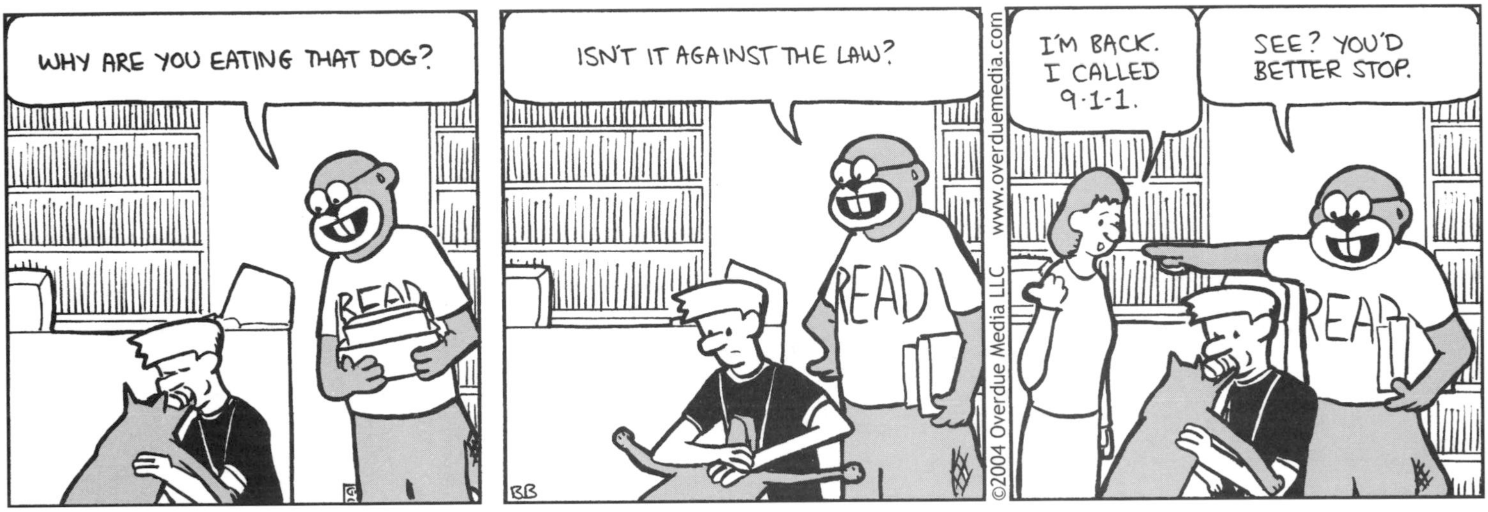
WHY ARE YOU EATING THAT DOG?
READ
ISN'T IT AGAINST THE LAW?
READ
©2004 Overdue Media LLC www.overduemedia.com
I'M BACK. I CALLED 9-1-1.
SEE? YOU'D BETTER STOP.

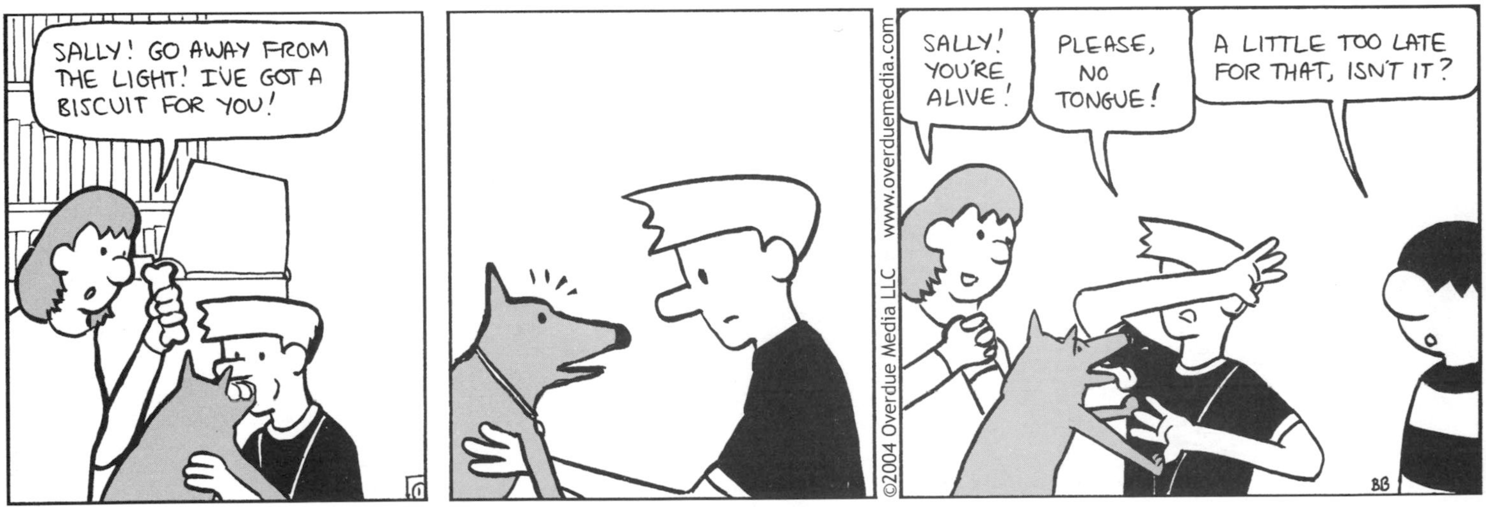
SALLY! GO AWAY FROM THE LIGHT! I'VE GOT A BISCUIT FOR YOU!
©2004 Overdue Media LLC www.overduemedia.com
SALLY! YOU'RE ALIVE!
PLEASE, NO TONGUE!
A LITTLE TOO LATE FOR THAT, ISN'T IT?

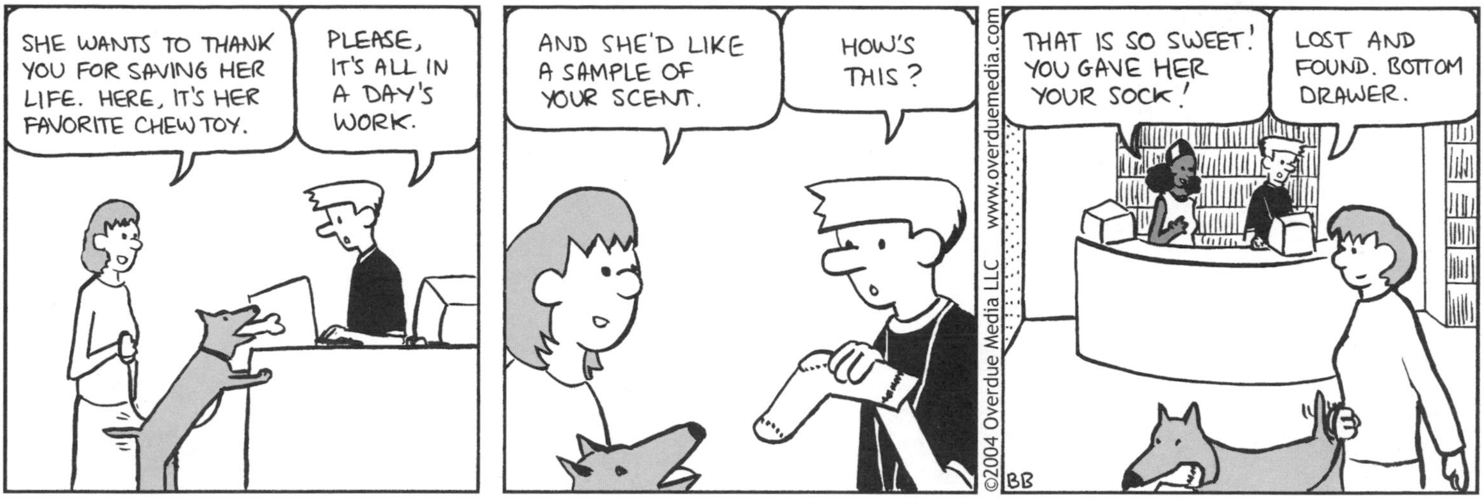
SHE WANTS TO THANK YOU FOR SAVING HER LIFE. HERE, IT'S HER FAVORITE CHEW TOY.
PLEASE, IT'S ALL IN A DAY'S WORK.
AND SHE'D LIKE A SAMPLE OF YOUR SCENT.
HOW'S THIS?
©2004 Overdue Media LLC www.overduemedia.com
THAT IS SO SWEET! YOU GAVE HER YOUR SOCK!
LOST AND FOUND. BOTTOM DRAWER.
BB

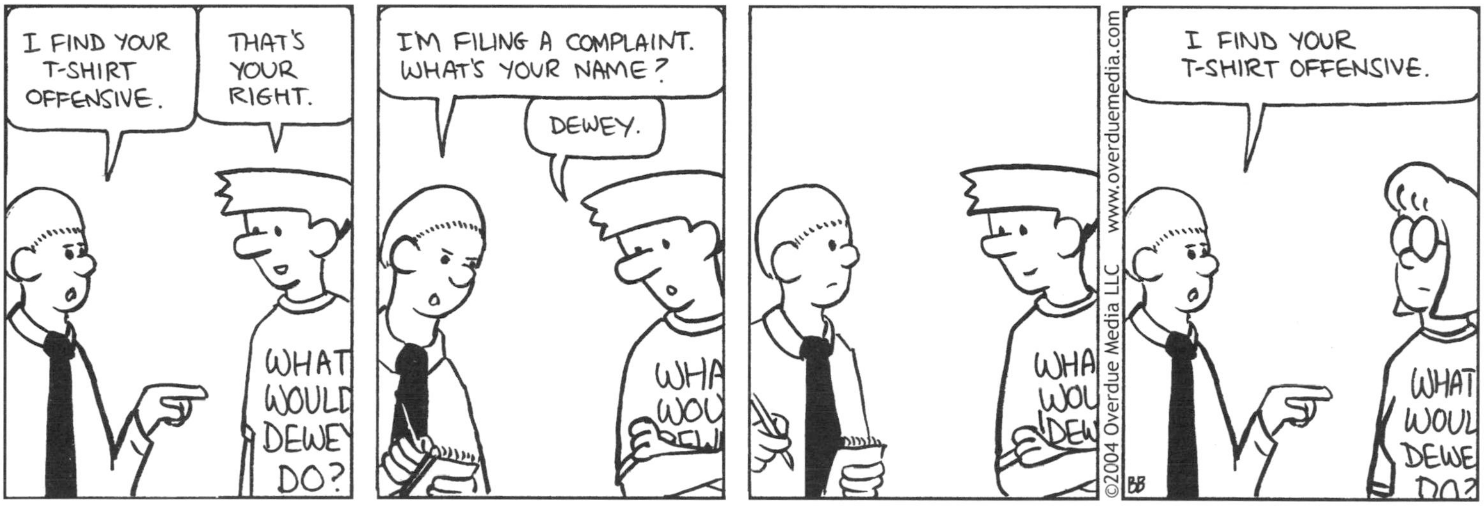
I FIND YOUR T-SHIRT OFFENSIVE.
THAT'S YOUR RIGHT.
WHAT WOULD DEWEY DO?
I'M FILING A COMPLAINT. WHAT'S YOUR NAME?
DEWEY.
©2004 Overdue Media LLC www.overduemedia.com
I FIND YOUR T-SHIRT OFFENSIVE.
BB

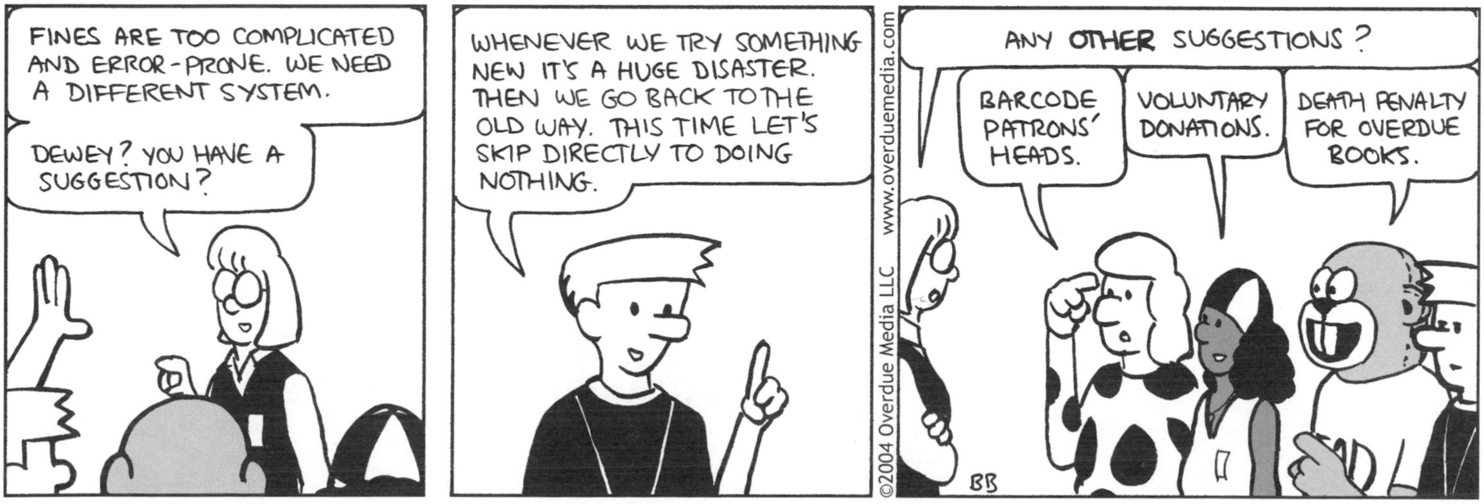
FINES ARE TOO COMPLICATED AND ERROR-PRONE. WE NEED A DIFFERENT SYSTEM.
DEWEY? YOU HAVE A SUGGESTION?
WHENEVER WE TRY SOMETHING NEW IT'S A HUGE DISASTER. THEN WE GO BACK TO THE OLD WAY. THIS TIME LET'S SKIP DIRECTLY TO DOING NOTHING.
©2004 Overdue Media LLC www.overduemedia.com
ANY OTHER SUGGESTIONS?
BARCODE PATRONS' HEADS.
VOLUNTARY DONATIONS.
DEATH PENALTY FOR OVERDUE BOOKS.
BB

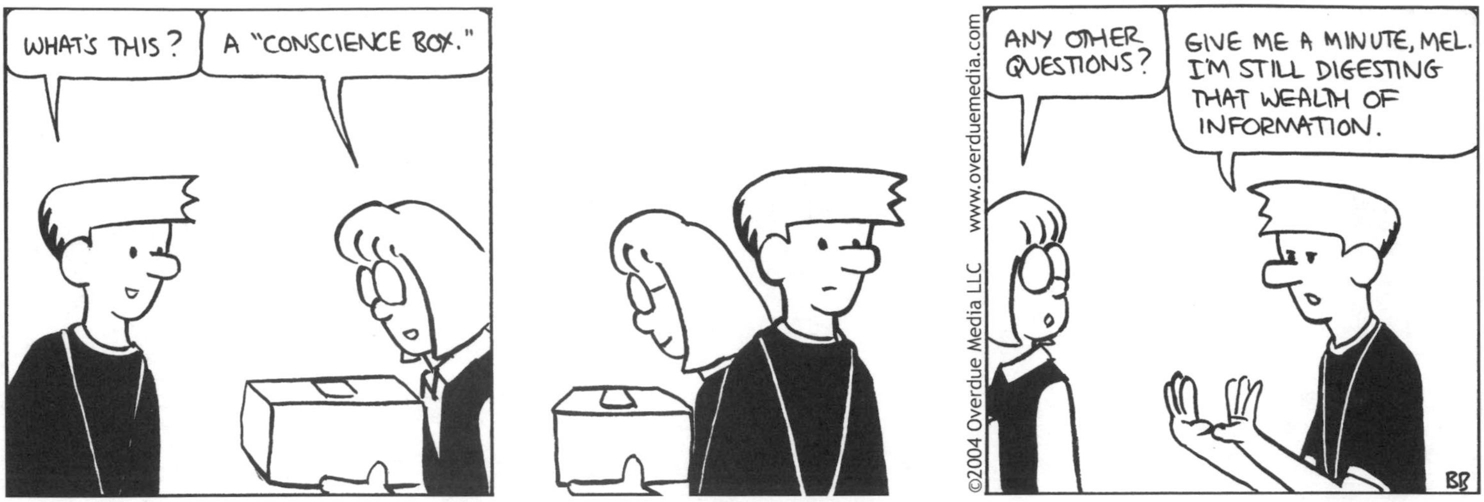
WHAT'S THIS?
A "CONSCIENCE BOX."
ANY OTHER QUESTIONS?
GIVE ME A MINUTE, MEL. I'M STILL DIGESTING THAT WEALTH OF INFORMATION.
©2004 Overdue Media LLC www.overduemedia.com


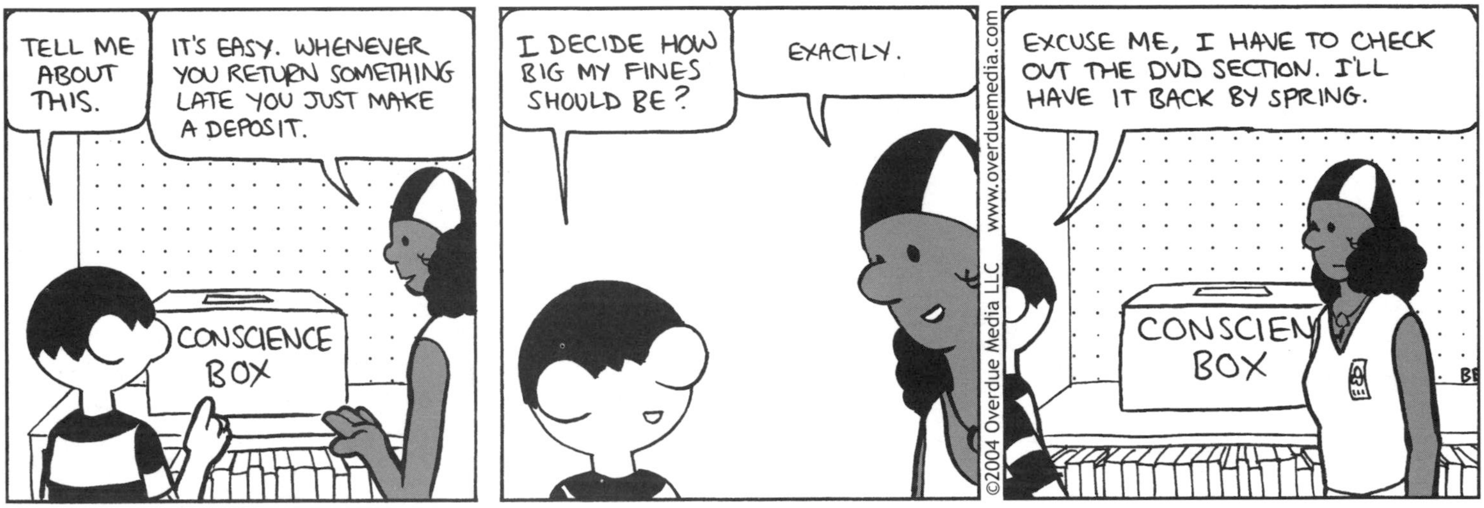
TELL ME ABOUT THIS.
IT'S EASY. WHENEVER YOU RETURN SOMETHING LATE YOU JUST MAKE A DEPOSIT.
CONSCIENCE BOX
I DECIDE HOW BIG MY FINES SHOULD BE?
EXACTLY.
EXCUSE ME, I HAVE TO CHECK OUT THE DVD SECTION. I'LL HAVE IT BACK BY SPRING.
CONSCIEN BOX
©2004 Overdue Media LLC www.overduemedia.com


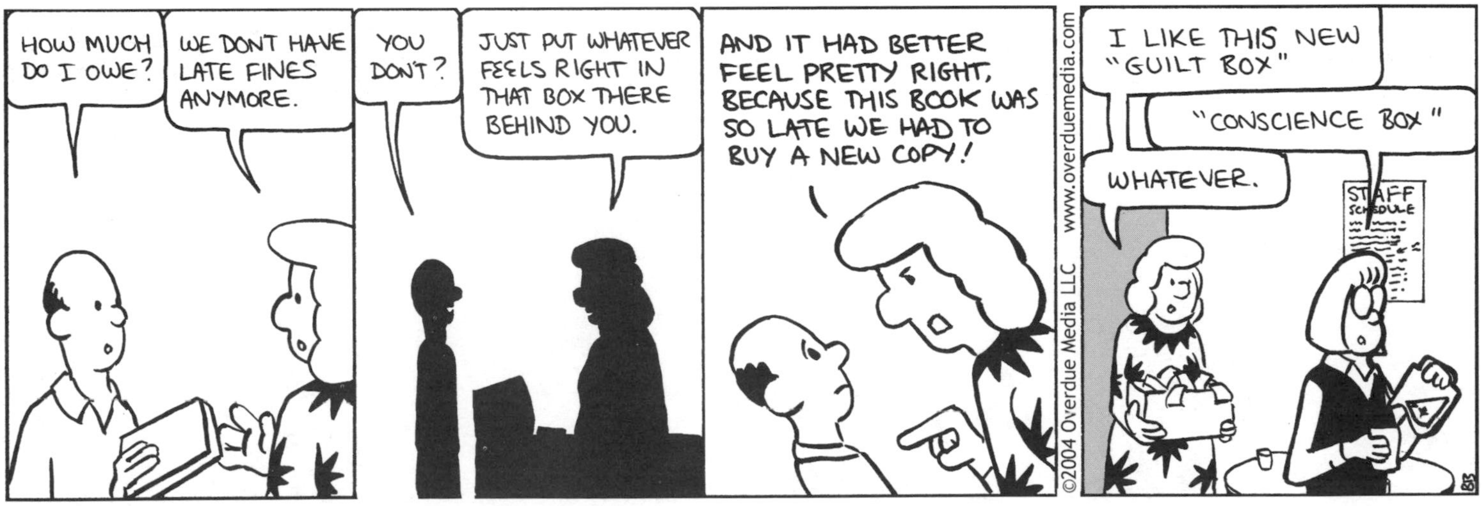
HOW MUCH DO I OWE?
WE DON'T HAVE LATE FINES ANYMORE.
YOU DON'T?
JUST PUT WHATEVER FEELS RIGHT IN THAT BOX THERE BEHIND YOU.
AND IT HAD BETTER FEEL PRETTY RIGHT, BECAUSE THIS BOOK WAS SO LATE WE HAD TO BUY A NEW COPY!
I LIKE THIS NEW "GUILT BOX"
"CONSCIENCE BOX"
WHATEVER.
STAFF SCHEDULE
©2004 Overdue Media LLC www.overduemedia.com

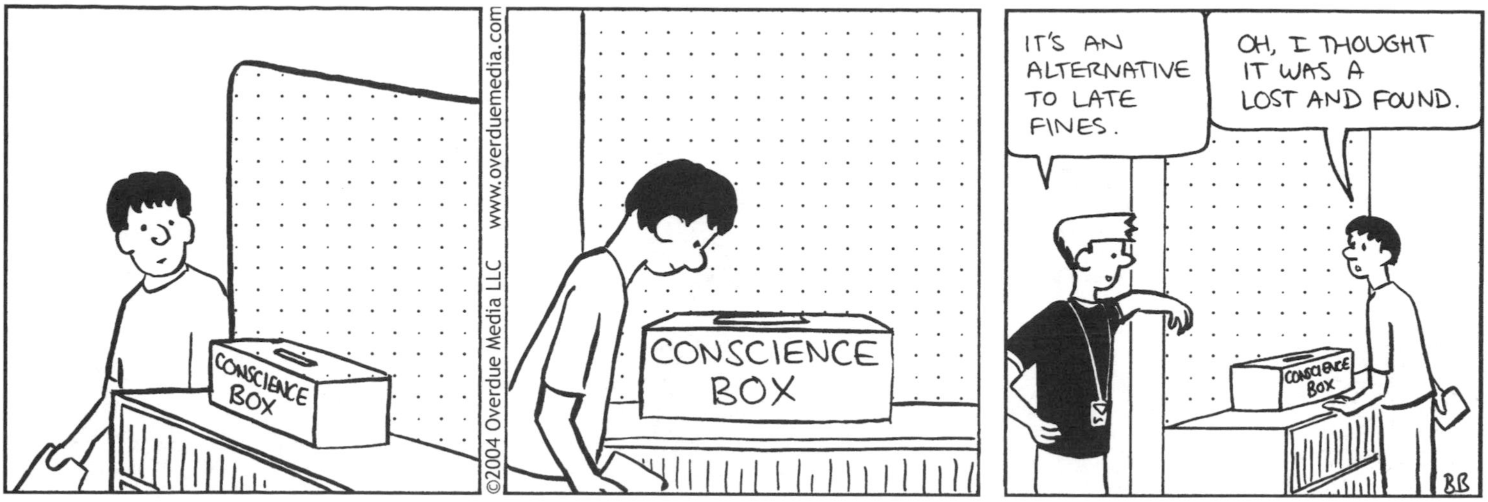
CONSCIENCE BOX
©2004 Overdue Media LLC www.overduemedia.com
CONSCIENCE BOX
IT'S AN ALTERNATIVE TO LATE FINES.
OH, I THOUGHT IT WAS A LOST AND FOUND.
CONSCIENCE BOX
BB

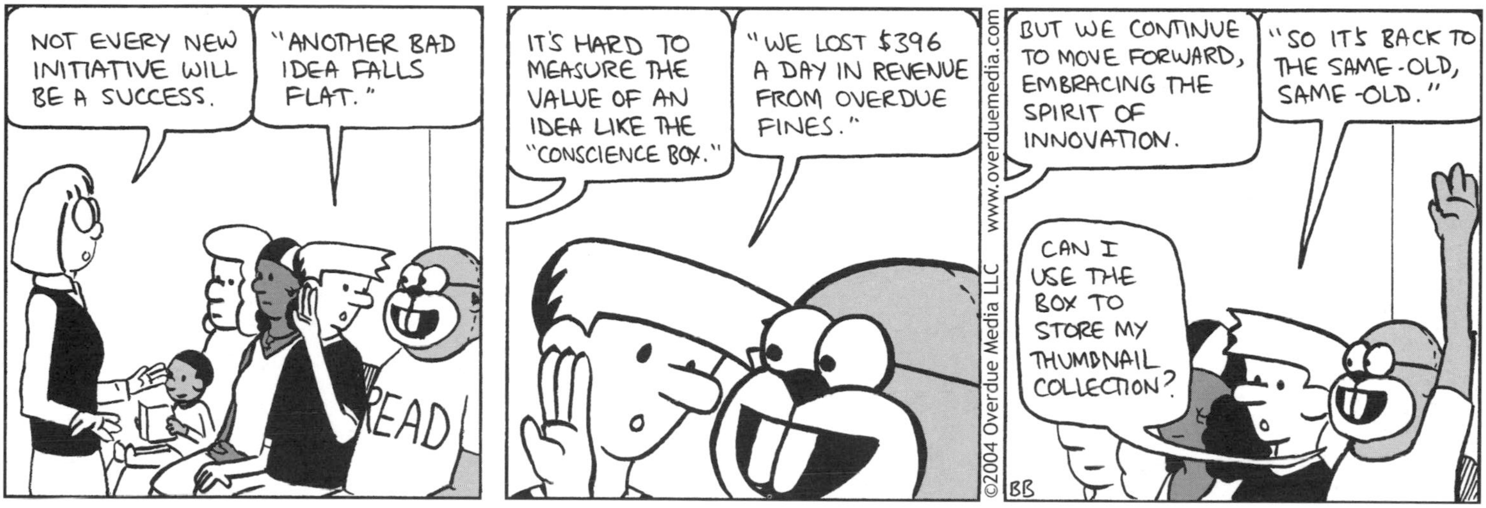
NOT EVERY NEW INITIATIVE WILL BE A SUCCESS.
"ANOTHER BAD IDEA FALLS FLAT."
READ
IT'S HARD TO MEASURE THE VALUE OF AN IDEA LIKE THE "CONSCIENCE BOX."
"WE LOST $396 A DAY IN REVENUE FROM OVERDUE FINES."
©2004 Overdue Media LLC www.overduemedia.com
BUT WE CONTINUE TO MOVE FORWARD, EMBRACING THE SPIRIT OF INNOVATION.
"SO IT'S BACK TO THE SAME-OLD, SAME-OLD."
CAN I USE THE BOX TO STORE MY THUMBNAIL COLLECTION?
BB

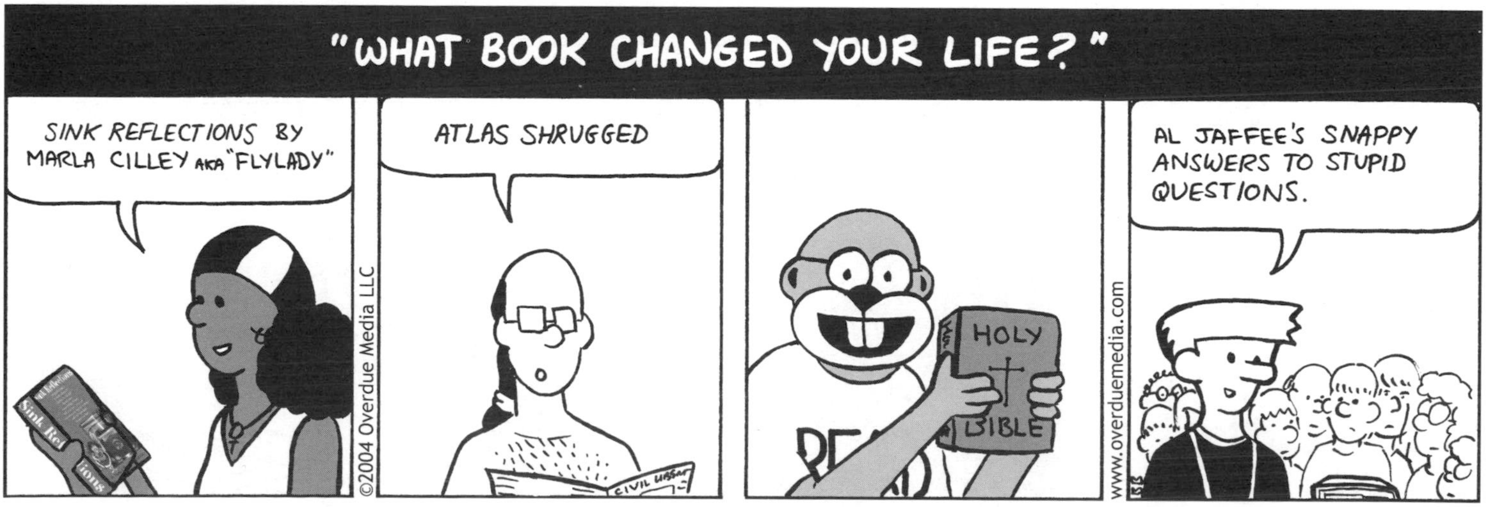
"WHAT BOOK CHANGED YOUR LIFE?"
SINK REFLECTIONS BY MARLA CILLEY AKA "FLYLADY"
©2004 Overdue Media LLC
ATLAS SHRUGGED
HOLY BIBLE
AL JAFFEE'S SNAPPY ANSWERS TO STUPID QUESTIONS.
www.overduemedia.com

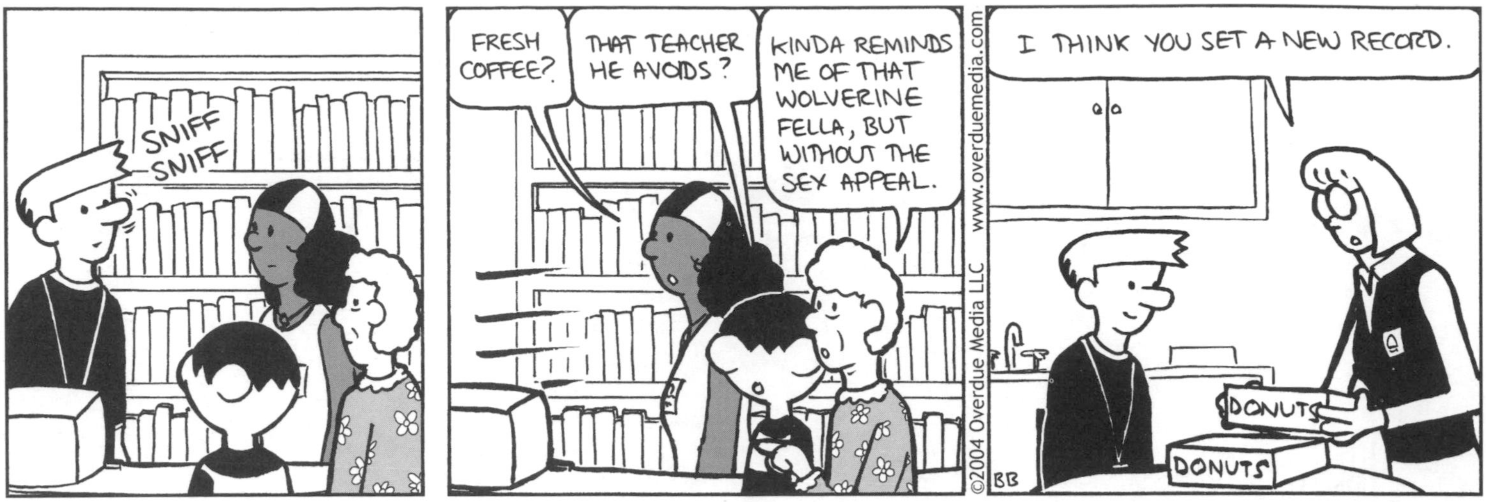
SNIFF SNIFF
FRESH COFFEE?
THAT TEACHER HE AVOIDS?
KINDA REMINDS ME OF THAT WOLVERINE FELLA, BUT WITHOUT THE SEX APPEAL.
©2004 Overdue Media LLC www.overduemedia.com
I THINK YOU SET A NEW RECORD.
DONUTS
DONUTS
BB

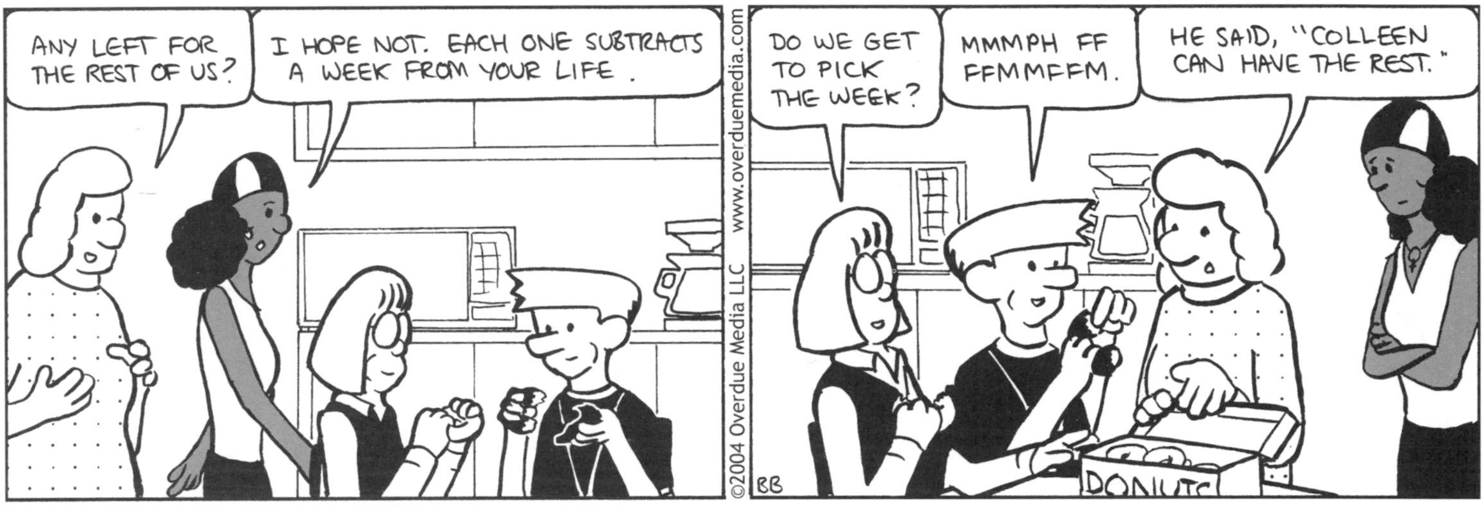
ANY LEFT FOR THE REST OF US?
I HOPE NOT. EACH ONE SUBTRACTS A WEEK FROM YOUR LIFE.
©2004 Overdue Media LLC www.overduemedia.com
DO WE GET TO PICK THE WEEK?
MMMPH FF FFMMFFM.
HE SAID, "COLLEEN CAN HAVE THE REST."
BB

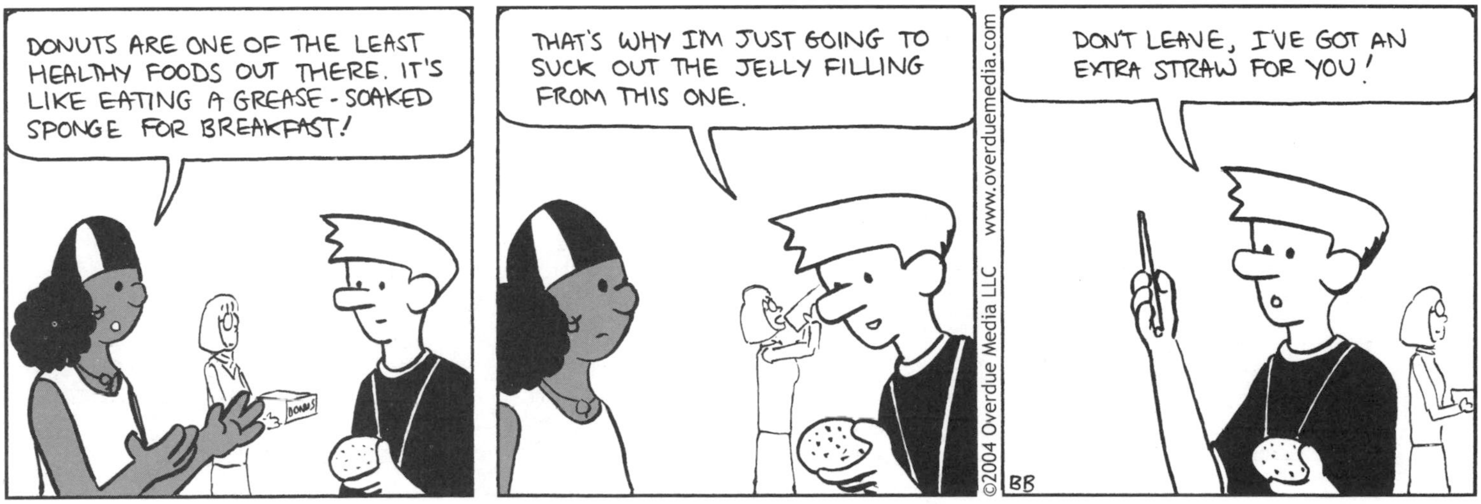
DONUTS ARE ONE OF THE LEAST HEALTHY FOODS OUT THERE. IT'S LIKE EATING A GREASE-SOAKED SPONGE FOR BREAKFAST!
THAT'S WHY I'M JUST GOING TO SUCK OUT THE JELLY FILLING FROM THIS ONE.
©2004 Overdue Media LLC www.overduemedia.com
DON'T LEAVE, I'VE GOT AN EXTRA STRAW FOR YOU!
BB

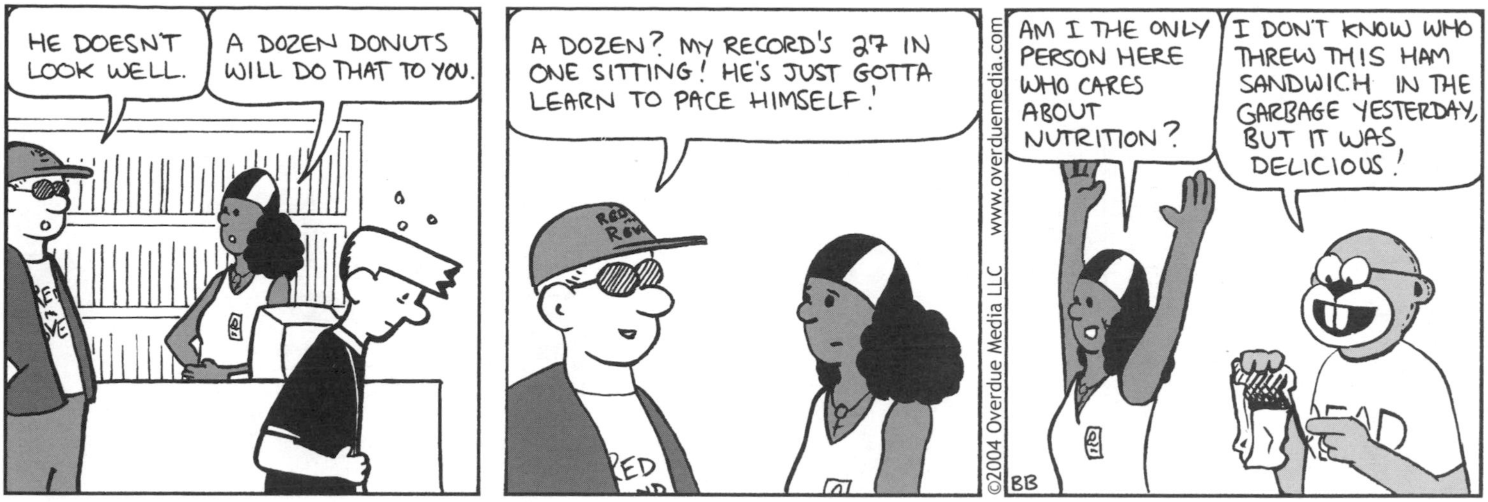
HE DOESN'T LOOK WELL.
A DOZEN DONUTS WILL DO THAT TO YOU.
A DOZEN? MY RECORD'S 27 IN ONE SITTING! HE'S JUST GOTTA LEARN TO PACE HIMSELF!
AM I THE ONLY PERSON HERE WHO CARES ABOUT NUTRITION?
I DON'T KNOW WHO THREW THIS HAM SANDWICH IN THE GARBAGE YESTERDAY, BUT IT WAS DELICIOUS!
©2004 Overdue Media LLC www.overduemedia.com

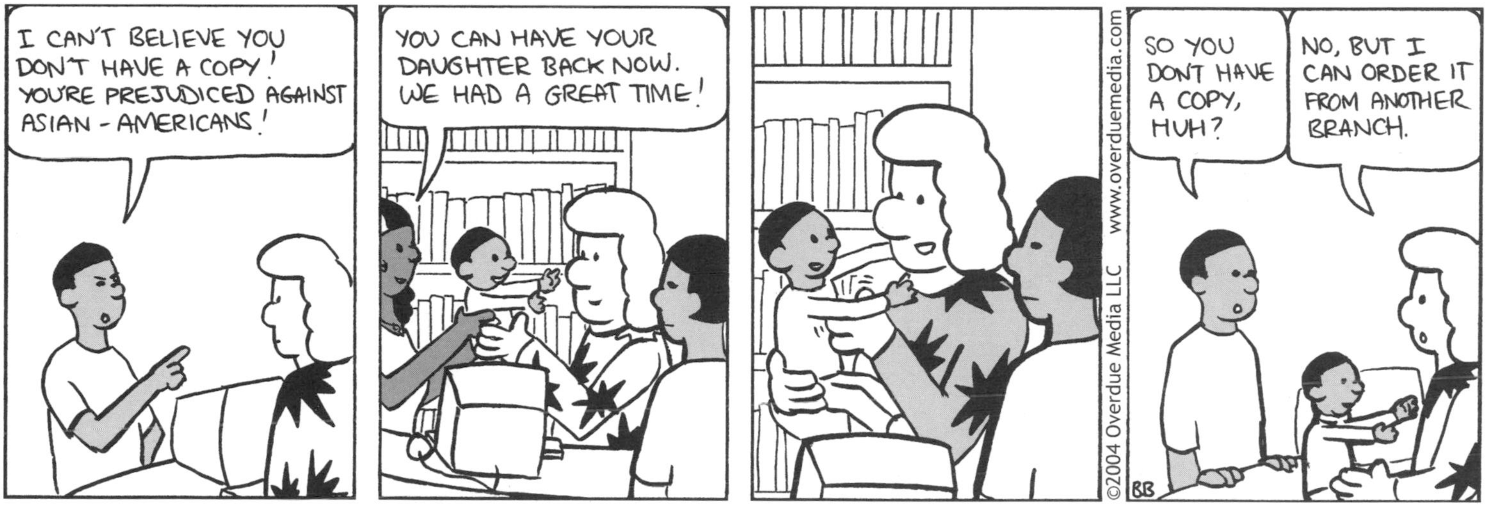
I CAN'T BELIEVE YOU DON'T HAVE A COPY! YOU'RE PREJUDICED AGAINST ASIAN-AMERICANS!
YOU CAN HAVE YOUR DAUGHTER BACK NOW. WE HAD A GREAT TIME!
SO YOU DON'T HAVE A COPY, HUH?
NO, BUT I CAN ORDER IT FROM ANOTHER BRANCH.
©2004 Overdue Media LLC www.overduemedia.com

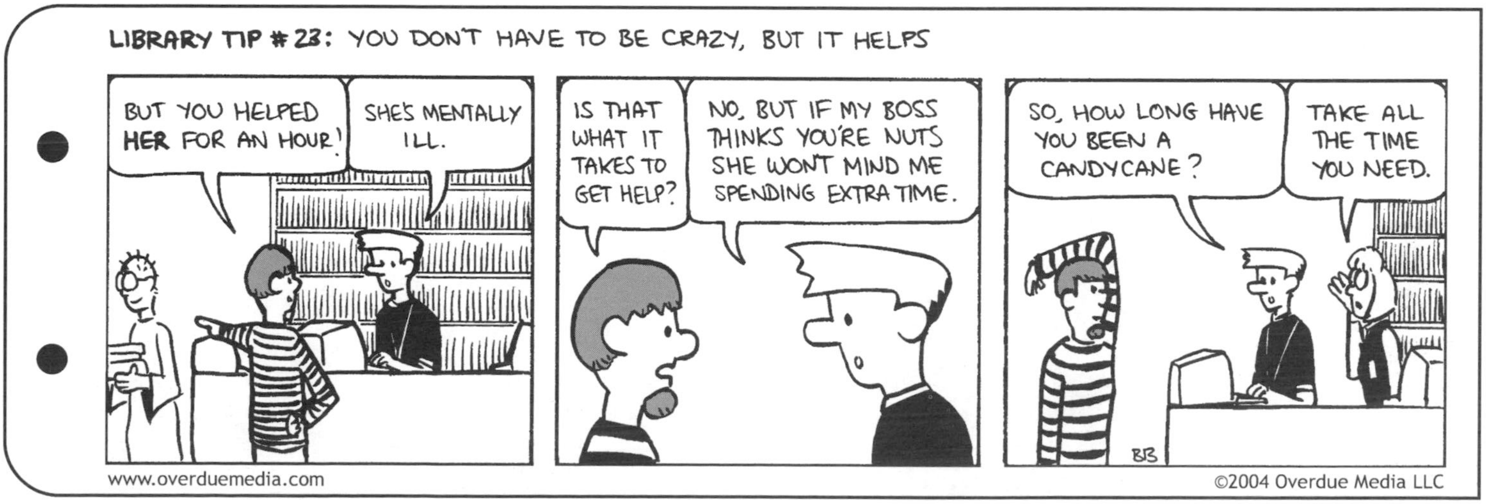
LIBRARY TIP #23: YOU DON'T HAVE TO BE CRAZY, BUT IT HELPS
BUT YOU HELPED HER FOR AN HOUR!
SHE'S MENTALLY ILL.
IS THAT WHAT IT TAKES TO GET HELP?
NO, BUT IF MY BOSS THINKS YOU'RE NUTS SHE WON'T MIND ME SPENDING EXTRA TIME.
SO, HOW LONG HAVE YOU BEEN A CANDYCANE?
TAKE ALL THE TIME YOU NEED.
www.overduemedia.com
©2004 Overdue Media LLC

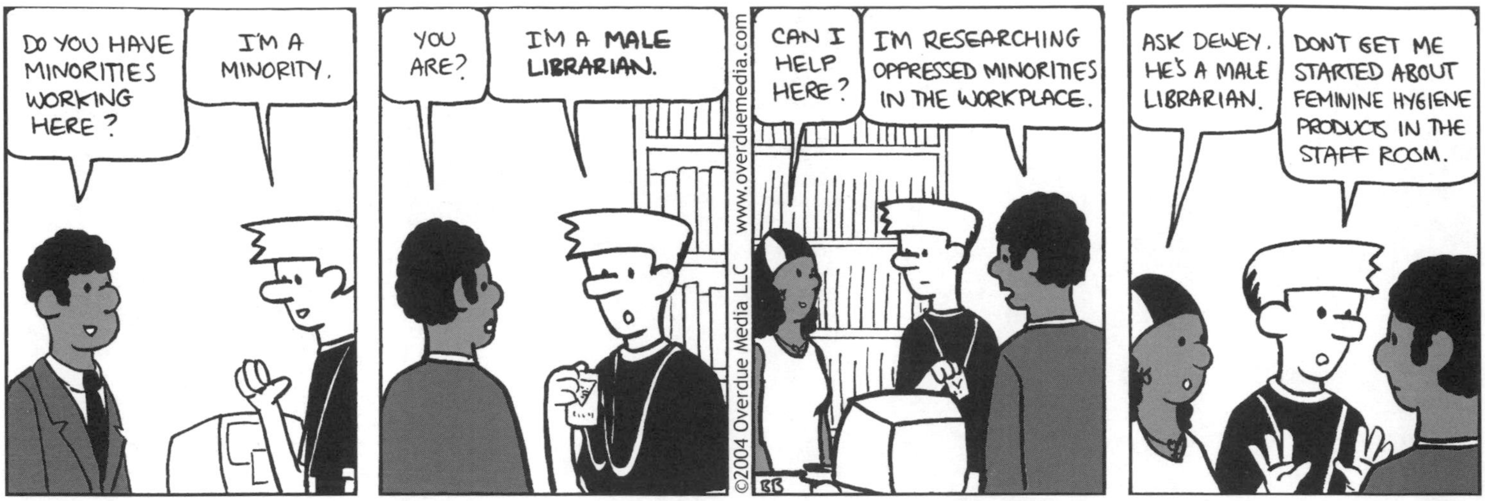
DO YOU HAVE MINORITIES WORKING HERE?
I'M A MINORITY.
YOU ARE?
I'M A **MALE LIBRARIAN.**
www.overduemedia.com
©2004 Overdue Media LLC
CAN I HELP HERE?
I'M RESEARCHING OPPRESSED MINORITIES IN THE WORKPLACE.
ASK DEWEY. HE'S A MALE LIBRARIAN.
DON'T GET ME STARTED ABOUT FEMININE HYGIENE PRODUCTS IN THE STAFF ROOM.

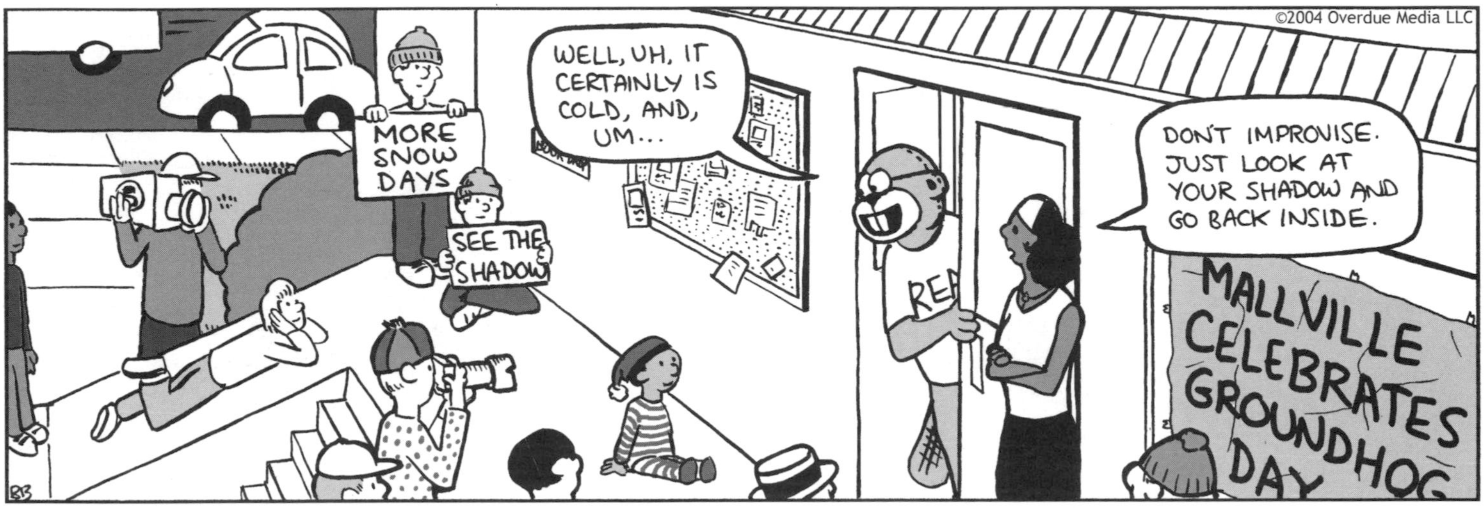
©2004 Overdue Media LLC
MORE SNOW DAYS
SEE THE SHADOW
WELL, UH, IT CERTAINLY IS COLD, AND, UM...
DON'T IMPROVISE. JUST LOOK AT YOUR SHADOW AND GO BACK INSIDE.
MALLVILLE CELEBRATES GROUNDHOG DAY

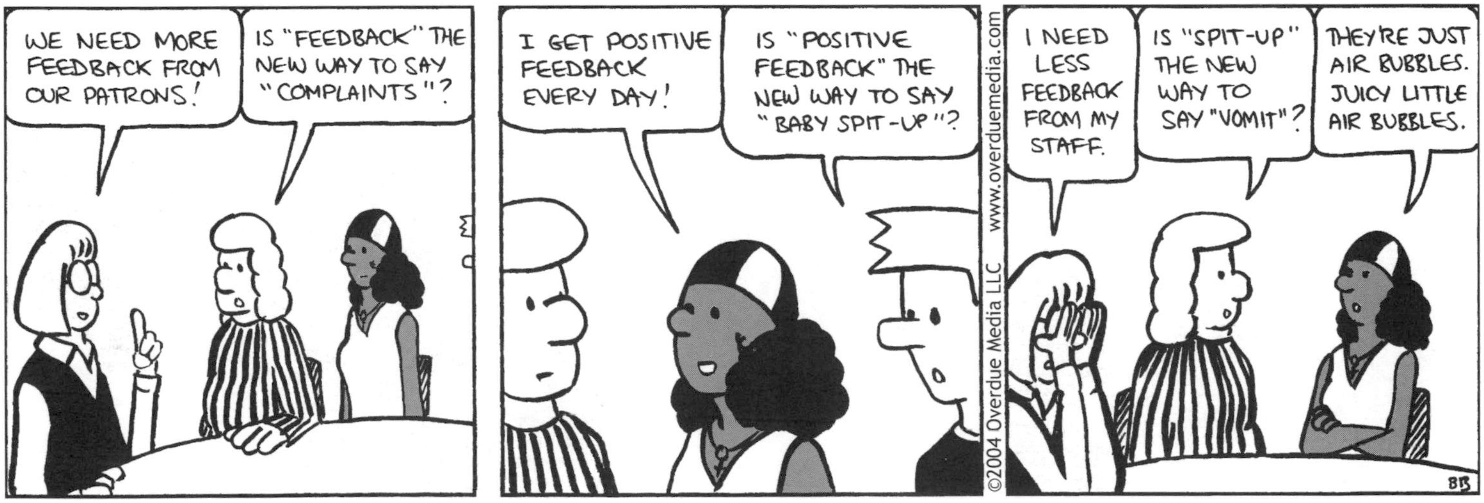
WE NEED MORE FEEDBACK FROM OUR PATRONS!
IS "FEEDBACK" THE NEW WAY TO SAY "COMPLAINTS"?
I GET POSITIVE FEEDBACK EVERY DAY!
IS "POSITIVE FEEDBACK" THE NEW WAY TO SAY "BABY SPIT-UP"?
www.overduemedia.com
©2004 Overdue Media LLC
I NEED LESS FEEDBACK FROM MY STAFF.
IS "SPIT-UP" THE NEW WAY TO SAY "VOMIT"?
THEY'RE JUST AIR BUBBLES. JUICY LITTLE AIR BUBBLES.

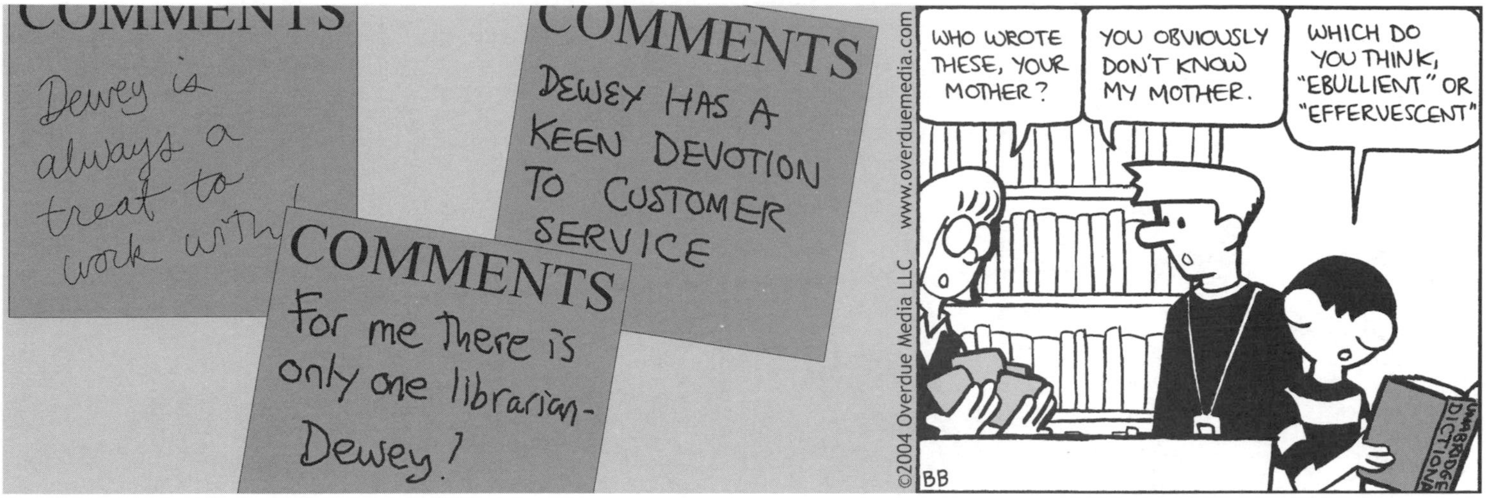
COMMENTS
Dewey is always a treat to work with!
COMMENTS
DEWEY HAS A KEEN DEVOTION TO CUSTOMER SERVICE
COMMENTS
For me there is only one librarian- Dewey!
©2004 Overdue Media LLC www.overduemedia.com
WHO WROTE THESE, YOUR MOTHER?
YOU OBVIOUSLY DON'T KNOW MY MOTHER.
WHICH DO YOU THINK, "EBULLIENT" OR "EFFERVESCENT"
BB

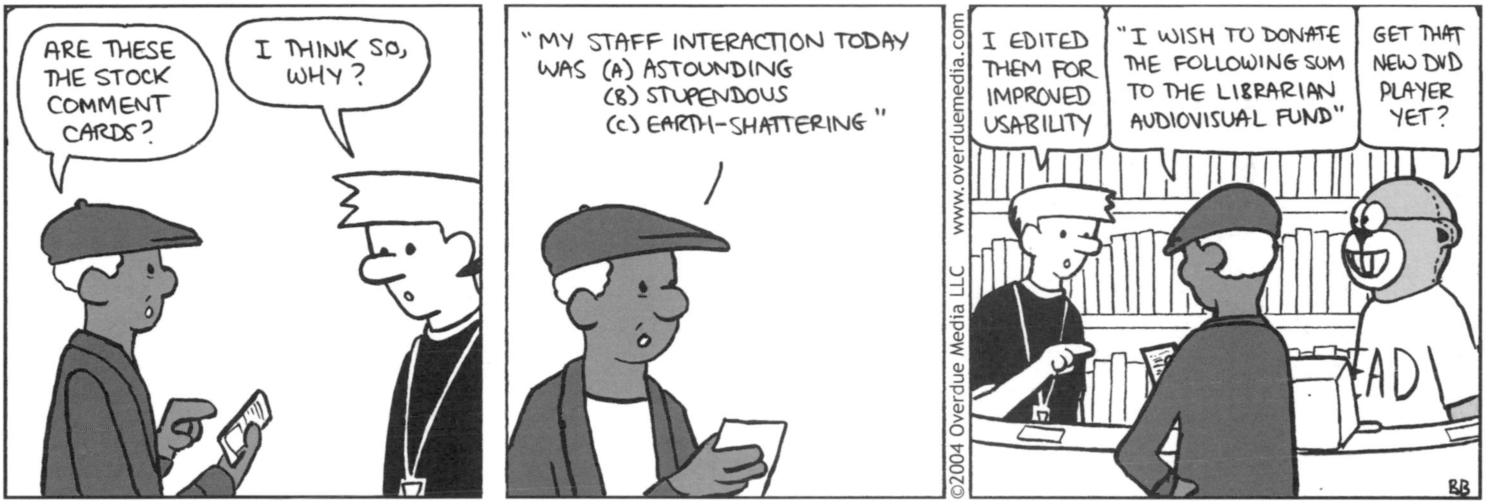
ARE THESE THE STOCK COMMENT CARDS?
I THINK SO, WHY?
"MY STAFF INTERACTION TODAY WAS (A) ASTOUNDING (B) STUPENDOUS (C) EARTH-SHATTERING"
©2004 Overdue Media LLC www.overduemedia.com
I EDITED THEM FOR IMPROVED USABILITY
"I WISH TO DONATE THE FOLLOWING SUM TO THE LIBRARIAN AUDIOVISUAL FUND"
GET THAT NEW DVD PLAYER YET?
BB

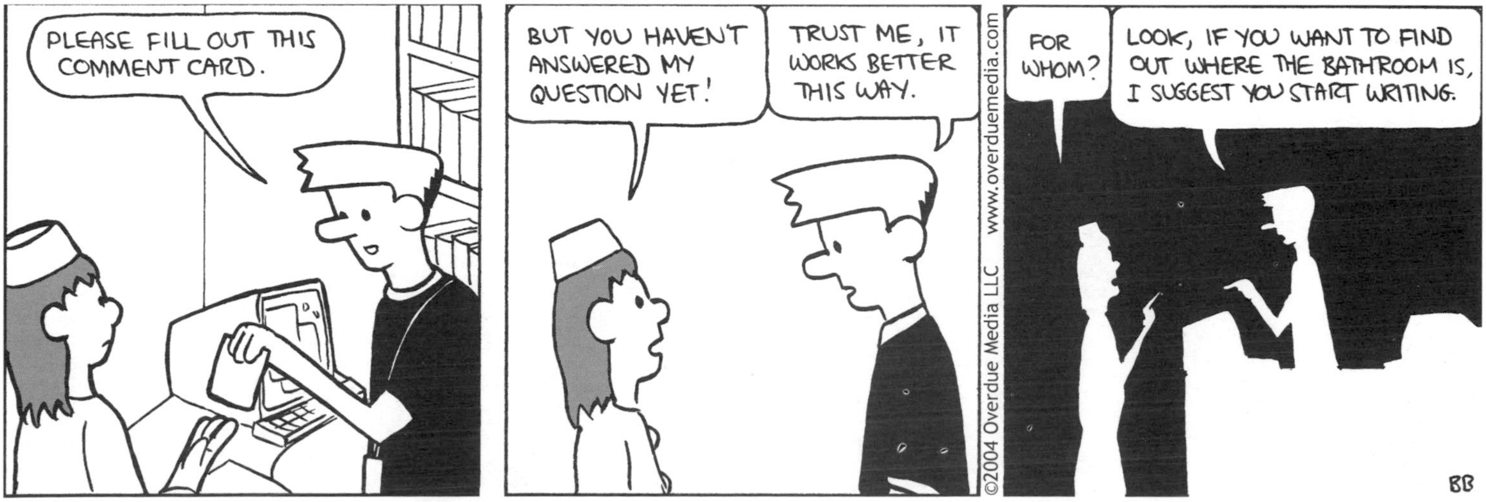
PLEASE FILL OUT THIS COMMENT CARD.
BUT YOU HAVEN'T ANSWERED MY QUESTION YET!
TRUST ME, IT WORKS BETTER THIS WAY.
©2004 Overdue Media LLC www.overduemedia.com
FOR WHOM?
LOOK, IF YOU WANT TO FIND OUT WHERE THE BATHROOM IS, I SUGGEST YOU START WRITING.
BB

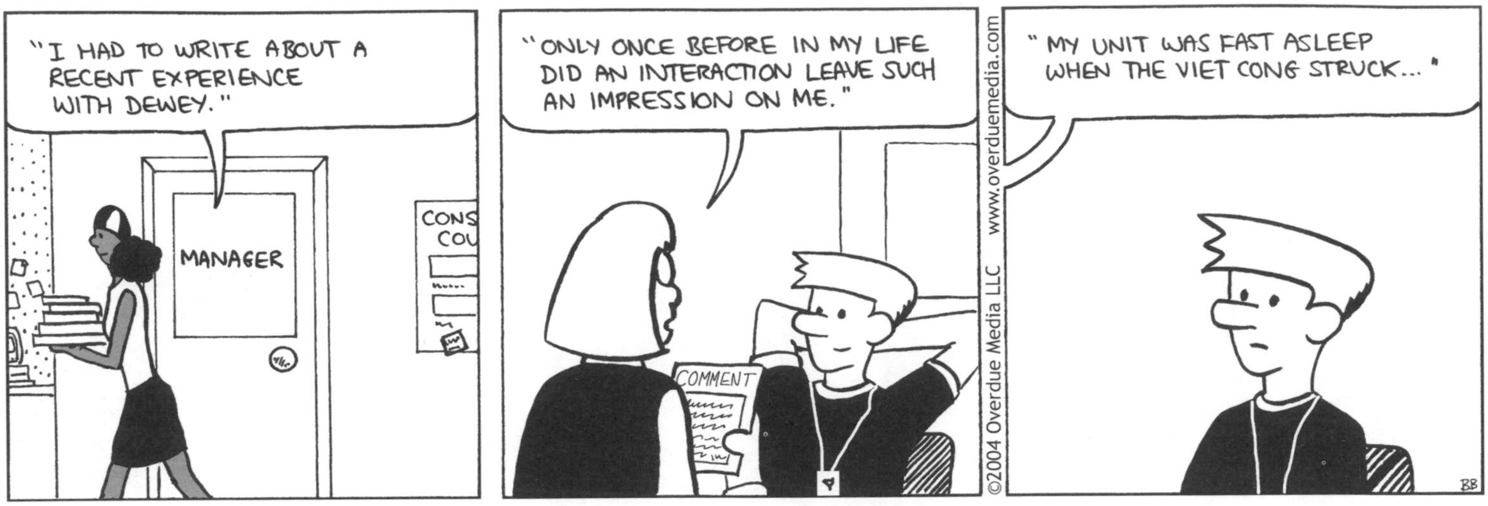
"I HAD TO WRITE ABOUT A RECENT EXPERIENCE WITH DEWEY."
MANAGER
"ONLY ONCE BEFORE IN MY LIFE DID AN INTERACTION LEAVE SUCH AN IMPRESSION ON ME."
COMMENT
©2004 Overdue Media LLC www.overduemedia.com
"MY UNIT WAS FAST ASLEEP WHEN THE VIET CONG STRUCK..."
BB

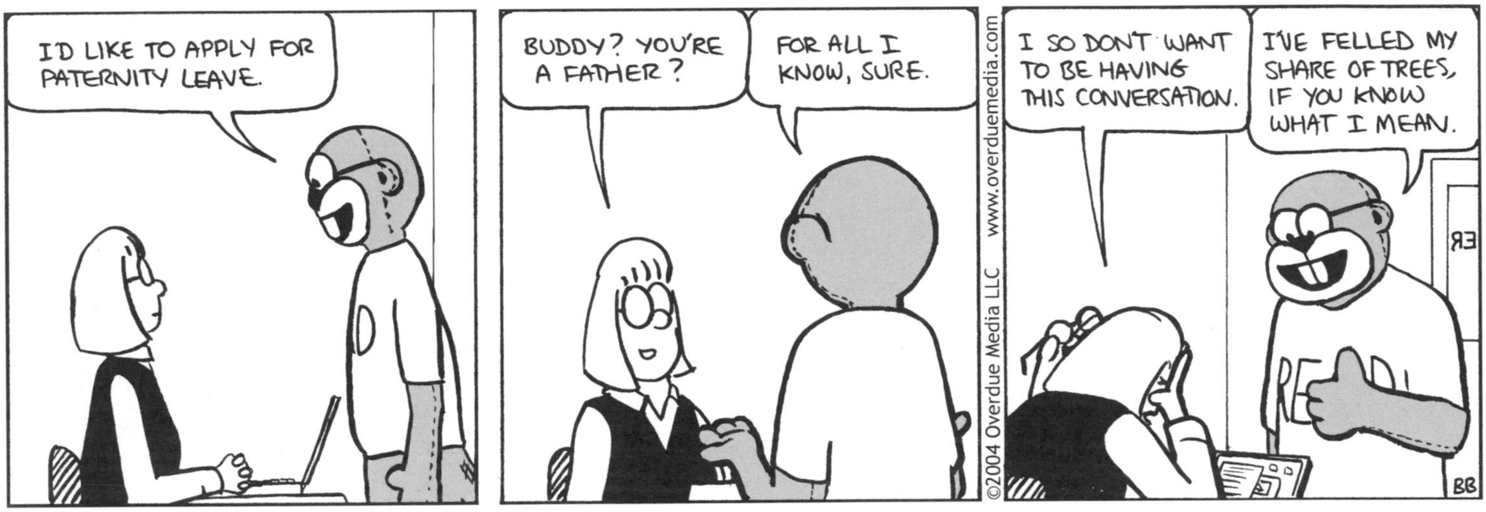
I'D LIKE TO APPLY FOR PATERNITY LEAVE.
BUDDY? YOU'RE A FATHER?
FOR ALL I KNOW, SURE.
©2004 Overdue Media LLC www.overduemedia.com
I SO DON'T WANT TO BE HAVING THIS CONVERSATION.
I'VE FELLED MY SHARE OF TREES, IF YOU KNOW WHAT I MEAN.
BB

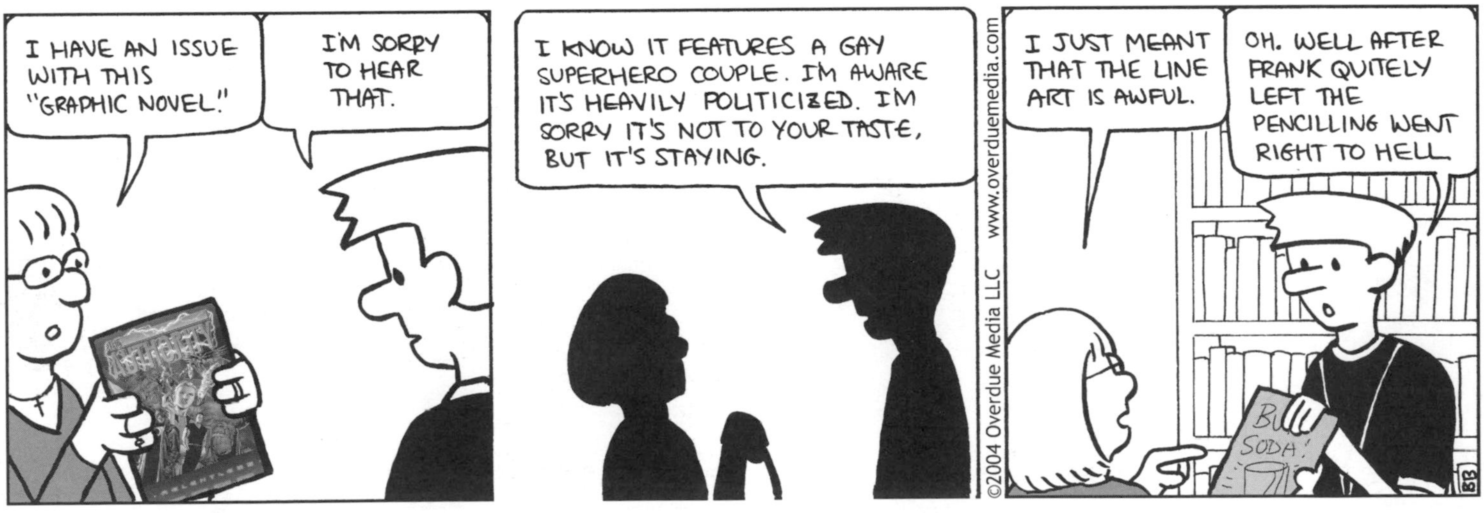
I HAVE AN ISSUE WITH THIS "GRAPHIC NOVEL."
I'M SORRY TO HEAR THAT.
I KNOW IT FEATURES A GAY SUPERHERO COUPLE. I'M AWARE IT'S HEAVILY POLITICIZED. I'M SORRY IT'S NOT TO YOUR TASTE, BUT IT'S STAYING.
©2004 Overdue Media LLC www.overduemedia.com
I JUST MEANT THAT THE LINE ART IS AWFUL.
OH. WELL AFTER FRANK QUITELY LEFT THE PENCILLING WENT RIGHT TO HELL.
SODA!
BB

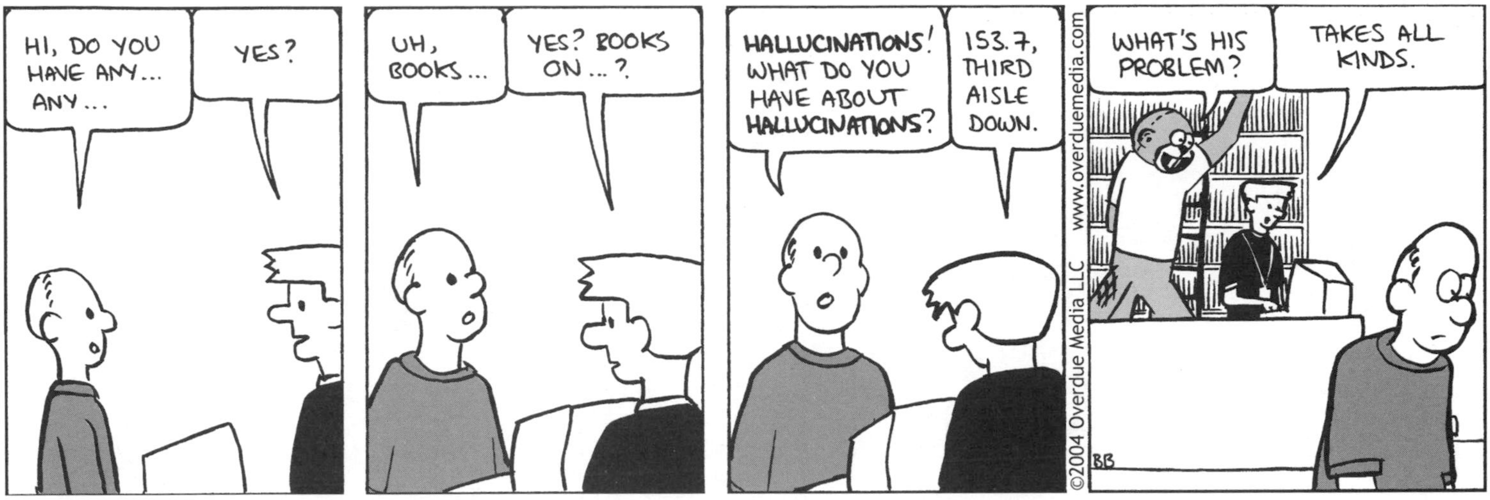
HI, DO YOU HAVE ANY... ANY...
YES?
UH, BOOKS...
YES? BOOKS ON...?
HALLUCINATIONS! WHAT DO YOU HAVE ABOUT HALLUCINATIONS?
153.7, THIRD AISLE DOWN.
WHAT'S HIS PROBLEM?
TAKES ALL KINDS.
www.overduemedia.com
©2004 Overdue Media LLC
BB

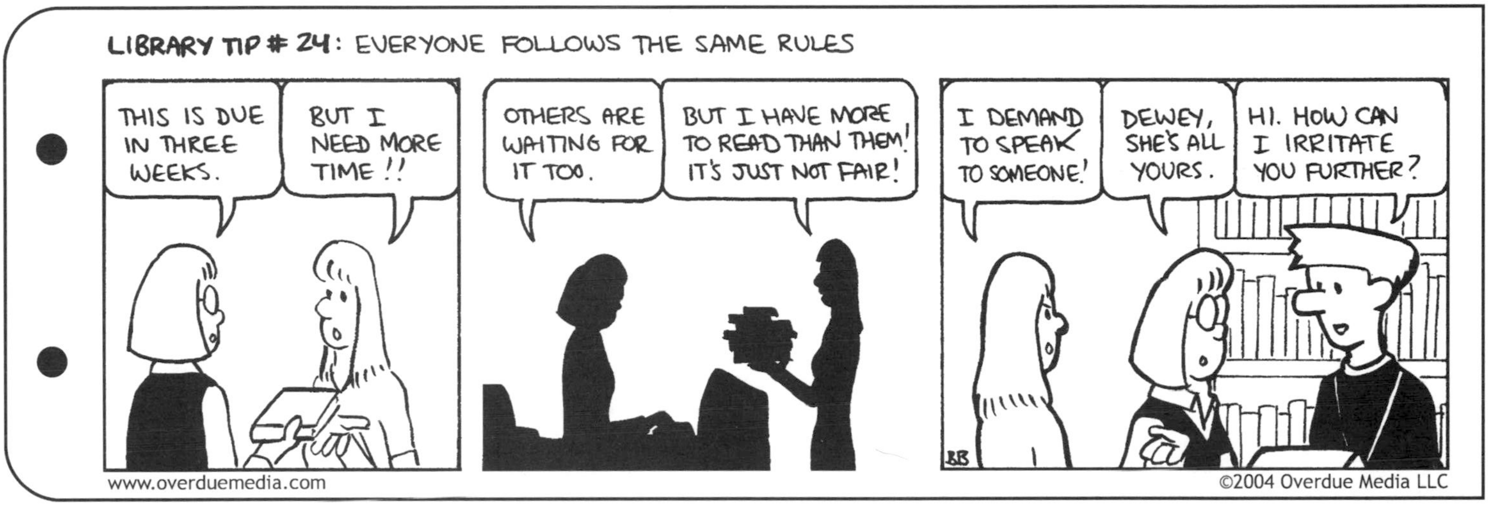
LIBRARY TIP # 24: EVERYONE FOLLOWS THE SAME RULES
THIS IS DUE IN THREE WEEKS.
BUT I NEED MORE TIME!!
OTHERS ARE WAITING FOR IT TOO.
BUT I HAVE MORE TO READ THAN THEM! IT'S JUST NOT FAIR!
I DEMAND TO SPEAK TO SOMEONE!
DEWEY, SHE'S ALL YOURS.
HI. HOW CAN I IRRITATE YOU FURTHER?
BB
www.overduemedia.com
©2004 Overdue Media LLC

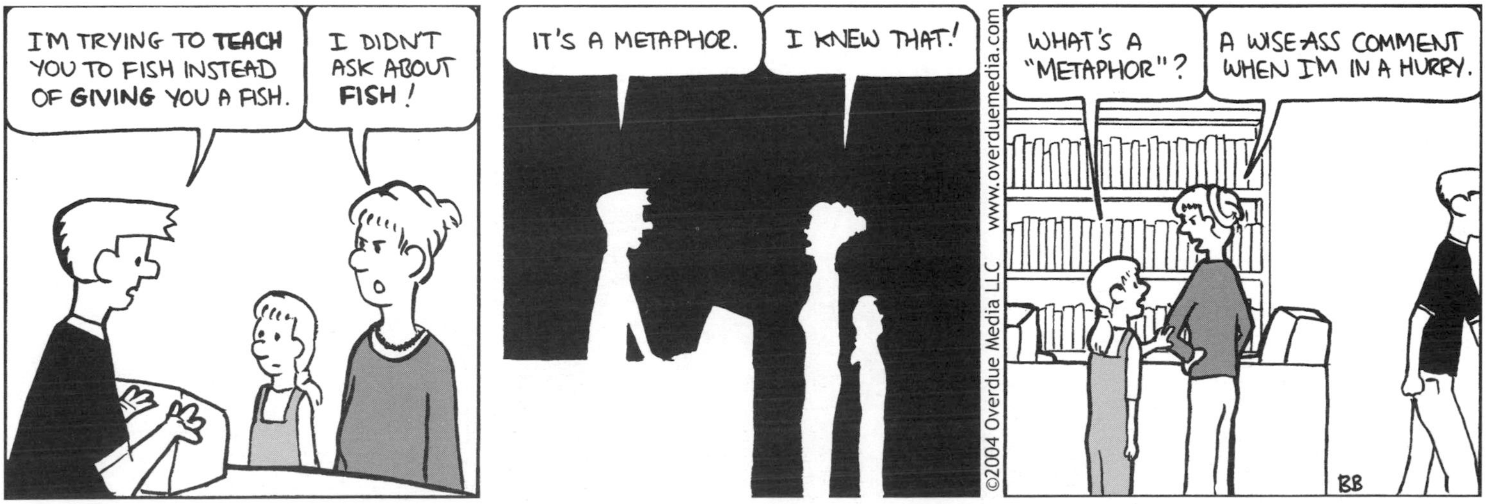
I'M TRYING TO TEACH YOU TO FISH INSTEAD OF GIVING YOU A FISH.
I DIDN'T ASK ABOUT FISH!
IT'S A METAPHOR.
I KNEW THAT!
WHAT'S A "METAPHOR"?
A WISE-ASS COMMENT WHEN I'M IN A HURRY.
www.overduemedia.com
©2004 Overdue Media LLC
BB

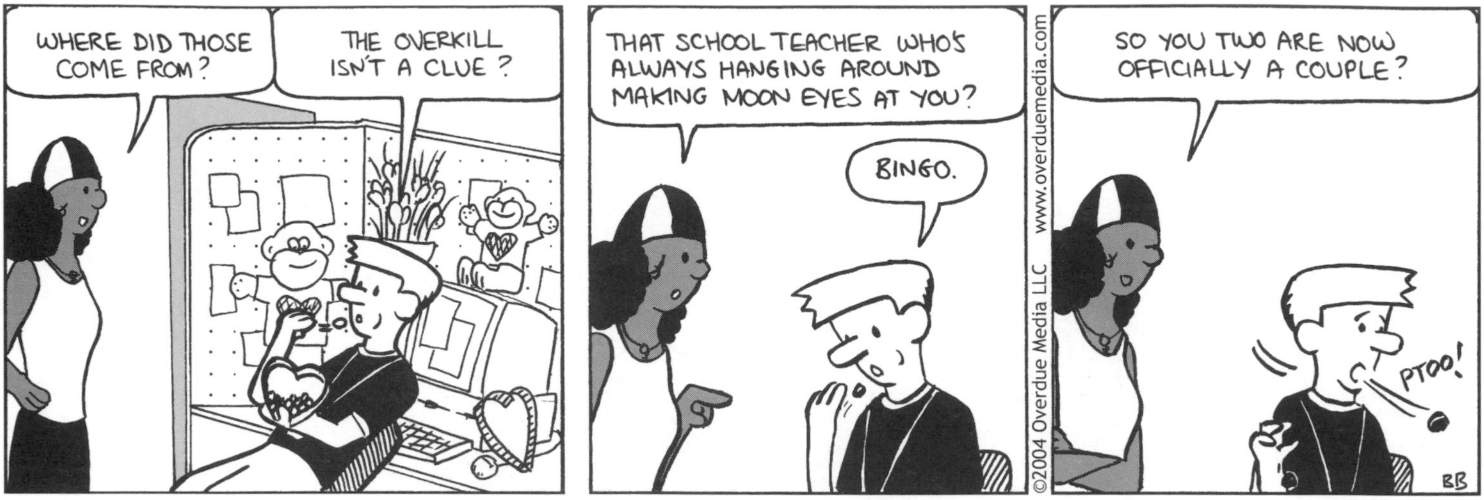
WHERE DID THOSE COME FROM?
THE OVERKILL ISN'T A CLUE?
THAT SCHOOL TEACHER WHO'S ALWAYS HANGING AROUND MAKING MOON EYES AT YOU?
BINGO.
©2004 Overdue Media LLC www.overduemedia.com
SO YOU TWO ARE NOW OFFICIALLY A COUPLE?
PTOO!
BB

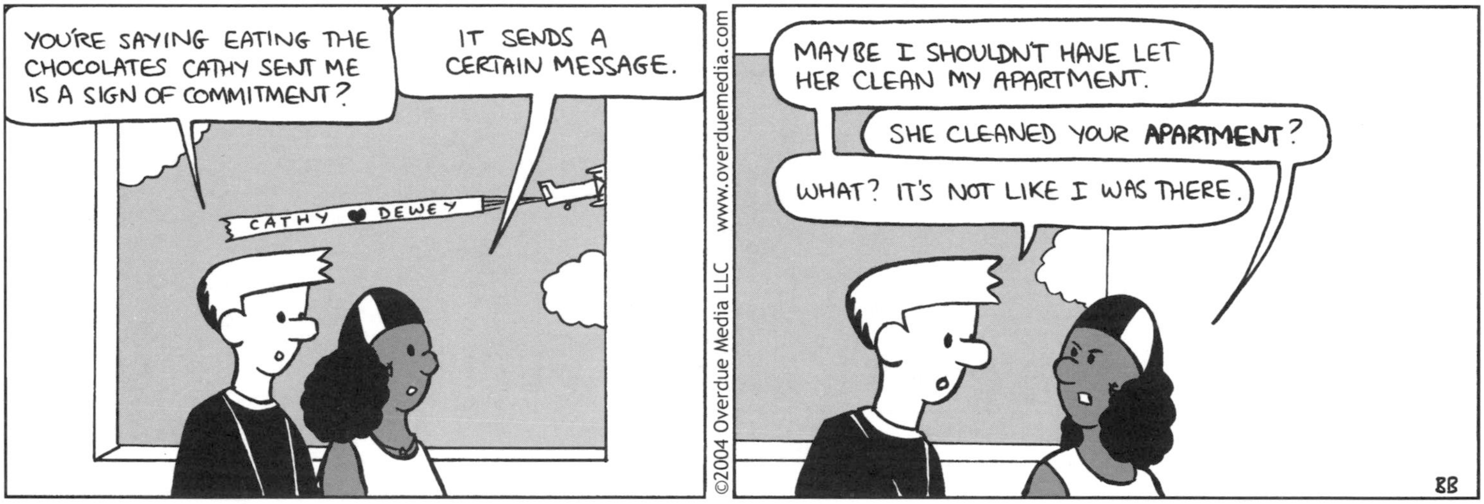
YOU'RE SAYING EATING THE CHOCOLATES CATHY SENT ME IS A SIGN OF COMMITMENT?
IT SENDS A CERTAIN MESSAGE.
CATHY ♥ DEWEY
©2004 Overdue Media LLC www.overduemedia.com
MAYBE I SHOULDN'T HAVE LET HER CLEAN MY APARTMENT.
SHE CLEANED YOUR **APARTMENT**?
WHAT? IT'S NOT LIKE I WAS THERE.
BB

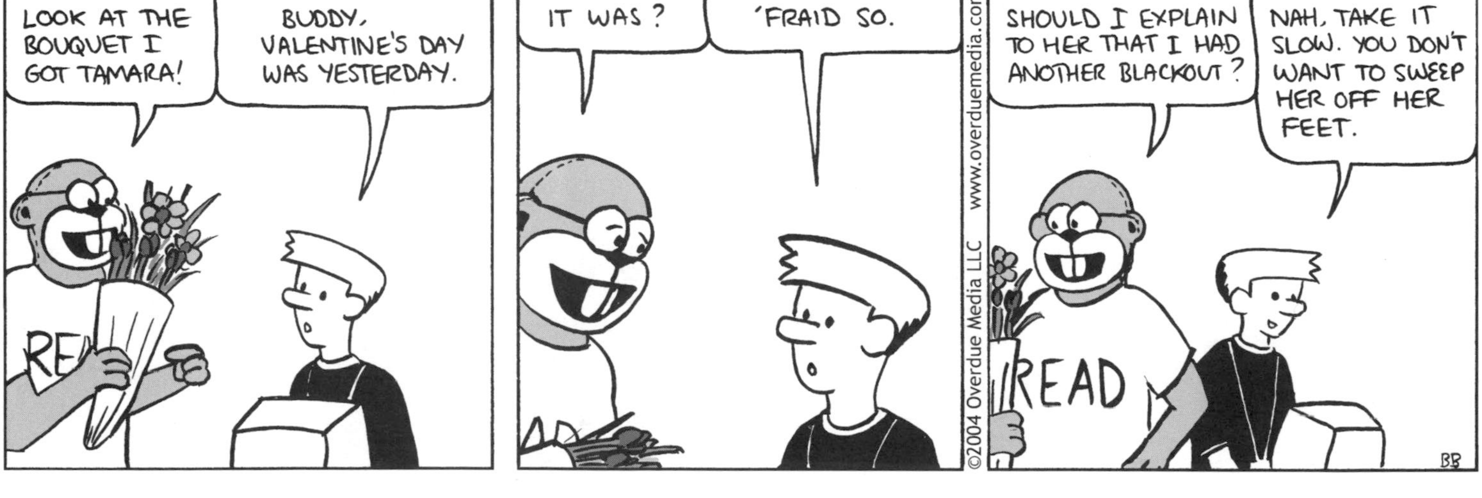
LOOK AT THE BOUQUET I GOT TAMARA!
BUDDY, VALENTINE'S DAY WAS YESTERDAY.
RE
IT WAS?
'FRAID SO.
©2004 Overdue Media LLC www.overduemedia.com
SHOULD I EXPLAIN TO HER THAT I HAD ANOTHER BLACKOUT?
NAH, TAKE IT SLOW. YOU DON'T WANT TO SWEEP HER OFF HER FEET.
READ
BB

# What did you do for your summer vacation?

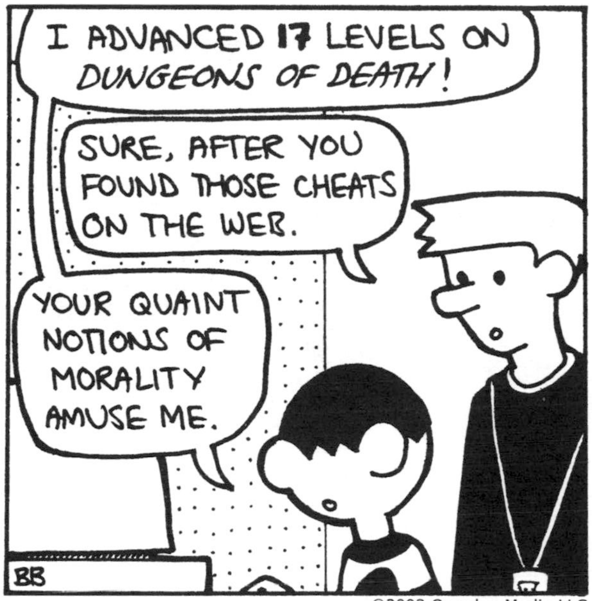
I ADVANCED 17 LEVELS ON DUNGEONS OF DEATH!
SURE, AFTER YOU FOUND THOSE CHEATS ON THE WEB.
YOUR QUAINT NOTIONS OF MORALITY AMUSE ME.
BB



Here's what *Unshelved* might look like as a single-panel cartoon à la *Family Circus* (except funny). We whipped this up for Seattle's Bumbershoot 2003 arts festival, where Bill was part of a panel on comics along with fellow Seattle cartoonists John Lustig (*Last Kiss*), Roberta Gregory (*Bitchy Bitch*), and Donna Barr (*Desert Peach*). Each panelist contributed a comic that answered the above question. Festival goers were invited to fill in their own answers and the best ones won prizes. The funniest ones, alas, aren't printable here.

# Conference Tips

These strips appeared in *CogNotes*, the daily newspaper of the American Library Association 2004 Midwinter Meeting. *Unshelved* strips have appeared in hundreds of publications worldwide (see our website for information about how to get *Unshelved* in yours) but this was the first time we wrote custom strips. It was kinda fun. Originally we were going to have Dewey on some sort of library conference adventure, but five strips didn't seem like enough space for such a juicy topic. So instead we gave a little advice.

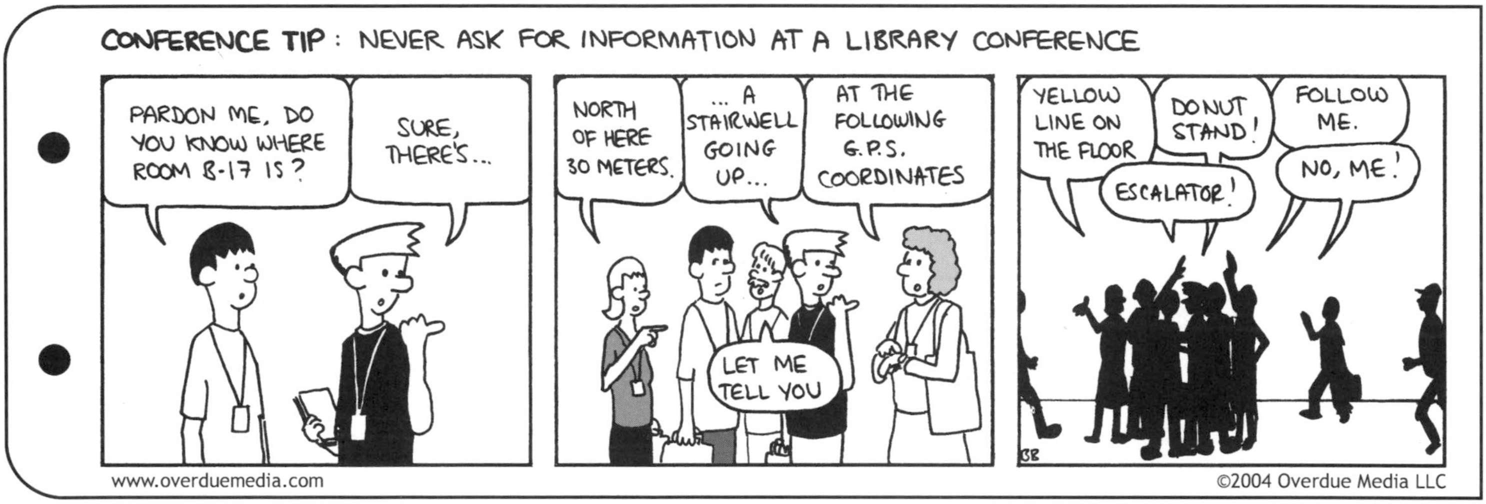
CONFERENCE TIP: NEVER ASK FOR INFORMATION AT A LIBRARY CONFERENCE
PARDON ME, DO YOU KNOW WHERE ROOM B-17 IS?
SURE, THERE'S...
NORTH OF HERE 30 METERS.
... A STAIRWELL GOING UP...
AT THE FOLLOWING G.P.S. COORDINATES
LET ME TELL YOU
YELLOW LINE ON THE FLOOR
DONUT STAND!
ESCALATOR!
FOLLOW ME.
NO, ME!
www.overduemedia.com
©2004 Overdue Media LLC

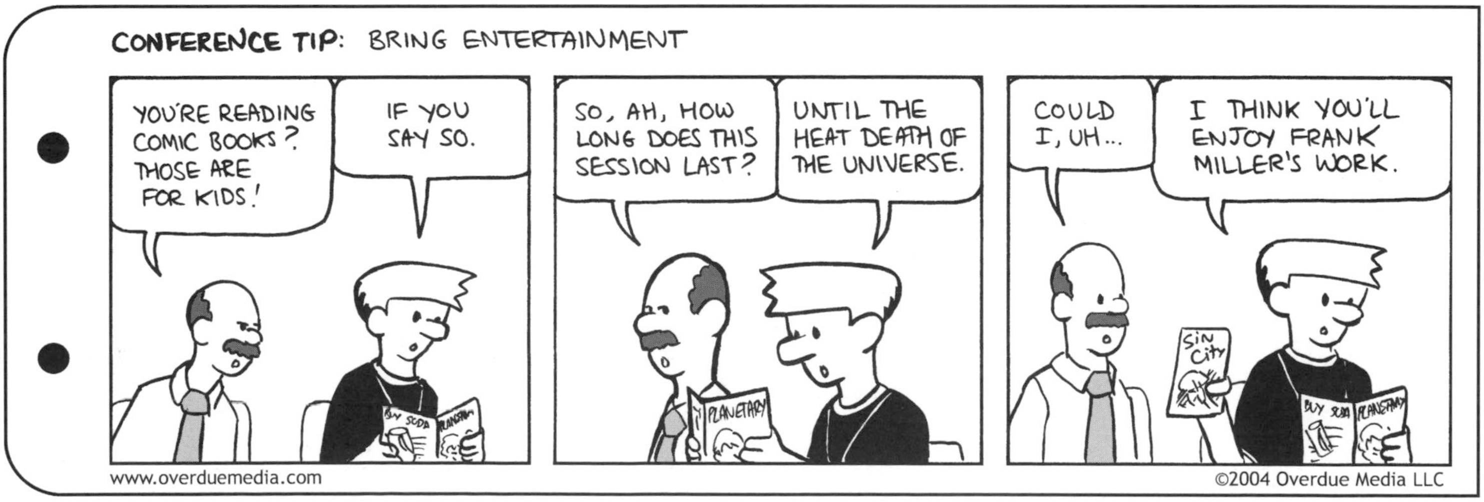
CONFERENCE TIP: BRING ENTERTAINMENT
YOU'RE READING COMIC BOOKS? THOSE ARE FOR KIDS!
IF YOU SAY SO.
SO, AH, HOW LONG DOES THIS SESSION LAST?
UNTIL THE HEAT DEATH OF THE UNIVERSE.
COULD I, UH...
I THINK YOU'LL ENJOY FRANK MILLER'S WORK.
SIN CITY
PLANETARY
www.overduemedia.com
©2004 Overdue Media LLC

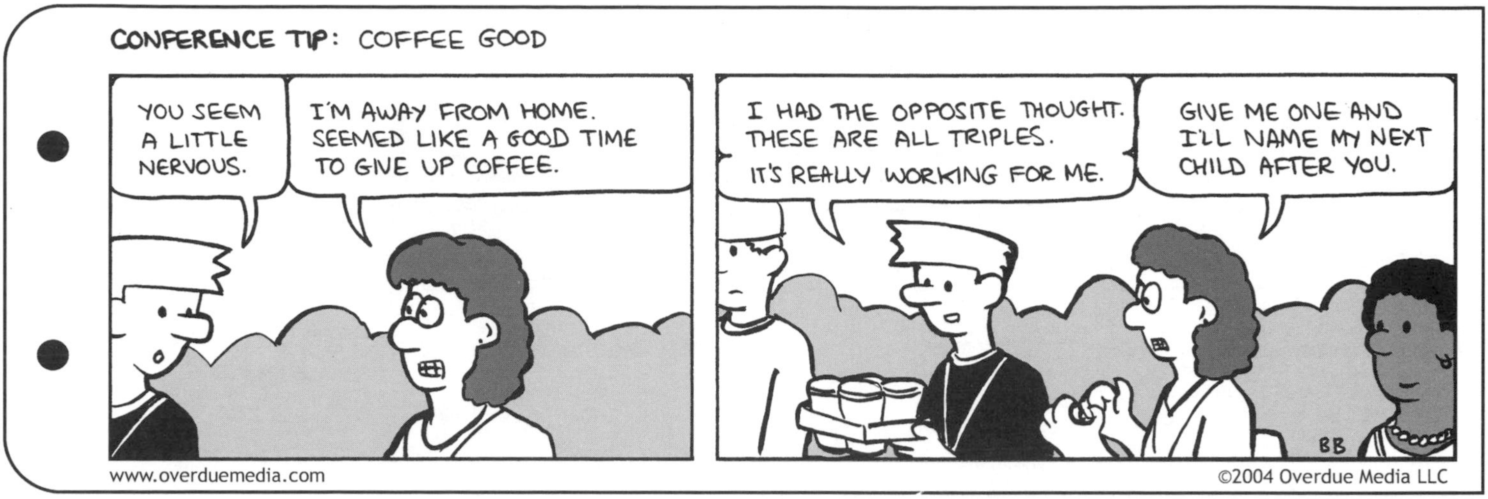
CONFERENCE TIP: COFFEE GOOD
YOU SEEM A LITTLE NERVOUS.
I'M AWAY FROM HOME. SEEMED LIKE A GOOD TIME TO GIVE UP COFFEE.
I HAD THE OPPOSITE THOUGHT. THESE ARE ALL TRIPLES.
IT'S REALLY WORKING FOR ME.
GIVE ME ONE AND I'LL NAME MY NEXT CHILD AFTER YOU.
BB
www.overduemedia.com
©2004 Overdue Media LLC

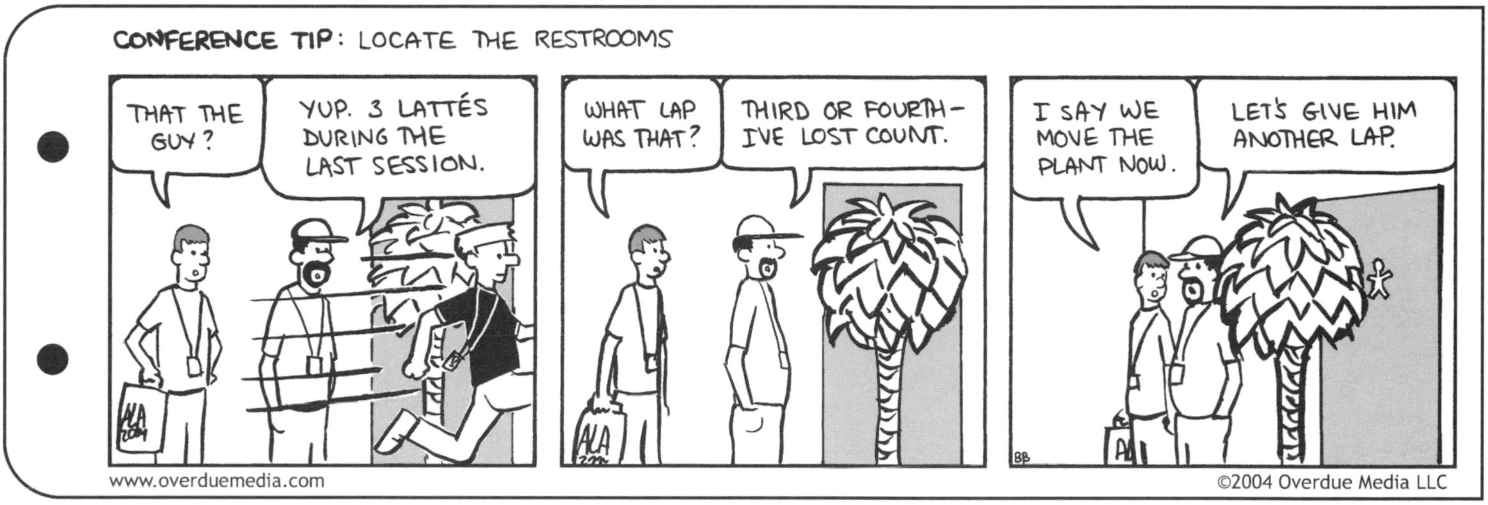
CONFERENCE TIP: LOCATE THE RESTROOMS
THAT THE GUY?
YUP. 3 LATTÉS DURING THE LAST SESSION.
WHAT LAP WAS THAT?
THIRD OR FOURTH– I'VE LOST COUNT.
I SAY WE MOVE THE PLANT NOW.
LET'S GIVE HIM ANOTHER LAP.
BB
www.overduemedia.com
©2004 Overdue Media LLC

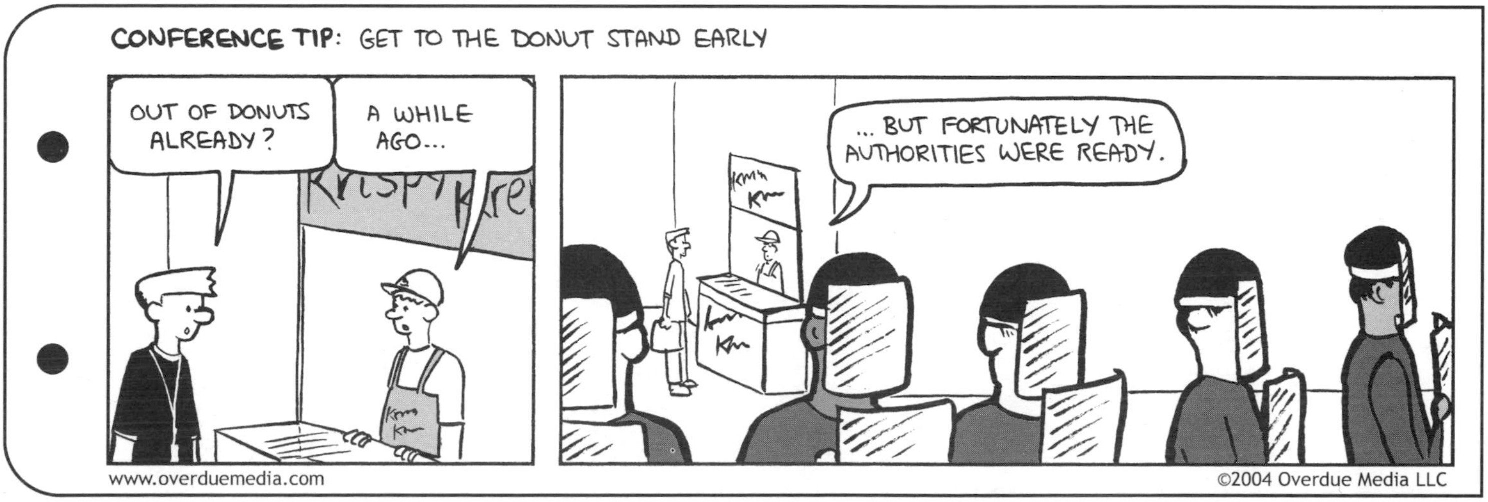
CONFERENCE TIP: GET TO THE DONUT STAND EARLY
OUT OF DONUTS ALREADY?
A WHILE AGO...
... BUT FORTUNATELY THE AUTHORITIES WERE READY.
www.overduemedia.com
©2004 Overdue Media LLC

# How we make
# Unshelved™
### a comic strip about a library

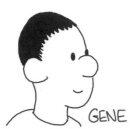
GENE

BILL

**STEP 1: PANIC**

We need a strip.

For next week? I'm in the middle of —

For today!

**STEP 2: WRITE**

#%&$@ !!

TAP TAP TAP

**STEP 3: DELIVERY**

PANT PANT !!!

RRIP!

OVERDUE MEDIA LLC

Haven't you ever heard of "email"?

**STEP 4: COMPLIMENT**

It's good...

**STEP 5: EDIT**

... but I'm taking out the poop jokes. This is a family comic strip.

Families poop.

Not in libraries they don't.

That's what you think.

How's this?

It's just like the version I gave you except you inserted the word "actually" four times.

I wanted to give you something to edit too.

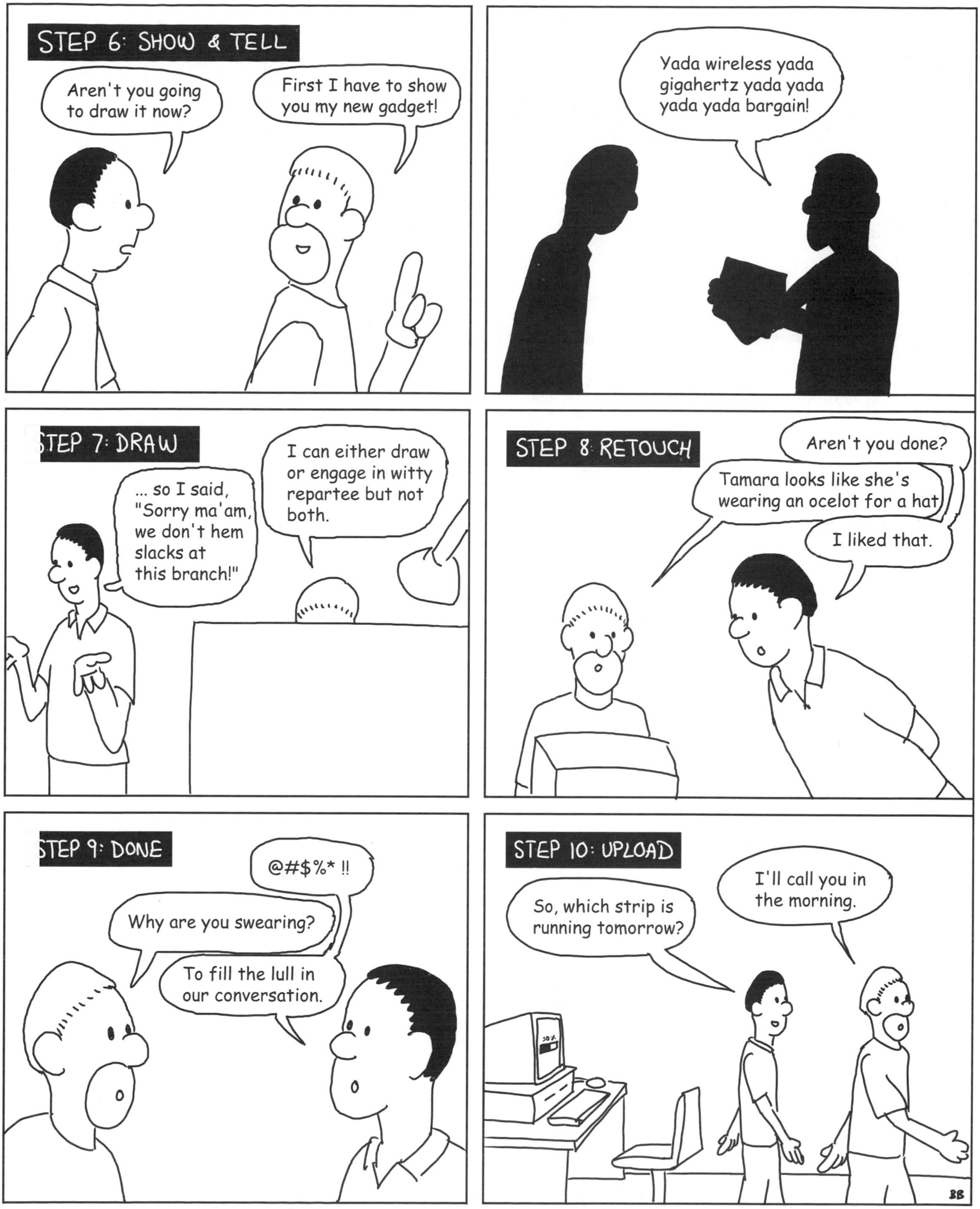
STEP 6: SHOW & TELL
Aren't you going to draw it now?
First I have to show you my new gadget!
Yada wireless yada gigahertz yada yada yada yada bargain!
STEP 7: DRAW
... so I said, "Sorry ma'am, we don't hem slacks at this branch!"
I can either draw or engage in witty repartee but not both.
STEP 8: RETOUCH
Aren't you done?
Tamara looks like she's wearing an ocelot for a hat
I liked that.
STEP 9: DONE
@#$%* !!
Why are you swearing?
To fill the lull in our conversation.
STEP 10: UPLOAD
So, which strip is running tomorrow?
I'll call you in the morning.
BB

# read Unshelved™ every day at
# www.overduemedia.com

- Strip archive
- Sign up for free daily & weekly email delivery
- RSS and Web syndication
- Buy *Unshelved* books and merchandise
- Authors' blog with news about the strip
- Upcoming appearances by Bill and Gene
- Special features
- ... and much more!

*Unshelved Volume 1* collects the first year of *Unshelved* in a book that otherwise greatly resembles this one.

You can order our books from our website and a variety of booksellers and comic shops - contact us if you're interested in stocking them. Libraries can purchase our books from major book wholesalers.

## contact us at
## unshelved@overduemedia.com